GLOBAL POLITICAL ECONOMY

third edition

EDITED BY JOHN RAVENHILL

OXFORD
UNIVERSITY PRESS

OXFORD
UNIVERSITY PRESS

Great Clarendon Street, Oxford OX2 6DP

Oxford University Press is a department of the University of Oxford.
It furthers the University's objective of excellence in research, scholarship,
and education by publishing worldwide in

Oxford New York

Auckland Cape Town Dar es Salaam Hong Kong Karachi
Kuala Lumpur Madrid Melbourne Mexico City Nairobi
New Delhi Shanghai Taipei Toronto

With offices in

Argentina Austria Brazil Chile Czech Republic France Greece
Guatemala Hungary Italy Japan Poland Portugal Singapore
South Korea Switzerland Thailand Turkey Ukraine Vietnam

Oxford is a registered trade mark of Oxford University Press
in the UK and in certain other countries

Published in the United States
by Oxford University Press Inc., New York

© Oxford University Press 2011

The moral rights of the authors have been asserted
Database right Oxford University Press (maker)

First published 2005

Second edition 2008

British Library Cataloguing in Publication Data
Data available

Library of Congress Cataloging in Publication Data
Data available

Typeset by Laserwords Private Limited, Chennai, India
Printed in Italy on acid-free paper by L.E.G.O. S.p.A

ISBN 978–0–19–957081–2

10 9 8 7 6 5 4 3

GLOBAL POLITICAL ECONOMY

Preface and Acknowledgements

The contributors to this book are delighted that it has proved sufficiently popular with instructors and students that the publishers have commissioned a third edition. For this edition, the chapters have been substantially revised to take into account the tumultuous developments in the global economy associated with the global financial crisis.

We are very pleased to welcome Professor Nicola Phillips as a contributor to this volume, although note with sadness the death of Professor Caroline Thomas who previously contributed the chapter on relations between developed and developing economies.

Students in IPE courses are often concerned about their lack of background in economics. While we provide concise explanations in this book for all of the key concepts that we use (and the book contains a comprehensive Glossary), students often want to go beyond this basic information to improve their knowledge of economics. The following books are useful introductions, written with the non-specialist in mind:

James Gerber, *International Economics*, 5th edn (Pearson Education, 2010).

John Black, Nigar Hashimzade, and Gareth Miles, *Oxford Dictionary of Economics*, 3rd edn (Oxford, 2009).

Donald Rutherford, *Routledge Dictionary of Economics*, 2nd edn (Routledge, 2002).

Donald Rutherford, *Economics: The Key Concepts* (Routledge, 2007).

For those who are comfortable with basic economic concepts, the following are the best introductory overviews of major theoretical approaches to international economics:

Paul Krugman and Maurice Obstfeld, *International Economics: Theory and Practice*, 8th edn (Addison-Wesley, 2008).

Peter B. Kenen, *The International Economy*, 4th edn (Cambridge University Press, 2000).

Preparation of a volume of this size is a major task, which would not have been possible without generous support from the Department of International Relations, College of Asia and the Pacific, Australian National University. The Department's publications editor Mary-Louise Hickey, began preparing the manuscript to Oxford University Press's requirements, and Jikon Lai completed the work to the meticulous standards that Mary-Louise has always maintained. Jikon also provided excellent research assistance for Chapter 6.

Figure Acknowledgements:

Figure 5.1 from Department of Trade and Industry (UK), 'Average Industrial Tariffs in Developed Countries since 1947', *The Government's Expenditure Plans* (Her Majesty's Stationery Office, 2000), chapter 8. Reprinted with the permission of Her Majesty's Stationery Office.

Figure 6.1 from World Trade Organization, 'Regional Trade Agreements: Facts and Figures', www.wto.org/english/tratop_e/region_e/regfac_e.htm (Geneva: World Trade Organization, 2010). Reprinted with the permission of the World Trade Organization.

Figure 6.2 from World Trade Organization, Committee on Regional Trade Agreements, 'Mapping of Regional Trade Agreements: Note by the Secretariat', WT/REG/W/41 (Geneva: World Trade Organization, 2000), Chart 2. Reprinted with the permission of the World Trade Organization.

Table 8.1 from World Bank, *Global Development Finance* (Washington, DC: World Bank, 2009), p. 50. Reprinted with the permission of the World Bank.

Table 9.3 from P. H. Lindert and J. G. Williamson, 'Does Globalization Make the World More Unequal?', in M. D. Bordo, A. M. Taylor, and J. G. Williamson (eds), *Globalization in Historical Perspective* (Chicago, IL: University of Chicago Press, 2003), Table 5.1. Reprinted with the permission of the University of Chicago Press and the authors.

Figure 12.1 and *Table 12.3* from B. Milanovic, *Worlds Apart: Measuring International and Global Inequality* (Princeton, NJ: Princeton University Press, 2005), figure 10.1 and table 7.3. Reprinted with the permission of Princeton University Press and the author.

Figure 12.5 from B. Milanovic, 'Global Inequality Recalculated: The Effect of New 2005 PPP Estimates on Global Inequality', World Bank Working Paper 5061 (Washington, DC: World Bank, September), figure 1. Reprinted with the permission of the World Bank.

Every effort has been made to trace and contact copyright holders but this has not been possible in every case. If notified, the publisher will undertake to rectify any errors or omissions at the earliest opportunity.

Crown copyright material is reproduced under Class License Number C01P0000148 with the permission of OPSI and the Queen's Printer for Scotland.

I am grateful to the authors for the work they have put into their chapters, and for complying with the tight schedule required in publishing a book of this type.

My principal debt, as always, is to my wife, Stefa Wirga, who has provided encouragement and support throughout the project from its original conceptualization.

JOHN RAVENHILL

Brief Contents

Detailed Contents

List of Figures

List of Boxes

List of Tables

Abbreviations

ACP	Africa, the Caribbean, and the Pacific
ACU	Asian Currency Unit
AFL–CIO	American Federation of Labor–Congress of Industrial Organizations
AFTA	ASEAN Free Trade Area
ANZCERTA	Australia–New Zealand Closer Economic Relations Trade Agreement
APEC	Asia-Pacific Economic Cooperation
ASEAN	Association of Southeast Asian Nations
BIS	Bank for International Settlements
BRICs	The 'new globalizers': Brazil, Russia, India, China
CACM	Central American Common Market
CAP	Common Agricultural Policy
CARICOM	Caribbean Community and Common Market
CEO	Chief executive officer
CER	Closer Economic Relations
CERDS	Charter of Economic Rights and Duties of States
CFA	Communauté Financière Africaine (African Financial Community)
CFCs	chlorofluorocarbons
CITES	Convention on International Trade in Endangered Species of Wild Flora and Fauna
COCOM	Coordinating Committee for Multilateral Export Controls
COMECON	Council of Mutual Economic Assistance
COMESA	Common Market for Eastern and Southern Africa
COP	Conference of the Parties
COREPER	Committee of Permanent Representatives
CPIA	Country Policy and Institutional Assessment
CPR	Common pool resources
CSAs	country-specific advantages
CUSFTA/CUSTA	Canada–US Free Trade Agreement
DAC	Development Assistance Committee
DDA	Doha Development Agenda

DSB	Dispute Settlement Body
DSF	Debt Sustainability Framework
DSU	Dispute Settlement Understanding
EC	European Community
ECLA	Economic Commission for Latin America
ECLAC	Economic Commission for Latin America and the Caribbean
ECOSOC	[United Nations] Economic and Social Council
ECOWAS	Economic Community of West African States
ECSC	European Coal and Steel Community
ECU	European Currency Unit
EEC	European Economic Community
EFTA	European Free Trade Association
EMS	electronic manufacturing service; also, European Monetary System; also Environmental Management System
EPA	Environmental Protection Agency
EPZs	Export Processing Zones
EU	European Union
FASB	Financial Accounting Standards Board
FDI	foreign direct investment
FSA	firm-specific advantages
FSB	Financial Stability Board
FSC	Forest Stewardship Council
FSF	Financial Stability Forum
FVA	fair value accounting
G7	Group of Seven
G8	Group of Eight
G10	Group of Ten
G20	Group of Twenty
G77	Group of Seventy-Seven
GATS	General Agreement on Trade in Services
GATT	General Agreement on Tariffs and Trade
GCC	Gulf Cooperation Council
GDP	gross domestic product
GEF	Global Environment Facility
GEIs	global economic institutions
GEMs	global economic multilaterals
GEMI	Global Environmental Management Initiative
GM	General Motors
GNP	gross national product
GPE	global political economy
GVCs	global value chains
HIPC	Heavily Indebted Poor Countries initiative

IAIS	International Association of Insurance Supervisors
IASB	International Accounting Standards Board
IBM	International Business Machines
IBRD	International Bank for Reconstruction and Development
ICCO	International Cocoa Organization
ICO	International Coffee Organization
ICP	International Comparison Program
ICSG	International Copper Study Group
ICSID	International Centre for Settlement of Investment Disputes
IDA	International Development Association
IDB	Inter-American Development Bank
IEPL	International extreme poverty line
IFC	[World Bank] International Finance Corporation
IFI	international financial institution
IFRS	international financial reporting standards
ILO	International Labour Organization
IMF	International Monetary Fund
IO	*International Organization*
IOM	International Organization for Migration
IOSCO	International Organization of Securities Commissions
IPCC	Intergovernmental Panel on Climate Change
IPE	international political economy
IR	International Relations
ISI	import-substitution industrialization
ISO	International Organization for Standardization; also, International Sugar Organization
ITA	Information Technology Agreement (WTO); also, International Trade Administration
ITO	International Trade Organization
ITTO	International Tropical Timber Organization
JFC	[World Bank–Civil Society] Joint Facilitation Committee
JV	joint venture
LAC	Latin America and the Caribbean
LDCs	less developed countries
LIC	Low-income country
LLDC	Landlocked developing countries
LMU	Latin Monetary Union
LTCM	Lon-Term Captial Management (American hedge fund)

M&As	Mergers and acquisitions
MAFF	Ministry for Agriculture, Forestry, and Fisheries (Japan)
MAI	[OECD] Multilateral Agreement on Investment
MDGs	Millennium Development Goals
MDRI	Multilateral Debt Relief Initiative
MEOs	multilateral economic organizations
MERCOSUR	Common Market of the South
MFA	Multifibre Arrangement
MFN	most-favoured nation
MIC	middle-income country
MIGA	[World Bank] Multilateral Investment Guarantee Agency
MITI	Ministry for International Trade and Industry (Japan)
MNC	multinational corporation
MNE	multinational enterprise
NAFTA	North American Free Trade Agreement
NAM	non-aligned movement
NAMA	non-agriculture market access
NASA	US National Aeronautics and Space Administration
NEC	Nippon Electric Company
NGOs	non-governmental organizations
NIDL	new international division of labour
NIEs	newly industrializing economies
NIEO	New International Economic Order
NTBs	non-tariff barriers
NTMs	non-tariff measures
ODA	Official Development Assistance
OECD	Organization for Economic Co-operation and Development
OEMs	original equipment manufacturers
OPEC	Organization of the Petroleum Exporting Countries
PC	personal computer
PD	Prisoner's Dilemma
PGA	Peoples' Global Action
PIER	politics of international economic relations
POPs	persistent organic pollutants
PPP	purchasing power parity
PRSPs	Poverty Reduction Strategy Papers
PSIA	Poverty and Social Impact Analysis
PTA	preferential trade agreement
PWC	Post-Washington Consensus

PWT	Penn World Tables
R&D	research and development
RNGMA	Regional Nature of Global Multinational Activity Survey
RTA	regional trading agreement
RTAA	Reciprocal Trade Agreements Act
SADCC	Southern African Development Coordination Conference
SAPs	structural adjustment programmes
SDR	Special Drawing Rights
SFM	sustainable forest management
SIDS	Small Island Developing States
SMEs	small and medium-sized enterprise
SMU	Scandinavian Monetary Union
SSA	Sub-Saharan Africa
SWFs	sovereign wealth funds
SWIFT	Society for the Worldwide Interbank Transactions
TNC	transnational corporation
TPRM	Trade Policy Review Mechanism
TRIMs	Trade-Related Investment Measures
TRIPs	Trade-Related Aspects of Intellectual Property Rights
UN	United Nations Organization
UNCED	United Nations Conference on the Environment and Development
UNEP	United Nations Environment Programme
UNCTAD	United Nations Conference on Trade and Development
UNDP	United Nations Development Programme
UNEP	United Nations Environment Programme
UNFCC	United Nations Framework Convention on Climate Change
UNIDO	United Nations Industrial Development Organization
USAID	United States Agency for International Development
USTR	United States Trade Representative
VW	Volkswagen
WC	Washington Consensus
WCED	World Commission on Environment and Development
WEU	Western European Union
WIDER	[UN] World Institute for Development Economics Research
WTO	World Trade Organization

About the Contributors

Vinod K Aggarwal is Professor of Political Science, Affiliated Professor of Business and Public Policy at the Haas School of Business, and Director of the Berkeley APEC Study Center at the University of California, Berkeley. His publications include *Liberal Protectionism* (University of California Press), *Debt Games* (Cambridge University Press), and *Bilateral Trade Agreements in the Asia-Pacific* (Routledge).

Peter Dauvergne is Professor of Political Science and Canada Research Chair in Global Environmental Politics, and Director, Liu Institute for Global Issues at the University of British Columbia, Vancouver, Canada. His publications include *Shadows in the Forest* (MIT Press) and *Loggers and Degradation in the Asia-Pacific* (Cambridge University Press).

Cédric Dupont is Professor of Political Science at the Graduate Institute of International Studies, Geneva. He is also Director of the Centre on Alpine Environment and Society at the Kurt Bösch University Institute in Sion, Switzerland. He has published in journals, including the *European Journal of International Relations* and the *International Political Science Review*.

Colin Hay is Professor of Political Analysis at the University of Sheffield, UK. His recent publications include *Why We Hate Politics* (Polity Press), *Political Analysis* (Palgrave), *The State* (Palgrave), *European Politics* (Oxford University Press), and *Demystifying Globalization* (Palgrave).

Eric Helleiner is CIGI Chair in International Governance at the University of Waterloo, Ontario, Canada. His publications include *States and the Reemergence of Global Finance* and *The Making of National Money* (both from Cornell University Press), as well as *Towards North American Monetary Union?* (McGill-Queen's University Press).

Michael J Hiscox is Professor of Government, Harvard University. His publications include *International Trade and Political Conflict* (Princeton University Press).

Anthony McGrew is Professor of International Relations and Head of the School of Social Sciences at the University of Southampton, UK. His recent publications include *Globalization/Anti-Globalization: Beyond the Great Divide,*

Globalization Theory, and *Globalization: Human Security and Development* (all published by Polity Press).

Louis W Pauly is Director of the Centre for International Studies, University of Toronto, Canada, where he also holds the Canada Research Chair in Globalization and Governance. His publications include *Opening Financial Markets* and *Who Elected the Bankers?* (both Cornell University Press).

Nicola Phillips is Professor of Political Economy and Director of the Political Economy Institute at the University of Manchester, UK. Her publications include *Development* (co-authored with Anthony Payne, Polity), *Globalizing International Political Economy* (Palgrave), and *The Southern Cone Model: The Political Economy of Regional Capitalist Development in Latin America* (Routledge).

John Ravenhill is Professor in the Department of International Relations, College of Asia and the Pacific, Australian National University. His publications include *Crisis as Catalyst: Asia's Dynamic Political Economy* (Cornell), *APEC and the Construction of Pacific Rim Regionalism*, and *The Asian Financial Crisis and the Architecture of Global Finance* (both Cambridge University Press).

Eric Thun is Peter Moores Lecturer in Chinese Business Studies at Oxford University's Saïd Business School. His publications include *Changing Lanes in China: Foreign Direct Investment, Local Governments and Auto Sector Development* (Cambridge University Press).

Robert Hunter Wade is Professor of Political Economy, Development Studies Institute, London School of Economics, UK. His publications include *Governing the Market* (Princeton University Press), *Village Republics* (Cambridge University Press), and *Irrigation and Agricultural Politics in South Korea* (Westview Press).

Matthew Watson is Professor of Political Economy, Department of Politics and International Studies, University of Warwick, UK. His publications include *The Political Economy of International Capital Mobility* (Palgrave Macmillan), while the argument in the current contribution is more closely related to his previous book, *Foundations of International Political Economy* (Palgrave Macmillan).

Gilbert R Winham is Emeritus Professor of Political Science and Adjunct Professor, Faculty of Law, Dalhousie University, Halifax, Nova Scotia, Canada. His publications include *International Trade and the Tokyo Round Negotiation* (Princeton University Press) and *The Evolution of International Trade Agreements* (University of Toronto Press).

Guided Tour of Textbook Features

This book is enriched with a number of learning tools to help you navigate the text and reinforce your knowledge of global political economy. This guided tour shows you how to get the most out of your textbook package.

Reader's guides

Reader's guides set the scene for upcoming themes and issues to be discussed, and indicate the scope of coverage within the chapter.

Boxes

Throughout the book boxes provide you with extra information on particular topics to complement your understanding of the main chapter text.

Key points

Each main chapter section ends with a set of key points that summarize the most important arguments developed.

Questions

A set of carefully devised questions has been
provided to help you assess your understanding
of core themes, and may also be used as the basis
of seminar discussion or coursework.

? Questions

1. What are the basic components of the international trade regime? Give examples.
2. What was the effect of the US Reciprocal Trade Agreements Act of 1934?
3. What does non-discrimination mean in international trade; and how is it put into effect the GATT?
4. Compare the results of the Kennedy and Tokyo Rounds of GATT multilateral trade negoti
5. What was the role of the developing countries in the Uruguay Round negotiation; an historically significant?
6. What were the challenges encountered in negotiating rules for trade in services in the U negotiation?
7. How does the WTO differ from the GATT?
8. What is the WTO Dispute Settlement Understanding (DSU); why is it necessary; and wh

Further reading

Take your learning further by using the reading
lists at the end of chapter to find the key literature
in the field, or more detailed information on a
specific topic.

→ Further reading

Trade

■ Destler, I. M. (1995), *American Trade Politics*, 3rd edn (Washington, DC: Institute for Economics). This is required reading for anyone interested in how US trade policy is made comprehensive analysis of American political institutions and policy-making.

■ Hayes, J. P. (1993), *Making Trade Policy in the European Community* (London: Macmill provides a thorough discussion of the processes of trade policy-making in the European Com

■ Hiscox, M. J. (2002), *International Trade and Political Conflict* (Princeton, NJ: Princet Press). An analysis of historical changes in levels of factor specificity in several Western na these changes to shifts in political alignments in trade politics.

■ Krueger, A. O. (1995), *Trade Policies and Developing Nations* (Washington, DC: Brooking An engaging discussion of trade liberalization in developing nations in recent years.

■ Rogowski, R. (1989), *Commerce and Coalitions* (Princeton, NJ: Princeton University Pres

Web links

At the end of each chapter you will find an
annotated summary of useful websites to help
you with further research.

:// Web links

■ www.isn.ethz.ch/linkslib Good links to security and global economy nexuses.
■ www.wto.org Official WTO site, with useful material about its policies and data on world
■ www.theglobalsite.ac.uk Good site for the globalization debate and related links.
■ www.tradeobservatory.org Unofficial site operated by non-governmental organizations (of the WTO and economic globalization.
■ www.polity.co.uk/global Good site for the globalization debate and many good links.
■ www.rgemonitor.com Excellent site for a whole range of material on global economy globalization.
■ www.indiana.edu/~ipe/ipesection Good site for general material on IPE.
■ www.nber.org Excellent studies of economic globalization in National Bureau of Econo (NBER) Working Paper series.

Glossary terms

Key terms appear in blue in the text and are
defined in a glossary at the end of the book
to aid you in exam revision.

apocalyptic predictions of the demise of the nation state. In such accounts, globalization is invariably cast in the role of prosecutor, judge, jury, and executioner. Yet, despite such doom-laden prognoses, government expenditure continues to account for a significant and, in many cases, rising share of **gross domestic product** (GDP), whilst the nation state remains the principal focus of political identification and the principal locus of political debate and contestation in an interdependent world. Given this seeming paradox, it is perhaps not surprising that the question of the impact of globalization on the development of the state has become a subject of considerable interest and intense controversy.

domestically, and whether or n state as having a present or, i have a very significant bearing political autonomy we perceive turn, has significant consequen which we might legitimately h accountable for their conduct i significance of the issues we a is important to proceed with caution.

We should perhaps be wary ically, as many have, that global (and the governments which power) with no alternative oth

Guided Tour of the Online Resource Centre

www.oxfordtextbooks.co.uk/orc/ravenhill3e/

The Online Resource Centre that accompanies this book provides students and instructors with ready-to-use teaching and learning materials. These resources are free of charge and designed to maximize the learning experience.

For Students

Timeline

Familiarise yourself with key events in global political economy by looking at the timeline.

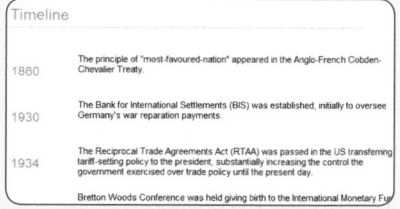

Flashcard glossary

A series of interactive flashcards containing key terms allows you to test your knowledge of the terminology of global political economy.

Web links

Additional web links have been provided and organized by theme.

For Lecturers

Case studies

Four case studies are included for use in seminar work, including one on financial crises in the last decade.

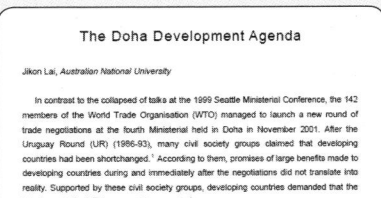

PowerPoint® slides

PowerPoint® slides complement each chapter of the book and are a useful resource for preparing lectures and handouts.

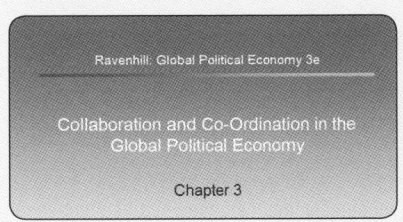

Boxes and Figures from the Text

Boxes and figures from the text have been provided in high resolution format for downloading into presentation software or for use in assignments and exam material.

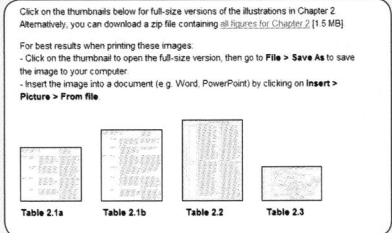

PART 1

Theoretical Approaches to Global Political Economy

The Study of Global Political Economy

John Ravenhill

1

 Reader's guide

The contemporary international economic system is more closely integrated than in any previous era. The recession of 2008–9 provides a clear illustration of the relationship between trade, finance, international institutions, and the difficulties that governments face in coping with the problems generated by complex interdependence.

Before 1945, the spectacular increase in economic integration that had occurred over the previous century was not accompanied by institutionalized governmental collaboration on economic matters. International trade patterns also changed very little over several centuries before 1945. The end of the Second World War marked a significant disjunction: global economic institutions were created, and the transnational corporation emerged as a major actor in international economic relations.

Since the emergence of international political economy (IPE) as a major subfield of the study of international relations in the early 1970s, IPE scholars have generated an enormous literature that has been the product of the employment of a wide variety of theories and methods. Most introductions to the study of IPE have divided the theoretical approaches to the subject into three categories: liberalism, nationalism, and Marxism. This threefold typology is of limited utility today, given the overlap between many of the approaches classified in different categories, and the wealth of theories and methodologies applied in the contemporary study of global political economy.

JOHN RAVENHILL

Prologue: The Great Recession of 2008–9

On 15 September 2008, the American financial services firm, Lehman Brothers, filed for bankruptcy, the largest single bankruptcy in United States history. The news triggered a massive sell-off of shares on Wall Street, the Dow Jones index shedding more than 500 points (4.4 per cent), the biggest fall since the terrorist attacks of September 11, 2001. The effects of the bankruptcy soon reverberated around the world, marking the start of what became known as the 'Great Recession'. In 2009, world output fell by 0.8 per cent, the first such fall since the 1930s; and world trade declined by more than 12 per cent. Inflows of **foreign direct investment (FDI)** fell by approximately 40 per cent in 2009.

The fall in global output masked substantial differences in national and regional performance: the industrialized economies were among the worst hit, with output in the European Union (EU) falling by 4 per cent and that in the United States by 3.2 per cent. Among the less developed economies, some of the worst affected were those such as Singapore and Taiwan which were most dependent on international trade. Although China and India continued to grow strongly (at 8.7 and 5.6 per cent, respectively), the 36 per cent decline in the price of oil, and the 19 per cent decline in the prices of non-fuel commodities in 2008, a repercussion of the drop in world manufacturing output, had a severe impact on many less developed economies. Output in Mexico slumped by nearly 7 per cent, in Brazil by 0.4 per cent, while that of Africa slowed from the 2008 figure of 5 per cent to under 2 per cent (all data from IMF 2010b: table 1.1). The dollar value of Africa's exports slumped by one-third in 2009 (Miller 2010).

The problems of Lehman Brothers stemmed in large part from its involvement in the sub-prime mortgage market. Lehman Brothers, like many other financial services firms, had become a substantial player in securitizing these mortgages (see Box 1.1).

Box 1.1 Sub-Prime Lending and Securitization

Loans characterized as 'sub-prime' are those that are regarded by the market as carrying a higher-than-usual element of risk. Typically, they have been contracted with borrowers who, for a variety of reasons that might include limited experience in borrowing, poor credit history, or low or unreliable income, are regarded as more likely than average to default on their loans.

To offset the increased risks of lending in the sub-prime market, financial institutions took advantage of the practice of securitization, which had initially developed in the 1970s. Before that period, providers of mortgage finance typically held the loans they had made until borrowers repaid them: in other words, they bore all the risk of the lending and typically financed the loans from their own resources. As the demand for mortgage finance rose, however, and lenders became increasingly concerned about risk, they developed the practice (often with the assistance of other financial institutions) of pooling the loans; the pool was then split into shares that were on-sold to investors as tradeable securities (bonds) that carried either a fixed or floating interest rate. The investors in the securities thereby assumed much of the risk attached to the loans. The practice of securitization spread from the United States to Europe in the late 1980s.

In the 1990s and the first decade of the current century, financial institutions developed ever more sophisticated means for pooling and on-selling loans. Individual securities were increasingly split into tranches, each of which carried a different level of risk: the higher tranches had the first claim on any income that the lender received; the lower tranches would be the first to absorb any losses. At the beginning of 2009, securitization accounted for approximately 28 per cent of outstanding credit in the United States: the figures for the UK and the euro zone were 14 and 6 per cent, respectively (IMF 2009b: box 1.2).

That problems which began in the home lending market in the United States could plunge the world into its worst recession since the 1930s, is powerful testimony to the integration of the contemporary global economy. Problems that began in the financial sector were quickly transmitted to the 'real' economy when banks curtailed their lending (and, in many instances, had to be bailed out by their governments): firms (and households) lacked the finance, not only to invest for the future, but even to conduct their daily operations. Finance for international trade dried up. The world economy quickly went into reverse. With the slowdown in production, the demand for and prices of raw materials fell substantially. Hit by falling prices for their exports and by a curtailment of inflows of public and private lending, output in many developing economies either went into reverse or declined below the rate of population growth. The World Bank estimated that the recession would increase the number of people living in poverty by 65 million (see Chapter 12 in this volume by Robert Hunter Wade), and further delay realization of the Millennium Development Goals (see Chapter 13 in this volume by Nicola Phillips).

The International Monetary Fund (IMF) (2009*b*: 5) suggested that the crisis-induced write-downs of bad loans by financial institutions will total around US$3.4 trillion (including $230 billion in mortgage lending in the US alone)—imposing a potentially massive burden on the public purse for the recapitalization of these institutions. Because governments had to issue bonds to cover the costs of bail-outs, risk was in effect transferred from private to public balance sheets. The bail-outs, coupled with the costs of the stimulus packages that most countries introduced to fight the recession, and with a steep reduction in tax revenues owing to the economic downturn, left public finances in most industrialized economies in a parlous state. The IMF anticipated that the average budget deficit in industrialized economies would be 10 per cent of **gross domestic product** (GDP) in 2009, and 8.5 per cent in 2010. As a consequence, the ratio of public debt to GDP was expected to jump by 40 percentage points to 115 per cent in 2014, the largest increase since the Second World War (IMF 2009*b*: box 1.3). The steep increase in sovereign debt threatened the credit ratings of some countries, particularly those in southern and eastern Europe, and left all governments with a challenge as to how to reconcile income and expenditure in the future.

On several key dimensions, the downturn precipitated by the recession in 2008 was sharper than that of the 1930s. In the first year of the recession, global output and global trade fell more rapidly than in the 1930s — by 13 per cent and 20 per cent, respectively. Similarly, global stock markets fell more precipitously — by 50 per cent in the first twelve months (compared with only slightly over 10 per cent in the 1930s) (Eichengreen and O'Rourke 2010). How the recession differed from the 1930s, however, was that at least the initial downturn was not so protracted — with recovery in global trade, output, and in stock markets beginning in the second half of 2009, this recovery in itself being a reflection of the effectiveness of concerted responses at the national and global levels (see below).

One reason for the severity of the recession that began in 2008 was that, unlike previous post-war downturns, all regions of the world were in economic decline simultaneously. The extent of the crisis provided evidence that, not just a quantitative increase in interdependence had occurred in recent years, but also a qualitative change. As the World Trade Organization (WTO) noted, the rapid spread of the recession worldwide was caused, in part, by the increasing presence of global supply chains in countries' trade (see Chapter 11 in this volume by Eric Thun). With components crossing national frontiers many times before a manufactured product reaches its final destination, a decline in the major global markets for finished products quickly affects trade — and then employment — in other parts of the world. Moreover, the extent of the recession, and the rapidity with which all regions of the world were affected, posed both practical and conceptual challenges for national and international governance. For the global financial institutions (the International Monetary Fund, the

World Bank), the cessation of private and public lending posed a severe challenge to their efforts to minimize the impact of the recession on developing economies (and exposes the inadequacies of their existing funding).

Few observers anticipated the recession (or, at least, the severity with which it would strike). The world economy had enjoyed a sustained long boom, continuing on an upward trajectory despite the bursting of the 'dot.com' bubble and the shock of the 2001 terrorist attacks. For students of global political economy, however, the possibility that the processes of globalization might be interrupted or even thrown into reverse should come as no surprise (see Chapter 9 by Anthony McGrew in this volume). The causes of the crisis are similar to those that have afflicted the world previously (albeit with some new twists, reflecting aspects of contemporary financial globalization).

The recession was triggered by the bursting of an asset price bubble—in this instance, the inflated US housing market. The term 'bubble' was coined in the United Kingdom in 1720, following the crash of the South Sea Company, and the passing in that year of the so-called 'Bubble Act'—more formally, 'An Act to Restrain the Extravagant and Unwarrantable Practice of Raising Money by Voluntary Subscription for Carrying on Projects Dangerous to the Trade and Subjects of the United Kingdom'. As in previous crises, the collapse of the bubble caused panic among investors, whose uncertainty over whether they could recoup their money caused them to flee the market (see Chapter 8 by Louis W. Pauly in this volume). Investor panic had significantly exacerbated the other major financial crisis to affect the global economy in the previous quarter of a century—that which afflicted East Asia in 1997/98 (Noble and Ravenhill 2000; Radelet and Sachs 2000). And, as with previous crashes, the bubble was associated with behaviour that was either outside the law or certainly contrary to its spirit—the 2,200-page report issued in March 2010 by Anton R. Valukas, an examiner appointed by the US Trustee to investigate the causes of the Lehman bankruptcy, for instance, found that Lehman had used accounting sleight of hand to conceal the extent of its bad loans (de la Merced and Sorkin 2010).

Globalization of finance did introduce some elements to the 2008–9 recession that had not been seen before. The growth of financial intermediation, of which an important aspect was the securitization of mortgage debt, had two important consequences. The first was that what began as a national problem (defaults on US mortgages) was quickly transformed into a global crisis. The new mortgage-backed financial instruments had been marketed globally by American and European investment banks—with the consequence that, once the bubble burst, various institutional investors, ranging from local councils in Australia and Norway to the London Metropolitan Police's pension fund, suffered significant losses. In a low-inflation environment, these investors had been attracted to financial instruments that offered potentially higher rates of return than those available on more familiar investments and, in doing so, had either discounted or not understood the risks involved.

The second consequence was that the complexity of the new financial instruments exacerbated the problem of panic because of the uncertainty created in transactions among financial institutions (for a detailed discussion of the new 'structured financial products' see IMF 2008: ch. 2). Financial institutions found it very difficult to determine exactly what their liabilities were. Once panic set in, they were reluctant to lend to one another—and, here, another dimension of financial globalization entered the equation: the increasing dependence of bank-lending on funds borrowed in the international wholesale market, rather than on their own deposits or capital. The extreme case was that of Iceland, where the country's banks had been the main source of its international debts, which were estimated in 2008 to amount to $276,622 for every resident. In 2008/9 alone, the three largest Icelandic banks had €11 billion of debt obligations maturing (Brogger 2008). When no new financing was forthcoming, the banks collapsed (although banks in Iceland staved off problems in the period between

2006 and 2008 by turning to the international retail market, offering savers in Europe online accounts with slightly higher rates than available from local institutions). The debts were so great that the private banks could not be bailed out by the country's central bank and the losses of the financial sector were expected to total $90 billion (Wade 2009*b*). Financial sector deregulation in Iceland had, in Robert Wade's words created an 'accident waiting to happen' (Wade 2009*b*: 14). The value of Iceland's currency measured against the euro more than halved during 2008. Iceland may have been the extreme case but similar instances of reckless behaviour by financial institutions were commonplace in Europe (especially the UK) and the United States (financial institutions in most other regions of the world had been more conservative in their approach, in part because of better regulatory frameworks introduced in response to crises in the 1980s and 1990s).

The recession undermined triumphalist notions that governments had learned to master the factors driving business or economic cycles more generally, or that unregulated markets would generate optimal outcomes. A striking feature of the early governmental response to the recession was the

acknowledgement of the inadequacies of previous policy approaches, particularly in the area of financial sector regulation ('Major failures in the financial sector and in financial regulation and supervision were fundamental causes of the crisis', admitted the Group of Twenty (G20) leaders in the communiqué from their London summit (G20 2009*a*: para. 13)). How significant a shift in regulatory frameworks, either nationally or internationally, will be introduced remains unclear. At the time of writing, in early 2010, lobbyists for the financial sector, particularly in the United States, were fighting hard against any intrusive government action.

The recession prompted unprecedented policy interventions at the national and global levels, and produced significant changes in global governance—with the emergence of the G20 as the principal intergovernmental body for global economic management (Box 1.2). The crisis also saw the revitalization of the International Monetary Fund when the G20 agreed to make an additional $850 billion available to the international financial institutions (IFIs) and to endorse a more flexible response from the Fund to countries experiencing financial problems (see Chapter 7 by Eric Helleiner in this volume).

Box 1.2 The G20

The Group of Twenty (G20) Finance Ministers and Central Bank Governors was established in 1999, following the financial crises that had primarily afflicted East Asia but had also spread to other developing economies, to bring together systemically important industrialized and developing economies to discuss key issues in the global economy. The inaugural meeting of the G20 took place in Berlin, on December 15–16, 1999.

The membership of the G20 comprises finance ministers and central bank governors of Argentina, Australia, Brazil, Canada, China, France, Germany, India, Indonesia, Italy, Japan, Mexico, Russia, Saudi Arabia, South Africa, Republic of Korea, Turkey, the United Kingdom, and the United States. The European Union, represented by the rotating Council Presidency and by the European Central Bank, is the twentieth member of the G20. To

facilitate policy co-ordination with the global financial institutions, the Managing Director of the International Monetary Fund and the President of the World Bank, plus the chairs of the International Monetary and Financial Committee and Development Committee of the IMF and World Bank, also participate in G20 meetings on an *ex officio* basis.

The G20 remained a relatively low-profile and low-key grouping until the 2008 recession, when an inaugural meeting of the political leaders of the G20 was held in Washington, DC in November. The elevation of the G20 was recognition on the part of the leaders of the principal industrialized economies that their own grouping (the Group of Eight (G8)—see below) was not sufficiently representative to effectively manage the problems of an increasingly globalized economy. In particular, it was acknowledgement of the growing importance of the major developing economies—especially China, India, and Brazil. At their meeting in Pittsburgh in September 2009, the G20 leaders formalized the status of the grouping by designating 'the G20 to be the premier forum for our international economic cooperation' (G20 2009*b*: para. 19).

The Group of Seven (G7) industrialized countries was established in 1975, the first of a series of annual meetings where politicians and officials from the world's leading economies discussed issues relating to macroeconomic policy co-ordination, trade, and financial policies, and relations with developing countries.

Six countries were present at the initial meeting in Rambouillet in France: Britain, France, (West) Germany, Italy, Japan, and the United States. Canada joined the group in 1976, at its second meeting. In 1977, the group allowed participation by a representative of the European Community. From 1994 onwards, the G7 met with representatives of Russia at each of its meetings; at the Birmingham meeting in 1998, Russia was accorded full membership, transforming the G7 into the G8. The G8 continues to exist alongside the G20.

For more details on the G20, see www.g20.org/; for the G7/G8, see www.g7.utoronto.ca/

At the national level, most G20 economies implemented stimulus packages that the IMF estimated were equivalent to 1.5 per cent of their GDP in 2009 and 1.25 per cent in 2010. Half of the G20 countries cut personal income taxes; a third cut indirect taxes such as value added taxes and excise duties. Three-quarters of the G20 members increased government expenditures on infrastructure, primarily on transportation networks (IMF 2009*a*: 18). Many also increased expenditures on programmes for the most vulnerable. The concerted international response was testimony to how the governance of the global economy had changed since the great depression of the 1930s. And although governments implemented measures designed to stimulate local industries, the widespread resort to beggar-thy-neighbour protectionist policies that characterized the 1930s was avoided. A report for the G20 estimated that protectionist measures introduced after the onset of the recession affected less than half of 1 per cent of global trade (OECD (Organisation for Economic Co-operation and Development), WTO, and UN (United Nations) 2010: 7).

For some observers, however, particularly those in Europe and the United States, the global recession did reflect one dimension of beggar-thy-neighbour policies that were at least as important in contributing to the recession as were regulatory failures: the mounting imbalances in international trade and payments, which they attributed primarily to

China's determination to avoid a rapid appreciation of its currency against the US dollar. One of the missions with which the G20 has tasked the IMF is to analyse 'whether policies pursued by individual G20 countries are collectively consistent with more sustainable and balanced trajectories for the global economy' (G20 2009*b*: para. 7), a co-ordinating role that the IMF has singularly failed to perform since its foundation.

The recession of 2008–9 and the responses of the international community to it provide an excellent illustration of many of the themes of this book:

- the growing interdependence of countries in a globalizing economy;
- the vulnerability of the contemporary global financial system to periodic crises;
- the speed with which developments in one part of the world economy are transmitted to others;
- the increased significance of private actors in the contemporary global economy, especially in the financial sector;
- the way in which crises prompt governments to seek collaboration to regulate international markets—but concurrently the difficulties that states have in co-ordinating their behaviours to take effective action;
- the significant and evolving role of international institutions in responding to crises; and

- the manner in which the increased severity of financial crises has had an impact on poverty and inequality.

Although, as will become evident in later chapters, contributors to this book hold a variety of perspectives on the question of whether there is such a thing as a 'global' economy, all would accept that we live in a *globalizing* economy that differs in some fundamental ways from anything that the world has previously experienced. The following section briefly sketches how the world economy evolved to reach its present state.

The World Economy Pre-1914

The 'modern world economy', most historians agree, came into existence in the late fifteenth and sixteenth centuries. This was a period in which despotic monarchs in Western Europe, seeking to consolidate their power against both internal and external foes, pushed to extend the boundaries of markets. In this era of mercantilism, political power was equated with wealth, and wealth with power (Viner 1948). Wealth, in the form of bullion generated by trade surpluses or seized from enemies, enabled monarchs to build the administrative apparatus of their states and to finance the construction of military forces. The new concentration of military power could be projected, both internally and externally, to extract further resources. The consolidation of the state went hand in hand with the extension of markets. Gradually, most parts of the world were enmeshed in a Eurocentric economy, as suppliers of raw materials and 'luxury' goods. Britain adopted domestic reforms largely pioneered by the Netherlands (which had the world's highest per capita income in the seventeenth and eighteenth centuries) to supplant the Dutch in many world markets: armed conflict and the use of the Navigation Acts (1651–1849), which restricted the use of foreign vessels in British trade, enabled it to monopolize trade with its ever-expanding empire.

The era of mercantilism did not, however, bring a notable increase in overall global wealth. Before 1820, per capita incomes in most parts of the world were not significantly different from those of the previous eight *centuries* (they increased by less than an average of one-tenth of 1 per cent each year between 1700 and 1820). And despite the striking extension of the global market during the seventeenth and eighteenth centuries, the vast majority of commerce continued to be conducted within individual localities until the advent of the Industrial Revolution. The introduction of steam power revolutionized transportation, both internally and internationally. And in the second half of the nineteenth century, further technological advances — the introduction of refrigerated ships, the laying of submarine telegraph cables — contributed to a 'shrinking' of the world and to a deepening of the international division of labour. The value of world exports grew tenfold (from a relatively small base) between 1820 and 1870: from 1870 to 1913, world exports grew at an annual average rate of 3.4 per cent, substantially above the 2.1 annual increase in world GDP (Maddison 2001: 262, table B–19, and 362, table F–4).

Trade was becoming increasingly important to world welfare, yet the pattern of international commerce in 1913 — indeed, even in 1945 — was not dramatically different from that of the eighteenth century. The industrialized countries of the world — essentially a Western European core to which had been added the United States and Japan by the turn of the twentieth century — exported principally manufactured goods, while the rest of the world supplied agricultural products and raw materials to feed the industrialized countries' workforces and to fuel their manufacturing plants (as a relative latecomer to industrialization, and an economy with significant comparative advantage in agricultural production, the United States was an exception to this generalization: cotton remained the single most important export for the United States in 1913, contributing nearly twice the value of exports of machinery and iron and steel combined; it was not until 1930 that machinery exports exceeded those of cotton, although by 1910 the US had become a net exporter of manufactured goods (data from Mitchell 1993: 504, table E3; and Irwin 2003)).

With the exception of the United States, trade among the industrialized countries in manufactured goods remained relatively unimportant. In 1913, for example, agricultural products and other primary products constituted two-thirds of the total imports of the United Kingdom. To be sure, some changes had occurred in the composition of imports. Although the 'luxury' imports of the previous centuries—sugar, tea, coffee, and tobacco—had become staples in the diet of the new urban working and middle classes, their aggregate importance in European imports had shrunk relative to other commodities, notably wheat and flour, butter and vegetable oils, and meat (Offer 1989: 82, table 6.1).

For the early European industrializers, trade with their colonies, dominions, or with the other lands of recent European settlement, such as Argentina, was more important than trade with other industrialized countries. For the United Kingdom, a larger share of imports was contributed by Argentina, Australia, Canada, and India together than by the United States, despite the latter's importance in British imports of cotton for its burgeoning textiles industry. These four countries also took five times the American share of British exports in 1913 (Mitchell 1992: 644, table E2). Similarly, Algeria was a larger market for French exports in 1913 than was the United States.

Tariffs continued to constitute a significant barrier to international trade, even in what is often termed the 'golden age' of liberalism before 1914. Most industrialized countries (the significant exceptions being the United Kingdom and the Netherlands) had actually raised the level of their tariffs in the last three decades of the nineteenth century

to protect their domestic producers against the increasing import competition that had been facilitated by lower transport costs. In 1913, the average tariff level in Germany and Japan was 12 per cent, in France 16 per cent, and in the United States 32.5 per cent (Maddison 1989: 47, table 4.4). The post-1870 increase in tariffs offset some of the gains from lower transportation costs. Lindert and Williamson (2001) estimate that nearly three-quarters of the closer integration of markets that occurred in the century before the outbreak of the First World War is attributable to these lower transport costs (see Table 9.3 in McGrew, Chapter 9 in this volume).

Governments continued to erect barriers to the movement of goods in the second part of the nineteenth century, but capital and people moved relatively freely across the globe, their mobility facilitated by developments in transportation and communication. From 1820 to 1913, 26 million people migrated from Europe to the United States, Canada, Australia, New Zealand, Argentina, and Brazil. Five million Indians followed the British flag in migrating to Burma, Malaya, Sri Lanka, and Africa, while an even larger number of Chinese are estimated to have migrated to other countries on the Western Pacific rim (Maddison 2001: 98). The opening up of the lands of 'new settlement' required massive capital investments—in railways in particular. By 1913, the United Kingdom, France, and Germany had investments abroad totalling over $33 billion: after the 1870s, Britain invested more than half its savings abroad, and the income from its foreign investments in 1913 was equivalent to almost 10 per cent of all the goods and services produced domestically (Maddison 2001: 100).

The spectacular growth in international economic integration was not accompanied by any significant institutionalization of intergovernmental collaboration. Even though the Anglo-French Cobden–Chevalier Treaty of 1860 had introduced the principle of most-favoured nation status (MFN) into international trade agreements (see Box 1.3), governments conducted trade negotiations on a bilateral basis rather than under the auspices of an international institution.

Box 1.3 Most-Favoured Nation Status (MFN)

Under the most-favoured nation (MFN) principle, a government is obliged to grant to any trading partner with which it has signed an agreement treatment equivalent to the best ('most preferred') it offers to any of its partners. For example, if France had a trade treaty with Germany in which it had reduced its tariffs on imports of German steel to 8 per cent, it would be obliged, under the most-favoured nation principle, if it signed a trade treaty with the United States, to reduce its tariffs on imports of US steel also to 8 per cent. The MFN principle is the foundation for non-discrimination in international trade, and is often asserted to be the 'cornerstone' of the post-1945 trade regime (see Winham, Chapter 5 in this volume). The MFN principle makes a significant contribution to depoliticizing trade relations because: (*a*) countries are obliged to give equivalent treatment to all trading partners, regardless of their economic power; and (*b*) countries cannot discriminate in their treatment of the trade of certain partners simply because they do not like the political complexion or policies of the governments of these countries.

The international financial system was similarly characterized by a lack of institutionalization. The rapid growth of economic integration was facilitated by the international adoption of the gold standard (see Box 1.4). The origins of the nineteenth-century gold standard lay in action by the Bank of England in 1821 to make all its notes convertible into gold (although Britain had operated a de facto gold standard from as early as 1717). The United States, though formally on a bimetallic (gold and silver) standard, switched to a de facto gold standard in 1834 and turned this into a de jure arrangement in 1900. Germany and other industrializing economies followed suit in the 1870s. Because every country fixed the value of its national currency in terms of gold, each currency had a fixed exchange rate against every other in the system (assume, for example, that the United States sets the value of its currency as $100 per ounce of gold, while the United Kingdom sets its value at £50 per ounce of gold: the exchange rate between the two currencies would be £1 = $2).

Box 1.4 The Gold Standard

A gold standard requires a country to fix the price of its domestic currency in terms of a specific amount of gold. National money (which may or may not consist of gold coins, because other metallic coins and banknotes were also used in some countries) and bank deposits would be freely convertible into gold at the specified price.

Under the gold standard, because the level of each country's economic activity is determined by its money supply, which in turn rested on its gold holdings, a disequilibrium in its balance of trade in principle would be self-correcting. Let us assume, for example, that Britain is running a trade deficit with the United States because inflation in Britain has made its exports relatively unattractive to US consumers. Because British exports do not cover the full costs of imports from the United States, British authorities would have to transfer gold to the US Treasury. This transfer would reduce the money supply,

and hence the level of economic activity in Britain, having a deflationary effect on the domestic economy, and depress its demand for imports. In the United States, the opposite would occur: an inflow of gold would boost the money supply, thereby generating additional economic activity in the United States and increasing inflationary pressures there. Higher levels of economic activity would increase the country's demand for imports. Changes in the money supplies in the two countries brought about by the transfer of gold, therefore, would bring their demand for goods back into balance and lead to a restoration of the ratio of the two countries' prices to that reflected in the exchange rate between their currencies.

In principle, the gold standard should act to restore equilibrium automatically in international payments. Central banks, however, were also expected to facilitate adjustment by raising their interest rates when countries were suffering a payments deficit (thereby further dampening domestic economic activities and making domestic investments more attractive to foreigners) and, conversely, to lower interest rates when their economies were experiencing a payments surplus. For most of the period from 1870 to 1914, the Bank of England played by the rules of the game fairly consistently. Other central banks—including those of France and Belgium—did not. They frequently intervened to attempt to shield the domestic economy from the effects of gold flows (to 'sterilize' their effects) by buying or selling securities (thereby reducing or increasing the volume of gold circulating in the domestic economy).

The gold standard was vulnerable to shocks, which were often transmitted quickly from one country to another. The discovery of gold in California in 1848, for example, led to an increase in the US money supply, domestic inflation, and an outflow of gold to its trade partners, which in turn raised their domestic price levels. Countries on the periphery were particularly vulnerable to shocks: interest-rate increases in the industrialized countries, for example, often drew capital from the periphery, leaving the peripheral countries with the major burden of adjustment.

For further discussion, see Eichengreen (1985) and Officer (2001).

The great contribution of the gold standard to facilitating international commerce was that economic agents generally did not have to worry about foreign exchange risks: the possibility that the value of the currency of a foreign country would change vis-à-vis their domestic currency and thus, for example, reduce the value of their foreign investments. British investors in American railways could be confident that the dollars they had bought with their sterling investments would buy the same amount of sterling at the date their investment matured, and that the US Treasury would convert the dollars back into gold at this time. Meanwhile, they received interest on the sums invested. Confidence in the gold standard did not rest on any international institution but rather on the commitment of individual governments to maintain the opportunity for individuals to convert their domestic currencies into gold at a fixed exchange rate. Ultimately, the implementation of the gold standard rested on the assumption that governments had both the capacity and the will to impose economic pain on their domestic populations when deflation was needed in order to bring their economy back into equilibrium. These domestic costs became less acceptable with the rise of working-class political representation, and with the growth of expectations that a fundamental responsibility of governments was to ensure domestic full employment.

Key points

- The modern world economy came into existence in the fifteenth and sixteenth centuries.
- Despite the significant changes that occurred in the three centuries before the outbreak of the First World War, the fundamental composition and direction of international trade remained unchanged.
- Neither in the field of trade nor of finance was any significant international institution constructed in the years before 1914.

- Advances in technology were the main driving force behind the integration of markets, and they facilitated the enormous growth in investment and migration in the nineteenth century.
- The great merit of the gold standard was that it provided certainty for international transactions because it largely removed the risk of foreign exchange losses.

The outbreak of the First World War was a devastating blow to cosmopolitan liberalism: it destroyed the credibility of the liberal argument that economic interdependence in itself would be sufficient to foster an era of peaceful coexistence among states. The war brought to an end an era of unprecedented economic interdependence among the leading industrial countries. As discussed in the chapters by McGrew and Hay in this book, for many industrialized economies, indicators of economic openness and interdependence did not regain their pre-First World War levels until the 1970s.

The war devastated the economies of Europe: subsequent political instability compounded economic disruptions. Economic reconstruction was further complicated by demands that Germany make reparations for its aggression, and that Britain and other European countries repay their wartime borrowings from the United States. The economic chaos of the inter-war years was a sorry reflection of the inability of governments to agree on measures to restore economic stability, and their resort to beggar-thy-neighbour policies in their efforts to alleviate domestic economic distress. Although the collapse of international trade in the 1930s is the feature of the inter-war economy that figures most prominently in stories of this era, the most fundamental problem of the period was the inability of states to construct a viable international financial system.

The international gold standard broke down with the outbreak of war in August 1914, when a speculative attack on sterling caused the Bank of England to impose exchange controls—a refusal to convert sterling into gold and a de facto ban on gold exports. Other countries followed suit. Leading countries agreed to reinstate a modified version of the international gold standard in 1925. They failed to act consistently, however, in re-establishing the link between national currencies and gold. The United Kingdom restored the convertibility of sterling at the pre-war gold price, despite the domestic inflation that had occurred in the intervening decade. The consequence was that sterling was generally reckoned to be overvalued by at least 10 per cent, making British exports uncompetitive. It proved very difficult for the British government to establish an equilibrium in its balance of payments without imposing severe deflation domestically. Other countries—notably France, Belgium, and Italy—restored convertibility of their currencies at a much lower price of gold than had prevailed before 1914.

The resulting misalignment of currencies was compounded by higher trade barriers than had existed before 1914, the absence of a country/central bank with the resources and the will to provide leadership to the system, and by a failure of central banks to play by the 'rules of the game' of the gold standard. Their inclination to intervene to 'sterilize' the domestic impact of international gold flows was symptomatic of a more fundamental underlying problem: in an era when the working class had been fully enfranchised, when trade unions had become important players in political systems, especially in Western Europe, and when governments were expected to take responsibility for maintaining full employment and promoting domestic economic welfare, the subordination of the domestic economy to the dictates of global markets in the form of the international gold standard was no longer politically acceptable. Polanyi (1944) is the classic statement of this argument; on the misguided attempts by Britain to restore the convertibility of sterling at pre-1914 levels, see Keynes (1925).

The abandonment of the international gold standard followed another speculative attack on sterling in the middle of 1931. The Bank of England lost much of its reserves in July and August of that year, and Britain abandoned the gold standard in September, a move that precipitated a sharp depreciation of the pound (testimony to its over-valuation in the brief period in which the gold standard was restored). Other countries again quickly followed in breaking the link between their currencies and gold. By then, the world economy was in depression, following the shocks to the world economy transmitted from the United States after the Wall Street collapse of October 1929. The gold standard almost certainly exacerbated the effects of the depression, because government efforts to maintain the link between their currencies and gold constrained the use of expansionary (inflationary) policies to combat unemployment and low levels of domestic demand (Eichengreen 1992).

The world economy was already in depression before the US Congress, in response to concerns about the intensification of import competition for domestic farmers, passed the Smoot–Hawley Tariff of 1930. This raised US tariffs to historically high levels (an average *ad valorem* tariff of 41 per cent, although tariff rates were already very high as a result of the Tariff Act of 1922, the Fordney–McCumber Tariff). Retaliation from US trading partners quickly followed, with the European countries giving preferential tariff treatment to their colonies. The value of world trade declined by two-thirds between 1929 and 1934, and became increasingly concentrated in closed imperial blocks.

As in the pre-1914 period, international institutions played no significant role in the governance of international economic matters. The League of Nations had established an Economic and Financial Organization with subcommittees on the various areas of international economic relations. It enjoyed success in the early 1920s in co-ordinating a financial reconstruction package of £26 million for Austria. It also held various conferences aimed at facilitating trade by promoting common standards on customs procedures, compilation of economic statistics, and so on. But the economic and political disarray of the inter-war period simply overwhelmed the League's limited resources and legitimacy: the move to restore international economic collaboration awaited effective action by the world's leading economy, the United States. This began with the passage by Congress in 1934 of the Reciprocal Trade Agreements Act (RTAA), which gave the president the authority to negotiate foreign trade agreements (without Congressional approval). The RTAA and the subsequent signature before 1939 of trade agreements with twenty of America's trading partners laid the foundations for the multilateral system that emerged after the Second World War (the reasons why US trade policy changed so dramatically between 1930 and 1934 have been a focus of significant recent work in international political economy; see Hiscox 1999; Irwin and Kroszner 1997).

Key points

- Misalignment of exchange rates contributed to the problems of economic adjustment in the 1920s.
- The world economy was already in recession before tariffs were raised in the early 1930s—but higher tariffs exacerbated the decline in international trade.
- States did not negotiate any significant institutionalization of international economic relations in the inter-war period.

The world economy that emerged after the Second World War was qualitatively different from anything experienced before. John Ruggie, a leading contemporary theorist of political economy, has identified two fundamental principles that distinguish the post-war economy from its predecessors: the adoption of what Ruggie (1982), following Polanyi (1944), terms **embedded liberalism**, and a commitment to **multilateralism** (Ruggie 1992).

Embedded liberalism refers to the compromise that governments made after 1945 between safeguarding their domestic economic objectives, especially a commitment to maintaining full employment on the one hand, and an opening up of the domestic economy to allow for the restoration of international trade and investment on the other. The 'embedding' of the commitment to economic openness—the liberal element—within domestic economic and political objectives was attained through the inclusion of provisions in the rules of international trade and finance that would allow governments to opt out, on a temporary basis, from their international commitments should these threaten fundamental domestic economic objectives. Moreover, an acknowledgement of the legitimacy of the principle that governments should give priority to the pursuit of domestic economic objectives was also written into the rules of the game. The adoption of the principle of embedded liberalism was a recognition by governments that international economic collaboration rested on their capacity to maintain domestic political consensus—and that international economic collaboration was, fundamentally, a political bargain. This recognition explains, for example, why the agricultural sector was for many years excluded from trade liberalization: the domestic political costs for governments of negotiating freer trade in agricultural products were judged to be so high as to jeopardize otherwise politically feasible trade liberalization in other sectors.

The institutionalization of international economic co-operation is another fundamental change in international economic relations in the post-war period. Neither in the period of relative stability of the pre-First World War gold standard era nor in the chaos of the 1930s did leading economies create significant international economic institutions. A commitment to multilateralism is one of the defining characteristics of the post-1945 order. For Ruggie (1992: 571), multilateralism is not merely a matter of numbers—it involves collaboration among three or more states, not necessarily all members of the system—but it also has a *qualitative* element in that the co-ordination of relations is on 'the basis of "generalized" principles of conduct—that is, principles which specify appropriate conduct for a class of actions, without regard to the particularistic interests of the parties or the strategic exigencies that may exist in any specific occurrence'. A classic example is the most-favoured nation principle, with its requirement that products from all trading partners must be treated in the same manner regardless of the characteristics of the countries involved. This principle for the conduct of trade contrasts, for example, with the largely bilateral trade agreements of the inter-war years, where governments, rather than applying a generalized principle to their trade relations, discriminated in their treatment of individual trading partners.

The commitment to multilateralism that developed in the late 1930s and during the Second World War bore immediate fruit in the founding of the **Bretton Woods** multilateral financial institutions: the International Monetary Fund and the World Bank (see Box 1.5). Note, however, that these global or universal institutions, membership of which is open to all states in the international system, are just one form of multilateralism. For the whole of the period since 1945, but especially since the mid 1990s, regional institutions have also played an important role in international economic (as well as security) affairs (see Ravenhill, Chapter 6 in this volume). States have increasingly enmeshed themselves in a dense web of multilateral institutions.

Box 1.5 Bretton Woods

In 1944, the Western allies brought together their principal economic advisers for a conference at the Mount Washington Hotel in the village of Bretton Woods, New Hampshire, to chart the future of the international economy in the post-war period. The forty-four governments represented at what was officially known as the United Nations Monetary and Financial Conference agreed on the principles that would govern international finance in the post-war years, and to create two major international institutions to assist in the management of these arrangements: the International Monetary Fund; and the World Bank (formally known as the International Bank for Reconstruction and Development). For details of the discussions at the conference see van Dormael (1978) (excerpted at www.imfsite.org/origins/confer.html; see also www.yale.edu/lawweb/avalon/decade/decad047.htm).

These institutions and the rules for managing international finance that were agreed became known collectively as the Bretton Woods regimes. In 1947, a United Nations Conference on Trade and Employment in Havana, Cuba, drew up a charter (www.globefield.com/havana.htm) for an International Trade Organization (ITO), to complement the Bretton Woods financial institutions. The ITO never came to fruition, however—see Winham, Chapter 5 in this volume.

The unprecedented rates of economic growth achieved in the years after 1945 attest to the success of the pursuit of multilateral economic collaboration in this period. Global GDP grew at close to 5 per cent in the period 1950–73. Although the recessions that followed the oil price rises of 1973–4 and 1979–80, and the debt crises that afflicted Latin America and Africa, contributed to a slowing of growth in the quarter-century after 1973, world GDP nonetheless grew at an average of 3 per cent per annum, a faster rate than during any period before 1945 (Maddison 2001: 262, table 8–19). Moreover, world trade grew more rapidly than world production: world exports expanded by close to 8 per cent per annum in the years 1950–73, and by 5 per cent annually in the subsequent twenty-five-year period (Maddison 2001: 362, table F–4). The internationalized sector consequently grew in importance in most economies, with important implications for the balance of domestic political interests on trade policy issues (see Hiscox, Chapter 4 in this volume).

Aggregate rates of growth, however, disguised substantial variations across different regions of the world economy. The gap between rich and poor widened substantially (see Figure 1.1). In 1500, little difference had existed in per capita incomes across various regions of the world. Incomes per head in the United States did not exceed those of China until the second quarter of the eighteenth century. By the third quarter of the nineteenth century, however, a marked gap had developed between incomes per capita in the United States and Western Europe on the one hand, and those of the rest of the world. Per capita incomes in Africa and in most parts of Asia stagnated (and in China actually regressed for a century). Despite the economic turmoil and slower rates of growth of the inter-war years, the absolute gap between the industrialized economies and the rest of the world continued to widen: the divergence increased rapidly in the post-1945 era. Only a handful of previously less developed countries (LDCs), mostly in East Asia, made significant progress in closing the gap. Africa, meanwhile, became increasingly detached from the globalizing economy: its exports, measured in constant prices, barely expanded in the years between 1973 and 1990. The poor export performance contributed to falls in per capita income that occurred in the majority of years between 1973 and 1998. By the latter date, the average per capita income in Africa was no more than Western Europe had experienced in 1820 (all data drawn from Maddison 2001). Growing international inequality has been a fundamental part of the modern globalizing economy (see Wade, Chapter 12 in this volume).

Another defining characteristic of the post-1945 international economy was the growth in the number of transnational corporations (TNCs) (also referred to in some chapters of this volume as multinational enterprises). A growth of significant private economic enterprises with international operations had accompanied the emergence of the modern world economy in the fifteenth century. These, however, were primarily trading companies, such as the East India Company, specializing in moving goods between national markets. And when foreign investment took off in earnest, in the half-century before the First World War, the vast majority of it was portfolio investment—that is, investment in bonds and other financial instruments that did not give investors management control over the borrowing company. Companies that engaged in foreign direct investment—that is, the ownership and management of assets in more than one country for the purposes of production of goods or services (the definition of a TNC)—were relative rarities before 1945 (with some notable exceptions, such as the major oil companies and IBM). In the post-Second World War years, FDI took off, and has grown more rapidly than either production or international trade (see Thun, Chapter 11 in this volume).

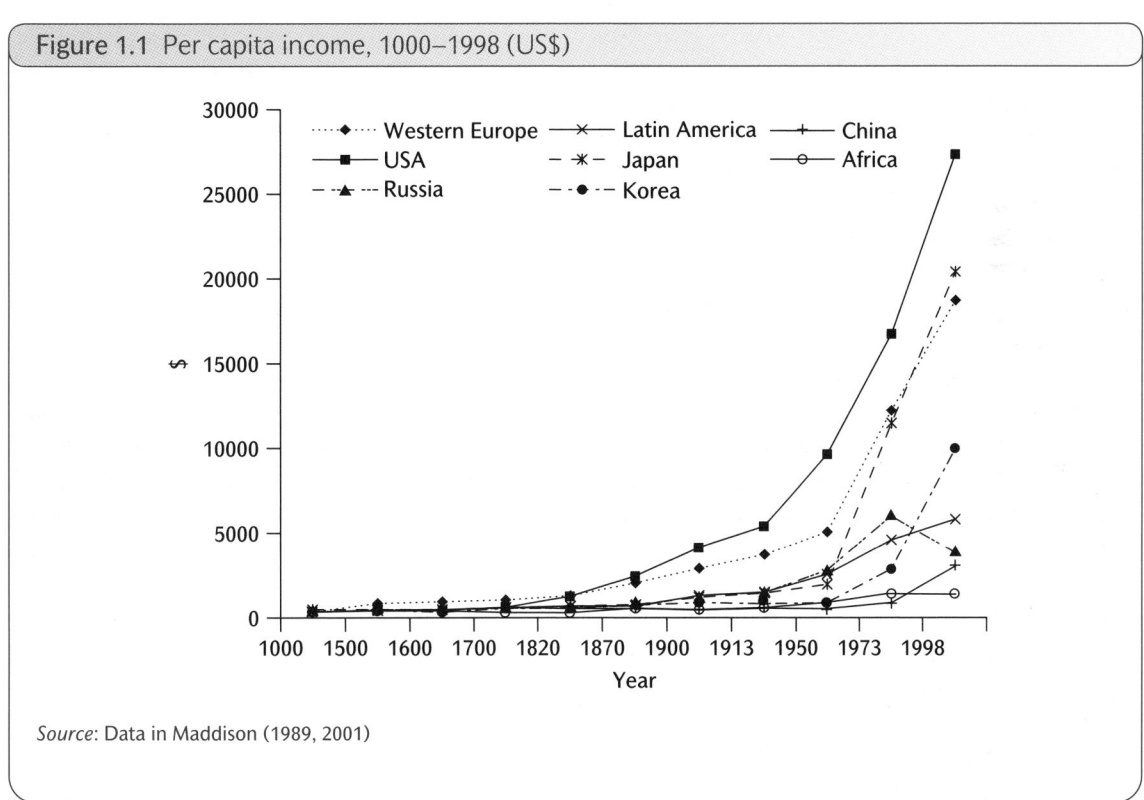

Figure 1.1 Per capita income, 1000–1998 (US$)

Source: Data in Maddison (1989, 2001)

The TNC has become the key actor in the globalizing economy. By 2009, it was estimated that there were 82,000 TNCs in operation, controlling more than 810,000 subsidiaries worldwide. The global stock of FDI amounted to about $15 trillion, and the value added by TNC subsidiaries was equal to about 10 per cent of the world's GDP. Moreover, sales by the subsidiaries of TNCs were nearly double the total value of world trade: an estimated $32 trillion compared to a figure of $17 trillion for all world exports (all data from UNCTAD 2009*b*: 18). Whereas in the period before 1960, the vast majority of FDI and TNCs came from the United States, in subsequent years the American presence has been supplemented by corporations with their headquarters in Europe, Japan, Korea, and, increasingly, in less developed countries such as Brazil, China, and India (for further discussion, see Dicken 2003).

The activities of TNCs, in turn, have transformed the nature of international trade fundamentally. In particular, the composition of trade has changed dramatically since 1945. Whereas in the inter-war years the composition of trade differed little from that of the previous centuries—that is, it was based on the exchange of raw materials and agricultural products for manufactured goods, since the post-war reconstruction of Europe and Japan, the principal component of trade has been the international exchange of manufactured goods. At first, this trade was primarily among the industrialized countries. In many instances, it involved intra-industry trade, that is, the international exchange of products from the same industry. For example, intra-industry trade occurs when Sweden exports Volvo cars to Germany and imports BMW vehicles from Germany. As this example suggests, product differentiation by brand name often provides the basis for intra-industry trade, and bears little resemblance to the comparative advantage-based explanation for trade that underlies conventional economic theory. This change in the composition of world trade has been associated with the growing role of TNCs. They now account for two-thirds of global trade: trade among the various subsidiaries of TNCs—that is, trade within the same firm—constitutes fully a third of all world trade.

Since the 1980s, in particular, less developed countries have also been integrated into the international production networks led by TNCs (see Thun, Chapter 11 in this volume). An increasing number of developing countries have changed the structure of their tariffs to give preference to the processing and assembling of components that are subsequently exported. The World Trade Organization estimates that such processing activities account for more than 80 per cent of the exports of the Dominican Republic, close to 60 per cent of the exports of China, and nearly 50 per cent of the exports of Mexico (WTO 2000*a*). This participation in global production networks is the most significant factor in a dramatic change in the commodity composition of the exports of less developing countries. Contrary to some popular impressions, by the end of the 1990s, manufactured exports constituted 70 per cent of the total exports from the developing world. The share of manufactures in their exports had increased threefold since the end of the 1970s (UNCTAD 2001: xviii).

Reference to these less developed economies provides a timely reminder of another dramatic change in international economic relations since 1945—a huge augmentation in the number of independent states in the system. As noted in Box 1.5, only forty-four countries were represented at the Bretton Woods conference, which was dominated by the industrialized countries of Europe and North America, but also included a few of the long-independent countries of Central and South America. Within two decades, almost all of the colonies of the European countries had gained their independence. This development had profound implications for the international system. One was simply the consequence of an increase in both the number of states and in the diversity of the international community: the number of states in the system more than doubled. Collaboration in international economic relations and the management of various dimensions of this collaboration became increasingly complex, illustrated very clearly in the trade sphere by the difficulties in negotiating the Uruguay and Doha Rounds of WTO talks (see Winham, Chapter 5 in this volume, for details of these discussions; and Aggarwal and Dupont, Chapter 3, for a discussion of the problems that larger numbers pose for collaboration). The growth in the number of less developed countries also brought institutional change, most notably in the foundation of the United Nations Conference on Trade and Development (UNCTAD) in 1964. And the new arithmetic in the international system generally, and particularly within the United Nations system, contributed to a change in international norms with the adoption, first, of decolonization (Jackson 1993), and then of development as core norms of the modern system.

Another defining characteristic of the contemporary system contributed to the enshrining of the development norm—the vast expansion in the number of non-governmental organizations (NGOs), many of which were focused on the alleviation of poverty (for further discussion of this topic, see the chapters in this volume by Wade and Phillips). NGOs have also been prominent in global environmental affairs (see Dauvergne, Chapter 14 in this volume). Relations between industrialized and less developed countries, and issues relating to global poverty and inequality, emerged as an important dimension of the study of international political economy, the evolution of which is discussed in the next section of this chapter.

Key points

The post-war international economy was qualitatively different from anything that preceded it, on several dimensions:

- states made a commitment to multilateralism, reflected in the construction of institutions at the global and regional levels;
- the world economy grew at unprecedented rates after 1945—the internationalized component of economies became more significant as trade and

foreign investment grew more rapidly than production;

- TNCs and foreign direct investment (FDI) emerged as key agents in the process of internationalization;
- the composition and direction of international trade changed dramatically, with intra-industry trade among industrialized economies constituting the vast majority of aggregate world trade; and
- the number of countries in the international system rose substantially.

The Study of Global Political Economy

The emergence of international political economy as a distinct subfield

International political economy (IPE) developed as a significant subfield in the study of international

relations in the 1970s. As has so often been the case in political science, the emergence of a new subject area was a response both to real world changes and to trends in theorizing within and outside the discipline (see Box 1.6).

When IPE emerged as a major focus for students of international relations, it inherited the rather misleading adjective 'international' as the leading word in its title. Commentators have often pointed out that 'international' relations is a misnomer for its subject matter in that it confuses 'nation' with 'state', and fails to acknowledge the significance of private actors in global politics. But labels, like institutions, are often 'sticky'—once adopted, it is difficult to displace them, even if a better alternative is available. The abbreviation, IPE, has become synonymous with the field of study. Even though we prefer 'global political economy' for the title of the book because it reflects more accurately the contemporary subject matter of this field, many of the contributors follow conventional usage in employing the abbreviation IPE and in referring to 'international' political economy.

While the study of international political economy achieved a new prominence in the 1970s, a variety of work in what would now be recognized as the field of IPE was published much earlier than this. A prominent example is Albert Hirschman's (1945) study of Germany's economic relations with its East European neighbours. Much of the work in the field of development economics that blossomed in the post-war period included significant political and international components. And the Marxist tradition of political economy remained vibrant, particularly in Europe.

To confuse matters, the study of economics was known in the eighteenth and nineteenth centuries as political economy (see, for example, John Stuart Mill's (1970), *Principles of Political Economy*). The titles of some leading journals in the field of economics—for example, the *Journal of Political Economy*, first published in 1892—reflect this older usage.

In the early 1970s, the global economy entered a period of turbulence following an unprecedented period of stable economic growth. The 'long boom' from the early post-war years through to 1970 benefited developed and less developed economies alike. Because of the comparative stability of this period, it was commonplace to regard international economic relations as a relatively uncontentious issue area that could be left to technocrats to manage. All this changed in the late 1960s, however, when the US economy encountered increasing problems because its commitment to a fixed exchange rate constrained its policy options at a time when domestic inflation was being fuelled by high levels of government expenditure—domestically, on social programmes, and internationally on the pursuit of the Vietnam War. In August 1971, a new era of instability in the global economy was ushered in when the Nixon administration unilaterally devalued the dollar (for further discussion, see Helleiner, Chapter 7 in this volume). In doing so, it set in train events that were to end the system of fixed exchange rates, one of the pillars of the Bretton Woods financial regime.

The new instability in international finance reinforced perceptions that the global economy was about to enter an era of significant upheaval. Commodity prices had risen substantially in the early 1970s; Western concerns about the future availability and pricing of raw materials were compounded by the success of the Organization of the Petroleum Exporting Countries (OPEC) during the Arab–Israeli war of 1973 in substantially increasing the price of crude oil. Less developed countries believed that they could use their new-found 'commodity power' to engineer a dramatic restructuring of international economic regimes, a demand they made through calls at the United Nations for a New International Economic Order (NIEO) (see Phillips, Chapter 13 in this volume). Industrialized economies were already having difficulty in coping with a surge in imports of manufactured goods from Japan and the East Asian newly industrializing economies (NIEs), causing them to revert to various measures to protect their domestic industries, in disregard of their obligations under the international trade regime. In trade and finance regimes alike, new pressures were causing governments to seek to rewrite the rules governing international economic interactions.

At this time of the greatest instability in international economic relations since the depression of the 1930s, inter-state relations in the security realm, which had been the principal focus of the study of post-war international relations, appeared to be on the verge of entering a new era of collaboration. The United States was winding down its involvement in Indo-China; Henry Kissinger was negotiating détente with the Soviet Union; and President Nixon's visit to China in 1972 appeared to presage a new epoch in which China would be integrated peacefully into the international system. For many scholars of international relations, the traditional agenda of the discipline was incomplete, and the preoccupation of the dominant, realist approach with security issues and military power seemed increasingly irrelevant to the new international environment (Keohane and Nye 1972; Morse 1976).

The new turbulence in international economic relations prompted political scientists to take an interest in a subject matter that had previously been left largely to economists. It was not, as some commentators have suggested, that international economic relations had suddenly become politicized. Politics and asymmetries in power had always underlain the structure of global economic relations, seen, for example, in the content of the various financial regimes negotiated at Bretton Woods. Rather, what was novel was that the turbulence of the early 1970s suggested that the fundamental rules of the game were suddenly open for renegotiation.

Political scientists' new interest in international economic relations also coincided with the abandonment by the economics profession of what had previously been taught and researched as institutional economics: as the discipline of economics aspired to more 'scientific' approaches through the application of statistical and mathematical models, so it increasingly abandoned the study of international economic institutions. Political scientists discovered a vacuum that they quickly filled: the field of international political economy was born.

What is IPE?

International political economy is a field of enquiry, a subject matter whose central focus is the interrelationship between public and private power in the allocation of scarce resources. It is not a specific approach or set of approaches to studying this subject matter (as we shall see, the full range of theoretical and methodological approaches from international and comparative politics has been applied to the study of international political economy).

Like other branches of the discipline, IPE seeks to answer the classic questions posed in Harold D. Lasswell's (1936) definition of politics: *who gets what, when, and how?* This definition identifies explicitly questions of *distribution* as being central to the study of politics. It also points implicitly to the importance of power—the concept that is at the heart of the study of political science—in determining outcomes. Power, of course, takes various forms: it is classically defined in terms of relationships—the capacity of one actor to change the behaviour of another (Dahl 1963). But power is also exercised in the capacity of actors to set agendas (Bachrach and Baratz 1970; Lukes 1974), and to structure the rules in various areas of international economic relations so as to privilege some actors and to disadvantage others (Strange 1988).

Consider, for example, the international financial regime. As the world's largest economy (and single most important market for many other countries in the global system), the United States has been able, over the years, to exercise relational power: to force changes in the behaviour of other countries—notably, to accept changes in their exchange rates (as, for example, in the Nixon administration's breaking of the fixed exchange rate between the dollar and gold, and the forced appreciation of the North-East Asian currencies against the dollar following the **Plaza Accord**). The rules of the international financial regime have also been structured so that they privilege the more economically developed states in the system: not only do the wealthy industrialized economies enjoy more votes within the IMF and the World Bank under the weighted voting system employed in the two major **international financial institutions (IFIs)** (Box 1.7), but the industrialized economies (in part because of arrangements they have negotiated among themselves) have also

largely escaped the discipline imposed by the IMF on countries that run persistent balance of payments deficits. Until the recession of 2008–9, no industrialized country had sought assistance from the IMF since Britain and Italy did so in 1976. Despite running huge deficits in its balance of payments, the United States has not been subject to IMF discipline, because it can take advantage of the international acceptability of the dollar and print more money to finance its trade deficits.

Box 1.7 Voting in the International Financial Institutions

When the allied powers decided at Bretton Woods to create two international financial institutions, they agreed on a formula for voting rights that represented a compromise between the principle of sovereign equality and the realities of markedly unequal economic power. Members' voting power has two components: 'basic votes', assigned equally to all members; and (a much larger number) of weighted votes that are linked directly to the money members subscribed to the two institutions. Quotas have been adjusted since the post-Second World War period (1940s) as the membership of the institutions has expanded, but the G7 industrialized countries still control 45 per cent of the votes in the IMF, while more than forty African countries together have less than 5 per cent of the total votes.

Eight countries—China, France, Germany, Japan, Russia, Saudi Arabia, the United Kingdom, and the United States—have their own representative on the twenty-four-member IMF Executive Board, which is responsible for the day-to-day running of the institution. Others are arranged in various groups, with a single executive director casting their collective votes. Five executive directors represent individual countries on the seventeen-member World Bank Executive Board: the United States, Japan, Germany, France, and the United Kingdom; the remaining twelve directors represent the Bank's other 180 member states.

In the IMF, 'Ordinary' Decisions require a simple majority, whereas 'Special' Decisions require an 85 per cent 'supermajority'. The United States, with 16.74 per cent of the total votes at the IMF, can unilaterally block 'Special' Decisions', such as changes in the IMF's Charter or use

of its holdings of gold. Voting, however, is relatively rare, with most decisions being carried by consensus.

Criticisms of the failure of IMF quotas and voting rights to reflect the growing significance of developing economies were increasingly voiced after the East Asian financial crises of 1997–8. This criticism led to proposals to reform quotas and to increase the number of basic votes assigned to each country. The first stage was an 'ad hoc' increase in the quotas of China, Korea, Mexico, and Turkey (ranging from about a 20 per cent increase for Turkey to about 80 per cent for Korea), to take effect in 2007. Further renegotiations of quotas are expected in the wake of the recession of 2008–9, given the greater influence it afforded developing economies through the elevation of the G20 to the status as the primary forum for global economic governance.

By convention, since the foundation of the two IFIs, the United States has nominated the president of the World Bank, and (West) European countries the managing director of the IMF. In an unusual move in 2000, however, the Clinton administration in the US vetoed the German government's first-choice nominee for the post of managing director of the IMF. Although the appointment of the nominees is subject to a formal vote within the Fund and the Bank, other members have only the option of either voting for or against the nominated candidate rather than proposing alternative names.

The Washington, DC location of the two IFIs facilitates US influence over their operations. For more detailed discussion of the representativeness and accountability of the IFIs, see Woods (2003).

A list of the members of the IMF and their voting rights can be found at www.imf.org/external/np/sec/memdir/members.htm. (Unlike the IFIs, the World Trade Organization operates on the principle of one member, one vote, but its members have never voted: decision-making is by consensus, see Winham, Chapter 5 in this volume.)

Besides a focus on questions of distribution and of power, two of the fundamental concerns of political science, students of international political economy have also been preoccupied with one of the central issues in the study of international relations: which conditions are more favourable for the evolution of co-operation among states in an environment where no central enforcement agency is present? For many observers, this problem of 'co-operation under anarchy' is even more pertinent in the economic than in the security realm. This is because greater potential exists in the economic sphere, particularly under conditions of interdependence, for co-operation on a win-win basis, but states have a considerable temptation to 'cheat' by attempting to exploit concessions made by others while not fully responding in kind (see Aggarwal and Dupont, Chapter 3 in this volume).

Much of the early IPE work in the 1970s and early 1980s, particularly in North America, married two of these central concerns—the distribution of power within the global economy, and the potential for states to engage in collaboration. Conducted at a time when many perceived US economic power to be waning, this work focused on the link between hegemony and an open global economy (see Box 1.8).

Box 1.8 Power and Collaboration

The theory of **hegemonic stability** suggests that international economic collaboration in pursuit of an open (or liberal) economic order is most likely to occur when the global economy is dominated by a single power (because this country, the hegemon, will have both the desire and the capacity to support an open economic system—the dominant economy is likely to benefit most from free trade; moreover, its relatively large size will give it leverage over other states in the system). Theorists pointed to the experience of the mid nineteenth century, when Britain was the hegemonic power, and to the period of US dominance from 1945 to 1971, as demonstrating the relationship between hegemony and an open world economy. In contrast, the inter-war period, when no single country enjoyed equivalent preeminence, was characterized by a breakdown in international economic collaboration. The decline in the relative position of the US economy in the 1960s, following the rebuilding of the Western European and Japanese economies, appeared to coincide with renewed closure (a rise in protectionism in response to imports from Japan and the East Asian NIEs) and the general turbulence in global economic regimes noted above.

Subsequently, however, the hegemonic stability argument was undermined both by trends in the real world and by new theoretical work. In the 1990s, countries extended their collaboration on international economic matters, especially in trade, despite a relatively more even dispersion of economic power in the global system.

For statements of the hegemonic stability argument, see Kindleberger (1973) and Krasner (1976); for alternative theoretical perspectives see Keohane (1984, 1997), Snidal (1985b), and Pahre (1999). For further discussion, see Aggarwal and Dupont, Chapter 3 in this volume.

Approaches to the study of global political economy

Following the publication of Robert Gilpin's (1987) magisterial overview of the then emerging field of international political economy, most introductions to the subject have identified three principal categories of theoretical approaches to IPE. In Gilpin's original terminology (he changed some of his labels in the updated version of his book (Gilpin 2001)), these were liberalism, nationalism, and Marxism. Of these three labels, only liberalism has been used universally in other categorizations. Other writers have substituted statism, 'mercantilism', 'realism' or 'economic nationalism' for nationalism. The approaches that Gilpin subsumed under the label Marxism have variously been identified as 'radical', 'critical', 'structuralist', 'dependency', 'underdevelopment', and 'world systems'.

In itself, the use of a variety of labels points to one of the problems with the 'trichotomous' categorization of approaches to the study of IPE: the (sometimes misleading) lumping together of substantially different perspectives within a single category. Moreover, the trichotomous categorization does not capture the wealth of methodological and theoretical approaches used in the contemporary study of IPE, or provide an accurate signpost to the breadth of fascinating questions that currently preoccupies researchers in the field. For these reasons, we do not use such conventional categorization in this book. So common is the trichotomy in introductions to IPE, however, that it is worth investing a little time in understanding the underlying foundations of the categorization. Matthew Watson's chapter in this volume examines the historical origins and subsequent intellectual lineage of the principal theoretical perspectives on IPE.

Much of the best work in international political economy in recent years has been less concerned with prescription than with explanation—for example, how differences in political institutions shape policy decisions, and why some sectors of the economy are more successful than others in seeking protection (see Hiscox, Chapter 4 in this volume); why it is easier for states to collaborate on some issues rather than others (see Aggarwal and Dupont, Chapter 3 in this volume); why states have increasingly pursued trade agreements at the regional instead of the global level (Ravenhill, Chapter 6 in this volume); why states have been unable to agree on an effective regime for dealing with international debt (Pauly, Chapter 8 in this volume); and why some global environments regimes are effective while others are not (Dauvergne, Chapter 14 in this volume). Of course, policy prescriptions often follow from such theoretically informed analysis, and they are far more specific than those of the 'get the state out of the market' variety.

Since the early 1980s, the study of international political economy has been enriched by the application of a diverse array of theoretical and methodological approaches, but neither their subject matter nor the methodologies employed allow easy categorization. Take, for example, the role of ideas in shaping policy agendas, in helping states to reach agreement in various international negotiations, and in legitimizing current economic, political, and social structures. Ideas have been the central focus of work firmly within the Marxist tradition, which builds on the arguments of the former Italian communist party leader, Antonio Gramsci, on how ideas help ruling classes to legitimate their domination (Cox 1987; Gill 1990). But ideas have also been pivotal to quite different approaches, drawing on the work of the German sociologist, Max Weber. Work from this perspective examines the role that ideas play in defining the range of policy options that governments consider, and in providing a focal point for agreement in international negotiations (Hall 1989; Goldstein and Keohane 1993; Garrett and Lange 1996). Also derived from Weberian analysis are constructivist approaches, which emphasize the significance of ideas in constituting actors' perceptions of their interests and identities, rather than taking these for granted—examples of the application of constructivist analysis to IPE include Colin Hay (Chapter 10 in this volume), Haas (1992), Hay and Rosamond (2002), Burch and Denemark (1997), Abdelal *et al.* (2010). And cross-fertilization has occurred across different approaches—for example, the Gramscian idea of hegemony has been used by writers from a non-Marxist perspective, such as Ikenberry and Kupchan (1990), and finds resonance in Joseph Nye's (1990) concept of 'soft' power.

Likewise, turning to **methodology**, we find similar methods employed by scholars from dramatically different theoretical traditions. Consider rational choice approaches, for example. Since the mid 1990s, rational choice has dominated many areas of the study of political science, particularly in universities in the United States. Its origins lie in economic theory; the focus is primarily on individuals, the factors that lead them to choose preferred courses of action, and how strategic interaction generates uncertainty. In IPE, rational choice analysis has been prominent in the recent study of why international institutions, including the European Union, take particular forms, what the effects of institutions are, and why some institutions survive longer than others (Frey 1984; Martin 1992; Garrett and Weingast 1993). Vaubel (1986, 1991) has applied rational choice analysis in an examination of the behaviour of the officials of the IMF. Such work is very much in the mainstream of contemporary political science. But rational choice methods have also been applied by theorists working within the Marxist tradition—for example, Roemer (1988), and Carver and Thomas (1995).

Although rational choice methods have become dominant in some circles within North American political science, a large number of scholars of IPE would find it difficult to accept the argument of one proponent of rational choice methods that IPE 'is today characterized by growing consensus on theories, methods, analytical frameworks, and important questions' (Martin 2002: 244). Diversity in **ontology**, **epistemology**, and methodology continues to characterize the international study of global political economy (see Box 1.9). Many scholars find this rich mix of theories and methodologies a cause

for celebration rather than concern. This is certainly the view of the contributors to this volume, which reflects much of the current lively debate in the study of IPE.

> **Box 1.9** Epistemology, Ontology, and Methodology
>
> Epistemology addresses the issues of what knowledge is and how it is acquired. Ontology is the study of being, addressing the question of what is there, what are the essential features of an object. Methodology refers to a procedure or set of procedures used to study a subject matter.

The first part of this volume looks at some of the approaches that have addressed the key concerns of theorists of IPE: what conditions are most conducive to the emergence of collaborative behaviour among states on economic issues, and what are the determinants of the foreign economic policies of states? It then examines the evolution of trade relations, first at the global and then at the regional level. Chapter 7 reviews the development of the global financial regime since 1944; the following chapter addresses the causes of financial crises and the reasons why international collaboration to date has been ineffective in devising strategies to combat them.

The chapters in the second half of the book that examine various aspects of the debate about globalization: whether in fact the contemporary economy is global and whether it differs, qualitatively or quantitatively, from previous eras of economic interdependence; the role of international production networks in driving globalization; the consequences of enhanced globalization for the policy options available to states; the impact of globalization on world poverty and inequality; how globalization has changed the relations between industrialized and less developed economies; and the impact of globalization on the environment.

JOHN RAVENHILL

Key points

- The field of international political economy emerged in the early 1970s in response to developments in the world economy, in international security, and in the study of economics and international relations.

- IPE is best defined by its subject matter rather than as a particular theory or methodology.

- Approaches to the study of IPE have conventionally been divided into the three categories of liberalism, nationalism, and Marxism.

- This trichotomous division is of questionable contemporary utility because of the variation in approaches included within each of the three categories.

- The contemporary study of IPE is characterized by the application of a wealth of theories and methodologies.

- Most of the contemporary work in IPE focuses on positive theory: that is, attempting to explain why things happen, rather than on policy prescription.

? Questions

1. What were the principal factors that determined the severity of the recession of 2008–9?

2. In what ways did the recession of 2008–9 change global economic governance?

3. What were the principal features of the classical period of mercantilism?

4. What were the reasons for rapid economic growth in the nineteenth century?

5. How did the gold standard operate automatically to bring the payments position of countries into equilibrium?

6. What were the principal reasons for the breakdown of international economic relations in the inter-war period?

7. What are the defining characteristics of the post-1945 world economy?

8. What factors led to the emergence of IPE as a significant field of study?

9. What is IPE?

10. What are the main weaknesses with the traditional threefold categorization of approaches to IPE?

→ Further reading

 Cohen, B. J. (1977), *Organizing the World's Money: The Political Economy of International Monetary Relations* (New York: Basic Books). The first major study from an IPE perspective of global financial relations.

■ Cohen, B. J. (2008), *International Political Economy: An Intellectual History* (Princeton, NJ: Princeton University Press). The most detailed examination of the development of contemporary international political economy.

■ Cooper, R. N. (1968), *The Economics of Interdependence* (New York: Columbia University Press). A pioneering work that laid the foundations for the emergence of IPE as a significant field of enquiry in the 1970s.

■ Crane, G. T., and Amawi, A. (eds) (1997), *The Theoretical Evolution of International Political Economy: A Reader*, 2nd edn (New York: Oxford University Press). An excellent compilation of selections from classical and contemporary writing on international political economy.

■ Gilpin, R. (1987), *The Political Economy of International Relations* (Princeton, NJ: Princeton University Press). The most theoretically sophisticated of the early introductory books on IPE.

■ Hirschman, A. O. (1945), *National Power and the Structure of Foreign Trade* (Berkeley and Los Angeles, CA: University of California Press). A pioneering study of the relationship between power and the foreign economic relations of Nazi Germany.

■ Keohane, R. O. (1984), *After Hegemony: Cooperation and Discord in the World Political Economy* (Princeton, NJ: Princeton University Press). The most thorough assessment of the relationship between the distribution of power and collaboration among states on international economic matters.

■ Maddison, A. (2001), *The World Economy: A Millennial Perspective* (Paris: Development Centre of the Organization for Economic Co-operation and Development). Excellent source of historical statistics on the development of the world economy.

■ Palan, R. (ed.) (2000), *Global Political Economy: Contemporary Theories* (London: Routledge). The most comprehensive survey of contemporary theoretical approaches to global political economy.

■ Schwartz, H. M. (2010), *States Versus Markets: The Emergence of a Global Economy*, 3rd edn (London: Macmillan). Provides an unusual historical perspective on the contemporary global economy by tracing its development since the 1500s, with emphasis placed on the links between the emergence of the modern state and the modern global economy.

■ Strange, S. (1971), *Sterling and British Policy: A Political Study of an International Currency in Decline* (London: Oxford University Press). A pioneering work on the relationship between politics and international financial policies.

■ Strange, S. (1988), *States and Markets* (London: Pinter). An idiosyncratic introduction to global political economy that is organized around the theme of structural power.

■ Wallerstein, I. (1974), *The Modern World-System* (New York: Academic Press). The first volume of a multi-part work examining the emergence of the modern world economy.

:// Web links

- www.g7.utoronto.ca   University of Toronto G8 Information Centre.
- www.imf.org   International Monetary Fund.
- www.worldbank.org   World Bank.
- www.unctad.org   United Nations Conference on Trade and Development (UNCTAD).
- www.opec.org   Organization of the Petroleum Exporting Countries.

JOHN RAVENHILL

- www.eh.net/encyclopedia/article/officer.gold.standard   Gold Standard—EH.Net Encyclopedia.
- www.amosweb.com/gls   Glossary of economic terms.

 Online resource centre

For additional material and resources, please visit the Online Resource Centre at:
www.oxfordtextbooks.co.uk/ravenhill3e/

The Historical Roots of Theoretical Traditions in Global Political Economy

2

Matthew Watson

 ## Reader's guide

This chapter focuses on the historical origins and the subsequent intellectual lineage of different theoretical positions within contemporary global political economy (GPE). The search for such origins is important in general, because it reminds the student of any subject field that contemporary perspectives are part of a longer tradition of thought. It is even more important in GPE because introductory textbooks to this particular field tend not to rework its historical roots from scratch. Instead, they often rely on populist intellectual histories, where the politest thing that can be said about the ensuing image of the origins of the field is that it is overly simplified. In addition to that, on many occasions, it is just plain wrong. By taking the alternative option of trying to present students with a clear idea of exactly what divided the main theoretical positions in contemporary GPE at their point of origination, this chapter provides important contextual evidence about the way in which those positions have subsequently evolved into their modern form. The discussion of historical roots acts as a precursor to reviewing a number of ways of thinking about the methodological divisions that are embedded within the field today, as well as a precursor to searching for a means of incorporating the core theoretical distinctions of GPE—realism versus liberalism versus Marxism—into an account of these methodological divisions. The result is that it is possible to collapse a number of the rigid lines of demarcation that are drawn in introductory textbooks between competing theoretical positions in GPE. The populist intellectual histories on which these demarcations are founded can therefore be shown to obscure many of GPE's most noteworthy theoretical subtleties. Appropriate ways of thinking about the major divisions in the field should avoid overly aggressive segmentation in order to capture the sense of being able to move fluidly between different positions that share similar historical origins.

Introduction

The purpose of this chapter is to provide a broad overview of the subject field of GPE as a whole, but without simply repeating the introductions to the field that dominate other textbooks. Indeed, those introductions will often appear in the pages that follow as objects of criticism. I take issue with them for their theoretical simplicity, for their lack of attention to the historical roots of GPE, and for allowing these two aspects of their underlying approach to contribute to the reproduction of a number of important historical myths about the subject field. My aim is to uncover a sense of the shared analytical commitments that make one researcher's work readily recognizable to another researcher as belonging to a shared intellectual tradition. This makes it possible to identify more clearly the primary theoretical and methodological divisions that fragment the field into one of competing approaches.

I shall attempt to do so by exploring the historical antecedents of various perspectives in international political economy (IPE), out of which the more recent designation of GPE has arisen. At most, then, this chapter should be read alongside the usual introductory textbook chapters on IPE theory and not as a direct substitute for them, because its aims are different to those of the introductory textbooks. The textbooks focus overwhelmingly on the character of the modern-day positions of realism, liberalism, and Marxism, as well as on what modern-day proponents of those positions say about their debts to

classic interventions in the history of their field. My focus, in the first instance, is on those interventions themselves and the arguments that their authors made in their own words.

At their core, GPE and IPE are very much the same; some researchers simply prefer one name rather than the other. The difference in terminology corresponds mainly to a matter of timing. The use of the name GPE is a recent phenomenon, reflecting the assumption that an important global dimension has been introduced into world economic affairs since the 1980s. For those who accept that the world economy has effectively been globalized in the intervening period, the designation of GPE makes a good deal of sense. In this chapter, though, as I will be focusing largely on the theoretical origins of the subject field and the historical antecedents of those origins, the GPE designation has less resonance. The origins of the subject field date to the early 1970s, a time before anyone talked in any systematic way about globalization. As a consequence, at that time, all the people working in the field called the subject international political economy. For this reason, in what follows, I shall use the designation IPE rather than GPE, albeit noting that as GPE is merely a recent manifestation of modern IPE, the historical antecedents of the two are exactly the same.

Exploring the historical roots of various perspectives in IPE is far from straightforward. First, any attempt to create self-contained categories that serve to synthesize many individuals' work into a single approach with a single label necessarily involves a process of both abstraction and generalization. At most, it is possible to provide heuristic categories in order to underscore the idea that there are particular, as well as discrete, ways of doing IPE. Second, and perhaps more importantly, the way in which IPE is taught is often different from the way it is researched, even though its teachers and researchers are the same people. In general, one set of (overwhelmingly theoretical) heuristic categories underpins the teaching of IPE and an altogether different set of (overwhelmingly methodological) categories underpins academic appraisals of what it means to be researching IPE. Both sets of categories will be discussed as the chapter unfolds, even though this serves to reinforce the sense that IPE possesses something of a dual identity.

I begin with the way in which IPE is traditionally taught. In International Relations (IR), almost all textbook guides to the field introduce students to the relevant subject material via the pedagogical distinction between realism, liberalism, and Marxism. Perhaps as a reflection of the way in which most international political economists were introduced to their subject field as a subset of IR, this same three-way distinction also features extremely prominently in IPE teaching. Indeed, Robert Gilpin—author of the best-selling IPE textbook, *The Political Economy of International Relations* (1987), as well as being one of the first generation of IPE scholars who, according to Benjamin Cohen (2008*b*), set the parameters within which the field continues to be located today—describes realism, liberalism, and Marxism as 'the three ideologies' of IPE (Gilpin 1987: 25). The choice of descriptor is important. He could have called them three separate starting points for IPE. However, this would have implied that, at some stage, students would be required to branch out from those starting points in order to comprehend what is at stake by beginning there. Equally, he could have called them three separate theoretical bases for understanding the world on which international political economists are asked to comment. However, the art of working within a theoretical perspective is always to question the limits that perspective imposes on original thought.

Gilpin is clear about why he instead uses the word 'ideology' to describe realist, liberal, and Marxist IPE. As he readily admits (1987: 25–6), he does so in an attempt to capture a sense of self-contained, coherent world views, capable of imposing meaning on any experience of the world, and equally capable of encapsulating whole systems of thought and belief. This may well be so, and students can turn to pretty much any introductory IPE textbook to find out how the subject field might be divided using this three-way split. My intention in this chapter is rather different. The textbook introductions generally display very little focus on the historical roots of these three competing traditions of IPE's orthodox pedagogy. In specifying these roots rather more precisely, it becomes possible to show the limitations of conceiving of Gilpin's three ideologies of IPE as self-contained, coherent world views. As such, it also undermines the reason for calling them 'ideologies' in the first place. The historical roots of each of these three traditions will now be subjected to critical scrutiny in turn, beginning with realism.

Why Realist IPE and Nationalist Political Economy are not Necessarily the Same Thing

The fact that scholars even consider it worthwhile to teach realism as one possible basis for IPE reveals something potentially interesting about the subject field's origins. Realism, of course, is a standard theoretical approach in International Relations, but a fair degree of creative licence is then required to transpose it into a readily recognizable political economy approach bearing an obvious history of ideas lineage. There might well be political economy underpinnings of the **methodology** that most realists adopt. In a subsequent section, I discuss the linkage between the central methodological premises of neoclassical economics and the decision to model state behaviour as utility maximizing in pursuit of the national interest. This is the starting point for the majority of work undertaken in the realist tradition, with its conscious embrace of rational choice theory. However, realism itself has no political economy *content*, even if it usually does appropriate a political economy *methodology*. The aim of realist IPE is simply to explain how one state seeks to impose its national interest at the expense of other states' national interests in bargaining situations that occur either bilaterally or multilaterally.

As there is every justification for tackling such a question with no regards whatsoever for theories of political economy — it is not, after all, a political economy question — this raises the issue of whether realist IPE, strictly speaking, should qualify for being called IPE at all. Is it possible to undertake international political economy with complete disregard for theories of political economy? Susan Strange, for one, believes that it is not. She argues (1998a) that realism reduces IPE to the economic branch of foreign policy studies and, for this reason, she withheld the designation of IPE when describing work conducted in the realist tradition. Instead, she prefers to call it the 'PIER' approach, where PIER stands for the politics of international economic relations. This is a bold and for some, no doubt, a controversial move, as it draws fairly strict boundaries around the subject field, telling some people that their work counts as IPE proper but others that it does not. In other words, by insisting that IPE has to have political economy foundations of a recognizable lineage if it is to be deserving of the name, Strange forcibly excludes many realists from consideration within the subject field, even though this is the intellectual home that they would instinctively nominate for their own work.

Is Strange justified in being so unforgiving? What to my mind makes her controversial intervention both plausible and important is this. When the surface of the realist name tag is scratched, it quickly becomes apparent that something altogether different is going on underneath. Perhaps in the search for some sort of political economy credibility — and almost certainly in an attempt to disarm the question of whether realism is genuinely IPE — significant efforts have been made to re-describe contemporary IPE realism as the logical heir of classical nineteenth-century political economy nationalism.

This is a standard refrain of pretty much all introductory textbooks in the subject field. Yet, in its own terms, it is an unconvincing claim, as I will now try to demonstrate. To treat the two as synonymous styles of study separated only by distance in time might well provide contemporary IPE realists with a post hoc image of historical roots. At the same time, though, it systematically distorts the objectives of classical nineteenth-century political economy nationalism.

The overwhelming statism of modern-day realist IPE

The intellectual lineage of IPE realism can be traced to the founding texts of modern IR realism. It represents an attempt to synthesize two separate strands of thought, described by R. B. J. Walker (1993: 108–22) as structural realism and historical realism. Modern structural realists tend to follow Hans Morgenthau's pioneering lead (1948/1960) in anthropomorphizing the state and therefore treating state behaviour as epiphenomenal of essential human characteristics. By making the further assumption that it is human nature to be self-serving and to chase gains solely for oneself, combatively self-interested actions are consequently inscribed into the very logic of state behaviour. It might well be necessary to differentiate Walker's designation of structural realism from Kenneth Waltz's 'neo-realist' variant of the same, because Waltz (1979) explicitly rejects Morgenthau's anthropomorphization of the state. However, his account of the nature of state behaviour and of its essential logic is much the same as that of Morgenthau. By contrast, modern historical realists work within a tradition that originates with E. H. Carr (1939/1946). Here, the emphasis is on developing historically contextualized explanations for how the instinct for combatively self-interested actions might be balanced in any given instance by the perceived need for a state to demonstrate to rival states that it is acting within the bounds of international political norms. The structural logic of state behaviour might therefore always be offset by historically conditioned concerns for turning away from exercising full-on aggression towards other states.

Any student who comes to this chapter already familiar with introductory textbook accounts of competing IPE approaches will doubtless immediately recognize what is being described here. The two IR realist traditions, one starting with Morgenthau (but with its Waltzian variant) and the other with Carr, translate readily into IPE realism, with both emphasizing the statist assumptions of the modern-day scholars following in their footsteps. On the one hand, it is assumed that states are concerned solely with their own interests when calculating their preferred stance in international economic negotiations (that is, the realist tradition that begins with Morgenthau and is taken on by Waltz). On the other hand, it is also assumed that states will want to avoid triggering retaliatory actions from other states, as this is likely to harm domestic producers and consumers, and thus work against the national economic interest (that is, the realist tradition that begins with Carr). The easiest way to prevent the precipitation of openly aggressive behaviour from other states is to show that one is acting in accordance with the prevailing international economic norms. These are the norms that are both inscribed

into and defended by the actions of international institutions, thereby setting the context for global economic governance. In contemporary times, they include respect for the right of others to engage in free trade (as enshrined in the operating credo of the World Trade Organization (WTO)) and a commitment to liberalizing financial flows and open capital accounts (as enshrined in the operating credo of the International Monetary Fund (IMF)).

In this sense, subject matters that link states economically can be talked about using exactly the same explanatory language of IR realism of the essential struggle between states for power, prestige, and influence in 'high' political arenas. Even the core IR realism concepts of diplomacy and warfare are translated into IPE by using the adjectival prefix 'economic'. The ontological basis of the theoretical claims that define the approach—that is, the common assumptions its adherents share about the fundamental nature of the world that deserves explanation—is very definitely the state. As Stephen Krasner, one of the leading proponents of this style of IPE, suggests (1994: 17), it is assumed that 'states are the ontological givens in the system'. The *only* world that realist IPE can adequately describe is a world of states, and every other aspect of that world is merely subsidiary to the existence, activities, and decisions of states. Other influential actors, such as large corporate bodies or regulatory institutions, are either constituted directly by states or have their capabilities delegated to them by the decisions of states. From this perspective, to focus on world economic affairs is necessarily to prioritize the study of the actions of states. The statist approach provides no new methods of understanding of its own, theorizing actual state behaviour in exactly the same way as realism. In IPE, then, 'realism' and **statism** serve as acceptable synonyms for one another.

The questions on which this style of IPE focuses are by no means insignificant questions. The state is clearly an important actor in shaping its citizens' experiences and expectations of the world economy, and to suggest otherwise solely in the search for intellectual space that transcends realist IPE would be unhelpful. It is clearly an issue of note for IPE scholars to understand how states position themselves against one another in international economic negotiations, as well as how they position themselves with respect to the balance of political forces within their respective societies in order to decide on the character of their negotiating positions in the first place.

However, realist IPE with its statist ontology drawn from its rational choice theory method makes an even starker claim than this. The rational choice theory method dictates that it is unnecessary to ask how states will form their interests in any particular set of circumstances because those interests will be an existential given. States will always act in a way that enhances their immediate power resources within the world economy because those power resources are crucial to shaping further bilateral and multilateral economic negotiations to their advantage. This acts to reduce drastically the time period over which states can be assumed to be forward looking in managing their economic affairs: in effect, forward-looking behaviour is oriented merely to the shortest of short terms. On this point, though, modern-day IPE realism is directly at odds with classical nineteenth-century political economy nationalism. In fact, it might well be possible to push the differences between the two to their logical conclusions in order to depict classical nineteenth-century political economy nationalism as an anti-realist perspective. Yet, this is not a claim that can be found within introductory IPE textbooks.

The political economy foundations of nineteenth-century economic nationalism

The most obvious and most famous account of classical nineteenth-century political economy nationalism is Friedrich List's *National System of Political Economy* (1841/2005*a*, *b*, *c*). For this reason,

it is perhaps understandable that so many introductory IPE textbooks have sought preemptive forms of analysis in List's work to act as a link to modern-day IPE realism (e.g., Gilpin 1987; Gill and Law 1988; Frieden and Lake 1995; O'Brien and Williams 2004). However, such a link requires that a disservice be done to List by forcing him to talk to modern-day intellectual agendas rather than his own by superimposing modern-day academic language onto his work. This is nowhere more apparent than on the question of how states derive their economic interests. For modern-day IPE realists, this is simply a matter of devising strategies to enhance short-term economic bargaining power, but for List it always involved complex trade-offs between emphasizing short- and long-term economic goals. It also involved successfully managing the expectations of society if the long-term goals of overall national economic development were to be prioritized over the short-term goals of the immediate enrichment of society. There are clear elements of anti-realism contained within this position.

The first is that List was adamant (1841/2005*a*: 18–22; 1841/2005*b*: 34–5) that what counted as the national economic interest changed with respect to the stage of development exhibited by a country. Stated straightforwardly in this way, List's claim does not appear to be something to which most realists would today object, but there is a subtle yet important difference of approach between the two. Modern-day realists assume that the national economic interest will change over time as the country's level of development changes, but that in each individual time period the national economic interest will cohere internally as a singular entity. In List's work, by contrast, 'the' national economic interest was actually a series of competing national economic interests played out at a single moment in historical time but over markedly different timeframes. The question he asked was how might a state balance its broad overall societal objective of developing as quickly as possible with ensuring the compliance of its citizens at every stage of the development trajectory?

List's specific concern (1841/2005*b*: 191–2, 216–18; 2005*c*: 44–52) was to show why a newly politically unified but still only partially industrialized Germany should revoke its commitment to Britain's nineteenth-century laissez-faire policy, even if this temporarily restricted ordinary Germans' consumption possibilities by stopping them from accessing cheap British imports. List is often treated as if he were a critic of free trade per se, but this was not so. His argument was only that free trade was wrong for Germany in the particular historical conjuncture in which he was writing. Germany, he wrote, should seek a better position to engage in free trade alongside Britain only once it had developed into Britain's industrial equal. Free trade was still the ultimate goal of List's nationalist political economy, then, only just not yet. His conclusion was that political attempts should be made to forge a nationalist economic identity by winning the German people over to the idea that their consumption of British goods in the short term was detrimental to German national economic self-determination in the long term.

The second big difference between List's work and that of modern-day IPE realists who try to enlist him as their intellectual antecedent is that he point-blank rejected their statist ontology. Instead, in clearly elaborated terms to introduce what is almost certainly the most important chapter of his most important book, List announced his commitment—both political and theoretical—to a nationalist ontology. He wrote that (1841/2005*b*: 70): 'Between each individual and entire humanity . . . stands THE NATION, with its special language and literature, with its peculiar origin and history, with its special manners and customs, laws and institutions.' He even placed the claim in capital letters in an attempt to make it impossible to miss, but still it *is* missed when introductory IPE textbooks claim an unproblematic lineage from List to modern-day state-centred IPE realism.

A new generation of List scholars in IPE highlight this neglect of the nation in their attempts to prise his *National System of Political Economy* from the clutches of modern-day realists and to ask what a nationalist economic ontology would look like today from a Listian perspective (e.g., Levi-Faur 1997; Crane 1998; Helleiner 2005). Their work suggests that there is no simple one-to-one correspondence between List's nationalist economic ontology and the sorts of protectionist policies that he advocated for Germany in the specific circumstances it faced in the middle of the nineteenth century. While List certainly did favour the introduction of barriers to trade because he believed such protection to be consistent with German national economic interests at that specific time, the realm of national economic interests is much broader than the single case that he described. Because it is much broader, it can lead to many different types of policies today. Indeed, one of the major lessons to emerge from the work of a new generation of List scholars within IPE is that economically liberal policies can be the preference derived from adopting an economically nationalist ontology. In other words, in an attempt to satisfy perceptions of the national interest today 'the nation' can be incorporated into liberal economic structures just as easily as into any other type of policy. The contextual factor of globalization leads many IPE scholars to assume that it is actually *easier* to construct liberal policies from a nationalist ontology today than it is the protectionist policies that List advocated for Germany in his day.

The continuing appeal of List's *National System*

The enduring appeal of List's work to contemporary scholars and students of IPE is that it provides a means of asserting the right to autonomy for developing countries seeking political shelter from the disruptive influence of international economic norms. Just as List had argued that the imposition of the British policy choice of laissez-faire served to frustrate German development aspirations, so, too, do many people today suggest that development space is systematically squeezed by the neoliberal agenda of global governance institutions (see Phillips, Chapter 13 in this volume). List's *National System* appears to be a valuable resource to appropriate in this respect, because introductory IPE textbooks draw a smooth line of descendence from Adam Smith's *Wealth of Nations* to contemporary neoliberalism, while List was a wholly uncompromising critic of Smithian liberalism. Once again, though, all is not what it seems on first appearance in constructing the historical roots of IPE in this way.

List's attack on Smith could hardly be described as reasoned—yet alone a reasonable—argument. It borders on the rabid in terms of the deliberately provocative language he used, all the time playing fast and loose with what Smith actually said if putting different words into his mouth served List's particular political purposes. The phrase 'laissez-faire' was not one that Smith used in his own work; moreover, at repeated points throughout *The Wealth of Nations* he presents his preferred policy solutions that are anything but laissez-faire in orientation (Viner 1928/1989: 141). Yet, still, it is laissez-faire inclinations that List consistently attributed to Smith. There is an irony in List being treated as the guru of realist IPE by so many modern-day realists in that there are clear anti-realist themes running throughout his work. In much the same way, he treated Smith as the doyen of the liberal laissez-faire economy, despite the many instances in which Smith's work presents clear anti-liberal arguments.

List turned his back on textual accuracy in the search for more convenient depictions of Smith's work. In doing so, he invited upon himself a rather different legacy in the minds of historians of economic thought to that which has been popularized within IPE. To the textbook authors and to many of the new generation of List specialists within IPE, he belongs amongst the very highest ranks of economic theorists (e.g., Winch 1998). To historians

of economic thought, by contrast, he deserves no such elevated status. Indeed, they generally relegate him to the company of political pamphleteers in the third or even fourth rank of economic theorists (e.g. Nicholson 1904/1977; Tribe 1995). List opened up space for his crusade against Smithian political economy by deliberately caricaturing Smith's economics and turning his often ambivalent comments on the exposure of everyday life to market dynamics into undiluted and largely unthinking support for laissez-faire. Would a top rank economic theorist really be expected to act in such a carefree manner with the historical roots of his or her subject field as List did?

The consensus opinion of historians of economic thought is that they would not, which leads them to conclude that List's distortion of Smith's work is a cause for regret. Particularly in terms of its textbooks, however, IPE is dominated by accounts of Smith's work that very much mirror List's in focus. Although on many points he was a highly sympathetic critic of the market economy, Smith was a critic, nonetheless, because of the way in which it turned a person's intrinsic worth into a monetary price. As will be demonstrated later in the chapter, he understood this outcome to be a regrettably dehumanizing effect of the market economy and a clear impediment to the sustenance of functioning social organisms. Smith was not the gung-ho advocate of the marketization of everything as he was made to appear in List's characterization of his rampant individualism (1841/2005*b*: 70). Instead, the whole of his economic theory begins from the premise of how first to construct and then reproduce a functioning society. The contents of the textbooks suggest that IPE is taught today with very few of its scholars having noticed this fact or, if they have, treating it as unimportant. As a consequence, the historical roots of liberalism are poorly specified and, thus, poorly understood within IPE.

Key points

- Despite the tendency to regard them as synonymous, the statist ontology of realist IPE bears no resemblance to List's nationalist ontology as outlined in his classic work, *National System of Political Economy*.

- Greater clarity would be brought to understanding IPE's historical roots by thinking of 'realism' as an umbrella term for a number of very different

approaches to explaining international economic affairs.

- State power lies at the heart of the explanatory frameworks of all these separate approaches, but they do not share a single conceptualization of what state power means, how it can be detected or what is important about it.

Why the IPE Textbook Account of Smithian Economic Liberalism is Usually Wrong

There is a further irony contained in Smith's treatment at the hands of List. List forced contrary opinions onto Smith to the ones that Smith actually held in order to outline his nationalist alternative to British laissez-faire policy in the nineteenth century. The integrity of Smith's original writing therefore suffers as List's exaggerated style of criticism eliminated all the subtleties and qualifications in his work and turned him into the defender of a clearly defined but equally clearly parodied liberal position. However, Smith was not wholly innocent of having done much the same to a previous generation of political economy writers. That is, he created the space for his liberal alternative to the dominant economic ideas of the day by reducing the complexities of other people's texts to a straightforward anti-liberal dogma.

List's *National System* is littered with accusations of nineteenth-century British hypocrisy, arguing that successive British governments had conveniently forgotten the country's own developmental history in trying to enforce laissez-faire as the developmental context for other countries trying to close the industrial gap with Britain (e.g., List 1841/2005a: 69–70; 1841/2005b: 87–9). He pointed to the multiplicity of protective legislations that the British

had introduced to facilitate their development, and noted that this was exactly the sort of legislation that adherence to laissez-faire ruled out for other countries. For current purposes, the most interesting aspect of List's account is the praise he heaped on seventeenth- and eighteenth-century writers of the British Mercantilist School for their advocacy of the system of tariffs and trade restrictions that supported their country's developmental aspirations. The irony is that no such self-conscious and self-organizing School existed in popular thought until Smith defined it in that way in *The Wealth of Nations*. However, Smith's definition was an entirely negative one, designed to show where economic theory had gone wrong before his day and based on fairly crude pigeonholing devices in order to falsely homogenize that theory into a single, internally consistent tradition of thought. Therefore, the historical roots of IPE liberalism do not necessarily have the most illustrious or pristine of origins.

Smith on mercantilism

Smith devoted a significant proportion of the 950 pages of *The Wealth of Nations* to refuting the core propositions of mercantilism. Arguably the two most important contributions to mercantilist thought—certainly in its anglophone variant—are to be found in Thomas Mun's *England's Treasure by Forraign Trade* (1664/1928) and Bernard Mandeville's *Fable of the Bees* (1714/1755). At the very least, these were the two publications that drew so much of Smith's attention in his efforts to construct what he viewed as a credible liberal counter-argument. Mun's treatise was a celebration of England's eminent position in seventeenth-century international trade relations, which he attributed to a strong state capable of structuring the country's commercial activities so as to produce continual trade surpluses. Imports were discouraged by the use of tariffs, quotas, and subsidies. However, the English used their state strategically—through military means if necessary—to ensure that similarly restrictive practices were not imposed against their goods. As a consequence, exports were not discouraged to the same extent as imports. The result was a net inflow of precious metals as other countries serviced their trade deficits with England. For many of the people whom Smith lumped together as a single Mercantilist School, the hoarding of precious metals made possible by trade surpluses was the measure of the nation's wealth, not the overall productive capacity of the economy as a whole.

Mandeville extended Mun's analysis to argue that, while hoarding of precious metals was the primary objective of the state's economic policy, the state should also ensure that its citizens did not follow its lead by attempting to hoard their wealth. He suggested that individual saving might well be seen as a private virtue, but that it was in fact a public vice. The impetus for export activity could only be maintained under the full utilization of domestic productive potential, and this, in turn, required the state to be on its guard against domestic under-consumption. Such situations were most likely to ensue when individuals chose to save rather than spend any new income they earned, so every effort had to be made to encourage spending, with the state acting coercively

if necessary. Mandeville's best-remembered text is most famous for its celebration of a host of individualistic and often anti-social character traits (Mandeville 1723/1997). He positively eulogized selfish behaviour aimed at rather tawdry acts of personal display, because he treated these as the lifeblood of the consumption mentalities that kept the growth rate of the economy high (Goldsmith 1990; Hundert 1994).

It is important to understand the historical context of why Mun and Mandeville were Smith's two principal targets in his critique of mercantilism. Such concern for appropriate contextualization of Smith's main claims is almost always absent from IPE, which shows how much work is to be done before the historical roots of liberal IPE can be specified adequately. Smith's liberalism is not a simple ideological argument in favour of transferring economic authority from the state to the market, as it is made to appear in so much of the discussion to be found in introductory IPE (and IR) textbooks (e.g., Dunne 2001; Steans and Pettiford 2001; Scholte 2005). It is at once both much more historically specific and much more subtle than that. Even though Smith presented his attack on mercantilism in terms of economics, it is not in fact an economic critique that is most prominent in this part of his work. Instead, it is a combination of political and moral critiques that most notably stands out.

Smith's liberal account of government

Starting with Smith's critique of Mun, the important historical fact to keep in mind here is that Mun was simultaneously a member of the Standing Commission on Trade established in Britain in 1622 and a member of the committee of the British East India Company. Smith's political critique of mercantilism—I will turn to his moral critique of mercantilism in due course—focused on the obvious conflict of interests contained in situations such as this. Smith is often wrongly judged to have been against the whole process of modern government as an unnecessary distraction to the otherwise natural workings of the market economy. Testament to the popularity of this misunderstanding was the proliferation of Adam Smith neckties worn around Washington, DC by political consultants complaining about the dynamics of 'Big Government' in the Reagan years. Yet, Smith repeatedly used his own texts to highlight the indispensability of government to the way in which markets form and are reproduced in everyday economic life (McLean 2006). Markets can function only in the presence of an institutionalized system of private property rights, he said, and that system requires the law-making authority of the government to be credible (Fleischacker 2004). It was not government per se that drew Smith's ire, so much as clear corruption of the process of government when it is captured by particular vested interests.

The British East India Company was granted an English Royal Charter in 1600 to act on behalf of the sovereign in meeting the country's commercial objectives as laid down by the government (Robins 2006). It, and other exclusive stockholding corporations like it, operated at a significant distance from the oversight that the government could apply to it. The East India Company's sphere of activities was nearly two years' sailing time removed from its home country when allowing for the whole of the round trip. This provided it with a large degree of autonomy, which it used to seize for itself monopoly rights in the territories in which it was active. It generally treated those territories as colonial possessions, stripping as and how the Company deemed fit each colony of its resources and each colony's people of their dignity and their ability to be economically self-sufficient. It imposed a form of martial law for this purpose, denying local people their social and economic rights in the interests of repatriating balance of trade surpluses to England. Smith made his feelings on this issue plain (1776/1981: IV.vii.b.44) by writing that to prohibit a people 'from making all that they can of every part of their own produce, or from employing their stock and industry in the way that they judge most advantageous to themselves, is a manifest violation of the most sacred rights of mankind'.

Always an opponent of colonization, Smith found the East India Company's activities particularly objectionable for the abuse of trust it displayed in the enactment of martial law (Muthu 2008). He called it, as well as other exclusive stockholding corporations like it, 'nuisances in every respect' (Smith 1776/1981: IV.vii.c.108). Perhaps feeling himself unable to take on directly the Company's supporters and paid employees in government, Smith set his sights instead on the economic *means* that the East India Company used to generate balance of trade surpluses: attacking the economic means through which it derived its political power also constituted an implicit attack on its political power. He endeavoured to cast 'odious imputation' upon the specific system of government in operation in England at the height of the East India Company's powers, whereby tariffs and other commercial restraints could be used to profit the Company at the expense of building the economic capabilities of the acquired territories, and so preventing them from enriching English consumers by trading lower-priced goods with them (Smith 1776/1981: IV.vii.c.107).

In one conceptual move, Smith was able to show that the political conflicts of interest sustaining the monopoly positions of exclusive stockholding corporations was bad both for the countries that the English colonized *and* for ordinary English citizens as well. He wrote that:

> Since the establishment of the English East India company, for example, the other inhabitants of England, over and above being excluded from the trade, must have paid in the price of the East India goods which they have consumed, not only for all the extraordinary profits which the company may have made upon those goods in consequence of their monopoly, but for all the extraordinary waste which the fraud and abuse, inseparable from the management of the affairs of so great a company, must necessarily have occasioned.

Smith 1776/1981: IV.vii.c.91

He described such a situation as an 'absurdity' (Smith 1776/1981: IV.vii.c.91).

Smith's political critique of mercantilism paved the way for his advocacy of free trade: the monopolizing spirit against which he set himself was specifically a mercantile monopoly. The theoretical case for free trade was subsequently taken up even more forcefully by David Ricardo, and it is from Ricardo's rather than Smith's perspective that IPE scholars today typically teach the liberal arguments for free trade (see Ricardo 1817/2002).

Ricardo assumed that different economies are differently endowed. Some countries have climates specifically suited to certain types of agricultural production; others have developed expertise in financial services and now have a solid banking structure; and others still concentrate the **capital accumulation** process in the production of manufactured goods. He further assumed that countries should specialize economically in what they already do best, thus increasing their existing lead over other countries in these areas.

This is the logic of **comparative advantage**, and Ricardo argued that modern economic production should be organized in each country on the basis of comparative advantage. To back this point, he showed—as a matter of logic, supported by elementary arithmetic—that welfare gains were available, both for the world as a whole and for every country in it, as long as a system of comparative advantage was supported by an institutionalized structure of free trade among nations. This was true even if one country had an **absolute advantage** over others in producing all categories of goods. The implication was that countries should specialize economically in what they do best, and reap the gains from this by trading the produce of their specialization in an unrestricted manner with other countries. Ricardo was writing only forty years after Smith, but the sheer scale of the difference between his position and previous mercantilist practice shows just how far opinion had shifted in the interim.

Smith's liberal account of human behaviour

Smith's moral critique of mercantilism centred on what he saw as the unfortunate, even disreputable, behavioural characteristics being advocated in Mandeville's *Fable of the Bees*. In order to make his displeasure absolutely clear he described Mandeville as the purveyor of a 'licentious system' of philosophy which was 'wholly pernicious' (Smith 1759/1982: VII.ii.4.6). At the time of writing his *Theory of Moral Sentiments*, Smith found himself caught between two very different accounts of the moral basis of the newly emergent commercial society with its attendant market economy. On the one side, there was Mandeville, armed with a completely functionalist defence of commercial and market-based ethics. In Smith's reading, Mandeville paid no attention at all to respectable manners, validating all sorts of anti-social behaviour as long as it helped to advance economic interests and caused the economy to grow. Gratuitous displays of personal wealth invited no moral condemnation, even if they were paraded in the context of other people's poverty, because it meant that more money was circulating within the economy. Higher degrees of monetary expenditure were consistent, in turn, with enhanced growth potentials. Likewise, obsequiousness to the rich, praising and then aspiring to emulate their consumption for no sake other than its own, was also considered fine, because this, too, triggered new economic activity. Whenever Mandeville identified greater levels of economic activity, he was able to rationalize whatever behavioural traits underpinned it. To him, the creation of a civilized market order was not the priority; the creation of a dynamic market economy was.

Smith disagreed. In his view, a dynamic market economy was not a reasonable objective in itself if it could only be bought at the cost of fundamentally anti-social behaviour. However, Smith did not disagree with Mandeville to such an extent that he allied himself with the chief proponent of the other side of the debate, Jean-Jacques Rousseau. In his *Discourse on Inequality*, Rousseau implied that human life was increasingly not worth living if economic expediency was to be raised above the public ethics of the pre-liberal classical republican tradition (Rousseau 1755/2003; see also Baron 1988). He was a strong supporter of the republican proposition that the virtue of the individual overshadows all other considerations, and certainly those of economic efficiency (Hörnqvist 2000). Rousseau went as far as to regret the entire move into the commercial stage of society, because for him this was associated with the unavoidable corruption of the individual as a moral entity. The very possibility of luxury consumption within such a society, he said, was sufficient to turn everyone away from the path of virtue and to glorify instead in the possession of commodities for its own sake. He depicted a future of socially obstructive individuals permanently on the lookout for the commendation of their fellows purely on the basis of the wealth that they could display in their acquisitions. His conclusion was that life surrounded by commerce and markets necessarily forced people to live in each other's opinions and to lose their virtue in doing so.

The historical roots of liberal IPE date to Smith's attempts to construct a middle way between the ethics-free zone of Mandeville's economics and the economic restrictions of Rousseau's ethics (e.g., De Marchi 1999). However, the ethical basis of Smith's thought has been almost completely written out of the IPE account of liberalism. As Stephen Rosow (1997) has argued persuasively, this is as narrow an understanding of liberalism as there has been in that approach's whole history. When IPE scholars talk about liberalism, it is almost always purely an economic liberalism of which they speak, even though Smith's work was built upon altogether different foundations. It is true that he sided with Mandeville against Rousseau on the latter's insistence that progress into the commercial stage of society was necessarily at odds with human happiness. Yet, he shared many of Rousseau's concerns

about the corrupting influence of luxury consumption and the need, contra Mandeville, to restate the value of virtue in the face of that corruption. He thus set out to construct a philosophical account of moral activity that would be specifically suited to the commercial stage of society. It is an account oriented to the articulation of what might be called the 'bourgeois virtues' (McCloskey 2006).

The enactment of bourgeois virtues entails learning how to exhibit a politeness of manners, deliberately reining in the urge for self-display in anything other than the most restrained way. Smith called this learning the virtue of self-command (Smith 1759/1982: VI.iii.11). Tutoring oneself to self-command means being able to understand the effects of other people's hardship and to respond accordingly to one's success with only muted celebrations. Moderation of emotions all round is the order of the day in such a world (Smith 1759/1982: I.ii.intro.2). This eliminates at a stroke the gratuitous parade of possessions so beloved of Mandeville's consumers, as well as the obsequiousness to the rich which encourages the parade of possessions in the first place. Throughout *The Theory of Moral Sentiments*, Smith suggested that whether or not society functions successfully under the influence of market-based economies depends on whether or not self-command is enacted successfully amongst the population as a whole.

Smith therefore praised deliberate acts of impartiality and insisted that all individuals should experience dutiful sensations to act conscionably with respect to other members of society. The purpose of government when understood from this perspective is to design social institutions to ensure that people live within the bounds of acceptable behaviour (Raphael and Macfie 1982). Partiality of the self is thereby juxtaposed with acting impartially through first having incorporated the image of the good society into one's most basic world view. When Smith's clear preference for a society populated by individuals who are capable of exercising self-command is taken into consideration, it becomes evident that it is very difficult to read his work as unequivocal endorsement of a market-based liberalism.

However, this is precisely how most IPE scholars and, to my knowledge, all introductory IPE textbooks *do* read his work (e.g., Strange 1994; Underhill 1994; Grieco and Ikenberry 2003; Brawley 2005; Oatley 2006). They typically focus on one throwaway comment in *The Wealth of Nations* about the 'invisible hand', deprive that comment of all its specific historical meaning, and then turn it into unstinting praise of the automatic adjustment mechanisms inherent in all markets. Smith himself, in contrast, was unwilling to put his name to any such claim. It might therefore lead to convenient scholarship to appeal to Smith's notion of the invisible hand in order to draw a direct lineage from his foundational work on economic liberalism to international financial institutions' preference today for neoliberalism. Yet, convenience alone does

not make it right to do so, just as it did not in the mid nineteenth century when List drew a direct lineage from Smith to the British preference for laissez-faire.

> ### Key points
>
> - Smith was guilty of artificially homogenizing existing writings in the mercantilist tradition, but he did so to support his political and moral critiques of mercantilism.
> - The IPE textbook account of *The Wealth of Nations* is a crude, often even slapdash, characterization of Smith's work as a whole.
> - Associating Smith solely with the populist rendition of the 'invisible hand' concept is a complete red herring as far as serious Adam Smith scholarship is concerned.

Why the Historical Roots of Marxist IPE are Closer to Liberalism than is Commonly Assumed

The historical roots of Marxist IPE are much more frequently and much more accurately discussed within the subject field as a whole than are the historical roots of either nationalist or liberal IPE. For whatever reason, IPE scholars in general appear to be more comfortable constructing positions that are recognizably part of a lineage which appeals in some way to Marx than they are doing likewise for either List or Smith. Nonetheless, an important division is still visible on the question of which Marx to hark back to.

Some contributions in Marxist IPE are rooted in the normative Marx, who makes the avowedly political case for a new type of society. The lineage here is usually to *The Communist Manifesto* (Marx and Engels 1848/1948). Others, however, are rooted in the analytical Marx, who makes the intellectual case for breaking with the liberal traditions of classical

economics. The lineage here is usually to the *Grundrisse* (Marx 1973) or to *Capital* (Marx 1890/1930). Despite this difference, all are united in their refusal to take the social basis of capitalism for granted, as well as in their determination to ask searching questions about the likely effects of the capitalist system on those who have to live their lives within it. The broad church of IPE scholars who find their inspiration in Marx ask why members of society should be expected to consent to the reproduction of the capitalist system. This is to be contrasted with what Marx called the 'bourgeois economics' of Smith and the other classical economists, whom he said were only interested in how the capitalist system might be organized to grow more effectively.

As has already been shown, though, this is not really to take Smith's texts at face value. Had he genuinely been interested solely in the capitalist accumulation imperative, Smith would have had no need to articulate his views quite so clearly in opposition to those of Mandeville. Marx was consequently partly right in his overall objection to Smith's work—after all, Smith exhibited no desire to leave behind the commercial stage of society in its entirety, only to civilize it—but not wholly so.

There is something quite noteworthy in the language that Marx used to describe Smithian theory. He was often quite rude about Smith and dismissive of his talents as an economic theorist. The label 'bourgeois economist' when used by Marx is, of course, something to be accused of and not something to be celebrated for being. It is a label issued in disparagement rather than in praise. Yet, behind this facade of outright rejection of what Smith stood for, there are a number of instances in his work when Marx borrowed his starting propositions directly from Smith. His rudeness was of the sort that is driven by exasperation that potentially important insights on the human condition of capitalism were not pushed to their logical political conclusion, rather than the suggestion that Smith's work was altogether devoid of insight. Understanding the historical roots of Marxist IPE requires at least some appreciation of the relationship between the two men's work.

The foundations of Marx's political economy

The whole of Marx's political economy is grounded in the opening premise that the capitalist system can only be a dynamic entity when the needs of that system are forcibly prioritized over the rights of individuals to live as autonomous human beings. The reproduction of the capitalist system overrides that autonomy by turning individuals into a functional part of the system. People might believe that they work to satisfy basic existential needs, that they work to be able to finance leisure time, or that they work to provide themselves with the material possessions they associate with a life of comfort. Yet, for Marx, this in itself is an element of false

consciousness: an inability to see things for what they really are and to form interests accordingly. Within a capitalist system, he said, people in fact work solely in order to preserve the smooth running of the system itself through preserving the momentum towards capital accumulation. In effect, no individual is more than a tiny cog in a huge economic machine, and it is the well-being of the machine that takes precedence over the defence of truly human existence. In Marx's view, the incorporation of the individual as a commodified input into the capitalist system necessarily comes at the cost of dehumanizing effects.

Interestingly, exactly the same conclusion shines through the later books of Smith's *Wealth of Nations*. In the earlier books, Smith outlined his model of the economy as it reached its commercial stage. He placed the concept of division of labour centre-stage in his model, showing that the growth of the economy and the consequent enrichment of the nation both depend on the degree to which work takes place within specialized units. The depth of the institutionalization of the market follows closely the incorporation of workers into ever-more finely detailed patterns of specialization (Smith 1776/1981: I.iii.1). This was socially beneficial, according to Smith, because the greater the scope of market relations the more chance there was of lifting people out of poverty. However, it was by no means an unequivocal social good, because there were palpable psychological costs involved when enforcing the division of labour onto people amid the move towards routinized factory work. Smith went as far (1776/1981: V.i.f.60, 61) as to call the ensuing psychological effects 'mental mutilation'; the division of labour forced the mind into a 'drowsy stupidity' (1776/1981: V.i.f.51).

On this most fundamental of assumptions about everyday experiences under capitalism there is thus very little to choose between Marx and Smith. Marx developed from first principles a thoroughly thought-through and conceptually robust notion of **alienation** to replace Smith's simple observation about mental mutilation (see, for instance, Mészáros 2005), but it would be difficult to prove that they were doing anything other than talking about the same essential process. The only real difference — major though it is — relates to what they inferred from these shared foundations. Smith offered state-financed education as a palliative to the psychological drudgery of repeating the same basic work tasks day-in, day-out. In other words, he envisaged a solution in which workers could have the dehumanizing effects of their incorporation into a division of labour balanced by state-financed mental stimulation outside of work hours. For Marx, this was Smith at his most bourgeois. The education palliative was merely a means of imposing false consciousness, he said, and it was therefore part of the problem through which workers failed to see that the interests of the capitalist system did not coincide with their own interests.

To ground this claim and to signal his break from Smith, Marx worked within the basic Hegelian position which states that individuals' activities in the world change both the world on which they act and who they themselves are. The novelty in his argument was in his insistence that it is the practical activities associated with the production process that matter most in this respect, thus rendering Smith's education palliative null and void. Individuals are socialized into the necessity of production before being coerced into a social structure that facilitates specifically capitalist production. Once there, the requirement is to live a regimented life, consisting primarily of the endless repetition of basic work tasks, so that standardized commodity production can take place. Obedience is paramount, and creativity in productive practices is discouraged for fear that it will corrupt the standardization of commodities.

Given this, it is easy to see why Marx thought that the act of labour was so important to life in a capitalist society. The subjugation of the needs of the individual to the reproduction of the capitalist system in effect reduces the essence of human life to mere labouring activities. Even then, Marx was eager to show that labourers do not receive full recompense for the value of their labouring activities. He drew a politically charged distinction between labour and labour power, arguing that the average capitalist will always seek to reduce wages as far as possible, until they become the equivalent of labour power, even though it is labour that is physically expended in the production process. Labour power represents the costs of sustaining the workers who have been incorporated into the capitalist system. Yet it is labour that adds value to the commodities being produced, and thereby creates the potential for the capitalist to take profits out of the system. The more that capitalists are able to enforce a structural difference between labour and labour power, the more assured are those capitalists of being able to reward themselves with handsome profits. Marx described this as the logic of surplus value extraction, and he believed it to be a fundamental logic inscribed into the very essence of the capitalist system. The basic idea here is that, in order to ensure the dynamism that guarantees its survival as a system, employers under capitalism must require employees to add more economic value in production than they are recompensed for in terms of wages.

This, of course, is also a logic of exploitation. The contractual basis of the wage labour nexus defends a situation in which workers remain unpaid for part of the work they are obliged to do. A procedural injustice is clearly perpetrated in this instance and, given that this experience is fundamental to the reproduction of capitalism as a functioning system, for Marx, capitalism could never be just. Indeed, from his perspective, the whole essence of capitalism is that it forcibly submits the vast majority of any given society — via the process of false consciousness — to implicit consent to the injustices that are committed against them. This is the point of departure for the political Marx to build upon the insights of the analytical Marx in order to advocate the move to a brand new society capable of transcending the logic of exploitation on which capitalism depends. The organizational basis for prosecuting such a move arises from the fact that exploitation and injustice are not solitary experiences under capitalism. Rather, they are experiences that are shared to a greater or lesser degree by everyone within society who has to work to finance their own subsistence. Marx thus depicted society as riven into two classes relating to their respective positions in the production process. On the one hand, there are the capitalists—the bourgeoisie—who benefit from the surplus value extraction that permeates right to the heart of the capitalist system. On the other hand, there are the workers—the proletariat—who bear the indignity of having surplus value forcibly extracted from them.

Modern 'structuralist' and 'critical' extensions of Marx's political economy

Proponents of Marxist IPE have stayed remarkably loyal to Marx's original analytical formulations in the 150+ years since they were initially devised. They seek to uncover exploitative dynamics in modern processes of international production, and they present such dynamics as infringements of global justice. Thus, they might investigate the way in which large companies with multinational operating facilities today make profits for themselves and their shareholders, focusing in particular on the potential for labour power to command different prices in different countries, as well as on how this creates opportunities for multinational corporations to enforce ever-greater discrepancies between the labour they command and the labour power they are obliged to recompense. The policy-making apparatus of the state might always be called upon to defend workers' rights and to meliorate the tendency towards proletarian exploitation. Yet, Marxist IPE scholars have pointed increasingly to the development of a transnational capitalist class as a byproduct of the contemporary trend towards globalization (see, for example, van der Pijl 1998; Sklair 2001). Members of a transnational capitalist class have allegiance to no state and are therefore able increasingly to escape the impact of regulatory policies introduced by state managers in the interests of workers' rights. If this is true, then the fundamental antagonism between

bourgeoisie and proletariat identified by Marx is likely to be experienced in its purest form today within specifically international production processes.

A 'structuralist' approach to Marxist IPE has developed in an attempt to capture this point, conceptualizing the world economy as a single, integrated capitalist system existing within a single, integrated political space of exploitation. Structuralists will often pay only limited attention to reconstructing Marx's explanatory framework in its own terms, because their real starting point is instead in Lenin's efforts to internationalize fundamental Marxian themes (Lenin 1917/1996). In a pamphlet of the same name, Lenin argued that imperialism had become the 'highest stage of capitalism' by the start of the twentieth century, and that, as such, the new dynamism within the capitalist system centred on the relationship between states. Marx's original class-based analysis was retained, but Lenin asked how class-based relationships had been transformed now that capitalism had become a world system.

He argued that domestic bourgeoisies in advanced European countries had increasingly become international bourgeoisies through their willingness to strike class compromises at home. Their acquiescence to the granting of workers' rights domestically was met by a need to increase the level of surplus value extraction overseas in the interests of maintaining underlying levels of profitability for the national economy as a whole. Colonial links provided the ideal political context in which this could be achieved. As a consequence, imperialism was seen to have important economic effects both at home and abroad. Given the willingness of many scholars to treat contemporary conditions of globalization as just the latest phase of economic imperialism (see, for example, Hoogvelt 1997; Hardt and Negri 2000; Petras and Veltmeyer 2001), the structuralist approach to IPE has retained many adherents. They are usually to be found today practising either World Systems Theory or Dependency Theory. In its most up-to-date guise, World Systems Theory is based on the assumption that the world divides into economic regions of core, periphery, and semi-periphery (see, for example, Wallerstein 1979), while Dependency Theory is based on the assumption that the continued distorted development of poorer countries results from the need to defend the conditions that have led to the development trajectory of more economically advanced countries (see, for example, dos Santos 1970).

There are numerous variants of self-styled 'critical' IPE competing against modern structuralist Marxism for space in the radical IPE literature (see also Box 2.1). Some of these retain strong filial links with their Marxist heritage, whereas others have tried to place as much distance as possible between themselves and Marx's political economy. Yet, all seem to be linked to some degree to the turn towards post-Marxist Critical Theory in IR from the 1980s onwards. As a philosophical movement, Critical Theory dates from the 1930s and the Frankfurt School interventions focusing on the essentially political nature of all social scientific explanations. However, in IR, the origins of Critical Theory are more usually traced to Robert Cox's selective appropriation of Frankfurt School

theory than to the foundations of that theory itself. In the early 1980s, Cox attempted to create renewed space for radical approaches to IR by juxtaposing the transformative intentions of radical approaches with what he termed the 'problem solving' goals of non-radical approaches (Cox 1981). Cox had detected an ever-sharper concentration of research activities in IR on increasingly technical questions of system management: how best to organize the relationship between states in order to minimize the potential for violence between them, and how best to integrate states into an international system whose emergent properties emphasized liberal concerns for co-operation in the interests of meeting common goals. In this way, IR had been focused on finding solutions to systemic problems which served to defend the most basic structure of world economic affairs. That is, it took the world increasingly as it found it, and stopped asking more profound questions concerning the political and moral legitimacy of the economic foundations of that world. Cox's appeal to a critical theoretical tradition should therefore be seen as an effort to refocus IR on these existential issues.

Box 2.1 Feminist International Political Economy

Feminists have every much the same entitlement to the labels 'radical IPE' and 'critical IPE' as have Marxists. Feminist approaches to the subject field are certainly radical in their assertions that the capitalist system is founded on the reproduction of patriarchal social relations and, as such, the system itself should be a focus for concerted political challenge. They are also certainly critical in their related concerns to show that the dual structures of a capitalist economy and a patriarchal society are anything but natural. Rather, the continued existence of these structures requires decisive political interventions on the part of those who have privileged access to public decision-making bodies. As such, they must both be seen as conscious political choices.

Many feminists accept the basic Marxist proposition that the capitalist economy is rooted inextricably in the exploitation of those whose labours are functional to

its reproduction. Indeed, for those feminists who seek to emphasize the economic basis of everyday life in their explanations of the subordinate social position of women, there is much to commend in an integrated Marxist–feminist perspective. Almost all feminists, however, wish to push beyond the Marxist conception of society, which overlooks the issue of gender in order to focus solely on the interaction of economic classes. In Marx's original analysis of the dynamics of capitalist reproduction, it is the male industrial working-class that is the main agent of historical change, and this focus has been retained by the majority of modern-day Marxists. The aim is to show how systems of ostensibly free exchange have been established on the back of the forced extraction of surplus value from the working class. The focus of feminist IPE is different. Here, the aim is to show how systems of ostensibly free exchange have been established on the back of social norms that involve deeply gendered assumptions about family role specialization.

The ability of women to participate fully in the economy—whether as consumers or as producers—is constrained by the tasks they are required to undertake in support of basic family structures. Whereas the Marxist conception of labour refers only to paid work in the formal economy, feminists' extended conception of labour also includes unpaid work undertaken in the home, without which the maintenance of the workforce in the formal economy could not be guaranteed. Economy and society are therefore not distinct entities but rather interdependent spheres of human existence. As a consequence, any attempt to reproduce economic relations in their distinctively capitalist form is also likely to involve reproducing social relations in their distinctively patriarchal form. According to feminists, to engage truly with either radical or critical IPE requires explicit and simultaneous theorization of both dimensions of reproduction—that is, economic and social—within the context of everyday life.

This appeal translated readily into IPE. Cox's own work asked how the basic structure of world affairs was predicated upon the forced institutionalization of social relations of production consistent with capitalist accumulation (see, for example, Cox with Sinclair 1996). As such, it was an attempt to get IR scholars to ask questions more usually associated with IPE. His aim was to show that the dominant problem-solving tradition in IR was inattentive to issues of economic organization, either nationally or internationally. It was consequently closed to political or moral critiques of capitalism and it had no basis to engage with radical perspectives on the social relations of capitalist production. In Cox's terms, it simply had to take the continued reproduction of capitalist accumulation for granted. It could ask how to manage the relationship between states so that possible tensions embedded within the very nature of accumulation might be alleviated. However, it had no basis from which to understand the social implications of those tensions as a need to argue for the move to an alternative type of society. Critical Theory's attraction was precisely that it was able to offer a grounding for such an argument.

Returning the discussion again to historical roots, twentieth-century extensions of Marxism are notable for the way in which they involve at least a partial break with Marx's own intellectual trajectory. This is by no means a complete break, because the aspiration for a better world free of the logic of economic exploitation remains visible in modern-day IPE literatures that trace their origins either to Lenin or to the Frankfurt School. In this respect, the political Marx remains alive and well in this work, thereby justifying the retention of the label 'Marxist' in order to describe it. However, the analytical Marx is not necessarily as prominent. As befits the continued presence of the political Marx, modern-day Marxist IPE seeks its normative essence in a fundamental challenge to prevailing neoliberal conditions of world order. Yet, it does not always reveal its historical roots in the analytical Marx's struggle to undermine the way in which Smith's liberal political economy came to colonize the concepts of orthodox economic discourse as a means of asserting his own distinctive conceptual terminology in its place. It certainly does little to show the struggle in which Marx had to engage in order to break free of Smithian thinking, given that he so often took Smith's conceptual starting points as his own. Smith's theory of the capitalist economy as an engine for the creation of economic value reappears, albeit in admittedly revised form, in Marx's work; exactly the same is true of his account of the way in which the focus on creating value has negative psychological effects on the capitalist workforce.

Key points

- Marx insisted that all economic experiences should be placed in their correct historical context and understood in relation to the evolution of the capitalist system from one time period to the next.
- Marxist IPE is an all-encompassing critique of capitalist society, from the exploitation it enforces upon its members to the false consciousness that masks the real dynamics of this exploitation within the normal workings of everyday life.

- In order to keep pace with changes to the economy, twentieth-century extensions of Marxism increasingly came to place more emphasis on the international dimension of economic affairs, but they have done so through partial divorce from their political economy origins in Marx's own work.

Methodological Distinctions to Sub-Divide the Field

So, where does this discussion leave us? The three-way distinction between realism, liberalism, and Marxism remains the standard fare of introductory IPE teaching. It is through the series of oppositions between the three approaches that students are taught the basic concepts of the subject field, and these continue to be the primary points of reference as students are gradually exposed to more complex concepts. Yet, is it defensible in its own terms? My argument is that it almost certainly is not. It matters, for a number of reasons, that one is accurate when it comes to specifying the historical roots of the contemporary theories on which modern-day work is based. If this specification is questionable, then the intellectual lineage that acts as a defence of the contemporary position is equally questionable. Contemporary theories are not free-floating entities, but are necessarily part of historically grounded traditions of thought. If the claim to belong to a certain tradition cannot be sustained under close textual scrutiny, then the contemporary theory immediately loses both its historical anchoring and part of its validation to talk authoritatively about the world as it is encountered today. By this measure, it must be doubted whether realism, liberalism, or Marxism hold the

clear-cut and tightly contained positions that they appear to hold in introductory IPE texts.

It is therefore time to move on, away from the focus on how IPE is taught, to an alternative focus on how IPE is researched. How might the distinctiveness of individual research strategies be understood in relation to one another? The first thing to note is that there is no single, generally accepted method of appraising the subject field in terms of basic themes of research. The specialist literature is rather sparse on this particular issue, and most of the people who have attempted overall appraisals of IPE have devised their own classificatory schema for identifying the major analytical and disciplinary divisions in IPE scholars' research. These appraisals tend to focus in particular on how the choice of methodology combines with the choice of analytical and disciplinary perspectives in order to define the nature of individual contributions.

One place to begin in the search for suitable heuristic distinctions to subdivide the field is with Craig Murphy and Douglas Nelson's desire to distinguish between an 'IO (*International Organization*) School' and a 'British School' of IPE (Murphy and Nelson 2001). The meanings of these labels are not self-evident and, at one level, they might even invite confusion. They certainly require more explanation, which is what they will receive in due course. For now, though, the important thing to note is that Murphy and Nelson's distinction is an attempt to divide the field analytically through focusing on the different methodological choices that IPE authors make. This is important in terms of recognizing divergent starting points within the subject field and of trying to understand how different interventions into IPE debates relate to one another on the basis of their underlying structure of argument.

Murphy and Nelson's 'IO' and 'British' Schools of IPE

As 'IO' refers to *International Organization*, the leading US-based journal in the field, and as the IO School is purposefully juxtaposed with the British School, notice is served of a possible 'transatlantic divide' in IPE. However, this does not mean that all US scholars share an unreflexive, almost preconscious, allegiance to the IO School; nor does it mean that all scholars working in US universities, irrespective of their country of origin, share a similar affiliation. It is merely to point to the fact that most scholarly IPE journals published in the US have followed the lead of *International Organization* in prioritizing a particular conception of research within the field.

Similarly, the label 'British School' should not be understood too literally, at least not to infer homogeneity of approach in all IPE that originates geographically in the UK. Once again, it is the editorial policy of leading journals that gives meaning to the label, and British School editorial policy attracts work submitted from all over the world. The label is intended to capture the sense that the major journals published in the UK have been set up in (often conscious) opposition to the style of IPE scholarship that features so prominently in the major journals published in the US. It therefore provides a potential home for work that might not otherwise be published, wherever in the world that work originates.

In the first instance, the division to which Murphy and Nelson want to draw attention is methodological. Authors whose work is consistent with the IO School approach tend to link economic outcomes to interests, and this is achieved most often through the application of a largely mechanistic rational choice framework. This is a relatively recent trend, even within *International Organization* itself, but it is, nonetheless, the trend enacted increasingly in modern-day scholarship. Economic agents are assumed to satisfy their interests in a manner that imposes the logic of utility maximization on their actions. What is true of individuals' economic behaviour is also considered to be true of economic policy. States are assumed to have readily identifiable interests, as well as to be constituted in such a way as to have the cognitive capacities of a utility-maximizing agent. As a consequence, policy decisions are treated as a rational response to a national interest that is relatively straightforward both to define and to act upon, and whose identification with the will of the people is thought to be largely uncontroversial.

IPE within the IO School tradition is able to focus on the standard political question of 'who gets what and how', but it reduces its answers to that question to those that are consistent with a rationalist framework that can say almost nothing about social influences on the construction of economic identities. As an individual's behaviour is conceptually indistinguishable from that of states in so far as both are orientated towards a pre-given structure of interests, every agent within the economy will be seeking to ensure that they emerge from economic activity with a sense of having enhanced their standing within society. Policy outcomes can therefore most often be reduced to the prevailing balance of interests within society—either domestically or internationally.

By contrast, British School scholars tend to focus less on matters of policy than do their IO School counterparts, and they reject the idea that all issues of concern to the student of IPE can be reduced to models of rational agential choice. They concentrate instead on how the choice of any particular agent is itself shaped by the social structures of the economic environment in which it is attempted. Individuals' economic behaviour is thus not understood as a purely rational response to external circumstances which in themselves do nothing to condition how economic agents think about the choices available to them. Rather, behaviour is assumed to reflect social aspirations, aspirations arise as a consequence of socially constituted identities, and the process of identity formation responds to complex dynamics of acculturation to embedded economic norms.

From this standpoint, neither individuals' interests nor the national interest can be discerned from observing the outcomes of economic behaviour that must be assumed, by definition, to be utility maximizing. Both identities and interests precede behaviour, and they are linked not to a process of rational calculation but to the place of the individual within the social life of the community. Of particular importance to the British School is the question of how both identities and interests reflect the structure of distribution within society. In this respect, British School scholars are equally happy to work with a conception of either national or international society. They ask either how the structure of distribution nationally affects economic identities and interests nationally (or vice versa), or how the structure of distribution internationally affects economic identities and interests internationally (or vice versa). An emphasis on issues of distributive justice is thereby enabled.

This is also to focus on the question of 'who gets what and how', but this might be the only underlying property shared by the IO and British Schools of IPE. The IO School asks how initial economic endowments are expended in an attempt to maximize utility, while the British School asks how those endowments arise in the first place from culturally specific relationships between economy and society. The IO School treats IPE generically as the study of constrained utility maximization problems under conditions of rational choice, while the British School treats IPE as the study of the philosophy of social organization across various spatial

scales of economic life. The IO School prioritizes exchange relations as the essence of the economy, and it models policy decisions as direct analogues of economic exchange. By contrast, the British School prioritizes distributive relations, and it theorizes policy decisions as reflections of the underlying balance of social forces.

Cohen's 'American' and 'British' Schools of IPE

Murphy and Nelson's account of what divides IPE scholars perhaps has not received the attention it deserves, because it has been largely overtaken in recent years by a further account that creates the image of a transatlantic divide in IPE. This is associated with the work of Benjamin Cohen (2007, 2008b, 2009), one of the most respected figures in the subject field for many years. Cohen posits the existence of an 'American' School of IPE in opposition to a 'British' School.

Although he makes his core argument in a different way, it is relatively easy to transpose Cohen's labels onto Murphy and Nelson's, and not only because both use exactly the same term to describe one half of IPE's principal division. The real underlying similarity between the two typologies is that both emphasize methodological differences as the important factor that causes the two Schools to diverge from one another. The main difference is that Murphy and Nelson talk about how different methodological choices cause journal editors to favour some styles of analysis over others in their decisions about how to allocate space in their publications, whereas Cohen talks about the methodological choices that individual IPE scholars make about how to undertake their analyses in the first place.

In general, Cohen places a 'follow-my-leader' interpretation on his explanation of what divides American School and British School IPE. He identifies seven highly influential scholars—he calls them the Magnificent Seven (2008b: 10)—who laid the methodological foundations for IPE in its earliest years. As befits the subsequent distribution of IPE scholars to their respective Schools, five of these 'first-generation' trailblazers paved the way for the development of the American School (Robert Keohane, Robert Gilpin, Charles Kindleberger, Stephen Krasner, and Peter Katzenstein), and two for the British School (Susan Strange and Robert Cox). Cohen's underlying point is that, although all seven agreed that there was a need for a field of International Political Economy to close the existing gap between International Relations and International Economics, they disagreed quite significantly about how the ensuing field of IPE should be constructed. The fact that the five first-generation American School scholars were in broad consensus about how to proceed sustained the possibility that such a School might be created; likewise, the broad consensus between the two first generation British School scholars. Cohen further argues that the two divergent roots of IPE's transatlantic divide as laid down in the first generation have themselves been magnified by the increasingly divergent second and third generations. The follow-my-leader approach appears to have been characterized by following the first generation to increasingly extreme articulations of their original differences in a manner that is consistent with path-dependent effects.

Cohen's arguably most controversial claim is that what has emerged over time is an American School that prides itself so much on its scientific method that this is willingly traded for the realistic nature of its underlying concepts and for its broader applicability to political debates about the content of world economic order; this co-exists in his opinion with a British School that is so attentive to its normative method that it generally overlooks the need for empirical testing or the desire to generate replicable results. As in the Murphy and Nelson account of the IO School, Cohen's American School has a much more restricted scope of study and a much narrower definition of what counts as political in IPE. Both variants of the British School are as inclusive as possible on each of these questions. Its proponents tend to rule out nothing a priori as a feasible object of study if it can be shown

that it relates to a site of human agency which has some demonstrable impact on economic life chances around the world. The objective of such studies is to show how the underlying structure of society shapes the state/market relationship in different contexts in order to produce distributional consequences worldwide. By contrast, the American School is more likely to focus solely on issues of policy formation, studying the success that particular actors have had in embedding their interests in international economic agreements and how they have shaped the state/market relationship accordingly. This applies equally to the achievement of national objectives by actors who work at the level of the state and to the maintenance of effective international institutions by actors who work at the level of global governance.

As with the Murphy and Nelson designation of a transatlantic divide, much depends in this respect on the willingness to adopt rational choice theory as the means of developing the explanatory framework. American School IPE exhibits underlying methodological preferences which appear to be ideally adapted to the embrace of rational choice theory. The abstract assumptions of utility-maximizing behaviour provide American School scholars with the degree of replicability and predictive capacity in their results that they treasure so highly. The use of rational choice theory provides a seemingly rigorous basis on which to claim that a particular type of policy will always be selected in certain circumstances, either because it reflects the generic enactment of self-interest that will always be in play, or because this is the type of policy consistently produced in similar circumstances in the past.

British School scholars have generally been much less sympathetic to the encroachment of rational choice theory within IPE. Their concern is that rational choice theory itself attempts to naturalize a specific conception of economic agency, one which is institutionally suited only to life lived within generally free market economies. To adopt that approach, they argue, is akin to turning IPE into an element of the free market hegemony that the subject field's scholars might otherwise wish to critique. It is simply not possible from this perspective to gain sufficient autonomous theoretical space to comment on the political structures of world order if the theory being used itself both reflects and reinforces those structures.

Cohen's self-confessed aim in describing the increasing divergence of three generations of American and British School scholarship is conciliatory. He sees himself very much as a bridge-builder, praising the American School for its commitment to scientific rigour but equally praising the British School for its focus on the bigger picture of why world economy dynamics impose themselves on life chances in the way they do. Mutual recognition of these competing strengths, he suggests, makes it much more feasible that IPE scholars might begin the profitable search for what exists in the intellectual space lying between the two Schools.

However, Cohen's intervention does not yet appear to have had his desired effect. It has generated much debate—most notably both a discussion section in and a whole special issue of the *Review of International Political Economy* (15/1 and 16/1, respectively), as well as a whole special issue of *New Political Economy* (14/3)—but so far, this has amounted to more heat than light. The content of the responses from both sides has arguably served to reinforce Cohen's original argument. By finding different ways to describe the distinctiveness of the work that goes on within their respective Schools, the proponents of both have merely confirmed Cohen's initial suspicion that both Schools are only too willing to define themselves in opposition to the other (see also Higgott and Watson 2008; McNamara 2009).

Drawbacks of the Murphy/Nelson and Cohen approaches

If there are problems with the Murphy and Nelson and the Cohen designations, then they are twofold. From the perspective of the current review, the most obvious one is that of over-homogenization

(in much the same way that the three-way theoretical distinction between realism, liberalism, and Marxism is guilty of over-homogenization). The concern when using the either/or distinction between the IO/American School and the British School is that many interventions into IPE debates will lose their individuality if they can only be thought of as reflecting one half or the other of a binary opposition. In practice, on both sides of the transatlantic divide, what is presented as a single position is in fact an amalgam of a large number of different positions, many of which will involve ignoring the other school altogether and instead challenging other positions from within the same school. What can be made to look like an internally homogeneous school for the sake of analytical abstraction subsequently fragments into a series of often mutually antagonistic theoretical claims when viewed more closely.

In addition to this, the Murphy and Nelson and the Cohen designations prioritize the contemporary practices of IPE and they understand these solely on their own terms. From my perspective, what is most obviously missing here is a ready way to link contemporary pursuits within IPE to their historical roots via a direct intellectual lineage. The two-schools approach refers only to ways in which IPE might be undertaken in the present. Its labels offer few clues about how the two schools correspond to established, yet competing, historical traditions in political economy. The designations emphasize contemporary theories, contemporary methods, and contemporary approaches, presenting the choice between the two schools as one that mirrors the most obvious methodological dispute in contemporary social science: will the convenience of rational choice theory be accepted as a modelling technique, or will a more philosophically reflexive account of human agency be demanded?

At one level, this focus on the contemporary is entirely understandable. After all, almost every appraisal of the subject field begins by commenting on IPE's youth relative to other fields (see, for example, Gill and Law 1988; Onuf 1997;

Pearson and Rochester 1998; Dash et al. 2003). It was forged amid attempts to explain events that were a particular feature of distinctively modern times. Specifically, the recent manifestation of IPE results from concerns to reflect on the future of world economic affairs following the collapse of the **Bretton Woods** system of international economic management in the early 1970s (see, for example, Krasner 1976; Gilpin 1987; Frieden and Lake 1995; Grieco and Ikenberry 2003). Given this intimate connection between the birth of IPE and the onset of the most recent phase of the modern world economy, it could conceivably be said that contemporary theories, methods, and approaches are all that is required to understand that world.

Yet, this would be to overlook an important point already raised on a number of occasions in the current chapter. This is that contemporary approaches are not free-floating entities; they are not without their own history and they cannot be understood other than in relation to the historical traditions of thought of which they are a part. To treat contemporary approaches in their own self-referential terms is to deny them their intellectual heritage, as well as to strip them of the historical anchoring that comes from recognizing their lineage. As such, the labels IO/American School and British School, while useful, are also not without their limits. Consequently, the search should probably continue for the most appropriate heuristic distinctions for understanding the subject field of IPE in its entirety.

Key points

- Murphy and Nelson's distinction between the IO School and the British School of IPE recognizes competing transatlantic methodologies and attempts to divide the field in relation to the major underlying analytical themes derived from these methodological differences; Cohen's distinction between the American School and the British School of IPE does exactly the same.
- Cohen contrasts the scientific pretensions of American School IPE (with its associated formal methodological rigour) with the non-scientific pretensions of British School IPE (with its associated concern for normative clarity); without using the same labels, Murphy and Nelson point to something very similar in their account of the IO School's embrace but the British School's rejection of rational choice theory.

- The Murphy and Nelson and the Cohen distinctions tell us a lot about what distinguishes one contemporary group of practitioners from another, but they do not tell us about the origins of those different practices and they therefore divorce contemporary IPE from its historical roots.

Disciplinary Distinctions to Sub-Divide the Field

My preference is to distinguish between two broad approaches to IPE, one of which is the 'international relations' approach, and the other the 'political economy' approach (Watson 2005: ch. 1). The advantage of using this classificatory schema is that it divides the subject field on the basis of its disciplinary starting point. As such, there is no necessary tendency to privilege modern forms of study, and thus to divorce those forms from their historical roots. In fact, the reason for using a heuristic distinction emphasizing disciplinary starting points is precisely to signal the importance of different intellectual lineages.

The disciplinary basis of the transatlantic divide

There are, of course, different ways of practising both IR and political economy. No simple mapping procedure exists, then, through which we can say that Murphy and Nelson's implied transtlantic divide—let alone Cohen's much more explicit transatlantic divide—translates into a dispute between those who treat IPE as a subset of IR and those who treat it as a subset of political economy. It is possible to detect both IR and political economy perspectives in either the IO School or the American School tradition. Equally, it is also possible to detect both IR and political economy perspectives in the British School tradition. The disciplinary distinction between IR and political economy perspectives can therefore be used alongside the analytical distinction between the IO/American School and the British School. The result is a two-by-two table (see Table 2.1).

Thus, there is no need to treat the disciplinary distinction between the IR and political economy perspectives and the analytical distinction between the IO/American School and the British School as being mutually exclusive. Indeed, by using the two distinctions in conjunction with one another, it is possible to devise a more nuanced picture of the subject field of IPE. The three different distinctions drawn by Murphy and Nelson, Cohen, and Watson in their different depictions of the field all share one important property: they are all 'either/or' characterizations, in which to be practising IPE is either to be doing one thing or another. A logic of opposition is thus implied, whereby alternative approaches must necessarily be at loggerheads with one another. Yet, as soon as we try to integrate these depictions into a single characterization the sense of an oppositional logic dividing the field in two immediately begins to recede.

Most obviously, such integration doubles the number of generic positions one can expect to find within IPE. Table 2.1, as is clear to see, is a four-cell rather than a two-cell table, suggesting that there are at least four generic types of IPE for the student to discover and to work with. Moreover, the movement between two adjacent cells in Table 2.1 is likely to be much more fluid than across a binary opposition. This is because adjacent cells share one important constitutive feature. Reading across the page, they are either both part of the IO/American School or both part of the British School, and, as such, they have underlying analytical and methodological assumptions in common. Reading down the page, adjacent cells are either both part of the IR perspective or both part of the political economy perspective, and, as such, they have an underlying disciplinary pedigree in common. This implies that there might well be significant IPE content to be found in the borderlands between adjacent cells, which is a possibility that immediately becomes less easy to contemplate if we revert to thinking about the subject field through the lens of an oppositional logic across a binary distinction.

Further reflections on the liberalism/realism/Marxism trichotomy

The four-cell approach to appraising IPE research also allows us to turn our attention back to the liberalism versus realism versus Marxism trichotomy used so extensively in teaching the fundamentals of the field. The trichotomy is usually presented as three mutually exclusive traditions of thought, which can only be understood in opposition to one another. In other words, we learn most about the arguments that proponents of one position are likely to make by knowing what proponents of the other two positions would *not* argue: each position thus becomes hermetically sealed in its distinctiveness from the other two. The mental map of the field that arises from this characterization is triangular

Table 2.1 A Four-Cell Approach for Appraising IPE

| | | Disciplinary heuristic distinctions (Watson 2005) | |
		International relations	Political economy
Analytical heuristic distinctions (Murphy and Nelson 2001; Cohen 2008)	IO/ American School	The aim is to model relationships between states as games played by rational actors. The substantive context in which the game takes place is international economic negotiations (at the World Trade Organization, for example; or at the G8). These contexts are not understood as dialogic forums in which negotiators come together in democratic discussions to decide what is best for the world as a whole. Any pronouncements of this nature are seen as a smokescreen to disguise the enactment of a narrowly defined national interest. International economic negotiations are therefore treated as competitive environments in which states struggle for supremacy. At times they might make concessions to one another, but only if this is seen as the most likely strategy to elicit the greatest gains.	The aim is to model relationships between economic agents on the assumption that they are both by instinct and by definition rational actors. The substantive context in which these relationships are explored is highly varied. They include the interactions between the firm and its shareholders, labour and management, consumers and consumption culture, development ideals and the World Bank/International Monetary Fund, etc. At all times, these interactions are understood as competitive struggles in which each side is trying to impose its interest on the other. Cessation of struggle only occurs in the event of interests being aligned. The goal of all actors is to maximize the utility arising from their economic activities, and they will act upon such a goal largely without reference to their long-term interests.
	British School	The aim is to uncover the sources of both the state's hard and soft power, with a view to demonstrating how these translate into important economic resources. As above, the substantive context of study is most likely to be international economic negotiations, but here it is believed that the outcomes of the negotiations are influenced by more than the representatives around the table enacting the national interest. Outcomes are also influenced by the prevailing ideological climate, so it is also necessary to show how the dominant world view arose, and how it is reproduced in the interactions between state and non-state actors. There are circumstances in which non-state actors might be the primary recipients of gains, and this could even be at the expense of states.	The aim is to explore the link between established modes of economic thinking and the practices of everyday economic life. In particular, it is to specify the mechanisms (political, cultural, cognitive) through which individuals are socialized into creating patterns of life that replicate directly the implied behavioural traits embedded in economic theory. Economic theory is thus presented as an ideological intervention into the world rather than a politically neutral description of relationships within that world. A range of actors carry the premises of economic theory in their intentions, and disseminate them more widely within society through their day-to-day practices. But these practices are also challenged by counter-cultural movements seeking to contest their influence on everyday life. The economy is thus necessarily an arena of social struggle.

in shape, with liberalism, realism, and Marxism occupying the three corners, and the rest of the field being pretty much barren land. A very different mental map emerges, however, if we try instead to locate the disaggregated view of the trichotomy outlined in earlier sections of the chapter on to the four-cell approach outlined in Table 2.1. The result is shown in Table 2.2. The single lines connecting different positions (both within cells and across the boundaries of adjacent cells) show positions which have much in common with one another, whereas the double lines connecting different positions show instances in which one position was created as a direct refutation of another.

As before, what emerges in this instance is a much more fluid conception of the field than is implied by the trichotomous structure of introductory IPE teaching. Many of the individual approaches to the subject field themselves traverse a boundary between adjacent cells, while many more are closely linked to approaches located in other cells. By re-presenting the liberalism versus realism versus Marxism trichotomy as a series of false demarcations between what are in any case amalgams of heterogeneous positions, it becomes much more possible to focus on the nature of those links than it is using the standard presentation of the trichotomy, in which no such links are presumed to exist. Even in those instances in which the fluidity of the subject field breaks down because one position is established in direct opposition to another, this is as likely to occur within the context of a single cell as across a boundary dividing two cells.

The result is a pictorial warning against the reification of simple clear-cut divisions in the complex and diverse theoretical underpinnings of the field as a whole. The image of IPE thus created is much messier than the one with which the chapter began as a reflection of what is to be found in other IPE textbooks by ways of introduction to the subject field. Yet, this in itself is no bad thing, because it provides a more representative characterization of the field than one that is guilty of pigeonholing contributions to the literature into neat, but incommensurable, little boxes. Academic instinct is

always to push the limits of theoretical arguments as far as they will go: to extend the previous analogy, to attempt to think outside the box. This is no less true of IPE than it is of any other subject field. The rigid reification of theoretical demarcations therefore deprives the analyst of IPE of a sense of the ebb and flow of theoretical arguments over time. None of the positions represented in Table 2.2 will be fixed beyond the short term. Their centres will remain pretty much where they are in their current cells, but their outermost boundaries will shift under the influence of future theoretical innovations. Some of the approaches will appear to move closer together in the future, as their respective boundaries converge on increasingly common theoretical underpinnings. However, it is just as likely that others will appear to move further apart.

Beyond heuristic distinctions altogether?

Having muddied the waters of clear-cut distinctions in the representation of the field outlined above, it is next necessary to ask whether IPE scholars should be thinking in terms of heuristic distinctions at all. By reflecting further on the Watson distinction between the IR and political economy perspectives, it is more than possible to conclude that they should not. That distinction appears to suggest that only half of IPE scholars work with political economy assumptions, yet by scratching the surface of this claim it is possible to show that this is not in fact the case. The question that needs to be asked of scholars working within the IR perspective is whether they fail per se to work with political economy assumptions when practising their IPE, or whether they merely fail to acknowledge the basis of their political economy assumptions in a consciously reflexive way?

When we read Table 2.1 across the page, we see that IO/American School IPE can be practised from both an IR and a political economy perspective. Yet, this does not mean that the IO/American School's IR perspective is devoid of all political economy

Table 2.2 Mapping IPE's Theoretical Divisions onto the Four-Cell Approach to the Field

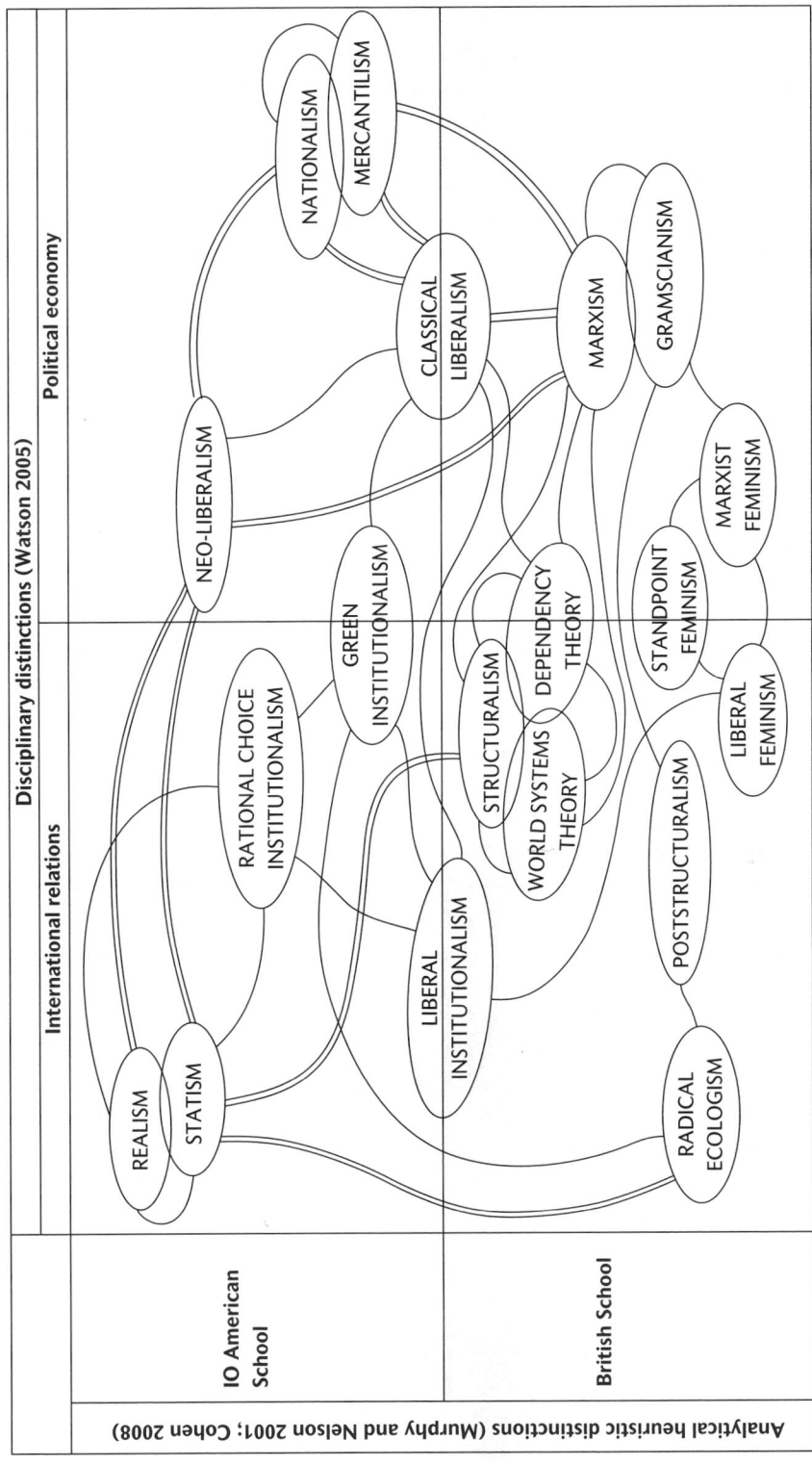

essence. In common with the IO/American School's political economy perspective, it treats IPE as the study of constrained utility maximization problems under conditions of rational choice. This most basic way of conceptualizing issues of concern within the subject field implies that it is rooted in a particular form of economic thinking, because it very much mirrors the patterns of scholarship encountered in neoclassical economics. The only difference between the two IO/American School cousins is that this intellectual lineage is more readily acknowledged in the political economy perspective than it is in the IR perspective. It would be much more usual, for example, for those adopting theoretical positions in the upper-right cell of Table 2.2 to comment openly on their historical roots in neoclassical economics than it would be for those adopting theoretical positions in the upper-left cell to do the same.

A similar story can be told in relation to British School IPE. It can also be practised from both an IR perspective and a political economy perspective, and here, too, there is more than initially meets the eye with the IR perspective. Both camps within the British School treat IPE as the study of the philosophy of social organization with respect to everyday economic life. This most basic way of conceptualizing the issues of concern within the subject field also leads us back to a particular form of economic thinking. It very much mirrors the patterns of scholarship we encounter in classical political economy, the tradition that was dominant before the onset of the era of neoclassical economics in the 1870s (Heilbroner 2000). As before, the big difference here is probably only one of emphasis, with those working in the political economy perspective of the British School more readily acknowledging the intellectual lineage of contemporary positions

than those working in the IR perspective. We would not expect, for example, modern-day Marxists to do anything other than acknowledge the intellectual debt that their specific brand of IPE owes to Marx's political economy. In contrast, it would be much less usual to see anyone adopting a theoretical position from the bottom-left cell of Table 2.2 reflecting openly on the classical political economy origins of their work.

It is a significant finding that both Murphy and Nelson's and Cohen's two schools of IPE have origins in, and replicate, the analytical style of two very different traditions of economic thought, because these historical differences feed through directly today into different scholarly intentions embedded right at the heart of contemporary IPE's two schools. It is important, then, to say a few words about the differences between classical political economy and neoclassical economics.

Historians of economic thought usually treat the shift from classical political economy to neoclassical economics as one from an outdated to a thoroughly state-of-the-art way of studying economic relations (see, for example, Blaug 1996; Backhouse 2002). After all, classical political economy was the dominant tradition until the so-called 'Marginalist Revolution' of the 1870s (see Box 2.2), whereupon economists have typically followed the premises of neoclassical theory (see, for example, Robinson 1964; Barber 1991). Yet, what counts as a pathbreaking moment in appraisals of economics should not necessarily lead us to dismiss the insights that can be gleaned about IPE from continuing to follow the original path. The two subject fields are orientated around different aims and different goals, so it is perfectly understandable that appraisals of them will emphasize different issues as being decisive to their respective historical developments.

Neoclassical economics has divergent origins, but it also has a distinctive core. That core emerges from the assumption that all economic actions result from 'constrained maximization' decisions. Agents are necessarily constrained, because they will not have a limitless supply of money, and they will also have competing claims on whatever money they do have. But within this context, it is assumed that they will attempt to allocate their available resources to the best possible outcome. According to neoclassical economics, this is the outcome that maximizes utility, where utility is a technical economic term for the degree of pleasure that can be derived from commodity consumption. It is not claimed that economic agents *actually* undertake the complex calculations required to show that choices always follow the fully rational utility maximizing option. Instead, it is simply assumed that it is human instinct to adopt necessarily mechanistically rational behavioural traits and, as a consequence, all actions must automatically be utility maximizing, whether the agent is conscious of having targeted such motivations or not.

This might sound familiar, even for someone who is approaching neoclassical economics for the very first time. This is because it is exactly the same structure of argument as for rational choice theory. While the latter's proponents do not always reflect explicitly on the intellectual origins of their position, the roots of rational choice theory in fact stem directly from neoclassical economics. The choices described by rational choice theory are not choices at all in the literal sense of the word, because they do not follow from a process of reflection about how best to orientate behaviour within the context of the social relationships in which it is contemplated. Instead, it is modelled as an instinctive selection of the utility maximizing option in the interests of self-preferment.

It is important that the link is made between rational choice theory and neoclassical economics when engaged in appraisals of the subject field of IPE, because so many contemporary international political economists adopt rational choice theory as their chosen methodology. This is particularly true of those researchers with North American training, which once again raises the possibility of a transatlantic divide in IPE. For its proponents, rational choice theory is a universal methodology that transcends the selection of key concepts and theoretical frameworks. By remaining steadfast in the assertion that all economic actions must necessarily entail the goal of utility maximization, it is possible to align almost any concept or framework with the core claims of rational choice theory.

For its critics, though, this can only be achieved by trying too hard to squeeze other arguments into a rational choice framework where they might not fit comfortably. The assumption of utility maximization leads to an entirely decontextualized theory of action, in so far as it removes the economic agent from the social relationships in which he or she is involved. Rational choice theoretical perspectives in IPE can only describe situations in which individuals can in some way be assumed to be beyond society. But there are no circumstances in which an individual can truly be said to exist in such a state. Rational choice theoretical perspectives can still be defended in pragmatic terms, because they provide a convenient means of constructing straightforward hypotheses against which to compare observations drawn from the real world. However, such hypotheses might always be susceptible to the charge of superficiality. As they can only ever be abstractions of the actual decisions with which people are faced in their everyday lives, they can never capture on their own the full complexity of the social totality in which international economic processes are embedded.

Starting with classical political economy, it developed historically as an open field of scholarship, whereby practitioners argued strongly for their own position but were content to accept a plurality of theories and methods for the field as a whole. The labour theory of value—which in general states that the one true price of a good reflects the quantity of labour expended in its production—provides a consistent point of departure for most classical political economists. However, it is specified in a variety of ways depending on the normative perspective adopted by the theorist. The labour theory of value has both intuitive and normative appeal, because it provides a means of passing judgement on the intrinsic value of a commodity, which can then be compared with its actual selling price to determine how power has been exercized in the market relationship. Analytical divergences arise within the labour theory of value, though, depending on what, precisely, is meant by labour, which is why the Smithian, Ricardian, and Marxian accounts of economic interdependencies contrast so markedly with one another.

For some, especially those whose classical political economy begins with Marx, the labour theory of value is just that: the intrinsic value of a commodity is determined by the inputs workers provide for the production process via their labour, and by nothing else. For others, though, entrepreneurial labour should also be reflected in the price of a commodity (this is a feature of Smith's concept of natural prices) and so should the organizational labour provided by the firm (this is a feature of Ricardo's defence of profits). Today, in order to emphasize the significance of the so-called knowledge economy, some would say that intellectual labour should also be accounted for in the dynamics of price formation. Discussions have also recently begun about the concepts of 'emotional' and 'affective' labour, through which service sector workers impose perceptions of value onto the products they are selling by managing their ostensible feelings for the product in a way that secures the sale. There is thus no single labour theory of value, and hence no scientific unity in the approach. But this did not matter to the classical political economists. For them, the search for scientific unity was less important than was the possibility of dialogue between theorists with different world views. The labour theory of value could not have taken its many divergent forms were it not for this sense of later generations of theorists engaging with and talking directly to the conceptual legacies of earlier generations of theorists.

This sense of priority is entirely reversed within neoclassical economics, where scientific unity is a much more important feature of the day-to-day practice of economists. Neoclassical economics is therefore more closed as a field of scholarship than is classical political economy. Its practitioners have

tended to coalesce around set theories and methods, and what internal debate there is bears little upon the core precepts of the field. Neoclassical economics focuses almost all of its attention on instances in which behaviour can have a rational calculus of costs and benefits imposed upon it.

The aim is to use this calculus to offer a detached, objective description of economic events that matches the standards of scientific rigour by being cleansed of the disruptive influence of philosophical debate (Schumpeter 1954/1994). The analyst is thus able to comment on economic affairs from beyond the boundaries of his/her own particular world view. Such concerns relegate the significance of clear normative position-taking, thus providing economic enquiry with a technical veneer. The methodologist of economics (and father of John Maynard Keynes), John Neville Keynes, once distinguished between the 'science' and the 'art' of economics, in order to emphasize that economists' attempts to engage in methodologically rigorous enquiry (the science) must also be set within the context of explicit acknowledgement that all economic enquiry is always undertaken with specific purposes in mind (the art) (Keynes 1891/1970). David Colander has picked up on this distinction to suggest that the current dominance of neoclassical theory has led to the disappearance of the 'art' of economics (Colander 2001). Economic theory always proceeds according to preconceived social ends but, in trying to emphasize the purely technical prerequisites of modern theory, this is something that neoclassical economics attempts to disguise.

The different degrees of openness between the two broad traditions of economic thought are also replicated in the two schools of IPE that they inform. Members of the IO/American School tend to construct their analyses of the world (whether loosely or more formally) on rational choice theory grounds. They might still disagree on their prescriptions for future political action, depending on which socioeconomic factors they choose to include in their understanding of the utility function. But there is broad agreement on questions of ontology (viewing the interaction between economic agents and their world as constrained utility maximization problems), questions of methodology (imposing implicit values on the costs and benefits of a particular decision in order to explain, after the event, how that decision conforms to a rational calculus), and questions of theory (reducing economic identity to an epiphenomenon of self-interest). This gives the appearance of a relatively closed body of thought, in which academic progress rests on the ever more precise specification of the dynamics involved, rather than reflexive analysis of the essence of political economy itself.

By contrast, the British School is much more avowedly a broad church. Perhaps the only unifying point for its practitioners is collective agreement on what it is not, which involves the conscious rejection of both the starting point and the style of analysis of neoclassical economics. Beyond that, though, there is considerable diversity of content between the different positions associated with the British School. These range from ontological disputes about the nature of the world (for example, between various strands of structuralist thought and an increasingly prominent post-structuralist trend building on the constructivist turn), to theoretical disputes about how to conceptualize the economy in its most fundamental form (for example, whether to start with the act of production or the social relations of production), and normative disputes about the most important aspect of the economy's social structure (for example, whether to emphasize gender, class, race, religion, and so on).

Much therefore hinges on recognizing the significance of the Marginalist Revolution in the 1870s, as it is this that divides the political economy roots of IO/American School and British School IPE. Neoclassical economics is itself a complex amalgam of positions that possess a familial resemblance but otherwise have different theoretical emphases (see Watson 2005: ch. 2). There are even three distinct starting points for neoclassical theory, to be found in the contrasting work of William Stanley Jevons (1871/1970), Carl Menger (1871/1950), and Léon Walras (1874/1984). As these three worked out of Manchester, Vienna, and Lausanne, respectively, there were rival English-speaking, German-speaking, and French-speaking traditions of neoclassical economics right from the start. However, despite these differences, all three traditions have a similar core in a recognized way of thinking, and it is this that has subsequently filtered through to influence the analytical style of contemporary IO/American School IPE.

The core of neoclassical economics is given its clearest enunciation in Jevons's *Theory of Political Economy*. It comes in the form of an anti-productionist reworking of the classical political economists' theory of value. The classical political economists had assumed that all commodities had an intrinsic value. Moreover, to the extent that this intrinsic value was a reflection of both the quantity and the different types of labour embedded in the commodity via the production process, they were happy to endorse a labour theory of value. The classical political economists therefore highlighted the significance of production to the inscription of value upon a commodity. Jevons took exception to this way of thinking, insisting that the intrinsic value of a commodity does not determine its price but, on the contrary, it is possible to use the price at which it was exchanged to make plausible inferences about its value. This is because the price at which it was exchanged will reveal the degree of utility the consumer will expect to enjoy from its purchase (that is, the higher the purchase price, the more the expected utility; the lower the purchase price, the less the expected utility). Jevons was adamant that value is entirely dependent upon utility (1871/1970: 77).

Hence, Jevons created an analytical framework in which little significance can be accorded to the process of production. It is for this reason that practitioners of contemporary British School IPE have to go back to pre-Jevonian political economy to discover ways of thinking that enable them to begin their analyses with the social relations of production. Instead, Jevons focused the gaze of subsequent generations of neoclassical economists on the process of consumption, as he believed that it is here that value is imposed on commodities through the price consumers are willing to pay in expectation of the utility they will subsequently experience. Rather than accept the classical political economists' emphasis on relations of production, then, Jevons devised a new analytical framework that emphasized the moment at which a commodity is exchanged (and, therefore, he emphasized exchange relations more generally).

Thus established, Jevons's framework had two crucial effects, and both of these can be detected clearly in contemporary IO/American School IPE. First, it embedded utility maximization as both the language of economics and the intuitive basis of economic enquiry. As outlined previously, proponents of the IO/American School tend to treat all issues in IPE as constrained utility maximization problems (that is, how one actor might be a successful utility maximizer in circumstances in which all other actors are trying to do the same). Second, Jevons's framework reduced all events of economic significance to the moment of exchange. Within contemporary IPE, IO/American School practitioners also attempt to model all events of economic significance in terms of their underlying exchange relations. International economic negotiations are certainly understood in this way, whereby the negotiating environment is one to which negotiators bring bargaining resources in an attempt to influence outcomes to their own advantage. International labour relations, international corporate governance issues, and international environmental treaties can also be thought of in this way: how can one side shape the exchange relation to enable that side to benefit the most?

The birth of neoclassical economics should therefore be seen as a decisive historical moment for contemporary IPE, even though it occurred exactly a century before the birth of IPE itself. The introduction of neoclassical theory into the subject field of economics created a decisive fissure there. Those who followed the key insights of neoclassical economics were performing a fundamentally different type of economic enquiry from their classical political economy forebears, and nothing has been achieved since the 1870s to reunite these two traditions. The same fissure also informs many of the key differences that create the sense of a heterogeneous field of IPE today. These are differences in analytical instincts, in fundamental ways of setting up problems of international economic significance, in the most basic view of the world, and in underlying methodology. At heart, these differences are rooted historically in the split between neoclassical economics and classical political economy.

Key points

- A more fluid and dynamic conception of the field arises from integrating methodological and disciplinary distinctions in an attempt to tease out the links between one position and another.

- Most people working from an IR perspective in IPE fail to recognize explicitly the political economy traditions in which they are located, but more can be learnt about their approaches by recognizing these links formally.

- The decisive break in the history of economic thought engendered by the Marginalist Revolution in the 1870s also has important implications for the way in which IPE is researched today.

Conclusion

So, what can be distilled from this tour around the subject field of IPE? Perhaps the most obvious thing to note is that it has not been presented in the same way as can be found in introductory textbooks in the field. The aim has even been to caution against many of the textbook accounts in order to signal to students what might easily be overlooked if the textbooks' simplistic characterizations are accepted at face value. The argument is that students must be much more attentive in particular to the historical roots of IPE if they are to make sense of the astonishing degree of growth of the subject field since its inception in the early 1970s. IPE now incorporates the work of so many people and creates bridges to so many other cognate social scientific subject fields, that it is impossible to do justice to every conceivable way of practising it within the confines of a single chapter. My only hope is that I might have whetted the appetites of students to find out more for themselves of what can be discovered within the IPE literature. Beyond that, two principal conclusions arise from the preceding pages.

First, it is clear that IPE is anything other than a united field of study. To my mind, this is a point in its favour rather than something to bemoan. There are some prominent scholars who might not agree, given their position that progress in the field will only be possible when there is consensus on key concepts, principles, and methods of enquiry. However, this plea for uniformity of approach comes with obvious costs. After all, united subject fields are ones in which the space for genuine intellectual debate is squeezed to a minimum. For me, IPE is not only about describing the world as it is at the present time; it is also about describing how the world might be in the future. This means that debate is the lifeblood of the field and that, to flourish, the field must necessarily stop short of being united. Moreover, subject fields that revolve around the reproduction of set themes, theories, and methods leave little to the creativity of individual theorists. It is surely something to celebrate that few IPE theorists could claim to have been seriously hampered in this way; they are free to display their intellectual creativity in whatever manner they deem best.

Recognizing the laudable nature of IPE's diversity is one thing. However, trying to impose typological order on those differences is an altogether more difficult task. As the preceding analysis has shown, this can be attempted in many ways, but each classificatory schema appears to run into its own problems. Moreover, they also all appear to share an even more important common drawback.

The second major conclusion of the chapter is that any attempt to impose typological order on the field runs the risk of introducing overly rigid, and often false, lines of demarcation which lead to the artificial segregation of the field. What emerges is often a stereotype of the positions that define the field, rather than an accurate account of the field itself. The stereotypes fall down in large part because they are insufficiently attentive to the historical roots of the positions under review and, once a discussion of those roots is reinstated, it can be shown that the movement between positions is often much more fluid than the rigid demarcations of the stereotypes allow.

This is not an argument against categorization per se—and, given the preceding analysis, how could it be? Rather, it is a plea for the open acknowledgement of the limitations of all typologies. They can only ever act as guides to further reflection and as means of opening up more sophisticated understandings of the field as a whole. In particular, they should be used to facilitate attempts to transcend overly homogenized depictions of the major divisions within the field, even though it is the typologies themselves that promote such images of homogeneity.

The main lesson to be learned in this respect—and, indeed, the main message of the chapter as a whole—is that awareness of the historical roots of contemporary IPE is a prerequisite for practising IPE successfully. Such awareness matters because, without it, it is impossible to trace the intellectual lineage of contemporary positions and, in the absence of the ability to do that, contemporary positions are stripped of their own origins. The result is positions with inadequate historical moorings, debates between which are always likely to be grounded inappropriately. History matters, then, and a historical turn to situate IPE more assuredly within the context of its political economy origins is very much to be advocated.

? Questions

1. Why might it be important to know how the major theoretical and analytical positions in IPE compare, sometimes linking directly to one another and sometimes being constructed in direct opposition to one another?

2. What can be gained in our understanding of contemporary IPE by attempting to uncover the historical roots of the political economy traditions in which modern positions are located? In other words, why should we read classic texts?

3. To what extent does the trichotomous structure of liberalism versus realism versus Marxism obscure the significance of societal cleavages such as gender, race, and religion?

4. To what extent do IPE theories take the development profile of Western market capitalism and treat it as a generic feature of economic life, thus implying that all other countries will also have the same experience?

5. What are the main features of nationalist political economy in both its original and reworked Listian forms? Is it possible to point to examples in the modern world of nationalist insights continuing to inform the management of international economic affairs?

6. Is Marxism still relevant in contemporary IPE? What features of the world that Marx described are still recognizably with us today?

7. Would it be appropriate to describe the economics of globalization simply as the operation of a global 'invisible hand'? If not, what does this do to the usual characterization of globalization as a liberal project?

8. Is it advisable to agree with Susan Strange, and argue that the study of foreign economic policy is not IPE proper, because it has no historical lineage to a recognizable tradition in political economy?

9. How convincing is the characterization of a 'transatlantic divide' within contemporary IPE?

10. To what extent do many IPE theorists incorporate the key insights of neoclassical economics without acknowledging explicitly that this is what they are doing?

→ Further reading

General

■ Watson, M. (2005), *Foundations of International Political Economy* (Basingstoke: Palgrave Macmillan). This is for students who find my account of the practice of IPE convincing, as the themes of the current chapter are surveyed in much greater depth in this book.

History of economic ideas

■ Backhouse, R. (2002), *The Penguin History of Economics* (London: Penguin). This book is written with the beginner student in mind, and, as such, it is a more accessible introduction to the history of economic ideas than those that address the student who already has some training in economics.

■ Barber, W. (2001), *A History of Economic Thought*, repr. edn (London: Penguin). This book attempts similar things to Backhouse, also assuming no prior economics training from its readership in presenting an accessible history of economic ideas.

■ Blaug, M. (1996), *Economic Theory in Retrospect*, 5th edn (Cambridge: Cambridge University Press). This is almost certainly the most comprehensive account of the different ways in which the economy has been studied in the history of economic thought. However, it is written from a perspective which assumes that the student has some prior background in economics debates, but this will not necessarily be the case for beginning IPE students.

■ Heilbroner, R. (2000), *The Worldly Philosophers: The Lives, Times, and Ideas of the Great Economic Thinkers*, 7th edn (London: Penguin). This is an accessible text where the author's aim is not to dazzle his readers with the technicalities of the argument, but to bring the basic ideas he is discussing to life. It performs the same sort of function as Backhouse and Barber, as it is aimed at the same sort of readership.

■ Landreth, H., and Colander, D. (1994), *History of Economic Thought*, 3rd edn (Boston, MA: Houghton Mifflin). This book covers much of the same territory as Blaug, and would serve as a more than acceptable substitute for it. Again, though, it is written assuming that the reader has some background training in the theories, methods, and language of economics.

■ Robinson, J. (1964), *Economic Philosophy*, revd edn (Harmondsworth: Penguin). This is written less as an introduction to the history of economic ideas and more as an attempt by the author to carve out her own view of how economic analysis should proceed. Nonetheless, it is a very good read and students will learn much from it.

■ Samuels, W., Biddle, J., and Davis, J. (eds) (2007), *A Companion to the History of Economic Thought*, 2nd edn (Oxford: Blackwell). This is a relatively new book, offering extensive commentary and criticism on existing attempts to provide a plausible historiography of economic ideas. Thirty-nine chapters cover nearly 700 pages of scholars writing on their research specialisms; but, as with Blaug and with Landreth and Colander, this is probably not for students who possess no prior knowledge of rudimentary economic debates.

Introductions to the classical political economists

■ Heilbroner, R. (1986), *The Essential Adam Smith* (New York: W. W. Norton). This is a very good introduction to the work of Adam Smith. Heilbroner provides excerpts from all of Smith's published work, each of which is preceded by a useful introduction.

■ Hollander, S. (1987), *Classical Economics* (Oxford: Basil Blackwell). This is a very good introduction to the field of classical political economy as a whole. However, there is a chance that beginning IPE students might find it a little bit daunting, as it is written by a respected economist for an audience that has some familiarity with the rudiments of economics.

■ Wheen, F. (1999), *Karl Marx* (London: Fourth Estate). This is perhaps the most readable of all biographies of Marx, and it tries to draw out the intellectual inspiration underpinning his work from a broader assessment of his life.

■ Wolff, J. (2002), *Why Read Marx Today?* (New York: Oxford University Press). This is an introductory book about Marx's ideas, and it will not present the non-economist with similar problems to those they might experience when reading Hollander. The content of the book follows directly from the self-explanatory title.

Classic texts

Despite all the above advice on further reading, nothing beats the rewards that come from going back to a classic text and discovering what is in it for oneself. I would very much advocate, then, that students attempt to familiarize themselves with at least some of the classic texts mentioned by name in this chapter.

MATTHEW WATSON

 Web links

■ www.unc.edu/depts/econ/byrns_web/EC434/HET/biographies.htm An electronic encyclopaedia, allowing students easy access to thumbnail sketches of the most important figures in the history of economic ideas. Further searching of the site reveals an extensive glossary of economic terms and theories.

■ www.blupete.com/Literature/Biographies/Philosophy/BiosEcon.htm Students can work their way around the alphabetical listings on this site to find the bibliographies of most of the great economists in history, plus excerpts from the work of all those mentioned by name in this chapter.

■ http://oll.libertyfund.org/ This is the link to the online library of the Liberty Fund, which holds fully searchable electronic versions of many of the most important texts in the history of liberal political economy. The Complete Works of Adam Smith, for instance, is amongst the deposits in the online library.

■ www.marxists.org/subject/economy/index.htm This is a comprehensive site that allows students to explore both Marx's work and his reflections on the context in which his work was written. Importantly, it also contains links to a detailed glossary of terms to be found in the writings of Marxist political economists.

■ www.epistemelinks.com/Main/Philosophers.aspx?PhilCode=Smit This is another comprehensive site, providing the student with a large number of links to further sites containing Adam Smith archives. A similar archive is available through the www.marxists.org website listed above.

 Online resource centre

For additional material and resources, please visit the Online Resource Centre at:
www.oxfordtextbooks.co.uk/ravenhill3e/

Collaboration and Co-Ordination in the Global Political Economy

Vinod K Aggarwal and Cédric Dupont

∗ Reader's guide

How can one understand the problems of collaboration and co-ordination in the global political economy? In situations of global interdependence, individual action by states often does not yield the desired result. Many argue that the solution to the problem of interdependence is to create international institutions, but this approach itself raises the issue of how states might go about creating such institutions in the first place. In this chapter, we examine the conditions under which states might wish to take joint action and provides an introduction to game theory as an approach to understanding interdependent decision-making. We next discuss the conditions under which international institutions are likely to be developed and how they may facilitate international cooperation. We then examine major dimensions of institutional variation, with a discussion of factors that shape the design of international institutions.

Introduction

It is now commonplace to hear about the phenomenon of globalization. Much of the current analytical debate on globalization has its roots in the international political economy literature on interdependence of the early 1970s (Cooper 1972; Keohane and Nye 1977). At that time, political scientists began to identify the characteristics of the changing global economy, including the increased flows of goods and money across national boundaries as well as the rise of non-state actors as a challenge to traditional conceptions of international politics.

Although increasing interdependence among states was a relatively new phenomenon when considered against the baseline of the 1950s, high levels of interdependence had existed in earlier historical periods, including the period prior to the First World War (Bordo et al. 1999; McGrew, Chapter 9 in this volume). This interdependence, however, was not matched by high levels of institutionalization, standing in stark contrast to the post-Second World War Bretton Woods organizations of the International Monetary Fund (IMF), the World Bank, and the General Agreement on Tariffs and Trade (GATT) (and now its successor, the World Trade Organization (WTO)). The problems that institutions such as the IMF faced with the breakdown of the Bretton Woods dollar-based standard in 1971, the movement toward trade protectionism that appeared to undermine the GATT, and

instability in the oil market with the 1973–4 oil crisis also drove the debate on interdependence in the early 1970s.

A key issue in considering the implications of interdependence revolves around the question of how to achieve collaboration and co-ordination among states. In particular, scholars have focused on how states respond to perceived problems in the global economy that they cannot deal with solely on their own. An important starting point is to distinguish interdependence from interconnectedness based on the costs of interaction. 'Where interactions do not have significant costly effects, there is simply interconnectedness' (Keohane and Nye 1977: 9). With costly effects (or high benefits), however, we can consider countries as mutually dependent on each other, or interdependent. In attempting to cope with interdependence, then, countries will be faced with making decisions that will affect their direct well-being, and thus the sharing of costs and benefits can be potentially controversial.

This chapter considers the problem of collaboration by first characterizing situations that might require states to work with each other to achieve a desired outcome. We then focus on basic game theory as an analytical tool to tackle the nature of collaboration and co-ordination efforts. Finally, we consider how institutions might play a role in enhancing the prospects for co-operative behaviour.

Globalization and the Need for International Co-Operation

According to international economics textbooks, worldwide economic openness has clear benefits. Integrated world markets help to ensure an optimal allocation of factors of production and therefore help to maximize both aggregate world

welfare and individual national welfare. By contrast, sealing off national borders fosters economic inefficiency and has negative consequences for poverty alleviation and development prospects. Yet, in practice, the benefits of globalization cannot always be realized by states pursuing independent policies: co-operative action is required.

The process of global integration forces significant adjustments in production patterns across states. In particular, the changing distribution of costs and benefits from trade liberalization can result in strong political opposition, both for and against further liberalization. Adjustment has been all the more difficult in that it leads to unpredictable outcomes and instability in the prices of traded goods. This has proven particularly problematical for many of the lowest-income countries because they often rely on one or two commodities for the bulk of their exports. Not only have the prices of most non-fuel commodities been volatile, but they have also been declining over the past decades due to both longer and deeper slumps than booms (Cashin et al. 1999). Ultra-specialization in some of those commodities has therefore, on the one hand, brought severe adjustment costs and, on the other hand, failed to provide stable and increasing revenues. Developing countries that rely on the manufactures of exports have also faced significant adjustment challenges. For example, many Latin American countries have increasingly faced a loss of market share in the United States and Europe with the rapid rise of the Chinese export juggernaut.

Liberal analysts often argue that countries will be able to manage the process of adjusting to a rapidly shifting division of labour. From their perspective, the prospect of growth in a large number of newly competitive sectors, combined with state capacity to provide social and fiscal transfers, should serve as means to address the challenges of world competition. Yet, developing countries, in particular the poorest among them, often have a pre-industrial economic structure. As a consequence, economic openness has brought about a radical transformation of their socioeconomic structures, particularly in rural areas, leading to massive migration flows to urban areas. The state structures of developing states are often simply unable to cope with such a rapid and radical transformation. This has led to chaos and, in many

instances, to famine and violence as well as to further political instability and insecurity. For their part, rich countries often face strong domestic lobbies in agriculture, textiles, steel, and other older sectors of the economy, creating pressure for trade-distorting restrictions of various kinds including subsidies, tariffs, quotas, voluntary export restraints, and the like (see Hiscox, Chapter 4 in this volume).

Given these political constraints, countries may either be unwilling or unable by themselves to sustain processes of economic liberalization. In that it would be difficult to renege openly and fully on previous commitments, they may be tempted to gain time by shirking on the implementation of their commitments. While others would continue to implement fully their market opening commitments, they could slow or halt theirs. But their counterparts may find this unacceptable, and react by reneging on their own commitments, leading to an action-reaction cycle that slows global integration and decreases economic welfare. International co-operative action may therefore be required to avoid the unfortunate effects of this temptation to free ride. This temptation varies according to the sociopolitical organization of countries and to their degree of economic flexibility. On the sociopolitical dimension, the political insulation of governments from lobbying by those who are affected by adjustment costs can ease the process of economic liberalization, as was the case in the first wave of globalization in the second half of the nineteenth century when few countries had democratic systems of government. But with the spread of democracy, such political insulation has drastically diminished, forcing governments to at best 'talk' protectionist or worse, adopt protectionist policies during economic recessions. Another way to make liberalization politically palatable has been the development in some countries of corporatist deals between the government, unions, and business to share the costs of adjustment. The temptation to free ride also depends on the economy of countries and on its flexibility, particularly regarding labour markets, as well as labour skill levels. More generally, countries with deregulated markets, and few and lean state-owned companies should be less tempted to free ride on the globalization process, because adjustment would be less costly.

International co-operation may also be required to remedy what we call the 'inhibiting fear' that countries may feel when facing a decision either to engage in economic liberalization or to continue it. Although countries may be convinced that liberalization will yield benefits, they may be hesitant to risk the instability that might come from the ebb and flow of the international market. This fear is particular problematical in the domain of financial liberalization. In contrast to trade integration, financial integration has produced sudden and violent shocks to national economies (see Pauly, Chapter 8 in this volume). The massive increase in capital flows in the last fifteen years has been accompanied by extreme volatility, particularly for developing countries that have been experiencing sharp fluctuations in the flow of short-term capital (Edwards 2005; Calvo and Talvi 2005). As Louis Pauly discusses in Chapter 8, the series of crises that hit South East Asia in the period 1997–8 led to drastic economic contractions. South Korea's growth rate dropped 7 percentage points below its pre-crisis, five-year average growth rate, Indonesia's performance was similar, and Thailand's was even worse (Bordo and Eichengreen 2002). Recent work following the Asian financial crises and the Argentinean crisis in 2001, both at the aggregate and case specific levels, has shown that governments are highly vulnerable to such profound economic contractions. On average, the chances of losing office in the six months immediately following a currency crash seem to be twice as likely as at other times (Frankel 2005). Economic globalization has created profound and far-reaching policy challenges to states that, in turn, have an impact on key pillars of their economic and political organization.

International co-operative action in the financial realm may reassure countries by promises of assistance either by individual states or international institutions before or during difficult times.

This may facilitate states' adjustment efforts in responding to shocks and prevent them from taking the wrong action at the wrong time, which could lead to massive negative contagion effects. As with trade, the need for international support varies across countries depending on the sociopolitical and economic characteristics that we have discussed. The inadequate response of rich states and financial institutions to the problems faced by countries affected by the financial crises of the late 1990s has led many countries to build up their holdings of foreign reserves rapidly to counter speculative attacks on their currency. Reserves now amount to more than 30 per cent of developing countries' GDP, enough to finance almost one year of imports. But this individual response has come at a significant price. Most central banks hold foreign exchange reserves in the form of low-yielding, short-term US Treasury (and other) securities; the accumulation of reserves by developing countries created an important opportunity cost (the difference between what governments might have earned by investing these assets elsewhere versus keeping them in low-yielding securities). In most cases, for instance, investing the same amount in the domestic economy would have yielded a significantly higher return. According to a recent study, the income loss due to this difference in yields amounts to close to 1 per cent of GDP (Rodrik 2006b). Leaving aside the question of whether this insurance against the vagaries of financial integration comes at an acceptable price, such a solution is only available to a small number of countries, and therefore is not a viable alternative to international action to provide liquidity to countries facing financial crises.

Finally, when countries address the issues of 'temptation to free ride' and 'inhibiting fear', they may encounter a third problem—how to negotiate the distribution of gains and losses from a possible agreement. This 'where to meet' problem can be seen in cases of international co-operation such as a decision on how much to contribute to common support funds, how and to what extent to intervene in currency markets, and in the trade-off between quotas, tariffs, and subsidies in trade negotiations. For example, as part of the bargaining over the creation of a common pool of resources to support financial stability, there is likely to be considerable debate about the criteria for which country should contribute how much. This burden-sharing decision has often been a problem historically. Intervention in currency markets is also controversial. Although some national intervention to maintain stable currencies may be warranted in that it helps governments to obtain various national economic objectives such as controlling the rate of inflation, the US has often accused Japan and China

(and other East Asian states) of manipulating their exchange rates to gain a competitive advantage in trade.

Burden-sharing problems may also be part of the problem of trade liberalization. A good example has been the ongoing conflict for many years with respect to the reduction of agricultural support schemes that have been used by developed countries (and often by developing countries as well) to protect their farmers. Addressing the free riding temptation has been hampered by the difficulty to find an agreement at a lower level of support.

Key points

- International co-operation can help to address three typical problems associated with the process of global integration: a temptation to free ride, an inhibiting fear, and a need to find meeting points in situations where collaboration will produce differing costs and benefits to governments.

- A country's need for international co-operation depends on its sociopolitical structure as well as on the structure and flexibility of its economy.
- Different types of problems associated with the process of global integration call for different solutions to address the three typical problems, ranging from the provision of binding rules to facilitating mechanisms.

International Co-Operation: A Strategic Interdependence Approach

Our discussion so far has highlighted the potentially important role of international co-operation in enhancing the prospects for global economic integration. Yet, as the 'where to meet problem' shows, such co-operation may itself entail varying costs and benefits for participating states and its successful negotiation is therefore not a foregone conclusion. To explore further the challenges of international co-operation, we can utilize a game theoretic approach to examine interdependent decision-making. A

country's choice depends both on its cost/benefit evaluation of the various outcomes and on its expectations regarding the choices of other actors. Game theory provides useful tools to analyze actors' behaviour in such a context. Key features of actors' interactions are captured through 'games' that describe the choices available to actors (players in the game), their evaluations of potential outcomes, as well as the information they have when they make their choices (see Box 3.1).

Box 3.1 Game Theory and its Critics

Game theory has become a standard tool for analysis of situations of interdependence in social sciences. Aside from its predictive aim, game theory has a strong appeal for anyone engaged in explanation, investigation, or prescription. It often makes ostensibly puzzling processes intelligible, without attributing causality to factors such as the incompetence, irresponsibility, or lack of concern of decision-makers.

Whatever its value, however, the use of game theory poses severe methodological problems that have prompted intense debates in the literature. Critics have traditionally emphasized: (*a*) the over-stretching of the concept of rationality; and (*b*) the gap between abstract theoretical concepts and real phenomena. Regarding the notion of rationality, most applications of game theory assume that players, interacting under conditions of imperfect information, possess a very high computational ability. To make their decisions, players must evaluate a host of possible worlds on the basis of the knowledge commonly shared with others or privately known. This kind of situation often implies that players engage in comparative reasoning about a large set of possible worlds. Leeway in their interpretation often leads to a myriad of possible equilibria, which significantly decreases the predictive power of game theory. To avoid this indeterminacy, most game theorists have refined the concept of 'rationality' to allow the selection of one or very few equilibria among the vast initial array. For example, one might assume that people always choose to buy the cheapest product available (even though we know that many people buy based on brand

name, reputation, or other factors) because it makes the choices of actors easier to map. Most of these refinements to the concept of rationality thus lack empirical grounding.

A more recent controversy has focused on the empirical contribution of rational choice approaches to politics, including game-theoretic work. A variety of pathologies have prevented rational choice theory from improving our understanding of politics. In particular, rational choice theorists are, according to these critics, method-driven rather than problem-driven. In other words, instead of focusing on building models that accurately reflect decision-making in the real world, game theorists (according to critics) are more concerned with constructing elegant models rather than matching the models to real world situations. As a consequence, game theorists tend to neglect issues of empirical testing and therefore to undermine the scientific value of rational choice theory.

Although there clearly remain weaknesses in most game theoretic analyses of international relations, the link between theory and empirics has improved over the last decade. Users of game theory have resorted to different techniques to check the validity of their models based on a comparison with reality. The dominant approach has been indirect testing through the statistical analysis using either large-N data sets or a series of case studies. Another approach has been to use case studies to trace the behavioural attitude of actors and check them with specific predictions of models.

To keep this chapter's discussion of game theory as parsimonious as possible, we focus on simple games with two persons and two strategies per person. We further assume that actors have extensive knowledge of the other actor's preferences but that they cannot observe his or her actual choices. Obviously, in real-life situations, actors may have less information about preferences and/or may be able to observe the other's behaviour. Our modelling choices may appear to oversimplify real-life examples but, as several authors have

already shown, simple models can clearly reveal the decisions that governments face in attempting to deal with fundamental aspects of interdependence (Cooper 1975; Snidal 1985*a*; Martin 1992; Zürn 1992; Aggarwal and Dupont 1999; Drezner 2007).

Each of the three typical problems discussed in the previous discussion can be depicted with a specific game. We address them in turn and then focus on situations that represent mixed situations.

Figure 3.1 Prisoner's Dilemma game (ordinal form)

		Player Beta	
		S1	*S2*
Player Alpha	*S1*	3, 3	1, 4
	S2	4, 1	**2, 2**

Note: Nash Equilibrium in bold type

'Free riding temptation': The Prisoner's Dilemma (PD)

As we have seen, global economic integration remains fragile due to countries' political difficulties in implementing potentially costly changes in economic policy. They may be tempted to free ride on others' policy changes to take advantage of their gains from their trading partners opening their markets, which may in turn affect others' policy choices, and possibly bring an end to global economic liberalization. This situation is nicely captured with the game called the Prisoner's Dilemma (PD).

The Prisoner's Dilemma models a situation in which two individuals are involved in a robbery and are then caught near the scene of the crime. The District Attorney (the DA or prosecutor) does not have sufficient evidence to convict either of the suspects of robbery unless at least one of them reveals additional information to him, but he has some evidence to convict both of them of a lesser crime (for instance, reckless driving or carrying a firearm). The DA wants more information to convict both suspects for a long period. The two prisoners are placed in separate interrogation rooms. The DA tells each prisoner that if they confess and reveal the truth, they will get a much lighter sentence. If both prisoners confess, however (strategy S2 in the game depicted in Figure 3.1 above) they each get a heavier sentence than they

would have received if they had both remained silent (strategy S1 in Figure 3.1) where they would have been charged with the lesser crime (when both confess, the DA has the evidence to convict both on the more serious offences). Confessing to the DA could bring the minimal sentence if the other one does not confess but could also lead to a lengthier sentence if the other also confesses. Remaining silent, on the other hand, may lead to either a moderate sanction if the other prisoner remains silent, or the maximum penalty if the other one speaks to the attorney. Facing this situation, and unable to communicate, the logical strategy for both prisoners is to choose to confess. They do so because confessing to the DA is individually always a safer strategy than remaining silent. The key point of the Prisoner's Dilemma game is that actors may face a structure of interaction that prevents them from reaching a co-operative solution, even though such a solution would be optimal for both of them.

This story can be generalized using the game depicted in Figure 3.1. The numbers in the various cells indicate the preferences of players on an ordinal ranking scale, with 4 being the most preferred situation and 1 the least preferred. In the following figures, the first number in each box refers to Player Alpha's preference, while the second number refers to Player Beta's preference (thus '4, 1' is Alpha's most preferred outcome and Beta's least preferred outcome).

As Figure 3.1 shows, both players have a dominant strategy (confess, Strategy 2) that leads to what is called the Nash Equilibrium outcome, which is in the lower-right cell of the matrix. A Nash Equilibrium is an outcome in which none of the players can improve his or her situation by changing their individual strategy. But if both switch to Strategy 1 (remain silent) together, both players will secure a better outcome (upper-left cell). Yet, ironically, this collectively optimal situation is unstable because each actor can improve his or her own welfare by individually switching strategy to the cells in the upper-right or lower-left corners of the matrix.

Within international political economy, the Prisoner's Dilemma has been widely used to illustrate the problem of reciprocal trade liberalization (Grossman and Helpman 1995; Hoekman and Kostecki 1995; Maggi 1999). The difficulties in monitoring partners' trade policies, and the potential political benefits to governments from open export markets and closed domestic markets often push states to back out of their commitments to reciprocate trade liberalization measures. As Conybeare shows (1984), this argument particularly applies to countries with large domestic markets, as these countries are less dependent on the success of trade liberalization (this makes the utilities of the lower-right cell in Figure 3.1 relatively acceptable) and such countries can also positively affect world prices through their tariff policy (imposing a tariff on imports lowers the price that other countries will receive for their exports). For smaller countries, though, the Prisoner's Dilemma is not an adequate depiction of their trade situations. Rather, smaller countries tend to have preferences that reflect the game of chicken, a situation which we discuss below.

Another typical application of the Prisoner's Dilemma in international political economy has been in examining the collective management of resources. Whereas countries producing particular commodities traded on world markets would prefer a situation where they all manage production so as to keep prices sufficiently high (by forming a cartel such as the Organization of the Petroleum Exporting Countries (OPEC)), individual countries face the temptation to 'cheat' by increasing extraction or production of those commodities so as to maximize their individual income. As a result, acting collectively to keep commodities prices stable (in commodities such as coffee, tin, and even oil) has been a daunting task, particularly for developing countries.

'Inhibiting fear': assurance games

The second typical problem that a country seeking to enter international co-operation faces comes from the uncertainty of benefits and costs linked to integration in the world economy. Global economic integration brings its full benefits when most countries are part of it and adopt appropriate policies. When some countries make mistakes, or if liberalization policies lose momentum, international markets may react abruptly. If states become paralyzed by this likelihood, the whole world may revert to a much lower level of integration. This situation is best modelled through another category of game—assurance games.

One specific example of an assurance game is 'Stag Hunt', depicted in Figure 3.2 below. The name of the game comes from the story of two hunters chasing a stag. They go out before dawn and take positions on different sides of an area where they think a stag is hiding. They have a mutual understanding to shoot only at the stag (strategy S1 in the game depicted in Figure 3.2). Shooting at any other wild animal, say a hare, (strategy S2) would lead them to miss shooting the stag because the stag would be frightened by the noise and stay put in its hiding place. As time goes by and as dawn arrives, however, both hunters start thinking that going back home with a hare might be better than continuing to wait for the stag to come out of hiding. If each of them thinks that the other one will eventually yield to the temptation to shoot at a hare, they will both end up killing a hare—a better outcome than not catching anything but clearly much less attractive than sharing a stag.

Figure 3.2 Assurance game (Stag Hunt) (ordinal form)

		Player Beta	
		S1	*S2*
Player Alpha	*S1*	**4, 4**	1, 3
	S2	3, 1	**2, 2**

Note: Nash Equilibria in bold type

In Stag Hunt, players share a single most preferred outcome but they do not have dominant strategies. As a result, there is a second, Pareto-deficient, equilibrium outcome. In such a game, reaching the Pareto-efficient equilibrium is not a foregone conclusion. Doubts about the willingness of one's counterpart to choose strategy S1 (shoot the stag) might push a player to choose strategy S2 (shoot a hare), which guarantees for that individual the highest minimal gain. Yet, such an outcome is rather unlikely because of the attraction of the upper-left cell. In contrast to the Prisoner's Dilemma game, it is not the temptation to reap additional gains that may prevent actors to be in the upper-left cell of the game but their anticipation of a possible mistake or unintentional move by the other one.

Financial globalization has features of a stag hunt game. With increasing capital flows among countries, global capital markets become deeper and provide greater opportunities for individual countries. Yet, policy mistakes by some countries may quickly destabilize markets. Fear of the potential negative impact of such a destabilization may lead countries to implement measures to slow down or restrict capital movements. Such a move may lead to changes in other actors' expectations and quickly drive the world, or at least a region of the world, to a much lower level of integration. This new situation could have the advantage of being less risky for countries but is unlikely to bring as many opportunities for investment and therefore reduce growth prospects.

'Where to meet': co-ordination games

Whereas market liberalization is essential for global economic integration and increased prosperity, sustainable global integration requires some market supervision. This supervision in turn requires co-operative action by countries. The difficulty, however, is that there are often many ways to supervise markets and countries may differ on their preferred co-ordination point because potential solutions vary in their costs and benefits. This strategic context corresponds to a game of co-ordination. In the specific game depicted in Figure 3.3, actors have to choose *among* Pareto-efficient outcomes (Pareto-efficient outcomes are defined as outcomes from which no actor could become better off without worsening the payoffs to another actor). Its name, 'Battle of the Sexes', comes from the story of a husband and wife who have to decide where to spend their evening after work. They can either go to the opera or watch a football match. Neither spouse derives much pleasure by being without the other one but they differ on the best choice. The husband would prefer to watch football (strategy S1 in Figure 3.3) whereas the wife would p the opera (strategy S2 in Figure 3.3). In the story, both are getting out of work and have to rush either to the stadium or to the opera. They cannot communicate with each other (say the batteries of their cellphones are dead!), and have to meet at one of the locations. If each of them follows their preferred solution, they end up at different locations, which both regard as a bad outcome. Perversely, if both of them want to please the other one by choosing the location that they know that their partner prefers, they also end up being separated. Thus, they have somehow implicitly to co-ordinate, with one making a concession and the other getting his/her first choice. Figure 3.3 provides a generalization of that story.

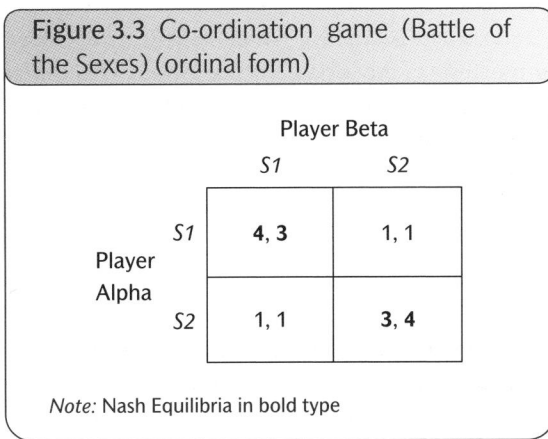

Figure 3.3 Co-ordination game (Battle of the Sexes) (ordinal form)

		Player Beta	
		S1	*S2*
Player Alpha	*S1*	**4, 3**	1, 1
	S2	1, 1	**3, 4**

Note: Nash Equilibria in bold type

In the Battle of the Sexes, none of the players has a dominant strategy. Player Alpha prefers to play Strategy 1 when player Beta chooses Strategy 1 and prefers Strategy 2 when player Beta chooses Strategy 2. With player Beta having the same preferences as Alpha, the game has two equilibrium outcomes—the upper-left and lower-right cells in Figure 3.3. These two outcomes are clearly Pareto-superior to the two other possible outcomes, but actors will disagree on which one to choose. Player Alpha prefers the upper-left cell, whereas player Beta prefers to end up in the lower-right cell. Both players want to avoid being separated but each player prefers a different outcome.

In international political economy, efforts by developed countries to choose mutually compatible macroeconomic policies typically reflect games of co-ordination (Putnam and Bayne 1987). For instance, when there is high volatility in financial and exchange rate markets, co-ordinated responses by leading countries would often be best but each country would like to choose the policy mix that fits best its own domestic constraints. Co-ordination was a key challenge in efforts to address the global financial crisis in 2008–9. Whereas major central banks were able to co-ordinate their actions to contain the stress in financial markets to a reasonable extent, governments had more difficulty in implementing concerted fiscal responses. Some countries, such as the United States, engaged in large fiscal stimulus, while others were more reluctant to use fiscal policy out of concern for the health of public finances. This asymmetry fuelled a concern for free riding where a country would benefit from the efforts of its neighbours, as their stimulus plans boost its exports without affecting its fiscal stance. As a result, countries resorting to large stimulus tended to adopt 'nationalist' or protectionist policies to channel government funding to national firms. To offset these suboptimal dynamics, major economies met in a series of meetings (particularly in London and Pittsburgh in 2009) under the heading of the G20 grouping with the major objective to implement concerted policies.

Another prominent example is the choice of international monetary system (Cooper 1975). Discussions between the US and Great Britain during the Second World War regarding the architecture of the future international economic order revealed that although both countries agreed on the absolute need for coordination, they fought over the details of the new order, with each trying to impose its own plan. A more recent example was the debate within the European Union (EU) over the design of the monetary union, which saw Britain, France, and Germany proposing different solutions for some economic and monetary convergence between member states as well as for rules of fiscal behaviour within the monetary union (Wolf and Zangl 1996). At the global level, in the aftermath of the recent global financial crisis, Russia and China have aired the idea of finding an alternative to the current dollar-dominated system.

Mixed situations: Chicken, Called Bluff, and Suasion

We now turn to games that capture situations in which more than one typical problem of co-operation may be present or in which the actors may view the structure of the problem differently. We begin with the game of Chicken that combines the features of the temptation to free ride as well as distributive tensions between the actors. This game, depicted in Figure 3.4, builds on the story of two cars, travelling in opposite directions, speeding down the middle of the road toward one another. Inside each car sits a driver who wants to impress his respective passenger that he is a tough person (i.e., demonstrate resolve). The best way to do so is to continue driving straight down the middle of the road (strategy S2 in the game depicted in Figure 3.4)—even when the car coming in the opposite direction comes dangerously close. Yet, if at least one driver does not swerve, the outcome will be disastrous and both cars will crash, killing everyone. To avoid this unfortunate outcome, at least one

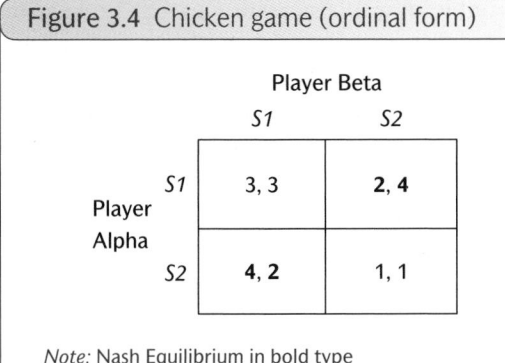

Figure 3.4 Chicken game (ordinal form)

Player Beta

		S1	S2
Player Alpha	S1	3, 3	**2, 4**
	S2	**4, 2**	1, 1

Note: Nash Equilibrium in bold type

driver will have to yield and swerve (strategy S1 in Figure 3.4), but both would like the other one to be the 'Chicken' who swerves.

The distributive tension between two equilibrium outcomes is a typical feature of the co-ordination games discussed above. But in contrast to those games, the game of Chicken has a third outcome that is collectively optimal — the compromise solution in the upper-left cell. As in the Prisoner's Dilemma, however, this outcome is not stable and actors have a strong temptation to revert to one of the two equilibria represented in boldface in Figure 3.4. As such, the Chicken game helps to capture more complex situations faced by countries attempting to engage in international co-operation (Stein 1982).

In the context of the global political economy, Chicken games are useful depictions of the complex structure of burden-sharing that occurs within a group of powerful players. For instance, when there is monetary and financial in stability in the global economy, the US and the EU may tend to resist making public commitments to international co-operation unless there is a clear sign that the other party will act similarly. Getting out of a trade negotiation stalemate or dispute can also be a Chicken-like situation in which each actor is unwilling to agree on any asymmetric solutions.

To this point, we have only considered cases where actors have symmetrical preferences. We now examine two interesting *asymmetric* games, the first of which has one player whose preferences are those of the Prisoner's Dilemma game, and a second player with a structure of preferences of the Chicken game. The resulting asymmetric game, known as the game of 'Called Bluff', is depicted in Figure 3.5.

Player Alpha has Prisoner's Dilemma preferences with a dominant strategy to play S2, whereas player Beta has Chicken preferences with a preferred choice of S2 if Alpha chooses S1 and a choice of S1 if Alpha chooses S2. Yet, in this game, owing to the asymmetry in payoffs, Beta knows that Alpha has a dominant strategy of S2, Beta therefore should choose S1, leading to the equilibrium outcome in the lower-left cell in Figure 3.5. Here, Player Alpha gets his/her most preferred outcome, whereas player Beta gets his/her second-worse outcome. This scenario can be used to analyse situations where stronger countries or actors can take advantage of the other's weakness and shift the burden of cost of co-operative action onto the weaker party. This outcome is caused by the difference in actors' sensitivity (vulnerability) to the need for co-operation itself. The player with the less dependence on the need for co-operation (Alpha in Figure 3.5) is able to free ride on the other player (Beta in Figure 3.5). Given the lack of capacity of the weaker actor to sustain co-operation alone, this often leads to a breakdown of international action.

Figure 3.5 Called Bluff (ordinal form)

Player Beta

		S1	S2
Player Alpha	S1	3, 3	1, 4
	S2	**4, 2**	2, 1

Note: Nash equilibrium in bold type

A good illustration of this situation is the monetary policy of Germany and Japan in the 1960s, in the context of the Bretton Woods fixed exchange rate system. The stronger player, the United States, asked these countries to revalue their currencies to help boost the competitiveness of US exports and relieve the pressure on the dollar. These countries refused to undertake significant reevaluations, which thus had increasingly costly implications for the US economy and, ultimately under the Nixon administration, the US simply forced the burden of adjustment on to the weaker countries by breaking the link between the dollar and gold and imposing a 10 per cent across-the-board tariff. This action led to the end of the Bretton Woods system (see Helleiner, Chapter 7 in this volume).

A second case of asymmetry is a game with one player having preferences oriented toward co-operation and the other one having Chicken preferences. In the game of 'Suasion', Player Beta has preferences similar to a player in the Chicken game, but Player Alpha has preferences that are typical of another game, the game of Harmony. The basic feature of Harmony games (see Figure 3.6) is that not only do both players dislike acting separately (as in the case of co-ordination games), but they also do not differ on the best outcome. They both therefore have a dominant strategy to do the same thing. Co-operation is, so to speak, naturally guaranteed (as, for instance, in nineteenth-century liberal assumptions about international economic relations).

Combining a player with Chicken preferences and a player with Harmony preferences yields the game depicted in Figure 3.7, known as the game of 'Suasion' (Martin 1992). The predicted outcome of the Suasion game shares some similarity with that of the game of Called Bluff that was illustrated in Figure 3.5 above. Both games feature a situation in which one player gets his/her most preferred outcome. However, the difference between these two games is that in Suasion, the 'stronger' player gets his/her second-best outcome, which results from the choice of a dominant strategy by Alpha. Put into the context of international co-operation, this clearly reflects a situation in which an actor perceives the benefits of international action to be much more than its associated costs. Because this actor (Alpha) absolutely wants to carry through action at the international level and is assumed to have the capability to do so, other actors (Beta) are in a situation whereby they will let him (Alpha) undertake the bulk of the effort, and will enjoy the benefits at low or no costs to themselves.

One can view this as a situation as one of the tyranny of the weak, which is in sharp contrast to the game of Called Bluff. Note, however, that the stronger player is not forced into an asymmetric outcome by the behaviour of the weak, but by his own preferences. From this perspective, the Suasion game features an opportunistic attitude by the weak rather than a deliberately tyrannical outlook. Martin (1992) argues that this game illustrates the

Figure 3.6 Harmony (ordinal form)

Player Beta

		S1	S2
Player Alpha	S1	**4, 4**	3, 2
	S2	2, 3	1, 1

Note: Nash Equilibrium in bold type

Figure 3.7 Suasion (ordinal form)

Player Beta

		S1	S2
Player Alpha	S1	4, 3	**3, 4**
	S2	2, 2	1, 1

Note: Nash Equilibrium in bold type

Western world's restriction of technology exports to the Soviet Union during the Cold War. Control of technology sales to the Soviet bloc was done through the Coordinating Committee for Multilateral Export Controls (COCOM). Within it, however, the United States had a dominant strategy to control technology whereas European states were more opportunistic. They could benefit from sales to the Soviet bloc without jeopardizing the overall balance of power between the two blocs. The US was dissatisfied with this situation and had to persuade Europeans to participate fully in COCOM.

More generally, this type of game relates to situations where one actor (or group of actors) can undertake actions that are immune (up to some degree) to the free riding behaviour of other countries. For example, tax havens in small countries were 'tolerated' by bigger countries as long as the latter could use capital movement restrictions to secure financial stability. When capital restrictions were dismantled, there were significant increases in the efforts to circumvent the free riding behaviour of tax havens. Such free riding became politically intolerable with the advent of the global financial crisis, which required global co-ordination efforts. The G20 countries put significant pressure on 'renegade' countries with the preparation of a black list by the Organization for Economic Co-operation and Development (OECD).

Key points

- Each of the typical problems of international co-operation can be viewed through the lens of strategic decision-making.

- Game theory can help us analyse interdependent decision-making.

- Co-operation can be expected to fail either due to actors' incentives to cheat, to actors' sensitivities to distribution issues, or to lack of confidence in the other actor's behaviour.

- Problems of distribution and free riding may be combined in real-world situations; some games are able to model these combinations.

- Differences in resources or in the perceived need for co-operation result in situations of asymmetric burden-sharing.

International Co-Operation: A Variety of Solutions

The discussion of co-operation problems in the global political economy highlights the varied nature of the challenges facing actors. We now turn to the question of how to address these challenges. In particular, we focus on the role that international institutions can play in addressing co-operation problems. Our analysis begins with situations where the problems can be addressed without institutions and then turns to cases where institutions help the process of co-operation.

International action without international institutions

In most of the games that we have examined, individual actions by both players lead, or may lead, to an outcome that we can characterize as collectively optimal because there is no welfare loss. Yet, this notion of optimality tends to be short-sighted because the asymmetric outcomes of the Called Bluff, Suasion, Chicken, and even co-ordination games

VINOD K AGGARWAL AND CÉDRIC DUPONT

are optimal only in terms of a narrow view of *collective welfare*. Such a conception of welfare does not obviate the problems of the distribution of gains that may either make the road to an agreement difficult or plague the likelihood of collaboration. As we discuss below, institutions may play useful roles in addressing these problems, but collaboration may also occur through individual actions.

Individual, decentralized, action can also be optimal in the thorny case of the Prisoner's Dilemma. Yet, for this to happen, we must relax the baseline assumption that players play the game only once, and allow them to have repeated interactions through time (Axelrod and Keohane 1986; Taylor 1987; Sandler 1992; Cornes and Sandler 1996). When players expect to meet again in the future, they may be more willing to co-operate. Yet, even under such conditions of iteration, however, co-operation is not a foregone conclusion. For example, if the expected net value of co-operation is too low (for example, actors may overly discount the importance of future iterations owing to a dire economic or political situation at home for governments), the temptation to free ride cannot be overcome. The Prisoner's Dilemma (PD) demonstrates that, if defection by one actor would generate high costs for the other actor (resulting in a lengthy prison sentence in PD), or if actors cannot gather information easily, actors may not reach a Pareto-optimal outcome.

Applied to the case of trade liberalization, repeated interaction is not sufficient to ensure co-operative behaviour for governments that are under heavy domestic pressure, as the temptation to reap immediate political gains through defection may simply be too great. Domestic pressure may be particularly high in democratic countries where economic groups or citizens have easy access to the political sphere, in countries with a political system that tends to favour coalitional governments, or in countries without strongly embedded social consultation mechanisms. Conversely, the cost of defection may be too high when actors invest heavily in co-operative efforts and value the outcome produced by co-operation. In such cases, they are significantly more reluctant to jeopardize

co-operation, even if others have undertaken free riding behaviour.

A world without international institutions is also not universally effective in securing the exchange of goods. As long as trading partners have access to other markets for their products, an institution-free world can work in the context of global trade, because countries can simply turn to another market if a breach in the trading relationship occurs. Yet, if there is only one partner that is interested in the goods produced, or if it would be more costly to trade with other partners, such an option does not exist. If a country cannot threaten to sell its goods elsewhere, another country may take advantage of it. Another important qualification for successful institution-free contexts is if one (or both) of the parties has made relation-specific investments. In such a case, these investments will discourage defection and may encourage cooperative behaviour.

What other factors might impede co-operation when actors cannot rely on international institutions? Monitoring will be much more difficult if states only have limited information gathering capability. If an actor has so little information that, for example, it is unsure whether the other actor 'defected' on the last round, then the prospect of repeated interactions does not increase the chances of co-operation. Similarly, an expanding number of states, with an expanding range of trade products that use increasingly sophisticated policies to intervene in markets, makes monitoring trade policies increasingly difficult. It is therefore more difficult to detect non-compliance without the help of a third party.

The role of institutions

As our discussion above suggests, actors may need help to sustain collectively optimal outcomes. One way that individuals might be able to co-ordinate their choices to achieve desired goals might be through the creation or use of international institutions or regimes. International regimes have been defined broadly as 'sets of . . . principles, norms, rules, and decision-making procedures around which actors' expectations converge' (Krasner 1983:2). To refine this definition, we can distinguish between the principles and norms—the 'meta-regime' (Aggarwal 1985)—and the regime itself, defined as the rules and procedures to allow us to distinguish between two very different types of constraints on the behaviour of states. In this case, we can use the term 'institution' to refer to the combination of a meta-regime and a regime—rather than Krasner's definition. Note that an institution is not the same thing as an international organization: one can find areas of international collaboration where there are well-defined principles, norms, rules, and procedures for actors' behaviour in the absence of an organization such as the IMF. We structure our discussion below around three major functions of institutions.

First, institutions can act as channels for the third-party enforcement of agreements. To overcome successfully players' temptation to free ride, international institutions should be strong, meaning that member countries should have specific and binding obligations. In particular, agreements that credibly restrain actors' temptation to free ride in trade and monetary policy, for instance, need to rely on some sort of enforcement mechanism delegated to an international institution. At its strongest expression, in the European Union or in the WTO, such a mechanism relies on an organization (the EU has two such entities, the Commission and the Court of Justice) with supranational power to monitor, evaluate, and sanction (if needed) the behaviour of its members.

The chances of a co-operative agreement can also be enhanced through a different kind of centralization—one that ensures a prompt and undistorted dissemination of information. This type of facility helps identify the requirements of multilateral action and protects against possible defections. Enforcement can also be achieved either through positive incentives, as when the International Monetary Fund provides funds to countries that are following its policy recommendations, or through punitive action, as when the World Trade Organization rules against a particular state policy.

Second, international institutions can help craft responses to situations characterized by distributive tensions among states. They can help states choose one among several collective outcomes and eliminate some sharply asymmetric outcomes. Institutions may also be useful for gathering information about the preferences of actors, and through appropriate use of agenda setting, may help find focal point solutions for both cost sharing and benefit splitting. Institutions with a firmly and widely established meta-regime tend to perform these tasks extremely well. In contrast, institutions lacking a strong meta-regime may have difficulty generating possible solutions that are attractive to all members. This has often been considered as the source of difficulties for the GATT, and its successor, the WTO. Deep disagreements among GATT members led to the creation of another forum, the United Nations Conference on Trade and Development (UNCTAD), in the 1960s, and to serious hurdles in the negotiations of the extension of the scope of GATT/WTO, as recently revealed during the Doha Round of negotiations (initiated in 2001 and still ongoing at the time of publication). The members of UNCTAD had shared principles and norms that they felt were not importantly addressed in GATT/WTO.

Third, international institutions can do a lot to allay actors' fear or reluctance to engage in co-operative behaviour. Rather than enforcing a particular outcome, institutions should enable actors to reach it (by pooling resources, for example). To help the integration of developing countries into the global financial system, the IMF provides cheap credit opportunities through the contributions subscribed by all members. The World Bank finances the development of basic infrastructure in developing countries to help them reduce poverty. At the European regional level, the European Monetary System (EMS) has relied on a decentralized system of very short lending facilities among members to help them defend the parity grid that tightened them together.

To address enforcement and distribution problems, institutions can establish rights for members that either define mechanisms of exclusion or determine compensation schemes. In relation to our previous discussion of games and co-operation, careful institutional design can sometimes 'privatize' the benefits of co-operation, reducing the temptation to free ride. The reduction of trade barriers almost always applies to countries that belong to particular clubs, be they regional (see Ravenhill, Chapter 6 in this volume) or global. Assigning rights and obligations can also produce decentralized co-operation when institutions also provide information about the preferences of actors and reduce the costs of their discussions to their minimum. When actors are more certain about who owns and is responsible for what (a result of the assignment of rights and obligations), co-operation may result.

Under these conditions, as Coase (1960) suggests, actors do not need any centralized power to remedy the problem of negative externalities (situations where an individual's action negatively affects the well-being of another individual in ways that need not be paid for according to the existing definition of property rights) (Conybeare 1980; Keohane 1984) but should find a mutually satisfactory solution through financial compensation. The crucial aspect, in the Coasian framework, is establishing liabilities for externalities. The history of international monetary agreements provides several examples of the difficulties associated with determining satisfactory schemes assigning responsibilities to the involved parties. For instance, the collapse of the

fixed exchange rate systems (in March 1973), was largely due to the inability of IMF members to redistribute the burden of adjustment from the US to Germany and Japan. Difficulties in the so-called European Snake in the early 1970s induced member states to design the EMS in such a way as to put the responsibility on strong currency members (in particular, on Germany) to intervene as much as weak currency members in defending existing parities.

Our brief discussion of the roles of institutions reveals the value associated with information-gathering and dissemination. Long-term enforcement requires identifying prospects for defection, finding a focal point based on the constellation of positions, and informing actors of the overall global context. Therefore, a major activity of international institutions is to collect information about actors' behaviour, preferences, and the state of the international environment.

Key points

- Institutions are key instruments for resolving enforcement, distribution, and assurance problems.
- Institutions help assign rights and obligations to benefactors of co-operation as well as in defining those benefactors.
- Institutions help make the international scene an information-rich environment.

The Formation and Evolution of Institutions

We have seen that institutions can help co-operation in several ways. But how might institutions be formed in the first place? And what factors may impact the design of institutions? We begin with a broad discussion from the literature on international relations and then turn to more specific issues. In examining institutions, five different approaches in international relations have been

brought to bear on this problem: neo-realism, neo-realist institutionalism, neoliberal institutionalism, cognitivism, and radical constructivism (Aggarwal 1998—the term radical constructivism was first used by Haas 1992; for a recent synthesis see Duffield 2007).

Neo-realists assume that in an anarchic international system, states must rely primarily on their own resources to ensure their security. Thus, for neo-realist scholars, regimes and international institutions have no significant role in international relations because power considerations are predominant in an anarchic world (Waltz 1979; Mearsheimer 1990). In this view, as we have discussed earlier, collaboration will only be sustainable if states value future interactions highly, have symmetric resources, and are highly interdependent.

Still within a power-based tradition, though, some scholars have examined changes in and the effects of international institutions. In this literature, labelled neo-realist institutionalism, the central concern is on how regimes affect the distribution of costs and benefits of state interaction. For analysts in this school (Krasner 1983, 1991; Aggarwal 1985; Knight 1992), institutions have distributional consequences (in other words, the benefits of co-operation may be unequal) and can be used as devices to seek and maintain asymmetric gains. They can more broadly help control other actors' behaviour, both at home and abroad (Aggarwal 1985). For example, within the domestic context, state elites can argue that their hands are tied and thus attempt to circumvent pressure for particular actions from domestic actors. Examples of this include the Mexican government signing onto the North American Free Trade Agreement (NAFTA) (tying the hands of the Mexican government to a more open market posture in the face of domestic protectionist groups) or the American use of the Multifibre Arrangement (MFA) to prevent textile and apparel interests from pressing for excessive protection.

A central theme in this literature has been the role of hegemonic powers in fostering the development of institutions through both positive and negative incentives (Kindleberger 1973; Gilpin 1975; Krasner 1985). Benevolent hegemons, for example, may provide public goods (a special type of good, for example, national defence, that cannot practically be withheld from an individual without withholding them from all (the 'non-excludability criterion') and for which the marginal cost of an additional person consuming them, once they have been produced, is zero (the 'non-rival consumption' criterion)), because their large size makes it worthwhile for them to take action on their own to overcome collective action problems (see Box 3.2). But while suggesting that regimes may form when powerful states desire them, this approach does not tell us much about the nature of regimes. Moreover, scholars in this school overemphasize tensions arising from the differences in the distribution of benefits between actors and downplay the possibility that actors may not necessarily and as acutely think in comparative terms, but focus on the positive impact of institutions on their situations. Finally, this approach has little to say about actors' desire to pursue multilateral versus bilateral solutions to accomplish their ends.

Box 3.2 Goods and the Problems of Co-Operation

In examining the problem of collaboration, we can use the concept of 'type of goods' to examine more rigorously the problem of incentives to free ride, fear that one's counterparts will fail to follow good policies, and the distributive conflicts that might ensue over where to meet. In a capitalist economy, private firms produce goods such as wheat, clothing, computers, and services such as financial products, insurance, and the like. Such goods are generally referred to as **private goods**, based on two characteristics: the goods are generally excludable and are not joint in consumption. The concept of *excludable* means that goods can be withheld from those who do not pay for them; *not joint in consumption* means that when a consumer utilizes the good, it is exhausted and cannot be used by others without there being additional production. In addition to private goods, other goods may be desired, such as national defence or parks. These goods are characterized by the lack of ability to create exclusion and the jointness of their consumption, and they are known as **public goods**. Because anyone can have access to these goods once they are produced, consumers will misrepresent their demand for such goods as they can obtain them once they are produced and 'free ride'. In such cases, the private sector will not produce public goods, and governments will coerce citizens to pay for such goods through mechanisms such as taxation. If a good is characterized by lack of exclusion and lack of jointness, then such a good is referred to as a common pool resource. Examples of such goods include fish in the oceans, or even, as a limiting case, a public park. Thus, if the ocean is overfished, fish will cease to reproduce and die out. Similarly, while parks are often seen as public goods, too many users of a park create crowding, which impairs the enjoyment of the good for others. Private actors will be particularly reluctant to produce such goods, and even governments will be concerned about the problem of too many users. Finally, **inclusive club goods** refer to goods that may be excludable and yet be joint in consumption. These include goods such as software, music, and literature, which the private sector has a great incentive to produce. Once a unit of the good is produced, it can be distributed at either little or no cost. Indeed, firms may quickly develop a monopoly in the production of such goods if they are the first movers who make the good, and thus face regulation. For example, if a firm launches a satellite to beam television programmes to consumers, while the initial cost of securing a rocket to put the satellite into orbit will be great, once the satellite is in operation, the programmes can be disseminated to large numbers of consumers. Private firms will generally attempt to regulate consumption by encoding the transmission to prevent free riding. Alternatively, governments may simply regulate the industry and consumer behaviour to prevent consumption without paying (for example, penalties for copyright infringement). Figure 3.8 summarizes the four types of goods.

How do the problems of creating various types of goods play out in the international arena, and what obstacles do states face in achieving co-operation? Consider the case of co-operation with respect to global warming. It is now well documented that emissions of greenhouse gas, in particular CO_2, due to human activity (in particular the burning of fossil fuels) have reached levels that lead to an important warming of average temperatures on earth with potentially dramatic impact on populations in the medium to long term.

Figure 3.8 Types of goods

		Jointness in production?	
		YES	NO
Exclusion possible?	NO	Public	Common pool resources
	YES	Inclusive club goods	Private

Yet, because reducing the emission of greenhouse gas is a costly process that may require deep restructuring of energy production and use, the negotiations over how much or how quickly to limit those gases has been an internationally contentious issue. The public goods nature of the problem can be seen in the incentives to free ride by various countries that wish to benefit from the reduction in emissions of greenhouse gases but do not want to bear the costs of reducing their emissions. There is a severe distributive conflict ('where to meet') as actors debate the levels of reduction for developed and developing countries. The latter fear to derail economic development to fight a phenomenon largely associated with the economic development since the mid 1800s of current developed economies. With respect to crowding, at the extreme, limiting global warming has common pool resource properties, because jointness may be impaired if one (or a small number of countries) produces a huge amount of emissions that then spread evenly in the atmosphere.

States recognized the need to take action to limit global warming in 1992 with the adoption of the United Nations Framework Convention on Climate Change (UNFCCC) that established the Conference of the Parties (COP) as its highest authority to develop an international climate change regime. So far, the most important pillar of this regime has been the Kyoto Protocol adopted in 1997 by the COP and entered into force in 2006. The Protocol set binding targets for the reduction of greenhouse gases by thirty-seven industrialized countries (the so-called Annex I countries) as well as a general commitment for all groups of countries. The originality of the protocol is that it defines 'flexible mechanisms' to help industrialized economies meet their targets, including the trading of emission 'rights', the transfer of 'clean energy' technology to developing nations (the so-called Clean Development Mechanism) as well as the possibility of joint implementation. But whereas the flexibility of implementation for industrialized economies and the lack of binding commitments for developing countries were essential for the adoption of the Kyoto Protocol, they have reduced its impact on curbing global warming. There is a clear need to do more, including by developing countries, and within a stronger monitoring framework but discussions have been impeded by severe distributive conflicts (on financial commitments in particular) both within industrialized countries and between industrialized and developing countries. At the December 2009 Copenhagen Summit, countries failed to reach a binding agreement and only set a target to reduce global warming by 2°C.

With respect to inclusive club goods, the debate over standards also illustrates the problem of 'where to meet'.

If a firm convinces its government to advocate the choice of its standard in international negotiations, the firm may be able to gain a significant advantage over its competitors. Even less firm-driven choices may influence costs and benefits, and lead to possible conflict. For example, the implementation of international financial reporting standards (IFRS) developed under the auspices of the International Accounting Standards Board (IASB) led to fierce debates and discussions within the European Union before its final implementation in January 2005. The IFRS cornerstone is the notion of fair value accounting (FVA) that aims at assigning market values to assets. Whereas this had been the standard adopted in the Anglo-Saxon world, continental European firms had relied on a more 'prudent' way, with a valuation based on the balance sheet and a low valuation of assets. The move toward a new standard increased significantly the risk of hostile takeover of companies that would become suddenly more attractive due to 'hidden' reserves.

Building on these criticisms of the neo-realist approach, neoliberal institutionalists have examined the specific incentives for states to create institutions—as opposed to simply engaging in ad hoc bargaining. This body of work, taking off from seminal research by Oliver Williamson, examines the role of institutions in lowering the costs involved in choosing, organizing, negotiating, and entering into an agreement (what he calls transaction costs), and has garnered a considerable following in the field of international relations (Keohane 1984). As we have seen, institutions provide many useful functions in helping actors to co-ordinate their actions or achieve collaboration. This theoretical approach assumes that collaborative action is primarily demand driven—that is, actors will create institutions because they are useful—but does not really specify a mechanism for how they would actually go about creating them.

An important theme of this work has been how existing institutions may constrain future institutional developments (Keohane and Nye 1977; Keohane 1984). One aspect of this constraint is the possibility that existing institutions with

a broad mandate will affect the negotiation of more specific institutions, leading to the 'nesting' of regimes within one another (Aggarwal 1985). Thus, while the notion of transaction costs and sunk costs (the investments that actors have made in specific institutions) are central elements in this thinking, the role of regimes in providing states with information and reducing organizational costs can be distinguished from the role of existing institutions in constraining future actions.

A fourth approach to examining institutional innovation and change puts emphasis on the role of expert consensus and the interplay of experts and politicians (Haas 1980; Haas 1992). New knowledge and cognitive understandings may lead decision-makers to calculate their interests differently. For example, work by Ernst Haas focused on the efforts of politicians to use linkages across various issues (sometimes from quite distinct areas) to create new issue packages in international negotiations. The objective is to provide benefits to all, in an effort to facilitate the formation of international regimes (Haas 1980).

Lastly, 'radical constructivists', while focusing on the role of ideas, argue that reality is in fact constructed in the minds of decision-makers. These scholars, drawing from Ernst Haas's work, go much further than Haas in suggesting that, 'power and interest do not have effects apart from the shared knowledge that constitutes them as such' (Wendt 1995: 74). Analysts in this school see norms and values as being dominant causal forces and ascribe considerable power to institutions, not only in constraining actors, but in fundamentally altering how they conceive of their basic interests. In summarizing their view, Peter Haas notes that this school argues that 'there is no "objective" basis for identifying material reality and all claims for objectivity are therefore suspect' (Haas 1992:21). The subjective element in states' decision-making makes it more difficult to evaluate objectively the role that institutions might play or how they might be constructed.

The characteristics of international institutions

The five general approaches discussed above are a useful starting point for the understanding of how institutions are created and of the key drivers of their subsequent evolution, but they are clearly of limited help in understanding specific variations in the forms of institutions. Based on the existing literature and on our own work, we characterize institutions in terms of their membership, the stringency of their rules (the degree to which they constrain state behaviour), their scope, their membership, the extent of delegation of power from member states to institutional bodies and the centralization of tasks within the institution.

The Bretton Woods institutions, the WTO, and UNCTAD have quasi-universal *membership* (see Box 3.3). By contrast, the Group of Seven most industrialized countries only welcomed one new member since the 1970s (Russia formally joined the Group in 1997, transforming it into the G8). Similarly, most regional integration arrangements have remained as select clubs with limited membership (see Ravenhill, Chapter 6 in this volume). Membership also varies in terms of the type of actors who can participate. While most institutions remain state-centric, some have started to include private actors. For instance, the Financial Stability Forum (FSF) was created in 1999 to promote international financial stability groups' representatives from national ministries, international financial institutions, and sector-specific groups (insurance, accounting standards, securities commissions). Controversy continues at the WTO over whether non-state actors should be permitted to participate in deliberations (for other efforts paying particular attention to membership issues see Sandler 1992; Koremenos et al. 2001; Aggarwal and Dupont 2002).

Box 3.3 IMF and WTO: Selected Organizational Characteristics

Created to promote international monetary co-operation, the International Monetary Fund exerts a surveillance function over member states' financial and economic policies and provides financial and technical assistance to member states. Day-to-day business is conducted by the Executive Board, a body with 24 Executive Directors representing directly or indirectly all members. The IMF's five largest shareholders—the US, Japan, Germany, France, and the United Kingdom—along with China, Russia, and Saudi Arabia have their own seats, whereas the other 16 Executive Directors are elected by groups of countries.

The Executive Board is empowered by the Board of Governors, the highest authority of the IMF in which each member has a seat. To assist it in the conduct of IMF affairs, the Executive Board in turn selects a Managing Director who is the chief of the operating staff of the Fund—roughly 2,800 employees with half of them being economists.

Within the Executive Board, the normal *de jure* decision-making mode is simple majority, but important issues are decided by qualified majority, either by 70 per cent (suspension of one member's rights in case of non-respect of obligations) or by 85 per cent (for instance, modification of quotas, change in the seats of the Executive Board, or provisions for general exchange arrangements). Qualified majority voting increases the power of the biggest contributors, in particular the US, which has a veto power over issues requiring 85 per cent majority decisions. *De facto*, however, voting rarely occurs in the Executive Board. Instead, Executive Directors use consensus to adopt decisions.

The institutional structure of the WTO differs significantly from the IMF model. It reflects very clearly what the organization considers to be its primary role—a forum for the negotiation of trade liberalization agreements. The WTO's principal institutional structures are a ministerial Conference meeting every two years, the General Council, and three councils in the area of goods, services, and intellectual property. All members have a seat on these councils. The default decision-making mode is consensus, but decisions may also be made by unanimity (suspension of MFN treatment), with a 75 per cent majority (interpretation of an existing multilateral agreement, or a waiver of an obligation for a particular country) or a two-thirds majority (for instance, the admission of new members).

The WTO General Council also serves as the Trade Policy Review Body that reviews member states' trade policies. Reviews are conducted on the basis of a policy statement by the member under review and a report prepared by economists in the WTO Secretariat. That Secretariat, headed by a director-general, has around 630 staff and its main function is one of administrative and technical support for WTO councils, committees, and working groups.

Delegation of authority in the WTO is therefore restricted to the mechanism for solving trade disputes between members. Delegation is conferred first to small groups of experts (3 or 5) who are established when members fail to settle disputes in conciliatory way. Panel members are independent individuals under instruction from no government. Their role is to make an objective assessment of the dispute and issue a report with findings and recommendations (establishing the legality of member states' policies in the case under dispute). This report has then to be adopted by the General Council serving as the Dispute Settlement Body. The latter, however, can only reject the panel report by consensus.

The second body with delegated authority from the member state is the Appellate Body, which reviews appeals made by member states on panel reports. The seven members of the Appellate Body serve for four-year terms and are legal experts with international standing. The appeal can uphold, modify, or reverse the panel's legal findings and conclusions. As in the case of panel reports, the appeal report must be endorsed by the Dispute Settlement Body. Rejection is only possible by consensus.

For more information, http://www.wto.org; and http://www.imf.org

The second dimension, *stringency of rules*, covers both the precision and the obligation of rules in the literature on legalization of world politics (see Aggarwal 1985 on regime strength; and Abbot and Snidal 2000 on legalization). From this perspective, authors have often contrasted the so-called European and Asian models of regional economic integration. The first one is built upon a wide set of specific and binding rules (called the *acquis communautaire* in the jargon of European integration) whereas the second is built upon declarations, intentions, and voluntary commitments (Ravenhill 1995, 2001). The lack of any precise and concise definition of a balance of payments problem in the IMF severely affected the constraining power of this institution on preventing its members from running imbalances.

Third, we consider the *scope* of agreements defined as issue coverage (Aggarwal 1985; Koremenos et al. 2001). The evolution of the GATT from its origins in 1947 to the creation of the WTO in 1995 reveals an important increase in the scope of the agreements. Whereas GATT initially focused on the liberalization of trade in goods, the WTO covers services and agriculture, as well as trade-related aspects of intellectual property rights and investment (see Winham, Chapter 5 in this volume). Similarly, the G7/G8 agenda has drastically expanded from a focus on macroeconomic management to a broad range of international security and economic issues, including terrorism, energy, environment, and arms control. At the other end of the range, one finds sector-specific institutions such as the International Organization of Securities Commissions (IOSCO), the International Associations of Insurance Supervisors (IAIS), and International Accounting Standards Board (IASB), as well as product-specific organizations such as the International Coffee Organization (ICO), the International Cocoa Organization (ICCO), the International Copper Study Group (ICSG), and the International Sugar Organization (ISO).

The fourth dimension is the extent of *institutional delegation*, the authority ceded by members to an institution, a dimension central to several existing studies (Abbot and Snidal 2000; McCall Smith 2000; Dupont and Hefeker 2001; Hawkins et al. 2006). International agreements may or may not include the creation of institutional organs, and these organs may or may not be given some autonomy from members for making new rules or monitoring and enforcing existing ones.

The extent of delegation may vary significantly across organs of the same institution. For instance, while the dispute settlement process in the WTO features an independent appellate body, the governing body of the organization — the General Council — relies upon consensus decision-making and the members have kept the size and prerogatives of the secretariat down to a minimum. At the regional level, the extent of delegation strongly distinguishes the European Union from the small secretariats found in other regional institutions. Whereas the EU includes organs with supranational power, governments remain in full control of negotiation and implementation processes in most other regional agreements, including NAFTA, the Association of Southeast Asian Nations (ASEAN), and the Asia-Pacific Economic Cooperation (APEC) grouping.

A fifth dimension is *institutional centralization* (Koremenos et al. 2001). Is there a concentration of tasks performed by a single institutional entity? Centralization may refer to such tasks as the diffusion of information, monitoring of members'

behaviour or the imposition of sanctions, as well as the adoption of new rules or modification of existing ones. Strong administrative bodies are natural candidates for the centralization of many tasks, as exemplified by the case of the European Commission in the European Union, or the administration of the IMF or the World Bank. Yet, in the latter two, key decisions and tasks go through the Executive Board with a limited membership of 24 countries or groups of countries represented by Executive Directors chosen by member states (see Helleiner, Chapter 7 in this volume).

It is often difficult to understand these five dimensions as being separate, but they are conceptually distinct. As an example, although it is hard to imagine an agreement with lax rules and high delegation, strict rules do not necessarily imply high delegation (good instances are the numerous bilateral treaties on investment and, to a lesser extent, bilateral free trade treaties). Similarly, centralization and delegation may reinforce each other, but neither requires the other one. Conferences or councils of heads of governments and states centralize most of the activities of several regional economic organizations (including monitoring, and dispute settlement). Yet, decision-making remains either consensual (where no state publicly dissents from the agreement) or based on unanimity.

Explaining institutional design

How can one account for institutional variation on these five dimensions? Consistent with a functionalist approach to the study of international institutions, we should expect the five dimensions to be affected by the type of problems that institutions should address (Stein 1982; Snidal 1985*a*; Aggarwal and Dupont 1999; Koremenos et al. 2001; Ostrom 2003). In Table 3.1, we link our three typical problems with specific roles for international institutions. Keeping these in mind, the 'temptation to free ride' problem is the one that clearly calls for strong rules, with delegation and centralization to

Table 3.1 From Problems to Institutional Solutions

	'Free riding temptation'	'Inhibiting fear'	'Where to meet'
Strategic game	Prisoner's Dilemma	Stag Hunt (assurance games)	Battle of the Sexes
Illustrations	Trade liberalization Debt rescheduling	Financial integration Trade specialization	Managing adjustments Multilateral negotiations
Role(s) of institutions	Channel to enforce contracts • monitoring/surveillance • sanctioning mechanisms • policy transfer	Enhancers of co-operation • pools of resources • suppliers of knowledge and capacity	Providers of solutions to distributive conflicts • negotiation forums • agenda setting • linkages
Examples of institutional solutions	*Monitoring/surveillance*: Articles IV and VIII of IMF; Trade Policy Review mechanism WTO *'Sanction'*: IMF Conditionality, WTO Dispute Settlement Body's (DSB) authorization of sanctions *Policy transfer*: Common Trade policy and Economic and Monetary Union in the European Union	*Pools of resources*: quota system in IMF *Suppliers of knowledge and capacity*: WTO (technical co-operation); World Bank; IMF; UNCTAD	*Negotiation forums*: WTO General Council; Executive Boards IMF and World Bank; UNCTAD *Agenda setting*: IMF and World Bank staff

international bodies. Co-operation is difficult and thus requires relatively strong institutions. In such cases, membership tends to be restricted to well-'socialized' governments. An inclusive membership makes monitoring more difficult and costly, and thus creates many opportunities for members to free ride.

As for scope, on the one hand, enforcement of the agreements is more likely to occur when institutions have a broad scope and are able to connect different issues ('issue linkage'). Linkages across issues help in deterring defection on a single issue when actors have broad interests (McGinnis 1986; Lohmann 1997). For example, members of the WTO cannot subscribe to the agreement on goods (GATT) without also accepting the agreement on services (General Agreement on Trade

in Services (GATS)), as well as the agreements on intellectual property rights (Trade-Related Aspects of Intellectual Property Rights (TRIPs)) and investment (Trade-Related Investment Measures (TRIMs)), and the dispute-settlement mechanism. On the other hand, adding issues to an institution's agenda requires strong capacity to monitor behaviour, which may often simply not be present.

The 'inhibiting fear' and 'where to meet' problems call for quite different institutional features. For these cases, there is a positive link with centralization for the pooling of resources, knowledge and information provision, or the reduction of costs of negotiations. Addressing the 'inhibiting fear' may require some clear and binding rules on access to resources and knowledge. Yet, in these cases, restricting the size of membership may not be a strong prerequisite for success. Solving distribution problems may require a softening of rules to allow some room for different interpretations of the agreements. Delegation of power is not essential in both situations, except for a potential benefit of agenda-setting power to find mutually acceptable solutions.

As for scope, there is no clear link between 'inhibiting fear' and issue coverage. But a diverse set of issues can provide greater ground for compromise when players have different preferences and when they do not assign equal value to all of the issues. For instance, trade liberalization and monetary co-operation in the European Community has often been facilitated by the development of social or regional policies or packages to 'compensate' countries that might not immediately be major beneficiaries of the other policies. But, as the case of agriculture in the GATT/WTO shows, having different issues on the agenda is not helpful when countries categorically exclude certain issues from consideration in making trade-offs. Finally, with respect to membership, selected, restrictive groupings tend to reinforce the fear of being left out and thus should be avoided to address the 'inhibiting fear' problem. As for problems of distribution, more members may on the one hand help in the quest for new solutions. Yet, new members may also add as many new conflicts as complementarities among players.

As we have seen, then, different types of problems call for appropriate institutional design. Although focusing on general tendencies in institutional design in view of the problems they need to address provides a useful first step, we are still faced with some anomalies. For instance, given that trade liberalization is widely portrayed as embodying a 'temptation to free ride', how can one explain that some institutions (for instance, European Free Trade Association) that focus on trade liberalization have remained informal and thus lack organs with delegated power? Why is it that some institutions do not have clear rules and preconditions for membership (for instance, GATT/WTO or the EU until

the early 1990s)? And lastly, why do some countries prefer very loose rules in designing institutions (such as ASEAN and APEC)?

To increase our ability to understand such choices, we can consider three other key influences. First, an important issue is what we call *potential participants* in the institution. In particular, the number of these actors and their relative power—two factors considered by Koremenos et al. (2001), as well as their overall financial and 'social' capital (Ostrom 2000), influence the design of institutions. Relatively little concern about membership rules in GATT 1947 can be accounted for by the fact that the international system was much smaller and more homogeneous than the one that emerged in the 1960s as a result of decolonization. Similarly, the need to define strict criteria for entering the EU only became salient when the iron curtain fell and former communist countries with still very different political systems expressed an interest in joining the EU. Turning to the financial and social capital among potential actors, the disparities in size of financial reserves held by East Asian economies surely explains the very decentralized form of the regional financing arrangement known as the 'Chiang Mai Initiative' (an East Asian institution that is intended to provide emergency finance to member economies facing a run on their currencies). In turn, the fact that there has been little formalization of relationships between central banks in the developed, democratic world, builds upon a joint understanding and on a high level of expertise on how to address problems.

Second, the *information and knowledge available to actors* affects institutional design. Institutions comprised of actors with rich and reliable information usually require less centralization or less delegation (Coase 1960; Williamson 1975; Koremenos et al. 2001), as illustrated with the loose structure of the European Free Trade Association from its creation in 1960 to its upgrading in 1993. The founding members of that association—the United Kingdom, Denmark, Norway, Sweden, Austria, Switzerland, and Portugal—did not have the mutual distrust that characterized French–German relationships in the EC and information from part-ner countries was thus considered by all members to be rich and reliable. Existing knowledge about the issue area(s) covered by the agreement may affect the stringency of rules, the delegation of power, is-sue scope, and membership. Poor knowledge about the issues at stake tends to make actors wary of mak-ing hard commitments (rules and delegation)—a tendency particularly present in the discussions in the domain of the environment (see Dauvergne, Chapter 14 in this volume). Better knowledge may affect issue scope and the contours of membership. Whereas the politics of trade liberalization may call for careful selection of members for inclusion in the WTO, the widespread belief in the veracity of international trade theory (which argues that global membership yields the greatest efficiency in the allocation of resources) helps to account for the pressure increasingly to universalize membership in this institution.

Third, and finally, we can focus on the *out-side institutional setting*. When actors create new institutions, they do not generally do so in a vac-uum. Thus, when new institutions are developed, they must often be reconciled with existing ones. One approach to achieving such reconciliation is by nesting broader and narrower institutions in hierarchical fashion. Another means of achieving harmony among institutions is through an insti-tutional division of labour, or 'horizontal' linkages (Aggarwal 1998). The challenge of institutional rec-onciliation is not, however, unique to the creation of new ones. In lieu of creating new institutions, policy-makers might also modify existing insti-tutions for new purposes. For instance, faced by seemingly intractable balance of payments prob-lems in Africa in the 1990s, the IMF developed new structural adjustment facilities that over-lapped substantially with those of the World Bank. When modifying institutions, therefore, members must also focus on issues of institutional com-patibility. Moreover, bargaining over institutional modification is likely to be strongly influenced by existing institutions.

A few examples will illustrate these ideas. One can think about the problem of reconciling institutions from both an issue-area and a regional perspec-tive (Oye 1992; Gamble and Payne 1996; Lawrence 1996a). Nested institutions in an issue-area are nicely illustrated by the relationship between the international regime for textile and apparel trade (the Long-Term Arrangement Regarding Interna-tional Trade in Cotton Textiles and its successor arrangement, the Multifibre Arrangement) with re-spect to the broader regime in which it is nested, the GATT. When the Executive Branch in the US faced pressure from domestic protectionist inter-ests simultaneously with international pressures to keep its market open, the American administra-tion promoted the formation of a sector-specific international regime under GATT auspices. This 'nesting' effort ensured a high degree of confor-mity with both the GATT's principles and norms as well as with its rules and procedures (Ag-garwal 1985, 1994). Although the textile regime deviated from some of the GATT's norms in permitting discriminatory treatment of develop-ing countries' exports, it did adopt and adapt the most-favoured nation (MFN) norm, which called for developed countries to treat all developing coun-tries alike.

The Asia-Pacific Economic Cooperation group-ing (APEC), created in 1989, illustrates the concept of regional nesting. APEC's founding members were extremely worried about undermining the GATT, and sought to reconcile these two in-stitutions by focusing on the notion of 'open regionalism'—that is, the creation of APEC would not bar others from benefiting from any ensuing liberalization in the region. APEC members saw this non-discriminatory liberalization as a better alternative to using Article 24 of the GATT, which permits the formation of discriminatory free trade areas and customs unions, to justify this accord (see Ravenhill, Chapter 6 in this volume). Rather than forming an institution that could conflict with the promotion of GATT initiatives, therefore, APEC founding members attempted to construct an institution that would complement the GATT. Furthermore, APEC members wanted to avoid undermining existing sub-regional organizations, in particular ASEAN. This clearly restricted the level of obligation and delegation that could have been transferred to the newly created pan-regional organization (Dupont 1998).

An alternative mode of reconciling institutions would be simply to create 'horizontal' institutions to deal with separate but related activities, as exemplified by the division of labour between the GATT and the Bretton Woods monetary system (IMF and World Bank). In creating institutions in the era after the Second World War, policy-makers were concerned about a return to the 1930s era of competitive devaluations, marked by an inward turn among states and the use of protectionist measures. These 'beggar-thy-neighbour' policies were found across economic issue areas, and individual action by each state worked to the detriment of all. As a consequence, the founders of the Bretton Woods monetary system also turned their focus to creating institutions that would help to encourage trade liberalization. By promoting fixed exchange rates through the IMF and liberalization of trade through the GATT, policy-makers hoped that this horizontal institutional division of labour between complementary institutions would lead to freer trade.

Finally, on a regional basis, one can see the development of the European Economic Coal and Steel Community and the Western European Union (WEU) as horizontal organizations. The first was oriented toward strengthening European cooperation in economic matters (which, of course, had important security implications), while the WEU sought to develop a co-ordinated European defence effort.

Conclusion

This chapter has sought to provide a systematic analysis of the problem of collaboration in global political economy through the lenses of types of problems, games, and institutions. We have seen that states may need to collaborate or co-ordinate their actions to keep economic globalization on track because they may face problems of free riding, an inhibiting fear that their efforts will lead to instability for their economy, and the need to find co-ordination points that have varying costs and benefits to the participants.

The problem of free riding or the difficulty of finding a co-ordination equilibrium is a common one on a number of issues, including trade, monetary cooperation, the environment, human rights, and the like. Despite some limitations, game theory provides useful insight into the diverse set of problems that states may face in collaborating or in co-ordinating their actions. One of the most commonly used games, the Prisoner's Dilemma, has been utilized to show that in many issue areas, actors have a strong incentive to defect, despite the potential joint gains that they may receive. Yet, as we have shown, many problems in international political economy are not PD games, but instead may be better characterized as Chicken, Assurance, Suasion, or even Harmony games. By carefully examining the types of problems that actors face in a particular issue area—the structure of payoffs—game theory provides insight into the constraints on joint action.

It is worth keeping in mind that the preferences that go into creating games are often assumed by many analysts—particularly those in the neorealist institutionalist and neoliberal institutionalist camps. Where do preferences come from and are such preferences amenable to change? It is on this dimension that constructivist arguments focusing on the role of experts, changing knowledge, and possible shifts in preferences through learning may provide significant insight that can help us to create more logically compelling games.

Once we can establish the basic game structure that actors face, we can better examine what role institutions might play in ensuring more favourable outcomes. In some cases, contrary to the perspective often taken by neo-institutionalists, institutions may not really be necessary for ensuring co-operative state action. Hence, we examined the types of situations in which self-help might lead to a positive outcome versus those in which institutions might play a genuinely useful role in overcoming collective action problems.

The role of institutions in fostering collaboration itself raises two puzzles: First, how might states collaborate in the first place to create institutions? This in itself raises an analytical problem that various theories have attempted to address. As we have seen, hegemons may have strong incentives to create institutions to constrain the behaviour of other actors and possibly their own domestic lobbies. Other approaches such as neoliberal institutionalism focus on the strong incentives that major states may have in creating institutions and suggest that small numbers of actors may be able to overcome the usual collective action problems that may lead to free riding behaviour. To understand better the process of institutional design, we focused on five dimensions to characterize institutions: membership, the stringency of their rules, their scope, their membership, the extent of delegation of power from member states to institutional bodies, and the centralization of tasks within the institution. The types of problems which actors face can partially account for specific institutional characteristics. Yet, other factors also influence the design of institutions. These include the potential participants in the specific issue area, the knowledge and information available to actors, and the pre-existing institutional context. In particular, with respect to the last factor, the Asian financial crisis of 1997–8 and the ongoing proliferation of trade agreements raises an important issue about reconciling new and old institutions. The Asian financial crisis generated considerable conflict when some Asian countries sought to create an Asian Monetary Fund. In the end, this effort faltered in the face of IMF and US opposition, but East Asian countries have since aggressively sought to create regional institutions. In trade, the problems of the Doha Round have been accompanied by a renewed push to shift away from broad multilateral institutions to bilateral free trade agreements and regional accords. The extent to which such arrangements will further undermine the WTO remains a crucial question that will have important implications for prospects of continued economic liberalization in the global economy.

? Questions

1. Why does globalization increase the pressure for international collaboration?
2. What is the most frequent problem of collaboration in global political economy?
3. What is the thorniest situation of collaboration in global political economy?
4. How can game theory help us understand problems of collaboration?
5. Can enforcement really be carried out in international political economy?
6. How can institutions help overcome obstacles to collaboration?
7. What is the link between the types of problems that countries face in the global economy and their choice of an institution?

8. What are some key characteristics that can be used to describe international institutions?

9. What theories or variables help to account for the choice of specific international institutional characteristics?

→ **Further reading**

■ Aggarwal, V. K. (ed.) (1998), *Institutional Designs for a Complex World: Bargaining, Linkages and Nesting* (Ithaca, NY: Cornell University Press). A collective volume that focuses on the relationships between institutions and the stability of dense institutional settings.

■ Aggarwal, V. K., and Dupont, C. (1999), 'Goods, Games and Institutions', *International Political Science Review*, 20/4: 393–409. The original and technical presentation of our theory that links goods, games, and institutions.

■ Cooper, R. N. (ed.) (1989), *Can Nations Agree?* (Washington, DC: Brookings Institution). An insightful collection of work on co-ordination attempts of economic policies among nations outside of institutional settings.

■ Hasenclever, A., Mayer, P., and Rittberger, V. (1997), *Theories of International Regimes* (Cambridge: Cambridge University Press). A collective volume on recent developments on theories of international regimes with application to all domains of international politics.

■ Kaul, I., Grunberg, I., and Stern, M. A. (eds) (1999), *Global Public Goods: International Cooperation in the 21st Century* (New York: Oxford University Press). A collective volume with a range of examples of global public goods in economics, politics, and environment with interesting lessons for the future provision of such goods.

■ Keohane, R. O. (1984), *After Hegemony: Cooperation and Discord in the World Political Economy* (Princeton, NJ: Princeton University Press). The classic work on the links between regime change and change in power distribution.

■ Koremenos, B., Lipson, C., and Snidal, D. (2001), 'The Rational Design of International Institutions', *International Organization*, 55/4: 761–99. Introductory article to the latest collective work on institutional design, using insights from game theory and considering various facets of institutions.

■ Krasner, S. D. (ed.) (1983), *International Regimes* (Ithaca, NY: Cornell University Press). The seminal collective volume on international regimes that includes the classic definition of regimes as well as a range of examples in various domains of international politics.

■ Olson, M. (1965), *The Logic of Collective Action: Public Goods and the Theory of Groups* (Cambridge, MA: Harvard University Press). Classic work on collective action and the conditions under which groups of actors may produce public goods.

■ Sandler, T. (1992), *Collective Action: Theory and Applications* (Ann Arbor, MI: University of Michigan Press). A comprehensive treatment of the problem of collective action using both basic and advanced formal analytical tools.

■ Snidal, D. (1985), 'Coordination versus Prisoners' Dilemma: Implications for International Co-Operation and Regimes', *American Political Science Review*, 79/4: 923–42. The seminal article on the contrast between PD and co-ordination games applied to international relations.

■ Taylor, M. (1987), *The Possibility of Cooperation* (Cambridge: Cambridge University Press). An advanced treatment of the problem of co-operation using repeated games.

■ Yarbrough, B. V., and Yarbrough, R. M. (1992), *Cooperation and Governance in International Trade: The Strategic Organizational Approach* (Princeton, NJ: Princeton University Press). An elegant analysis of the problem of governance in trade approached through the lens of transaction costs.

 ## Web links

■ www.gametheory.net/ Game theory.
■ http://www.globalpublicgoods.org Global public goods.

 ## Online resource centre

For additional material and resources, please visit the Online Resource Centre at:
www.oxfordtextbooks.co.uk/ravenhill3e/

4

The Domestic Sources of Foreign Economic Policies

Michael J Hiscox

 Chapter contents

- Introduction
- Policy Preferences
- Institutions
- Conclusions, Extensions, and Complications
- Appendix 4.1

 Reader's guide

How should a nation manage its economic ties with the rest of the world? How should the government regulate the flow of goods, people, and investment to and from foreign nations? Debates over foreign economic policies are a recurring, often volatile, feature of national politics in all countries. Indeed, how governments should now be dealing with the multiple facets of 'globalization' is perhaps the single most pressing political issue of our time. It is an issue that has been debated in international institutions, national legislatures, and lecture halls across the world; it has mobilized nationalist populist movements at one end of the political spectrum, and transnational environmental and human rights organizations at the other; and it has led to violent protests and demonstrations in the streets of Seattle, Melbourne, Washington, Genoa, and New York. What are the battle lines in these political debates? How are policies decided in different countries? How do differences in political institutions shape these policy decisions? And how do new ideas and information about policy options filter into politics? This chapter examines each of these questions, focusing on the domestic politics of trade, immigration, investment, and exchange rates.

Each government must make choices about how best to manage the way its own economy is linked to the global economy. It must choose whether to open the national market to international trade, whether to liberalize trade with some nations more than with others, and whether to allow more trade in some sectors of the economy than in others. Each government must also decide whether to restrict international flows of investment in different sectors, and whether to regulate immigration and emigration by different types of workers. And it must either fix the exchange rate for the national currency or allow the rate to fluctuate to some degree, in response to supply and demand in international financial markets.

Of course, if every government always made the same choices in all these areas of policy, things would be very simple for us as scholars (and much more predictable for the citizens of the world). But governments in different countries, and at different moments in history, have often chosen radically different foreign economic policies. Some have closed off their national economies almost completely from the rest of the world, imposing strict limits on trade, immigration, and investment—an example is China in the 1960s, which kept itself isolated almost completely from the rest of the world's economies. In other situations, governments have adopted the opposite approach, allowing virtually unfettered economic exchange between their citizens and foreigners—ironically, Hong Kong in the 1960s may be the best example of this type of extreme openness. Most governments today adopt a mixture of policies that fall somewhere in the middle ground between these two extremes, imposing selective controls on activities that affect some sectors of their economy, and restricting exchanges with some foreign countries more than with others. Understanding why governments make the particular choices they do requires careful attention to the political pressures they face from different

domestic groups and the political institutions that regulate the way collective decisions are made and implemented.

Politics, we know, is all about who gets what, when, and how. Different individuals and groups in every society typically have very different views about what their government should do when it comes to setting the policies that regulate international trade, immigration, investment, and exchange rates. These competing demands must be reconciled in some way by the political institutions that govern policy-making. To really understand the domestic origins of foreign economic policies we thus need to perform two critical tasks:

1. Identify or map the policy preferences of different groups in the domestic economy.
2. Specify how political institutions determine the way these preferences are aggregated or converted into actual government decisions.

The first step will require some *economic* analysis. How people are affected by their nation's ties with the global economy, and thus what types of policies they prefer to manage those ties, depends primarily on how they make their living. Steelworkers, for example, typically have very different views from wheat farmers about most foreign economic policies, because these policies rarely affect the steel and wheat industries in a similar fashion. Of critical importance here are the types of assets that individuals own, and how the income earned from these assets is affected by different policy choices.

The second step calls for *political* analysis. How political representatives are elected, how groups organize to lobby or otherwise influence politicians, and how policies are proposed, debated, amended, and passed in legislatures, and then implemented by government agencies, all depend on the structure of political institutions. Democratically elected leaders face very different institutional constraints from military dictators, of course, and even among democracies there is quite a wide range of institutional variation that can have a large impact on the behaviour of policy-makers.

These two analytical steps put together like this, combining both economic and political analysis in tandem, are generally referred to as the *political economy* approach to the study of policy outcomes. In the next two sections, we shall consider each of the two analytical steps in some detail, examining the domestic sources of policies in the areas of trade, immigration, investment, and exchange rates. We shall then shift gears a little, and consider

the ways in which ideas and information might affect policy-making. We shall also discuss linkages between the different policy dimensions and non-economic issues, focusing on environmental and human rights concerns, and how they feature in debates over foreign economic policies. Finally, in the conclusion, to link all this to the discussion of international collaboration and co-ordination in the previous chapter, we shall briefly consider the impact of domestic politics on bargaining over economic issues between governments at the international level.

Policy Preferences

The guiding assumption here is that, when it comes to taking positions on how to regulate ties with the global economy, individuals and groups are fundamentally concerned with how different policy choices affect their incomes. Of course, people may also have important non-material concerns that affect their attitudes toward foreign economic policies. Many people are concerned about the ways in which globalization affects national security, for example, and they worry about its impact on traditional cultures, on the world's environment, and on human rights; and these concerns may have a direct impact on their views about the regulation of international trade, immigration, and investment. We shall discuss some of these important considerations in more detail later in the chapter. But we begin here with the simplest possible framework in which economic policies are evaluated only in terms of their economic effects. Given that organized producer groups have almost always been the most vocal participants in domestic debates about foreign economic policies, and the debates themselves have been couched mainly in economic terms, this seems an appropriate way to begin.

Trade

The dramatic growth in international trade over the last few decades has intensified political debate over the costs and benefits of trade openness. In the United States, the controversy surrounding the creation of the North American Free Trade Agreement (NAFTA) in 1993 was especially intense, and similar arguments have arisen in Europe over the issue of enlargement of the European Union, and over attempts to reform the Common Agricultural Policy (CAP). Rapid trade policy reforms have also generated a significant political backlash in many developing nations, and recent years have witnessed violent protests and demonstrations by groups from a variety of countries that hope to disrupt meetings of the World Trade Organization (WTO). Political leaders around the world frequently voice concerns about the negative effects of trade, and the need to protect their firms and workers from foreign competition.

What is behind all this political fuss and bother? At first glance, it may seem puzzling that there is so much conflict over trade. After all, the most famous insight from international economics is the proof that trade provides mutual gains; that is, when countries exchange goods and services they are all generally better off. Trade allows each country to specialize in producing those goods and services in which it has a comparative advantage, and in doing so world welfare is improved (see Appendix 4.1).

While there are gains from trade for all countries *in the aggregate*, what makes trade so controversial is that, among individuals within each country, trade creates winners and losers. How trade affects different individuals depends on how they earn their living. To flesh out this story, economists have traditionally relied on a very simple theory of trade devised by two Swedish economists, Eli Heckscher and Bertil Ohlin. In the Heckscher–Ohlin model of trade, each nation's comparative advantage is traced to its particular endowments of different factors of production: that is, basic inputs such as land, labour, and capital that are used in different proportions in the production of different goods and services. Since the costs of these inputs in each country will depend on their availability, differences in factor endowments across countries will create differences in comparative advantage. Each country will tend to export items whose production requires intensive use of the factors with which it is abundantly endowed relative to other nations; conversely, each country will import goods whose production requires intensive use of factors that are relatively scarce. Countries well endowed with land, such as Australia and Canada, are expected to export agricultural products (for example, wheat and wool), while importing products that require the intensive use of labour (for example, textiles and footwear) from more labour-abundant economies like China and India. The advanced economies of Europe, Japan, and the United States, well endowed with capital relative to the rest of the world, should export capital-intensive products (for example, automobiles and pharmaceuticals), while importing other types of goods from less developed trading partners where supplies of capital are scarce compared to supplies of labour and land.

Building on this simple model of trade, Wolfgang Stolper and Paul Samuelson (1941) derived a famous theorem in 1941 that outlined the likely effects of trade on the real incomes of different sets of individuals within any economy. According to the Stolper–Samuelson theorem, trade benefits those who own the factors of production with which the economy is relatively well endowed, but hurts owners of scarce factors. The reasoning is straightforward: by encouraging specialization in each economy in export-orientated types of production, trade increases the demand for locally abundant factors (and bids up the earnings of those who own those factors), while reducing demand for locally scarce factors (and lowering the earnings of owners of such factors). In Australia and Canada, the theorem tells us, landowners should clearly benefit from trade, while workers can expect lower real wages as a consequence of increased imports of labour-intensive goods. In the United States, the theorem predicts that trade should benefit owners of capital and landowners at the expense of workers. The converse should hold in relatively labour-abundant (and capital-scarce) developing economies such as China and India, where trade will raise the wages of workers relative to the profits earned by local owners of capital.

By revealing how trade benefits some people while making others worse off, the Stolper–Samuelson theorem thus accounts for why trade is such a divisive political issue. The theorem also provides a neat way to map the policy preferences of individuals in each economy. In each nation, owners of locally *abundant* factors should support greater trade openness, while owners of locally *scarce* factors should be protectionist (see Box 4.1).

MICHAEL J HISCOX

Box 4.1 The Repeal of the Corn Laws

The story of the repeal of Britain's protectionist Corn Laws in 1846 is perhaps still the best-known example of a political clash over trade policy that fits nicely with the **Stolper–Samuelson theorem**. With the revival of foreign trade after the Napoleonic Wars, policy debates in Britain began to focus on the protectionist Corn Laws that restricted importation of various grains (wheat, rye, barley, and oats, as well as peas and beans), defended resolutely by the landowning elite. Pressure for reform came most strongly from manufacturers, especially textile producers in Leicester and Manchester, anxious to reduce labour costs (see McCord 1958). It was these manufacturers who formed the leadership of the Anti-Corn Law League in 1838, and a cotton manufacturer, Richard Cobden, became the League's most famous advocate. The push for reform soon drew a larger following among both the urban middle and working classes, and attracted support from the working-class Chartist reform movement, which organized the 'bigger loaf' campaign in the 1840s. The effects were soon felt in Parliament, transformed by the Great Reform Act of 1832 and the enfranchisement of voters in the large industrial centres of the West Riding. Cobden himself entered Parliament in 1841, campaigning with the cry, 'You must untax the people's bread!' and

the League stepped up its campaign with a storm of pamphlets, petition drives, public meetings, and addresses to labour unions. The widespread economic distress of the early 1840s had a great impact on the Tory prime minister, Robert Peel. He introduced a sliding scale for grain duties in 1841 and then reduced those rates in 1842 and 1844, in an attempt to ease the food crisis, but this aroused fierce opposition from landed interests and from within Conservative ranks. The failure of the potato crop in 1845, and the ensuing food crisis, gave Peel the pretext to go further. Amid reports of widespread starvation, the prime minister pushed through a bill to repeal the Corn Laws altogether, with support from both Liberals and Radicals. The conflict over repeal split the Conservatives irrevocably. Once 'purified' of their Peelite faction, the Tories (known for years as the Protectionists) were increasingly isolated on the trade issue in Parliament. Peel's supporters, including William Gladstone, gravitated to the Liberals, and their free trade platform drew on an immense base of support among urban industrialists, the middle classes, and workers. Gladstone's first budget as prime minister in 1860, effectively eliminated all remaining protectionist duties in Britain.

There is a good deal of evidence in the histories of political conflict over trade in a variety of nations that fits with this simple prediction (see Rogowski 1989). In Australia, for example, the first national elections in 1901 were fought between a Free Trade party representing predominantly rural voters, and a Protectionist party supported overwhelmingly by urban owners of capital and labour. A very similar kind of political division characterized most debates over trade policy in Canada in the late nineteenth century, with support for trade openness emanating mainly from farmers in the western provinces. In Europe and Japan, in contrast, much of the opposition to trade over the last century or so has come from agricultural interests, anxious to block cheap imports of farm products from abroad. In the United States and Europe, at least since the 1960s, labour unions have voiced

some of the loudest opposition to trade openness and called for import restrictions aimed at protecting jobs in labour-intensive industries threatened by foreign competition.

On the other hand, political divisions and coalitions in trade politics often appear to contradict this simple model of preferences. It is quite common to see workers and owners in the same industry banding together to lobby for protective import barriers, for example, in contemporary debates about policy in the United States, even though the Stolper–Samuelson theorem tells us that capital and labour are supposed to have directly opposing views about trade in these economies. So what is going on here? The critical problem is that the theorem is derived by assuming that factors of production are highly mobile between different industries in each economy. An alternative approach to mapping the effects of trade on incomes, often referred to as the specific factors model allows instead that it can be quite costly to move factors of production between different sectors in the economy. That is, different types of land, labour skills, and capital equipment often have a very limited or specific use (or range of uses) to which they can be put when it comes to making products. The plant and machinery used in modern manufacturing industries is very specialized: the presses used to stamp out automobile bodies are designed only for that purpose, for example, and cannot be adapted easily or quickly to perform other tasks. Steel factories cannot easily be converted into pharmaceutical factories or software design houses. Nor can steelworkers quickly adapt their skills and become chemical engineers or computer programmers.

In the specific factors model, the real incomes of different individuals are tied very closely to the fortunes of the particular industries in which they make their living. Individuals employed or invested in export industries benefit from trade according to this model, while those who are attached to import-competing industries are harmed (see Jones 1971; Mussa 1974). In the advanced economies of Europe and the United States, the implication is that owners and employees in export-orientated industries such as aerospace, pharmaceuticals, computer software, construction equipment, and financial services, should be much more supportive of trade than their counterparts in, say, the steel, textiles, and footwear industries, which face intense pressure from import competition. There is much evidence supporting these predictions in the real world of trade politics, especially in the debates over trade in the most advanced economies, where technologies (and the skills that complement them) have become increasingly specialized in many different manufacturing and service industries, and even in various areas of agriculture and mining production (see Magee 1980; Hiscox 2002). In the recent debates over regional and multilateral trade agreements in the United States, for example, some of the most vociferous opposition to removing barriers to trade has come from owners and workers aligned together in the steel and textile industries.

The leading research on the political economy of trade now assumes routinely that the specific factors approach is the most appropriate way to think about trade policy preferences, at least in the contemporary context in the advanced economies (see Grossman and Helpman 1994; Rodrik 1995), so we shall rely on it for the most part in the discussions below. This model, it is worth noting, is still nested within the broader Heckscher–Ohlin theory that explains trade according to differences in factor endowments. Newer theories of trade, motivated by some clear evidence that not all trade seems to fit well with this simple endowments-based theory (for example, Europe, Japan, and the United States all importing automobiles from each other), have made some significant departures from the standard Heckscher–Ohlin framework. One innovation is to allow that technologies of production and tastes among consumers may vary substantially across countries. Such differences might affect the types of products an economy will be likely to export and import, but the predictions about trade policy preferences derived from the specific factors approach are not otherwise affected: individuals engaged in export industries favour trade, while those in import-competing industries oppose trade. A more complicated innovation in trade theory allows for the possibility of economies of scale. In some industries requiring large investments of capital, the largest firms may enjoy such a dramatic cost advantage over smaller firms that those markets tend to be dominated by only a few, very large, corporations. In such cases, in which firms compete with one another and with foreign rivals for different market niches, trade may have different effects for firms in the same industry. These types of complexities are difficult to incorporate into a broadly applicable model of trade, however, so we shall not pursue them here. Although it might be pointed out that large firms that enjoy economies of scale in production also tend to engage in foreign investment, locating parts of their enterprise in different nations. Below, we shall discuss the political implications of this type of multinational investment in more detail.

Immigration

Of course, globalization is not simply a matter of trade in goods and services; it also involves international flows of the factors of production themselves—the migration of workers between nations, and international investment and lending that transfers capital across borders. There is not a radical difference between how we analyse these phenomena and how we examine trade, but neither is the analysis identical in terms of the economic effects and the policy preferences we anticipate for different sets of individuals within each nation.

Political debates about immigration policy have been rising in volume and intensity in recent years in almost all Western economies. On the one hand, immigration is seen by many as an economic and cultural lifeline that can supply firms in key industries with skilled workers while also injecting new artistic and intellectual life into the nation. On the other hand, many people are concerned that immigrants take jobs away from local workers and create ethnic enclaves that can Balkanize a nation and lead to more crime and other social ills. These latter concerns have encouraged the recent imposition of much tighter immigration controls in many countries, while also nurturing the growth of extremist anti-immigrant political movements in several European countries and increasing the incidence of hate crimes directed toward immigrants. The debate seems certain to continue in the years ahead, and to grow fiercer.

Historically, immigration has almost always been more politically controversial than has trade. The issue is still so sensitive that tight restrictions on immigration are nearly universal. Again, as with limits on trade, such restrictions make little sense if we look only at the *aggregate* welfare effects of international labour flows. It is easy to demonstrate that when labour is free to migrate to countries where it can be more productive (and earn correspondingly higher wages), there will be an increase in total world output of goods and services (see Krugman and Obstfeld 2000: ch. 7). And total output must also increase in any economy that allows more immigrants to enter. This expansion in production makes it possible, in principle, for everyone to enjoy higher standards of living. Migration flows can actually serve the same economic purpose as trade flows, responding to price signals to improve economic efficiency. Indeed, in the standard Heckscher–Ohlin model of trade described above, trade is simply a function of country differences in endowments of labour and other factors, and so international movements of goods and factors are, in fact, substitutes for one another. Countries abundantly endowed with labour, such as China and India, and in which wages are thus quite low compared to wages paid elsewhere, are not only natural suppliers of labour-intensive exports for the world market, but are also natural suppliers of labour itself (that is, emigrants).

As we already know, however, what matters most for politics is not that aggregate welfare gains are possible from exchanges (of goods or factors) between economies; what matters most is that some people gain and others lose. Which individuals are most likely to oppose immigration? Again, the standard economic analysis emphasizes the importance of the different types of productive factors—including land and capital, as above, with an additional distinction made between high-skilled labour (or 'human capital') and low-skilled or blue-collar labour. What is critical, as you will have already guessed, is the impact that immigration can have on relative supplies of factors of production in the local economy. If immigrants have low skill levels, as is typically assumed when discussing the effects of immigration in the advanced economies of Europe and North America, allowing more immigration will increase the local supply of low-skilled labour relative to other factors. The effect is to lower the real wages of all low-skilled workers, as the new arrivals price themselves into employment by accepting lower pay, while raising the real earnings for local owners of land, capital, and skills, as demand for these other factors increases. Of course, if a nation only allows *high-skilled* workers to immigrate, the effect will be lower real wages for high-skilled workers, but higher real earnings for low-skilled workers and owners of land and capital.

The basic results from this simple model of the impact of immigration—often referred to as 'factor-proportions' analysis (see Borjas et al. 1996; Borjas 1999)—are widely applicable. Immigration always harms local workers with similar skill levels to those of the arriving workers, while benefiting local owners of other factors. Even if we allow for high levels of trade, which can partially offset the impact of immigration as economies adjust to the change in factor supplies by importing less of some goods that can now be produced locally at a lower cost, the effects are always in the same direction—although they may become very small in size, and even disappear altogether, if the local economy is small relative to other economies (Leamer and Levinsohn 1995). The effects are even generally the same if we allow that the skills of workers can be highly 'specific' to particular industries, though the impact of immigration on earnings will be larger for high-skilled (specific) workers in some industries than in others. Any inflow of unskilled labour will be especially valuable for high-skilled workers in sectors that use unskilled labour more intensively, for example, but it will still benefit all high-skilled workers since output (and demand for their skills) will rise in each industry. Conversely, an inflow of any type of high-skilled labour will generate the largest decline in earnings for high-skilled workers in the same industry (those who own the same specific skills as the immigrants). But it will also hurt high-skilled workers in other industries in the local economy whose earnings will suffer, albeit in a relatively minor way, as demand for their types of specific skills falls in response to the expansion taking place in the industry into which the skilled immigrants have moved.

So, again, we have a very simple and generally applicable way of identifying the policy preferences of individuals. Individuals can be expected to oppose any policy that would permit immigration of foreign workers with similar skill levels, but they will support other types of immigration. Individuals who make their living from ownership of land and capital are likely to be the strongest supporters of more open immigration laws. If we look at the political debates over immigration laws in particular countries, the general alignment of interests seems to fit rather well with these expectations. Typically, the most vocal opposition to changes in immigration laws that would permit more low-skilled immigration comes from labour unions representing blue-collar workers. In the United States, for example, the AFL–CIO has traditionally taken a very tough stance in favour of restrictive immigration laws and border control measures aimed at stemming illegal immigration into the country from Mexico (Tichenor 2002: 209). American business and farm associations have taken a very different position, often lobbying for more lenient treatment of illegal immigrants and for larger quotas in various non-immigrant working visa categories. In similar fashion, trade union federations in Britain, France, and Germany have raised protests about enlargement of the European Union and the possible influx of low-skilled workers into their economies from new member countries in Southern and Eastern Europe. High-skilled workers have not shied away from immigration politics either, often lobbying to restrict inflows of immigrants with skills that match their own and would thus pose a competitive threat in the local labour market—the American Medical Association, for example, the organization that represents doctors in the United States, has pushed hard to limit the number of foreign doctors granted visa status while also making it more difficult for them to obtain licences to practice (see Box 4.2).

Box 4.2 The 'New World' Closes its Doors to Immigrants

Beginning in the 1840s and 1850s, there was a huge surge in emigration from England, Ireland, and other parts of Europe and Asia to the 'New World' economies in North and South America and Australasia, where labour was relatively scarce and wage rates comparatively high. The rudimentary border controls and open policy towards immigrants in these frontier economies meant that labour flows responded quite quickly to economic events—and, in particular, to gold rushes and other 'booms' associated with the construction of railways and the birth of new industries. Over time, however, as labour unions became more organized and politically influential in the New World economies, greater restrictions were imposed on immigration. The political pressure for limits on immigration became especially strong during economic recessions, when local rates of unemployment often rose swiftly, and labour groups blamed new immigrants for taking jobs away from 'native' workers (see Goldin 1994). Between the 1880s and the 1920s, all the New World economies gradually closed themselves off to immigration (see O'Rourke and Williamson 1999). In the United States, the first bans were imposed on Chinese immigrants in 1882, and then on all Asian immigrants in 1917, when a tough literacy test was also introduced as a way of limiting inflows of low-skilled workers. In 1921, the Emergency Quota Act placed severe restrictions on all new arrivals. The strongest political support for these measures came from north-eastern states with highly urbanized populations working in manufacturing industries, where labour unions were particularly well organized and vocal.

This simple approach to the political economy of immigration restrictions is very useful, at least as a first step towards understanding the political forces that are likely to shape policy outcomes. It is extremely difficult, however, to analyse the politics of immigration without examining non-economic concerns among individuals related to questions of culture and identity. Immigration policy, after all, has a profound impact on who makes up the nation itself. In this way, it is quite different from trade policy. A great deal of recent research suggests that divisions among individuals over immigration policy are most strongly related to fundamental differences in cultural values associated with ethnic and racial tolerance and cosmopolitanism (for example, Espenshade and Calhoun 1993; Citrin et al. 1997; McLaren 2001). This question of whether preferences related to non-economic issues have a profound effect on attitudes towards foreign economic policies is one that we shall return to below.

Foreign investment

Capital can also move from one country to another. These movements usually do not take the form of a physical relocation of some existing buildings and machinery from a site in one nation to another site abroad (the equivalent to worker migration). Instead, they take the form of financial transactions between citizens of different nations that transfer ownership rights over assets: a firm in one country buys facilities abroad that it can operate as a subsidiary, for example, or individuals in one country buy shares in foreign companies, or a bank in one country lends money to foreign firms. All such transactions increase the stock of capital available for productive use in one country, and decrease the stock of capital in another country.

The dramatic increase in the volume of international capital flows since the 1960s, outstripping the increase in trade, has had a profound impact on the international economy. Short-term flows of capital in the form of portfolio investment (purchases of company shares and other forms of securities, including government bonds), which can change direction quite rapidly in response to news and speculation about changing macroeconomic conditions and possible adjustments in exchange rates, have had a major impact on the choices governments can make when it comes to monetary and exchange rate policies (see Pauly, Chapter 8 in this volume). Longer-term capital flows in the form of 'direct foreign investment' (where the purchase of foreign assets by a firm based in one country gives it ownership control of a firm located on foreign soil), have perhaps been even more politically controversial since the activities of these multinational firms have had major and highly visible effects in the host nations in which they manage affiliates (see Thun, Chapter 11 in this volume). Many critics of multinational corporations fear that the economic leverage enjoyed by these firms, especially in small, developing nations, can undermine national policies aimed at improving environmental standards and human rights. The political debate over direct foreign investment is thus highly charged.

Tight restrictions on both short- and long-term investment by foreigners have been quite common historically, although the controls have been much less strict than those typically imposed on immigration. Clearly, these controls cannot be motivated by a desire for economic efficiency. If such controls are removed and capital is allowed to move freely to those locations in which it is used most productively (and where it will be rewarded, as a result, with higher earnings), it is easy to show that the total output of goods and services will be increased in both the country to which the capital is flowing and in the world economy as a whole. Again, this expansion in aggregate production makes it possible, in principle, to raise the standard of living for people everywhere. International investment, just like the migration of workers examined above, can serve the same economic purpose that is otherwise served by trade. International flows of capital substitute for the exports of capital-intensive goods and services in the benchmark Heckscher–Ohlin model. In general, then, we can expect that the advanced industrial economies of Europe and the United States, which have abundant local supplies of capital for investment, and in which rates of return on capital are thus quite low compared with earnings elsewhere, are the natural suppliers of capital (as well as capital-intensive goods) to poorer nations, in which capital is in relatively scarce supply (see Box 4.3).

Box 4.3 Investment, Imperialism, and the 'Race for Africa'

Beginning in the 1870s, vast quantities of investment capital flowed from the centres of finance in Western Europe to the rest of the world, providing the capital necessary to develop railways and telegraph networks, ports, and new mining industries in eastern and central Europe, the Americas, and much of Asia. In the following decade, the political context in which these foreign investments were made began to change drastically as an intense race developed among the major powers for political control of territories in Africa and Eastern Asia. Governments in Britain, France, Germany, and Belgium made imperial expansion in these regions their most urgent foreign policy priority. Seizing political control of territories in which there was often no clear or stable governing authority, or at least not one capable of defending the area from conquest by outside force, was a way to safeguard the investments that were being made in these territories (mostly in the production of raw materials, such as cotton, silk, rubber, vegetable oils, and other products of tropical climates, as well as railways and ports, that were all very vulnerable to seizure). These imperial policies were supported most strongly by financial interests and conservative parties, typically backed by commercial and shipping industries as well, and by military leaders anxious about the security implications of falling behind rivals in the control of strategic territories and ports. British economist, J. A. Hobson (1902/1948), and following him, Lenin (1917/1996), famously interpreted the imperial expansion of this time as the natural consequence of owners of capital needing access to new investment opportunities overseas; imperialism was, in Hobson's terms, 'excessive capital in search of investment'.

One point worth making here about the likely direction of capital flows concerns the distinction between lending and portfolio flows of capital and direct foreign investment (see Ravenhill, Chapter 1 in this volume). It is reasonable to imagine that the former types of international investment are driven purely by the quest to maximize (risk-adjusted) rates of return on capital, in line with the Heckscher–Ohlin model. With the caveat that capital-poor developing countries are often politically unstable, and high levels of risk can deter investors, we should, nevertheless, expect large flows of capital from the industrial nations to the developing world. It is much less clear that economy-wide differences in rates of return are critical for explaining patterns in direct foreign investment. There is certainly a considerable amount of direct investment by European, American, and Japanese firms in developing nations, with many firms setting up a 'vertical' multinational structure of enterprises that locates land or labour-intensive parts of the production process in developing nations. But the vast bulk of direct foreign investment in the modern world economy, in fact, takes the form of capital flows between the industrial economies themselves, with firms creating 'horizontal' structures in which similar functions are performed in facilities in different locations (see Graham and Krugman 1995: 36). This type of investment does not fit well with the standard Heckscher–Ohlin predictions based on factor endowments, and is best explained instead by the special advantages that firms in some industries gain by jumping borders (and trade barriers), and by internalizing transactions within the firm itself. Firms that rely heavily on specialized technologies, and management and marketing expertise, may have a hard time selling these kinds of intangible assets to foreign companies it would like to work with as suppliers or distributors; instead, it may make far more sense to keep all these relationships within the firm (see Hymer 1976; Caves 1982). Many of these types of horizontal multinational firms also appear to have been established to secure access to foreign markets into which they might not otherwise be able to sell because they

faced trade barriers. This 'tariff-jumping' motive was a big factor in motivating Japanese auto firms to set up manufacturing facilities in both Europe and North America beginning in the 1980s. The implication is that there is often a strong connection between the effects of trade policies and investment (and investment restrictions), a topic we shall return to in the final section of the chapter (see also Thun, Chapter 11 in this volume).

Now, putting aside the aggregate welfare gains that international movements of capital make possible, which individuals are likely to benefit from such capital flows, and which individuals will lose out? Here, we can simply apply the logic of the same 'factor proportions' approach we used above to outline the effects of immigration. We might distinguish between different types of capital, in the same way that we distinguished between low- and high-skilled labour above, and set apart lending and short-term or portfolio investment flows from direct foreign investment. But to keep things simple here, we shall just consider them all as a single form of capital. What is critical here, of course, is the impact that inflows of any foreign capital have on relative supplies of factors of production in the local economy. Allowing more inflows of capital from abroad will increase the local supply of capital relative to other factors, and thus lower real returns for local owners of capital. At the same time, inflows of investment will raise the real earnings of local owners of land and labour by increasing demand for these other factors of production.

Again, even allowing for the fact that trade flows can partially offset the impact of international movements of factors of production—economies may adjust by importing lower quantities of some goods that are now less costly to produce at home—the direction of the effects on the incomes of different groups is always the same. Local owners of capital are disadvantaged by inflows of foreign capital; while local landowners and workers (in all categories) are better off. These effects may diminish in size in cases in which the local economy is small relative to others, as we noted above when discussing the income effects of immigration, but they are always working in the same direction. And, again, in parallel with the analysis of immigration flows, these income effects are not affected drastically by allowing that capital can take forms that are highly 'specific' to particular industries—though the effects may be larger for owners of some types of capital than others. This is especially relevant when we think about direct foreign investment, which typically involves the relocation of a particular set of manufacturing or marketing activities that require very specific types of technologies in a particular industry. An inflow of any type of specific capital will, of course, result in a decline in earnings for local owners of capital in the same industry; it will also hurt all others who own specific types of capital used in different industries—in a more marginal way, of course—as demand for their assets will fall in response to the expansion taking place in the industry favoured by foreign investment.

We can thus expect that policies allowing greater inflows of foreign capital will be strongly opposed by individuals who own capital in the local economy, but such policies will be supported by local landowners and workers. There is some evidence that does fit well with these basic predictions. Perhaps the best example involves the way European and American auto companies have supported restrictions on the operations of local affiliates of their Japanese rivals since the 1980s. In Europe, auto firms pushed hard for an agreement with Japan that included cars produced in Japanese affiliates within the limits set on the total Japanese market share of the European auto market. In the United States, after some initial hesitation (perhaps reflecting the fact that they had themselves set up numerous foreign transplant firms around the world), the US auto firms supported a variety of proposals for 'domestic content' laws that would have placed local affiliates of Japanese auto makers at a considerable disadvantage by disrupting their relationships with parts suppliers at home (Crystal 2003). The 'big three' American firms (Ford, General Motors, and Chrysler) also seized the opportunity to demand high local content requirements in the rules of origin for autos in the negotiations over the 1993 North American Free Trade Agreement, ensuring that they would have a major advantage over Japanese transplants producing cars in Mexico for the North American market. Interestingly, the workers we would expect to be strongly supportive of incoming Japanese investment in the auto industry, represented by the United Auto Workers union, were in fact quite lukewarm—perhaps because they had long advocated that tough domestic content rules be applied to American firms, to prevent them from transplanting their parts manufacturing facilities to Canada and Mexico, and perhaps also in response to concerns that the foreign transplants setting up in southern American states such as Tennessee (Nissan) and Kentucky (Toyota) were not employing union members.

Foreign investment tends to be even more politically controversial in developing nations, where the behaviour of large foreign corporations can have profound effects on the local economy and on local politics. One particular concern among critics of multinational firms has been the role that several large corporations have apparently played in supporting authoritarian governments that have restricted political organization among labour groups, limited growth in wage rates, and permitted firms to mistreat workers and pollute the environment (see Evans 1979; Klein 2002). While the evidence is not very clear, in some cases, local owners of capital may well have muted their opposition to investments by foreign firms in order to support authoritarian policies adopted by military regimes: in Nigeria, for example, where Shell (the European oil company) has long been the major foreign investor, or more recently in Myanmar, where Unocal (an American oil and gas firm) is the key foreign player. But the basic competitive tension between local capitalists and foreign firms (whose entry into the economy bids down local profits) is typically very obvious even in these unstable and non-democratic environments, as local firms have often encouraged their governments to impose severe restrictions on foreign investments, including onerous regulations stipulating that foreign firms use local rather than imported inputs, exclusion from key sectors of the economy, and even nation- alization (seizure) of firms' assets (Jenkins 1987: 172). Newer evidence suggests that, as we might ex- pect given the preferences of labour in capital-poor developing nations, left-wing governments backed by organized labour have made the strongest efforts to lure foreign firms to make investments (Pinto 2003).

So far, we have considered only the issue of whether governments relax restrictions on *inflows* of foreign capital. Of course, governments can and often do act to influence how much investment flows out of their economies. And the same holds for labour flows, as governments often try to affect *emigration* as well as immigration—many govern- ments, in countries as diverse as Australia, Canada, and India, are worried about a 'brain drain' of skilled workers and professionals, for example, and have adopted a range of policies to discourage or tax such labour flows. But the issue of outward direct investment, often involving the 'outsourc- ing' of jobs by multinational firms to their affiliates in labour-abundant (low-wage) nations, has be- come an especially salient political issue recently in Europe and the United States. The political di- visions over the issue are largely what we expect from the factor proportions theory: those who own capital are strongly opposed to any restrictions on their ability to invest it abroad in order to earn higher profits, but restrictions on outward invest- ment are strongly supported by local workers, who understand that capital outflows will reduce their real earnings. In the United States, for example, the most ardent advocates of legislation that would raise the tax burden on profits earned abroad by Ameri- can corporations has been the AFL–CIO and those workers among its membership that have been hit hardest by outsourcing (for example, labour unions in the textile and auto industries). Interestingly, these labour unions have often had support from environmental and human rights groups concerned that competition among developing countries to attract new investments from multinational firms may produce a race to the bottom in environmental and labour standards. Coalitions of labour unions and human rights groups have waged campaigns to try to force US corporations to adhere to strict codes of conduct abroad. We shall discuss these types of multi-issue political coalitions below.

Exchange rates

Of course, a critical difference between transactions that take place between individuals living in the same country and transactions between people in different countries is that the latter require that people can convert one national currency into an- other. If a firm in Australia wants to import DVDs from a film studio in the United States, for example, it will need to exchange its Australian dollars for US dollars to pay the American company. The rate at which this conversion takes place will obviously affect the transaction: the more Australian dollars it takes to buy the number of US dollars required (the price of the DVDs), the more costly are the imports for movie-loving Australian buyers. All the trade and investment transactions taking place every day in the world economy are affected by the rates at which currencies are exchanged.

Before the First World War, almost all govern- ments fixed the value of their currency in terms of gold, thereby creating an international monetary system in which all rates of conversion between individual currencies were held constant (for fur- ther discussion of this international gold standard, see Ravenhill, Box 1.4 in this volume). Between the Second World War and 1973, most currencies were fixed in value to the US dollar, the most important currency in the post-war world economy. In this system, often referred to as the Bretton Woods system (see Ravenhill: Box 1.5 in this volume), the United States agreed to guarantee the value of the dollar by committing to exchange dollars for gold at a set price of $35 per ounce. Since 1973, when the Nixon administration officially abandoned the fixed rate between the dollar and gold, all the major currencies have essentially been allowed to fluctuate freely in value in world financial markets (see Helleiner, Chapter 7 in this volume). Among developing nations, however, many governments continue to fix the value of their currency in terms of dollars or another of the major currencies (see Frieden et al. 2001). And groups of nations in different regions of the world, including the members of the European Union, have made separate efforts to stabilize exchange rates at the regional level, even progressing to the adoption of a common regional currency.

The fundamental choice each government must make involves deciding whether to allow the value of the national currency to fluctuate freely in response to market demand and supply, or instead fix the value of the currency in terms of some other currency or external standard—typically, the

currency of a major trading partner or, as was common in the past, gold (a precious metal valued highly in most societies throughout history). When a government chooses to fix the value of the national currency, it sets the official rate of exchange and commits itself to buy the currency at that fixed rate when requested to by private actors or foreign governments. Between a 'pure float' and a fixed exchange rate there are intermediate options: a government can choose a target value for the exchange rate and only allow the currency to fluctuate in value within some range around the target rate. The wider this range, of course, the more policy approximates floating the currency (see Box 4.4).

Box 4.4 The Politics of the Rising Dollar

Between 1980 and 1985, the US dollar rose by approximately 50 per cent in value against the Japanese yen and by roughly similar amounts against the German Deutschmark and the British pound. The rapid dollar appreciation placed immense strain on US producers of traded goods and services, and by 1985 the Reagan government was being lobbied strenuously by a large variety of groups asking for some kind of action to halt the rise (see Destler and Henning 1989). The strongest pressure came from groups in a broad collection of export-orientated sectors, including grain farmers, firms such as IBM and Motorola in the computer industry, and Caterpillar, a large exporter of construction equipment and machinery. The voices of these exporters were swelled by protests coming from firms in import-competing industries, including the major auto companies and the steel-makers. The initial reaction from the Reagan administration was to sit tight and characterize the rise of the dollar as a sign that the rest of the world held the United States and its economy in high esteem. The government had set a course to restrain inflation when entering office in 1981, and had raised US interest rates considerably. Taking action to devalue the dollar would have thrown into substantial doubt this commitment to

defeat inflation. After their initial pleas were rebuffed by the White House, however, many groups from the steel, auto, and textiles industries began demanding new forms of trade protection instead, bombarding Congress with calls for trade barriers that would make up for the competitive effects of the dollar appreciation. It was this threat of runaway protectionism in Congress that finally prompted the government to take action on the dollar. In 1985, the White House reached an agreement with the governments of Japan, Germany, Britain, and France, which became known as the Plaza Accord (a reference to the lavish New York hotel in which it was negotiated). This deal provided for a co-operative effort to manage a gradual depreciation of the dollar against the other currencies, with each government agreeing to alter its macroeconomic policies in such a way as to ease demand for the dollar compared with other currencies (for example, the Reagan government agreed to lower interest rates and to make a new effort to reduce the size of the US budget deficit). By giving up some control over macroeconomic policy, in co-ordination with other governments, the White House was able to reverse the rise of the dollar and ease the strain imposed on US producers of traded goods and services.

When it comes to trade, immigration, and investment, economists agree almost universally on the policy choice that is best for maximizing national (and world) output, and hence general standards of living: removing barriers to all types of international exchange is optimal, because it allows resources to be allocated in the most productive way. There is no similar consensus, however, on the best approach to currency policy. Fixing the exchange rate has both pros and cons, and it is not always clear which are larger. By eliminating fluctuations in the exchange rate, fixing makes international trade and investment less costly for firms and individuals, since they will not need to worry that the benefits from these international transactions will be affected adversely by some sudden, unexpected shift in exchange rates. By doing away with exchange rate risk, fixing allows the economy to benefit more fully from international trade and investment. But what is the downside? What does the government give up by pledging to buy or sell its own currency on request at the official rate of exchange? The answer, in short, is control over monetary policy.

A nation's monetary policy regulates the supply of money (and the associated cost of credit) in order to manage aggregate levels of economic activity, and hence levels of inflation and unemployment. Governments typically use monetary policy to counter economic cycles: they expand the supply of money and lower the cost of credit during recessions to increase economic activity and promote job creation, and restrict the supply of money and raise the cost of borrowing during 'booms' to slow economic activity and control inflation. When a government commits to fixing the exchange rate, it effectively gives up the ability to tailor monetary policy to manage domestic economic conditions. To see why, just imagine what happens to money supply if, at the given exchange rate, the nation's residents spend more on foreign goods, services and assets in any given period than foreigners buy from firms and individuals in that nation: the country's balance of payments, which registers the value of all transactions with the rest of the world, will be in deficit. This means that that there is less overall demand

for the country's currency than for the currencies of other countries (needed for residents to buy foreign products and assets). To satisfy this excess demand for foreign currencies and to maintain the exchange rate at the fixed level, the government will be a net buyer of its own currency, selling off its reserves of foreign currencies (or gold). The automatic effect of maintaining the fixed exchange rate in these conditions, then, is to reduce the total supply of the nation's money in circulation and slow domestic economic activity. Just the opposite should occur when the nation runs a balance of payments surplus: excess demand for its currency compared to other currencies will require that the government increases the supply of its money in circulation, thus stimulating economic activity.

In effect, then, fixing the value of the currency makes monetary policy a hostage to exchange rate policy. Even if a government sets the exchange rate at a level that it hopes will generate no balance of payments deficits or surpluses, since the balance of international transactions in any period will depend heavily on external economic conditions and events in foreign countries, it has very little control. A recession abroad, for example, will reduce purchases of a nation's products by foreigners and lead to a deficit in the balance of payments, and so, if currency values are fixed firmly, this recession will be 'transmitted' to the home nation by the subsequent reduction in its money supply.

The crux of the choice between fixed and floating exchange rates is the choice between stability and policy control: a stable exchange rate will increase the economic benefits attainable from international trade and investment, but this requires giving up the ability to adjust monetary policy to suit domestic economic conditions. Governments in the most advanced economies have generally decided that policy control is more important to them than exchange rate stability, at least since the early 1970s. Governments in smaller, developing nations have mainly chosen exchange rate stability over policy control. In part, this is because these countries tend to rely more heavily on trade and foreign investment as sources of economic growth. This choice is also more attractive for governments in smaller countries trying to defeat chronic inflation. Government promises to deal with runaway inflation in these countries may not be regarded as credible by private actors if governments in the past have shown a tendency to act irresponsibly (for example, by printing and spending large amounts of money) when facing electoral challenges. Since the expectations that private actors have about government policy feed directly into the prices (and wages) set, inflationary expectations can have devastating effects. In such circumstances, fixing the nation's currency in terms of the currency of a major trading partner with a comparatively low rate of inflation can serve an important function, providing a way for the government to commit itself more credibly to a low-inflation monetary policy. In essence, by committing to keep the exchange rate fixed, the government is ceding control of monetary policy in a very clear and visible way, and anchoring inflation at home to the inflation rate in the partner country (see Giavazzi and Pagano 1988; Broz and Frieden 2001).

In terms of the effects on aggregate welfare, the wisdom of fixing exchange rates is thus not always crystal clear. The best or most preferred policy for different sets of individuals within each country can similarly be difficult to identify. Consider first the case in which we assume that factors of production are mobile between sectors in the domestic economy (they are not 'specific' to particular sectors), and so we can apply the logic of the Stolper–Samuelson theorem and factor-proportions analysis. Since exchange rate volatility serves, in effect, as an added barrier or cost to international trade and investment flows, we have a place to begin when trying to map the policy preferences of individuals: in each economy, owners of locally abundant factors are more likely to support a fixed exchange rate, while owners of locally scarce factors are more likely to prefer a floating rate. In the capital-abundant, labour-scarce advanced economies of Europe and the United States, we might thus expect a simple class division over exchange rate policy: fixed rates benefit owners of

capital at the expense of workers. We could expect the reverse alignment of class interests in the labour-abundant, capital-scarce economies of, say, China and India. In such countries, greater exchange rate certainty should encourage more trade and greater inflows of foreign investment, and both types of international flows will benefit workers at the expense of local owners of capital.

But, here, we cannot think about exchange rate stability without also thinking about monetary policy control. In general, workers might be expected to oppose fixed exchange rates in most circumstances, since they are likely to bear greater costs than others when monetary policy can no longer be used to avert economic downturns resulting in higher levels of unemployment. Owners of capital, on the other hand, care less about unemployment rates than they do about keeping inflation in check, which is typically much easier for the government to achieve (as noted above) when monetary policy is committed to keeping the exchange rate fixed. Just as in the case for the nation as whole, then, owners of labour and owners of capital may have to make a difficult choice about where they stand in terms of the trade-off between the effects of greater currency stability and less monetary policy control. In contemporary, labour-scarce Europe, for example, workers would seem to be better off along both dimensions if exchange rates were more flexible, while owners of capital should prefer fixed rates. There is some evidence that fits in with this interpretation. Labour unions in Western European countries generally provided the most vocal opposition to government policies aimed at fixing or stabilizing exchange rates in the 1970s and 1980s, particularly in France and Italy. But the record is mixed. While the labour-backed Socialist government that came to power in France in 1981 initially abandoned exchange rate stability as a goal, by 1983 it was committed to a fixed currency peg (see Oatley 1997). In fact, during the inter-war period in Europe, left-wing governments tended to keep their currencies fixed to the gold standard longer than other governments (Simmons 1994). And looking across a broader range of countries, in which labour is the locally abundant factor and capital is scarce, the preferences of these broad classes of individuals when it comes to exchange rates becomes even more difficult to predict.

Perhaps one major reason why it is difficult to find compelling evidence to support simple class-based interpretations of exchange rate politics is that individuals tend to see things very differently depending on the industries in which they are employed and invested. If we allow, as in previous discussions above, that factors of production are typically very specific to particular industries, we get a very different picture of the alignment of individual preferences on the exchange rate issue. And the picture is also much clearer. Individuals employed or invested in sectors that invest or sell in foreign markets are likely to favour exchange rate stability, since fluctuations in rates impose costs on their international transactions and because they have a relatively small economic stake in domestic (versus foreign) macroeconomic conditions. Those individuals associated with firms and banks that invest heavily in foreign markets, for example, and export-orientated sectors that sell a large proportion of their output abroad, should thus tend to support fixed exchange rates. On the other hand, owners and employees in import-competing industries and those producing non-traded services (for example, building, transportation, sales) whose incomes depend overwhelmingly on domestic economic conditions, are likely to favour flexible exchange rates that allow the government more control over monetary policy. There is some compelling evidence supporting these predictions, especially in the debates over exchange rate policy in the most advanced economies. In Europe in recent decades, for example, the strongest support for fixing exchange rates (and ultimately, for creating a common European currency) has come from the international banks, multinational firms in a diverse range of industries (including auto firms such as BMW and Mercedes), and from export-orientated sectors. The strongest opposition to fixed rates has tended to come from owners and labour unions associated with import-competing industries such

as coal, steel, and textiles, especially in nations such as France and Italy that have battled relatively high rates of inflation (see Frieden 1994). In developing nations, recent studies have indicated that governments are more likely to float their currency when the import-competing manufacturing sector accounts for a large proportion of the local economy (Frieden et al. 2001).

Finally, when a government does decide to fix or stabilize its currency, it must also decide the level at which to set the exchange rate. Whether the currency should be 'stronger' (that is, take a higher value versus other currencies) or 'weaker' (a lower value) is a second, important dimension of exchange rate policy. Even when the currency is floating, in fact, if it happens to move strongly in one direction or another, the issue can become a salient one, since the government may be called upon to intervene in an effort to raise or lower the exchange rate towards some new target. What is interesting in this regard is that the alignment of the various groups in terms of preferences for fixing versus floating the currency are not quite the same as the way they are positioned on the issue of the actual rate that should be set or targeted. A stronger currency will harm those in both export-orientated and import-competing industries, since it will make their products less attractive to consumers relative to the foreign alternatives. Individuals in these sectors should prefer a weaker currency. But a weaker currency will harm all others in the local economy by eroding their purchasing power when it comes to buying foreign goods and services. Owners and employees in non-traded sectors should prefer a stronger currency, as should any multinational firms or international banks that are investing abroad and purchasing foreign assets (Frieden 1994). In the real world of politics, in cases in which the level of a nation's exchange rate has, in fact, become a salient political issue, these types of coalitions do appear to emerge. Devaluation of the US dollar became a major election issue in the 1890s, for example, with the rise of the Populist movement, supported predominantly by export-orientated farmers who demanded a break from the gold standard in order to reset the dollar exchange rate at a lower level. The Populists were opposed most strongly by banking and commercial interests in the north-eastern states, who favoured a strong dollar (see Frieden 1997).

> ## Key points
>
> - According to the Stolper–Samuelson theorem, trade benefits those who own the factors of production with which the economy is relatively well endowed, and hurts owners of scarce factors.
> - In the alternative 'specific factors' model, individuals employed or invested in export industries are the ones who benefit from trade, while those who are attached to import-competing industries are disadvantaged.
> - The leading research assumes that the specific factors approach is the most appropriate way to think about the effects of trade in the contemporary advanced economies.
> - Immigration harms the real earnings of local workers with similar skill levels to those of the arriving workers, while benefiting everyone else in the host country.
> - Inflows of foreign capital will hurt individuals who own capital in the local economy, while benefiting all local landowners and workers.
> - Individuals attached to firms and banks that invest abroad or export a large proportion of their output are likely to favour a fixed exchange rate. On the other hand, owners and employees in import-competing industries and those producing non-traded services are likely to favour a flexible exchange rate.
> - A stronger currency will harm those in both export-orientated *and* import-competing industries, while benefiting all others in the local economy.

Institutions

Once we have specified the preferences of different individuals and groups on any particular issue, we need to think about how much influence they will have over policy outcomes. This is where political institutions come in to play. Political institutions establish the rules by which policy is made, and thus how the policy preferences of different groups are weighed in the process that determines the policy outcome. It is appropriate here to start with the broadest types of rules first, and consider the formal mechanisms by which governments and representatives in legislative bodies are elected (or otherwise come to power). These broad features of the institutional environment have large effects on all types of policies. But, then, we can move on to discuss more specific aspects of the legislative process and administrative agencies that have implications for the formulation and implementation of trade, immigration, investment, and exchange rate policies.

Elections and representation

Perhaps it is best to start with the observation that the general relationship between democratization and foreign economic policy-making is a matter that is still open to considerable theoretical and empirical doubt. Part of the puzzle is that there is a great deal of variation in the levels of economic openness we have observed among autocratic nations. In autocratic regimes, the orientation of policy will depend on the particular desires and motivations of the (non-elected) leadership, and there are different theoretical approaches to this issue. Non-elected governments could pursue trade and investment liberalization, on the one hand, if they calculate that this will increase their own power or wealth (for example, through taxation) by increasing national economic output. Such policies may be easier to adopt because autocratic leaders are more insulated than their democratic counterparts from the political demands made by any organized domestic groups that favour trade protection and limits on foreign investment (Haggard 1990). Perhaps this is an apt description of the state of affairs in China, as it has been opening its economy gradually to trade and investment since the 1980s, and non-democratic governments in Taiwan and South Korea pursued trade liberalization even more rapidly in the 1960s. On the other hand, autocratic governments may draw political support from small, powerful groups that favour trade protection. Many such governments appear to have used trade and investment barriers in ways that were aimed at consolidating their rule (Wintrobe 1998). The experience in Sub-Saharan African nations since the 1960s, and in Pakistan and Myanmar, seems to fit this mould. Without a detailed assessment of the particular groups upon which a particular authoritarian regime depends for political backing, it is quite difficult to make predictions about likely policy outcomes under non-democratic rule.

In formal democracies that hold real elections, the most fundamental set of political rules is the set that defines which individuals get to vote. If the franchise law gives more weight to one side in a policy contest compared to others, it can obviously have a great impact on policy outcomes. Where only those who own land can vote, for example, agricultural interests will be privileged in the policy-making process. If this landowning elite favours trade protection, as it did in Britain in the years before the Great Reform Act of 1832, then such a policy is almost certain to be held firmly in place. By shifting political power away from landowners and towards urban owners of capital and labour, extensions of the franchise had a major impact on all forms of economic policy during the late nineteenth and early twentieth centuries in Europe, America,

and elsewhere. In England, the extension of voting power to the middle and working classes, achieved in the reforms of 1832 and 1867, had the effect of making free trade politically invincible—with a huge block of workers along with the urban business class supporting trade openness, and only a tiny fraction of the electorate (the traditional rural elites) against it, a government that endorsed tariffs or restrictions on investment would have been committing electoral suicide. In the United States and Australia, on the other hand, where labour and capital were in relatively scarce supply, the elimination of property qualifications for voting and the extension of suffrage had exactly the opposite effect, empowering a larger block of urban voters who favoured high tariffs. In general, extensions of the franchise to urban classes tend to produce more open policies toward trade, immigration, and investment in labour and capital-abundant countries, but more closed or protectionist policies in labour- and capital-scarce economies.

The precise rules by which representatives are elected to national legislatures are the next critical feature of the institutional environment. Scholars have suggested that, in parliamentary systems in which legislative seats are apportioned among parties according to the proportion of votes they receive ('proportional representation'), narrowly organized groups have far less impact on policy-making in general than they do in electoral systems in which individual seats are decided by the plurality rule (see Rogowski 1987). Parliamentary systems with proportional representation tend to encourage the formation of strong, cohesive political parties which appeal to a national constituency and have less to gain in electoral terms by responding to localized and particularistic demands in marginal or contested districts (McGillivray 1997). Other types of systems, in contrast, tend to encourage intra-party competition among individual politicians and the development of a 'personal vote' in particular electoral districts, and are thus more conducive to interest-group lobbying. The implications for foreign economic policies are usually spelt out in very clear terms: we expect that proportional representation systems with strong political parties (for example, Sweden) will typically produce lower levels of trade protection and other restrictions than alternative types of electoral systems (for example, Britain, the United States) in which particular local and regional interests have a greater influence.

These conclusions about the impact of particularistic groups in different types of electoral systems rest upon a critical insight derived from theoretical work on collective action in trade politics: that there is a fundamental asymmetry between the lobbying pressure generated from groups seeking protectionist policies, and the lobbying pressure that comes from groups who oppose such restrictions. The main reason for this is that restrictions on imports and other types of exchange, when imposed one at a time, tend to have very uneven effects. As we know from the analysis of the specific factors model above, the benefits of a tariff on a particular good are concentrated on the owners of capital and labour engaged in that particular industry. If the tariff is substantial, these benefits are likely to be quite large as a share of the incomes of those individuals, and thus they will typically be willing to spend a good deal of their time and energy (and savings) lobbying to ensure they get the tariff they want. The stakes are very high for them. In contrast, the costs of the tariff are shared among all the owners of other types of specific factors in the economy; they are dispersed so broadly, in fact, that they tend to be quite small as a fraction of the incomes of these individuals. Thus, it is unlikely that those hurt by the new tariff will be prepared to devote resources to lobbying against the policy proposal. Collective political action will always be much easier to organize in the relatively small groups that benefit from a particular trade restriction than in the much larger groups (the rest of the economy) that are hurt by the restriction (see Olson 1965). Perhaps the best

example of this logic is the extraordinary political power that has been demonstrated by the small, highly organized agricultural groups in Europe, the United States, and Japan since the 1950s. These groups, which together represent a tiny fraction of the population in each political system, have been able to win extremely high (if not prohibitive) rates of protection from imports and lavish subsidies (see Tyers and Anderson 1992).

Other aspects of electoral institutions may also play a role in shaping policy outcomes (see Box 4.5). In general, smaller electoral districts in plurality systems may be expected to increase the influence of sectoral or particularistic groups over elected representatives, and thus lead to higher levels of protection (Rogoswki 1987; Alt and Gilligan 1994). In larger districts, political representatives will be forced to balance the interests of a greater variety of industry groups when making decisions about policies, and will be less affected by the demands of any particular industry lobby, and a larger share of the costs of any tariff or restriction will be 'internalized' among voters within the district. From this perspective, upper chambers of parliaments, which typically allocate seats among representatives of much larger electoral districts than those in lower chambers, tend to be less inclined toward trade protection and other types of restrictive foreign economic policies. Meanwhile, in legislative chambers in which seats are defined along political/geographical lines without regard for population (for example, in the United States Senate, where each state receives two seats), agricultural, forestry, and mining interests in underpopulated areas typically gain a great deal more influence over policy-making than they can wield in chambers (for example, the United States House of Representatives) where legislative seats are defined based on the number of voters in each district.

Box 4.5 The Institutional Foundations of the Gold Standard

Why was the gold standard, the system of fixed exchange rates that appeared to work so well in bringing order and stability to the global economy between the 1880s and 1914, so difficult to re-establish in the 1920s? One very important reason has to do with the major changes in political institutions that took place in Western nations around the time of the First World War. The gold standard required that governments give up control of monetary policy in order to keep the value of their currencies fixed in terms of gold (and one another). In essence, macroeconomic policy was held hostage to exchange rate policy, so that currency values were stable. This was especially difficult for small economies that happened to run large balance of payments deficits at the set rates of exchange. To maintain their exchange rates, they were forced to reduce the supply of their money in circulation and raise interest rates, thereby reducing economic activity at home and increasing unemployment. If they were already in the middle of an economic recession, this meant making the downturn even worse. Governments could only follow through with this type of commitment to a fixed exchange rate if the economic costs of recession—which fell predominantly upon workers who lost jobs and income, and small businesses and farmers driven into debt—did not have direct political consequences in terms of their ability to remain in office. This changed in many nations around the start of the twentieth century, when electoral laws were reformed, extending the franchise to larger proportions of the population (including workers who had previously been denied the right to vote in many places). Around the same time, labour organizations, including trade unions and labour parties, grew in political strength in almost all the Western economies, using strikes to push for political reforms while gaining significant electoral representation for the first time. Given these profound changes in the lie of the political land, the attempts to recreate the gold standard in the inter-war period appear to have been doomed from the outset. Governments elected by much broader segments of the population were increasingly unwilling to give up their ability to manage domestic economic conditions, especially during recessions, in order merely to maintain the gold parity. Eventually, after weathering several smaller crises, the system collapsed when governments began to abandon the gold standard completely after 1929 in response to the onset of the Great Depression.

We have generally been focusing on trade policies, since most of the past research on the effects of institutions has tended to concentrate on tariff levels. But recent studies also suggest that differences in electoral institutions can have a significant impact on exchange rate policies. In particular, in plurality systems in which elections are all-or-nothing contests between the major parties, governments appear to be far less likely to fix exchange rates and give up control over monetary policy than governments in proportional representation systems (see Clark and Hallerberg 2000). It appears that the costs of having ceded control over monetary policy in plurality systems, should the government face an election contest during an economic slump, are much higher than elsewhere. This difference also appears to be more pronounced for governments in plurality systems, in which the timing of elections is predetermined by law (Bernhard and Leblang 1999).

Legislatures and policy-making rules

The rules that govern the way national legislatures go about making laws can have profound effects on the way the preferences of individuals and groups are aggregated into different types of foreign economic policies. These rules determine the way new policies are proposed, considered, amended, and voted upon. They structure the interactions among different legislative and executive bodies, and establish which branches have what types of agenda setting and veto power over policy.

Most of the recent research on the impact of legislative institutions on foreign economic policies has been focused on American trade policy. The point of departure for many studies is the infamous Smoot–Hawley Tariff Act of 1930, which was such a disaster that it helped to inspire a fairly radical change in the rules by which Congress has dealt with trade policy ever since. The core of the legislative problem, as many see it, is the possibility for logrolling or vote-trading between protectionist interests. The benefits of a tariff or trade restriction can often go to an import-competing industry located almost entirely in one electoral district, with the costs borne generally by individuals across the rest of the economy. In such cases, lobbying pressure by these industries can generate a protectionist logroll when tariffs are being set by voting among members of a legislature: each member of the legislature will propose generous protective measures for industries in his or her own district without accounting for the costs they impose on individuals elsewhere. To gain support for these measures, each member will vote in favour of similar measures proposed by other legislators. If members can vote indefinitely on a sequence of such proposals, a policy that includes every new tariff can be the equilibrium outcome (supported by each legislator's belief that a vote against another's proposal would induce others to retaliate by offering an amendment to withdraw protection from the defector's district). The result of such unchecked logrolling is a vast array of protective measures, such that all individuals are far worse off than they were before the bill was passed (see Weingast et al. 1981).

According to conventional wisdom, the Smoot–Hawley tariff was just such a logrolling disaster, and Congress reacted to it in a remarkably sensible way by redesigning the rules governing the way trade policy was made. Specifically, Congress delegated to the executive branch the authority to alter US trade policy by negotiating reciprocal trade agreements with other countries. This practice of delegating negotiating authority to the president has been continued since 1934. By delegating authority over policy to the president, who would presumably set trade policy to benefit all individuals within the one, *national* electoral district, this innovation eliminated the spectre of protectionist logrolling completely, and ensured that all the costs of trade protection were fully 'internalized' by a decision-maker accountable to all voters. In addition, by empowering the president to negotiate

trade agreements that elicited reciprocal tariff reductions from other countries, the change helped to mobilize support for trade liberalization among export interests who could now expect improved sales abroad as a result of tariff reductions at home.

The lessons drawn from this case are almost certainly overstated, and the conventional account has some gaping inconsistencies. In particular, there appears to have been no learning at all on the part of members of Congress between 1930 and 1934: the congressional voting records indicate that, among the members voting on both bills, almost all those who voted for Smoot–Hawley in 1930 voted against the Reciprocal Trade Agreements Act (RTAA) (see Schnietz 1994). Moreover, it is not at all clear that protectionist logrolls have been an otherwise unsolvable problem for tariff legislation in the US Congress (or elsewhere)—what of all the cases in which *liberalizing* bills were passed by legislatures in the absence of delegation? In the US Congress itself, the major acts passed by the Democrats when in control of government before the 1930s (the Wilson Tariff of 1894 and the Underwood Tariff of 1913) stand out in this regard. Examples also abound in the legislative histories of other Western democracies. It should not be a mystery as to why. In parliamentary systems, political parties play critical roles in controlling the legislative agenda. In proportional representation systems these parties compete for a share of the national vote, and so legislation designed to appease district-specific interests holds little appeal. Even in plurality rule systems, however, the majority party that forms a government typically imposes strict control over the policy agenda in a way that prevents such self-defeating logrolls. Finally, the notion that presidents, simply by dint of having a large (national) constituency, must be champions of freer trade, is hopelessly ahistorical. Here, again, we cannot ignore the critical role played by political parties. In the US case, the Republican base of support between the 1840s and 1940s was concentrated among manufacturing interests in the north-east and Midwest states and was staunchly protectionist, and a long list of Republican presidents championed high tariffs in election campaigns and backed the most protectionist of Republican tariff bills in Congress (see Hiscox 1999). More generally, in all the Western democracies, political parties typically have very distinct core constituencies among the electorate, defined in regional or class terms, to whom they are principally accountable when designing policies. Whether a government allows protectionist amendments during legislative deliberations of policy, and whether a president supports trade liberalization, will depend on their partisan affiliation and the preferences of their party's core electoral base.

Despite the distortions, the story of the RTAA does still hold some valuable lessons for thinking about ways in which legislative rules can affect foreign economic policies (see Box 4.6). The explicit institutional connection that the RTAA forged between tariff reductions at home and reciprocal reductions in tariffs abroad certainly played a role in generating increased support for trade policy reform among export-orientated industries, and thus made it easier for all policy-makers to support trade liberalization. This link is now more or less routine, of course, for policy-making in most Western governments, as a consequence of their membership commitments in the WTO. For nations outside the WTO, however, most of them being developing countries, where attempts to liberalize trade policy have a poor political track record, this does suggest that governments are more likely to succeed with trade reform if they can do so as part of a bilateral or regional free trade agreement with major trading partners.

Box 4.6 The Reciprocal Trade Agreements Act of 1934 (RTAA)

In 1930, the US Congress passed the infamous Smoot–Hawley Tariff Act, which raised import duties on a vast array of manufactured and agricultural goods (some to over 200 per cent), and was dubbed the 'worst tariff bill in the nation's history' even before it was passed. Retaliation from other countries, in the form of higher tariffs, was swift and substantial, and the subsequent sharp decline in world trade and the collapse of the fragile international monetary system increased the depth and scope of the Great Depression. The 1930 tariff bill was widely regarded as a case of protectionist logrolling run wild. The Senate alone made 1,253 amendments to the original House bill, and duties on over 20,000 items were altered (see Pastor 1980: 77–8). When the Democrats won control of the White House, and majorities in Congress, in 1932, they looked for a way to make a change. Rural interests still made up a large part of the Democrats' electoral base, especially in the south, and still strongly favoured trade and the party's traditional anti-tariff platform. Unilateral tariff reductions were politically sensitive in the middle of a recession, however, and were not popular at all among workers, who had thrown their support behind the Democrats in the 1932 campaign. Franklin D. Roosevelt's secretary of state, Cordell Hull, a long-time advocate of free trade, instead designed new legislation that would permit the president to negotiate bilateral treaties with trading partners, to restart trade by making reciprocal reductions in import duties. Passed as the Reciprocal Trade Agreements Act in 1934 (RTAA), the legislation granted the president authority (for three years) to negotiate alterations of up to 50 per cent in the existing import duties. When that initial authority expired in 1937, Congress renewed it and continued to do so in the decades that followed. Beginning in 1974, the president's authority was expanded to cover negotiations over a range of non-tariff barriers to trade (NTBs), although various procedural and monitoring provisions were also introduced to constrain executive behaviour, and the Congress maintained the power to approve or reject any trade agreement by vote (under the so-called 'fast-track' provision that prohibited amendments and set a firm time limit for a ratifying vote). The delegation of policy-making power to the executive branch, which can aggregate the costs and benefits of protection across the entire nation and bargain for reciprocal changes in the policies of other governments to open foreign markets to American exports, is credited with reorientating US trade policy away from protectionism in the decades since 1934 (see Destler 1995; Gilligan 1997).

The RTAA also offers a lesson about group access to lawmakers that is often overlooked. Up to 1934, congressional committee hearings were pivotal in shaping the trade legislation voted on in the US House and Senate. The hearings format, which assigned particular days for receiving testimony on the duties to be levied on different commodities, was especially convenient for industry group lobbying. This system was changed completely in 1934. After the RTAA, hearings were typically limited to general discussions about whether to extend the president's negotiating authority and, after 1974, whether to implement previously negotiated agreements (under 'fast-track' provisions that prohibited amendment). Closing off this very direct channel by which groups had been able for years to lobby for changes in duties on particular items may have had the most profound effect on trade policy-making in the United States. In general, *any* type of policy-making rule that provides routine access for organized groups to exert lobbying pressure to change particular features of legislation will make trade protection and other forms of restriction more likely—including open legislative hearings and 'commissions' or industry advisory panels set up within government agencies to gather opinions from producer and labour groups (see Alt and Gilligan 1994; Verdier 1994).

Legislative institutions can also influence other types of foreign economic policies. One line of work by scholars has been focusing on the general differences between multi-party coalition governments and single-party majority governments. Coalition governments appear to have less incentive than majority governments to alter their monetary policy prior to elections, to try to boost economic activity in an 'opportunistic' fashion, since voters find it difficult to assign blame or credit to any single party within the coalition. An implication seems to be that coalition governments are also much more likely than other types of government to adopt fixed exchange rates and give up control over monetary policy (see Bernhard and Leblang 1999).

Bureaucratic agencies

Lastly, there is the issue of how foreign economic policies are implemented or administered by the bureaucratic agencies of each government. The rules that are established to regulate these agencies, and the way they make decisions, can play a powerful part in shaping policy outcomes. Legislatures delegate the responsibility for implementing their laws to these agencies, establishing the rules by which they are to operate, the ways in which their performance is monitored and evaluated, and so on. Built into these relationships between the legislature and the bureaucracy, however, there is always some measure of 'slack'—that is, some room for bureaucrats to manoeuvre, free from legislative interference. This bureaucratic independence can have important effects in terms of foreign economic policies.

When it comes to the implementation of trade policies, for example, there is often a real fear that the bureaucratic agencies that administer various aspects of trade laws may develop far too cosy a relationship with the sectors of the home economy that they are supposed to be regulating. This danger of bureaucratic 'capture' appears to be very real. In the US case, the Departments of Commerce and Agriculture are both regarded as unapologetic advocates of protection for their 'clients'—American business firms and farmers. Indeed, the International Trade Administration (ITA), located within the Department of Commerce, is renowned for having 'gone native'. Charged with making rulings on petitions from US companies claiming that foreign firms are dumping products below cost in the American market, the ITA finds in favour of local firms in around 99 per cent of cases (see Bovard 1991).

This problem is by no means unique to the American system. In Japan, the Ministry of International Trade and Industry (MITI), and the Ministry Agriculture, Forestry, and Fisheries (MAFF), have long been known for their extremely close ties with Japanese industry, and the farming and fishing communities (see Okimoto 1988: 310).

While MITI was for many years applauded by Western observers as the model for a new kind of autonomous state bureaucracy, capable of targeting subsidies expertly to particular manufacturing industries that would excel in competition with foreign producers (Johnson 1982), comprehensive evidence from recent studies indicates that MITI, in fact, allocated support to favoured industries in a highly political and ineffective way, a situation much like that it bureaucracies elsewhere (see Beason and Weinstein 1993).

In general, extreme cases aside, the interplay between bureaucratic independence and accountability is complex. In some issue areas, greater independence is generally regarded as desirable. Central banking is perhaps the most important case. The general problem, which we have discussed briefly above, is often referred to as the time inconsistency of monetary policy. Governments have an incentive to allow an unexpected rise in inflation that boosts economic activity, especially when facing an election. But since private actors know this, any promises a government may make to keep inflation in check may not be considered credible. Even if the government has all the best intentions, private actors might, nevertheless, keep inflation expectations high. By delegating control over monetary policy to an independent central bank that is insulated from any political temptations to alter monetary policy, the government can beat the problem. Moreover, independent central banks also appear to play an important part in shaping currency policies. Recent studies have indicated that governments in countries with independent central banks are less likely to engage in electorally motivated manipulations of exchange rates (Clark and Reichert 1998). And a related claim is that governments that can commit credibly to low inflation by establishing an independent central bank are less likely to need to fix their exchange rate in order to gain anti-inflationary credibility. Central bank independence and fixed exchange rates, in other words, can function as policy substitutes (see Clark and Hallerberg 2000).

Key points

- Restrictions on the franchise can give more weight to one side relative to others in contests over foreign economic policies. Extensions of the franchise to urban classes tend to produce more open policies toward trade and investment in labour and capital-abundant countries, and more closed or protectionist policies in labour and capital-scarce economies.

- Collective action is easier to organize in the relatively small groups that benefit from a particular trade restriction than in the much larger groups that are hurt by the restriction, so the strongest lobbying pressure tends to come from protectionist groups.

- Proportional representation systems with strong political parties typically generate lower levels of trade protection and other restrictions than plurality rule systems, in which particular local and regional interests have a greater influence.

- Small electoral districts in plurality rule systems tend to increase the influence of sectoral or particularistic groups over elected representatives when compared to larger districts, and thus lead to higher levels of protection.

- In plurality rule systems, in which elections are all-or-nothing contests between the major parties, governments are less likely to fix exchange rates than governments in proportional representation systems.

- Whether a government allows protectionist logrolling in a legislature, and whether a president supports trade liberalization, will depend on their partisan affiliation and the policy preferences of their party's core electoral constituency.

- An explicit institutional connection that links tariff reductions at home with reciprocal reductions in tariffs abroad (for example, a free trade agreement), can generate much stronger support for trade policy reform among export-orientated industries.

- Rules that provide access for organized groups to exert lobbying pressure to change particular features of legislation make trade protection and other forms of restriction more likely.
- The delegation of policy-making authority to bureaucratic agencies or bodies independent from national legislatures may not produce policies less affected by lobbying from protectionist interests, since groups may gain privileged access to decision-makers in such agencies.
- The existence of an independent central bank makes it less likely that a government will choose to fix the exchange rate.

Conclusions, Extensions, and Complications

There is really no such thing as the 'national interest' when it comes to foreign economic policy—or rather, there is no single national interest; there are many. Different individuals have very different conceptions of what is best for the nation and, not coincidentally, best for themselves, when it comes to setting foreign economic policies. This chapter has attempted to outline the principal divisions that usually characterize domestic political battles over trade, immigration, investment, and exchange rates. These divisions, as we have seen, tend to fall along either class or industry lines. Owners of capital and workers are typically pitted against one another when it comes to restrictions on inflows of labour or capital, for example, but they tend to take the same position in each industry on trade and exchange rate issues since the effects of policy can be very different for different sectors of the economy.

Once we know who wants what, the next task involves figuring out who gets what they want from the political process. This second step involves understanding how policies are decided in different countries, and thus how differences in political institutions affect economic policy choices. Our ultimate goal is to work out why governments in different countries often choose very different types of trade, immigration, investment, and exchange rate policies. We might also hope to form some reasonably accurate predictions about what our governments are likely to do in the future. Understanding why governments make the choices they do, and predicting what they will do next, requires careful attention to the political pressures they face from domestic groups, and to the ways in which the preferences of these groups are aggregated into collective decisions by political institutions. But there are at least three additional complications to this simple analytical picture that we should discuss briefly here. The first is related to the knowledge or information that individuals have about the effects of different policies, and about the preferences of others; the second extension involves allowing for linkages between the various policy issues, and between these issues and other non-economic policy concerns; and the third complication involves international bargaining, and the ways in which we might think about the connection between domestic politics and international politics.

Information and the role of ideas

Who gains and who loses? And who wins the political contest between those who gain and those who lose? Answering these questions in each issue area is at the heart of the standard political economy approach we have outlined above. In keeping with traditional assumptions, we have been taking it for granted that individuals know what they want, know what others want, and know what types of policies will have what kinds of effects. These are heroic assumptions. A great deal of the most recent research in both economics and political science has, in fact, tried to depart from this notion that people have full or complete information about their world, examining the effects of uncertainty, asymmetry in information among actors, and changes in knowledge that might be attributable to learning and the impact of new ideas. It is useful in this respect to distinguish between two basic types of information that individuals may be missing: people may be lacking knowledge about the effects of different policies on economic outcomes, or they may not have full knowledge about other people (including government leaders) and their preferences. We can discuss each of these informational problems separately.

What if we allow that individuals are not sure about the effects of different types of policies? It took us some time to disentangle the various effects of trade, immigration, investment, and exchange rate policies above, with the help of several simplifying assumptions, so this does seem an important question to pose. This clearly provides a large window through which new ideas, in the form of new beliefs about cause-and-effect relationships between policies and outcomes, might have a significant impact on policy-making. This is the view espoused by John Maynard Keynes (1936: 383) in his famous contention that 'the ideas of economists and political philosophers, both when they are right and when they are wrong, are more powerful than is commonly understood. Indeed the world is ruled by little else.'

Several prominent scholars have, indeed, argued that foreign economic policies have changed markedly in response to new ideas about these policies and their effects. The abandonment of mercantilist restrictions on trade and investment by most European governments in the nineteenth century has been attributed, in large measure, to the ideas of Adam Smith and David Ricardo and the development of classical trade theory (Kindleberger 1975; Bhagwati 1988) (see Box 4.7). The multilateral liberalization of trade and investment among Western economies in the era after the Second World War, allowing governments considerable scope for managing their domestic economies to avoid recessions, has similarly been traced to the refinement of classical and neoclassical economic theories and the ideas of Keynes himself (Ruggie 1982; Goldstein 1993). More recently, the rush to liberalize trade by governments in developing nations has been attributed to a learning process and the discrediting of the idea that rapid development could be achieved by import-substitution policies (see Krueger 1995). Competing ideas about cause-and-effect relationships often appear in policy debates, and dominant ideas are frequently embedded within policy-making institutions as the foundations for rules followed by bureaucratic agencies (Goldstein 1993). Yet, there remains much debate about the degree to which these types of ideas are independent of the interests that might be served by them. Max Weber's famous analogy compared ideas to 'switchmen' who determine the tracks along which human behaviour, pushed by interests, travel (Weber 1913/1958). From a more sceptical perspective, one might suggest that the individuals who gain and lose the most from any economic policy, such as tariffs on trade, have all the knowledge they need about its effects, and need no new ideas from economists to help them out; the policies just reflect the wishes of those interested actors who have the most political clout, and the ideas that attract our attention are just the ones sprinkled like holy water over the new legislation (to borrow an equally memorable metaphor from Kindleberger (1975: 36)). The relationship between ideas and interests is still very murky, and will remain so until we have a better understanding of where new ideas about policy come from, and what explains which ideas catch on and spread.

Box 4.7 The Rise of Free Trade in Europe

The publication of *The Wealth of Nations* by Adam Smith in 1776 stands out as an intellectual landmark in the history of thinking about international trade, pointing out the critical role that trade plays in encouraging specialization, and the resulting gains in efficiency and wealth. Smith adroitly punctured the old doctrine of mercantilism, which favoured expanding exports while restricting imports and hoarding gold, making it clear that national wealth is defined not by stocks of gold but by how much citizens can consume with the resources they have at their disposal. But the modern theory of international trade really began with the arrival of David Ricardo's *Principles of Political Economy and Taxation* in 1817. Ricardo demonstrated that trade is mutually beneficial for all countries, even a country that cannot produce anything more efficiently than other nations in terms of the costs of its inputs. As long as the costs of production are different in different nations, Ricardo's analysis showed that it must be true that, in terms of the opportunity costs of production (the value of other things that might have been produced with the inputs used to make a given item), each nation will be better at producing some things than others, and thus there is a basis for specialization and exchange that will leave both countries better off. This 'law of comparative advantage', which Paul Samuelson has called the most beautiful law in economics, has had a profound impact on all scholarly and political debates about trade ever since. That the cause of free trade was taken up enthusiastically by the leading English political economists, including John Stuart Mill, all inspired by Ricardian theory, and that these ideas also spread rapidly throughout Europe during the nineteenth century, has led many scholars to suggest that the broad shift away from trade protectionism in Europe (which began in 1846 with the repeal of the Corn Laws that Ricardo himself had attacked) was a result in large measure of a profound change in the way leaders understood the economic effects of trade (see Kindleberger 1975; Bhagwati 1988).

But by focusing only on the role of new ideas and how they might change knowledge about policies, we may be missing the bulk of the iceberg here when it comes to the impact of incomplete information. We noted in the discussions above that while foreign economic policies such as tariffs on imported goods generate real costs for a large set of owners and workers in all the other (non-protected) sectors of the economy, these costs are dispersed across such a large number of individuals that the 'per person' losses can be extremely small. Not only will it not pay for those affected to take political action to oppose the tariff in these cases, it may not even pay for them to spend any time or resources acquiring accurate information about the policy and its effects. Public opinion experts typically regard foreign economic policies as a particularly complex set of issues, about which survey respondents have very low levels of information (see Bauer et al. 1972: 81–4). Survey responses to questions about these issues tend to vary drastically with simple changes in question wording, making it very difficult to pinpoint where the public stands on any given policy question at any particular point in time (see Destler 1995: 180). One implication is that voters may be very susceptible to issue-framing or manipulation by political leaders and organized lobby groups whenever these issues become more prominent. Recent research on political communication and public opinion has highlighted this possibility (for example, Manheim 1991; Zaller 1992: 95). To the extent that this type of influence can be exercised, the politics of globalization may be regarded, at least to some degree, as a competition in issue framing among organized interests on different sides of the debate trying to sway public opinion to their side. This did appear to be an important dimension of the intense debate over NAFTA in the United States in 1993 (Holsti 1996: 52).

Another interesting implication of incomplete information among voters is that it may provide an explanation for why governments so often seem to do very inefficient things when setting foreign economic policies. Economists are fond of pointing out that if a government really wanted to redistribute income to particular groups of owners and employees, using restrictions on trade is a very inefficient way to go about it. It would be far better just to make a direct, lump-sum payment to these individuals and avoid the inefficiencies generated by trade barriers that prop up uncompetitive industries. But if the costs to taxpayers of such direct payments are more visible (because they must appear, say, in the government's annual budget), they are more likely to generate a backlash among the voters on whom the burden falls. If this is true, it may make sense for a government to use trade policies to redistribute income to favoured groups, because these policies provide an effective disguise in a low-information environment (see Tullock 1983). From this perspective, the use of trade protection can be characterized as 'optimal obfuscation' (Magee et al. 1989).

Finally, what happens if we allow that individuals, even if they are fully informed about the effects of foreign economic policies, may, nevertheless, be uncertain about the motivations or intentions of the government managing them. One circumstance in which this type of incomplete information can become important is when setting exchange rate policy, as we have discussed above. Since governments have an incentive to print money and allow a burst of inflation when facing an election, any promises they make to keep inflation in check may not be considered credible by private actors, who understand that the government has an incentive to bluff and portray itself as 'tougher' on inflation than it really is. The problem is that no one can be sure that the government values its low-inflation reputation enough (relative to how much it wants to gain reelection) to keep its pledge; even if the government had followed through with its promises, private actors might, nevertheless, keep inflation expectations high. If there is no independent central bank to which control of monetary policy can be ceded, governments in these circumstances are likely to be drawn more to fixing the exchange rate, especially in countries that have a history of chronic inflation. Fixing the value of the currency is a way for the government to signal to private actors that it is committed to keeping inflation under control by raising the potential costs to itself should it fail.

Another important context in which incomplete information about the government may play a key role in shaping policies is the case in which a government is attempting to reform trade policy in the face of stiff opposition from groups in import-competing industries. In such cases, since the government may, indeed, have an incentive to back down if it encounters a major political revolt, any promises it makes in advance to hold fast to the reforms may not be considered credible by the groups (who know very well that the government could just be trying to bluff its way through the painful reforms). Thus, even if the government does fully intend to stick with the reforms, it might have to weather a long and costly (and perhaps even violent) political protest. Again, tying its own hands in some clear and visible way can be an especially attractive policy option for a government in this situation, and by signing an international trade treaty with a major regional partner, it might be able to do the trick. This desire to make a credible commitment to trade reform is widely held to have been one reason why the Mexican government initiated the negotiations that produced the NAFTA agreement in 1993, after two decades of failed efforts to lower trade barriers unilaterally (see Whalley 1999).

Combinations of policies and issue linkages

Up to this point, we have been examining one type of foreign economic policy at a time. It is clear, however, that the effects of different policy instruments often depend on how *other* policies are set. In the basic Heckscher–Ohlin model, trade and factor movements are *substitutes* for one another — more of one type of international flow will generally mean less of another, and vice versa. If exports of labour-intensive products can move easily across a border between a labour-abundant economy (where wages are low) and a labour-scarce economy (where wages are high), this will tend to equalize labour costs over time, reducing the incentives for workers themselves to try to migrate between countries. If exports between the countries are blocked or impeded, more workers are likely to try to cross the border into the country that pays higher wages. When a dam is placed in front of flows in one channel it tends to divert flows into other channels.

This interaction among policies can become very interesting, because we know that while trade and factor flows are substitutable in general terms, they, in fact, have different types of effects on individuals. Individuals may thus have preferences for different combinations of policies. Perhaps the best example concerns the relationship between trade flows (and trade barriers) and direct investment. There is a great deal of evidence that firms engage in direct investment in markets as a way of 'jumping' trade barriers that would inhibit exports, and they even seem to reduce exports and invest more to stave off anticipated pressure for tariffs among local firms—a phenomenon known as 'quid pro quo foreign investment' (Bhagwati et al. 1987; Blonigen and Feenstra 1996). Local firms may be able to raise trade barriers, since they should have the lobbying support of their workers, whose jobs are endangered by high levels of imports, but they are less likely to win restrictions on inward direct investment by foreign firms, since workers in the industry will benefit from any new inflows of capital. Indeed, the best *policy combination* for local workers in an industry facing competition from a (relocatable) foreign producer is a high tariff *and* no restrictions on inward foreign investment. Local firms would prefer restrictions of *both* types of exchange, but would accept any restrictions rather than none at all if these are the politically feasible options. This political logic helps to explain the common pattern in policies towards the automobile industry in Europe and North America, where restrictions on imports were negotiated with Japanese auto firms but no restrictions were imposed to block the same firms from investing heavily in production facilities within both markets.

Exchange rate policy can also be 'in play' at the same time as trade policy. Trade policy and exchange rate policy are partially substitutable: a 1 per cent depreciation of the currency is equivalent to a 1 per cent across-the-board tariff on imports and a 1 per cent subsidy for all exports. But, clearly, the coalition that supports depreciation—those invested and employed in both import-competing and exporting industries—is different from the coalition that would support higher tariffs (import-competing interests). Exchange rate policies tend to be more rigid than trade policies, in general, mainly because the credibility of monetary policy commitments is undermined by frequent shifts in policy. But when there is an opportunity for the government to alter the exchange rate, intense lobbying for protection by import-competing groups (or even just the threat of it), may induce export interests to help persuade the government to weaken the currency—an outcome that would ease the competitive pressure on producers threatened by imports, while not harming (benefiting, in fact) those engaged in export industries. This seems to have been the case in the United States in the early 1980s, as the value of the US dollar rose dramatically. While the White House appeared to prefer to leave both its currency and trade policies unchanged, fearing a spate of protectionist legislation from Congress in response to lobbying by firms and unions in import-sensitive sectors, and hearing support for depreciation from export interests as well, it moved in 1985 to weaken the value of the dollar. Similarly, in many Latin American countries in the 1980s and 1990s, governments attempting reforms aimed at lowering barriers to trade were able to render these changes more politically palatable to threatened sectors by devaluing exchange rates at the same time (see De Gregorio 2001).

Perhaps even more important, in some ways, than these connections between different foreign economic policies are the linkages that have been made with increasing frequency in recent policy debates between these policies and a variety of *non-economic* issues. Some of these linkages are not new.

Trade and investment policies have always been connected in various ways to the issue of national security. Most governments place tight controls on trade in weapons and dangerous chemicals, for example, and restrictions on foreign investment in strategically important industries (such as, energy, airlines, and broadcasting) are also common. And governments have strong incentives to lower barriers to trade and investment more rapidly among alliance partners than with other nations in the international system, as the experience in Europe after the Second World War (and among the industrialized democracies more generally) makes clear (see Gowa 1994). All individuals within an economy tend to share similar concerns about national security, so this form of issue linkage tends to affect policy-making in a fairly straightforward way, generating more support among all citizens for policy options that contribute most clearly to national security. But foreign economic policies are now linked more regularly with a range of other non-economic issues, about which individuals tend to have more varied opinions. Most importantly, trade and investment are now frequently linked to discussions of environmental policy and to human rights issues in the political debates about globalization in Western democracies.

How do these issue linkages affect the analysis of the politics of trade and investment? The clearest impact is the involvement of a variety of organized environmental and human rights groups in recent debates over regional trade agreements and the WTO (see Destler and Balint 1999). The members of these groups care deeply about addressing environmental and human rights problems in their own countries and in other countries around the world; and they either believe that globalization is making these problems worse and thus should be restrained in some way, or they argue that trade and investment provide economic leverage which can and should be used to persuade governments in developing nations to improve environmental and labour standards and democratic institutions. The position taken by many of these groups is that all trade agreements, including the WTO itself, should include provisions for minimum environmental and labour standards that would be enforced (if necessary) by the imposition of trade sanctions. Many environmental groups have also lobbied for changes to the existing rules of the WTO, so that laws that discriminated against foreign products on environmental grounds (for example, import bans on tuna caught using nets that also endanger dolphins) would be permissible. But environmentalists and human rights activists have also expressed grave concerns about the behaviour of multinational firms in developing nations, with much of the focus being on whether these large corporations are moving production to areas in which they can pollute and otherwise damage the environment, or run 'sweatshop' factories in which they mistreat and underpay workers, avoiding the regulatory supervision that would prevent such behaviour in their home countries. The policies recommended by these groups, and in particular by human rights organizations worried by the lack of democratic institutions in countries such as China, typically involve a more proactive use of economic sanctions—that is, Western governments cutting off trade with, and investment to, such 'problem' nations until their leaders make significant political reforms. Consumer boycotts aimed at particular corporations that are investing in such nations are usually warmly recommended too (although these types of consumer actions represent private market behaviour and are thus not a question of public policy).

One important general development has been the formation of what might be called 'Baptist and bootlegger' coalitions between some of these issue groups, and the business and labour organizations that have an economic stake in restricting international trade and/or investment. This type of coalition gets its name from American politics in the era of Prohibition, when strong support for the ban on alcohol sales came from Baptists, on moral grounds, and from bootleggers, who made large fortunes selling alcohol on the black market (see Yandle 1984). In recent debates over the NAFTA in the United States, for example, environmental groups such as the Sierra Club joined with labour unions in lobbying against the agreement, on the grounds that it did not contain provisions that would ensure a substantial improvement in environmental and labour standards in Mexico (see Destler and Balint 1999: 42–5). And recent 'anti-sweatshop' campaigns, organized by human rights groups and student activists, and targeting foreign investment and outsourcing by US apparel manufacturers to nations such as Vietnam and China, have been backed financially and supported enthusiastically by American textile unions and firms producing locally.

The concern among many analysts, especially among those who generally support international economic integration for its ability to raise living standards in all countries, is that these types of political coalitions may be hijacked by their protectionist members who support restrictions on international trade and investment, *regardless* of whether they have any positive (or negative) long-term effects on environmental conditions or human rights standards. It would be far better, many argue, to pursue improvements in environmental and human rights standards by working towards separate international treaties dealing with those precise issues in a more direct way, perhaps by compensating developing nations for making costly improvements to their environmental and labour laws. Sanctions could severely limit economic growth in the very poorest developing countries, where governments are likely to resist making political concessions (especially democratic reforms that increase the risk that they will be toppled from power). The issues are complex, however, and the political problems difficult. The 'Baptists' are drawn to supporting economic sanctions rather than other policy instruments (for example, new international treaties, or foreign aid grants to nations that improve their environmental standards), because they have calculated that these alternatives are politically infeasible. With the support of the 'bootleggers' for restrictions on trade and investment, however, they might stand a greater chance of getting something done that will have beneficial effects.

The general point here is that our simple, one-issue-at-a-time approach to the analysis of foreign economic policies becomes much more complicated when we allow that different policy instruments are often up for grabs at the same time and have partially substitutable effects, and if we take into account the fact that a variety of groups are often interested in using the tools of foreign economic policy to advance non-economic types of goals. Often, it is the institutional context in which government decisions are made (many of the features of which we have discussed above) that determines which types of policy instruments are more adjustable than others, and which types of political coalitions are more viable than others. The most comprehensive and persuasive accounts of economic policy-making will take all these complexities into account.

International bargaining and domestic politics

Finally, recalling the discussion by Aggarwal and Dupont in the previous chapter, it is worth pausing here briefly to consider the ways in which the domestic politics of foreign economic policies may be translated into international-level bargaining over these same issues. What we really require here is a theoretical model of the policy-making process that takes into account all the incentives and constraints operating among actors at both domestic and international levels. This is the type of model that Putnam (1988) famously envisioned, using the metaphor of the two-level game. A government engaged in international economic negotiations, in fact, plays two different political 'games' at the same time, he suggested, with its actions constituting 'moves' that must be seen, not only in the context of the demands made by individuals and groups in *domestic* politics, but also in view of the bargaining power it has when negotiating *international* agreements with other governments. Government leaders negotiate with other leaders at the international level over the terms of economic agreements, and in those negotiations the relative size and strength of the economy can make a tremendous difference to the terms that can be demanded. But the leaders must be attuned to the preferences of the domestic groups whose support they need to remain in office, and the set of international deals that would be ratified or supported by these groups at home.

To date, theoretical work along these lines has focused mainly on differences between the preferences of legislative and executive branches of government, and their different agenda-setting and vetoing powers, and how these features of domestic politics affect the outcomes of international negotiations and agreements (see Evans et al. 1993; Milner 1997a). Much of the attention has been directed to the so-called 'Schelling conjecture', which holds that a hawkish domestic constituency — represented in the simplest models as a legislature that prefers very little international co-operation — can, in fact, improve the bargaining power of the executive branch in its dealings with foreign counterparts (Schelling 1960: 28–9). Recent work has also focused on how executive–legislative divisions affect the credibility of governments during international negotiations (for example, Martin 2000), and whether international agreements are negotiated to allow for greater flexibility in cases when future changes in domestic political coalitions might lead to substantial shifts in the types of policies a government can implement (Downs and Rocke 1995).

While being full of insights about the effects of domestic political institutions on the prospects for international co-operation, this line of work has so far paid very little attention to the roles played by organized interests and voters in shaping legislative and executive preferences on particular policy issues. In fact, to date, standard political economy models of trade politics, emphasizing the role played by organized lobby groups in the formulation of policy, have not at all been linked to two-level game models of negotiations over trade and other economic agreements. Moreover, the existing work on two-level games tends to concentrate overwhelmingly on parameters that operate only on one level — domestic politics in the home nation. Features of the strategic relationship between nations, such as the economic and military asymmetries that might affect relative bargaining power, or common ties to alliances or international institutions that might affect incentives to co-operate, are largely ignored. We clearly need a better two-level mousetrap: a model that incorporates a fuller representation of organized interests and lobbying at the domestic level, while also allowing for the ways in which incentives and constraints are generated at the international level.

In practice, most international political economists work with partial theories that focus on one set of causal variables operating at one level. Some argue that the features of the international system, such as the distribution of economic power, and any specific nation's position within it, impose broad but important constraints on what governments can and cannot do when setting policies. Others, in keeping with the orientation of this chapter, argue that the prime focus of our attention should be placed on what is going on within nations — their particular sets of political institutions, and the preferences and lobbying activities of different group of individuals — since it is these things that primarily determine the policies chosen by governments. But, in principal, almost all scholars recognize that politics at both the domestic and international levels should be a feature of any complete analysis of foreign economic policy. Integrating theoretical insights about politics at these two levels is an extremely complex and challenging task that still remains, to a very large extent, undone.

Key points

- To understand the domestic origins of foreign economic policies, we need to perform two main tasks: first, to map the policy preferences of different groups in the domestic economy; and then to specify how political institutions affect the way that these preferences are aggregated into government decisions.

- Policy preferences depend mainly on the types of assets people own, and how the income earned from those assets is affected by different policies.

- Political institutions affect policy outcomes by defining who has a vote, how political representatives are elected, and how policy-making takes place in legislatures, and is delegated to presidents and government agencies.

- New ideas about cause-and-effect relationships appear to have had a large impact on foreign economic policies in different eras. The relationship between ideas and interests is far from clear, however, and we need a better understanding of where new ideas about policy come from, and what explains which ideas catch on and spread.

- Foreign economic policies involve a complex set of issues about which most voters have very low levels of information. As a result, the politics of globalization may be regarded to some degree as a competition in issue framing among organized interests.

- If private actors have incomplete information about the degree to which the government is committed

to policy reforms, the government may have an incentive to tie its own hands in some visible way (for example, by fixing the exchange rate, or signing a trade treaty) to signal its intentions in a credible way.

- Since the effects of a change in one type of foreign economic policy may depend on choices made about other types of policy, individuals may have preferences over different combinations of policies that are closely related (for example, tariffs and restrictions on inward investment induced by tariffs).

- Trade and investment policies are also linked to discussions of *non-economic* issues. One important development has been the formation of 'Baptist and bootlegger' coalitions between environmental and human rights groups concerned about globalization, and business and labour organizations that have an economic stake in restricting international trade and investment.

- Governments may be thought of as playing political games at two levels, their actions constituting moves that are both responses to demands made by groups in *domestic* politics, and responses to offers made by other governments in *international* negotiations.

- We need a better theory of two-level games that incorporates fuller representations of both domestic and international politics. In practice, most international political economists employ partial theories that focus only on variables operating at a single level.

? Questions

1. If the economic case for trade liberalization is so strong, why is it that governments continue to impose barriers to trade and are engaged so frequently in trade disputes?

2. Trade theory does not imply that every individual within each nation will benefit from the lowering of trade barriers, just that aggregate benefits will exceed aggregate losses. Who stands to benefit most from trade liberalization in the advanced economies of Europe, Japan, and the United States, and who is most likely to be disadvantaged? What about the situation in developing nations with different types of factor endowments?

3. Can these different groups of individuals reach some kind of agreement so that trade liberalization can benefit everyone? What are the political obstacles to this type of agreement?

4. Is it inappropriate to think only, or primarily, in terms of economic gains and losses when evaluating the effects of increased international trade? How important are other types of concerns (for example, national security, income inequality, environmental hazards, human rights abuses) in the political debates that determine policy outcomes?

5. What types of electoral and policy-making institutions tend to mitigate the effects of lobbying by protectionist groups when it comes to the determination of trade policy? Are electoral systems based on proportional representation likely to generate less protection than plurality systems?

6. Do the economic effects of immigration shape the political struggles over changes in immigration law? Or do the politics of immigration reflect other types of cultural and social divisions within host countries?

7. What are the economic effects of foreign investment for the source country and for the host country? Does foreign investment generate a 'race to the bottom' in labour and environmental standards in developing countries? Does it inhibit democratic reform?

8. What economic and political changes during the twentieth century led to the abandonment of fixed exchange rates among the advanced economies? Why do many developing countries continue to fix their exchange rates?

 Further reading

Trade

▨ Destler, I. M. (1995), *American Trade Politics*, 3rd edn (Washington, DC: Institute for International Economics). This is required reading for anyone interested in how US trade policy is made. It provides a comprehensive analysis of American political institutions and policy-making.

▨ Hayes, J. P. (1993), *Making Trade Policy in the European Community* (London: Macmillan). This book provides a thorough discussion of the processes of trade policy-making in the European Community.

▨ Hiscox, M. J. (2002), *International Trade and Political Conflict* (Princeton, NJ: Princeton University Press). An analysis of historical changes in levels of factor specificity in several Western nations, relating these changes to shifts in political alignments in trade politics.

▨ Krueger, A. O. (1995), *Trade Policies and Developing Nations* (Washington, DC: Brookings Institution). An engaging discussion of trade liberalization in developing nations in recent years.

▨ Rogowski, R. (1989), *Commerce and Coalitions* (Princeton, NJ: Princeton University Press). A sweeping analysis of coalitions in trade politics in a variety of historical contexts, based on an application of the Stolper–Samuelson theorem.

Immigration

▨ Borjas, G. J. (1999), *Heaven's Door: Immigration Policy and the American Economy* (Princeton, NJ: Princeton University Press). A provocative analysis of the effects of immigration in the United States in recent decades.

▨ Fetzer, J. S. (2000), *Public Attitudes toward Immigration in the United States, France, and Germany* (Cambridge: Cambridge University Press). This book uses available survey data to compare public attitudes towards immigration in the United States, France, and Germany, and the determinants of anti-immigrant sentiments.

■ Tichenor, D. J. (2002), *Dividing Lines: The Politics of Immigration Control in America* (Princeton, NJ: Princeton University Press). A very impressive history of immigration politics in the United States.

Investment

■ Crystal, J. (2003), *Unwanted Company: Foreign Investment in American Industries* (Ithaca, NY: Cornell University Press). An excellent study of political debates about inward direct foreign investment in the United States.

■ Graham, E., and Krugman, P. R. (1995), *Foreign Direct Investment in the United States* (Washington, DC: Institute for International Economics). This book provides a comprehensive analysis of the economic and political effects of inward foreign investment.

■ Moran, T. (1998), *Foreign Direct Investment and Development* (Washington, DC: Institute for International Economics). An excellent study of the effects of direct foreign investment in developing nations.

Exchange rates

■ Frieden, J., Ghezzi, P., and Stein, E. (eds) (2001), *The Currency Game: Exchange Rate Politics in Latin America* (New York: Inter-American Development Bank). A very interesting collection of research on the politics of exchange rate policies in Latin America.

■ Henning, R. C. (1994), *Currencies and Politics in the United States, Germany, and Japan* (Washington, DC: Institute for International Economics). This book provides a clear and detailed discussion of exchange rate policy-making in the United States, Germany, and Japan.

■ Simmons, B. A. (1994), *Who Adjusts? Domestic Sources of Foreign Economic Policy during the Interwar Years* (Princeton, NJ: Princeton University Press). An impressive analysis of the political determinants of exchange rate policies adopted by Western nations in the inter-war period.

Institutions

■ Gilligan, M. (1997), *Empowering Exporters: Reciprocity and Collective Action in Twentieth-Century American Trade Policy* (Ann Arbor, MI: University of Michigan Press). A fine study of the importance of institutionalizing reciprocity in trade policy-making.

■ Hiscox, M. J. (1999), 'The Magic Bullet? The RTAA, Institutional Reform, and Trade Liberalization', *International Organization*, 53/4: 669–98. A critical review of research on the RTAA that emphasizes the role of political parties and their core constituencies in the of politics institutional change.

■ Rogowski, R. (1987), 'Trade and the Variety of Democratic Institutions', *International Organization*, 41/2: 203–23. A classic analysis of the ways in which different types of electoral institutions affect trade policy outcomes in democracies.

■ Wintrobe, R. (1998), *The Political Economy of Dictatorship* (Cambridge: Cambridge University Press). An excellent analysis of policy-making in non-democratic regimes.

Extensions and complications

■ Elliott, K. A., and Freeman, R. (2003), *Can Labor Standards Improve under Globalization?* (Washington, DC: Institute for International Economics). This book provides a comprehensive review of the debates about whether trade and investment policies should be linked to agreements about improving labour standards in developing nations.

■ Goldstein, J., and Keohane, R. O. (eds) (1993), *Ideas and Foreign Policy: Beliefs, Institutions, and Political Change* (Ithaca, NY: Cornell University Press). An important collection of essays discussing the impact of new ideas on foreign policy outcomes.

■ Graham, E. (2000), *Fighting the Wrong Enemy: Anti-Global Activists and Multinational Enterprises* (Washington, DC: Institute for International Economics). A compelling analysis of the effects of direct foreign investment in developing nations that argues that criticisms made by environmental and human rights groups are misguided.

■ Irwin, D. (1996), *Against the Tide: An Intellectual History of Free Trade* (Princeton, NJ: Princeton University Press). A sweeping account of theoretical developments in economics that support the case for trade liberalization.

 ## Web links

■ For regular research reports and briefs on policy issues:
www.iie.com   Institute for International Economics.

■ For theoretical background on international economics and helpful beginner guides:
www.internationalecon.com   International Economics Study Center.
www.amosweb.com/gls   Amos World Economics Glossary.

■ For data and analysis of public opinion on international economic issues:
http://pewglobal.org   The PEW Global Attitudes Project.
www.pipa.org   The Program on International Policy Attitudes (PIPA).

■ For data on world trade, migration, and investment:
www.wto.org/english/res_e/statis_e/statis_e.htm   WTO's International Trade Statistics.
www.ilo.org/public/english/protection/migrant/info/ilm_dbase.htm   ILO's International Labour Migration Database.
www.unctad.org/Templates/Page.asp?intItemID=3204&lang=1   UNCTAD's World Investment Directory.

■ For information and statistics on trade, immigration, investment, and exchange rate policies:
http://r0.unctad.org/trains_new/database.shtm   UNCTAD's TRAINS Database of Trade Control Measures.
www.wto.org/english/tratop_e/dda_e/tnc_e.htm   WTO's Negotiations Committee.
www.ustr.gov   United States Trade Representative (USTR).
http://europa.eu.int/comm/trade   European Union Trade Policy.
www.meti.go.jp/english/index.html   Japanese Trade Policy.
www.migrationpolicy.org   The Migration Policy Institute.
www.imf.org/external/np/tre/tad/exfin1.cfm   IMF's Country Finances and Exchange Rates.
www.federalreserve.gov   Federal Reserve Board.
www.bankofengland.co.uk   Bank of England.
www.ecb.int   European Union Central Bank.
www.boj.or.jp/en   Bank of Japan.

 ## Online resource centre

For additional material and resources, please visit the Online Resource Centre at:
www.oxfordtextbooks.co.uk/ravenhill3e/

Box 4.8 The Theory of Comparative Advantage

The case for free trade was stated succinctly by Adam Smith. In *The Wealth of Nations* , he wrote: 'If a foreign country can supply us with a commodity cheaper than we ourselves can make it, better buy it of them with some part of the produce of our own industry, employed in a way in which we have some advantage' (Book iv, Section ii: 12). The idea here is simple and intuitive. If a country can produce some set of goods at lower cost than can a foreign country, and if the foreign country can produce some other set of goods at a lower cost, then clearly it would be best for the country to trade its relatively cheaper goods for the foreign economy's relatively cheaper goods. In this way, both countries can gain from trade. This is the theory of trade according to absolute advantage.

David Ricardo, working in the early part of the nineteenth century, realized that absolute advantage was a limited case of a more general basis for international trade (the idea was originally stated by another economist, Robert Torrens, in *Essay on the External Corn Trade* , published in 1815, but most historians of economic thought believe that Ricardo reached his conclusions independently). Consider Table 4.1. Portugal can produce both cloth and wine more efficiently, that is, with less labour input than England (it has an absolute advantage in the production of both commodities). Ricardo argued that, nonetheless, it could still be mutually beneficial for both countries to specialize and trade.

Table 4.1 Comparative Costs of Production (Cost Per Unit in Person Hours)

Country	Cloth	Wine
England	15	30
Portugal	10	15

The logic of comparative advantage rests on the *opportunity costs* of producing goods across countries; that is, the amount of one good that has to be given up to produce another good. In Table 4.1, producing a unit of wine in England requires the same amount of labour as required to produce two units of cloth. Production of an extra unit of wine means forgoing production of two units of cloth (that is, the opportunity cost of a unit of wine is two units of cloth). In Portugal, the labour required to produce a unit of wine would only produce 1.5 units of cloth (that is, the opportunity cost of a unit of wine is 1.5 units of cloth in Portugal). To concentrate on wine production in Portugal requires giving up relatively less cloth output than would be the case in England. Similarly, if England produced only cloth, the amount of wine production forgone would be relatively smaller than if Portugal did so.

Portugal is thus relatively better at producing wine than is England: if Portugal concentrated on producing wine, it would give up a smaller volume of cloth production than would England. Portugal is said to have a *comparative advantage* in the production of wine. England is relatively better at producing cloth than wine, so, England is said to have a comparative advantage in the production of cloth.

Because relative or comparative costs differ, it can still be mutually advantageous for both countries to trade *even though Portugal has an absolute advantage in producing both commodities* . For international welfare to be maximized, Portugal should specialize in the product in which it is relatively most efficient; and England, in the commodity in which it is relatively least inefficient.

Table 4.2 shows how trade might be advantageous. Costs of production are as set out in Table 4.1. In this example, England is assumed to have 270 person hours available for production. Before trade takes place, it produces and consumes eight units of cloth (requiring 120 person hours of labour input) and five units of wine (150 person hours). Portugal has fewer labour resources, with a total of 180 person hours of labour available for production. Before trade takes place, it produces and consumes nine units of cloth (requiring 90 person hours of labour input) and six units of wine (90 person hours). Total production for the two economies combined is seventeen units of cloth and eleven units of wine.

Table 4.2 Production Before and After Trade

Country	Production before trade		Production after trade	
	Cloth	Wine	Cloth	Wine
England	8	5	18	0
Portugal	9	6	0	12
Total	17	11	18	12

If both countries now specialize, with Portugal producing only wine and England producing only cloth, and all their labour resources are devoted to the single product, England can produce (270 divided by 15) units of cloth and Portugal (180 divided by 15) units of wine. Total production by the two economies is eighteen units of cloth and twelve units of wine. Specialization, according to comparative advantage and international trade, therefore, has enabled overall welfare to increase because total production has gone up by one unit of cloth and one unit of wine.

For trade to take place, the ratio of the price of the two goods must be lower than the domestic opportunity costs of production; that is, a bottle of wine will have to sell for somewhere between 1.5 and 2 bales of cloth. Note that the theory says nothing about distributional questions; that is, where in this range the price will settle, and thus who will gain most from trade.

The simple theory of comparative advantage makes a number of important assumptions:

- There are no transport costs.
- Costs are constant and there are no economies of scale.
- There are only two economies producing two goods.
- Traded goods are homogeneous (that is, identical as far as the consumer is concerned).
- Factors of production (labour and capital) are perfectly mobile internally but not internationally.
- There is full employment in both economies.
- There are no tariffs or other trade barriers.
- There is perfect knowledge, so that all buyers and sellers know where the cheapest goods can be found internationally.

Despite the lack of correspondence between the contemporary globalized economy and these assumptions, most economists believe that the fundamental principle that Ricardo identified still holds.

PART 2
Global Trade

The Evolution of the Global Trade Regime

5

Gilbert R Winham

 Reader's guide

The twentieth century witnessed a remarkable growth in international institutions, and nowhere was this growth greater than in the international trade system. Out of the ashes of a world economy torn by war and depression, a world trading regime was initiated at mid century with the creation of the General Agreement on Tariffs and Trade (GATT) in 1947, which began with a few simple procedures and rules designed to promote the idea that if someone in one country can produce something that people in another country want to buy, they should have the right to sell it to them. From this simple beginning, the world trade regime developed by the end of the century into the most prominent example of co-operation between countries in the entire international system. This chapter reviews the history of this extraordinary development.

Introduction

Today, the global trade regime is a rules-based political system where the rules flowing from international agreements that seek to promote and stabilize economic exchanges between countries are ranged against the regulations of national governments that often seek to restrict those exchanges. The purpose of the international rules is to reduce the protectionism of national regulations, but even more, to reduce the uncertainty and unpredictability of international trade relations, and to promote stability. The task of this chapter will be to show how the global trade regime has been established through the actions of trading countries over the past 150 years, and how it became institutionalized in the World Trade Organization (WTO).

The global trade regime of the late twentieth and early twenty-first centuries is based on three components: trade, national regulations, and international agreements. Trade and national regulations have been a theme and counterpoint throughout much of history, in the sense that when national regulations receded, trade flourished; and when those regulations intensified, trade languished. To this combination can be added the third factor of international agreements, by which countries attempt to establish international rules that would restrict their own (and other countries') capacity to interrupt international trade through national regulation. Rules and regulations appear to be inherent in our highly ordered lives, and the irony is that in order to reduce regulation of one kind, it requires the intercession of rules of another kind. The important issue is where the rules or regulations come from, and whether their purpose is to reduce or expand the scope of our economic activity.

Trade, which is a staple of our modern global political economy, is also a historic, and even prehistoric, phenomenon. It was important to many ancient and medieval powers. Trade lay at the centre of state revenue and state power in ancient Athens; Ptolemaic Egypt; the Italian city states of Venice, Florence, and Genoa; and the German Hanseatic League. Nowhere was this clearer than in ancient Athens, which developed through commercial activities and at its height was totally dependent on trade. Athens exported silver and olive oil, and the boundaries of its trade have been charted over time by the shards of pottery urns that have been discovered throughout the

Mediterranean region. In return, the Athenians were dependent on the import of grain, which was essential to maintain the population of Athens in an arid region.

In examining the global trade regime, trade is by necessity the starting point, but government is equally part of the story. This point has been observed by many writers, but perhaps was expressed most effectively by John Condliffe, as follows:

> The beginnings of trade are to be found in the enterprise of groups and individuals, but regulation and taxation of trade are almost as old as trade itself. In tracking history, if enterprise is the theme, regulation is the counterpoint. As soon as the track begins to be beaten out, established authority intervenes to control and levy tolls upon the traders.
>
> Condliffe (1950: 27)

Early trade was a primitive exercise in economic enterprise. The means of regulating trade were equally primitive. The earliest means were tolls, exacted by local leaders for permission to pass through territory, or to trade, or simply for protection. From the earliest times, tolls were an expression of military control and political sovereignty, and if one controlled territory, one could exact tribute through tolls at will. This resulted in a great hindrance to trade, especially in Europe, which was divided into many small jurisdictions during the Middle Ages.

A more modern method of regulation than tolls was the tariff, or customs duty, which we now recognize as a percentage tax added to the price of imported goods. Tariffs are still with us today, but they are among the oldest functions of government. The purpose of early tariffs, whether on imports or exports, was to raise revenue. Tariffs were effective for this purpose, because, by the beginning of the eighteenth century, duties on imported goods had come to be the chief source of revenue in European countries. A further function of the tariff was to protect domestic producers from foreign competition.

Today, protectionism is the main purpose of the tariff. The revenue function is less important in developed countries, as governments have found other, more effective, means to raise revenues, although the tariff is still an important source of revenue in some developing countries. However, as if to demonstrate the ingenuity of government regulators, new forms of protection have arisen, collectively known as non-tariff measures (NTMs) (also, non-tariff barriers (NTBs)). These measures have now become more important than tariffs, the latter having been greatly reduced (again, mainly between developed countries) by successive trade agreements under the General Agreement on Tariffs and Trade (GATT).

The regulations that have restricted trade in recent decades have been the work of national governments. But those same governments have also reached international agreements with other governments attempting to constrain the extent to which domestic policies would restrict the free flow of international trade. These agreements started as simple undertakings between peoples as to how their commercial relations would be conducted, and trade agreements are almost as old as trade itself. For example, commercial treaties have been discovered between the kings of ancient Egypt and Babylonia, giving the parties the right to exact duties on the merchandise of traders or travellers. In more modern times, such treaties have been instrumental in establishing the rules whereby trade could be carried on between different political jurisdictions.

There has been a close relationship between trade and commercial treaties throughout history, to the extent that it accounts for much of the diplomatic practice between countries. An important watershed in this relationship occurred in the mid nineteenth century with the Cobden–Chevalier (or Anglo-French) Treaty of 1860. This treaty initiated a brief period of liberalized trade between the United Kingdom and the Continent, which ended with the world depression of 1873–96. However, the treaty demonstrated that trade agreements could serve as an effective means of trade liberalization by alleviating some of the worst effects of competitive national regulation, and it set the stage for the deployment of trade negotiation in the twentieth century.

Key points

- The international trade regime is based on three components: trade, national regulations, and international agreements.

Historical Antecedents: 1860 to 1945

War and depression

The impact of government regulation on trade was well understood by the nineteenth century from the writings of Adam Smith and other political economists. Smith noted that, in addition to raising revenue, tariffs also had the effect of protecting domestic producers from foreign competition, something Smith and other reformers generally viewed with disfavour. As a political movement, however, the effort to curtail protectionist regulation did not begin until the Reform Act of 1932 in England. A campaign for free trade had begun among British merchants in the second quarter of the nineteenth century. The campaign was part of a broader effort of political reform in British society, and its eventual success resulted in part from the political realignment introduced by the Reform Act. The campaign was led by Richard Cobden, who demonstrated the importance of pragmatic leadership in promoting the ideal of free trade. In 1848, Britain repealed the Corn Laws, which provided high protection to agricultural products, and followed up this action with a series of administrative and diplomatic measures over the next two decades that put free trade into practice. Meanwhile, on the Continent, the French free trade movement had sought to convince the government of Louis Napoleon to reciprocate the British move towards free trade that was initiated by the repeal of the Corn Laws. No action was taken until the opportunity arose to incorporate a tariff negotiation in a commercial and political treaty with Great Britain. The Cobden–Chevalier treaty of 1860 was the result, which later helped to open the French market to British manufacturers (Rosecrance 1986).

The European system enjoyed a brief period of liberal commercial exchange that started in the 1830s and lasted until the 1870s. This period was dominated economically by Great Britain. The Napoleonic Wars of the early 1800s had left British manufacturing capabilities unscathed, and following the wars, Britain's economic strength allowed it to become the leading creditor country in the world. Britain provided aid and loans to European nations and had large exports of foreign investment, mainly to the United States and British colonies in Asia. In sum, the mid-century period of free trade essentially originated in the domestic politics of Britain and spread to the nations of Europe through the mechanism of international commercial treaties. The European commitment to free trade was considerably less enduring than the British, and it turned around quickly in the face of depression after 1870. For the British, however, free trade was the principal commercial policy of the nation until well after the First World War.

Protectionism reasserted itself in Europe as a straightforward response to hard times. As a result of a series of rapid technological improvements in the mid 1850s, the comparative advantage in grain growing shifted decisively to the New World, with the result that grain prices fell sharply in European markets. At the same time, a slump occurred in industrial production, which continued for over two decades in the form of low prices and low return on

capital for manufactured products. International competition became severe, and in all countries there were strong pressures for protection against imports. One by one, national governments succumbed to the pressures, and reversed the period of relatively free trade that had been established prior to the 1850s. Austria-Hungary raised tariffs in 1876, and Italy followed in 1878. In 1879, Germany shifted to a protectionist policy and, because of its size in the European economy and its philosophy of nationalism and mercantilism, it set a protectionist tone for the overall system. France responded to German protectionism with restrictions of its own and, for its part, the United States continued the protectionism it had pursued throughout the nineteenth century. The United Kingdom, the Low Countries, and Switzerland, however, resisted the move toward higher tariffs, but by the end of the century, the UK was the only major nation practising free trade (Kindleberger 1951).

The depression that began in the 1870s also ushered in a lengthy period of protectionism that never really changed until after the Second World War. In the early part of the twentieth century, growing nationalism, and then war in 1914, exacerbated the protectionist trend that was already well established in response to the economic conditions of the late 1800s. The war broke up an imperfect but workable equilibrium between internal economic policies, trade, and payments that had existed under the gold standard of the nineteenth century. The war produced enormous dislocation that was even more serious in economic terms than the destruction that had occurred. The results were maladjustments to the free flow of labour, capital, and goods, which created impediments to economic activity that lasted well into the 1920s. But continued war planning also played an important role in the European mentality after 1919. In the realm of economic policy, war planning took the form of mercantilism, and later a bilateralism (that is, a focus on negotiating agreements with individual trade partners rather than through an international organization), inspired by Nazi Germany but copied by many other countries.

Both mercantilism and bilateralism were designed to place the interests of the nation ahead of the wider community, and they inevitably took their toll on the economic performance of the overall system. The practice of both mercantilism and bilateralism, like war itself, was an expression of nationalism in economic policy.

The breakdown of the international economic system from war undoubtedly deepened the depression within national economies, and nations made efforts at the international level to repair the damage. Two such efforts stand out. The first was the World Economic Conference of 1927, and the associated Conference on Import and Export Prohibitions and Restrictions (Shonfield 1976). These meetings were aimed at countering the trend towards increased tariffs that was occurring in all countries during the 1920s. Countries initially agreed on a tariff truce and an agreement that would regulate quotas and other restrictions. However, the agreement failed to receive sufficient signatures to become binding, and the tariff truce was later discarded by individual country actions. The second effort was the World Economic Conference of 1933, at which time countries tried to achieve an international currency stabilization agreement amid wildly fluctuating exchange rates that were perceived to be causing significant disruptions to international trade. This plan failed to attract the Americans and, in the wake of the collapsed conference, countries engaged in a period of competitive exchange rate devaluations during the mid 1930s.

Reciprocal Trade Agreements Act of 1934 (RTAA)

The United States had emerged from the First World War as the largest trading nation in the world; hence, it was likely that domestic events affecting US trade capabilities would have a wide impact on commercial relations in the international system. This was the case with two events of the early 1930s: the Smoot–Hawley tariff of 1930, and the Reciprocal Trade Agreements Act of 1934 (RTAA) (Tasca 1938). The former was the culmination of a trend toward protectionism that had begun in the late nineteenth century, while the latter was the beginning of a trend toward liberalism that was interrupted by the Second World War but then continued into the present. These two events were major watersheds in commercial policy, and probably more important than the Second World War because they were economic events originating in the world economic system, rather than being the economic results of upheaval in the international political system.

The Smoot–Hawley Act of 1930 raised US duties to historic levels and increased the scope of tariff coverage as well. The Act was not a dramatic turnabout in protectionism, since US tariffs were already high, and all major trading nations were protectionist at that time. Rather, it represented a new level in the long movement by nations toward closing off their economies to foreign imports. In the wake of the Smoot–Hawley tariff and the retaliation by foreign countries that it precipitated, world trade fell by about two-thirds by the mid 1930s. The breakdown of trade after 1930 was alarming to Western governments, but even more alarming was the process that had led to that breakdown. The Smoot–Hawley Act was written in congressional committees that were essentially unable to master the detail that had become inherent in any major tariff legislation. Because of this economic illiteracy, and because of the general sympathy toward protectionism that had been created by the Depression, Congress essentially extended protection to all those groups that demanded it. The spectacle was that of a gross excess of the democratic process and a loss of control over the economy by both the US president and the congressional leadership.

The breakdown of trade took its toll on public sympathy toward protectionism. The tariff became an issue in the presidential election of 1932, and was attacked by Democratic candidate Franklin D. Roosevelt as contributing to the Depression. Following his election, Roosevelt appointed Cordell

Hull as secretary of state, a man committed to the view that free trade was an essential ingredient in world prosperity, and an even more important ingredient in international peace and stability. Hull and his officials began working with Congress to prepare new tariff legislation, and two years later the legislation was enacted under the title Reciprocal Trade Agreements Act (RTAA) of 1934.

The RTAA produced a revolution in US and even international trade policy. The central element of the RTAA was that it empowered the president to lower (or raise) tariffs up to 50 per cent from Smoot–Hawley levels in the course of trade negotiations with other countries. From the standpoint of American politics, the RTAA transferred tariff-setting policy to the presidency, which could organize itself bureaucratically for the task, and away from the Congress, which had ultimately proven to be incapable of managing the tariff or of discriminating between the many appeals brought by constituents for protection. This transfer substantially increased the control the government exercised over trade policy, and it has been an essential part of the US trade policy structure ever since 1934. From the standpoint of international politics, the RTAA was revolutionary in that it accepted implicitly that setting tariff rates could no longer be exclusively a unilateral policy by a nation state, but, rather, was a bilateral matter to be settled through negotiation. This action was reminiscent of the efforts by Michel Chevalier in the previous century to use commercial and political negotiation to reduce trade restrictions between France and Britain, and it began the changeover from a protectionist trade policy that had existed since the 1870s.

The US government pursued reciprocal trade agreements with other countries as far as economic circumstances after 1934 would allow. By 1939, the United States had concluded twenty-one agreements, which made reductions in about a thousand duties. All agreements were made on a **most-favoured nation (MFN)** or non-discriminatory basis, which slowed the negotiation because it engaged more parties, but also for the same reason extended the impact of the agreements more widely. The RTAA agreements were successful in increasing the flow of international trade, but the greatest value of the programme was that it provided a corpus of experience in trade liberalization that became integrated after the Second World War. The act of reaching bilateral agreements gave governments the opportunity to create mechanisms for liberalizing trade, which was demonstrated by the fact that most of the GATT articles drawn up in 1947 were taken from various agreements reached during the previous decade under the RTAA system. For example, the escape clause that was written into Article XIX of the GATT was drawn from an agreement the United States reached with Mexico in 1942.

The reciprocal trade programme was concurrent with a sea change in US and world public opinion regarding protectionism and free trade. In 1930, the passage of the Smoot–Hawley tariff took place in an environment favourable to protectionism, and within a legislative system that encouraged protectionist pressure groups to press their demands vigorously. This can be contrasted with the climate that existed in 1953–4, when the Republican Party under Dwight Eisenhower reversed its historic policy of protectionism by extending the RTAA of 1934. In the second case, public opinion was much more supportive of free trade, and there was relatively little effective protectionist pressure on the legislators, particularly from the more important economic interest groups in the country (Bauer et al. 1972). What appeared to have changed, not only in the United States but also elsewhere, was the principle of free trade versus protectionism, or more precisely, the expectations that people held as to which principle was just and would ordinarily prevail as a general rule. This change created a more favourable economic context for the major changes in the world trade regime that occurred after the Second World War.

> ## Key points
>
> - Organized efforts to establish freer trade in Europe began in the middle of the nineteenth century.
> - A lengthy period of protectionism was initiated by the world depression that began in the 1870s, and then continued as a result of the world wars
>
> and depression of the first half of the twentieth century.
>
> - Efforts to establish a liberal international trading system were begun with the US Reciprocal Trade Agreements Act of 1934.

The ITO and the GATT: 1947 to 1948

Post-war economic situation

The ascendancy of the United States in the early post-war period was immediately evident in the play of international policy-making. In terms of security policy, the United States took over the leadership of the Western alliance. The United States enjoyed a preponderant position in the formation of the United Nations and other post-war international organizations. Reconstruction aid to Europe through the Marshall Plan further demonstrated the primacy of the United States in the Western system. In addition, US economic hegemony could be demonstrated by figures representing three important areas of the international economic system, namely international monetary payments, trade, and foreign investment. In 1947, the United States held about 70 per cent of the monetary gold stock of the world. Even a decade later, this figure had not dropped below 59 per cent of the world's stock (Cooper 1968). There was an acute shortage of US dollars over this period, and the dollar itself began to serve as a reserve currency for international payments. Regarding trade, by 1950 the United States accounted for nearly 17 per cent of world trade, and its share was about one and one-half times the share of the United Kingdom, the next leading nation (Krasner 1976). Throughout the decade of the 1950s, the United States increased its preponderance in world trade. By 1960, US trade was

20 per cent of overall world trade, over twice as large as that of the next leading nation (the UK), and roughly equal to the combined total of the three leading European economies, namely the UK, France, and West Germany. Finally, with regard to foreign investment, the United States went from an initial accumulated stock of foreign investment of $7 billion in 1946 to over $100 billion in 1973. The latter figure represented 51 per cent of total world foreign investment in that year (UN Commission on Transnational Corporations 1978). The second-ranking nation in foreign investment in 1973 was the United Kingdom with 13.5 per cent, or about a quarter of the US total. In sum, all the major indicators of international economic performance demonstrate that the United States was in a unique position of leadership in the first two decades of the post-war period.

United States' leadership rested relatively easily on other Western nations because the security concerns of the Cold War with the Soviets encouraged those nations to be more willing to follow than they might otherwise have been. However, any system where one nation is dominant is likely to reflect the values of that nation, which was the case of the trade regime set up under the GATT after 1947. One American value that was carried forward to the international system was a relatively liberal pro-business, anti-government approach to international trade, which to the Europeans was problematic because of the uncertain circumstances facing European economies after the war, and their emphasis on maintaining low levels of unemployment. For the Americans, however, trade liberalization was an attractive goal in ideological terms, and it was also consistent with the US national interest, since the United States was favourably positioned to benefit from freer trade.

A second American value was that of multilateralism, intended to guarantee non-discrimination between all countries participating in the trade regime. The Americans blamed the collapse of international trade in that period on the 'closed' imperial trading blocs the Europeans created in the inter-war years, and saw in multilateralism a means of removing trade restrictions. However, the Europeans were much more guarded, fearing that their weaker economies would be unable to withstand the strain of multilateral trade liberalization. In the place of multilateralism, the Europeans promoted the virtues of regionalism, which later came to fruition in the formation of the institutions that led to the present-day European Union (EU). Yet another American value was a legal approach to international trade relations, complete with the conception of a code of international trade law backed up by a mechanism for settling disputes between parties. For their part, the Europeans were wary of a code approach to international trade relations, and sought instead to preserve their right to administrative discretion. They preferred to build up a post-war trading system on practice rather than formal legal commitments (Gardner 1969).

The result of the different approaches taken by the United States and its allies is that the trade regime was, and has always been, based on compromise in the face of policy disagreements. Because of its predominant position, the US approach prevailed on most issues, but the rules that were negotiated were often riven with exceptions that weakened the legitimacy and effectiveness of the regime. It is important when assessing the trade regime to recall that it has always been based on a negotiated consensus, and that in the real world consensus is often only achieved through compromises that are unpalatable to the purists.

The rules of the GATT

Led by the United States, the Second World War allies attempted to create a new structure for the international system following the war. An essential part of this attempt was the Bretton Woods Conference of 1944, which established the International Bank for Reconstruction and Development (World Bank) and the International Monetary Fund (IMF). Along with these efforts in the development and monetary fields, the allies met in several conferences to establish the architecture of an international trade regime. To that end, countries concluded and signed an agreement to establish an **International Trade Organization (ITO)** in 1948, which was to complete the triad of functional organizations in the area of international economic relations. However, the US Congress failed to ratify the agreement, and without US involvement the ITO would have been irrelevant. In place of the ITO, countries relied on the General Agreement on Tariffs and Trade (GATT), established in 1947, to provide structure for the rapidly expanding trade system. The GATT itself was simply a contract embodying trade rules that were negotiated during a multilateral tariff negotiation in 1947. The GATT rules were partly a mechanism to ensure that countries that reduced protection by lowering tariffs did not reinstitute that protection through other measures. The GATT was never intended to function as an international organization. The fact that the GATT came to look and function like an international organization is the result of a largely unplanned and incremental accretion of political and legal powers. It was institution building by accident.

The GATT rules are contained in the thirty-five articles of the General Agreement (Jackson 1969). Perhaps the most important rule was that of non-discrimination, which is found in Articles I and III of the GATT. Article I is known as most-favoured nation principle (see Box 5.1). It required that any advantage—such as a lowered tariff—granted to another contracting party would immediately be accorded to all other contracting parties. This obligation—strongly promoted by the United States—attacked the practice of bilateral tariff preferences, which were commonly employed for political reasons before the Second World War, and which compartmentalized and therefore reduced the flow of trade between nations. The United States prevailed on this matter, but not before it compromised with the Europeans on preferential trade arrangements for their colonies. Another aspect of non-discrimination was found in Article III, which obliged nations to treat foreign products—once they had been imported and duty paid—no less favourably than domestic products with respect to taxes and other requirements. In general, Article I ensured that a country could not discriminate externally, and Article III ensured it could not discriminate internally.

Box 5.1 Most-Favoured Nation Principle (MFN)

The most-favoured nation principle (MFN) was introduced into the trade agreements of the 1930s and incorporated as Article I of the General Agreement on Tariffs and Trade in 1947. It required GATT Contracting Parties to extend to all signatories the benefits of any agreement that it might reach with any other country (that is, the 'most-favoured nation') in the GATT. The GATT provided a forum, and a legal regime, within which countries were encouraged to negotiate and to reach agreements to lower tariffs on a reciprocal basis. Normally, a country (for example, Great Britain) would conclude such an agreement on a bilateral basis with the principal supplier of a good (for example, an agreement with Canada to lower the tariff on winter boots), but the resulting lowered tariff would be accorded to all countries exporting winter boots to Great Britain. In this example, it would be assumed that Canada might reciprocate by

lowering its tariff on another good, of which Great Britain was the principal supplier to Canada.

The effect of the MFN principle was to eliminate discrimination between trade partners, as countries were in principle obliged to have one MFN tariff that applied to all other countries, and therefore were prohibited from applying different tariffs on the same product coming from different countries. Non-discrimination introduced the problem of free riding, where a country might take unreciprocated benefits from a lowering of tariffs by other countries, but this was regarded as a lesser problem than that caused by overtly discriminatory tariff policies. The overall purpose of MFN and non-discrimination was to create a unified multilateral trading system, and to prevent the international trade system from degenerating into a Balkanized system of regional preferences.

The principles of external and internal non-discrimination were not easy to establish in international trade. For example, in the 1930s, Article I non-discrimination, or most-favoured nation treatment, would have required a country such as Great Britain to give another country (even Nazi Germany) that did not discriminate against British trade the same tariff preferences it might have negotiated with a third country. This principle had the effect of elevating economics over politics in international relations, and was the subject of internal debate in Western countries in the years leading up to the Second World War. Similarly, Article III non-discrimination was also difficult for nations to accept, because it removed a whole range of policy tools (such as internal taxes or distribution requirements) that governments traditionally used to extend preferential treatment to domestic products.

Non-discrimination continues to be the cornerstone of the international trade system. Article I remains a basic building block of the GATT, and even though it has been somewhat compromised by preferential free trade agreements, nations negotiating those agreements have been careful to ensure that preference arrangements did not introduce new protectionism into the broader system. As for Article III, its relevance is demonstrated by the frequency with which it has been tested in GATT, and now World Trade Organization dispute settlement panels. An early example is the 1988 case on Canadian Liquor Board practices, where a panel found that discriminatory markup and listing practices by Canadian provincial liquor boards were inconsistent with Canada's obligations to its trading partners under Article III. This decision created pressure for reform of the Canadian practices.

A second important GATT rule was the prohibition in Article XI against quantitative and other non-tariff restrictions to trade (Dam 1970). The theory of the GATT was to delegitimize the use of protectionist measures other than tariffs, hence Article XI contained the stark obligation that 'no restrictions other than duties (that is, tariffs)' shall be maintained on the importation of any product. Article XI is increasingly regarded by trade lawyers as a key constraint on governments. For example, confrontations between trade and environmental concerns are a staple of contemporary trade policy, and Article XI obligations are the crux of this debate, as was illustrated in a 1991 GATT panel decision on tuna. At issue was environmental legislation in the United States which prevented the sale of tuna caught by methods that also kill dolphins, which served as the rationale for a ban on imports of tuna from Mexico. The United States lost the case when the GATT panel determined that the US restrictions violated that nation's obligations to Mexico under Article XI.

A third GATT rule deals with the methodology adopted by the GATT for reducing trade restrictions. This methodology was the sponsorship from time to time of tariff negotiations to be conducted 'on a reciprocal and mutually advantageous basis' and 'directed to the substantial reduction of tariffs' (Article XXVIII bis). The concept of reciprocity is the most interesting aspect of this methodology. Reciprocity can be seen as a normal aspect of negotiation in general, which in international trade has been promoted as a political imperative where nations give tariff reductions in order to get similar benefits from their partners, although economists often deride this concept, arguing that it is countries offering tariff reductions that make their economies more efficient and hence realize the benefit. Nevertheless, in the GATT's early history of trade negotiations, reciprocity was a guiding beacon as countries began the process of dismantling tariff protectionism. However, reciprocity as a concept ran into difficulties when developing countries acceded to the GATT. Because it is questionable whether equal treatment of unequal partners in trade negotiations could be considered reciprocal, numerous exceptions from full reciprocity were granted by industrialized GATT partners in favour of developing countries. For example, in various negotiations, an attempt was made to mitigate the obligations of GATT membership for developing countries through the concept of special and differential treatment. In the end, the efforts to water down GATT reciprocity for developing countries have produced very little in concrete terms, which demonstrates how difficult it is in international trade to depart from the notion of 'equal treatment under the law'. Nevertheless, demands for special treatment are a continuing aspect of the trade regime, as evidenced in the Doha trade negotiations (discussed later in this chapter).

Two other basic norms of the GATT are safeguards and the concept of 'commercial considerations'. Safeguards were based on the operational plan of the GATT framers that restrictive measures on trade would be converted to tariff protection, and then tariffs would be reduced through multilateral negotiations. In a situation where tariff reductions created an especially difficult political problem in any contracting party, the GATT also allowed (in Article XIX) for nations to backtrack on their commitments (that is, to raise tariffs) for a period of time to permit the orderly adjustment of domestic markets. The intent was to ensure that problems in specific industries did not compromise the general process of liberalization. The fact that the GATT has accommodated itself to protectionist pressures over the years has often been viewed positively by governments and commentators as an example of pragmatism and resilience.

The other rule of 'commercial considerations', or support for the values of the free market versus government interventionism, is implicit in the entire framework of the GATT. The term is mentioned specifically in Article XVII, where state-controlled enterprises are enjoined to act according to 'commercial considerations', and it is implicit in Article XVI, where the harmful effect of subsidies on efficient production is mentioned. Because the GATT represents commercial, free-market values, it has been a successful organization in a world that has recently moved in the same direction, and continues to move in that direction following the dissolution of international communism in the early 1990s.

In sum, the rules of the GATT provided a basis for governance in a narrow, but fundamentally important, sector of international relations. In any regime, or even government, the test of the regime is that the rules are understood, and that they guide behaviour. Without doubt, the rules of the GATT were known in the main, and they were

usually followed by the contracting parties to the Agreement (Hudec 1975).

> **Key points**
>
> - Following the Second World War, the United States was a preponderant presence in the world economy, and took a leadership role in post-war planning.
> - Trading nations established the General Agreement on Tariffs and Trade (GATT) in 1947, and attempted in 1948 to create an International Trade Organization (ITO), which failed to receive ratification by the US Congress.
> - The GATT obliged importing countries not to discriminate in favour of products coming from one country over those from another, or in favour of domestic products over foreign products, once the latter had paid any duties required and entered the importing country.
> - The principles and rules of the GATT provided a rudimentary basis for the regulation of international trade.

Multilateral Trade Negotiations: 1950s to 1980s

Post-war negotiations and the Kennedy Round

The main role of the GATT was to liberalize trade, and most decisions to that end were initiated in trade negotiations. The GATT was established to support the trade negotiations in 1947, and following that date the GATT sponsored multilateral negotiations in 1949 (Annecy), 1951 (Torquay), 1956 (Geneva), 1960–1 (the Dillon Round), and in 1963–7 (the Kennedy Round). Further negotiations were the Tokyo Round (1973–9), the Uruguay Round (1986–93), and the WTO Doha 'Round', initiated in January 2002, and continuing at the time of writing. Of these nine negotiations,

the first four after 1947 took up some important institutional matters, such as the accession of new members, but they did not make significant progress in liberalizing trade. One reason is that the European countries relied heavily on non-tariff measures throughout the mid 1950s, and hence any tariff concessions given during GATT negotiations were not meaningful in trade terms. Furthermore, European recovery from the war did not occur as quickly as expected, as evidenced by the fact that European currencies were not made fully convertible until 1958, which made it difficult for these countries to increase their exposure to international competition. In practice, the United States was the preponderant actor in the early negotiations, and offered most of the tariff concessions.

The GATT incorporated the bilateral negotiation process established by the RTAA, and simply multi-lateralized it (Diebold 1952). However, this change was not accomplished in a single stroke. The early GATT tariff negotiations were multilateral in name, but the real action occurred bilaterally between nations that served as principal suppliers and principal consumers of each other's products. Bilateral agreements were then multilateralized automatically through the most-favoured nation principle. If a country were, say, to halve its tariff of 10 per cent on Country A's widgets following bilateral negotiations with A, it would be obliged to extend the new tariff of 5 per cent on all imports of widgets from any other GATT contracting party. Nations could, and often did, remain aloof from the bilateral negotiating process, while nevertheless taking advantage—as free riders—of reductions concluded by other nations. Over time, the emphasis in the GATT shifted from the negotiation of tariff reductions to the negotiation of legal codes of behaviour. The latter negotiations are more fully multilateral, and are carried out in a process reminiscent of domestic parliamentary legislation, with a structured committee process leading to decisions in broader forums.

The Kennedy Round of 1963–7 emerged as the first significant negotiation in GATT after the initial negotiation in 1947 (Preeg 1970). It led to an average tariff reduction among the participants of about 35 per cent, in sharp contrast to the reduction of less than 10 per cent on a much smaller volume of trade in the Dillon Round that preceded it, or even the 20 per cent reduction achieved in the negotiation of 1947. The negotiation also produced an anti-dumping code (see Box 5.2) designed to help standardize national policies in this difficult and contentious area, and an international grain agreement that established price ranges for wheat and provided for multilateral sharing of food aid to developing countries. The Kennedy Round was, moreover, the first GATT negotiation at which the nations of the European Community (EC) participated as a single unit, which was the first time Europe and America engaged in a major negotiation across the Atlantic on an apparent basis of equality and reciprocity. It is interesting to note the historical correlation between a successful outcome in trade negotiation and the increasing equality of the major actors in those negotiations, for it is a trend that continued through the Kennedy Round and on into the Tokyo Round of the 1970s.

Box 5.2 Dumping and Anti-Dumping Duties

Dumping in international trade is generally understood as selling a product to another country for less than its sale price in the exporting country. Dumping is defined more precisely in Article VI of the GATT as exporting below the 'normal value' of a product, and is determined through a comparison of the price of the product in both the exporter's and importer's markets, or through an analysis of the exporter's costs of producing the product versus what it sold for on export. Determining 'normal value' through an examination of production costs can be uncertain and can lead to high anti-dumping duties, especially in non-market economies, where prices may not have the same meaning as in market economies.

Dumping is 'condemned' by the GATT if it causes injury to a domestic industry producing a 'like product' in the importing country. In the event a product is dumped and causes injury, as determined by an anti-dumping investigation conducted by the government of the importing country, the importing country can impose an 'anti-dumping duty' (in other words, an additional tariff) equal to the margin of dumping, meaning the difference between the normal value of the product and its export price.

In plain terms, dumping amounts to underselling, which is acceptable competitive behaviour within countries, but which is generally considered objectionable in the politically sensitive terrain of international commerce.

Anti-dumping actions are widely sought after by import-competing industries as a convenient means of protection against foreign competitors, especially since trade laws in most countries make it relatively easy to establish a case against foreign dumping. As a result, there has been a sharp increase in the incidence of anti-dumping actions by GATT and WTO Members since the 1980s. For example, worldwide anti-dumping initiations rose from around 150 a year in 1981 to 366 a year in 2001, before falling to about 200 by 2004 (Jones 2006). It is possible that the drop after 2001 resulted from a disinclination to initiate actions during the negotiation of the Doha Round. Developing countries have increased their own use of anti-dumping investigations, and between 1995 and 2005 seven of the ten heaviest users of anti-dumping actions were developing countries.

To sum up, anti-dumping duties can be viewed as a harassing and objectionable impediment to legitimate trade, and consequently countries have negotiated Anti-Dumping Codes in the Kennedy, Tokyo, and Uruguay Rounds designed to discipline the actions governments can take to protect domestic industries from foreign dumping. National legislation and international treaties on dumping and anti-dumping duties can be traced back to the beginning of the twentieth century, and these practices have been perhaps the most highly litigious and politicized area of the trade regime since its inception.

Apart from the economic results of the Kennedy Round, there were important political results that flowed from the successful completion of this major negotiation. The negotiation of trade liberalization in GATT was always a continuing struggle between liberalizing and protectionist forces. Those governments favouring liberalization have used negotiation, especially multilateral negotiation, as the principal means to trade free from protectionist restrictions. Those favouring protectionism have been more ascendant, and more effective, between major trade negotiations. This increased the salience and importance of any given negotiation over time, because there would be an increasing number of policy issues riding on the outcome. Thus, the pressure at the Kennedy Round to reach an acceptable settlement was increased, and ensured that any deadlock would constitute a failure that would go beyond the issues at the table.

The upshot was that the Kennedy Round took on enormous importance as a symbol as it went along. It became a test of the national will of the major participants to continue the post-war trend towards trade liberalization. Even more important, it was a test of the willingness of nations to avoid a breakdown that would lead to increased protectionism. The main reason the Kennedy Round succeeded is that governments feared what the implications of failure might mean for the international economic system, and because they wanted to avoid blame for causing such implications. In a strict sense, of course, it is clear that a deadlock in the Kennedy Round would have meant only that nations did not agree to reduce tariffs or other restrictions; this would have had no necessary consequences for increased protectionism. However, the situation was not framed in such terms. The political reality was that nations felt under great pressure to avoid a breakdown of a dialogue that had extended for five years, and of a settlement that would help to structure trading relations in the foreseeable future. Among these general concerns, the positions that delegations took on individual tariffs or products ultimately became less important. Thus, the main political result of the Kennedy Round was the achievement of the agreement itself, especially since the agreement was significant in trade terms.

Tokyo Round

At the close of the Kennedy Round in 1967, the GATT secretariat, led by Director-General Sir Eric Wyndham-White, sought to convince the major trading nations to extend liberalization into the area of non-tariff barriers to trade (Evans 1971). This initial effort was unsuccessful, but by the early 1970s chaos in the international monetary system and increasing use of non-tariff barriers in response to the surge of exports from Japan and the newly industrializing economies (NIEs) resurrected fears of trade protectionism and convinced national governments to begin a new negotiation in the GATT. This negotiation, named after the city in which it was initiated, started slowly because of the need to gather and classify enormous amounts of trade data with respect to NTBs. The negotiation was delayed further by the need for the United States to pass legislation authorizing the president to negotiate (an event that was not completed until January 1975), and by the US election of 1976. The negotiation effectively got under way in 1977, and comprehensive offers from delegations were in place by early 1978. Serious bargaining took place during the following year, and in April 1979 the final agreements were signed, subject to later ratification.

The agreements reached at the Tokyo Round were the most comprehensive and far-reaching results achieved in trade negotiations since the creation of the GATT (Winham 1986). The results fell into three categories: six legal codes (plus a sectoral code for trade in aircraft) that dealt with NTBs; tariff reductions; and a series of revisions of GATT articles primarily of interest to developing countries. The six codes updated and expanded aspects of the trade law of the GATT, and were the most important part of the Tokyo Round accords. These covered, respectively, customs valuation procedures, import licensing, technical standards for products, subsidies and countervailing duty measures, government procurement, and anti-dumping duty procedures. However, negotiations on a safeguards code failed.

The general thrust of the code negotiations was to effect a 'constitutional reform' of GATT law, and as well to improve the openness, certainty, and non-arbitrariness of the rules governing international trade. In some areas, this was accomplished without appreciable controversy. In codes on customs valuation, import licensing, and technical barriers, nations proceeded from the widely shared philosophy that government regulations in these areas should not be used to provide protection for domestic producers, by design or otherwise.

In other areas, agreement was more problematic. The attempted code on Article XIX safeguards encountered a determined insistence by the European Commission regarding the right to apply safeguards selectively on a targeted basis, rather than non-discriminatorily or across the board. Selectivity, in particular, was resisted by the developing countries, which would be the primary targets of this tactic. Also, the code on subsidies and countervailing duties triggered deeply held disagreements between the United States and the Commission over the appropriateness of agricultural export subsidies in modern government practice, but in the end this disagreement was reconciled by limiting the actions taken on agriculture, and the code was signed.

The second category of results from the Tokyo Round was tariff reductions. To put these results in perspective, tariff negotiations were the main item of business in the six multilateral negotiations that were held under GATT auspices through the Kennedy Round of 1967. Tariffs were not the major focus of the Tokyo Round, yet the average reductions of about 35 per cent of industrial nations' tariffs achieved in this negotiation were comparable to the reductions of the Kennedy Round. The reductions covered more than $100 billion of imports, and were phased in over an eight-year period beginning in 1980 (Cline 1983).

A major controversy in the tariff negotiation was to arrive at a tariff-cutting formula for manufactured products. A similar controversy had occurred in the Kennedy Round, at which time nations settled on a linear approach (50 per cent cut across the board, less exceptions) supported mainly by the United States. In the Tokyo Round, proponents of a tariff-harmonizing formula carried the day, and nations agreed to table offers according to a compromise Swiss formula that generally required tariff cuts to be proportional to the size of the tariff. The final bargaining produced a number of exceptions to the general formula, particularly in industries where imports were already high, and 'sensitive' domestic interests were threatened. For example, in the United States, where the average tariff cut was 31 per cent, the duties for leather imports were reduced by only 4 per cent; for apparel, 15 per cent; for automobiles, 16 per cent; and tariffs for footwear and colour televisions were exempted from any cuts. Similar exceptions were made by other trading nations.

The third category of Tokyo Round results was a proposed series of revisions to GATT Articles known as the 'framework' agreements. Negotiations on this subject were initiated by Brazil, intending to clarify GATT obligations and ease those obligations for developing countries. The framework agreements covered subjects such as safeguard actions for development purposes (or infant industry promotion), trade measures taken to correct payments deficits, export controls, and deviations from most-favoured nation procedures for developing countries. One important accord in the framework package was the Understanding regarding Notification, Consultation, Dispute Settlement, and Surveillance, which required GATT members to notify trading partners of the trade measures they adopt, and thus to provide an early warning for all countries of actions that might affect their interests adversely. The framework agreements did not substantially rewrite GATT law to advantage developing countries, and as a result many of those countries felt the results were 'frustrating and incomplete' (UNCTAD 1979: 34). However, the agreements did improve GATT language on matters related to developing countries, and therefore probably improved the capacity of the GATT legal machinery to mediate and reduce trade disputes.

The Tokyo Round underscored the extent to which multilateral negotiation had become a point of departure for managing the international trade system. In contrast with past GATT negotiations, which were largely limited to the reduction of tariffs,

the Tokyo Round was a rule-making exercise of major proportions. Furthermore, the agreements of the Tokyo Round constituted legal rules that reached further into the nation state and impacted more deeply on individual human behaviour than was the case with most international agreements. The process of negotiating these rules was extraordinarily complex, and arguably the code negotiations of the Tokyo Round were the most advanced, in terms of bureaucratic complexity, of any multilateral negotiations occurring at that time. The greatest complexity lay in attempting to integrate the conflicting trade legislation of many nations into a co-ordinated set of international rules. In their efforts to mesh the rule-making apparatus of different countries into a single structure, the Tokyo Round negotiators faced problems that became commonplace a decade later as nations coped with the implications of an increasingly interdependent world.

Key points

- Multilateral trade negotiations were conducted in the GATT to reduce tariff protectionism on a reciprocal basis.
- In the Tokyo Round (1973–9), countries focused on the more difficult task of reducing non-tariff measures that afforded protection in international trade. These measures were regulated through the negotiation of international codes of behaviour.
- The Tokyo Round demonstrated the importance of multilateral negotiation to the management of the international trade system.

The Uruguay Round and the WTO: 1986 to 1994

Background

The next major effort to establish further the world trade regime was the Uruguay Round

negotiation, which was launched at a GATT ministerial meeting in Punta del Este, Uruguay, in September 1986 (Croome 1995). The path to the

Uruguay Round was difficult, indeed. The previous GATT multilateral negotiation had made considerable progress in reducing protectionism from non-tariff barriers. Pressure began to build up shortly after 1979 to expand the GATT regime to include new issues—such as services, investment, and intellectual property—in addition to the old issues that dealt with trade in goods. In particular, the United States argued that a new negotiation was necessary to make the GATT relevant to a changing world economy, and in 1982 a GATT ministerial meeting was convened to consider this possibility. The idea met sharp resistance, particularly from developing countries that were overwhelmed by the global debt crisis and mainly concerned to expand traditional exports to developed countries to service debt obligations to the International Monetary Fund, Western governments, and private banks. Led by India and Brazil, the developing countries insisted that they were not sufficiently developed to negotiate the new issues, such as services, on an equal footing with the developed countries. Moreover, developing countries held that the developed countries had evaded their obligations in some of the traditional goods, such as textiles or agricultural products, which were of particular importance to developing countries, and demanded further liberalization in these areas as a precondition to any new negotiations. The result was that the 1982 ministerial meeting was a failure for the proponents of new negotiations, although the meeting did establish important work programmes that generated the data needed for future negotiation.

The most dramatic part of the lead-up to the Uruguay Round negotiation came in the week-long special ministerial session at Punta del Este in September 1986 (Winham 1998*a*). At the eleventh hour, it was agreed between the Americans and the Indians that the session would launch negotiations on a range of issues, including services, but that negotiations on services would be undertaken in a separate structure from those on goods, which presumably would lessen the prospects that developed countries could force trade-offs between services and the traditional subjects in the negotiation.

Once the breakthrough on services occurred, it was clear that the remaining issues did not warrant holding up the prospect for a new negotiation, and settlement quickly followed on investment and intellectual property, which had also been major sticking points between the developed and developing countries.

New issues

The agenda of the Uruguay Round (Box 5.3) comprised fifteen negotiating groups arranged initially in four principal categories: market access (including the critical areas of agriculture and textiles); reform of GATT rules; measures to strengthen the GATT as an institution; and the new issues, specifically services, investment, and intellectual property (Preeg 1995). The new issues were included in the negotiation in order to make the GATT more relevant to developments in the world economy, and to respond to strong pressures coming from industry in developed countries. By the late 1980s, services had come to account for well over half of the gross domestic product (GDP) of developed countries, and they were beginning to account for an increasing proportion of international trade. For the GATT, the incorporation of services was not a straightforward matter. Services are not goods, which had always been the focus of GATT rules, but rather are processes in which skills and knowledge are exchanged in order to meet a particular consumer need. They can include processes as widely differentiated as engineering consulting, financial intermediation, tourism, or legal advice. Services often require the movement of the factors of production (for example, the establishment of a bank branch in a foreign country to sell financial services), a condition that is constantly affected by changes in technology that decrease the barrier separating non-traded from traded services. For its part, the GATT had identified many services as 'non-traded goods', although this characterization was dropped and services became recognized as an integral part of the international economy. There are many obstacles that can prevent a free exchange of services between countries, but an important one is the reluctance of domestic authorities to grant foreign firms the right to establish and do business in their markets. Such a refusal may be motivated by protectionist impulses, but it may also be inspired—for example in the case of prudential banking legislation—by a desire to protect the consumer, who is often viewed as being at a disadvantage with respect to the foreign service provider.

Box 5.3 Uruguay Round Agreements

The GATT Multilateral Trade Negotiation known as the Uruguay Round began in September 1986, effectively concluded in December 1993, and formally concluded with official signatures at the Marrakesh (Morocco) Ministerial Meeting in April 1994. The Uruguay Round produced a wide range of agreements integrated under a common legal system. What is usually thought of as the 'WTO system' is contained in the Marrakesh Agreement Establishing the World Trade Organization (WTO) and the Dispute Settlement Understanding (DSU). The WTO Agreement established the WTO as an international organization, and ensured that all the agreements negotiated at the Uruguay Round were accepted as a **single undertaking**, thus increasing the legal integration of the WTO trade regime. The dispute settlement system established by the DSU was also intended to apply to all areas of the Uruguay Round Agreements, hence it is an integral part of the architecture of the new WTO system.

The Uruguay Round Agreements comprise about sixty agreements totalling some 550 pages, covering subjects as widely diversified as agriculture, safeguards, trade in intellectual property, **rules of origin**, textiles and clothing, and technical barriers to trade. These agreements can be accessed on the WTO website www.wto.org under the title 'Legal Texts of the WTO Agreements'. In addition, the Uruguay Round Agreements also included the General Agreement on Tariffs and Trade 1994, which effectively incorporated the GATT of 1947 into the WTO system. There were some additional agreements interpreting various provisions of the GATT, such as the meaning of 'other duties and charges' in Article II, which covers tariff schedules, but there is historical and legal continuity from the basic rules and provisions of the GATT to the modern WTO trade regime.

Because countries have different regulatory objectives and standards, the result is that the global services market is essentially protectionist. GATT principles required non-discrimination among trade partners, national treatment of foreign suppliers, and transparency in the process by which domestic rules are developed, but the provision of services often requires the opposite behaviour if the consumer is to be protected and provided with a reliable and quality service. Governments generally seek to provide consistent regulation over their own markets; again, arguably, this might require discrimination against trade partners that apply different standards from trade in services. Because services are processes, defining them is difficult unless a strict functional definition is employed. The stricter the definition, however, the greater the chance that discrimination will occur. Yet, without strict definitions, domestic regulation may more easily be circumvented.

The tasks for the negotiators at the Uruguay Round were to incorporate GATT principles of transparency, national treatment and reciprocity, as well as newer principles such as market access, into an area of trade that was conceptually dissimilar from trade in goods, the normal milieu of GATT principles and practice (Arup 2000). Given the paucity of information on trade in services, the first task was to develop a common database on which substantive decisions could later be made. Second, a code of principles (which later became known as the General Agreement on Trade in Services (GATS)) would have to be negotiated to provide for a standard of treatment between countries of trade in services. Finally, the code of principles would have to be applied to specific sectors of services trade. To do this, negotiators needed to analyse existing measures that restricted trade in services in order to propose measures that would liberalize trade in specific services sectors.

The two other new issues on the Uruguay Round agenda were investment and intellectual property. Investment was included because by the 1980s, it had become apparent that investment was interchangeable with trade, and, more important, that trade liberalization might be less valuable in stimulating international economic exchanges unless it is accompanied by the liberalization of investment regimes. However, investment has always attracted considerable regulation in importing countries because of the risk to sovereignty associated with high levels of foreign investment in sensitive industries. In the Uruguay Round, the negotiation of a multilateral investment agreement eventually proved to be an unreachable goal, and the agreement that was reached on Trade-Related Investment Measures (TRIMs) dealt with only a small proportion of the issues raised in the negotiation.

Trade-Related Aspects of Intellectual Property Rights, better known as TRIPs, was the third of the new issues. Intellectual property rights grant state protection to producers of new ideas, but this protection was not well established in the international economy (Maskus 2000). Producers of high-tech products sought to internationalize the intellectual property protections they enjoyed in their home country, and producers' associations such as the Pharmaceuticals Manufacturers Association demanded constraints on generic industries that arguably did not recognize legitimate patents on drugs. Negotiations in the Uruguay Round began by addressing the problem of counterfeit goods in international trade, but developed countries—which asserted that inadequate protection of intellectual property rights was a serious non-tariff barrier to trade—quickly pressed for a broader negotiation over patents and copyrights. Developing countries, led by India and Brazil,

viewed TRIPs protection as a potential barrier to trade in its own right, but they were more concerned over the monopolies effectively granted in developed countries for products such as pharmaceuticals, which they considered crucial to the public interest. The developing countries acquiesced on this issue because they felt their losses were compensated by gains elsewhere in the overall accord, and an agreement was concluded that set international standards for certain protections dealing with copyrights and patents (Winham 1998a). However, the controversy over the TRIPs Agreement continued as a mainstay of WTO politics, as developing countries saw intellectual property rights as a mechanism by which developed countries could maintain a competitive edge relative to countries that lacked a sophisticated technological infrastructure.

Developing countries

For most of the history of the GATT, the developing countries have been marginal players. The GATT itself was largely a creation of the United States and its Western allies, and focused mainly on trade rather than economic development, which was the central concern of the poorer countries of Africa, Asia, and South America. Above all, the GATT took aim at the high level of tariffs in the trading system, and promoted the reduction of these tariff levels in developing countries (see Figure 5.1). By comparison, in terms of trade policy, most developing countries pursued a policy of import-substitution industrialization (ISI), which called for high protective tariffs to force consumers to purchase domestic-made products at the expense of imports. These policies encouraged developing-country governments to pursue trade policies of self-sufficiency, and to seek 'special and differential' benefits in GATT negotiations in lieu of accepting the multilateral rules of the GATT based on reciprocity. The upshot was that, as the GATT system matured, it became clear that one of the major threats to that system was its inability to be relevant to traders and governments

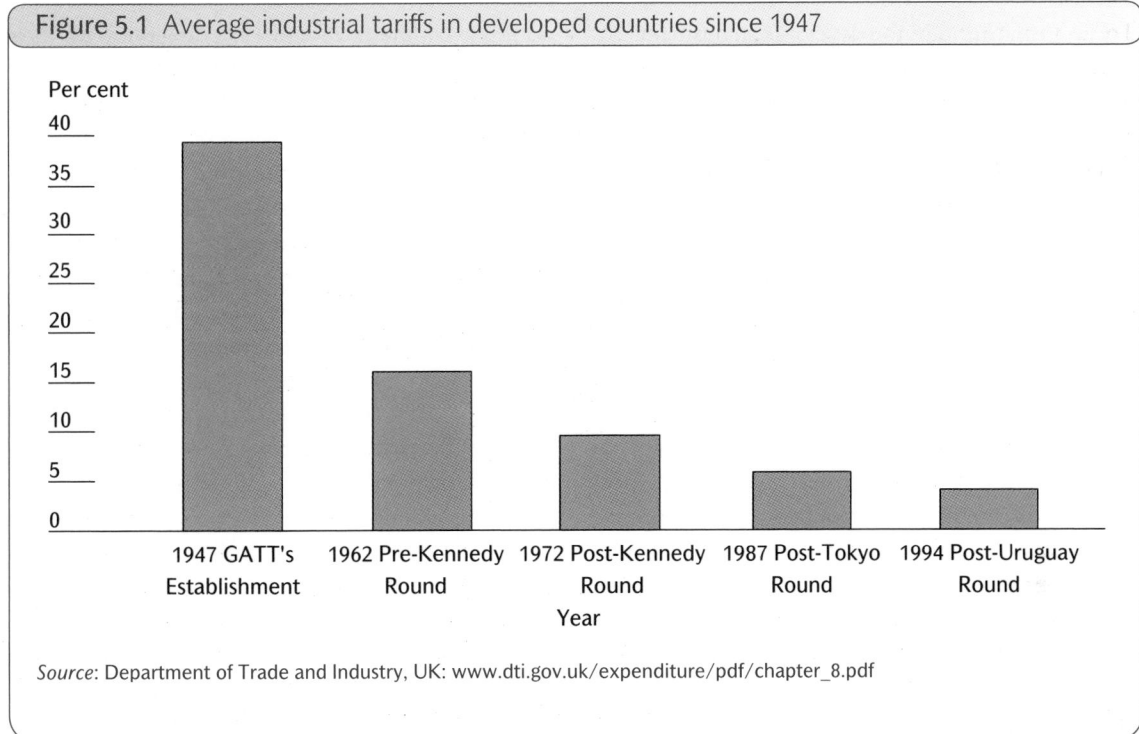

Figure 5.1 Average industrial tariffs in developed countries since 1947

Per cent

Source: Department of Trade and Industry, UK: www.dti.gov.uk/expenditure/pdf/chapter_8.pdf

in countries representing over two-thirds of the world's population. This threat was largely overcome in the Uruguay Round negotiation, for one of the results of the negotiation was that, for the first time, developing countries became fully integrated into the world trade regime.

The developing countries did not support the initiation of the Uruguay Round. Led by India and Brazil, they insisted that they were not sufficiently developed to negotiate the new issues such as services on an equal footing with the developed countries. Also, they argued that developed countries had not honoured their past commitment in traditional goods such as textiles or agriculture, and that further liberalization in these areas would be a precondition for any new negotiation. However,

once developing countries relented and agreed to negotiate, they quickly engaged in all the issues before the negotiation. As the negotiation continued, it became clear that the capacity to determine the outcome of the Uruguay Round fell mainly to the two major trading powers: the United States and the European Union. At this point, a curious change took place: the major powers that had been so insistent on a new negotiation reached a deadlock, largely over agriculture, while the developing countries that had fought so hard against a new negotiation for most of the 1980s became the greatest advocates for its successful conclusion in the early 1990s. From 1991 until the conclusion of the Uruguay Round in December 1993, the developing countries kept the pressure on the majors to settle their differences, which was an important element in the multilateral agreement that was eventually reached.

The turnaround in the developing countries' position was one of the most interesting stories of the Uruguay Round (Winham 1998a). It occurred, first, because developing countries were advantaged by two negotiating principles that underlay the Uruguay Round; namely, consensus and the single undertaking. Single undertaking meant that all issues of the negotiation were treated as a single package, with no exceptions, unlike the Tokyo Round, where agreements were signed on a plurilateral (or pick and choose) basis, with the result that countries were subject to differing rights and obligations. Consensus — which was a traditional GATT principle — meant that multilateral agreement required the passive support (that is, no formal opposition) of all participants. These principles combined to increase the power of small and middle-sized powers at the Uruguay Round, which was demonstrated dramatically at the 1988 ministerial meeting in Montreal when five Latin American countries withheld consensus from an interim package agreement because their concerns over agriculture were not being met by the major countries. This action emboldened the developing countries, and led them to take a greater interest in the overall negotiation.

Second, despite the reality that developing countries continued to be economically disadvantaged in comparison to developed countries, the agreements reached at the Uruguay Round were favourable to the interests of the former. Developing countries as a group benefited from agreements on agriculture, textiles, and clothing (and probably services), while they may have lost out on intellectual property and anti-dumping practices. Most important, however, developing countries were advantaged by the institutional arrangements resulting from the Uruguay Round Agreements, namely the strong dispute settlement mechanism and the creation of the World Trade Organization itself. On balance, these advantages encouraged the developing countries to support the Round.

Finally, and most important, the market-based economic reforms that took place in many developing countries in the 1980s encouraged their governments to look more favourably on the market-based principles and objectives of the GATT. That these changes were concurrent with pressures to liberalize economies from Western countries and international financial institutions (IFIs) is undeniable, but in the end the fall of communism and the obvious success of certain free market countries such as Singapore or Taiwan led to an internal policy revolution in many countries. For example, India suffered a severe financial crisis in 1991, following which it introduced reforms designed to deregulate the national economy and increase its economic efficiency. In the wake of these domestic reforms, India revised its negotiating strategy at the Uruguay Round from opposition to support for a multilateral agreement. In India and in many other developing countries, the impact of internal reform was to increase the congruence between domestic policies and the principles of the international trade regime.

The United States and the European Union

The structure of the contemporary international trade regime is centred mainly around the US–EU bilateral relationship (Bergsten 1999). However, this was not always the case. Until the early 1960s, the United States held a preponderant position in relation to other members of the GATT, and in multilateral negotiations it offered most of the concessions and expected little in return from other countries. This situation began to change in the Kennedy Round, when the six European Common Market countries negotiated as a single bloc. The change was largely completed by the Tokyo Round, when the European Community (now the European Union) had expanded to include the United Kingdom, making the EC the largest trading entity in the international system.

Negotiations in the Tokyo Round and subsequently could be characterized as a pyramidal process. This means that agreements were usually initiated between the principal players, namely the United States and the European Union, and then presented successively to middle-sized and smaller parties to establish a multilateral consensus. Pyramidal negotiation operates when there is a wide disparity of power among negotiating parties, and in particular when the negotiating structure is bipolar. On the positive side, pyramidal negotiation places the onus for initiating agreement on the parties that have effective power to veto a multilateral agreement. A drawback, however, is that this negotiation structure leaves less scope for smaller powers involved in large multilateral negotiations to influence the outcome or to protect their particular interests. As a result, criticism from smaller actors, including in particular developing countries, is endemic in multilateral trade negotiations.

The negotiation over agriculture in the Uruguay Round offered a good example of pyramidal negotiation. At the outset of the negotiation, a group of approximately fourteen agricultural exporters from among the developed and developing countries formed under Australian leadership to promote the liberalization of global agricultural markets. Known as the Cairns Group, these countries played an important role in the early stages of the negotiation in bridging the differences between the United States and the European Union over agricultural trade. However, by January 1992, it became clear that the Uruguay Round was blocked, and the reason was the agricultural negotiation between the major players. Agricultural trade had long been a difficult problem for many countries in the GATT system, but in the Uruguay Round the inherent problems of agriculture was compounded because this issue pitted the interests of the United States and the European Union against one another. The US–EU differences stemmed mainly from the fact that, since the 1960s,

Europe had established a protectionist policy under the Common Agricultural Policy (CAP), while the United States was moving towards a comparative advantage in agricultural exports. The Uruguay Round thus turned into a politicized contest between the major players, and for eighteen months the main activity of the multilateral negotiation was a series of bilateral encounters between US and EU officials. This blockage halted progress in areas other than agriculture, and even between other countries. The United States and the European Union eventually reached a resolution of their differences in the 'Blair House' accords on agriculture, but agriculture continued to be the major stumbling block to a general agreement until very late in the negotiation. This whole affair re-emphasized the importance of the major players in multilateral trade negotiation.

Results

The Uruguay Round Agreements were concluded on 15 December 1993. In comparison to the results achieved in previous negotiations, they represented an enormous accomplishment for the world trading system (see Table 5.1). These agreements created the World Trade Organization, which represented institutional progress in that the WTO is a formally constituted international organization and not — as the GATT was — mainly a contract regarding trade rules between countries. The WTO had enormous symbolic importance for the world trade regime, but it also had practical significance as well. Internally, the WTO and the Uruguay Round Agreements provided for clearer rules on trade, and reduced the fragmentation and inconsistency that had existed between various GATT-sponsored agreements. Externally, the WTO reinforced the role of trade in international economic relations, and it permitted trade concerns to be represented more fully in relations with the World Bank and the International Monetary Fund.

Table 5.1 Results of GATT Negotiations: 1960–94

Negotiation	No. of countries	Results
Dillon Round 1960–1	26	• Average tariff cut of 10% on $4.9 bn of trade
Kennedy Round 1963–7	62	• Average tariff cut of 35% on $40 bn of trade • Anti-dumping code
Tokyo Round 1973–9	102	• Average tariff cut of 35% on more than $100 bn of trade • Six codes dealing with non-tariff measures, plus aircraft code • Revision of GATT articles for developing countries
Uruguay Round 1986–94	128	• Average tariff cut of 39% on $3.7 tr of trade • Twelve Agreements (including Agriculture, Textiles, Subsidies, Safeguards) • New issues: Agreements on Trade in Services (GATS) and Trade-Related Aspects of Intellectual Property Rights (TRIPs) • Dispute Settlement Understanding (DSU) • Creation of WTO, new legal footing for the multilateral trade regime

Second, the various agreements reached at the Uruguay Round greatly expanded the rules of the international system of trade. New issues such as services were brought under multilateral rules for the first time, while old issues such as agriculture and textiles, which had long been essentially outside GATT disciplines were brought under multilateral rules, thereby beginning the lengthy process of reducing protectionism in two sectors that had for a long time resisted the progression towards a more liberal world trade regime (Paarlberg 1997). Third, the Uruguay Round Agreements were accepted by the developing countries engaged in the negotiation, and represented the most far-reaching commitments those countries had made in the international trade regime. Effectively, they brought the developing countries into that regime. The Uruguay Round concluded at a time when many developing countries were undergoing substantial

liberalization, and the confluence of change in the developing world and the deepening of the multilateral regime will engage trade more fully in the progress towards international development.

Finally, the Uruguay Round Agreements represented a further step towards a system based on rules rather than power in international trade. The agreements advanced the rules-based nature of trade relations between countries, and thereby increased the economic security of smaller and middle-sized countries in their relations with larger powers. In particular, the agreements established a formal, integrated dispute settlement system to replace the largely *ad hoc* mechanism that had evolved under the GATT. The agreements created an obligation for countries to adjudicate an issue if a trading partner seeks this recourse. Conversely, countries are obligated not to use unilateral trade sanctions as an alternative to multilateral dispute settlement actions under the WTO. Both provisions were intended to increase the prospects that countries, regardless of their size and power, would be equal before the law in trade disputes.

Key points

- Developing countries resisted efforts by developed countries to establish a new GATT negotiation following the Tokyo Round.
- The Uruguay Round (1986–93) comprised a lengthy negotiating agenda, including new issues such as trade in services and Trade-Related Aspects of Intellectual Property Rights (TRIPs).
- The most difficult issue in the Uruguay Round was trade in agriculture, particularly between the major parties, the European Union and the United States.

- The Uruguay Round was an enormous accomplishment for the international trade system. International rules were established in most important areas of international trade, the World Trade Organization (WTO) was created, and a more effective dispute settlement system established. The developing countries became full participants in the WTO system.

The WTO in Action: 1995 and Beyond

The structure of the WTO

The WTO was created as part of the results of the Uruguay Round negotiations that concluded on 15 December 1993, and it came into existence on 1 January 1995. Also included in the Uruguay Round results were a series of agreements that established rules dealing with agriculture, services, textiles and clothing, intellectual property, as well as a number of other issues related to trade. These agreements advanced substantially the rules-based nature of the trade regime originally established under the GATT. As Raymond Vernon (1995: 330) observed shortly after the conclusion of the Uruguay Round, 'The agreements, if taken at their face value, show promise of reshaping trade relationships throughout the world.' This statement surely reflects the stunning accomplishment of the negotiation, which was all the more remarkable given the low expectations held at the start of the round.

The WTO portion of the Uruguay Round Agreements created an unusual international organization. Most international organizations have specified procedures for making decisions in the name of the collectivity, but instead the WTO continued many of the consensual practices of the GATT. Essentially, the WTO represented a contract between its members, the purpose of which was to establish trade rules and then to back up those rules with a powerful dispute settlement system. To understand the WTO, it is necessary to examine important legal elements drawn from the WTO Agreement and the Dispute Settlement Understanding (DSU).

At the outset, the WTO Agreement explicitly established a new international organization that was to provide symbolic visibility and permanence for international trade policy in the international system (Jackson 1998). The WTO was vested with legal personality, which the GATT did not have, and which placed the WTO on the same footing as other organizations such as the IMF or the World Bank. The WTO Agreement further stated that the WTO should be the 'common institutional framework' for trade relations among its members, and should 'facilitate the implementation' of the various Uruguay Round Agreements. These provisions were important in that they centralized the governance of the trade system far more than had existed under the GATT. By comparison, the GATT in the 1990s was rapidly becoming a potpourri of decentralized separate agreements, which risked creating a watering down of the central obligations of the trade regime.

Second, the WTO Agreement provided that members would accept the WTO and the various other Agreements as a single piece, and would be obliged to bring their domestic laws into conformity with those Agreements. This commitment incorporated the well-known concept of 'single undertaking' that crystallized during the Uruguay Round negotiation. The single undertaking meant that countries were not free to pick and choose among the various agreements, as in the Tokyo Round, but were required to accept and implement the agreements as a package deal. This stratagem ensured that negotiators would make trade-offs in arriving at their final offers in the negotiation, and it also helped to clarify the obligations of members at the implementation stage that followed.

Third, the WTO Agreement provided for institutional structure and decision-making procedures for the new organization, which was more complex than the GATT had been to take into account the greater complexity of the subject matter in the Uruguay Round Agreements. On one point, however, the WTO continued the practice of the GATT, namely in the provision of decision-making by consensus. The WTO Agreement in Article IX defined consensus as existing 'if no Member, present at the meeting when the decision is taken, formally objects to the proposed decision'. This procedure meant that the WTO would continue mainly as a contract organization that would not create obligations for individual countries beyond those it had accepted

under the consensual decision-making practices of the WTO.

As for the DSU, it is first necessary to note that the Uruguay Round negotiators were aware that they were creating a vast addition to international trade laws, and they further recognized a legal system needed to be backed up with judicial procedures for the laws to have any real impact. In practical terms, this meant that a WTO member embroiled in a dispute with another member should have a right to proceed to a judicial process, and that the result of that process should be (legally) binding on the parties. The DSU provided for this basic right, and its significance can be appreciated by the fact that similar rights are practically non-existent in international law.

The practice of dispute settlement was begun on a customary basis under the GATT, and certain procedures, such as the establishment of adjudicatory panels to hear cases, were well in place prior to the creation of the WTO. The WTO's DSU improved the system in a number of ways. First, whereas the GATT had required the consent of both parties for a panel to be established (thereby allowing the party complained against to quash the panel procedure), the DSU provides in Article 6 that: 'If the complaining party so requests, a panel shall be established.' Furthermore, for the panel decision to become legally binding (or 'adopted' by the Council, the plenary body of the GATT's Contracting Parties), the GATT required consensus of all parties, meaning that the party that lost the case would have to acquiesce if the report were to be adopted. This procedure was not as meaningless as it might seem, as dispute settlement was a valued concept under the GATT, and consensual adoptions were the normal outcome of disputed cases. Nevertheless, GATT practice was an example of weak law, which was strengthened under the DSU by the requirement that a panel report would be adopted unless members decided by consensus *not* to adopt the report. This meant that a winning party would have to oppose adoption if the report was to be rejected, which is unlikely; hence, the DSU rules virtually provide that panel reports are automatically binding (Palmeter and Mavroidis 1999).

Second, the DSU strengthened the scope and mechanics of dispute settlement in the WTO. An Appellate Body was established to improve the consistency of legal decision-making. The coverage of dispute settlement was extended to all areas of the Uruguay Round Agreements, which provides for an integrated legal system and removes the competition that previously existed between differing dispute settlement mechanisms. Finally, the DSU makes it obligatory for members engaged in a dispute to use the WTO system and not resort to unilateral measures, as in the past, to settle the matter themselves. Taken in sum, the DSU represented an extraordinary step forward in the application of legal principles and methods in international law. That it would happen in the trade regime is an indicator of how much that regime has become governed by rules established in multilateral negotiations.

The WTO as an organization

The WTO is described most accurately as a formally contracted body of rules backed up by a judicial system and a minimum of political structure (Winham 1998*b*). The GATT, which was mainly a contract between parties, had provided for the possibility of joint organizational action by the 'Contracting Parties', but such actions were not emphasized in the General Agreement. By contrast, the WTO Agreement outlines a number of specific functions to be taken by the WTO as a collective body. These include: the implementation and administration of the Uruguay Round Agreements; maintenance of a forum for further negotiations; administration of the dispute settlement system; administration of the Trade Policy Review Mechanism (TPRM); and liaison with the World Bank and the IMF. With the exception of liaison with international financial institutions, these functions had first been established under the GATT on a customary basis.

Table 5.2 WTO Ministerial Conferences

Singapore, 9–13 December 1996
Geneva, 18–20 May 1998
Seattle, 30 November–3 December 1999
Doha, 9–13 November 2001
Cancun, 10–14 September 2003
Hong Kong, 13–18 December 2005

Source: WTO
(www.wto.org/english/thewto_e/minist_e/minist_e.htm)

The principal structures established to carry out the functions of the WTO are a Ministerial Conference meeting every two years (see Table 5.2); a General Council, which is a continuation of the Council of the GATT, and which can also meet as a Dispute Settlement Body and TPRM Review Body; and three councils in the area of goods, services, and intellectual property. Various other organs are mandated in the WTO Agreement, such as the Committee on Trade and Development, and additional bodies can be created by the Ministerial Conference as it deems necessary.

The WTO Agreement provided for a secretariat, which in the GATT had developed on an informal and customary basis. The WTO secretariat is small compared to the tasks it is expected to perform, and it is certainly small in relation to other international economic organizations. For example, in 1996, the complete staff of the WTO numbered 513, whereas comparable figures for the World Bank and the International Monetary Fund were 6,781 and 2,577, respectively (Blackhurst 1998). This same research showed that the WTO personnel numbers were exceeded by some fifteen international organizations, including some, such as the UN Industrial Development Organization (1,758 individuals) and the World Intellectual Property Organization (630 individuals), that have a much lower profile than the WTO.

As noted previously, decision-making in the WTO is based on consensus, the practice that had developed by custom in the GATT. Consensus is not the same as unanimity, and it is clear that the legal definition in Article IX of the WTO Agreement, as well as past and contemporary practice, permits countries to abstain and therefore to allow decisions to go forward in cases where not all members are in agreement with the issue under consideration. Consistent with the requirement for consensus, most organs of the WTO are plenary, and all members are able to participate.

The tasks of the WTO are carried out by its professional staff, and by the vigorous involvement of the Geneva delegations of the WTO members, which allows the WTO to function with a small secretariat. The WTO is usually described as a 'member-driven' organization, meaning that the members and not the secretariat are mainly responsible for setting the agenda and carrying out the functions of the organization. In the important routine tasks of the organization—including judgements on waivers of obligations, initiation of disputes or complaints, accession of new members, or working parties on free trade areas—action can only be taken by officials from member governments. Research from 1997 indicates that, to cover this workload, there were some 97 members with representation in Geneva, with an average of about five professional officers per delegation (Blackhurst 1998). These officials, plus their back-up support in home capitals, slightly exceeded the manpower available in the WTO secretariat in the same year.

In addition to the principal structures of the WTO mentioned previously, there are over twenty-five committees and working groups, and a fluctuating number of working parties on accessions of new members, all of which in principle are plenary bodies. In addition, there are organs with limited membership, including the Textiles Monitoring Body, plurilateral committees, dispute settlement panels, and the Appellate Body. Additionally, multilateral trade negotiations occasionally create further structure and tasks, and during the Tokyo and Uruguay Rounds a parallel structure under a Trade Negotiations Committee was struck to service those negotiations. Finally, there is an informal and fluid structure of consultation groups designed to bring 'like-minded' members together to discuss issues of common concern. The work associated with the various organs of the WTO is carried out mainly by the Geneva delegations of the members, with assistance from the WTO secretariat. The frequency of meetings is large and growing, and countries with small delegations are hard-pressed to monitor, let alone direct, the activities of the organization. Indeed, many of the least developed countries have no representation in Geneva, and have little capacity to pursue their own interests independent of the positions taken by developing countries as a bloc.

One of the important tasks of the WTO is to monitor and research the trade policies of the members. An important element in this task is the Trade Policy Review Mechanism (TPRM) which was begun by the GATT in 1989, roughly midway through the negotiation of the Uruguay Round. The TPRM is simply a review of a member's trade policy regime, conducted in part by the member itself and by officials of the GATT/WTO secretariat. Major trading countries such as the United States can expect a review once every two years, but for smaller countries the rotation will be less frequent. The main purpose of a TPRM review is information dissemination and transparency, but the reviews are also a valuable tool to evaluate whether members are in full compliance with their obligations under various WTO Agreements. The TPRM reviews are an example of collective executive action in an organization that has very much played down the executive function in comparison to the rule-making and rule-adjudication functions. Depending on the development of the international trade system and the politics conducted within that regime, the executive function of the WTO could become a much more important factor in the future.

The politics of the WTO

It is common to describe the WTO as a 'rules-based' system. Like the GATT before it, the WTO consists mainly of a set of rules intended to promote trade between member countries, and in particular

to provide for non-discrimination in trading relations. In any system of rules, a mechanism for
handling disputes is a natural and logical extension
of that system. In the GATT, a dispute settlement
system developed by customary practice, but in the
WTO it was mandated by international agreement
in the form of the DSU, and included in the Uruguay
Round Agreements. The DSU is a particularly powerful form of international dispute settlement, and
the management of this system has created political
controversy among the members of the WTO.

At the outset, it should be noted that dispute
settlement procedures have been frequently used
in the WTO. World Trade Organization statistics
(WTO 2000b) indicated that, in slightly more than
five years of operation, there had been some 193
member complaints to the WTO on 151 distinct
trade issues. By October 2003, total complaints
numbered over 300. Approximately half of the
complaints are settled or dropped in the consultation phase that precedes formal dispute settlement
(Davey 2000). Once a case is formally engaged, it
proceeds to a three-person panel comprising trade
experts for a legal decision, and then, if requested,
it will continue to the Appellate Body on appeal.
Once a decision has been reached, the next issue
is implementation. This is a problem the WTO
accepted in moving to a legally binding dispute settlement system compared to the more diplomatic
and political system that existed previously in the
GATT, where countries could avoid a legal decision
they could not live with. In the WTO, countries are
legally obliged to accept and implement a negative
dispute settlement decision, and it is possible for
an injured party to take retaliatory action, even
though such an action is counterproductive from
the standpoint of liberalizing the trade regime, in
that it erects further barriers to trade. But for the
largest WTO members, it is usually impossible to
oblige a powerful country—even through retaliatory sanctions—to implement an adverse decision
that it is determined to ignore. This was particularly the situation with the *Hormones* and *Bananas*
cases, two disputes that divided the United States
and the European Union (see WTO 2008, 2009c).

The problem is that if major powers are able to
circumvent the obligation to implement adverse
panel decisions, the WTO dispute settlement system will quickly lose the moral authority to secure
implementation from any countries. This could be
a fatal blow to the WTO rules-based regime.

There are other problems with dispute settlement
that have been raised by developing countries. One
is the costs of litigation before WTO panels and
the Appellate Body. There has been a tendency for
disputes to grow in legal complexity, a problem that
was already evident in the GATT in the late 1980s.
There are now more agreements to consider, and
the prospect of appeal to the WTO Appellate Body
has increased the importance of factual evidence
and precise legal argument. The complexity and
costs are especially hard to manage for developing
countries, which generally have small delegations
in Geneva and may therefore be forced to choose
between hiring expensive counsel or simply forgoing the opportunity to pursue a dispute settlement
case. These difficulties can impel developing countries towards a defensive rather than an offensive
posture in dispute settlement, and may reduce the
market-opening possibilities that the dispute settlement system may hold for more affluent WTO
members.

A second problem is what some countries have
called the 'politicization' of the dispute settlement
system. One issue is the tendency, in some countries that have lost WTO cases, for governments to
come under political criticism for permitting unwarranted foreign interference in domestic policies.
Such criticism inevitably forces government officials to take political acceptability (as well as WTO
law) into account when deciding how to implement
dispute settlement decisions. A second issue is the
decision of the Appellate Body to accept *amicus curiae* briefs from environmental non-governmental
organizations (NGOs) in the Shrimp–Turtle case
between the United States and a number of developing countries. The Appellate Body took this
action to address criticisms that by refusing to accept inputs from NGOs (such as, for example, the
World Wildlife Fund or Greenpeace), the WTO

dispute settlement system was undemocratic and not inclusive. However, the action of accepting legal briefs from NGOs undercut the concept of the WTO as an organization having nation states as members, especially when some poorer WTO members might not have the capability or financial resources to submit *amicus curiae* briefs themselves, even if they had the legal right to do it. Thus, in attempting to increase the democratic inclusiveness between developed country governments and the NGOs that are their domestic constituents, the democratic inclusiveness and juridical equality of the developing country members of the WTO is called into question.

In spite of such problems, dispute settlement is functioning reasonably well in the WTO, and, indeed, it is the cornerstone of the regime. Any system of rules requires a judicial function to interpret and apply the rules to specific cases, and the WTO system continues to serve the interests of the members. However, the rules are not always clear, and some judicial interpretation will be necessary to apply the rules to specific cases. As a result, panels and the Appellate Body will continue to face difficult decisions in which criticism is inevitable but outright condemnation is unlikely.

Negotiations

One of the major tasks of the WTO is to promote trade negotiations. This task is mandated in the WTO Agreement, which calls on the organization 'to provide a forum for negotiation' on matters arising under the Uruguay Round Agreements, and on further issues concerning the multilateral trade relations of the members. This mandate is more precise than that which existed under the GATT. However, the sponsorship of negotiations did arise by customary practice under the GATT, and in time those negotiations proved their value in terms of forwarding the agenda of trade liberalization. Hence, the WTO Agreement effectively codified GATT customary practice, and built negotiation of new issues into the organizational mission of the WTO.

The WTO moved quickly after 1995 to carry out its mandate to sponsor negotiations. In the area of trade in services, the Uruguay Round had concluded without commitments forthcoming from members in financial or telecommunications services. These became subjects of new negotiations, and by 1997 the WTO was able to announce major new agreements in both areas. The telecom agreement produced new liberalizing commitments from sixty-nine governments covering 90 per cent of global telecom revenues, while the financial services agreement included fifty-six scheduled offers from seventy countries (counting the EU as fifteen countries). Most important, the United States participated in both agreements, and dropped its previous refusal to apply concessions to all other participating countries on the basis of the most-favoured nation principle.

Further, in 1997, another negotiation concluded that was novel and not a continuation of the Uruguay Round. In March of that year, some forty governments concluded the WTO Ministerial Declaration on Trade in Information Technology Products (ITA) that freed trade on computer and telecommunications equipment. This agreement was concluded very quickly and it is significant because, together with the telecom agreement, it covers trade of a value equal to that of agriculture, automobiles, and textiles combined. These agreements represent the new economy in terms of commerce between nations, and it is clear that that commerce is now more liberalized than the commerce of the old economy.

In the areas of agriculture and trade in services, the Uruguay Round Agreements had included a 'built-in agenda' that called for new multilateral negotiations to start in 2000. These negotiations got under way, despite the failure of the Seattle Ministerial Conference in December 1999, which attempted to establish a mandate for a new round of negotiations in all areas. Thus, even allowing for the setback of Seattle, the WTO demonstrated it was capable of sponsoring new negotiations on a sectoral basis following the conclusion of the

Uruguay Round. Over time, it appears that negotiation has become less an exceptional part of the GATT/WTO regime and more part of the normal business of multilateral trade relations. The WTO is moving towards a regime of 'permanent negotiation', in which the organization begins to look more like a typical national legislature and less like the occasional diplomatic encounters of international relations.

The WTO Agreement calls for a ministerial meeting every two years, and the Seattle meeting of December 1999 provided an opportunity for some members to press for the commencement of a major new round of trade negotiations. As had been the case with the Uruguay Round, calls for a new negotiation occasioned a major rift in the multilateral trade regime. The European Union enthusiastically supported a new negotiation, and proposed a set of new issues including the controversial subjects of investment and competition policy. It was, however, less forthcoming on agricultural subsidies. The United States also favoured a new negotiation and proposed reductions in trade barriers in industrial goods, but it insisted on introducing trade sanctions to protect domestic policies related to labour and the environment. On agriculture, Washington continued its long-standing policy of making maximum demands on the European Union. For their part, the developing countries were opposed to the idea of a new negotiation, largely on the grounds that there was unfinished business from the Uruguay Round in the areas of agriculture, textiles, and TRIPs. Led by India and Brazil, the developing countries made the case that they had received a bad deal from the Uruguay Round, and that before any new negotiation could begin, some effort should be made to redress the inequities of the previous negotiation.

The Seattle Ministerial Conference was thus compromised by the conflicting positions of the various WTO members (Odell 2002). To this was added a bitter fight over the selection of the WTO director-general, which took place over the six months prior to Seattle and compromised the preparations normally required for success in any major ministerial

meeting. The meeting itself in Seattle was also compromised by street protests from groups opposed to the WTO and to globalization, and even by mismanagement of the negotiating agenda at the meeting itself. These factors combined to make the Seattle Ministerial Conference a spectacular failure. Ministers left Seattle without agreeing to launch a new round, and the collapse was so complete that no communiqué was produced promising the usual efforts at co-operation in the future.

Members were alarmed at the failure at Seattle, and recognized it as a test of the success of the WTO itself. Following the Seattle meeting, work continued at the technical level to bridge the many gaps between WTO members. It was recognized that the two-year cycle of ministerial meetings provides a stern test for the political viability of the organization, and members were determined to resolve as many problems as possible before the next meeting in the autumn of 2001.

Gradually, the major participants introduced concessions into their negotiating positions. The European Union reduced its expectations for new rules on investment and competition policy, and the US dropped its contentious demands on labour rights and the environment. There was also some promise of movement in agriculture, which has traditionally been the sticking point in GATT negotiations. Coupled with the increased flexibility shown by the participants, the WTO secretariat itself was better organized to mediate political differences and to manage the enormous detail associated with a large multilateral trade negotiation.

By September 2001, the most extreme positions had been modified and the parties had achieved a single negotiating text, which is the *sine qua non* for success in multilateral negotiation. By this time, it was clear that the major issues in the negotiation for the WTO membership were those of particular importance to the developing countries, mainly agriculture, and as well as a concern that had suddenly arisen on the world stage—the access to medicines needed to combat disease in poorer countries. Developing countries were fearful that the Intellectual Property Agreement (ie., TRIPs) negotiated in the Uruguay Round would prevent access to cheaper generic drugs to fight AIDS and other diseases that poorer societies were prey to, and they demanded a modification of the TRIPs agreement to permit discretion to override drug patents in the event of a national health emergency. Developed countries were generally unwilling to forgo concessions that had been achieved in the Uruguay Round, and the issue had festered for several years while the AIDS epidemic gathered momentum, particularly in Africa. The severity of the AIDS crisis brought moral pressure to bear on developed country governments and the pharmaceutical industry that had supported strong patent rights in the Uruguay Round.

The ministerial conference was held in Doha, Qatar, in November 2001 (see Box 5.4). The conference agenda was pre-negotiated and well prepared. In comparison to the Seattle draft declaration that had 402 pairs of square brackets in the text (which indicate disagreement), the draft declaration for the Doha meeting had only thirteen pairs of brackets remaining for ministerial decisions (Odell 2002). The Doha draft reflected the continuing effort at compromise that had characterized the discussions

since September. However, the TRIPs/health issue remained outstanding, and it was important enough that it threatened to cause the meeting to break down in disagreement. The stakes were high: for the developed countries, the TRIPs agreement represented an important security against the misappropriation, and even theft, of intellectual property, but for the developing countries, access to lower-cost generic medicines could easily be translated into lives saved or lost in the fight against AIDS and other diseases. An end to this impasse was eventually reached through an agreement to extend the date until 2016 for least developed countries to provide patents on pharmaceuticals, and by a formal affirmation that 'the TRIPs agreement does not and should not prevent Members from taking measures to protect public health'. The latter statement only reiterated rights that were already contained in the TRIPs agreement itself, but it was accepted by developing countries because it created a presumption that WTO members would be able to exercise their rights to procure generic medicines, and more important, that other members (particularly the US) would be unlikely to take dispute settlement actions against members that exercised those rights.

Box 5.4 Doha Round

The Doha Round was initiated by the WTO Doha Ministerial Declaration of 14 November 2001. It is the ninth multilateral trade negotiation to be conducted under the auspices of the GATT or WTO, and was originally scheduled to conclude not later than 1 January 2005. This deadline was compromised by the impasse that occurred between developed and developing countries at the Cancun WTO Ministerial meeting in September 2003. Following this setback, delegations managed to restore progress through the adoption of a Work Programme that focused the work of the negotiation on issues especially promoted by developing countries, namely agriculture, NAMA (non-agricultural market access, i.e., industrial tariffs), and to a lesser extent, trade in services. The Work

Programme also established a new deadline, December 2005, to occur concurrently with the Hong Kong Ministerial meeting.

The negotiation ran into difficulties in 2005, and was barely kept alive at the Hong Kong meeting. The main accomplishment of the meeting was to set a deadline in mid-2006 for the tabling of full modalities, as well as schedules of commitments, in the agricultural and NAMA negotiations. This task proved impossible. A new deadline was set for June 2007, and the negotiating parties once more failed to reach agreement. The scenario was repeated again in July 2008 in Geneva, with again the same result. In November 2009, at a regularly scheduled Ministerial meeting, the parties declined to negotiate the Doha Round issues at all. As the WTO entered the second decade of 2000, knowledgeable observers were claiming that the potential settlement on the table at the Doha Round was worth between $180 billion and $520 billion annually in trade benefits, but the parties were still unable to close the deal (Adler *et al.* 2009).

The mixture of *parties*, *issues*, and *negotiating environment* has helped to make the Doha Round irresolvable. First, parties. The 153 WTO Members at the Doha Round have organized themselves into many informal negotiating groups. However, in terms of negotiating behaviour, there are principally three parties responsible for the success or failure of the Round: the US, the EU, and a group of developing countries led mainly by Brazil and India. The developing countries are remarkably disparate, and range from least developed countries to economic giants such as China, India or Brazil. Developing countries are no longer powerless, and in terms of trade flows, which are an important indicator in the WTO, five of the developing country members are included in the world's top ten exporters and five are included in the top ten importers. The fact that the developing countries negotiate as a group makes it difficult to find proposals which Doha Round parties can support on the basis of consensus.

Second, issues. As the Doha Round moved forward, the main issues became further defined as agricultural subsidies, agricultural market access (mainly tariffs), and NAMA (again, mainly tariffs). In trade volume terms, the latter category simply dwarfs the former two. From the perspective of reaching an agreement, it is regrettable that the Doha Round has had a contracting agenda (unlike the Tokyo and Uruguay Rounds that had expanding agendas) that has come down as much as it has to tariffs. Tariffs are a tax, and money changes hands more clearly when tariffs are lowered than when other forms of restrictions are removed. They are hard to negotiate at any time. One would have to go back to the Kennedy Round of the 1960s to find a trade negotiation as much concerned over tariffs as the Doha Round. That negotiation was conducted mainly between like-minded developed countries, and it nearly failed to end in an agreement.

Third, negotiating environment. The environment of a negotiation is largely established by its objectives, which in GATT/WTO negotiations are usually set out in the ministerial declaration creating the negotiation. In the Doha Declaration, the objectives specified by all signatories clearly identified the main concern to be the betterment of developing and least developed countries. This was expressed in statements of belief, such as that trade could play a major role in economic development and the alleviation of poverty; and in statements of action, such as the intent to place the needs of the developing countries at the heart of the Doha Work Programme. The effect of these statements was to place the development goals, and moreover the related trade policies, at the centre of the concerns of the Doha Round negotiations. These statements were surely intended to be inspirational, but their effect has been to legitimize the aspirations of developing countries and to delegitimize the aspirations of developed countries. In negotiations, parties usually have offensive and defensive interests, and they attempt to balance off the losses on one side with the winnings on the other. In the Doha Round, the developed countries generally have not succeeded in achieving their requests made to developing countries (such as for the liberalization of trade in services), which is reflected in US President Barak Obama's call in late 2009 for greater market access from developing countries. Whatever else, a negotiated agreement must be sold in any country on the basis of gains versus losses, which is true of developed as well as developing countries.

In addition to the parties, issues, and negotiating environment, the Doha Round has also been bedevilled by the procedures adopted for this negotiation. Most multilateral tariff negotiations have ultimately been conducted bilaterally or plurilaterally by countries that have complementary interests as exporters or importers, and the results were recorded and accumulated at the end of the negotiation. This was known as an 'item-by-item approach'. In the Doha Round, the parties pursued a formula approach, which called upon parties: first, to negotiate a formula; second, to negotiate the numbers (for example, coefficients) to be inserted in the formula; and, third, to accept the implications of the formula for their national tariff schedule. For example, in the NAMA negotiation, parties agreed to a 'Swiss' formula for cutting industrial tariffs, as follows:

$Z = AX/(A + X)$, where X = initial tariff rate, A = coefficient, and Z = resulting lower tariff rate.

This formula provides that the lower the coefficient that is introduced, the greater is the tariff reduction, and the lower is the final tariff. It goes without saying that different groups of countries (for example, developed vs developing) would seek to select as coefficients those numbers that advantaged them in the negotiation. Analogous procedures were introduced for handling other areas of the negotiation, such as agricultural tariffs or subsidies.

It was said in support of the formula approach that, once the formula and coefficients had been selected, the major task of the negotiation was completed. This may have been true, but the fact remains that negotiating parties have been extraordinarily reluctant to commit to the formula approach and the results that it produces for countries' tariff schedules. The process of placing numbers into the formulas has been referred to by the WTO as the achievement of 'modalities', and this process has been the major hang-up in the negotiation since 2006. The modalities that are currently used in the WTO are taken from the best estimates of acceptable values by chairpersons of Doha Round negotiating groups (for example, the NAMA negotiating group), but they have not yet been accepted by the parties themselves. Until this happens, the Doha Round will not move into the final phase of the negotiation, which is to apply the agreed formulas (plus any agreed exceptions) and calculate the resulting new tariffs.

The resolution of the TRIPs/health issue ensured the success of the Doha meeting, although it would take another twenty-one months to eliminate the final obstacles to cheaper drug imports (WTO 2003*b*). With the success of the Doha meeting, the WTO members formally initiated a new multilateral negotiation, with a deadline of December 2004. The agenda comprised twelve wide-ranging issues, the focus of the negotiation was development, and in keeping with this focus the WTO members eschewed the term 'Round' in favour of the title Doha Development Agenda (DDA). However, despite this effort to promote change, the term 'Doha Round' soon reappeared in the vocabulary of the new WTO negotiation.

In its short history, the WTO suffered a serious setback in the Seattle Ministerial Conference, and then rebounded to launch a new multilateral negotiation in the Doha Ministerial Conference. The latter meeting laid out an agenda for the negotiation, and the negotiation went forward, but it was met with frequent delays and progress was slow. The first major deadline for the DDA was the ministerial meeting in Cancun, Mexico, in September 2003, at which time the Declaration from the meeting was to take the form of an updated agenda and progress report on the DDA. In Cancun, the WTO members were unable to reach consensus on a Ministerial Declaration. Once again, the WTO met with failure.

The issues on which the negotiation broke down were investment and competition policy, which were pressed by the European Union and Japan, but opposed vigorously by a group of mainly African developing countries. However, behind these issues was the far greater problem of agriculture, where, again, developing countries were intent to register their displeasure at the agricultural subsidy practices of the United States and the European Union. For example, four West African producers of cotton demanded a sectoral initiative to eliminate cotton subsidies in countries such as the US, the EU, and China, but they received a response suggesting that African countries should diversify their production, a message they interpreted as telling them to stop growing cotton. This response inflamed the Africans, and added to the antipathy that threatened to spiral out of control at the conference.

The deadline for the Doha Round was made impossible to achieve by the impasse that occurred between developed and developing countries at the Cancun meeting. Following this setback, delegates managed to get the negotiation back on the rails with a new approach to the Doha Work Programme adopted in the 'July Package' by the WTO General Council on 1 August 2004. The July Package extended the Doha Round deadline beyond January 2005, and established December 2005 for the next Ministerial Conference in Hong Kong. Most importantly, it singled out the subjects of agriculture (subsidies and tariffs), non-agricultural market access—NAMA (mainly, industrial tariffs), and, to a lesser degree trade in services, for priority attention in the negotiation. Additionally, the July Package reaffirmed the importance of a sectoral negotiation on cotton, and agreed to pursue the matter in the negotiations on agriculture.

The negotiation slowed in early 2005, with developing countries pressing developed countries, mainly regarding agriculture, while the latter insisted they could not take unilateral action on agriculture without receiving reciprocal concessions on industrial tariffs and services from developing countries. In the Hong Kong Ministerial Conference in December 2005, gruelling negotiations kept the Round alive, but they failed to produce the specific numbers or formulas needed to move to the next level of bargaining over tariffs and subsidies. The Meeting produced an agreement to eliminate agricultural subsidies by the year 2013, but beyond that its major accomplishment was to set a deadline of 30 April 2006 for the tabling of full modalities (that is, the numbers inserted into tariff and subsidy-cutting formulas) in agriculture and NAMA. The WTO director-general, Pascal Lamy, claimed this action had put the troubled Doha Round 'back on track'.

Negotiators failed to solve the problem of modalities by the 30 April deadline, however, and they failed in subsequent meetings over the following months. By most accounts, the major blockage occurred over agriculture, with the European Union unwilling to make substantial reductions on agricultural tariffs, and the United States unprepared to offer significant concessions on agricultural subsidies. Then, too, developing countries as a group were disinclined to make much movement on industrial tariffs or services. By 2007, a profound malaise had enveloped the negotiation.

Beneath the difficulties of the Doha Round lay a subtle change in the politics of the WTO. The GATT was the creation of developed countries, and up to the Uruguay Round the developing countries were largely passive bystanders in the evolution of the international trade regime. This changed with the creation of the WTO, and this change has since accelerated, particularly with the accession of China to full WTO membership (WTO 2001b). At the Cancun Ministerial Conference, a group of developing countries formed a coalition, known generally as the G20 countries, that succeeded in polarizing much of the debate into a North–South struggle. The basis for this polarization was the firm belief of the G20 that the benefits of the trade regime have not been proportioned equitably between developed and developing countries, especially in terms of the results of the Uruguay Round Agreements. This is a belief that is increasingly given some credence by observers of international economics, and will have to be addressed by the organization in the future if progress is to be achieved in the international trade regime (*Economist* 2003).

Key points

- The WTO is a rules-based international organization that operates on the basis of consensus. Members are legally bound to act in ways that are consistent with the rules they have negotiated, as interpreted by the dispute settlement mechanism.

- The work of the WTO is carried out by a series of committees supported by a small international secretariat. The dispute settlement mechanism has been especially active.

- The WTO has promoted further negotiated agreements in financial and telecommunications services, and in trade in information technology products.

- The WTO Agreement calls for a Ministerial Conference every two years. In December 1999, in Seattle, Washington State, US, some members sought support to commence a new multilateral negotiation, but the meeting concluded without agreement. In November 2001, in Doha, Qatar, following lengthy pre-negotiations between developed and developing countries, WTO Ministers agreed to initiate a new negotiation with a deadline of December 2004.

GILBERT R WINHAM

Conclusion

The start of the Doha negotiation was a reaffirmation of the direction the world trade regime has taken since the middle of the twentieth century. The focus of the regime has been to create rules whereby countries can exchange goods and services with a minimum of interference from national governments, and the means to accomplish that task has been to reach agreements through international negotiation. Such agreements are an important form of regulation, or system management, in the international economy. Trade has always been regulated, but in the past that regulation has mainly been done unilaterally by national governments, and has always posed a potential threat to trade and the stability of the international economy, as events of the 1930s amply demonstrated. Today, the regulation of trade is carried out as much through the negotiation of trade agreements as through the actions of domestic agencies, the purpose being to replace inward-looking national regulation with a broader conception of international rules. There is a need to keep the trade system moving in a liberal direction consistent with an open international society, because the alternatives to an open society—witnessed in the inter-war period in the twentieth century—were so damaging to the interests of all countries.

The GATT, and now the WTO, are central features of the international trade system. Through negotiations in these institutions, analogous to lawmaking in domestic parliaments, countries have been able to establish a rules-based regime for regulating international trade. The negotiation process is critically important to the success of the WTO, but it is a fickle and sometimes fragile process. When it is successful, the rules of the regime are advanced, and all countries can be said to benefit from the greater stability and predictability that comes from a regime based on rules rather than on the play of power politics. But the negotiation process is not always successful, and just as an absence of consensus occasionally paralyses the legislative agenda in domestic parliaments, the absence of consensus also stops the WTO from dealing with problems that many members think need to be addressed. If there is a major difference between domestic parliaments and the WTO, it is that an impasse in the former rarely calls into question the survival of the institution, whereas when an impasse occurs in the WTO, there is always the fear that the organization will be eclipsed, and that countries will use other means, including unilateral actions, to resolve the problems they face in the trade system. Thus, an analogy is often made between the WTO and a bicycle: both need to maintain forward momentum in order to remain stable.

As it looks to the future, the greatest challenge facing the WTO will be to incorporate the developing countries fully into a liberal international trade regime. Included in the Preamble to the WTO Agreement is a statement expressing the need that developing countries should 'secure a share in the growth in international trade commensurate with the needs of their economic development'. The Cancun Meeting was a political wake-up call that the developing countries will use their negotiating power to realize their aspirations in the Doha negotiation and beyond. Since the 1950s, the GATT and WTO have endured despite many challenges, but the task of implementing a global and inclusive trade regime will be the most imposing test of all.

Key points

- A Ministerial Conference in September 2003, in Cancun, Mexico, failed to find consensus on a Declaration designed to advance the work of the Doha negotiation.
- The greatest future challenge to the WTO is to find consensus between the developed and developing members of the organization.

? Questions

1. What are the basic components of the international trade regime? Give examples.

2. What was the effect of the US Reciprocal Trade Agreements Act of 1934?

3. What does non-discrimination mean in international trade; and how is it put into effect by the rules of the GATT?

4. Compare the results of the Kennedy and Tokyo Rounds of GATT multilateral trade negotiations.

5. What was the role of the developing countries in the Uruguay Round negotiation; and why was it historically significant?

6. What were the challenges encountered in negotiating rules for trade in services in the Uruguay Round negotiation?

7. How does the WTO differ from the GATT?

8. What is the WTO Dispute Settlement Understanding (DSU); why is it necessary; and what are some of the difficulties with its operations?

9. What are the challenges for the WTO in conducting the multilateral trade negotiation known as the Doha Development Agenda?

→ Further reading

■ Bhagwati, J. (1988), *Protectionism* (Cambridge, MA: MIT Press). A short but incisive review of the history, ideology, and practice of the trade policy of protectionism.

■ Bhagwati, J. (1991), *The World Trading System at Risk* (Princeton, NJ: Princeton University Press). An analysis of the challenges to the trading system that the Uruguay Round negotiation was intended to counter.

■ Condliffe, J. B. (1950), *The Commerce of Nations* (New York: W. W. Norton). A penetrating history of international trade that makes use of the memorable concept of the contest between enterprise and regulation.

■ Croome, J. (1995), *Reshaping the World Trading System: A History of the Uruguay Round* (Geneva: World Trade Organization). An official history of the Uruguay Round noted for its detail and accuracy.

■ Jackson, J. H. (1998), *The World Trade Organization: Constitution and Jurisprudence* (London: Pinter). An analysis of the WTO legal regime by a foremost scholar of international trade law.

■ Jones, V. C. (2006) 'WTO: Antidumping Issues in the Doha Development Agenda', CRS Report for Congress (Washington, DC: Congressional Research Service, Library of Congress). An up-to-date and informative review of anti-dumping practices.

■ Ostry, S. (1997), *The Post-Cold War Trading System: Who's on First* (Chicago, IL: University of Chicago Press). A masterful history of international trade from 1945 onwards that blends economics, politics, and law into a rounded analysis of the subject.

■ Preeg, E. H. (1995), *Traders in a Brave New World: The Uruguay Round and the Future of the International Trading System* (Chicago, IL: University of Chicago Press). A well-organized review of the major events of the negotiation that created the current international trade regime.

■ Rosecrance, R. (1986), *The Rise of the Trading State: Commerce and Conquest in the Modern World* (New York: Basic Books). A comprehensive treatment of the history of trading relations.

■ Winham, G. R. (1992), *The Evolution of International Trade Agreements* (Toronto: University of Toronto Press). A review of trade agreements from antiquity to the mid Uruguay Round, based on the 1991 Bissell Lectures at the University of Toronto.

■ WTO Secretariat (2000), *From GATT to the WTO: The Multilateral Trading System in the New Millennium* (Geneva: World Trade Organization). A collection of authoritative papers by noted experts on international trade and trade policy.

:// Web links

■ The main link for international trade is the WTO link: www.wto.org.

Other useful links are national ministries of international trade that can be found via Google, such as www.ustr.gov (United States) or www.international.gc.ca/menu.aspx (Canada).

Online resource centre

For additional material and resources, please visit the Online Resource Centre at: www.oxfordtextbooks.co.uk/ravenhill3e

6

Regional Trade Agreements

John Ravenhill

 Chapter contents

- Introduction
- Why Regionalism?
- The Rush to Regionalism
- The Political Economy of Regionalism
- The Economic Consequences of Regional Integration
- Regionalism and the WTO: Stepping Stone or Stumbling Block?

 Reader's guide

The number of regional trade agreements has grown rapidly since the World Trade Organization (WTO) came into existence in 1995. Roughly one-half of world trade is now conducted within these preferential trade arrangements, the most significant exception to the WTO's principle of non-discrimination. Governments have often entered regional economic agreements primarily motivated by political rather than economic considerations. Nonetheless, they may prefer trade liberalization on a regional rather than a global basis for several economic reasons. This chapter reviews the political economy of regionalism: why regional trade agreements are established, which actors are likely to support regional rather than global trade liberalization, the effects that regionalism has had on the trade and welfare of members and non-members, and the relationship between liberalization at the regional and global levels.

Introduction

When the Japanese prime minister, Junichiro Koizumi, and his Singaporean counterpart, Goh Chok Tong, signed a bilateral trade agreement in January 2002, Japan departed from the rapidly depleting ranks of WTO members that were not parties to a discriminatory trade arrangement. By the end of 2006, of the WTO's 150 members only one, Mongolia, was not a party to one or more regional trade agreements (RTAs). These take various forms ranging, in scope of cooperation, from free trade areas to economic unions (Box 6.1).

For most of the post-war period, the concept of regional economic integration has usually been associated with an arrangement between three or more geographically contiguous states. The EU is the best known of such arrangements, but consider also East African Cooperation (Kenya, Tanzania, and Uganda), and the Andean Community of Nations (Bolivia, Colombia, Ecuador, Peru, Venezuela). In recent years, however, a large number of preferential trade agreements (PTAs) have been signed that involve only two parties (for example, China–Hong Kong), and sometimes these bilateral agreements link parties that are not geographically contiguous (for example, Korea and Chile). Because non-global agreements are subject to the scrutiny of the WTO's Committee on Regional Trade Agreements, however, they are also frequently labelled 'regional'. Whether such terminology is appropriate is questionable (some commentators suggest that since many of the recent agreements are not regional in the conventional geographical sense and do not free all trade between the parties, they are better termed 'preferential' rather than 'regional' or 'free' trade agreements). But it is not just the terminology that is problematic: the arguments of the large body of theoretical work on regional integration, which was developed with groupings involving multiple members from the same geographical region in mind, may not be applicable to arrangements that involve only two parties or those that involve states that are not geographical neighbours.

Table 6.1 demonstrates the complexity of the current configuration of 'regional' arrangements—essentially all strategies for trade liberalization that fall between unilateral action at the one extreme and negotiations at the global level in the WTO at the other. Bilateral agreements can occur either between neighbours or between countries that are far removed from one another. Regionalism, as conventionally understood, is a *minilateral* relationship, that is, one that involves more than two countries, on a geographically concentrated basis, for example, NAFTA or the Association of Southeast Asian Nations (ASEAN) Free Trade Area (AFTA) (Table 6.5, at the end of the chapter, lists the principal minilateral regional trade groupings). In recent years, however, two other forms of minilateral groupings have emerged among members that are geographically dispersed. *Transregional* groupings link individual countries located in different parts of the world. A good example is the Asia-Pacific Economic Cooperation (APEC) grouping, whose membership comprises twenty-one countries from the Americas, Asia, Oceania, and Europe (Russia). Many of the recently negotiated bilateral RTAs, for instance, US–Jordan, Singapore–New Zealand, link countries from different geographical areas. *Interregional* arrangements join two established minilateral economic arrangements, as between the European Union and MERCOSUR (Argentina, Brazil, Paraguay, and Uruguay), and ASEAN and the Australia–New Zealand Closer Economic Relations Trade Agreement (ANZCERTA). By the end of 2006, more than twenty-five transregional and interregional agreements were operational.

Regional integration arrangements are usually categorized as a hierarchy that runs from free trade areas through customs unions and **common markets** to economic unions. The terminology of 'hierarchy' is used because each level incorporates all the provisions of the lower level of integration. This does not imply that particular regional arrangements will necessarily progress from a lower to a higher level of integration. Nor is it the case that regional partnerships inevitably begin at the lowest level and then move to 'deeper' integration: some arrangements, for instance, have been established as customs unions.

A *free trade area* exists when countries remove tariffs and **non-tariff barriers (NTBs)** to the free movement of goods and services between them. Governments, meanwhile, are free to choose how they treat goods and services imported from non-regional-partner states. Membership in one free trade area therefore does not prevent a country from establishing or joining other free trade areas: Mexico, for example, is a party to agreements with more than thirty countries. Because free trade areas impose relatively few constraints on national decision-making autonomy, they are the easiest of the regional arrangements to negotiate. More than 90 per cent of regional partnerships take the form of free trade areas. Examples include signatories to the North American Free Trade Agreement (NAFTA), the Japan–Singapore Economic Partnership Agreement, and the Baltic Free Trade Area.

A **customs union** goes beyond the removal of barriers to trade within the region to adopt a common set of policies towards imports from countries outside the region. This includes agreement on a common level of tariffs (often referred to as a 'common external tariff') on all extra-regional imports. Such agreements inevitably cost governments autonomy in their foreign economic policies (joint institutions are usually required to negotiate and administer the common external trade policies). They will also have distributive effects, depending on the level at which the common external tariff is set for various items. Consequently, customs unions are usually more difficult to negotiate than are free trade areas. The relatively small number of customs unions includes the Andean Community, Caribbean Community and Common Market (CARICOM), Common Market of the South (MERCOSUR, comprising Argentina, Brazil, Paraguay, and Uruguay), and the Southern African Customs Union. Many have experienced difficulties in negotiating a common external tariff. Even in the European Union (EU), individual states maintained different tariffs on some products for more than thirty years after its formation. MERCOSUR's negotiation of a common external tariff took fifteen years longer than anticipated, it applied to only three-quarters of total products, and even then was not accepted by two of its associate members, Bolivia and Peru.

A *common market* includes a customs union and also allows for free movement of labour and capital within the regional partnership. Such free flows of factors of production inevitably require governments to collaborate in additional policy areas to ensure comparable treatment in all countries within the common market. Historically, few governments have been willing to accept the loss of policy-making autonomy that occurs in a common market. The Andean Community, CARICOM, the COMESA (Common Market for Eastern and Southern Africa) grouping, and MERCOSUR have committed themselves to work for the establishment of a common market but it is too early to judge whether their aspirations will be realized.

An *economic union* includes a common market plus the adoption of a common currency and/or the harmonization of monetary, fiscal, and social policies. Only the European Union has reached this level of economic integration.

Many of the free trade agreements signed in recent years also include provisions for 'deeper' integration, the most common of which relate to the removal of restrictions on investment flows. But even though these are elements often found in common markets, these free trade areas do not aspire to the creation of a common external tariff or to the free flow of labour within the regional grouping.

Table 6.1 Example of the Geographical Scope of Trade Liberalization Strategies

Unilateral	Bilateral		Minilateral			Global
	Geographically concentrated	Geographically dispersed	Geographically concentrated	Geographically dispersed		
	Bilateral within region	Bilateral trans-regional	Regionalism	Trans-regionalism	Inter–regionalism	
Trade liberalization in SE Asia, Australia, and NZ in 1980s and 1990s	Australia–New Zealand CER[b] Trade Agreement	Singapore–USA	NAFTA	APEC[a]	EU–MERCOSUR CER[b]–AFTA	GATT/WTO

[a]Unlike the other RTAs discussed in this chapter, APEC is not a discriminatory arrangement (its members have pledged to reduce their trade barriers on imports from all sources).

[b]CER = Closer Economic Relations *Source*: Adapted from Aggarwal (2001: 238)

One of the few issues on which writers on regionalism agree is that there is no such thing as a 'natural' region. Regions are social constructions whose members define their boundaries. Consider, for instance, the European Union: in its successive incarnations—European Economic Community, European Community, and, now, the European Union—its membership has risen from its six founders to the current total of twenty-seven. And debates over EU membership for Turkey show that no consensus exists on either geographic or cultural criteria that could be used to distinguish the 'European' from the 'non-European'.

Regional trade agreements are one example of regionalism, which is a formal process of inter-governmental collaboration between two or more states. It should be distinguished from *regionalization*, which refers to the growth of economic interdependence within a given geographical area. RTAs are the most important exception that the WTO permits to the principle that countries should not discriminate in their treatment of other members. Parties to regional arrangements are obliged to notify the WTO of the details of their agreements; the Committee on Regional Trade Agreements has responsibility for ensuring that the agreements comply with the WTO's provisions (for agreements only involving developing economies, the responsibility lies with the Committee on Trade and Development). World Trade Organization data reflect the explosion in the number of regional arrangements that has occurred since the early 1990s. Throughout its entire existence from 1948 to 1994, the General Agreement on Tariffs and Trade (GATT) received 142 notifications of regional trade agreements, of which only 65 were still in force when it was replaced by the WTO. Between 1995 and December 2008, the WTO received notification of a further 279 agreements. Of this total of 421 agreements, 230 were in force at the end of 2008. The WTO estimated that if agreements that had not been notified to it—those currently under negotiation and discussion were taken into account—a total of close to 400 RTAs were scheduled to be operational by 2010 (www.wto.org/english/tratop_e/region_e/region_e.htm, accessed 21 February 2010). This growth in the number of arrangements has led to a marked increase in the share of global trade conducted within RTAs, now accounting for roughly one-half of world trade (but note that not all trade between regional partners benefits from treatment better than that offered to non-members—the most-favoured nation tariff may be zero; moreover, companies may decide not to do the paperwork required to gain the preferential access these agreements afford (see below).

Three sets of rules in the WTO permit the creation of RTAs:

- Article XXIV of the GATT lays down conditions for the establishment and operation of free trade agreements and customs unions covering trade in goods.

- The Enabling Clause, formally the 1979 Decision on Differential and More Favourable Treatment, Reciprocity and Fuller Participation of Developing Countries, permits regional agreements among developing countries on trade in goods.

- Article V of the General Agreement on Trade in Services (GATS) establishes conditions that permit liberalization of trade in services among regional partners.

At the end of 2006, of the 214 RTAs in force, 147 came under the auspices of Article XXIV, 45 were under GATS Article V (the most rapidly growing category of agreement), and 22 under the Enabling Clause (WTO 2006*b*). The last of these categories includes what could become the world's largest preferential market, the China–ASEAN Free Trade Area.

Why do governments choose to pursue their foreign economic policy objectives through regionalism rather than through other strategies? What explains the recent growth in regionalism? What economic and political interests are driving trade agreements at the regional level? What impact do regional agreements have on the economies and on the political systems of participants? And what are the consequences of the growth of RTAs for the global trading system? These are the principal questions that this chapter addresses (our focus is on trade rather than the recent growth in regional collaboration on finance).

Why Regionalism?

Economists assert that an economy's welfare can be maximized, other than in exceptional circumstances, if governments lower trade barriers on a non-discriminatory basis (either through unilateral action or through negotiations at the global level that adhere to the WTO's principle of non-discrimination). Regional trade agreements, on the other hand, can reduce global welfare by distorting the allocation of resources, and may even lead to welfare losses for their members (see Box 6.2). Moreover, from the political scientist's perspective, it is usually more efficient to negotiate a single agreement with a large number of states than to undertake a series of negotiations with individual states or with small groupings

(because it both economizes on the resources needed for negotiations and increases the opportunities for trade-offs in reaching a package deal).

Why, then, has regionalism not only been attractive to governments throughout the post-war period but has apparently become increasingly so in the last two decades? Governments usually have multiple motives in entering an arrangement as complex as a regional partnership: it would be naive to expect to find a single factor that explains governments' actions across all regional agreements. Moreover, governments often enter regional economic agreements primarily for political rather than economic reasons.

Box 6.2 The Costs and Benefits of Preferential Trade Agreements: Trade Diversion and Trade Creation

Jacob Viner (1950) was the first author to present a systematic assessment of the economic costs and benefits of regional economic integration, and to demonstrate, contrary to the then conventional wisdom, that a selective removal of tariffs might not be welfare enhancing. He argued that increased trade between parties to a regional arrangement can occur through two mechanisms. Trade creation occurs when imports from a regional partner displace goods that have been produced domestically at higher cost, goods that can no longer compete once the tariffs on imports from the regional partner are removed. Trade diversion occurs when imports from a regional partner displace those that originated outside the regional arrangement, the displacement occurring because the extra-regional imports are no longer price competitive when the tariffs on trade within the region are removed. Consider, for instance, a hypothetical example of what might happen with the implementation of the North American Free Trade Agreement (Table 6.2 below). Let's assume that Indonesia was the lowest-cost source of imported cotton T-shirts for the United States. Before the implementation of NAFTA, when all countries faced the same level of tariffs on their exports to the US market, its T-shirts were preferred to the higher-cost production of Mexican firms. Assume that the tariff on T-shirts was 10 per cent, the cost of manufacturing and delivering an Indonesian T-shirt to the US was $5 while that for a Mexican T-shirt was $5.40. Adding the 10 per cent tariff to the costs of manufacturing and delivery, the price paid by the importer before NAFTA would be $5.50 for an Indonesian shirt and $5.94 for a Mexican shirt.

Following the implementation of NAFTA, however, the tariff on imported T-shirts from Mexico is removed.

For the importer, the Mexican T-shirt is now the least expensive ($5.40) because it is no longer subject to tariffs, while the Indonesian product will still face a 10 per cent tariff and still costs the importer $5.50. Assuming that the importer chooses the lowest-cost product, imports will be switched after the regional scheme goes into effect from the lowest-cost producer (Indonesia) to Mexico, a relatively expensive producer, which now benefits from zero tariffs in the US market.

Several consequences follow from this trade *diversion*. The consumer in the USA *may* gain because the cost to the importer of purchasing a T-shirt falls from $5.50 to $5.40 (although the producer/wholesaler/retailer may be able to capture some or all of this gain). The US government, however, loses the tariff revenue (50 cents for each imported T-shirt) that it previously derived from taxing Indonesian T-shirt imports (the new imports from Mexico not being subject to a tariff). For the US economy as whole, therefore, the potential gain to consumers is significantly exceeded by the loss of tariff revenue (which is, of course, a form of taxation income for the government). Considered again from the perspective of the US economy, real resources are wasted because more money is being spent than would be the case if free trade prevailed ($5.40 compared with $5.00 for each imported T-shirt). And, unless exceptional circumstances prevail, the Indonesian economy will also suffer a welfare loss because of the decline in export revenue it experiences (and with the loss of the US market, it may also have to lower the price of its T-shirt exports to compete in other markets).

If trade diversion outweighs trade creation, then the net effect of a regional scheme on its members' welfare can be negative.

Table 6.2 The Potential for Trade Diversion after the Removal of Tariffs on Intra-Regional Trade ($)

	Cost of production	Tariff cost pre-NAFTA	Cost to importer pre-NAFTA	Tariff post-NAFTA	Cost to importer post-NAFTA
Indonesia	5.00	0.50 (10%)	5.50	0.50(10%)	5.50
Mexico	5.40	0.54 (10%)	5.94	Zero	5.40

Political motivations for entering regional trade agreements

Economic co-operation and confidence building

Regionalism frequently involves the use of economic means for political ends: the improvement of inter-state relations and/or the enhancement of security within a region. In international relationships that have a history of conflict or where no tradition of partnership exists, co-operation on economic matters can be a core element in a process of confidence building.

The origins of post-war European economic integration provide an excellent example. The European Coal and Steel Community (ECSC), created by the 1951 Treaty of Paris, was the first of the institutions of what eventually was to evolve into the European Union. The ECSC, founded by France, West Germany, Italy, Belgium, the Netherlands, and Luxembourg, pooled the coal and steel resources (perceived as critical to any military capacity) of its members by providing a unified market for these commodities; it also created a unified labour market in this sector. The underlying objective was to manage the rebuilding of Germany's economy post-war and to integrate it with those of its neighbours, thereby helping to restore confidence amongst countries whose conflicts had embroiled the world in two major wars.

In a similar fashion, the Association of Southeast Asian Nations, ASEAN, was founded in 1967 to promote economic co-operation in an attempt to build confidence and avoid conflict in a region that was the site of armed struggles in the Cold War era. Two of its founding members, Indonesia and Malaysia, had engaged in armed conflict in the period 1963–6 as the Indonesian government of President Sukarno attempted to destabilize the newly independent Malaysia. Over the years, ASEAN membership expanded and the organization successfully used co-operation on economic matters to overcome deep-seated inter-state rivalries and suspicions. In 1998, one of the visions of ASEAN's founders was realized when its membership was expanded to include all ten of the countries of South East Asia (including Vietnam and Cambodia that had in the previous quarter of a century been at war with other ASEAN states and with one another).

In some instances, regional economic integration has been stimulated by a desire to enhance the security of regional partners against threats emanating from *outside* the membership of the regional arrangement. The Southern African Development Coordination Conference (SADCC), for instance, was founded in 1980 in an attempt to reduce members' dependence on South Africa during the apartheid era.

Regional economic co-operation and the 'new security agenda'

Offers by industrialized countries in recent years to extend regional economic co-operation to their less developed neighbours have frequently been encouraged by concerns about 'non-traditional' security threats emanating from less developed partners. Such threats include environmental damage, illegal migration, organized crime, drug smuggling, and international terrorism. Regional co-operation may help address these issues directly, for example, through NAFTA's provisions on the environment, or, proponents hope, indirectly by promoting economic development and thereby ameliorating the conditions that were perceived as fostering the security threats. Concerns about new security threats played a part in European enthusiasm for new agreements with Mediterranean states, and in US interest in extending NAFTA to other Western Hemisphere countries.

Regionalism as a bargaining tool

Many of the regional economic agreements that developing countries established in the 1950s through the 1970s were motivated by a desire to enhance their bargaining power with transnational corporations (TNCs) and with trading partners. They were often inspired by the work of the UN's Economic Commission for Latin America, and its principal theorist, Raul Prebisch, whose ideas were subsequently taken up by writers from the dependency school. Prebisch (1963, 1970) had argued that regional integration was essential to provide a sufficiently large market to enable the efficient local production of goods that had previously been imported. Moreover, a regional partnership would enhance bargaining power with external actors if the partners negotiated with one voice. One approach, as in the Andean Pact (founded in 1969 by Bolivia, Chile (which withdrew in 1976), Colombia, Ecuador, and Peru) was to adopt a system of region-wide industrial licensing. The intention was to prevent TNCs from gaining concessions by playing off governments of the region against one another, and to use the carrot of access to a larger regional market to extract concessions from potential investors.

Less developed countries (LDCs) have also used regional partnerships as a way of gaining more aid from donor countries and organizations. Over the years, various governments and international organizations have encouraged regional economic integration among developing countries and have set aside some of their aid budgets to promote regional projects. The European Union has been a particularly enthusiastic supporter of regionalism in other parts of the world, providing both financial assistance and technical support for other regional schemes.

Moreover, a World Bank study (2000: 20) notes that by pooling their diplomatic resources in a regional arrangement, less developed countries are sometimes able to achieve greater prominence in international relations and to negotiate agreements that would not be available if they had acted individually, and to ensure election of their representatives to key positions in international organizations. The best example of successful pursuit of this strategy, the Bank suggests, is the Caribbean Community and Common Market (CARICOM).

But it is not just developing countries that have perceived regional economic partnerships as a means for enhancing their bargaining power. The Japanese Ministry of Economy, Trade and Industry, for instance, in advocating participation in discriminatory regional arrangements, pointed to the possibility that by facilitating partnerships with like-minded countries they could increase Japan's leverage within the WTO (METI 2000). The foundation of APEC (in 1989) was linked to perceptions that it could help to pressure the European Union into trade concessions during GATT's Uruguay Round of trade negotiations (Ravenhill 2001). And some authors have suggested that the negotiation of the Treaty of Rome, which established the European Economic Community in 1957, was at least in part motivated by European countries' desires to increase their leverage against the United States in the upcoming GATT talks (Milward 1984, 1992).

Regionalism as a mechanism for locking-in reforms

Regional trade agreements can enhance the credibility of domestic economic reforms and thereby increase the attractiveness of economies to potential foreign investors (Rodrik 1989). Such considerations have become more important in an increasingly integrated global economy where countries are competing to stake their claims as preferred partners in global production networks (see Thun, Chapter 11 in this volume).

Commitments made within a regional forum can be more attractive to potential investors than those made in global institutions for several reasons. Countries' compliance with their commitments is likely to be more closely scrutinized within a regional grouping: the numbers of partners to be monitored is smaller than within the WTO with its 150 members, and any breaking of commitments is more likely to have a direct impact on regional partners and lead to swift retaliation. Some regional arrangements provide for regional institutions to monitor the implementation of agreements. Moreover, repeated interactions with a small number of partners within regional arrangements may make governments more concerned about their reputations (their credibility as collaborators) than they would be within more diffuse multilateral forums (Fernandez and Portes 1998).

Regional arrangements may be particularly effective in enhancing the credibility of commitments when less developed countries enter partnerships with an industrialized country as, for instance, in Mexico's participation in NAFTA (Haggard 1997). And the possibility that the policy coverage of the RTA may be more comprehensive than agreements at the global level—embracing, for instance, rules on competition policy and on the treatment of foreign investment—further enhances the potential of regional arrangements as a device for signalling to potential foreign investors the seriousness of a government's commitment to reform.

Regionalism to satisfy domestic political constituencies

Often, the choice of trade policies faced by governments is not between liberalization at the global level and liberalization at the regional level, but between entering a regional agreement and undertaking unilateral liberalization. In contrast to a unilateral lowering of tariffs, which is usually politically difficult for governments because domestic groups believe that the government is giving something away (tariff protection) and not receiving anything in return from other countries, a regional trade agreement provides a means for a government to ensure that it receives concessions (reciprocity) from its partners in return for those that it has offered. And, insofar as a regional agreement makes it easier politically for governments to undertake liberalization, and therefore enhances such activities, it may be beneficial not just to regional partners but to the wider international community.

Ease of negotiating and implementing agreements

The larger the number of states, the more likely it is that they will have a greater diversity of interests that will complicate negotiations. Moreover, the larger the number of members, the more difficult it is to monitor behaviour and to enforce sanctions in the event of non-compliance (Oye 1985; Keohane 1984). A regional agreement with a limited number of partners accordingly might be easier to negotiate and implement than one at the global level. This logic is particularly applicable to bilateral trade agreements.

On the other hand, numerous cases exist of large numbers of governments successfully concluding international agreements (within the United Nations, for instance, on issues that range from arms control to the environment to human rights (see, for example, Osherenko and Young 1993: 12)). Kahler (1992) has argued persuasively that success in solving the numbers problem depends upon institutional design (a problem that the WTO has yet to address effectively). Mechanisms for discussing issues and voting procedures can be adapted to counter the problems of numbers and diversity. A larger numbers of participants may bring potential for greater gains and more opportunities for trade-offs among the parties.

In short, the international relations literature is inconclusive on the relationship between the number of participants and the successful negotiation and implementation of agreements. There are plenty of instances where regional negotiations have failed to produce agreements or have taken a very long time to complete (for instance, a free trade agreement between Japan and Korea was proposed in 1998 but negotiations had not been successfully concluded by 2010). Of greater importance to shaping state action, however, are the perceptions that governments hold on this issue. And there is little doubt that many *believe* that regional agreements are easier to negotiate than those at the global level, given the numbers and diversity of WTO membership. The failure to conclude the Doha Round nearly a decade after negotiations began reinforced these beliefs.

Economic motivations for regionalism

Here, we can distinguish between two possibilities: (*a*) where governments, for economic reasons, prefer a regional economic agreement to unilateral liberalization or to a non-discriminatory multilateral agreement; and (*b*) where they prefer a regional agreement to the status quo.

Economic reasons for choosing regionalism over multilateralism

Regionalism enables continued protection of sectors that would not survive in global competition

Even though mainstream economic theory suggests that welfare gains will be maximized when trade liberalization occurs on a non-discriminatory basis, governments may, nonetheless, prefer a regional (discriminatory) trade agreement. This alternative is attractive, for instance, when they (and interest groups, such as manufacturers' or farmers' associations, which almost certainly will be actively lobbying the government) believe that domestic producers will be successful in competition with regional partners and will benefit from the larger (protected) market that a regional scheme creates, but that they would not survive a competition with producers located outside the region. Added to this, is the possibility (discussed in more detail later in this chapter) that governments will be able to exclude completely 'politically sensitive' non-competitive domestic sectors from the trade liberalization measures negotiated within a regional agreement, whereas such exclusion would be more difficult at the global level.

A more benign variant of this argument is that a reform-minded government may seek to enter a regional agreement as a way to expose inefficient domestic producers gradually to international competition, with the expectation that competition from regional partners will generate reforms that will eventually enable the sector to be exposed to full international competition. In this scenario, regionalism is a steppingstone to broader liberalization.

Regionalism provides opportunities for 'deeper integration'

Regionalism may be more attractive than a multilateral treaty to pro-liberalization governments because it enables agreement on issues that would not be possible in the WTO where membership is more diverse. Since the early 1990s, a number of governments, such as those of the United States, Singapore, Chile, and Australia, which have been seeking to raise the tempo of trade liberalization, have turned to regional agreements in an attempt to promote 'deeper integration'. This concept refers to co-operation that goes beyond the traditional liberalization menu of removing tariff and non-tariff barriers. It may include, for instance, agreements on the environment, on the treatment of foreign direct investment (FDI), on domestic competition (anti-trust) policies, on intellectual property rights, and on labour standards. The North American Free Trade Agreement was one of the first free trade agreements to incorporate provisions on many of these matters. As trade liberalization within the WTO reduced the significance of border barriers so matters of 'deeper integration' have grown in importance as governments seek to establish a level playing field with their partners.

A regional approach is more likely to facilitate reaching agreement on these politically sensitive issues if the partner states share certain characteristics, for example, similar levels of economic development. Regional agreements, especially bilateral free trade areas, may also enable more powerful states to bring their weight to bear more effectively on weaker parties, for whom the price of gaining security of access to a larger market may be to accept undertakings on issues of 'deeper integration', such as their treatment of foreign investment, etc. (on this issue of unequal bargaining power in regional agreements see Helleiner 1996; and Perroni and Whalley 1994).

Economic reasons for preferring regionalism to unilateralism or the status quo

Larger markets and increased foreign investment

Governments may not have the option of choosing between a regional agreement and an agreement at the global level: the latter may simply not be available at the time. The choice that governments face is to stick with the status quo, to liberalize on a unilateral basis, or to seek a regional agreement. Besides the political advantages, noted above, that a regional agreement often has over unilateral action, economic advantages may also come into play. Co-ordinated liberalization on a regional basis broadens the geographical scope of liberalization and may also enable a widening of the product coverage of the agreement, thereby increasing the potential economic gains.

Compared with the status quo, a regional economic agreement can confer two principal economic benefits. First, it provides a larger 'home' market for domestic industries, possibly enabling them to produce more efficiently because of economies of scale (see Box 6.3). How significant an advantage is gained from regionalism will depend on the number of partner economies and their

relative size: a firm in a large economy is unlikely to make significant gains in economies of scale if the regional partnership is with only a couple of much smaller economies.

Second, regionalism can increase the attractiveness of an economy to potential investors. Companies that previously supplied the separate national markets through exports from outside the region may now find that the unified regional market is of sufficient size to make local production (and hence foreign investment into the region) attractive. Gains from foreign direct investment may be particularly significant when a less developed country enters into a regional partnership with one or more industrialized economies. Companies may be able to take advantage of the relatively low-cost labour in the less developed country to supply the whole of the regional market from factories established there. A frequently cited example is the dramatic increase that occurred in foreign direct investment into Mexico following the signature of NAFTA in 1994. Inflows of FDI to Mexico, which averaged $8 billion per year in the period 1990–5, rose to $14 billion in 1997 and to $24 billion in 2001 (UNCTAD 2002: 304, annex table B.1). Some evidence also exists of similar effects elsewhere, for example, foreign direct investment inflows to ASEAN increased after it negotiated its free trade area (UNCTAD 2003: 47, box II.5).

Box 6.3 Economies of Scale

In modern manufacturing, which frequently depends on the use of expensive machinery and on very large investments in research and development, large-scale production often enables firms to produce at a lower average cost per unit. These *economies of scale* can result, not just from a more efficient use of machinery and of labour, but also because specialist managers and workers can be employed, savings can be made in borrowing on financial markets (which generally charge higher rates of interest to smaller borrowers), raw materials can be purchased more cheaply when bought in bulk, and advertising costs are spread across a higher volume of output.

A related concept is *economies of scope*. These occur when firms can spread various costs (including, for instance, research and development, accounting, marketing) across various products, which may—although not necessarily—be related (for instance, production of calculators and of LCD screens for laptop computers).

A related strategy is for governments to attempt to establish their economies as regional hubs. For a number of activities, companies will wish to establish only one office in a geographical area (it might, for instance, be a central office responsible for procurement, or for providing management services to all of the company's regional subsidiaries). One of the reasons why some governments appear to have chosen to negotiate multiple regional trade agreements is that this strategy enhances the prospects for attracting companies' 'regional' headquarters as the economy becomes a 'hub' for multiple regional 'spokes'. Singapore, an active proponent of regional trade agreements is a good example—it has a larger number of regional corporate headquarters than any other developing economy. Regional hubs may also be attractive to subsidiaries of **multinational enterprises (MNEs)** seeking to take advantage of the preferential access the RTAs provide to third-country markets. For instance, US subsidiaries operating in Singapore enjoy duty-free access to the Japanese market for their production (subject to meeting the rules of origin in Singapore's economic partnership agreement with Japan—see Box 6.4), something not always available to them if they exported to Japan from their home base in the US.

Key points

- Governments often enter regional trade agreements for political reasons. These include: enhancing security; improving their international bargaining positions; signalling to potential investors the seriousness of their commitment to reforms; to satisfy domestic constituencies' demands for 'reciprocity'; and because they perceive regional agreements are easier to negotiate than those within the WTO.

- Economic motivations for regionalism include access to a larger 'domestic' market; possibilities for attracting additional foreign direct investment; the possibility of engaging in 'deeper integration'; and the opportunity afforded to continue to protect politically sensitive, globally uncompetitive industries.

Box 6.4 Rules of Origin

Countries that enter into a free trade agreement inevitably are concerned that non-members should not exploit the benefits they provide to their partners. In particular, they fear that because free trade areas (unlike customs unions) do not have a common external tariff, non-members will send goods into the free trade area through the country with the lowest tariff, and then use the free trade provisions of the grouping to access other members' markets. This *trade deflection* will lead to a loss of tariff revenue for the economies with higher tariffs and possibly to greater competition for their domestic producers.

Consider, for instance, the following hypothetical example. Assume that Mexico has a 5 per cent tariff on cameras whereas Canada and the United States both have a 12 per cent tariff. If they were able to take advantage of the introduction of free trade under NAFTA, Japanese camera manufacturers would export their cameras to Mexico and supply Canada and the United States from these exports. Both the Canadian and US governments would lose tariff revenue that they would otherwise collect on imports of Japanese cameras. And Japanese cameras (now subject to a lower tariff) would become more competitive than they otherwise would have been with cameras produced in Canada and the United States.

To prevent free trade areas from causing trade deflection of this type, their members typically adopt what are called rules of origin. These are intended to ensure that goods will only benefit from the provisions of the free trade agreement if they can be considered to have 'originated', that is, to have been produced primarily in the partner country. Goods that are merely passing through the partner or, for instance, have been restamped as 'Made in Mexico', will not qualify for duty-free access to other members' markets. Determining where a product has originated has become increasingly difficult in an integrated global economy with goods often being assembled from components manufactured in various countries.

Rules of origin typically take one or more of the following forms:

(a) *A value-added criterion.* This specifies that a particular percentage of the value of the export must have been generated within the partner country. For instance, to qualify as a local product for the purposes of NAFTA, 62.5 per cent of the value of an automobile must have been generated locally.

(b) *A change of tariff heading criterion.* The World Customs Organization has developed a 'Harmonized System Nomenclature' of tariff headings that classifies all products according to their degree of processing, ranging from raw materials through semi-processed products to finished manufactures. Under this criterion, a good is considered to have been produced domestically if a change in tariff heading results from the local processing/manufacture.

(c) *A specific processing criterion.* This stipulates that particular stages in the production of the export must be undertaken locally. For instance, cloth may only be considered a local product if weaving has been conducted locally.

(d) *A specific components criterion.* This establishes that particular parts of the finished good must have been manufactured locally for it to qualify for duty-free treatment. In NAFTA, colour television sets are considered to be local products only if their picture tubes have been manufactured locally. Usually, rules of origin allow for 'cumulation' so that components sourced from partner countries are counted as if they have been produced domestically (so that, for instance, a colour TV manufactured in Mexico which contains a picture tube manufactured in the US would be classed as a local product for NAFTA rules of origin purposes).

As is evident from these examples, rules of origin are usually product-specific and can be very complex. Specification of the rules of origin often constitutes the bulk of the agreements that establish free trade areas. Those for NAFTA, for instance, run to close to 200 pages of small print. They require detailed, complex negotiations. The complexity of rules of origin is often viewed as a barrier to developing economies' participation in international trade, especially when they have to cope with multiple sets of rules that govern trade with different partners.

The negotiation of rules of origin, moreover, whose product-specific provisions often appear to be arbitrary, offers an opportunity for domestic interests to attempt to seek protection against the effects of regional trade liberalization. Setting a high value-added criterion may make it impossible for rival producers in partner countries to qualify for duty-free access to the domestic market. And the requirement that a specific component be produced locally may increase the discrimination against non-members and exclude them from the enlarged regional market. For instance, Schiff and Winters (2003: 80) cite the example of tomato ketchup. Under the 1988 Canada–US Free Trade Agreement (CUSFTA/CUSTA), ketchup produced from imported tomato paste qualified as a local product and received duty-free treatment. When the CUSFTA was converted into NAFTA, however, the new rules of origin stated that ketchup would be considered a local product only if it contained tomato paste manufactured within NAFTA. The result was *trade diversion* from Chile to Mexico: whereas Chile accounted for more than 80 per cent of US imports of tomato paste before NAFTA, after the introduction of the NAFTA rules of origin Chile's share dropped to 5 per cent whereas that of Mexico rose to 75 per cent.

The rush to regionalism that began in the mid 1990s is the second major wave of RTAs since the Second World War: the first occurred in the early 1960s, largely in response to the 1957 establishment of the European Economic Community (regionalism, however, has a much longer history, dating back several centuries: the previous peak in regional activity occurred in the inter-war period, when industrialized countries responded to the great depression by attempting to form closed trading blocs with less developed countries, in the case of European countries, with their colonies).

Many of the agreements negotiated in the 1960s linked less developed countries together. In Africa, the growth of regionalism followed former European colonies gaining their independence in the late 1950s and early 1960s. As in South America, the other continent where regionalism took off in this period, the principal objectives of the regional agreements were to promote local import-substitution industrialization (ISI), and to enhance the bargaining power of participants vis-à-vis external actors (in Asia, few regional economic partnerships, with the exception of ASEAN, emerged, not least because of Cold War conflicts that divided countries in this part of the world). In marked contrast with the most recent wave of regionalism, the agreements among less developed countries in the 1960s aimed to restrict imports from outside the region (in other words, they deliberately sought trade diversion—see Box 6.2—and to control foreign investors).

The landscape of interstate relations in South America and particularly in Africa soon became littered with the debris of failed regional arrangements. One reason was that few of the parties to regional arrangements were significant economic partners for one another. This was especially the case in Africa where the economies had been shaped in the colonial era to produce primary commodity exports for the European market. The share of intraregional trade (that is, trade with regional partners) in countries' overall trade was often less than 5 per cent. A consequence was that liberalization of trade on a regional basis in itself brought the participants few immediate benefits.

Moreover, liberalization of trade within a region often exacerbated existing inequalities among the partner states. Where companies had a choice of a single country location to serve the unified, protected, regional market, they usually preferred the city where infrastructure was most developed. Industries therefore tended to cluster around 'growth poles' and shunned the poorer-resourced towns and cities in the least developed parts of the region. The less developed countries in a regional partnership frequently found that they faced significant costs from trade diversion as imports from outside the region were replaced by relatively high-cost production from their partner states. They also lost tariff revenue, on which many less developed economies depended heavily as a source of government funding (the loss occurring both because of the removal of intra-regional tariffs and from the diversion of imports from outside the region to goods sourced from regional partners).

Some regional arrangements (including ASEAN and the Andean Pact) attempted to address the problems caused by this unbalanced growth by pursuing a policy of industrial licensing: the location of new industrial plants would be agreed by governments and allocated across different parts of the region to ensure that the less developed gained a share of the benefits from integration. But such an approach was politically unpopular with the governments of the more developed partners. They perceived the losses in investment forgone and the generally negative responses from foreign partners as exceeding any gains they made from collaboration with their less developed regional partners.

Arguments about the distribution of benefits from regionalism led to the collapse of many of the schemes established in the 1960s, and to a heightening of tensions between regional partners. Contrary to the idea that regionalism might improve inter-state security, disputes over the distribution of benefits from regional partnerships contributed in some instances to the onset of armed conflicts between former regional partners, for example, the 'soccer war' between former Central American Common Market members Honduras and El Salvador in 1969, and hostilities between former East African Community members Uganda and Tanzania in 1979.

New Patterns in Regional Trade Agreements

The failure of many regional trade agreements among less developed countries in the 1970s (Figure 6.1 shows how few schemes from the 1960s and 1970s are still in force today) occurred at a time when there was a considerable degree of pessimism about the prospects for the European Community. There, integration had proceeded more slowly than many had anticipated, and progress had been punctuated by increasingly acrimonious disputes among the member governments. By the middle of the 1970s, when worldwide economic conditions were more turbulent than at any time since 1945 because of the Organization of the Petroleum Exporting Countries (OPEC)-induced oil price rises and subsequent recession, regional integration no longer appeared to be a viable solution to the problems of interdependence that governments faced. To political leaders and academics alike, regional integration appeared increasingly obsolescent—the terminology the intellectual father of European integration studies, Ernst B. Haas (1975), applied at the time to theories of integration.

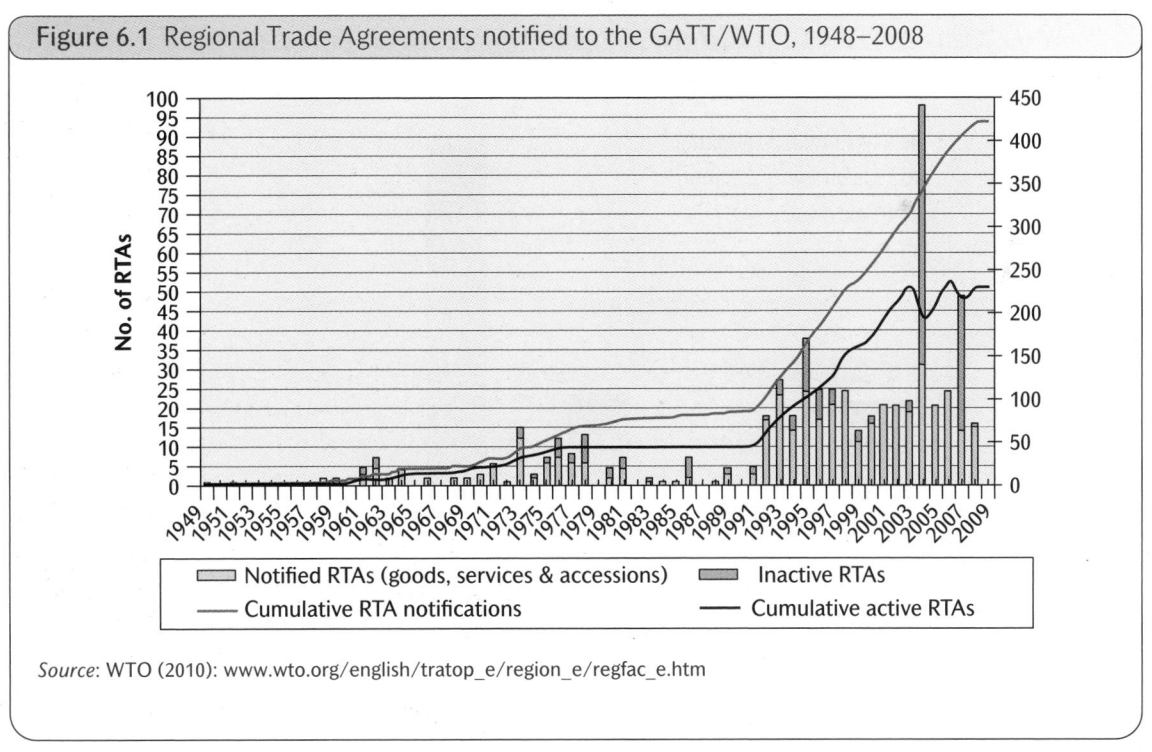

Figure 6.1 Regional Trade Agreements notified to the GATT/WTO, 1948–2008

Legend:
- Notified RTAs (goods, services & accessions)
- Inactive RTAs
- Cumulative RTA notifications
- Cumulative active RTAs

Source: WTO (2010): www.wto.org/english/tratop_e/region_e/regfac_e.htm

Two factors were to change the global context to make it far more favourable to regionalism in the 1990s. The first was the end of the Cold War. Regional economic agreements, like other aspects of international economic relations, are, in Aggarwal's (1985) terminology, 'nested' within the overall security context. A dramatic change in the security environment opened up new possibilities for partnerships among countries that had previously been on opposite sides of the Cold War divide. In Europe, the disintegration of the former Soviet Union and the 1991 break-up of the Council of Mutual Economic Assistance (COMECON; founded in 1949 by the Soviet Union as an alternative to the assistance that the US was providing Western Europe through the Marshall Plan, its membership expanded to include Czechoslovakia, East Germany, Poland, Hungary, Romania, Bulgaria, Mongolia, and Albania), opened the way for East European countries to enter into economic agreements with the European Union (and, for some, eventual membership

in the EU). It also required new arrangements to be established amongst former Soviet bloc members if economic co-operation was to be sustained. Georgia, for instance, signed six free trade agreements with other former Soviet republics in the 1990s.

The concentration of new regional agreements in Europe in the 1990s underlines the importance of the East European fragmentation for the growth in the number of regional trade agreements (the enlargement of the EU in 2004 and 2007 subsequently made many of these treaties redundant). In Asia, also, the end of the Cold War broke down the barriers that had previously prevented regional economic integration. In 1991, China joined the APEC grouping, which included its former Cold War foes Japan, the US, and South Korea. In 2001, demonstrating the enormous improvement of relations that had occurred in East Asia over the previous decade, China began to negotiate a free trade agreement with ASEAN (see Figure 6.2).

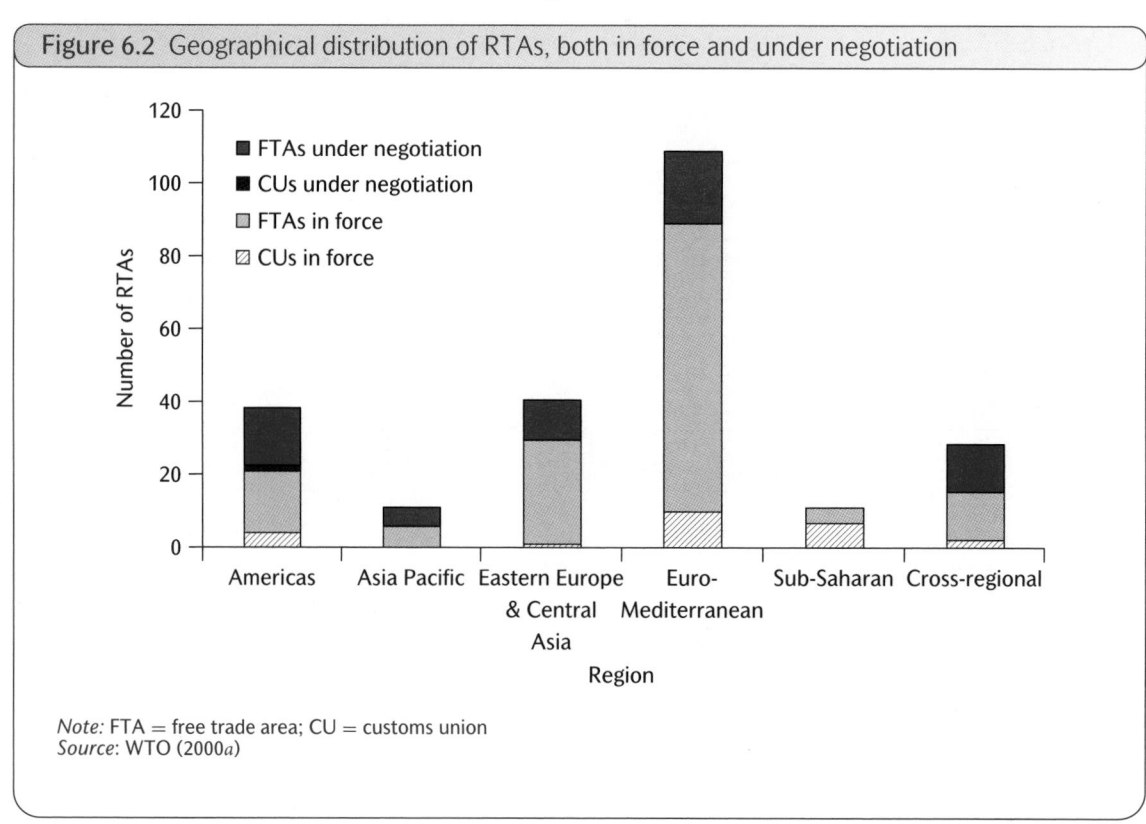

Figure 6.2 Geographical distribution of RTAs, both in force and under negotiation

Note: FTA = free trade area; CU = customs union
Source: WTO (2000*a*)

The second contextual factor was the growth in global interdependence, and the ascendancy of neo-liberal ideas in Western governments and in the international financial institutions (IFIs). The growing integration of markets—for goods, services, and finance—placed increasing pressure on governments to pursue market-friendly policies. Potential foreign investors quickly voted with their feet when faced by governments that attempted to impose conditions on them: indeed, from the early 1980s onwards, the balance of bargaining power between investors and governments shifted dramatically so that investors were increasingly able to demand concessions from host governments on issues such as taxation, rather than accepting restrictions on their activities. Similarly, financial markets were quick to punish governments that were perceived to be inward-looking or inclined towards interventionist measures.

In this new context, the regional arrangements that developed were often designed to enhance states' participation in the global economy, to signal their openness to foreign investment, and to seek access to the markets of industrialized countries. Unlike the arrangements from the 1960s and 1970s, the new regionalism frequently involved partnerships between industrialized and less developed economies, that is, they were often North–South rather than South–South in orientation. The North American Free Trade Agreement is the most prominent example; meanwhile, many less developed economies sought free trade agreements with the European Union, and by the early years of the new millennium, Japan had begun to negotiate free trade agreements with less developed economies in South East Asia and South America.

It was not just less developed countries that responded to the increased market integration through seeking regional economic partnerships. The decision by European member states to deepen integration and to complete the implementation of a single internal market (brought into being by the Single European Act, signed in 1986), has been widely interpreted as an attempt to strengthen the capacity of European companies to compete in the new global market place (Sandholtz and Zysman 1989; Schirm 2002).

Table 6.3 illustrates a number of the factors contributing to the explosive growth in regionalism in the 1990s. Transition economies (the former Soviet bloc countries) were involved in more than one-half of all RTAs signed in the 1990s (including forty RTAs that only involved other transition economies). Reflecting the desire of Southern countries to seek alliances with Northern partners, there was also a dramatic jump in the number of RTAs linking developed with developing countries in the 1990s. In contrast, few of the agreements signed in the 1990s linked two or more developed economies. In the new century, however, with the proliferation of bilateral agreements (and the rise of China and India), developing countries began once more to negotiate a significant number of agreements among themselves. A variety of other factors also contributed to the growth of regionalism in the 1990s.

Frustration with the difficulties of negotiating global agreements

The GATT began as a relatively small international institution dominated by Western industrial countries (see Winham, Chapter 5 in this volume). As more countries joined the GATT, so the difficulties of reaching agreement among an increasingly diverse group on an agenda that was becoming more complex were intensified. The consequence was that it took much longer to bring successive rounds of GATT talks to a conclusion.

Table 6.3 Notified RTAs in Goods by the Date of Entry into Force and Type of Partners (as of February 2010)

	Developed–Developed	Developed–Developing	Developed–Transition	Developing–Developing	Developing–Transition	Transition–Transition	Total
1958–1964	2	0	0	1	0	0	3
1965–1969	0	0	0	0	0	0	0
1970–1974	5	1	0	2	0	0	8
1975–1979	0	2	0	1	0	0	3
1980–1984	2	1	0	1	0	0	4
1985–1989	1	1	0	2	0	0	4
1990–1994	2	3	0	6	1	5	17
1995–1999	3	7	0	7	0	17	34
2000–2004	1	20	4	19	3	6	53
2005–2009	6	29	3	23	1	3	65
Total	**22**	**64**	**7**	**62**	**5**	**31**	**191**

Note: Developed countries include Canada, the United States, EU, European Free Trade Association (EFTA), Japan, Korea, Australia, and New Zealand; transition countries include the former Soviet Union, Eastern and Central Europe, the Baltic States, and the Balkans; the remaining countries are (self-) classified as developing.

Source: The WTO's Regional Trade Agreements Information System online (accessed in February 2010), available at http://www.wto.org/english/res_e/reser_e/discussion_papers_e.htm#n8

When the Uruguay Round of GATT negotiations stalled over issues relating to trade in agricultural products, governments turned to regional agreements both as a substitute for a global agreement and as a means of increasing pressure on other countries to attempt to persuade them to make concessions in global talks. Similar considerations applied a decade later when the WTO prepared to launch a new round of global trade negotiations: membership of the WTO was approaching 150 economies and the agenda was yet more complex. The 'debacle in Seattle', the failure of the WTO's ministerial meeting in December 1999, convinced many governments (including some that had previously been hostile towards RTAs, for example, Japan, see METI 2000), that negotiation of a new global agreement would not bring early results and that they should therefore look to RTAs if they wished to advance their trade agendas. The failure

of the Cancun WTO ministerial meeting in September 2003 and the suspension of the Doha Round negotiations in July 2006 reinforced these beliefs.

Bandwagoning and balancing: 'contagion' effects

The fact that post-war regional integration has come in two waves points both to the likelihood that common responses have occurred across various parts of the globe to the same stimuli (especially to increased economic interdependence), and to the possibility that regionalism in one part of the world triggers regionalism elsewhere through 'demonstration', 'emulation', or 'contagion' effects.

The establishment of the European Common Market in 1957, with its apparently positive impacts both on inter-state relations and on the economies of its members, inspired a wave of imitations among less developed countries. Similarly, the completion of the single internal market in the EU in 1992 and the establishment of NAFTA in 1994 led governments elsewhere to take a keener interest in becoming participants in regional agreements. The Japanese government report cited above, for instance, presented a detailed review of academic studies of existing regional arrangements, concluding that they generally had a positive effect on the welfare of member states. For many governments, therefore, the new interest in regionalism was primarily a defensive response to developments elsewhere. And some governments that were already party to regional arrangements sought new ones in an attempt to reduce their dependence on existing regional partners. Mexico, for instance, began negotiations for free trade arrangements with the European Union and Japan as a means of reducing its heavy reliance on its NAFTA partners.

It was not just governments, however, that were prompted into action by regionalism elsewhere. The essence of preferential trade agreements is that they are discriminatory: non-members do not share the benefits they provide. Companies located in non-members therefore find that RTAs place them at a competitive disadvantage. They have an incentive to lobby their governments either to bandwagon by joining existing regional arrangements where such possibilities exist, or to negotiate a treaty that provides them with equivalent access to markets (Baldwin 1993). For instance, following the implementation of NAFTA and the signature of the Mexico–EU Free Trade Agreement, Japanese manufacturers found themselves at a disadvantage in competing in the Mexican market. Whereas their American and European counterparts enjoyed duty-free access to Mexico, Japanese companies faced tariffs that averaged 16 per cent. The main business grouping, the Japan Federation of Economic Organizations, *Keidanren*, lobbied the government to sign a free trade agreement with Mexico that would give Japanese companies equivalent access to that enjoyed by their competitors (Ravenhill 2003).

The proliferation of preferential trade agreements across the globe, with the potential competitive disadvantages they bring for non-participants, increases the incentives for governments either to join existing agreements or to seek similar arrangements for their own exporters (Baldwin 1997; Oye 1992).

The change in the US attitude towards preferential agreements

The United States government was the strongest supporter of a non-discriminatory multilateral approach to trade in the negotiations that led to the creation of GATT at the end of the Second World War. Not only had it been a victim of the discriminatory colonial trading blocs that the European powers had created in the inter-war period, but it believed that their closing off of international trade had made a significant contribution to the global recession of the 1930s. It was largely at US insistence that non-discrimination was enshrined as the cornerstone of the post-war global trade regime.

Washington, however, was willing to tolerate regional trading groupings that discriminated against its exports where it believed that these helped to achieve its political objectives through, for example, facilitating reconciliation between former enemies and strengthening the economies of the participants so that they would be less susceptible to the perceived communist threat. Security concerns trumped economic principles. The primary example was the European Economic Community (EEC). Washington had encouraged European recipients of Marshall Plan assistance (Box 6.5) to co-ordinate their plans (which led to the formation of the Organization for European Economic Cooperation, the forerunner to the OECD, the Organization for Economic Co-operation and Development). It put pressure on France to accommodate the rebuilding of Germany's industry and to devise a mechanism that would allay French concerns (which ultimately became the Schuman Plan for the European Coal and Steel Community).

The US government supported the formation of the EEC in 1957, even though it was obvious that the new Community, like the ECSC, would not be fully compatible with GATT requirements for regional agreements and would discriminate against US exports. At the same time, it exerted pressure on the Europeans not to introduce any provisions that would increase discrimination against US economic interests. Its support for European integration was also accompanied by American initiatives in the GATT for new rounds of global negotiations with the objective of reducing overall tariff levels and thus the discrimination its exporters would face in the European market (the 'Kennedy Round', 1963–7, was the response to the EEC's creation, and the 'Tokyo Round', 1973–9, the response to the first enlargement of the Community when it admitted Denmark, Ireland, and the United Kingdom in 1973).

Box 6.5 The Marshall Plan

Under the Marshall Plan, the US government provided $11.8 billion in grants and a further $1.5 billion in loans to assist in the rebuilding of European economies (and, in some instances, those of their colonies) in the years 1948–52. The United Kingdom received the largest volume of grants ($2.8 billion), followed by France ($2.5 billion), Italy ($1.4 billion), and West Germany ($1.2 billion). The Plan was an outgrowth of Washington's concerns about the perceived growth of Soviet influence in Europe. Funds were used for purposes such as purchasing new machinery for factories, providing technical assistance to enable Europeans to become familiar with new technologies, and the rebuilding of roads, railways, and ports. The bilateral assistance provided to Europe under the Marshall Plan far exceeded the funds available from the **International Bank for Reconstruction and Development (World Bank)**. The Organization for European Economic Cooperation (which subsequently evolved into the Organization for Economic Co-operation and Development (OECD)) was created to manage the Marshall Plan aid.

Washington's attitude towards regional economic agreements among less developed countries was more ambivalent. Although it appreciated the possibility that regionalism might improve the security of the participants, its enthusiasm was tempered because of the anti-import and pro-interventionist frameworks that figured prominently in many of the regional schemes among less developing countries in the 1960s. Its support for regional economic integration among South American countries, therefore, was at best lukewarm. And, in other parts of the world, especially Asia, Washington opposed any movement towards a regional agreement from which it would be excluded.

The US attitude towards regional economic agreements changed in the early 1980s, as it despaired of the slow progress in global trade liberalization and bristled at the growing trade distortions generated by the European Community's Common Agricultural Policy (CAP). United States Trade Representative William Brock announced in 1982 that Washington was willing to enter into regional trade agreements. Negotiation of a free trade agreement with Israel quickly followed. The US also launched the Caribbean Basin Initiative, a programme of trade preferences for the island states of the region. Far more significant, however, was Washington's positive response to a Canadian proposal for negotiation of a free trade agreement. In one sense, this was not a dramatic departure in American trade policy. Washington had offered such an agreement to Canada on several occasions over the previous century, only to be rebuffed by a Canadian government concerned about maintaining its economic independence. Nonetheless, the signature of the Canada–US Free Trade Agreement in 1988 sent a dramatic signal to other members of the international community. This was reinforced in the following years when the first Bush administration indicated its willingness to construct a 'hub and spokes' framework that would link the US in a series of free trade agreements with partners in Central and South America, Oceania, and East Asia.

The new approach to trade policy in the early 1990s was succinctly stated by Lawrence Summers, who became under-secretary of the Treasury for International Affairs in the first Clinton administration: that there should be a 'presumption in favor of all the lateral reductions in trade barriers, whether they be multi, uni, tri, plurilateral' (quoted in Frankel 1997: 5). In other words, the policy was one of 'anything goes' in trade policy as long as it contributed to trade liberalization, there no longer being a presumption that discriminatory regional agreements would be barriers to liberalization at the global level.

With the United States itself in the second half of the 1990s actively pursuing regionalism through NAFTA and advocating its extension into a Free Trade Area of the Americas, it would have been difficult for Washington to maintain its opposition to regionalism in other parts of the world. The change in attitude was particularly important in facilitating the development of preferential trade arrangements in East Asia. Whereas Washington had vigorously opposed a proposal from Malaysian Prime Minister Mahathir Mohamad in the early 1990s for the creation of an East Asian Economic Group, which would have excluded the countries of North America and Oceania that were members of the rival APEC grouping, by the late 1990s it acquiesced in the creation of an equivalent grouping (ASEAN Plus Three, the ten ASEAN members plus China, Japan, and South Korea), and in numerous East Asian moves to negotiate bilateral free trade arrangements.

Making existing preferential trade arrangements compatible with WTO requirements

Some of the new free trade areas came into being because industrialized countries perceived that they needed to make their trade agreements with less developed countries compatible with the WTO's regulations. Here, the European Union has again been the most important actor.

The European Union had previously constructed a network of preferential trade arrangements with the countries of the southern Mediterranean, and with Africa, the Caribbean, and the Pacific grouping (ACP), which comprises over seventy countries, many of which had formerly been European colonies. These agreements had been negotiated in contexts entirely different from that prevailing in the second half of the 1990s. The arrangements with the ACP grouping were codified in the Lomé Conventions, the first of which had come into effect in 1975 at the height of the demands from less developed economies for the creation of a New International Economic Order (NIEO). Reflecting a context in which industrialized countries were responsive to the demands from less developed economies for special treatment, the Conventions offered duty-free access to the European market for most ACP exports, without obliging the ACP countries to provide similar preferential treatment to European exports: in other words, they were non-reciprocal arrangements. (Treaties with southern Mediterranean countries, signed in 1975–7, offered similar duty-free access to the European market: the Mediterranean countries committed themselves to lower their tariffs on imports from the European Community but the timetable for this process was not specified.)

Besides their general trade provisions, the Lomé Conventions also included special arrangements for specific products, including bananas, beef, rum, and sugar, on which some countries' export earnings were heavily dependent. These typically enabled their sale in European markets at prices much higher than those prevailing elsewhere. In some instances, they rested on a segmentation of the European market, with, for instance, exports of ACP bananas being subject to different treatment in the United Kingdom and in France than they received in Germany and the Netherlands. The European Union, in fact, operated three different tariff regimes for bananas, even though, as a common market, it had supposedly adopted a common external tariff. The new commitment to realizing a single internal market in the EU in 1992 made it impossible to maintain this arrangement for ACP bananas.

In an attempt to preserve the special position of ACP bananas, the European Union introduced an interventionist system of import licensing that discriminated against bananas coming from non-ACP countries (primarily Central and South America). Several of these producing countries challenged the new EU banana regime in the GATT; they were supported by the US government, which had been lobbied by the two giant US agribusiness firms, Dole and Chiquita, which handled most of the trade in Central and South American bananas. The outcome of the lengthy and convoluted dispute, which spanned the time period during which the WTO took over from the GATT, and which at one stage threatened to trigger a 'trade war' between the United States and the European Union, was that a WTO Dispute Settlement Panel found that the European provisions on bananas contravened several of its articles. The Europeans eventually backed down, committing themselves to introducing arrangements that were compatible with their WTO obligations (Ravenhill 2004).

The dispute illustrated how the WTO makes it possible for less developed countries to initiate a successful challenge against an aspect of the trade policies of an economic superpower, the EU. It also demonstrated the significance of the changed arrangements for dispute settlement with the transition from the GATT to the WTO: unlike the

situation under the GATT, when countries simply ignored dispute settlement judgements that they did not like, the EU had no viable alternative but to conform to the WTO's requirements. More important than the specifics of the banana dispute itself, are the implications of the WTO's judgement for rules governing the relations between industrialized and less developed economies.

In finding that the EU's banana regime contravened several of its provisions, the WTO rejected European arguments that the trade arrangements with the ACP were legitimized by WTO rules on RTAs and on special treatment for less developed economies. The WTO found that the Lomé Convention did not conform to its rules for regional trade arrangements because the ACP countries were not required to remove their tariffs on European imports (under the requirements of Article XXIV, all parties to a regional economic agreement must liberalize 'substantially all trade' between them). Moreover, the Convention did not conform to the rules on preferences for less developed economies because it gave special treatment to one group (the ACP) but not to other economies at similar levels of development. These rulings left the EU with only one other avenue for seeking WTO legitimacy for the Convention: to apply under Article IX of the WTO for a special waiver from the most-favoured-nation rule. But the requirements for such a waiver are more stringent under the WTO than they were in the GATT; the waiver is only for a fixed term and would not prevent WTO members from subsequently challenging specific elements of the arrangements. In other words, a waiver would have provided little assurance to the ACP states that the provisions would not be disrupted in the future.

Faced with this dilemma, the EU decided that the only means through which it could provide long-term trade security for the ACP would be to abandon its previous approach and to negotiate arrangements that were compatible with WTO rules on regional trade agreements (Article XXIV). It proposed to do this through concluding a series of economic partnership agreements with groupings of ACP countries, which were to be negotiated by the end of 2007. A similar decision had been made earlier regarding the trade agreements with the countries of the southern Mediterranean: in its Barcelona Declaration of 1995, the EU stated its intention to negotiate WTO-compatible free trade agreements with these countries. These were subsequently concluded with Tunisia (1995), Israel (1995), Morocco (1996), Jordan (1997), Egypt (1999), Algeria (2001), and Lebanon (2002).

Key points

- The regional trade agreements of the 1960s and 1970s aimed to promote regional industrialization behind tariff walls.
- They often broke down because of disagreements over the distribution of benefits and costs from regional co-operation.
- The new regionalism differs from this previous wave in that participating countries are typically using agreements to increase their integration into the world economy.
- Its origins lie in the end of the Cold War; the perceived success of RTAs elsewhere; frustrations with the pace of trade liberalization at the global level; a desire to make existing preferential trade relations compatible with WTO rules; and a change in US attitudes towards regionalism.

The Political Economy of Regionalism

Private sector interests

Previous sections of this chapter have identified several reasons why governments and private sector actors might wish to pursue regional economic integration. It is straightforward, for instance, to suggest that when companies face high tariffs in markets where their competitors' products enter duty free because of the existence of free trade arrangements, they will lobby their governments to obtain similar arrangements. But other than for these defensive reasons, when might companies support the establishment of a regional free trade area rather than prefer either continued protectionism or non-discriminatory liberalization?

To address this question requires a starting point that is far removed from the assumptions of trade theory as developed in neoclassical economics (which assumes constant returns to scale and immobile factors of production, that is, unit costs of production are the same regardless of the size of the production run, and factors of production — capital, for example — will not move across national boundaries). In particular, it rests on the possibility that companies will be able to produce more efficiently for a regional rather than a domestic market because they are able to capture economies of scale, on the increasing mobility of capital, and on observations regarding the geographical distribution of subsidiaries of transnational corporations.

The economies of scale argument assumes that regional integration is able to provide firms with the minimum market size required for them to capture scale economies, whereas the domestic market alone is too small for this to happen. But why would firms not prefer multilateral liberalization so as to gain access to even larger global markets? The reason is that a regional agreement will provide an opportunity to retain tariff and other barriers against competitors from outside the region. The logic is that of strategic trade theory, one component of which asserts that it is possible for governments to provide an advantage to their domestic companies if they offer a protected domestic market that enables them to realize economies of scale (Krugman 1990; for an application of the argument to the regional level see Milner 1997b; and Chase 2003, 2005).

The other departure from conventional trade theory rests on an acknowledgement that contemporary manufacturing often involves conducting various stages of production in different geographical locations to take advantage of local characteristics such as relatively low-cost labour or a concentration of product- or industry-specific skills. From the 1980s onwards, United States and European firms, facing intense competition in their domestic market from imports from East Asia, established subsidiaries in relatively low-labour-cost neighbouring countries, from which they sourced components (see the discussion in Thun, Chapter 11 in this volume). The establishment of regional free trade areas facilitates this corporate strategy (and, here, it is appropriate to remember the North–South architecture of many of the new regional arrangements of the 1990s, for example, trade agreements between the European Union and Eastern European and Mediterranean countries, NAFTA, and the Caribbean Basin Initiative). Moreover, the rules of origin, in NAFTA for instance, that allow components sourced from US companies to be counted towards requirements that goods must meet if they are to be deemed to have been manufactured in Mexico, serve as a protectionist device that provides further advantage to US-based corporations (for further discussion see Cox 2000).

Even though TNCs disperse their activities to capitalize on local characteristics, their production and sales are frequently concentrated within one geographical region. This geographical concentration of activities is likely to cause many TNCs to put their efforts into lobbying for regional trading agreements rather than for liberalization at the global level, because their principal interest is in removing barriers to trade between those countries in which their manufacturing plants are located. This concentration on the regional level is encouraged by the better prospects there, compared with the global level, of pursuing the 'deeper integration' that MNEs need for efficient integration of their production networks—for example, agreements on the treatment that foreign investment will receive, protection of intellectual property rights, and facilitation of the movement of skilled workers and management.

Economies of scale and regionalization of production may both incline companies towards lobbying for regional trade agreements but their impact on the attitudes of labour is likely to be more ambiguous. On the one hand, the possibility of gaining larger market share, longer production runs, and higher profits through the realization of economies of scale offers the prospect to labour of additional employment, higher wages, etc. On the other, the opportunity that the negotiation of a free trade area provides companies to regionalize their production will be likely to worry labour unions in relatively high-wage countries that will fear that labour-intensive stages of production will be moved to those parts of the region with lower labour costs. It was not surprising, therefore, that companies with regionalized production networks lobbied in favour of NAFTA, whereas labour unions (together with American firms that produced solely within the US for the domestic market) expressed their concern that the agreement would generate, in the words of H. Ross Perot, a 'giant sucking sound' as US jobs were lost to Mexico (Chase 2003).

The politics of regional deepening in the European Union: neo-functionalist and intergovernmental explanations

As indicated in Box 6.1, governments that enter regional agreements that involve more than the creation of a free trade area inevitably have to agree to establish institutions that 'pool their sovereignty' on policies that have to be determined at the regional level—for instance, the determination of common external tariffs and other common foreign economic policies in customs unions. The deeper the integration—that is, the broader the scope of policy issues on which members agree to co-operate—the greater will be the number of policy areas on which regional institutions will have to be given competence (unless members agree to a policy of mutual recognition whereby they accept policies/standards in other members as if they were their own).

Political scientists have long been fascinated by the question of whether, once a regional arrangement is established, it generates its own momentum towards not only closer economic but also closer political integration. The vast majority of regional economic agreements take the form of free trade areas, which, because they do not require setting a common external tariff, provide little stimulus for the establishment of a regional institution to co-ordinate policies. Most free trade areas do provide a process for the resolution of disputes between the parties over the interpretation and/or implementation of the free trade area's rules, but this is usually managed by secretariats within the governments of the member countries. For instance, although there is a NAFTA secretariat, which administers the dispute resolution procedures created by the agreement, this is a 'virtual' secretariat comprised of three sections located within the respective national governments. Very limited scope is available to such national agencies to act to promote deeper regional integration: indeed, the very lack of the creation of any alternative source of authority at the regional level is one of the attractions of free trade areas to many national governments. Even in those free trade areas where member governments have agreed to create a central secretariat, as in ASEAN, they often deliberately keep such institutions weak so that they do not develop as challengers to national governments.

With deeper integration, the scope for regional institutions to act autonomously may increase. The best example is the European Union, the only regional agreement that has fully implemented a common market and moved beyond this to form an economic union. It has by far the most complex of governance arrangements of any regional grouping. As Helen Wallace (2000: 44) suggests, 'much of what makes the EU so interesting . . . is the density of institutions and the evidence of institutional creativity. EU institutions provide both opportunities and constraints, and they serve to channel and to structure the behaviour of political actors from the participating countries.'

The principal political organs at the regional level are a supranational secretariat, the European Commission ('supranational' because it is autonomous from the governments of the member states and its officials have the responsibility of promoting the interests of the EU as a whole rather than those of specific members), an institution comprised of ministers from the national governments (the Council of Ministers, which is supported by a committee of senior officials, known by its French acronym, COREPER, the Committee of Permanent Representatives), the European Parliament (directly elected since 1979 by voters in the member states), and the European Court of Justice (which is charged with interpreting the various EU treaties that member states have signed). The EU treaties now extend far beyond the liberalization of internal trade and the establishment of common foreign economic policies to include competition policies, environmental policies, common foreign and security policies, justice and home affairs (including human rights), and regional development. The European Union and its member states now constitute a complex web of multilevel governance, with authority for making and implementing policies on various issues being split between institutions at the regional level, at the national level and, in some instances, at the subnational level (for further discussion see Bomberg and Stubb 2003; and Wallace et al. 2005).

Most of the theorizing in international relations on regionalism has concentrated on the European experience. The early years of European integration inspired the development of neo-functionalist analysis (Haas 1958; Lindberg 1963). This approach suggested how a regional grouping could generate a momentum of its own that would lead to a deepening of co-operation. The logic was that co-operation in one area of economic activity would produce pressures for co-operation in other areas as the costs of pursuing unco-ordinated policies became increasingly evident to member states and their private sector actors, a process that the *neo-functionalist* theorists termed 'spillover'. Entrepreneurial leadership by regional institutions could intensify the pressures for further co-operation.

In the European Union, the European Commission has the power to take initiatives in the various areas where the members have agreed that the EU has competence; it thus has the capacity to shape agendas and to push for further co-operation at the European level. The European Court of Justice's responsibility for interpreting the treaties and for adjudicating disputes between member states affords it an opportunity that extends into the realm of policy-making; over the last quarter of the twentieth century, some of its judgements significantly extended the scope of European competence.

One element of neo-functional theorizing emphasized the significance of the unintended consequences of previous actions and decisions. For instance, member states did not anticipate the important role that the Court of Justice would come to play in extending the scope of integration when they created a body that was intended to arbitrate disputes on the implementation of treaties. For theorists in the neo-functionalist tradition, the logic of spillover and the creative leadership provided by regional institutions can provide the integration process with a dynamic of its own (Sandholtz and Stone Sweet 1998 provide an example of theorizing from this perspective).

The neo-functionalist approach has consistently been challenged by scholars who assert that national states have primacy in the integration process. Stanley Hoffmann (1966) pioneered this challenge; the economic historian, Alan Milward (1992), subsequently developed the theme that integration in Europe is best interpreted as a strategy pursued by national states to strengthen their own positions. Andrew Moravcsik (1998) presents the most theoretically sophisticated articulation of this 'liberal intergovernmental' argument, suggesting that the major steps forward in European integration were driven not by the European Commission or the Court of Justice but by member governments that were responding in a rational way to domestic economic interests. Key decisions on integration reflect bargains struck among member states; the most significant European institution therefore is not the supranational Commission but the intergovernmental Council of Ministers. For writers in this tradition, to the extent that member states delegate authority to community institutions, such moves are 'calculated, rational, and circumscribed' (Bomberg and Stubb 2003: 11).

In this hotly contested debate, as is often the case in international relations theorizing, authors writing from one perspective have been reluctant to acknowledge that the arguments of the competing school have any legitimacy. Because the EU embraces such a wide array of activities, and the competencies of its various actors and the balance of power between them have evolved over time, it is possible for both sides to this debate to find compelling examples that support their case. Rather than perceiving this issue as a dichotomy of government preferences versus the actions of supranational institutions, it would be more helpful to focus on the interaction between these two. Sandholtz (1993) has argued persuasively that state preferences themselves are not formed in a vacuum: membership in the EU itself has become an important influence on how governments define their interests—they are socialized into particular ways of thinking.

To date, the failure of those other regional schemes that aspire to become common markets to realize their aspirations inevitably limits to the European context debates about the role that supranational institutions can play in driving integration forwards. Meanwhile, it is too early to tell definitively whether the neo-functional logic of spillover will apply to some of the more significant free trade areas—most notably NAFTA—that were established in the l990s, although little evidence has emerged to date to support such ideas (for discussion of the NAFTA case, see Capling and Nossal 2009).

Key points

- Corporations may prefer regionalism to global trade liberalization if it enables them to capture economies of scale while avoiding exposure to global competition.

- Regionalism may be particularly attractive to companies that seek 'deeper integration' to facilitate the operation of regional production networks (through, for instance, provisions to safeguard investments).

- Unskilled labour in industrialized economies is likely to oppose regional integration if this includes less

developed economies with significantly lower labour costs.

- Because most RTAs are free trade areas, they require little pooling of sovereignty and afford little scope for the emergence of sources of power at the regional level that rival national governments.

- In the EU, evidence from different sectors at different periods of time supports arguments from both the intergovernmental and the neo-functionalist perspectives.

The Economic Consequences of Regional Integration

The discussion of trade diversion in Box 6.2 reminds us that no assumption can be made that regional trade agreements will necessarily enhance the welfare of their participants. It is not straightforward to estimate the effect that RTAs have had on members' trade and their welfare more generally because the impact of many other variables has to be taken into consideration.

Regional agreements and members' trade

That the share of world trade conducted within RTAs has risen, as noted at the beginning of this chapter, reflects both an increase in the number of RTAs and an increase in the share of their total trade that members of RTAs conduct with one another. Table 6.4 shows for the major minilateral RTAs how the share of intra-regional trade in

members' total trade evolved in the last quarter of the twentieth century.

The share of intraregional trade in the total trade of members of some regional agreements rose dramatically: most notable here were NAFTA, CARICOM, and MERCOSUR. In contrast, ASEAN states were little more important as trading partners for one another in 2008 than they had been thirty-five years before, despite implementing a free trade agreement in the interim. The record of many African RTAs was mixed: the Southern African Development Community (SADC) was notably successful in increasing intra-regional trade, a reflection of the reintegration of the post-apartheid South Africa into the regional economy.

Simple statistics of this type, however, do not tell us whether the RTA itself has been a significant influence on trade among the member economies. Multiple factors other than the existence of a regional trade agreement can influence the volume of trade between any two countries. Among the most important of these are the size of the two economies, the levels of per capita income, the geographical distance between the two countries (and hence the transportation costs in trading), whether or not they share a common boundary, and whether or not their populations speak the same language. Such factors have to be built into any model that attempts to isolate the impact of the regional agreement itself on trade. Jeffrey Frankel (1997) has undertaken the most comprehensive modelling of this type. He finds that after allowing for the various factors identified above, regional trade agreements have had a (statistically significant) positive impact on the trade between their members. This positive effect is particularly pronounced for agreements among less developed economies, including ASEAN and MERCOSUR, but trade among EU member states was also 65 per cent above the level that would otherwise have been expected in the absence of a regional trade agreement. These results echo those in several other studies. The evidence points strongly to preferential trade agreements having caused changes in patterns of international trade.

These results in themselves, however, do not distinguish between trade creation and trade diversion effects, and thus tell us little about the welfare effects of the regional trade agreements. Again, isolating the causes of the increased trade is no easy task. The new preferences created for regional partners have to be viewed in the context of other changes in the participants' trade policies including, for instance, any reduction of their tariffs towards non-members of the regional agreement (as occurred in the 1980s and 1990s, both through unilateral liberalization and through implementation of GATT/WTO agreements).

Table 6.4 Changes in the Share of Intra-Regional Trade in Selected RTAs, 1970–2008

	1970	1980	1985	1990	1995	2000	2005	2008
EU (1957)	59.5	60.8	59.2	65.9	62.4	66.2	66.5	65.4
NAFTA (1994)	36.0	33.6	43.9	41.4	41.5	46.4	43.0	40.0
CACM (1961)	26.0	24.4	14.4	15.4	21.7	13.7	15.0*	15.2*
Andean Group (1988)	1.8	3.8	3.2	4.2	7.5	8.5	10.0	8.4
CARICOM (1973)	4.2	5.3	6.3	8.1	12.1	14.6	9.4*	10.2*
MERCOSUR (1991)	9.4	11.6	5.5	8.9	19.2	20.6	15.7	16.0
ECOWAS (1975)	2.9	9.6	5.1	8.0	9.0	9.6	10.0*	7.9*
SADC (1992)	4.2	0.4	1.4	3.1	10.6	11.9	9.2*	10.4*
ASEAN/AFTA (1992)	22.4	17.4	18.6	19	22.0	22.8	25.1	25.0
GCC (1981)	4.6	3.0	4.9	8.0	6.8	5.0	5.8*	5.9*

Note: Figures in parentheses refer to year in which the RTA came into force

Source: WTO (2003c: table 1B.11); updated with author's calculations from data in WTO 2009: appendix table A3, www.wto.org/english/res_e/statis_e/its2009_e/its09_appendix_e.htm, except for figures marked with an asterisk (*), which were calculated using data extracted from the IMF DOTS online database (accessed in February 2010) and may not therefore be directly comparable.

A major study by the World Bank (2000) finds that, although the ratio of intra-regional trade to gross domestic product (GDP) increased in all regional groupings reviewed, so too did the ratio of trade with extra-regional partners to GDP. In other words, not only did trade with regional partners grow in economic importance but so too did trade with countries outside the region. Consequently, the Bank concluded, while studies suggest that some trade diversion occurred in the EU, European Free Trade Association, and NAFTA, 'the picture is sufficiently mixed that it is not possible to conclude that trade diversion has been a major problem' (World Bank 2000: 48), a finding consistent with Frankel's (1997) comprehensive study (see also Krueger 1999).

That RTAs may distort members' trade patterns to a limited extent only is consistent with the lowering of MFN tariffs (and thus the preferential margins enjoyed by partner countries) that has occurred in the last two decades. In Canada, half of all MFN tariff lines are duty free; in the United States, the figure is 35 per cent. As noted in the previous chapter, the average tariff level in industrialized countries on imports of manufactured goods is less than 5 per cent. A similar trend towards tariff reduction is also evident in most less developed countries, with an inevitable consequence for the preferential margins that RTAs create. In ASEAN, for instance, in roughly two-thirds of the tariff lines, MFN and preferential tariffs are identical. For many of the others, the preferential margin is so small in the more developed economies (Singapore and Malaysia) that few companies have found it worthwhile to meet the rules of origin requirements and file the necessary paperwork: less than 5 per cent of all intra-ASEAN trade is estimated to take advantage of the preferential tariffs provided under the ASEAN Free Trade Agreement. Not only do many RTAs create few advantages for partners for many exports, but they also seldom help in the most heavily protected areas: when 'sensitive' sectors are protected by high MFN tariffs, governments frequently also exempt them altogether from the regional agreement or minimize the liberalization provided.

Scale economies and competition effects

Regional trade agreements affect the welfare of their participants through impacts beyond those on trade itself. One argument made in support of RTAs is that they will lead to increased investment flows for participants. As noted earlier, inflows of foreign direct investment into Mexico increased substantially after the signature of NAFTA. Similarly, the establishment of the European Community and the subsequent deepening of European integration through the completion of the single internal market led to substantial increases in foreign direct investment in the EU, both intra-regionally — that is, from one member state to another, and from external countries (Motta and Norman 1996).

The other means through which RTAs are often assumed to improve the welfare of participating countries is by increasing the size of the 'home' market. As noted earlier, this can be particularly important for firms dependent upon access to a market larger than that available within one country to achieve economies of scale. Moreover, regionalism may generate increased competition for domestic companies, thereby forcing them to become more efficient. Again, estimating these effects requires complex economic modelling with often 'heroic' assumptions. Although the computer simulations reach dramatically different conclusions depending on the assumptions they use, the most frequent finding is that regional integration produces only a very limited positive aggregate effect on the welfare of the economies of participants (on the Asia-Pacific region, for instance, see Scollay and Gilbert 2001). Supporters of regionalism suggest that these findings reflect the inability of the models to capture the 'dynamic' effects of regional integration, those that develop over time as companies benefit from scale economies and other efficiencies. Others argue that the majority of benefits from regionalism come from the beneficial effects of companies responding to increased competition rather than from realizing economies of scale, and that these competitive benefits can be achieved more effectively through non-discriminatory liberalization that exposes domestic companies to worldwide competition (Schiff and Winters 2003: 51–2).

In short, the verdict on the economic effects of regional trade arrangements is mixed and frequently inconclusive. Economic models suggest that there is little evidence that RTAs have generated significant

trade diversion. They do appear, at least in the years immediately following their signature, to have been associated with increased inflows of foreign direct investment. Yet, their overall effects on the economic welfare of participants, if positive, have been of limited magnitude. And in the most sophisticated of regional schemes, the European Union, welfare benefits arising from improved competitiveness in manufacturing have been at least partially offset by the welfare losses caused by the EU's Common Agricultural Policy.

Key points

- Although considerable complexity is involved in attempting to isolate the economic effects of RTAs, evidence suggests that they have led to more trade among members than would otherwise be the case.
- RTAs do appear to have encouraged increased investment in member states.

- Economic simulations suggest that RTAs have had little aggregate effect on members' economic welfare.
- Little evidence exists that RTAs have produced significant trade diversion.

Regionalism and the WTO: Stepping Stone or Stumbling Block?

The advent of the new regionalism has been accompanied by a lively debate about its relationship to trade liberalization at the global level. Will regional trade agreements facilitate or obstruct global trade liberalization or, as in Bhagwati's (1991) terminology, are regional agreements stepping stones or stumbling blocks?

Several arguments suggest how regional agreements might facilitate global negotiations:

1. Global negotiations that take place among regional groupings reduce the number of actors involved.

2. Reaching agreement on issues of deeper integration will be easier within regional groupings; these agreements can serve as models for global treaties.

3. Regional agreements can enhance the competitiveness of domestic industries, paving the way for full liberalization.

4. Regional agreements improve the financial position of export-oriented interests, thereby providing them with the means and incentive to lobby governments for broader liberalization, which will translate into support for global trade talks.

5. When regional agreements provide companies from some countries with preferential access to a foreign market, their competitors in other countries will lobby their governments to sign agreements that will provide them with equivalent access. This attempt 'to level the playing field' will produce what Baldwin (1997, 2006)

has called a 'domino' effect in regionalism, in effect, broadening the scope of liberalization. Baldwin (2006) has extended the argument by suggesting that, with the proliferation of RTAs, each with their own rules of origin, corporations will press for a rationalization of agreements because of the adverse consequences that they had on managing their supply chains.

The intuitively attractive argument that regional groupings simplify global negotiations by reducing the number of parties is counteracted by the difficulties that regional groupings often have in reaching a common position (witness the European Union on agricultural issues in global negotiations). Moreover, once a regional grouping has reached internal agreement on its own position, it may have little flexibility in bargaining with other actors. And there is no assurance that the common position adopted by a regional grouping will not be more restrictive than that held by a majority of its member states: in other words, the regional grouping can end up throwing its combined weight behind policies that might not have been supported by a majority of its members (or possibly the largest economies in the region), had they acted individually in the global negotiations. The recent proliferation of regional trade arrangements, many of which have overlapping memberships, suggests further complications should negotiations occur between 'regions' rather than between individual countries.

Until recently, little evidence existed to support arguments that agreement on contentious issues or on matters of 'deeper' integration could be reached more easily at the regional level. The European Union, for instance, has found it very difficult to liberalize the most politically sensitive areas of trade, especially in agriculture. In the OECD's words, 'regionalism has often failed to crack the hardest nuts' (2002: 20). And few regional agreements have moved beyond the basics of removing tariffs to address the 'behind-the-border' barriers that many economists believe are more significant impediments to contemporary trade than tariffs themselves. Nonetheless, the recent wave of regionalism has provided greater encouragement for the argument that deeper integration on issues such as investment and the environment is more easily accomplished through negotiations among a limited subset of countries (for further discussion see OECD 2002). Developments at the regional level on these issues, however, have yet to be translated into global agreements, so the idea that regional agreements will subsequently have a positive influence on global negotiations has yet to be substantiated.

The argument that regional agreements will enable industries to become internationally competitive, and therefore that an RTA will ease the path towards non-discriminatory liberalization, assumes that the level of competition at the regional level will be similar to that in the global marketplace to which firms will then be able to graduate. An alternative proposition is also intuitively plausible: that the regional market will be of sufficient size to enable firms to realize economies of scale, and that they will prefer to operate with the comfort provided by the external tariff of the regional grouping rather than be exposed to enhanced competition. Companies content with operating in the regional market may be financially strengthened through regional integration, and therefore may have an incentive to lobby against extending trade liberalization beyond the region.

Baldwin's arguments that RTAs create a virtuous circle in which companies will press governments for additional liberalization appears persuasive in the European context. It rests, however, on the proposition that these agreements create significant advantages for corporations in countries that have these agreements and, consequently, substantially disadvantage companies in countries that do not. In other parts of the world, however, where RTAs are shallower and less comprehensive, their effects are far more limited. Consequently, the political logic of Baldwin's argument has less force: because the agreements do not significantly disadvantage excluded parties, then these corporations may have little incentive to lobby for equivalent agreements; and, because of exceptions in the agreements, protectionist interests are not necessarily weakened (Ravenhill 2010).

Critics who see regional agreements as stumbling blocks in the path of global liberalization assert that:

- They magnify the influence of power disparities in international trade relations, enabling larger economies to impose their will on smaller partners, gaining them advantages through rules of origin that would not be achieved if liberalization occurred on a global basis, and thereby enhancing popular resentment in smaller, less developed economies against trade liberalization.

- They lead to a diversion of scarce bureaucratic resources and political leadership away from global trade negotiations towards those at the regional level.

- They give rise to what Bhagwati (1995) has termed a 'spaghetti bowl' effect of numerous, crisscrossing preferential arrangements with a multiplicity of tariff rates and different rules of origin. The complexity of regulations provides opportunities for special pleading by interest groups and generally increases the costs of engaging in international trade. With countries being members of several RTAs, each with its own set of rules, companies face difficult decisions on where to establish subsidiaries and where to source their inputs (OECD 2002: 18).

- They provide exporters with the access to markets that they desire, thereby removing their incentive to lobby the government either for further liberalization at the global level, or for a further opening up of their domestic markets.

- They enable governments to exempt sensitive political sectors from liberalization, thereby energizing protectionist forces and strengthening political resistance against liberalization at the global level.

The exemption of sensitive sectors from liberalization rests on the possibility that regional arrangements will not be comprehensive in their product coverage because members are able to exploit the ambiguity of the WTO's rules on RTAs (Box 6.6 summarizes these rules). For the WTO to regard regional trade agreements as legitimate, average duties at the regional level must not be higher than those imposed by individual members before the agreement, and the arrangements must cover 'substantially all the trade' between the parties. The first of these obligations is ambiguous because it takes no account of rules of origin and non-tariff barriers; moreover, a substantial gap often exists between the tariff levels that countries have committed to in the WTO (so-called 'bound' rates) and the actual ('applied') tariffs (which are usually lower) they have put into force. In entering a regional agreement, countries can therefore keep the regional tariffs below their bound levels while actually imposing higher rates than they previously applied to non-members.

Box 6.6 The World Trade Organization and Preferential Trade Agreements

Article XXIV of the GATT lays down the criteria that regional arrangements must meet to be regarded as legitimate by the WTO. Members' customs duties under the new agreement must not 'on the whole' be higher or more restrictive than those previously imposed by the individual countries. The preferential agreement, according to Article XXIV.8, must also eliminate duties and other restrictions on 'substantially all the trade' between participants.

These provisions have generated enormous controversy over the years. In particular, members have failed to reach agreement on defining and applying the phrase 'substantially all the trade'. The WTO notes 'there exists neither an agreed definition of the percentage of trade to be covered by a WTO-consistent agreement nor common criteria against which the exclusion of a particular sector from the agreement could be assessed'. The European Union, a pioneer in negotiating preferential trade agreements, has argued that the Article XXIV.8 requirement has both a quantitative and a qualitative element, with at least 90 per cent of the trade between parties being covered and no major sector excluded. But other members have contested this interpretation, which raises its own problems of definition: how is the 90 per cent of trade to be measured (does it only refer to existing trade or to that which might take place should restrictions be removed)? And how does one define a 'major' sector? A reinterpretation of Article XXIV.8 is one of the items on the agenda in the current Doha Round of multilateral negotiations, but one on which few observers believe there will be agreement.

The lack of consensus on the provisions of Article XXIV.8 has stymied the work of the WTO's Committee on Regional Trade Agreements, created in February 1996 to examine preferential trade agreements and their implications for the multilateral trading system. Members have been able to agree that only one of the large number of PTAs notified to the Committee since 1996 (the customs union between the Czech Republic and the Slovak Republic after the break-up of Czechoslovakia) is fully compatible with the relevant rules. Lack of consensus has prevented the Committee from finalizing its other reports. The WTO's record on this matter is similar to that of the GATT, which was able to agree on the compatibility with Article XXIV of only four of the more than fifty RTAs submitted to it for consideration. Political factors have dominated decision-making on this issue. Nowhere was this more evident than when a GATT Working Party was convened to consider whether the Treaty of Rome, which established the EEC in 1957, met the requirements for RTAs. Faced with a threat by the Europeans to quit GATT should their integration arrangements be found incompatible with the full requirements of Article XXIV (which they clearly were), the GATT Working Party failed to reach consensus in its deliberations. Ultimately, contracting parties' desire (as much for security as for economic reasons) for integration in Europe to proceed outweighed their concerns about the legality of the agreements. Subsequently, GATT and the WTO have simply failed to pass judgement on the vast majority of RTAs they have examined, including CUSFTA and NAFTA.

The rules relating to the establishment of preferential trading arrangements among less developed economies under the 'Enabling Clause' are even less restrictive than those under Article XXIV. They make no reference to coverage of trade, the complete elimination of duties or to a timetable for implementation. They require only that the regional agreement not constitute a barrier to most-favoured-nation trade reductions or cause 'undue difficulties' for other members. RTAs notified to the GATT/WTO under the Enabling Clause include AFTA and MERCOSUR.

As part of the Doha Round negotiations, WTO members agreed on a new 'transparency mechanism' for regional trade agreements. Members negotiating regional agreements are now obliged to provide early notification of an RTA to the WTO: the WTO Secretariat will have a new role in preparing a factual presentation on the agreement for consideration by the Committee on Regional Trade Agreements or the Committee on Trade and Development. How effective this new scrutiny of agreements will be remains to be seen.

The ambiguities of the second obligation—the requirement that RTAs should cover substantially all trade—are of even greater import because they have enabled countries to exclude politically sensitive sectors from regional agreements. The European Union, for instance, did not include most of Mexico's and South Africa's agricultural exports in the free trade agreements it signed with these countries. Similarly, the Japanese government excluded the few agricultural products that Singapore exported to it from its free trade agreement with the island state.

The political significance is that free trade agreements that provide partial liberalization can provide exporters with what they want (access to foreign markets), while enabling governments to avoid tackling the problem of inefficient domestic industries. The result is a process of 'liberalization without political pain'. The continued protection that uncompetitive domestic industries enjoy by being exempted from regional liberalization may encourage them to lobby against any liberalization, whether at the regional or the global level. Meanwhile, the wider the network of preferential trade agreements, the less incentive will domestic exporters have for lobbying for liberalization at the global level (Ravenhill 2006*b*). Take Mexico as the current extreme example. It has more than thirty preferential trade agreements with partners on all continents that collectively account for more than 60 per cent of global GDP and more than 97 per cent of its exports (the vast majority, of course, going to the United States). The signature of RTAs has substantially reduced the incentive for Mexican exporters to expend resources in lobbying for global liberalization. Some observers have suggested that the difficulties in negotiating the Doha Round have been exacerbated by its becoming an 'agriculture' round because manufacturing and service sectors showed little interest in lobbying for liberalization at the global level (in contrast to the Uruguay Round).

The evidence

The sometimes contradictory arguments on the relationship between regional trade agreements and global trade liberalization rest on intuitively plausible hypotheses, but ones that are not easy to test. Moreover, the relatively brief period for which many of the new regional agreements have been operating makes it difficult to reach conclusions about their effects (and generalization is hazardous when the agreements themselves differ so markedly in their scope and content).

Two pieces of evidence support those who believe that regional trade agreements have not been barriers to liberalization at the global level. The first is the successful conclusion of the Uruguay Round of GATT negotiations which, as documented in the previous chapter, produced major steps forward in liberalization at the global level (although most of the Uruguay Round's negotiations took place *before* many of the agreements that are part of the new wave of regionalism came into being). The second is that members of many of the regional trade agreements, particularly those in South America, have lowered their barriers to non-member states more rapidly than did countries that were not members of regional agreements (Foroutan 1998). Although it is impossible to demonstrate a causal relationship here, the logic is straightforward: lowering barriers to non-members at the same time as entering a preferential trade arrangement reduces the risk of welfare loss through trade diversion. Critics of the new regionalism, however, point to evidence that after joining regional arrangements, Israel, Mexico, and MERCOSUR members, when encountering economic difficulties, all raised their tariffs against non-members but exempted their regional partners. Like so many other issues relating to the new regionalism, the link between RTAs and global liberalization remains inconclusive. (See Table 6.5 for a list of websites maintained by most regional trade agreements.)

Table 6.5 Membership of Minilateral Regional Trading Agreements

AFTA	ASEAN Free Trade Area www.aseansec.org/12025.htm	Brunei, Darussalam, Cambodia, Indonesia, Laos, Malaysia, Myanmar, Philippines, Singapore, Thailand, Vietnam
APEC	Asia-Pacific Economic Cooperation www.apecs.org	Australia, Brunei, Darussalam, Canada, Chile, China, Hong Kong, Indonesia, Japan, Korea, Malaysia, Mexico, New Zealand, Papua New Guinea, Peru, Philippines, Russia, Singapore, Chinese Taipei (Taiwan), Thailand, United States, Vietnam

Table 6.5 (*continued*)

207

REGIONAL TRADE AGREEMENTS

APTA	Asia-Pacific Trade Agreement www.unescap.org/tid/apta.asp	Bangladesh, China, India, Republic of Korea, Laos, Sri Lanka
CAFTA-DR	Dominican Republic–Central America–United States Free Trade Agreement	Costa Rica, Dominican Republic, El Salvador, Guatemala, Honduras, Nicaragua, United States
CAN	Andean Community www.comunidadandina.org	Bolivia, Colombia, Ecuador, Peru
CARICOM	Caribbean Community and Common Market www.caricom.org	Antigua & Barbuda, Bahamas, Barbados, Belize, Dominica, Grenada, Guyana, Haiti, Jamaica, Monserrat, Trinidad & Tobago, St Kitts & Nevis, St Lucia, St Vincent & the Grenadines, Suriname
CACM	Central American Common Market www.sice.oas.org/trade/camertoc.asp	Costa Rica, El Salvador, Guatemala, Honduras, Nicaragua
CEFTA	Central European Free Trade Agreement	Albania, Bosnia and Herzegovina, Croatia, Kosovo, Macedonia, Moldova, Montenegro, Serbia
CEMAC	Economic and Monetary Community of Central Africa www.cemac.cf	Cameroon, Central African Republic, Chad, Congo, Equatorial Guinea, Gabon
CER	Closer Economic Relations Trade Agreement www.dfat.gov.au/geo/new_zealand/ anz_cer/anz_cer.html	Australia, New Zealand
CIS	Commonwealth of Independent States www.cis.minsk.by	Azerbaijan, Armenia, Belarus, Georgia, Kazakhstan, Kyrgyz Republic, Moldova, Russian Federation, Tajikistan, Turkmenistan, Ukraine, Uzbekistan
COMESA	Common Market for Eastern and Southern Africa www.comesa.int	Burundi, Comoros, Democratic Republic of Congo, Djibouti, Egypt, Eritrea, Ethiopia, Kenya, Libya, Madagascar, Malawi, Mauritius, Rwanda, Seychelles, Sudan, Swaziland, Uganda, Zambia, Zimbabwe
EAC	East African Community	Burundi, Kenya, Rwanda, Tanzania, Uganda
EAEC	Eurasian Economic Community	Belarus, Kazakhstan, Kyrgyz Republic, Russian Federation, Tajikistan
ECO	Economic Cooperation Organization www.ecosecretariat.org/	Afghanistan, Azerbaijan, Iran, Kazakhstan, Kyrgyz Republic, Pakistan, Tajikistan, Turkey, Turkmenistan, Uzbekistan
ECOWAS	Economic Community of West African States www.ecowas.int	Benin, Burkina Faso, Cape Verde, Côte d'Ivoire, Gambia, Ghana, Guinea, Guinea Bissau, Liberia, Mali, Niger, Nigeria, Senegal, Sierra Leone, Togo
EEA	European Economic Area http://ec.europa.eu/external_relations/eea	EC, Iceland, Liechtenstein, Norway

Table 6.5 (*continued*)

EFTA	European Free Trade Association www.efta.int	Iceland, Liechtenstein, Norway, Switzerland
EU	European Union http://europa.eu/	Austria, Belgium, Bulgaria, Cyprus, Czech Republic, Denmark, Estonia, Finland, France, Germany, Greece, Hungary, Ireland, Italy, Latvia, Lithuania, Luxembourg, Malta, Netherlands, Poland, Portugal, Romania, Slovakia, Slovenia, Spain, Sweden, United Kingdom
GCC	Gulf Cooperation Council www.gcc-sg.org/	Bahrain, Kuwait, Oman, Qatar, Saudi Arabia, United Arab Emirates
GSTP	Global System of Trade Preferences among Developing Countries www.unctadxi.org/templates/Page—1879.aspx	Algeria, Argentina, Bangladesh, Benin, Bolivia, Brazil, Cameroon, Chile, Colombia, Cuba, Democratic People's Republic of Korea, Ecuador, Egypt, Ghana, Guinea, Guyana, India, Indonesia, Islamic Republic of Iran, Iraq, Libya, Macedonia, Malaysia, Mexico, Morocco, Mozambique, Myanmar, Nicaragua, Nigeria, Pakistan, Peru, Philippines, Republic of Korea, Singapore, Sri Lanka, Sudan, Thailand, Trinidad & Tobago, Tunisia, United Republic of Tanzania, Venezuela, Vietnam, Zimbabwe
LAIA	Latin American Integration Association www.aladi.org	Argentina, Bolivia, Brazil, Chile, Colombia, Cuba, Ecuador, Mexico, Paraguay, Peru, Uruguay, Venezuela
MERCOSUR	Southern Common Market www.mercosur.int	Argentina, Brazil, Paraguay, Uruguay
MSG	Melanesian Spearhead Group	Fiji, Papua New Guinea, Solomon Islands, Vanuatu
NAFTA	North American Free Trade Agreement www.nafta-sec-alena.org	Canada, Mexico, United States
PAFTA	Pan-Arab Free Trade Area	Algeria, Bahrain, Egypt, Iraq, Jordan, Kuwait, Lebanon, Libyan Arab Jamahiriya, Morocco, Oman, Palestinian Authority, Qatar, Saudi Arabia, Sudan, Syrian Arab Republic, Tunisia, United Arab Emirates, Yemen
PICTA	Pacific Island Countries Trade Agreement	Cook Islands, Fiji, Kiribati, Micronesia, Federated States of, Nauru, Niue, Papua New Guinea, Samoa, Solomon Islands, Tonga, Tuvalu, Vanuatu
PTN	Protocol relating to Trade Negotiations among Developing Countries	Bangladesh, Brazil, Chile, Egypt, Israel, Mexico, Pakistan, Paraguay, Peru, Philippines, Republic of Korea, Serbia, Tunisia, Turkey, Uruguay

Table 6.5 (*continued*)

SADC	Southern African Development Community www.sadc.int/	Angola, Botswana, Democratic Republic of Congo, Lesotho, Madagascar, Malawi, Mauritius, Mozambique, Namibia, Seychelles, South Africa, Swaziland, Tanzania, Zambia, Zimbabwe
SACU	Southern African Customs Union www.sacu.int/	Botswana, Lesotho, Namibia, South Africa, Swaziland
SAFTA	South Asian Free Trade Agreement http://www.saarc-sec.org/userfiles/ saftaagreement.pdf	Bangladesh, Bhutan, India, Maldives, Nepal, Pakistan, Sri Lanka
SPARTECA	South Pacific Regional Trade and Economic Cooperation Agreement Trans-Pacific Strategic Economic Partnership	Australia, New Zealand, Cook Islands, Fiji, Kiribati, Marshall Islands, Micronesia, Nauru, Niue, Papua New Guinea, Samoa, Solomon Islands, Tonga, Tuvalu, Vanuatu Brunei Darussalam, Chile, Singapore
TRIPARTITE	Tripartite Agreement	Egypt, India, Yugoslavia
UEMOA/WAEMU	West African Economic and Monetary Union www.uemoa.int	Benin, Burkina Faso, Ivory Coast, Guinea Bissau, Mali, Niger, Senegal, Togo

Key points

- A lively debate amongst writers on RTAs has produced several plausible arguments suggesting that regionalism can facilitate or hinder trade liberalization at the global level.

- The new regionalism is of such recent origin that the evidence on its effects remains inconclusive.

- The success of the Uruguay Round refuted the popular arguments in the late 1980s that the world economy was about to fragment into three rival trading blocs. But the results of the Doha Round will be a more significant indicator of the effects of the new regionalism on liberalization at the global level.

? Questions

1. How does the pattern of recent RTAs differ from that of the 1960s and 1970s?

2. For what economic reasons might governments prefer trade liberalization at the regional rather than the global level?

3. What political benefits might membership of a regional agreement bring?

4. What are the likely sources of domestic political opposition to regionalism?

5. Why might companies lobby for liberalization at the regional rather than the global level?

6. What is 'deeper' integration?

7. What were the sources of the failure of many of the regional trade agreements of the 1960s and 1970s?

8. Why did the United States government change its mind in the early 1980s on the desirability of regional trade agreements?

9. How does trade creation differ from trade diversion?

10. Why are rules of origin regarded as a protectionist device?

11. What evidence is there that regional integration has had a positive impact on the economies of participating economies? And what has been its impact on non-members?

12. For what reasons might regionalism assist or impede trade liberalization at the global level?

 Further reading

General

■ Bhagwati, J., and Panagariya, A. (eds) (1996), *The Economics of Preferential Trade Agreements* (Washington, DC: AEI Press). An accessible overview of arguments by economists against regionalism.

■ Crawford, J.-A., and Florentino, R. V. (2005), 'The Changing Landscape of Regional Trade Agreements', WTO Discussion Paper 8 (Geneva: World Trade Organization), www.wto.org/english/res_e/booksp_e/discussion_papers8_e.pdf. A comprehensive assessment of recent RTAs by two members of the WTO Secretariat.

■ Fawcett, L., and Hurrell, A. (eds) (1995), *Regionalism in World Politics: Regional Organization and International Order* (Oxford: Oxford University Press). An initial exploration of the new regionalism with overviews and case studies.

■ Fawn R. (ed.) (2009), *Globalising the Regional, Regionalising the Global* (Cambridge: Cambridge University Press). A contemporary overview of developments in regionalism in various parts of the world.

■ Frankel, J. A. (1997), *Regional Trading Blocs in the World Economic System* (Washington, DC: Institute for International Economics). The most comprehensive examination of the effects of regional trade agreements.

■ Haas, E. B. (1975), *The Obsolescence of Regional Integration Theory* (Berkeley, CA: Institute of International Studies, University of California). A reconsideration of the relevance of early integration theory.

■ Mansfield, E. D., and Milner, H. V. (eds) (1997), *The Political Economy of Regionalism* (New York: Columbia University Press). A recent collection of articles from a political economy perspective on regionalism in general; it includes case studies of the principal geographical regions.

■ Moravcsik, A. (1998), *The Choice for Europe: Social Purpose and State Power from Messina to Maastricht* (Ithaca, NY: Cornell University Press). The most sophisticated statement of the liberal intergovernmental approach to regionalism.

■ World Bank (2000), *Trade Blocs* (New York: Oxford University Press). A review of the evidence on the economic and political effects of regionalism and their relevance to less developed economies.

Africa

■ Bach, D. (ed.) (1999), *Regionalisation in Africa: Integration & Disintegration* (Bloomington, IN: Indiana University Press). A collection that examines the relationship between regionalism, regionalization, and state disintegration in Africa.

■ Lee, M. C. (2003), *The Political Economy of Regionalism in Southern Africa* (Boulder, CO: Lynne Rienner). Examines the history of regionalism in the southern part of Africa, with a especial emphasis on SADC.

The Americas

■ Cameron, M. A., and Tomlin, B. W. (2000), *The Making of NAFTA: How the Deal was Done* (Ithaca, NY: Cornell University Press). Analyses the negotiating process leading up to the signature of the NAFTA treaty.

■ Hufbauer, G. C., and Schott, J. J. (2005), *NAFTA Revisited: Achievements and Challenges* (Washington, DC: Institute for International Economics). The most comprehensive analysis of the effects in various sectors of NAFTA's implementation.

■ Roett, R. (ed.) (1999), *Mercosur: Regional Integration, World Markets* (Boulder, CO: Lynne Rienner). A collection of articles on integration among MERCOSUR members and their relations with the global economy.

Asia-Pacific

■ Aggarwal, V. K., and Morrison, C. E. (eds) (1998), *Asia-Pacific Crossroads: Regime Creation and the Future of APEC* (New York: St Martin's Press). A collection of articles on the foundation of APEC, the objectives of its founders, and its early impact.

■ Aggarwal, V. K., and Urata, S. (eds) (2006), *Bilateral Trade Agreements in the Asia-Pacific: Origins, Evolution, and Implications* (London: Routledge). Reviews the recent spate of bilateral agreements in the Asia-Pacific region.

■ Ravenhill, J. (2001), *APEC and the Construction of Asia-Pacific Regionalism* (Cambridge: Cambridge University Press). Applies the theoretical literature on regionalism to APEC's foundation and operating principles.

Europe

■ Bomberg, E. E., Peterson, J., and Stubb, A. C. G. (eds) (2008), *The European Union: How Does it Work?* 2nd edn (Oxford: Oxford University Press). An up-to-date introductory text on the EU.

■ Milward, A. S. (1992), *The European Rescue of the Nation-State* (London: Routledge). A historical review of European integration from an intergovernmental perspective.

■ Wallace, H., Wallace, W., and Pollack, M. (eds) (2005), *Policy-Making in the European Union,* 5th edn (Oxford: Oxford University Press). The most comprehensive and theoretically sophisticated overview of the various dimensions of EU integration.

JOHN RAVENHILL

 Web links

Table 6.5 lists addresses for the websites maintained by most regional trade agreements.

www.wto.org/english/tratop_e/region_e/region_e.htm   The WTO website's gateway to the Organization's material on regional trade agreements.

 Online resource centre

For additional material and resources, please visit the Online Resource Centre at:
www.oxfordtextbooks.co.uk/ravenhill3e/

PART 3
Global Finance

The Evolution of the International Monetary and Financial System

Eric Helleiner

7

 Reader's guide

The international monetary and financial system plays a central role in the global political economy. Since the late nineteenth century, the nature of this system has undergone several transformations in response to changing political and economic conditions at both domestic and international levels. The first was the collapse of the integrated pre-1914 international monetary and financial regime during the inter-war years. The second transformation took place after the Second World War, when the Bretton Woods order was put in place. Since the early 1970s, another period of change has been under way as various features of the Bretton Woods order have unravelled with the globalization of finance, the collapse of the gold exchange standard and the move to a floating exchange rate regime among the major economic powers. These various changes have important political consequences for the key issue of who gets what, when, and how in the global political economy.

Introduction

It is often said that money makes the world go round. In this age of globalization, the saying appears more relevant than ever. International flows of money today dwarf the cross-border trade of goods. And the influence of these flows seems only to be enhanced by their unique speed and global reach.

If money is so influential, it is fitting that it should have a prominent place in the study of global political economy, and that scholarly research on the political economy of international monetary and financial issues has grown very rapidly in recent years. While perspectives vary enormously within this literature, scholars working in this field share the belief that the study of money and finance must embrace a wider lens than that adopted by most economists.

Economists are trained to view money and finance primarily as economic phenomena. From their standpoint, money serves as a medium of exchange, a unit of account, and a store of value, while financial activity allocates credit within the economy. Both of these functions are critical to large-scale economic life, since they facilitate commerce, savings, and investment.

These descriptions of the economic role of money and finance are certainly accurate, but they are also limiting. Money and finance, after all, serve many political purposes as well (not to mention social and cultural ones). In all modern societies, control over the issuing and management of money and credit has been a key source of power, and the subject of intense political struggles. The organization and functioning of monetary and financial systems are thus rarely determined by a narrow economic logic of maximizing efficiency. They also reflect various political rationales relating to the pursuit of power, ideas, and interests (Kirshner 2003).

The interrelationship between politics and systems of money and finance is particularly apparent at the international level, where no single political authority exists. What money should be used to facilitate international economic transactions and how should it be managed? What should the nature of the relationship between national currencies be? How should credit be created and allocated at the international level? The answers to these questions have profoundly important implications for politics, not just within countries but also between them. It should not surprise us, then, that they provoke domestic and international political struggles, often of an intense kind.

This chapter highlights this point by providing an overview of the evolution of the international monetary and financial system since the late nineteenth century. The first section examines how changing political circumstances, both internationally and domestically, during the inter-war years undermined the stability of the globally integrated financial and monetary order of the pre-1914 era. The next section describes how a new international monetary and financial system—the Bretton Woods order—was created in 1944 for the post-war period, with a number of distinct features. The following three sections analyse the causes and consequences of challenges to that order which have emerged since the early 1970s with the globalization of finance, the collapse of the gold exchange standard, and the move to a floating exchange rate regime among the major economic powers. In the next chapter, Louis W. Pauly addresses another feature of the contemporary international financial order: its vulnerability to crises.

The Fate of a Previous Globally Integrated Financial and Monetary Order

Debates about contemporary economic globalization often note that this trend had an important precedent in the late nineteenth and early twentieth centuries. This is certainly true in the monetary and financial sector (see McGrew, Chapter 9, and Hay, Chapter 10 in this volume). Cross-border flows of money increased dramatically in this earlier period and, according to some criteria, even surpassed those in the current era in significance for national economies. Some of these flows involved short-term capital movements that responded primarily to interest rate differentials between financial centres around the world. Others involved long-term capital exports from the leading European powers to international locations. The United Kingdom, in particular, exported enormous amounts of long-term capital after 1870, sums that were much larger

as a percentage of its national income than any creditor country is exporting today (James 2001: 12).

These capital flows were facilitated by the emergence of an international monetary regime that was also highly integrated, indeed, much more so than in the current period (Gallarotti 1995). By 1914, the currencies of most independent countries and colonized regions around the world were linked to the same gold standard (see Box 7.1). The result was a fixed exchange-rate regime with an almost global reach. Indeed, some European countries went even further, to create regional 'monetary unions' in which the currencies of the member countries could circulate in each others' territory. A high-level international conference was even held in 1867 to consider the possibility of a worldwide 'monetary union' of

---

Box 7.1 The Theory of the Adjustment Process under the International Gold Standard

In theory, the international gold standard was a self-regulating international monetary order. External imbalances would be corrected automatically by domestic wage and price adjustments, according to a process famously described by David Hume: the 'price–specie flow mechanism'. If a country experienced a balance of payments deficit, Hume noted, gold exports should depress domestic wages and prices in such a way that the country's international competitive position—and thus its trade position—would be improved. Hume's model assumed that most domestic money was gold coins, but the domestic monetary system of most countries on the gold standard during the late nineteenth and early twentieth centuries was dominated by fiduciary money in the form of bank notes and bank deposits. In this context, the

monetary authority that issued notes and regulated the banking system had to stimulate the automatic adjustments of the gold standard by following proper 'rules of the game'. In the event of a trade deficit, it was expected to tighten monetary conditions by curtailing the issue of notes and raising interest rates. The latter was designed, not just to induce deflationary pressures (by increasing the cost of borrowing), but also to attract short-term capital flows to help finance the payments imbalance while the underlying macroeconomic adjustment process was taking place. In practice, however, historians of the pre-1914 gold standard note that governments did not follow these 'rules of the game' as closely and consistently as the theory of the gold standard anticipated (Eichengreen 1985).

this kind. As the scramble for colonies intensified after 1870, many imperial powers often encouraged the circulation of their currencies in the newly acquired colonies during this period (Helleiner 2003: chs 6, 8). These currency unions and imperial currency blocs were designed to make economic transactions within each union or bloc easier to conduct.

The end of globalization

What can we learn from this era in our efforts to understand the political foundations of international money and finance? Perhaps the most interesting lesson is the fact that this globally integrated financial and monetary order did not last. In the contemporary period, globalization is sometimes said to be irreversible. Studying the fate of this earlier globalization trend reminds us to be more cautious. In particular, it highlights the importance of the *political* basis of international money and finance.

The first signs of disintegration came during the First World War, when cross-border financial flows diminished dramatically and many countries abandoned the gold standard in favour of currencies whose value fluctuated vis-à-vis each other. After the war ended, there was a concerted effort — led by the United Kingdom and the United States — to restore the pre-1914 international monetary and financial order, and this initiative was initially quite successful. Many countries did restore the gold standard during the 1920s, and international capital flows — both short-term and long-term — also resumed on a very large scale by the late 1920s (Pauly 1997: ch. 3).

But this success was short-lived. In the early 1930s, a major international financial crisis triggered the collapse of both international lending and the international gold standard. This development signalled what Harold James (2001) has called 'the end of globalization'. The international monetary and financial system broke up into a series of relatively closed currency blocs. Within each

bloc, some international lending continued and the value of currencies was usually fixed vis-à-vis each other. But between the blocs, international flows of capital was limited, and often regulated tightly by new government controls on cross-border financial movements (or 'capital controls'). The value of currencies between the blocs also fluctuated considerably for much of the decade and some governments introduced fully fledged exchange controls which restricted private actors from converting the national currency into other currencies freely.

Hegemonic stability theory

What explains this dramatic change in the nature of the international monetary and financial regime? A prominent explanation within international political economy (IPE) scholarship has been that the transformation was related to a change in the distribution of power among states within the international monetary and financial arena (see, for example, Kindleberger 1973). According to this hegemonic stability theory, the pre-1914 international financial and monetary regime remained stable as long as it was sustained by British hegemonic leadership. Before the First World War, the United Kingdom's currency, sterling, was seen to be 'as good as gold' and it was used around the globe as a world currency. Britain was also the largest creditor to the world and London's financial markets held a pre-eminent place in global finance. The United Kingdom's capital exports helped to finance global payments imbalances and they were usefully counter-cyclical; that is, foreign lending expanded when the UK entered a recession, thus compensating foreign countries for the decline in sales to the UK. During international financial crises, the Bank of England is also said to have played a leadership role in stabilizing markets through lender-of-last-resort activities (see Pauly, Chapter 8 in this volume).

After the First World War, however, the United Kingdom lost its ability to perform its leadership role in stabilizing the global monetary and financial order. The United States replaced it as the lead creditor to the world economy, and the US dollar emerged as the strongest and most trustworthy world currency. New York also began to rival London's position as the key international financial centre. In these new circumstances, the United States might have taken on the kind of leadership role that the United Kingdom had played before the war. But it proved unwilling to do so because of isolationist sentiments and domestic political conflicts between internationally orientated and more domestically focused economic interests (Frieden 1988). The resulting leadership vacuum is blamed for the instability and eventual breakdown of the gold standard and integrated financial order during the inter-war period.

Hegemonic stability theorists criticize several aspects of US behaviour during the 1920s and early 1930s. Its capital exports during the 1920s were pro-cyclical; they expanded rapidly when the US economy was booming in the mid-to-late 1920s, but then came to a sudden stop in 1928, just as the growth of the US economy was slowing down. The collapse of US lending generated balance of payments crises for many foreign countries that had relied on US loans to cover their external payments deficits. The United States then exacerbated these countries' difficulties by raising tariffs against imports with the passage of the 1930 Smoot–Hawley Act. As confidence in international financial markets collapsed in the early 1930s, the US also refused to take on the role of international lender-of-last-resort, or even to cancel the war debts that were compounding the crisis.

Changing domestic political conditions

This interpretation of the evolution of the international monetary and financial system from the pre-1914 period into the inter-war period is not universally accepted (see, for example, Calleo 1976; Eichengreen 1992; Simmons 1994). A particularly important critique has been that the transformation of the international financial and monetary system was generated more by a change in the distribution of power *within* many states than between them. According to this perspective, the stability of the pre-1914 international monetary and financial order was dependent on a very specific domestic political context: governments were strongly committed to the classical liberal idea that domestic monetary policy should be geared to the external goal of maintaining the convertibility of the national currency into gold at a fixed rate.

This commitment stemmed not just from liberal ideology, but also from the fact that governments before 1914 were less responsive to domestic popular pressures. Deflationary policies required to maintain the fixed currency peg in the face of a trade deficit or capital outflows could be very painful for domestic groups, particularly the poor whose wages were forced downwards (or who experienced unemployment if wages did not fall). These policies were politically viable only because many low-income citizens had little voice in the national political arena. In most countries, the electoral franchise remained narrow before 1914. In many countries, central banks were not even public bodies in this period, and in colonial or peripheral regions, monetary authorities were often controlled by foreign interests.

After the First World War, the domestic political order was transformed in many independent states. The electoral franchise widened, the power of labour grew, and there was increasing support for more interventionist economic policies. These changes generated political pressures for monetary policy to be geared more towards domestic goals, such as addressing domestic unemployment, rather than the goal of maintaining external convertibility of the currency into gold. As governments ceased to play by the 'rules of the game', the 'self-regulating' character of the gold standard began to break down (see Box 7.1). Short-term international financial flows also became more volatile and speculative, as investors no longer had confidence in governments' commitment to maintain fixed rates. Faced with these new domestic pressures, central banks also found it more difficult to co-operate in ways that promoted international monetary and financial stability.

In the context of the international financial crisis of 1931 and the Great Depression, many governments then chose simply to abandon the international gold standard altogether in order to escape its discipline. In countries facing external payments deficits, the depreciation of the national currency provided a quicker, less painful, method for adjusting the country's wages and prices vis-à-vis those in foreign countries in order to boost exports and curtail imports. Abandoning the international gold standard was also attractive to many governments in the early 1930s because the move helped insulate the country from deflationary pressures emanating from the US at this time. In addition, allowing the national exchange rate to fluctuate provided governments with greater national policy autonomy to pursue expansionary monetary policies that could address pressing domestic economic needs. This policy autonomy was reinforced by capital controls which insulated countries from the influence of speculative cross-border financial movements. For this reason, it was not surprising to find such controls supported by John Maynard Keynes, the leading advocate of domestically orientated, activist macroeconomic management, who famously urged in the early 1930s 'let finance be primarily national' (Keynes 1933: 758).

Key points

- In the late nineteenth and early twentieth centuries, a highly integrated global financial and monetary order existed. By the early 1930s, it had collapsed, and was replaced by a fragmented order organized around closed economic blocs and floating exchange rates.

- Some believe the reason for the breakdown of the pre-1914 order was the absence of a state acting as a hegemonic leader to perform such roles as the provision of stable international lending, the maintenance of an open market for foreign goods, and the stabilization of financial markets during crises.

- Others argue that the pre-1914 order was brought down more by a domestic political transformation across much of the world, associated with expansion of the electoral franchise, the growing power of labour, and the new prominence of supporters of interventionist economic policies.

The Bretton Woods Order

If an integrated international monetary and financial order was to be rebuilt, it would need to be compatible with the new priority placed on domestic policy autonomy. An opportunity to create such an order finally arose in the early 1940s, when US and UK policy-makers began to plan the organization of the post-war international monetary and financial system.

Embedded liberalism

At the time, it was clear that the United States would emerge from the war as the dominant economic power, and US policy-makers were determined to play a leadership role in building and sustaining a more liberal and multilateral international economic order than the one that had existed during the 1930s. The closed economic blocs and economic instability of the previous decade were thought to have contributed to the Great Depression and the Second World War. But US policy-makers did not want to see a return to the classical liberal international economic order of the pre-1930s period. Instead, they hoped to find a way to reconcile their commitment to an open multilateral world economy with the new domestically orientated priorities to combat unemployment and promote social welfare that had emerged with the New Deal.

This objective to create what Ruggie (1982) has called an **embedded liberal** international economic order was shared by policy-makers in many other countries, including Keynes who had emerged as the policy-maker in charge of UK planning for the post-war world economy during the early 1940s. Keynes and his American counterpart, Harry Dexter White, took the lead in producing a detailed blueprint for the post-war international monetary and financial order that was soon endorsed by forty-four countries at the 1944 Bretton Woods conference (van Dormael 1978; Gardner 1980).

At first sight, the blueprint seemed to signal a return to a pre-1930s world. Signatories to the Bretton Woods agreements agreed to peg their currency in relation to the gold content of the US dollar in 1944. At the time, the US dollar was convertible into gold at a rate of $35 per ounce. By pegging their currencies in this way, countries appeared to be establishing an international gold standard—or, to be more precise, a 'gold exchange' standard or 'gold-dollar' standard. And at one level, the objectives underlying the Bretton Woods agreements were, indeed, similar to those of the gold standard. The Bretton Woods architects sought to re-establish a world of international currency stability. Floating exchange rates were associated with beggar-thy-neighbour competitive devaluations, speculative financial flows, and the general breakdown of international economic integration.

A different kind of gold standard

But several other features of the Bretton Woods agreements made clear that this commitment did not signal a return to the kind of gold standard of the 1920s or the pre-1914 period. First, although countries agreed to make their currencies convertible for current account transactions (that is, trade payments), they were given the right to control all capital movements. While the Bretton Woods architects welcomed productive international investment flows, this provision was designed to enable governments to control speculative and 'disequilibrating' private financial flows which could disrupt stable exchange rates and national economic policy autonomy. The new support for capital controls signalled a dramatic change of views towards private cross-border financial movements from the 1920s. As John Maynard Keynes put it, 'What used to be a heresy is now endorsed as orthodox' (quoted in Helleiner 1994: 25).

The Bretton Woods conference also established two public institutions to assume some aspects of international lending that had previously been left to private markets: the International Monetary Fund (IMF) and the International Bank for Reconstruction and Development (IBRD) (known as the World Bank). The IMF was to provide short-term loans to help countries finance their temporary balance of payments deficits, thus providing deficit countries with greater breathing space than they had had under the pre-1930s international gold standard (see Box 7.2). The IBRD was designed to provide long-term loans for reconstruction and development after the war, a task that the private markets were not trusted to perform well. Support for the new 'development' function of the IBRD was particularly strong among those delegates from non-industrialized countries who made up well over half of the countries represented at the conference (Helleiner 2009).

Box 7.2 Quotas and Decision-Making in the IMF

While the World Bank can borrow from the private markets to fund its lending, the IMF's capacity to lend comes primarily from the contributions of member governments. On joining the IMF, all member governments pay a 'quota' to the institution that largely reflects their relative size within the world economy. The amount of money they can borrow from the Fund is then determined by their quota size. Quotas also play a very significant role in determining voting shares within the Fund. All countries are allocated 250 'basic votes', but the bulk of their voting share is determined by their quota size. At the time of the founding of the IMF, 'basic votes' made up 11 per cent of total votes, but they have fallen to a far lower share more recently because of the entrance of new members and quota increases.

Quotas are reviewed at least every five years, and the relative share of various countries has changed over time in response to these reviews. The US quota share, for example, has fallen from more than 30 per cent of the total votes in 1944 to roughly 17 per cent today, while the shares of countries such as Japan, Germany, and Saudi Arabia have increased considerably. One of the key issues on the international policy agenda today is the need to adjust IMF quotas to reflect the growing economic significance of rapidly industrializing countries.

The IMF is governed by its Board of Governors, which meets annually. Day-to-day decision-making, however, is delegated to the Executive Board, which meets several times a week. The Executive Board started with only twelve executive directors, with the five largest country contributors being assigned a single seat and other members being represented by 'constituency' groups. Today, the number of executive directors has risen to twenty-four and, in addition to the five largest contributors, single-country constituencies have been created for Saudi Arabia, China, and Russia.

Finally, rather than trust the automatic self-regulating adjustments of the gold standard, the Bretton Woods architects assigned public authorities with a more conscious and active role in the management of international economic imbalances. Particularly important was the fact that national governments were given the option of changing the peg value of their national currencies whenever their country was in 'fundamental disequilibrium' (a term whose precise meaning was left ambiguous). In other words, this was to be a kind of adjustable peg system, in which countries could substitute exchange rate devaluations for harsh domestic deflations when they experienced sustained payments deficits.

More generally, the IMF was to promote global monetary co-operation and encourage countries to 'shorten the duration and lessen the degree of disequilibrium in the international balances of payments of members'. To discourage international economic imbalances, the IMF's lending capacity gave it some potential influence over deficit countries. Another provision in its charter—the scarce currency clause—provided a means for official pressure to come to bear on surplus countries; if the Fund's ability to supply a surplus country's currency was threatened (because of excessive demand for it from other members), the IMF could declare that currency 'scarce' and member governments would then be permitted to impose temporary restrictions on trade with that country.

For the first decade-and-a-half after the Second World War, the Bretton Woods system, it has been said, was in 'virtual cold storage' (Skidelsky 2003: 125). It is certainly true that the IMF and IBRD played very limited roles during this period, and that European countries did not make their currencies convertible until 1958 (the Bretton Woods agreements had allowed for a 'transition' period of no specified length, during which countries could keep currencies inconvertible). At the same time, however, most governments outside the Soviet orbit were committed to the other principles outlined at Bretton Woods: namely, support for capital controls, the gold exchange standard, and the maintenance of an adjustable peg exchange rate regime. Moreover, although the IMF and World Bank were sidelined, other bodies—particularly the US government, but also regional institutions such as the European Payments Union—acted in the ways that Keynes and White had hoped the Bretton Woods institutions would. Public international lending was provided for temporary balance of payments support, as well as for reconstruction and development. United States policy-makers also encouraged international monetary co-operation and promoted 'embedded liberal' ideals when they were engaged in monetary and financing advisory roles around the world (Helleiner 1994: ch. 3; 2003: ch. 9).

During the heyday of the Bretton Woods order, from the late 1950s until 1971, the IMF and World Bank became more active lenders but they had a less central role in the system than Keynes and White had hoped for. Governments remain committed to the other key features of the order. What, then, became of the Bretton Woods order? In some respects, it seems to be still alive. The IMF and World Bank still exist (although their purpose has been altered, as described below); most countries' currencies are convertible for current account transactions; the dollar is still the key international currency; and the broader commitment to multilateralism has endured. In the following sections, however, I explore the key causes and consequences of challenges that have emerged to other features of the Bretton Woods regime with the globalization of finance, the collapse of the gold exchange standard, and the move to a floating exchange rate regime among the major economic powers.

Key points

- The Bretton Woods Conference in 1944 created a new international monetary and financial order that was inspired by an 'embedded liberal' ideology and backed by US leadership.

- Governments joining this order committed themselves to: currency convertibility for current account payments; a gold exchange standard; an adjustable peg exchange rate regime, an acceptance of capital controls, and support for the IMF and World Bank.

- Many of the features of the Bretton Woods order were in place between 1945 and 1958, but this order reached its heyday between 1958 and 1971.

The Globalization of Financial Markets

The globalization of private financial markets was one of the more dramatic developments of the last few decades. Recall that the Bretton Woods architects endorsed an international financial order in which governments could control cross-border private financial flows, and public international institutions were assigned a key role in allocating short-term and long-term credit at the international level. Today, this world appears to be turned upside down. Enormous sums of private capital flow around the world quite freely on a twenty-four-hour basis. And the size of these flows dwarfs the lending activities of the IMF and World Bank (whose loans have become focused exclusively on poorer countries).

Explaining financial globalization

How did we get from there to here? The globalization process began in the 1960s, but really accelerated after the early 1970s. Some analysts emphasize the technological and market explanations.

There is no question that the growth of global telecommunications networks in this period enabled money to be moved around the world much more easily than in the past. The dramatic expansion of international trade and multinational corporate activity during this period also encouraged growing demand for private international financial services. Private international financial flows also accelerated particularly after the 1973 oil price rise when private banks took on the role of recycling the new wealth of oil-producing countries. In addition, private actors were encouraged to diversify their assets internationally by the increasingly volatile currency environment after the breakdown of the Bretton Woods exchange rate system in the early 1970s (see below). The costs of international financial activity were also lowered throughout this period by various market innovations, such as the creation of derivatives products including futures, options, and swaps.

The globalization of finance was also a product of political choices by governments to support the emergence of a more liberal environment for cross-border financial flows (Helleiner 1994; Abdelal 2007). The first step in this direction took place when the British government encouraged the growth of the 'euro-market' in London during the 1960s where international financial activity in foreign currencies — primarily US dollars in the early years — could be conducted on a largely unregulated basis. After the early 1970s, many governments then fully dismantled capital controls they had employed at various times during the post-war years. The United States and United Kingdom led the way, abolishing their national capital controls in 1974 and 1979, respectively. They were soon followed by other Organization for Economic Co-operation and Development (OECD) countries. Indeed, by the 1990s, an almost fully liberal pattern of financial relations had emerged among wealthy 'Northern' countries, giving market actors a degree of freedom in cross-border financial activity unparalleled since the 1920s. Many poorer 'Southern' countries also abolished capital controls, including many small jurisdictions — such as the Grand Caymans — that

offered their territories as locations for 'offshore' international financial activity via loose regulatory environments (Palan 2003).

What explains states' growing support for financial globalization? The increasing influence of more free market or 'neo-liberal' ideology among financial policy-makers in this period played a part. Neo-liberals criticized the fact that capital controls interfered with individual freedom and prevented markets from efficiently allocating capital internationally. Many neo-liberals were also less sympathetic to Bretton Woods' 'embedded liberal' goal of protecting the policy autonomy of governments. From their standpoint, international financial markets could play a useful role imposing an external discipline on governments pursuing inflationary or fiscally unsustainable policies.

The liberalization of capital controls has also been seen by some policy-makers as a kind of competitive strategy to attract mobile financial business and capital to their national territory (Cerny 1994). The British government's support for the euromarkets and its decision to abolish capital controls in 1979 were both designed to help rebuild London's status as a leading international financial centre in this way. The US support for financial liberalization (both at home and abroad) was also designed to bolster New York's international financial position, as well as to attract foreign capital to the uniquely deep and liquid US financial markets in ways that could help finance US trade and budget deficits. The smaller, offshore financial centres also saw the hosting of an international financial centre as a development strategy that could provide employment and some limited government revenue (from such things as licenses and fees). Once governments such as these had begun to liberalize and deregulate their financial systems, many other governments also felt competitive pressure to emulate their decisions in order to prevent mobile domestic capital and financial business from migrating abroad. As their country's firms became increasingly transnational and had access to foreign financial markets, policy-makers also recognized that national capital controls could only be enforced in very rigid ways that would be costly to the national economy (Goodman and Pauly 1993).

Alongside governments' unilateral decisions to abolish capital controls, there have been some efforts to codify a more liberal set of international rules to govern cross-border financial flows (Abdelal 2007). Some of these efforts have been successful, such as a 1988 European Union directive to liberalize capital controls and a 1989 amendment to an OECD code which committed OECD countries to liberalize all financial flows. But the most ambitious initiative formally to overturn the restrictive Bretton Woods rules ultimately failed. In the mid 1990s, the IMF management began to seek to amend the Fund's Articles of Agreement to assign it in the purpose of promoting financial liberalization and to give it jurisdiction over capital movements. While the initiative initially met with support, it was ultimately defeated at the height of the 1997–8 East Asian financial crisis which highlighted to many policy-makers, including key figures in US Congress as well as many Southern countries, the potential risks associated with financial globalization.

Implications for national policy autonomy

What have been the implications of the globalization of finance? One set of implications is addressed in the next chapter: the vulnerability of global financial markets to financial crises. A second set of implications relates to the concerns of the Bretton Woods negotiators. As noted above, they worried that a liberal international financial order would undermine their efforts to create a stable exchange rate system and to protect national policy autonomy. We will see below how financial globalization did complicate the task of maintaining fixed exchange rates. But what about its implications for the autonomy of national governments to pursue their preferred economic policies?

This question has generated much debate in the field of IPE. Some have argued that financial globalization has severely undermined national policy autonomy, since it gives investors a powerful 'exit' option to exercise against governments that stray too far from their preferences. Proponents of this view argue that this discipline is felt particularly strongly by governments that pursue policies disliked by wealthy asset holders, such as large budget deficits, high taxation, expansionary macroeconomic policies that risk inflation, or, more generally, policies that reflect left-of-centre political values (Gill and Law 1989; McKenzie and Lee 1991; Kurzer 1993; Cerny 1994; Sinclair 1994; Harmes 1998). These new constraints—what Thomas Friedman (2000) calls the 'Golden Straightjacket'—are said to help explain why governments across the world have shifted away from these kinds of policies since the 1970s.

Southern governments are seen to be especially vulnerable to the discipline of global financial markets. This is partly because their financial systems are so small relative to the enormous size of global financial flows. It is also because investors tend to be more skittish about the security of their assets in contexts where economic and political instability is higher and there is a possibility of sovereign defaults. The 1994 Mexican peso crisis and the 1997–8 East Asian financial crisis are cited to show how entire countries' economic prospects can be devastated overnight by a sudden loss of confidence among private actors in international financial markets. More generally, Southern countries have also suffered from the fact that their wealthy citizens have taken advantage of the new global markets to park their assets in safer Northern financial markets. During debt crises, the size of this 'flight capital' from many debtor countries has often equalled or surpassed that of the country's external debts. In other words, these countries were often creditors to the world economy at the very moment that their governments were managing a severe debt crisis; if this flight capital could be repatriated, these countries would have experienced no debt crisis and associated loss of policy autonomy (Helleiner 2001; Lissakers 1991).

Other scholars suggest that these arguments about the declining policy autonomy of national governments are overstated. They point to open macroeconomic theory which explains that governments face trade-offs among an 'impossible trinity' of monetary policy autonomy, cross-border capital mobility, and stable exchange rates. Governments can achieve two of these goals, but never all three (see Box 7.3). As they liberalized cross-border capital movements, governments could still maintain monetary policy autonomy if they were willing to allow their national currency's exchange rate to fluctuate in value (Andrews 1994). Governments could, for example, continue to pursue autonomous expansionary monetary policies as long as they were willing to accept depreciation of the national currency. The importance of exchange rate policy in providing a degree of macroeconomic autonomy has also been highlighted in the case of capital flight from Southern countries. Jonathan Crystal (1994) has shown how Latin American countries maintaining overvalued exchange rates have suffered much more serious capital flight than those that have not, and how government decisions to maintain overvalued exchange rates reflected domestic political constraints rather than the influence of global financial markets.

Box 7.3 The 'Impossible Trinity' of Open Macroeconomics

Economists have pointed out that national governments face an inevitable trade-off between the three policy goals of exchange rate stability, national monetary policy autonomy, and capital mobility. It is only ever possible for governments to realize two of these goals at the same time. If, for example, a national government wants to preserve capital mobility and a fixed exchange rate, it must abandon an independent monetary policy. The reason is straightforward. An independent expansionary monetary policy in an environment of capital mobility will trigger capital outflows—and downward pressure on the national currency—as domestic interest rates fall. In this context, it will be possible to maintain the fixed exchange rate only by pushing interest rates back up and thereby abandoning the initial monetary policy goal. If, however, the government chooses to maintain the expansionary policy, it will need either to introduce capital controls or to embrace a floating exchange rate, thereby sacrificing one of the other goals within the 'impossible trinity'.

Historically, during the era of the gold standard, governments embraced fixed exchange rates and capital mobility, while abandoning national monetary policy autonomy. During the early post-1945 years, national policy autonomy and fixed (although adjustable) exchange rates were prioritized, while capital mobility was deemed to be less important. Since the early 1970s, the leading powers have sacrificed a global regime of fixed exchange rates in order to prioritize capital mobility and preserve a degree of monetary policy autonomy. Many governments within this system, however, have embraced fixed rates at the regional or bilateral level by using capital controls or by abandoning national policy autonomy.

Other authors suggest that the disciplining effect of global finance on governments with high levels of government spending, high taxation, or a more general left-of-centre political orientation has also been exaggerated (see the discussion in Hay, Chapter 10 in this volume). Garrett (1995) has highlighted how many OECD governments have been able to use borrowing in international capital markets to finance increased government spending (see also Swank 2002). In a detailed study of the preferences of international financial market actors, Mosley (2003) found that these actors were concerned primarily with national inflation rates and aggregate levels of fiscal deficits; they did not worry about governments' overall level of spending, taxation, or political orientation when considering investment decisions (although this result was less true when they considered investments in Southern countries). Other scholars have also noted that the policy autonomy of the US, in particular, has been boosted by the globalization of finance for the reasons noted above: private investors around the world have been attracted to its uniquely deep and liquid financial markets in ways that have helped fund US current account and fiscal deficits (for example, Strange 1986; Helleiner 1994).

IPE analysts have also argued that Southern countries faced with international financial crises are not always disciplined by international bankers. Argentina's experience in 2001–5, showed how debtor governments can exploit creditor divisions and place the burden of adjustment back onto international investors (Cooper and Momani 2005). Many poor countries have also found their policy autonomy boosted by an aspect of the financial globalization trend that has received less attention from IPE scholars: flows of remittances from rich to poor countries. These flows have been growing rapidly in recent years, and they are often more stable than the lending of rich-country investors. Indeed, they are sometimes even counter-cyclical; that is, they increase when the recipient country is undergoing difficult economic times (see, for example, Kapur and McHale 2003).

Finally, the increasing significance of 'sovereign wealth funds' (SWFs) within the last decade has also challenged the thesis that global financial markets are undermining government's policy autonomy. That thesis rested on the assumption that the key investors in global markets were private actors. But in the last decade, these state-controlled funds have emerged as increasingly influential international investors, with combined assets larger than the entire hedge fund industry. In this context, the analytical distinction between 'global markets' and 'states' has becomed blurred; the governments that control the largest funds (especially Abu Dhabi, China, Kuwait, Norway, and Singapore) are suddenly significant market actors. Their policy priorities, rather than being constrained by global markets, now play a role in shaping the behaviour of those markets. For example, Norway's SWF is mandated to invest in ways that uphold various international social and environmental conventions that Norwegian politicians have prioritized. Concerns have

also been raised about the overseas investments of other SWFs being used to gain economic or political leverage abroad (see the discussion in Helleiner and Kirshner 2009b; Helleiner and Lundblad 2008).

Distributive and environmental implications of financial globalization

Scholars of international political economy have also been interested in some other implications of financial globalization that attracted less attention at Bretton Woods, one of these being its distributive impact within countries. Neo-Marxist scholars have argued that financial globalization has bolstered the power of an emerging, internationally mobile capitalist class, while eroding that of labour. The emerging transnational capital class has gained 'structural power' through its new ability to exit—or simply to threaten to exit—domestic political settings. This power has been used to reinforce neo-liberal ideology and a kind of 'internationalization of the state' which serves the interests of this new class (Gill and Law 1989).

Jeffrey Frieden (1991) has also highlighted new political divisions that have emerged within the business sector. While **transnational corporations** (TNCs) and owners of financial assets and services have gained from financial globalization, businesses that are more nationally based often have not. In a world of heightened capital mobility, he argues, these two groups are, in fact, increasingly at loggerheads over policy choices within the 'impossible trinity'. The former generally prefer exchange rate stability because of their involvement in international trade and finance, even if this involves a cost of abandoning monetary policy autonomy. Those in the non-tradable sector are inclined to defend monetary policy autonomy, even if this involves accepting a floating exchange rate.

Some scholars have also analysed the gendered implications of financial globalization (Singh and Zammit 2000; van Staveren 2002). To the extent that global financial integration has been associated with the retrenchment of the welfare state, the costs have often been borne more by women than men. Cutbacks to government spending in areas such as health, education, public transportation, and other social services frequently have the effect of increasing the role played in these areas by the unpaid sector of the economy, a sector traditionally dominated by women. When countries experience international financial crises, other aspects of the burden of adjustment can also be strongly gendered. During the 1997–8 Asian financial crisis, incomes in the informal sectors—where women are heavily represented—fell particularly sharply, and job cuts in the formal private sector often fell more heavily on women. Aslanbeigui and Summerfield (2000: 87, 91) also note how 'across the region, migrant workers, the majority of whom were women, were expelled from host countries and they quote the World Bank's observation that 'child labour, prostitution and domestic violence' increased during the crisis. Other analysts have also highlighted how even global financial markets themselves are made up overwhelmingly of male traders and they operate with a culture and discourse that is hyper-masculinized (McDowell 1997; De Goede 2000).

A final issue that received little attention at the time of the Bretton Woods conference concerns the environmental implications of global financial markets. Scholarship on this topic has been fairly limited within the field of IPE to date, but some interesting themes have been put forward by those who have addressed it. Some analysts have suggested that speculative and volatile international financial flows reward instant economic results and short-term thinking in ways that greatly complicate the kind of long-term planning that is required for the promotion of environmental values. During the East Asian financial crisis, for example, governments scrapped environmental programmes and there was an intensification of deforestation, mining, and other economic activities that put pressure on natural ecosystems (Durbin and Welch

2002). Two analysts working with the World Business Council on Sustainable Development have also argued 'financial markets discount the future routinely and heavily' in ways that are damaging to environment (Schmidheiny and Zorraquin 1996: 8). As an example, they argue that 'it is clear that the globalization of investment flows is speeding the destruction of natural forests' (Schmidheiny and Zorraquin 1996: 10). International investors, they note, push firms to harvest an entire forest for a short-term windfall profit rather than manage the forest in a sustainable fashion over the long term.

On the other hand, one powerful actor in global finance—the global insurance sector—does have a longer-term perspective that has led it to lobby for action on climate change in order to reduce the risk of future claims in this area (Paterson 2001; Haufler 1997). A number of initiatives have also been launched in recent years by investor groups, banks, and accountants to push firms to act in more environmentally sustainable ways. These have been driven, not just by growing environmental worries, but also by economic concerns that the failure of markets to account fully for the growing significance of environmental risks can lead to poor business decisions. In addition to shareholder activism and steering their own investments away from firms involved in environmentally damaging activities, these groups have pressed for greater disclosure of environmentally related material risks from potential borrowers. Proponents argue that this disclosure could transform financial markets into a useful tool of discipline, punishing firms with poor environmental records while shifting capital towards those with good ones. They have developed a number of voluntary codes for firms to adopt, and these initiatives have received some official support, including from the World Bank in the case of the 'Equator Principles' and United Nations Environment Program through its Finance Initiative (Pattberg 2005; Wright and Rwabizambuga 2006; MacLeod 2007). Whether these voluntary codes will be followed by more mandatory rules remains to be seen.

Key points

- The globalization of financial markets has been driven, not just by technological and market pressures, but also by the decisions of states to liberalize capital controls that had been popular in the early post-war years.

- A hotly contested subject among IPE scholars concerns the question of whether, and to what extent,

global financial markets have eroded the policy autonomy of national governments.

- Financial globalization has also had important distributive consequences along class, sectoral, and gender lines. The environmental implications of global financial markets are also attracting growing attention.

The Collapse of the Gold Exchange Standard and the Future of the Dollar

While the globalization of financial markets took place in a gradual fashion, the Bretton Woods' gold exchange standard broke down in a more decisive way. In August 1971, the United States suddenly suspended the convertibility of the US dollar into gold. Since other currencies had been tied to gold only via the US dollar, this move signalled the end of gold's role as a standard for other currencies as well.

This collapse of the gold exchange standard had in fact been predicted as far back as 1960, when Robert Triffin (1960) had highlighted its inherent instability. In a system where the dollar was the central reserve currency, he argued that international liquidity could be expanded only when the United States provided the world with more dollars by running a balance of payments deficit. But the more it did so, the more it risked undermining confidence in the dollar's convertibility into gold.

One potential solution to the Triffin Dilemma was to create a new international currency whose supply would not be tied to the balance of payments condition of any one country. Keynes had, in fact, proposed such a currency—which he called 'bancor'—during the negotiations leading up to the Bretton Woods Conference. In 1965, the United States began to support the idea that the IMF could

issue such a currency as a means of supplementing the dollar's role as a reserve currency, and Special Drawing Rights (SDRs) were finally created for this purpose in 1969. The SDR was not a currency that individuals handled; it was used only by national monetary authorities as a reserve asset for settling inter-country payments imbalances (and subject to certain conditions). Subsequently, however, IMF members refused to approve the issuance of significant quantities of SDR to enable it to play much of a role in the global monetary system.

During the 1960s, and in particular after the mid-1960s, Triffin's predictions were increasingly borne out. US currency abroad did grow considerably larger than the amount of gold the US government held to back it up. In one sense, the situation was beneficial to the United States: the country was able to finance growing external deficits associated with the Vietnam War and its domestic Great Society programme (which produced rising imports) simply by printing dollars. Indeed, the United States was doing much more than providing the world with needed international liquidity by the late 1960s; it was actively exporting inflation by flooding the world with dollars. In another sense, however, the country was becoming increasingly vulnerable to a confidence crisis. If all holders of dollars suddenly decided to convert the US currency into gold, the US would not be able to meet the demand. Another cost to the US was the fact that the dollar's fixed value in gold was undermining the international competitiveness of US-based firms. If major trading partners in Europe and Japan had been willing to revalue their currencies, this problem could have been addressed, but these governments resisted, preferring to keep their exports to the US market competitively priced.

A crisis of confidence in the dollar's convertibility into gold was initially postponed when some key foreign allies—notably Germany and Japan—agreed not to convert their reserves into gold (sometimes as part of an explicit trade-off for US security protection: Zimmermann 2002). But other countries that were critical of US foreign policy in this period—France in particular—refused to adopt this practice, seeing it as a reinforcement of American hegemony (Kirshner 1995: 192–203). Private speculators also increasingly targeted the US dollar, especially after sterling was devalued in 1967. When speculative pressures against the dollar reached a peak in 1971, the United States chose simply to 'close the gold window' in order to free itself from the constraint on its policies that gold convertibility imposed (Gowa 1983).

The dollar's enduring global role

In the eyes of many observers, the breakdown of the gold exchange standard reflected declining US power, thus providing further evidence to support the hegemonic stability theory. Others, however, suggested US hegemonic power in the international monetary system remained and all that had changed was the country's willingness to lead (for example, Strange 1986; Calleo 1976). Defenders of the latter position pointed to the fact that the US dollar remained the unchallenged dominant world currency after 1971.

When US policy-makers ended the dollar's convertibility into gold, some predicted that the US currency's role as the dominant world currency would be challenged quickly, since the dollar was no longer 'as good as gold'. In fact, however, the dollar's central global role has endured up to the present day. It has continued to be the currency of choice for settling international economic transactions and for denominating international trade and investments across most of the world. Among countries that peg their currencies, the dollar is also the most popular anchor currency. In addition, the greenback has also remained the most common currency held by most governments in their foreign exchange reserves. The US dollar has even been used to an increasing degree by market actors within many poorer countries as a unit of account, a store of value, and even a medium of exchange since the 1980s (Helleiner and Kirshner 2009a).

In some respects, the US dollar's enduring central global position is a product of inertia. There are many 'network externalities' that reinforce the continued use of existing currencies, particularly when the issuing country is such a major player in the global economy; the more a currency is used, the greater the incentive for others to use it for convenience reasons. Some foreign governments have also continued to hold their reserves in US dollars and denominated their international trade in dollars because of economic and political ties with the US. Perhaps most important in explaining the dollar's enduring global role, however, has been the fact that US financial markets, particularly the short-term markets, have remained among the most liquid, large and deep in the world. This has made the holding and use of US dollars particularly attractive to private actors and foreign governments. Although some predicted that the yen and Deutschmark might challenge the dollar after 1971, neither Japan nor West Germany has been willing and/or able to cultivate the kinds of domestic markets, in which yen-denominated or Deutschmark-denominated assets could be held, to rival their dollar-based counterparts (Helleiner and Kirshner 2009a).

Emerging challenges to the dollar's dominant position?

Will the dollar's global role continue? There is enormous disagreement on this question among IPE scholars (see Helleiner and Kirshner 2008, 2009*a*). Some argue that the dollar's global status is now more precarious than at any time in the post-war period. The US's large current account and fiscal deficits, combined with its growing external debt, have raised concerns about whether the currency can continue to earn the confidence of global markets and foreign governments. The continued political loyalty of some of the latter to the dollar-based international monetary order has also been questioned as their economic and political ties to the US have weakened. The largest foreign official holders of US dollar reserves today are, after all, a more heterogenous group than the close US allies of the previous decades, including some countries often considered potential geostrategic rivals to the US such as China (see next section). In this uncertain context, some predict that a 'tipping point' could be reached where expectations of both market and government actors rapidly change.

This risk is heightened by the fact that the dollar is now facing what appears to be a more serious challenger than in the past: the euro. Is noted below, one goal behind the creation of the euro in 1999 was that it could rival the dollar's international role (Henning 1998: 563–5). When outlining the official rationale for Europe's monetary union, the European Commission (1990: 194, 191) praised how the euro could bring greater 'symmetry' to the global monetary order, and force the United States to become 'more conscious of the limits of independent policy-making'. It predicted that the euro would be a particularly attractive international currency because it would be backed by a conservative central bank dedicated to price stability, and because it would be able to be held in unified European money markets that would be 'the largest in the world'.

Since the euro's creation in 1999, however, the euro's challenge to the dollar has proved to be less significant than this prediction. One reason has been that European financial markets are not yet fully integrated and no central equivalent exists to the uniquely liquid and deep US Treasury bill market which helps sustain the dollar's global role. European governments have also so far shown little interest in actively cultivating the euro's international role beyond their immediate neighbours. Cohen (2003) argues that the euro's international use has also been held back by uncertainties regarding the governance structure, and thus the broader political credibility of the whole initiative. These uncertainties were highlighted particularly dramatically during the 2007–10 financial crisis which revealed both unclear pan-European crisis management procedures (leaving national governments to rescue financial institutions in a rather unco-ordinated manner) and the weak financial position of some euro members such as Greece. At the height of the crisis, some even questioned whether Europe's financial integration and even the euro-zone itself might unravel. If European co-operation continues to deepen and these issues are addressed, however, the euro's challenge to the dollar will likely grow.

What other challenges might the dollar face in the coming years? In the wake of the East Asian financial crisis of 1997–8, Japanese policy-makers became more interested in promoting the international use of the yen, especially in the East Asian region (Grimes 2009). The crisis had highlighted East Asian's reliance on the US dollar and Japan's limited monetary influence in the region, despite its rapidly growing trade and investment ties. To cultivate the yen's international role, the Japanese government began to pursue various initiatives such as fostering a more attractive short-term money market in Japan and encouraging the growth of yen-denominated lending from Japan. The internationalization of the yen, however, has continued to be held back by problems in the Japanese financial system, and by resistance from countries such as China to the idea of Japanese regional monetary leadership (Katada 2002).

As China has emerged as an increasingly important economic force in the world, some have speculated about whether its currency, the renminbi (RMB), might begin to challenge the dollar's international dominance. These speculations have been encouraged by the sudden interest shown by the Chinese government in internationalizing the RMB in response to the 2007–10 global financial crisis. The crisis highlighted to the Chinese leadership the vulnerabilities associated with its dependence on the dollar, particularly those stemming from the fact that the vast bulk of its foreign assets are held in US dollar-denominated assets. While some argue that China has gained power over the US through its large holdings of these assets, most powerful creditor countries in the past have lent abroad in their own currency in order to avoid exposure to kinds of exchange rate risks to which China now faces (Drezner 2009; Chin and Helleiner 2008). Because of the scale of Chinese reserve holdings (discussed in the next section), a 10 per cent decline in the dollar has the effect of generating Chinese financial losses equivalent to approximately 3 per cent of China's gross domestic product (GDP) (Cohen 2008c: 462). While this vulnerability has left Chinese officials with strong incentives in the short-term to defend the dollar in order to protect the value of its existing assets, it has also encouraged them to explore ways of reducing their dependence on the dollar over the medium term.

But the transformation of the RMB into a leading international currency will not happen quickly. The currency is not yet even fully convertible. And even if it was, the attractiveness of China's currency to foreigners would be inhibited by the absence of well-developed, liquid, and open RMB financial markets that are backed by a stable legal infrastructure and property rights. Like the United States in the late nineteenth century, China's ability to emerge as an international monetary leader lags very far behind its newfound industrial power (De Cecco 2009).

Expanded Role for the SDR?

Perhaps recognizing this fact, Chinese officials have also begun to support the strengthening of the SDR's role in the international monetary system. In March 2009, Chinese central bank governor Zhou Xiaochuan (2009) released a prominent paper which, citing Keynes and Triffin, argued for a 'super-sovereign reserve currency' such as the SDR which could be managed 'according to a clear set of rules' in order to 'ensure orderly supply' without reference to any individual country's distinctive domestic goals or balance of payments situation. To promote the SDR's use, Zhou recommended various ideas such as the issuing of SDR-denominated bonds, the establishment of a 'settlement system between the SDR and other currencies', as well as the creation of a fund at the IMF where governments could swap their existing reserve currencies for SDRs. Zhou also recommended that the SDR's value be determined by a wider basket of currencies than the existing four: the US dollar (which is weighted 44 per cent of the currency basket), the euro (34 per cent), the yen (11 per cent), and sterling (11 per cent).

Zhou's ideas found considerable support among national policy-makers from some other countries, including the other large dollar reserve holding countries such as Brazil and Russia. The United Nations' Stiglitz Commission, tasked with investigating the global financial crisis, also put forward some similar ideas in its 2009 report and it added that SDRs should be allocated on the basis of GDP or some measure of need instead of the existing method of using countries' IMF quotas (which ensures that new SDR allocations benefit most the wealthy industrialized countries who need SDRs least) (UN 2009a).

While other policy-makers were more skeptical of Zhou's ambitious ideas, they recognized the usefulness of the SDR for addressing an immediate short-term problem in 2009: the need to bolster the IMF's resources to help buffer countries from balance of payments shocks in the context of the global financial crisis at the time. With this goal in mind, the IMF membership as a whole backed the largest allocation of SDRs ever. While previous allocations in 1970–2 and 1979–81 totalled SDR 21.4 billion, the new amount approved in 2009 was approximately SDR 150 billion (US$250 billion) and it raised the share of SDRs in the world's non-gold official reserves from less than 0.5 per cent to about 5 per cent (Williamson 2009). The IMF also agreed to issue non-marketable SDR-demoninated bonds to countries such as China for the first time.

These developments have raised the profile of the SDR, but its role remains a relatively minor one in the international monetary system. For the SDR to become more important, much more would need to be done to cultivate its attractiveness as a reserve currency. To increase its liquidity, Barry Eichengreen (2009) has suggested that the IMF could take on the role of promoting a private market for SDRs by acting as a market-maker, buying and selling SDR claims at narrow spreads that are competitive with those for dollars. Even ambitious initiatives such as these, however, are not likely to achieve quickly the realization of the goal outlined in the second amendment of the IMF's Articles of Agreement of making the SDR the 'principal reserve asset in the international monetary system'. Instead, the SDR's role is likely to remain that of simply supplementing existing international reserve currencies for some time to come.

Consequences of the dollar's declining role?

The question of whether and how the dollar's international role may be challenged in the coming years thus remains controversial among IPE scholars, although they agree that its future will be determined by a combination of market and political developments. If the dollar's dominant global position is, in fact, challenged in the coming years, what would be the consequences? To begin with, the United States would lose some benefits it has derived from the currency's status. In addition to the international prestige that comes from issuing a dominant world currency, the US dollar's use abroad has produced extra **seigniorage** revenue for the US government (see Box 7.4). When foreigners hold dollars, they provide the equivalent of an interest-free (in the case of Federal Reserve notes) or a low interest (in the case of US Treasury securities) loan to the US. According to some estimates, this seigniorage profit has totalled between $16 billion and $22 billion per year recently (Cohen 2008a: 258).

Box 7.4 What is 'Seigniorage'?

Seigniorage is usually defined as the difference between the nominal value of money and its cost of production. This difference is a kind of 'profit' for the issuer of money. In mediaeval Europe, this source of revenue was often very important for ruling authorities. They could earn it either openly by adding a 'seigniorage' charge (above the normal mint charge that offset the cost of minting) when producing metallic coin, or more secretly by debasing their coin through a reduction of its weight or its 'fineness' (by increasing the proportion of non-precious alloy). If the surreptitious strategy were to be detected by the public, its effectiveness would be undermined, as people would either not accept the coins or accept them only at a discount. In more modern times, metallic coins no longer dominate the monetary system, and governments now earn seigniorage also through the issuing of paper currency as well as indirectly through their regulation of the creation of bank deposit money. National monetary authorities earn seigniorage not just from the use of the money they issue by citizens within their borders; the international use of their currency will augment the seigniorage revenue they earn even further.

The dollar's global role has also bolstered the US capacity to finance current account deficits as well as to deflect the costs of adjustments onto foreigners by depreciating its currency. In addition, US authorities have been able to use the dependence of market actors on dollar-clearing networks to encourage worldwide co-operation with US regulatory initiatives (for example, anti-money laundering regulations) as well as to enforce sanctions against foreign states. As the sole producer of the world's key currency, the US also plays a decisive role during international financial crisis because of its unique ability to make advances of dollars to foreign governments or private institutions in distress (see Pauly, Chapter 8 in this volume). Foreign dependence on an international currency may also benefit the issuer by encouraging foreigners to identify their interests more closely with those of the issuing country (Andrews 2006).

The erosion of the dollar's central global position would also have consequences for the world as a whole. In particular, it would raise the question of whether the international monetary system would be more or less stable without a dominant monetary power. Drawing on the inter-war experience, supporters of the hegemonic stability theory have predicted that increasing global monetary instability lies ahead. But others have suggested the opposite. David Calleo (1987: ch. 8) has long argued that a world monetary order based on more 'pluralistic' or 'balance of power' principles may be more likely to produce stability over time than one based on hegemony. A hegemonic power, in his view, is inevitably tempted to exploit its dominant position over time to serve its own interests rather than the interests of the stability of the system. Then European Commission president, Jacques Delors, advanced a similar argument in defending the euro project in 1993; in his words, the creation of the euro would make the EU 'strong enough to force the United States and Japan to play by rules which would ensure much greater monetary stability around the world' (quoted in Henning 1998: 565). Even if we accept that a more pluralistic international monetary order may be more stable, however, the transition away from a dollar-centred order is likely to contain risks for the world economy.

Key points

- In 1971, the United States ended the gold convertibility of its currency, and, by extension, that of all other currencies. The US decision reflected its desire to free itself from the growing constraint on its policies that gold convertibility was imposing.

- The US dollar continued to be a dominant global currency after it ceased to be convertible into gold in 1971 for a variety of economic and political reasons.

- The US dollar's global role may face new challenges from the euro, and to a lesser extent from the yen, the renminbi, and the SDR.

- These challenges will impose new constraints on US policy-making, but their wider systemic implications for global monetary stability are hard to predict.

Alongside the gold exchange standard, another feature of the Bretton Woods monetary order that broke down in the early 1970s was the adjustable peg system. This development took place in 1973, when governments allowed the world's major currencies to float in value vis-à-vis one other. The new floating exchange rate system was formalized in 1978, when a second amendment of the IMF's Articles of Agreement came into force which legalized floating exchange rates, and declared that each country could now choose its own exchange rate regime.

The end of the adjustable peg system was partly triggered by the growing size of speculative international financial flows which complicated governments' efforts to defend their currency pegs. Equally important, however, was the fact that influential policy-makers began to re-evaluate the merits of floating exchange rates. We have already seen how the Bretton Woods architects took a very negative view of the experience of floating exchange rates before the Second World War. Indeed, the drawbacks of floating exchange rates were deemed to be so obvious, that there had been very few serious defences of them at the time. By the early 1970s, however, floating exchange rates had attracted a number of prominent advocates, particularly in the United States (Odell 1982).

These advocates argued that floating exchange rates could play a very useful role in facilitating smooth adjustments to external imbalances in a world where governments were unwilling to accept the discipline of the gold standard. The idea of using exchange rate changes for this purpose had, of course, been endorsed at Bretton Woods; governments could adjust their currency's peg when the country was in 'fundamental disequilibrium'. But, in practice, governments had been reluctant to make these changes because exchange rate adjustments often generated political controversy, both at home and abroad. Governments usually made these adjustments only when large-scale speculative financial movements left them no option. The result had been a rather rigid and crisis-prone exchange rate system, in which countries often instead resorted to international economic controls to address imbalances. A floating exchange rate system would allow external imbalances to be addressed more smoothly and continuously, and without so much resort to controls.

It was also argued that floating exchange rates had unfairly been given a bad name during the 1930s. Advocates argued that floating exchange rates need not necessarily be associated with either competitive devaluations or a retreat from international economic integration, as they had been in the 1930s. Their role in encouraging destabilizing speculative financial flows during the 1930s was also questioned. Financial movements in that decade, it was argued, had been volatile, not because of floating exchange rates, but because they were responding properly to the highly unstable underlying economic conditions of the time (for example, Friedman 1953).

Has the floating exchange rate system performed in the ways that its advocates had hoped? The proponents of floating exchange rates were certainly correct that this exchange rate regime has not prevented the growth of international trade and investment, both of which expanded rapidly since the early 1970s. Floating exchange rates have undoubtedly often also played a useful role in facilitating adjustments to international economic imbalances. But critics have argued that this latter role should not be overstated.

From Plaza to Louvre

Some have echoed the argument made in the 1930s, that floating exchange rates have encouraged destabilizing speculative currency trading which has distorted currency values. It is certainly true that currency trading has grown very dramatically since the early 1970s; the size of daily foreign exchange trading increased from $15 billion in 1973 to $3.2 trillion by 2007 (Gilpin 2001: 261; BIS 2007). As foreign exchange trading has grown dramatically, exchange rates have sometimes been subject to considerable short-term volatility and longer-term misalignments. In these circumstances, floating exchange rates have often been the source of, rather than the means of adjusting to, external economic imbalances.

One of the more dramatic episodes of a longer-term misalignment involved the appreciation of the US dollar in the early-to-mid 1980s. Speculative financial flows, attracted by the US's high interest rates and rapid economic expansion after 1982, exacerbated the US current account deficit at the time, and generated widespread protectionist sentiments within the United States by 1984–5. This episode led the United States and other major industrial countries to consider briefly a move back towards more managed exchange rates. In September 1985, the G5 (the United States, the United Kingdom, the Federal Republic of Germany, France, and Japan) signed the Plaza Agreement which committed these countries to work together to encourage the US dollar to depreciate against the currencies of its major trading partners. After the dollar had fallen almost 50 per cent vis-à-vis the yen and Deutschmark by February 1987, they then announced the Louvre Accord, which established target ranges for the major currencies to be reached through closer macroeconomic policy co-ordination (Henning 1987; Funabashi 1988; Webb 1995).

This enthusiasm for a more managed exchange rate system between the world's major currencies proved to be short-lived. The three leading economic powers—the United States, West Germany, and Japan—were not prepared to accept the kinds of serious constraints on their macroeconomic policy autonomy that were required to make such a system effective. Many policy-makers in West Germany and Japan also argued that the US interest in macroeconomic policy co-ordination seemed designed primarily to reduce its own external deficit by encouraging changes in macroeconomic policy abroad rather than at home. This complaint had been heard before, during the late 1970s, when the US policy-makers last pressed Germany and Japan to co-ordinate macroeconomic policies. In both instances, US policy-makers sought to address their country's external payments deficit by pressing Germany and Japan to revalue their currencies and pursue more expansionary domestic economic policies. These moves would enable the United States to curtail its deficit without a domestic contraction by boosting US exports.

Bretton Woods II

Arguments for macroeconomic co-ordination among the leading powers have emerged at other moments, most recently in the context of the growth of East Asian trade surpluses since 2000. In this instance, criticism has been directed, not at speculative pressures in foreign exchange markets, but rather at many East Asian governments—particularly China—which are alleged to have deliberately undervalued their national currencies for competitive advantage in ways that have exacerbated global economic imbalances. They are accused, in other words, of not allowing their exchanges rates to float enough. The rapid accumulation of foreign exchange reserves by these governments is cited as evidence that they have been intervening in foreign exchange markets for this 'mercantilist' purpose, purchasing foreign exchange (usually dollars) in order to keep the value of their currency low. China's reserves have grown particularly dramatically, expanding approximately tenfold within a decade to a massive total of over $2 trillion in 2009 (of which approximately 70 to 80 per cent are estimated to be in US dollar-denominated assets). Its reserve holdings are now by far the largest in the world.

Some have argued that the recent East Asian accumulation of dollar reserves has recreated the situation that existed in the 1960s, when Europe and Japan built up dollar holdings as a result of their efforts to keep their exchange rates competitive vis-à-vis the US under the Bretton Woods exchange rate system. Proponents of this viewpoint have argued that the contemporary 'Bretton Woods II' system might be quite durable because it provided the major participating countries with economic benefits (Dooley et al. 2003). East Asian countries have been able to support their export-oriented industrialization strategies, while the US gains cheap imports and low cost foreign funding—in the form of foreign dollar holdings of its large trade and fiscal deficits.

Others have been less sure of the political sustainability of this system, particularly in the wake of the 2007–10 global financial crisis. Protectionist pressures within the US call into question that country's willingness to continue to provide an open market to exports from the new industrializing 'periphery'. US officials have also blamed surplus countries, especially China, for generating the crisis with their excessive savings, and called for a rebalancing of the US–Chinese macroeconomic relationship. Chinese officials have responded forcefully to these accusations of blame for the crisis, describing them as 'extremely ridiculous and irresponsible' and 'gangster logic' (quoted in Wolf 2009; see also Wolf 2008). From their standpoint, the crisis has been more a product of US policy mistakes and it has highlighted the vulnerabilities associated with their economy's high dependence on export-led growth. The costs of holding such large reserves have also become increasingly politicized with China, as citizens have asked why more of their country's savings are not being invested domestically. More generally, analysts in many countries have worried about whether the world economy's large payments imbalances will continue to be financed smoothly in the context of international financial instability.

Addressing Contemporary Global Imbalances

These various developments have placed the issue of addressing 'global imbalances' prominently on the international public policy agenda once again. It is clear, however, that the G5 or G7 can no longer be effective bodies within which this issue is addressed since many of the key surplus countries are not members. The IMF is an obvious possible alternative forum, particularly given the mandate it was assigned at Bretton Woods to address international economic imbalances. But the Fund's ability to be influential in the ways that the Bretton Woods architects imagined is limited. The major deficit country—the United States—is not borrowing from the Fund, while surplus countries are unlikely to be threatened by the 'scarce currency' clause since it has never been invoked because of the political controversies it would provoke.

Despite these constraints, some still hope the Fund could play an important role of facilitating macroeconomic co-ordination to address global imbalances. When the Bretton Woods exchange rate regime broke down in the early 1970s, many questioned the IMF's future. The outbreak of the international debt crisis in the early 1980s soon gave the Fund a new life as an institution focused on crisis management vis-à-vis poorer countries (see Pauly, Chapter 8 in this volume). But the Fund was also reborn in a second fashion after the early 1970s. In an effort to maintain some semblance of multilateral rules over the new floating exchange rate system, IMF members assigned the institution a new mandate to 'exercise firm surveillance over the exchange rate policies of members' under the second amendment to its charter that came into effect in 1978 (quoted in Pauly 1997: 105). The

IMF's 'surveillance' activities have since become an important part of its overall operations.

Although the Fund has focused mainly on bilateral consultations with individual member countries, it initiated a 'multilateral consultation' on global imbalances in 2006 involving China, the Euro area, Japan, the United States, and Saudi Arabia. Its thirty-year-old policy framework for bilateral 'surveillance' activities vis-à-vis exchange rates was also strengthened in 2007. Some hoped that these kinds of initiatives might allow the IMF to take an active role in reinvigorating the kind of multilateral exchange rate management that characterized the Plaza to Louvre period. But others have been more skeptical, particularly given the fact that many governments in the East Asian region distrust this international institution. Its tough conditionality on loans during the 1997–8 East Asian crisis was widely seen in that region as unhelpful, too intrusive, and overly influenced by US policy-makers' goals. Many analysts argue that distrust of the IMF is, in fact, an important reason why governments in this region have been trying to accumulate such large reserves in recent years. Those governments have preferred to protect themselves against external financial pressures through precautionary 'self-insurance' rather than rely on an institution with this record (Grimes 2009).

Another body that could play a role in addressing global imbalances is the new G20 leaders forum that was created in November 2008 at the height of the global financial crisis. All the world's major economies are members of this grouping, and it has already met regularly at the level of finance ministers and central bankers since 1999. During their first two summits, the G20 leaders focused primarily on international regulatory issues designed to minimize future crises (see Pauly, Chapter 8 in this volume). But at their third summit in September 2009, they widened the agenda, announcing that the G20 was now 'the premier forum for our international economic cooperation' and committing to a 'Framework for Strong, Sustainable and Balanced Growth'. This Framework includes a new 'consultative mutual assessment process' to evaluate whether national economic policies are consistent with shared goals outlined by the G20 as a whole. The IMF (along with the World Bank) is assigned a role of supporting this process through analyses which build on its existing bilateral and multilateral surveillance activities. This commitment to strengthened macroeconomic co-ordination lacks teeth and whether it will achieve results remains to be seen. The fundamental political challenge identified at Bretton Woods of reconciling countries' desire for national policy autonomy with their commitment to open multilateral world economy remains. And it is now being met in a context which is less 'hegemonic' than the early post-war years, raising new political challenges.

The creation of the euro

Although international efforts to co-ordinate the relationship between the values of the world's major currencies have been limited since the early 1970s, some governments have moved to create stable monetary relations in smaller regional contexts. The most elaborate initiative of this kind has taken place in Europe. At the time of the breakdown of the Bretton Woods exchange rate system, a number of the countries of the European Community (EC) attempted to stabilize exchange rates among themselves. These initial efforts were followed by the creation of the European Monetary System in 1979, which established a kind of 'mini-Bretton Woods' adjustable peg regime in which capital controls were still widely used and financial support was provided to protect each country's currency peg vis-à-vis other European currencies. Then, with the Maastricht Treaty in 1991, most members of European Union went one step further to commit to a full monetary union in 1999.

The long-standing resistance of many European governments to floating exchange rates within Europe has been driven partly by worries that exchange rate volatility and misalignments would disrupt their efforts to build a closer economic community. Exchange rate instability was deemed to be disruptive, not only to private commerce, but also to the complicated system of regional public payments within Europe's important Common Agricultural Policy. But why go so far as to abandon national currencies altogether in 1999?

One answer is that the adjustable peg system of the EMS became unsustainable after European governments committed themselves to abolish capital controls in 1988. The latter decision left European currency pegs vulnerable to increasingly powerful speculative financial flows, a fact demonstrated vividly in the 1992–3 European currency crisis. By commiting to a monetary union, they eliminated the possibility of future intra-regional exchange rate crises altogether.

Some policy-makers outside of Germany also saw the currency union as a way to import the German central bank's anti-inflationary monetary policy. Like the German Bundesbank, the new European central bank was given a strict mandate to pursue price stability as its primary goal. For neo-liberal policy-makers, whose influence had been growing across Europe, this mandate promised an end to activist national monetary policies which were often associated inflation (McNamara 1998). Some neo-liberals also hoped that the euro, by eliminating the possibility of national devaluations, might encourage greater price and wage flexibility within national economies as workers and firms were forced to confront the impact of external economic 'shocks' in a more direct fashion.

Interestingly, for a related reason, some European social democrats and unions saw the euro as an opportunity to reinvigorate national corporatist social pacts in which co-operative wage bargaining, employment friendly taxation schemes, and other social protection measures could assume a key role in the process of adjusting to external economic shocks. Because the euro could protect a country from speculative currency attacks, some of these interests also saw monetary union as creating a more stable macroeconomic environment in which progressive supply-side reforms could be undertaken to promote equity, growth, and employment. In some countries, adopting the euro was also seen

as a way to lower domestic interest rates by reducing risk premiums that the markets were imposing, a result that improved governments' budgetary positions and prevented cuts to the welfare state. Some on the left also hoped that the euro project might eventually help to dilute the monetary influence of the neo-liberal Bundesbank across Europe, and encourage co-ordinated EU-wide expansionary fiscal policies (Josselin 2001; Notermans 2001).

The monetary union project also had a broader political meaning. In addition to challenging US power (as noted above), the creation of the euro has been seen as an important symbol of the process of fostering ever-closer European co-operation. Many analysts also argue that the decision to create the euro was linked to a broader political deal between Germany and other European countries at the time of the Maastricht Treaty. Many European countries—especially France—had become increasingly frustrated by the domination of the European monetary system by the German Bundesbank, and they pressed for EMU as a way to dilute its influence. Germany is said to have accepted EMU when it came to be seen as a trade-off for European (and especially French) support for German reunification in 1989 (see, for example, Kaltenthaler 1998).

Currency unions elsewhere?

The European experiment in creating a currency union has triggered talk of a similar move in some other regions. Is this likely to happen? Economists try to help address this question by analysing whether each region resembles an 'optimum currency area' (see Box 7.5). In practice, though, this kind of economic analysis has had little predictive power in the European context, or elsewhere. One of the longest-standing monetary unions in the world is the CFA franc zone involving many former French colonies in West and Central Africa, and its member countries do not come close to resembling an 'optimum currency area'. Like the EMU, that monetary union was formed and has been sustained by certain political conditions. Particularly important in that case have been the power and political interests of France in the colonial and post-colonial context (Stasavage 2003).

Box 7.5 Monetary Unions and the Theory of Optimum Currency Areas

The theory of optimum currency areas was first developed by the Nobel Prize-winning economist, Robert Mundell (1961), to evaluate the pros and cons of forming a monetary union among a selected group of countries. While assuming the union will produce microeconomic benefits in the form of lower transaction costs for cross-border commerce, the theory focuses its analytical attention on the potential macroeconomic costs associated with abandoning the exchange rate as a tool of macroeconomic adjustment. If these costs are low, the region is said to approximate more closely an 'optimum currency area' that should be encouraged to create a monetary union.

To evaluate how significant these costs are in each regional context, the theory examines a number of criteria.

If selected countries experience similar external shocks, for example, the theory notes that they are more likely to be good candidates for monetary union, since they will each have less of a need for an independent exchange rate. Even if they experience asymmetric shocks, the macroeconomic costs of abandoning national exchange rates may still be low if wages and price are very flexible within each country, if labour is highly mobile between countries, or if there are mechanisms for transferring fiscal payments among the countries. Each of these conditions would enable adjustments to be made to external shocks in the absence of an exchange rate.

At the time of the euro's creation, there was a brief debate about constructing a monetary union either in North America or the Americas as a whole based on the US dollar. Two countries that were already extensively dollarized—Ecuador and El Salvador—introduced the US dollar as their national currency, in 2000 and 2001, respectively, but the idea of formal dollarization attracted little serious political support elsewhere, particularly after Argentina's spectacular financial crisis in late 2001. Between 1991 and 2001, Argentina managed its national currency on a 'currency board' basis, which tied the value of the currency tightly to the US dollar and encouraging dollarization. When the country began to experience growing current account deficits after the mid 1990s, the only way it could correct the problem—while retaining this monetary regime—was to undergo a costly deflation. This deflation produced high unemployment and dramatic cuts to government spending, and contributed to the country's massive financial crisis (Blustein 2005).

At a more political level, critics of formal dollarization were also helped by the fact that US

policy-makers made it clear that dollarized countries would not be offered any role in the decision-making of the US Federal Reserve, and that Fed officials had no intention of taking the concerns of dollarized countries into account when they set US monetary policy. United States policy-makers made it clear that they were not even willing to consider providing lender-of-last-resort support to institutions in dollarized countries. The only support they discussed seriously was the sharing of the seigniorage revenue that the United States would earn from the dollar's circulation in countries that formally dollarize (see Box 7.4). Even this idea, however, did not pick up enough support to be endorsed by US Congress or US financial officials when it was debated briefly in 1999–2000. While European countries shared sovereignty in creating the euro, countries in the Americas had only the choice of becoming a monetary dependency (Helleiner 2006).

There has also been some talk of monetary unions in the East Asian region in recent years. This talk builds on a decade of closer monetary and financial co-operation, which began in the wake of the

East Asian financial crisis. The crisis exposed the vulnerability of the region to outside market and political pressures, encouraging policy-makers to explore ways to boost East Asia's monetary and financial independence. The first major co-operative venture was the Chiang Mai Initiative, created in 2000 to provide short-term financial assistance to East Asian countries suffering from balance of payments crises. In 2003, the ASEAN countries, plus China, Japan, and South Korea, created the Asian Bond Markets Initiative, which seeks to encourage East Asian savings to be reinvested in the region. In 2006, alongside these initiatives, this same group of countries backed the creation of an Asian Currency Unit (ACU) whose value is made up of a weighted average of a basket of the region's currencies. Modelled on the European Currency Unit (ECU) that was a precursor to the euro, supporters hope the ACU could reduce the influence of the dollar and bolster monetary co-operation by acting as a unit of account for public and private actors in the region. While this initiative is important, the prospect of its leading to a fully fledged East Asian monetary union any time soon is considered remote by most observers. In addition to the usual concerns about monetary sovereignty, this initiative—like all the others—would be complicated by difficult relationship between Japan and China, each of which appears to have leadership aspirations in this area.

Key points

- The adjustable peg exchange rate regime of Bretton Woods was replaced in 1973 by a system of floating exchange rates between the currencies of the leading economic powers. The change was caused by heightened capital mobility and by a reconsideration of the merits of floating exchange rates among leading policy-makers, particularly in the United States.

- Floating exchange rates have performed an important role in facilitating balance of payments adjustments, but critics argue that they have also been subject to short-term volatility and longer-term misalignments.

- There have been occasional intergovernmental efforts since the 1970s to manage the relationship between the values of the world's major currencies through macroeconomic co-ordination. The most recent has been driven by a desire to address global imbalances that arose in the years leading up to the 2007–10 global financial crisis.

- Since the breakdown of the Bretton Woods exchange rate system, there have also been initiatives to create more stable monetary relations at the regional level, most notably in Europe where co-operation culminated in the creation of a monetary union in 1999. Political prospects for the creation of regional monetary unions soon in other regions such as the Americas or East Asia are remote.

Conclusion

The international monetary and financial system has undergone three important transformations since the late nineteenth century, in response to changing economic and political conditions. During the inter-war years, the global integrated monetary and financial order of the pre-1914 period broke down. At the Bretton Woods Conference of 1944, a new order was built on 'embedded liberal' principles. Since the early 1970s, the third change has been under way as a number of the features of the Bretton Woods system have unravelled with the globalization of finance, the collapse of the gold exchange standard, and the move to a floating exchange rate regime among the major economic powers.

The emerging international monetary and financial system cannot be characterized in simple terms. The highly globalized nature of financial markets is reminiscent of the pre-1914 era. The floating exchange rate regime between the major powers and new challenges to the dominant currency's international role remind some of the inter-war period. The legacy of the Bretton Woods order also clearly lives on in the enduring role of IMF and World Bank, current account convertibility, the dollar's global prominence, and the broader commitment to multilateralism.

Each of the recent transformations in the nature of the international monetary and financial system has had important consequences for the key question of who gets what, when, and how in the global political economy. Monetary and financial systems—at both the domestic and international levels—do not just serve economic functions. They also have implications for various political projects relating to the pursuit of power, ideas, and interests. For this reason, the study of money and finance cannot be left only to economists, who have traditionally dominated scholarship in this area. It also needs the attention of students of international political economy who have an interest in these wider political issues.

? Questions

1. Is a hegemonic leader necessary for a stable international monetary and financial system to exist?

2. To what extent has financial globalization undermined the power and policy autonomy of national governments? Is financial globalization irreversible?

3. How important has financial globalization been in influencing class, sectoral, and gender relations within countries? What are its environmental consequences?

4. For how much longer will the US dollar remain the world's key currency?

5. Will the SDR ever become the dominant reserve currency in the world? What would be the costs and benefits?

6. Has the floating exchange rate system created an unstable global political economy? Should the leading powers attempt to stabilize the relationship between the values of the major currencies?

7. How will current global economic imbalances be resolved and with what consequences? Should the IMF or G20 (or even just a G2 of the US and China) take the lead in addressing this issue?

8. Has the creation of the euro been a positive move for Europeans? Should other regions emulate the European example, and are they likely to do so?

→ Further reading

 Abdelal, R. (2007), *Capital Rules: The Construction of Global Finance* (Cambridge: Harvard University Press). A history of the changing norms regarding the liberal capital flows in the post-1945 years.

■ Andrews, D. (ed.) (2006), *International Monetary Power* (Ithaca, NY: Cornell University Press). A collection of essays concerning the relationship between state power and international money.

■ Best, J. (2005), *The Limits of Transparency: Ambiguity and the History of International Finance* (Ithaca, NY: Cornell University Press). A history of the evolution of the international monetary and financial governance since Bretton Woods.

■ Cohen, B. (2004), The *Future of Money* (Princeton, NJ: Princeton University Press). An analysis of key issues relating to the changing currency relations and the nature of money in the contemporary world.

■ Eichengreen, B. (2010), *Global Imbalances and the Lessons of Bretton Woods* (Cambridge, MA: MIT Press). An analysis of the political economy of global imbalances in historical perspective.

■ Helleiner, E., and Kirshner, J. (eds) (2009), *The Future of the Dollar* (Ithaca, NY: Cornell University Press). Contrasting views on the future of the dollar as an international currency.

■ Kirshner, J. (ed.) (2002), *Monetary Orders* (Ithaca, NY: Cornell University Press). A collection that highlights the political foundations of national and international monetary systems.

■ Porter, T. (2006), *Globalization and Finance* (Oxford: Polity Press). An overview of the politics and governance of global financial markets.

■ Schwartz, H. (2009), *Subprime Nation: American Power, Global Capital, and the Housing Bubble* (Ithaca, NY: Cornell University Press). An analysis of the political economy of global imbalances and their relationship to the pre-2007 US housing bubble.

■ Strange, S. (1998), *Mad Money: When Markets Outgrow Government* (Ann Arbor, MI: University of Michigan Press). A survey and critique of the contemporary international monetary and financial system.

:// Web links

■ www.bis.org   The website of the Bank for International Settlements. The Bank is the 'central bankers' bank' and it provides detailed analyses of international monetary and financial developments.

■ www.ft.com   World's leading newspaper addressing global monetary and financial developments.

■ http://ifiwatchnet.org/   The website of an international network of NGOs concerned with the activities of the IMF, World Bank, and other international financial institutions

■ www.imf.org   The website of the International Monetary Fund.

Online resource centre

For additional material and resources, please visit the Online Resource Centre at:
www.oxfordtextbooks.co.uk/ravenhill3e/

8

The Political Economy of Global Financial Crises

Louis W Pauly

 Chapter contents

- Introduction
- National Politics and International Markets
- The Nature and Variety of International Financial Crises
- The Changing Global Context
- Crisis Prevention
- Crisis Management and Resolution
- A New Global Architecture?

 Reader's guide

The world economy today reflects an experiment involving, on the one hand, the opening and deepening of financial markets and, on the other hand, the dispersion of the political authority required to ensure the stability of those markets. The resulting governance dilemmas are nowhere clearer than in the circumstances surrounding financial crises capable of spilling more readily across national borders. In recent decades, most such crises began in emerging-market countries. In the summer of 2008, however, the experiment encountered its biggest shock when policy mistakes in the United States combined with an economic downturn to spawn a global emergency. This chapter explores the political economy of crisis prevention, management, and resolution in an increasingly decentralized system.

Introduction

Promoting interdependence among the economies of the world was a key strategic objective of the United States and its main allies after 1945. During the 1970s, the logic of interdependence was extended from real economies, where tangible goods are produced, to markets for capital and financial services (Helleiner, Chapter 7 in this volume, and Helleiner 1994). From that point on, crises in financial markets began to spill more readily across national borders.

The collapse of the Bretton Woods exchange rate system in the early 1970s occurred in tandem with a broadening movement toward more open financial markets around the world. In fact, financial innovation and policy change had been gradually undermining the kinds of capital controls many countries put in place during the 1930s and especially during the Second World War. Although economists still argue over the precise effects this movement had on the efficiency of real economies, its most obvious negative effect was to make it easier for intermittent financial shocks to spread misery beyond the localities where they originated. Not wanting to repeat the worst experiences of the pre-1914 era, when depressions and instability were common, but also not wanting to bear the costs of wartime controls, policy-makers in the leading states in the system engaged in simultaneously competitive and co-operative efforts to enhance both efficiency and safety in more open and interdependent markets. In other words, they sought the benefits widely associated with freedom for capital flows, while also seeking ways to limit the risks thereby incurred. A policy experiment with deregulation at the national level went hand in hand with collective efforts to liberalize financial conditions globally while encouraging prudent risk-taking by banks and other financial intermediaries. With those institutions and their clients ever more able to diversify their balance sheets internationally, and with countries across the industrial and developing worlds becoming ever more dependent on the success of the modern experiment with openness, financial crises came to demand statecraft of the highest order.

As they did during the pre-1914 era of financial market openness, financial panics recurred with some regularity after the 1970s, and they now spread rapidly across both functional and geographic borders. Markets that once again were more integrated across national boundaries exhibited the behaviour of a manic depressive. Periods of ecstatic euphoria were almost routinely followed by periods of black despair. Financial assets much in demand one day, that is, 'liquid' or easy to sell, suddenly attracted no buyers. The political consequences would be profound and would no longer easily be kept within national boundaries.

In the late 1990s, this is precisely what occurred as panic spread from stock to bond to banking markets in East Asia, and then to their counterparts in Russia, Latin America, and eventually to Wall Street. Ten years later, the same syndrome recurred, but this time it originated in American housing markets. The building blocks of the post-1945 system themselves seemed threatened as bankers and investors around the world simultaneously lost the confidence necessary to make long-term investments. Looming over economic policy-makers in the United States and elsewhere was the spectre of the terrible decade spanning the US stock market collapse in 1929 and the start of the Second World War in 1939, when economic depression brought widespread unemployment and political extremism in its wake.

Notwithstanding the post-1945 movement toward freer international capital flows, the desire to avoid a repeat of the 1930s prompted governments throughout the world to reinforce their vital national payments systems by extending implicit or explicit guarantees to banks at the core of those systems. It also focused their attention on the linkages connecting those systems to one another. Still, especially after the multilateral commitment to pegged exchange rates was finally abandoned in 1973, one cross-border crisis followed another, prompting one of the world's leading financial speculators to offer a startling diagnosis: 'Financial markets are inherently unstable; left to their own devices, they are liable to break down. More importantly, many social values are not properly represented by market forces' (Soros 1997b; see also Soros 1997a, 1998). A former chief economist of the World Bank took the criticism further,

> While money should be flowing from the rich to the poor and risk from the poor to the rich, the global financial system is accomplishing neither. With poor countries left to bear the brunt of risk, crises have become a way of life—with more than a hundred crises in the last three decades.

(Stiglitz 2006: 246)

Even more fundamental questions about the wisdom of financial liberalization followed the crisis that began in 2007. Most remarkably, Alan Greenspan, a strong promoter of free markets who had recently retired as the head of the American central bank, conceded his 'state of shocked disbelief' that a system that for forty years had been 'working exceptionally well' came very close to collapsing (Greenspan 2008). In fact, such observations simply revived a long line of thinking inspired by the pioneering insights of

John Maynard Keynes (Minsky 1986; Skidelsky 2009).

The preceding chapter set out the broad context for understanding the changing monetary dimension of our contemporary global economy. This chapter looks in depth at the political economy of recurring financial crises therein. For students of international relations and international economics, such moments in time are worth considerable attention. They open a unique window on the fragile political structures and networks that underpin globalizing markets. Those markets seem to promise prosperity and peaceful interaction among the world's still distinctive societies, but they quite obviously cannot and do not in themselves ensure such outcomes. In this regard, the early chapters of the book drew attention to the importance of collaboration among the political authorities leading that system. International financial crises demonstrate both the continuing importance of such collaboration and the profound difficulty of achieving it with a degree of certainty.

National Politics and International Markets

Financial markets exist to support the development of 'real' economies. The prices of most financial assets and liabilities continuously fluctuate. Every such price signal is meaningful to someone, somewhere. But rapid and severe fluctuations in the value of financial claims can disrupt the fundamental mechanisms through which jobs are created or destroyed and goods and services are actually produced. In the democratic systems currently lying at the heart of an integrating global economy, financial market ups and downs are typically quite constructive. When they promote growth and innovation, they stabilize underlying social and political orders, even though their specific political effects can be difficult to predict (see

Hiscox, Chapter 4 in this volume). Economic resources are surely distributed and redistributed as financial prices move, but the process usually occurs in such a way that no particular group or groups with overwhelming political power become aggrieved enough to seek fundamental systemic change. In this regard, it is also worth noting that, with the exception of wartime, highly controlled financial markets tend to be associated with authoritarian governments and official corruption. Not always, but very often, this 'repression' of financial markets correlates with deepening poverty. The challenge then for those seeking to maximize the economic, social, and political benefits of financial liberalization is to find ways to limit the scope of market instability and more fairly to share residual burdens.

Extreme instability in financial markets is socially destructive. In modern history, it is associated with man-made disasters of the first order. In fact, from the 1870s until today, the global economy has grown rapidly and consistently, except during periods characterized by financial crises and subsequent wars. On a world scale, the only significant downturns in real economic growth occurred after the financial panic of 1907, during the First World War, between 1929 and 1931, and during the Second World War (IMF 2009d: 129). Crisis conditions can engender and generalize inflation or deflation, both of which can bring spiralling declines in disposable incomes and life prospects. When panic imposes costs deemed unbearable by the politically weak, the local effects can be traumatic for all concerned. But when it brings in its wake general contractions in real economies and imposes costs deemed unbearable by the politically strong and mobilized, it can rapidly destabilize social and political orders (see Box 8.1).

Box 8.1 The Policy Challenges of Financial Openness: The Case of Argentina

Blessed with abundant natural resources, diversified industries, and a well-educated labour force, Argentina might have become a regional beacon of prosperity during the twentieth century. It was not to be. After decades of troubles, hyperinflation struck in 1989. In April 1991, the government embarked upon a bold policy experiment to reverse the economy's course. The Convertibility Plan rigidly pegged the value of the peso to the US dollar and thereby constrained the ability of the central bank to print money. Simultaneously, the government announced a wide range of structural reforms to make the economy more flexible, competitive, and open. Initially, the plan achieved dramatic results. Inflation fell, international capital flowed in, and the economy grew by an average of 6 per cent through 1997. Late in 1998, however, a surprisingly severe recession began, and its effects were compounded by the unusual turbulence in global financial markets. As capital inflows dried up, some observers say the government did not react quickly enough with domestic policy adjustments. Others point to large loans from the IMF inadequately conditioned on such adjustments, and to a currency devaluation by Brazil that undercut Argentina's export competitiveness. Still others blame the Asia-focused panic then gripping private foreign lenders and investors. In any event, bank runs, the suspension of IMF loans, and severe political and social unrest ensued. In December 2001, the country began defaulting on its international debts; the next month it abandoned its currency peg, and as the peso's value plummeted, the value of its debt, now largely denominated in US dollars, exploded. In 2002, the economy contracted by 20 per cent and unemployment exceeded 20 per cent of the workforce.

In retrospect, it became clear that either the currency regime should have been abandoned during more halcyon days in 1996 or 1997 or that its continuation should have been supported by tighter fiscal policies, a reduction in international borrowing, and lower labour costs. At the time, neither course of action gained any political traction. Even so, according to a key IMF staffer, in 1998 'a crisis might have been avoided with good luck—for example, had the dollar depreciated against the euro, had Brazil not been forced to devalue, or had international capital markets not deteriorated—but Argentina's luck ran out' (Allen 2003: 131; Blustein 2005).

By 2004, a distinct lack of solidarity among Argentina's external creditors provided the policy space necessary to rekindle some domestic production. The government then took several desperate measures to stay afloat, including borrowing from Venezuela at very high interest rates and nationalizing state pension funds. Early in 2010, it engaged in an intense political struggle with its own central bank over the use of the bank's foreign currency reserves and with recalcitrant foreign creditors who refused to accede to an IMF-sponsored plan to restructure its debts. Shut out of international capital markets for over a decade, Argentina remained a symbol of lost opportunities.

In contrast, the globalizing political economy gradually and intentionally built up after 1945 rested on the assumption of a widening circle of shared prosperity. International economic interdependence formed a core element in the strategy of systemic stabilization and development designed mainly by the United States and the United Kingdom. The central idea of a more secure world based on open-market principles was not new, but its realist architects this time tried to limit the extent to which the strategy depended on a deregulated banking industry. Certainly, they could not forget the disappointed hopes of liberals like Norman Angell, whom in the halcyon days before 1914 had famously opined:

> Commercial interdependence, which is the special mark of banking as it is the mark of no other profession or trade in quite the same degree . . . is surely doing a great deal to demonstrate that morality after all is not founded upon self-sacrifice, but enlightened self-interest . . . And such a clearer understanding is bound to improve, not merely the relationship of one group to another, but the relationship of all men to other men, to create a consciousness which must make for more efficient human co-operation, a better human society.

(Keegan 1998: 12)

Alas, the interdependence of bankers did nothing to prevent the coming war and may even have made its sequel more likely by discouraging decisive early action against fascism (Kirshner 2007). The architects of the post-1945 system did not entirely discount the strategic value of commercial liberalism, but they excluded financial activity that was not trade-related by opting for a pegged exchange rate system and for tight bank regulation at the national level. In time, as we shall see, Angell's view once again became the common wisdom, albeit with a twist born of repeated financial crises and repeated reminders that the machinery of finance capitalism required attentive political oversight.

The die was cast in favour of the gradual loosening of restrictions over banking when those same architects decided to rely on the private sector for the provision of the vast amounts of capital required to help rebuild economies broken by war and then to promote development in the rest of the world. Public funds, such as those allocated by the United States through the Marshall Plan, kick-started that process, but they were soon dwarfed by private capital flows in the form of export proceeds, foreign bank borrowing, private remittances, and foreign direct investment. By the 1970s, changing official and private preferences in advanced industrial countries lay behind a series of explicit and implicit policy choices that cumulatively pushed the system back toward freer international capital movements mediated mainly by financial institutions able to engage in a widening range of commercial and investment activities.

Within twenty years, a similar shift in preferences would be well underway in much of the developing world, notwithstanding many emergencies that reminded policy-makers and market participants of certain historical lessons. Stable, well-functioning financial markets require stable, well-functioning regulatory authority underneath them. Market actors need clear operating rules. Property rights have to be established, and adjudicated when conflicts arise. Predictable procedures have to be in place to handle inevitable bankruptcies. Someone has to provide the degree of insurance necessary to limit the chance that specific debt defaults cascade and engulf otherwise healthy borrowers and lenders. Some agency has to be entrusted with the responsibility and endowed with the capability to act as lender-of-last-resort. In light of the risk that the very existence of such ultimate insurance facilities can tempt potential beneficiaries to act imprudently, a risk that economists call 'moral hazard', this last-resort lending function has to be complemented by the official supervision of financial intermediaries. Finally, to deal with extreme instability, the lender-of-last-resort has to be backed by an investor-of-last-resort, an investor with unlimited access to the currency required to stop financial contagion from spreading. Despite recurrent dreams of a substitute that might limit the risk of igniting another great inflation, and despite the budgetary constraints faced by even the wealthiest countries, no such institution has yet been invented—except for legitimate national governments with access to fiscal accounts and printing presses.

After 1945, all advanced industrial states applied just such lessons within their national financial markets. Some gave the bulk of regulatory and supervisory responsibilities to their central banks, while some split them between central banks and other official agencies. Most initiated some kind of deposit insurance scheme to ameliorate the risk of domestic bank runs, and they all tried to leave as much scope as domestic circumstances would allow for prudent self-discipline by market actors themselves. They, nevertheless, all constructed procedures to prevent or, at worst, to resolve financial emergencies. When no one else would lend sufficiently to institutions whose survival was deemed vital to larger national interests, or in the extreme when no one else would hold their stock, some arm of the state was endowed with the mandate to do so. Across the developing world, a challenge repeatedly confronted in more recent decades has been to create similar facilities. When they could not meet that challenge, and especially when financial distress threatened global order and other states refused to provide direct assistance, the International Monetary Fund (IMF) was now available to supplement the resources of indebted and troubled member-states. Since the Fund's underlying authority was of a limited and delegated nature, however, myriad economic and political controversies were always associated with its crisis management role.

National polities can certainly establish national regulators to govern national financial markets. When they fail to do so, it is appropriate to inquire into the reasons for internal political weaknesses or whether external political pressures were mainly to blame. But when those markets become ever more open, and ever more integrated, how can political authority and accountability be transnationalized? Deeply integrated financial markets promise no escape from the periodic necessity of reliable emergency stabilization measures. What is missing, of course, is a global polity capable in a crisis of sustaining last-resort lending and investing instruments analogous to those established at the national level. Therein lies the central political dilemma posed by the contemporary move toward broader financial openness.

Key points

- Financial markets have always been prone to bouts of instability.
- During the twentieth century, leading states built up national regulatory and supervisory systems to limit the dangers of financial crises.
- Cross-national regulatory coordination became necessary after international capital movements accelerated in the 1970s, but remained politically difficult to sustain and expand.

The Nature and Variety of International Financial Crises

Financial crises commence with sharp breaks in the prices of key financial instruments. The expectations of market participants suddenly change. 'Shocks' course through markets, and participants seek to adjust their positions rapidly. Historically, the consequences of crisis moments have varied in their severity and scope. The moments that particularly interest us here are those defined most often by plummeting prices in the value of a nation's banking assets at the core of its payments system (referred to as a 'banking crisis') and/or in the value of its currency relative to other currencies (referred to as a currency crisis).

Risk and uncertainty

Capitalist economies rest on foundations of debt. Borrowing and lending fuel economic growth. In principle, the aggregate financial claims created by the interaction of consumers, producers, savers, and investors in an economy are eminently supportable as long as expected future incomes exceed expected future debt repayments. The same logic applies internationally when once-separated economies become more integrated. At base, this involves the integration of markets for information.

Since we cannot know the future, expectations of future income flows are always doubtful. When enough borrowers and lenders share the perception that the extent of such doubts can reasonably be estimated, it becomes appropriate to speak of knowable probabilities, or risks (Knight 1921). Risks can be managed. Indeed, this is precisely what banks do when they accept deposits from savers in the short run, pool the proceeds, and make loans to borrowers in the long run. Through such activities, financial claims are generated, priced, and exchanged. The different time horizons of savers and borrowers are 'mediated'. In the absence of financial intermediaries, the ability of a particular firm, or of a particular country, to invest would be limited to the amount that firm or that country could save out of its own resources at any given moment in time

Even when financial intermediation occurs smoothly, say through efficient and prudent banks, specific financial claims (assets from the point of view of banks, liabilities from the point of view of borrowers) become insupportable all the time. Mistakes are made, misjudgements occur, market

conditions change unexpectedly. In the wake of such shocks, the expectations of creditors can shift and assets can be sold off and losses written off. If such shocks become generalized and creditors are uncertain about the limits of future losses, panic can ensue. Debtors and creditors, especially creditors late through the exit door, suffer reductions in their wealth and restraints on their economic prospects. When national markets are open, such uncertainty can easily spread like a contagious virus.

The history of capitalism is replete with such financial shocks. As Kindleberger put it in the title of a famous book, manias, panics, and crashes are endemic in a private market-based system (Kindleberger 1978). Few close observers deny that modern financial markets can sometimes be excessively volatile. Nevertheless, few participants are prepared to concede that alternative non-market or public allocation mechanisms in complex social systems are feasible. The massive human failures associated with planned economies in the twentieth century are not easy to forget.

The theoretical debate over whether the financial crises associated with market capitalism are self-correcting is a perennial one. Since the 1930s, however, the Keynesian side has apparently proved irresistible to policy-makers, except, as we shall see below, at one crucial moment in 2008. The near disaster that followed reinforced the Keynesian position. A financial crisis widely perceived to be severe simply requires some kind of decisive leadership if it is to be managed and resolved with the least possible social damage. In short, someone widely perceived to be acting with authority must administer a counter-shock capable of bringing market makers psychologically out of the realm of uncertainty and back into the realm of risk. Early on in the post-1945 period, the United States was the obvious leader. As the financial integration project proceeded and American economic power waned, more intense collaboration among diverse national and regional authorities were required. Questions concerning the reliability of such collaboration, moreover, rose in tandem with doubts about the distributive justice of a system that ever more tightly linked financial markets across rich and poor countries (Sen 2009).

Notwithstanding the difficulty of imagining radically different financial systems conducive to truly global prosperity in the long run, contemporary history highlights two crucial facts. First, financial crises, and especially banking crises, remain recurrent, their only reliable predictor an increasingly shared sense that they will not recur because 'this time is different' (Reinhart and Rogoff 2009). Second, when financial markets cross legal and political borders, the probability of crisis increases as the information embedded in prices becomes less readily accessible for all market participants. In the deep structure of contemporary financial markets, the information asymmetries analyzed by economists and the power asymmetries analyzed by political scientists overlap.

Incidence of international financial crises

Economic historians commonly depict the period 1870 to 1914 as the first to witness the rapid expansion of cross-border financial markets (Flandreau and Zumer 2004). Although few countries were involved, by some measures the scale of international financial intermediation far exceeded anything that has developed since then. A golden age only for some, the purchase and sale of financial claims to foreigners boomed, albeit only at various points

during this period. So, too, did defaults, especially around 1875, and then again when the world began marching toward what became known as the Great War. In an era when the values of the main currencies were meant to be firmly pegged to one another (recall the discussion in the previous chapter of the gold standard, which itself never worked perfectly), such defaults often translated into bank failures. After 1919, the incidence of banking crises escalated, but so, too, did currency crises when repegged exchange rates would not hold. The disastrous decade commencing in 1929 was characterized by the awful coincidence and global explosion of banking and currency crises (Kindleberger 1973).

Currency crises continued to plague the system that eventually emerged from the ashes of the Second World War. Efforts by the United States and its victorious allies to ensure internal financial stability did succeed in reducing the incidence of banking crises in the decades immediately following the war. But even after 1945, recurrent currency crises strained efforts to restore a stable exchange rate system reminiscent of the pre-1914 gold standard era. Those efforts failed in the early 1970s, when the link between the world's leading currency and the price of gold was decisively broken. After 1973, banking crises once again became a fact of international economic life; so, too, did their coincidence with currency crises mainly in the developing world. As we shall see, a powerful reminder that advanced industrial countries remained far from immune to twin crises came in 2008.

Key points

- The most damaging financial crises occur when banking markets and currency markets simultaneously come under pressure.
- After the breakdown of the Bretton Woods exchange rate system in the early 1970s and before the cross-border crisis of 2007, banking and currency crises occurred with most frequency in emerging market countries.

The Changing Global Context

In 1974, the failure of a German bank, Bankhaus I. D. Herstatt, to honour its foreign exchange contracts had knock-on effects globally, which ultimately even caused the Franklin National Bank of New York to fail as well (Spero 1980). Long memories recalled the collapse of the Credit-Anstalt Bank in Austria in 1931 and the contagion it spread through world markets (Schubert 1992). The post-1945 international economic system as a whole, however, did not revert to depression, and lessons for avoiding systemic crises were certainly learned in the years after the Bretton Woods exchange rate system collapsed. We return to them below.

Banks based in advanced industrial countries rapidly expanded their international lending operations throughout the 1970s, and multinational corporations diversified their investment activities. Gradually, individual investors expanded their appetites and capacities for buying bonds and other financial instruments issued by governments and firms in certain developing countries, mainly in Central and South America. Some associated capital flows were trade related, some investment related, and some simply reflected the kind of financial speculation inherent in a capitalist system now becoming more global. An explosion of international financial intermediation after the 1980s brought in its train financial crises with cross-border effects (Martinez-Diaz 2009). For policy-makers in relatively poor and rich countries alike, the main political question became both obvious and difficult to answer. When real economic growth rates were sought in excess of those capable of being generated by domestic savings, how were the benefits and costs of financial openness to be distributed?

In principle, inward flows of privately owned capital make it possible for real economies to grow more rapidly than if they rely solely on domestic resources. In practice, the extra costs associated with crisis-induced capital outflows, bank bailouts,

and the lost confidence of investors occasionally threatens to undermine real economies, set back the process of industrialization, and disrupt underlying political and social orders. Behind the immediate economic costs of financial crises, for example, in terms of lost economic output, lies a human story repeated time and again. It is the story of unemployment, increasing tax burdens, personal despair and hopelessness, family breakdown, and rising crime rates. In developing countries, it is the story of deepening poverty, *coups d'état*, and military dictatorship. Who would deny that it is best to avoid such outcomes? But their very possibility is inherent in the macro-policy choices both leading states and those aspiring to their level of prosperity made in the post-1945 period. With the final collapse in 1989 of the only alternative system once attractive to some, that of state socialism and central planning, financial openness apparently marked the only feasible road to the future. To be sure, nevertheless, all but the most dependent states retained the ability to determine the speed with which they went down that road, and all but the weakest retained levers of power sufficient to influence the internal distribution of the benefits and costs thereby incurred.

National policy reform, international systemic consequences

In essence, by the 1980s, it had become clear that states constituting the international economy had collectively moved away from one set of policy trade-offs and toward another. Immediately after the Second World War, they sought to reconcile their newfound desire for exchange rate stability with their interest in maintaining independent monetary policies. Both as a matter of logic and of policy, they therefore had to tolerate limits on inward and outward capital flows—the 'unholy trinity' idea discussed in Helleiner, Chapter 7 in this volume. Four decades later, their priorities had changed. Capital mobility and monetary autonomy were privileged, and they were willing to tolerate floating exchange rates as well as a degree of volatility in their expanding financial markets (Obstfeld and Taylor 2004).

In the 1970s, to be sure, some developing countries sought to limit the future role of privately owned international capital, and they demanded a new international economic order, which would have greatly expanded state interference in international markets. By the 1980s, most of them had abandoned such a quest, a phenomenon referred to by one close observer as a 'silent revolution' (Boughton 2001). Few, however, joined the leading states in embracing a clearer trade-off between financial openness, monetary independence, and exchange rate stability. In the latter regard, the painful earlier experience of leading states in attempting to hold onto exchange rate pegs would be repeated. So, too, would be the experience of bank failures.

Over time, exchange rates measure the relative price levels across economies that are linked together by trade and investment. They can, however, also gyrate wildly in the face of speculative pressures or unanticipated economic or political shocks. As real economies become more open to trade and foreign investment, such volatility can be difficult to manage, both economically and politically. In the short run, exporters, importers, and investors may be able to hedge their foreign exposures, but this is costly and gets more problematic as time horizons expand. Standard economic theory, if still disputed, suggests that the way to ameliorate excessive currency volatility is to co-ordinate a range of national monetary and fiscal policies. Industrialized economies demonstrated only intermittent interest in doing so after the move to floating exchange rates, despite rhetorical expressions to the contrary at successive high-profile meetings of the G7/G8 and other collaborative bodies (Baker 2006). They have, instead, left it to financial markets to attempt to impose on national societies the economic discipline necessary to stabilize the system

as a whole. In practice, the stronger the country—that is, the more it was capable of generating and retaining its own domestic savings and/or the more it was capable of attracting foreign capital flows despite its pursuit of fiscal and monetary policies that might, in principle, be expected to have the opposite consequence—the lower such disciplinary effects turned out to be. In any event, through such macro-policy choices, industrialized economies constructed a system that relied on the possibility of sharp reversals in capital flows to force on themselves and others that modicum of co-ordination required for the interdependence of real economies to deepen.

Partly in reaction, as Helleiner notes in the previous chapter, European states sought to restore internal discipline through the establishment of a regional currency union. Moreover, especially in the aftermath of the Asian crisis of the late 1990s, China and other states with robust export sectors sought to build a buffer against externally generated financial shocks through building high levels of foreign exchange reserves. Still, the system as a whole increasingly relied on more open financial markets to promote the cross-border policy adjustments entailed by deepening economic interdependence (Abdelal 2007).

Political sovereignty and economic interdependence

During periods of euphoria in financial markets, participants tend to forget historical lessons. When a fund manager is earning 5 per cent a year for a client, it is difficult to stay employed when colleagues elsewhere are earning 20 per cent for theirs. But only the most ideological of participants in global markets choose entirely to ignore the past. Perhaps this helps explain why, despite their new-found preference for financial openness, no governments have unambiguously embraced the principle that capital has an inviolable legal right to cross borders. In this regard, their evident reluctance clearly to match global treaties

on trade with robust agreements on capital movements or to designate an international overseer for systemically significant cross-border financial intermediaries is telling. The architects of the post-1973 order will simply not lodge ultimate political authority over international financial markets at the level where it logically belongs. No international agency has been authorized to regulate or supervise international capital flows, not the International Monetary Fund, not the World Bank, and not the Bank for International Settlements (BIS). None has been provided with the resources necessary to act as true lender-of-last-resort. States have instead opted to allow the financial institutions they themselves continue to license and supervise to expand their international operations on the understanding that national regulators would informally co-ordinate their supervisory policies and emergency practices to the extent necessary. At moments of confidence-withering crises, who would ultimately be responsible for bailing out financial institutions confronting the prospect of collapse? In the wake of actual financial crises in the decades following the breakdown of the Bretton Woods exchange rate system, the answer became clearer and clearer (Kapstein 1994). Last-resort facilities remain under the exclusive purview of individual states themselves, and the home states of financial intermediaries therefore bear primary regulatory and supervisory responsibilities. At most, preemptive or precautionary credit is made available to others by key states acting jointly through treaty-based intergovernmental organizations like the International Monetary Fund or through less formal regional understandings and bilateral reserve-swap arrangements (Henning 2002). In any event, trust between home and host states remains both crucial and tenuous. Every cross-border financial crisis therefore refocuses attention on the systemic risk and the ultimate fragility of the post-1970s policy experiment in financial openness (see Box 8.2).

Box 8.2 The Global Financial Panic of the Late 1990s

In the mid 1990s, interest rates fell and stock markets boomed in North America and Western Europe. Banks and portfolio investors, including rapidly expanding mutual funds and so-called 'hedge' funds that pooled the capital of institutional and wealthy investors, increasingly looked abroad for higher returns. With those higher returns came higher risks. At the same time, Japanese banks, confronting stagnant demand in a slumping home market, sought the higher earnings promised in neighbouring countries. Both public sector and private sector borrowers in emerging markets suddenly found new and ready sources of funds, and they borrowed heavily.

In Thailand, much of this new debt was denominated in the local currency, which the Thai government valued at a pegged, not floating rate. By buying Thai debt, investors and creditors, in essence, bet that the baht would hold its value. Early in 1997, however, Japanese banks, which then held about half of the country's foreign debt, began to lose confidence. They sought to reduce their exposures in Thailand as well as in a number of neighbouring countries. Their pullback prompted a regional liquidity crunch. Soon, generalized fears of a devaluation of the baht became self-fulfilling, and other Asian nations needed to defend the competitive edges of their own exporting industries by allowing their own currencies to depreciate.

Capital suddenly flew out of South Korea, Indonesia, and Malaysia, a phenomenon now exacerbated by the panicked reactions of hedge fund investors globally. Just as a bank hit by a run of depositors is forced hurriedly to raise cash by calling in loans, these hedge funds had to meet demands for withdrawals by liquidating their assets. As their Thai assets declined in redeemable value, they withdrew what they could as quickly as possible from their Asian portfolios. Liquidity dried up across the region, and very quickly the solvency of local banks recently considered sound came into question.

The government of Malaysia tried to stem the panic by doing what foreign investors had come to consider unthinkable: it risked its future ability to re-enter global markets by imposing capital controls to forbid the repatriation of what its prime minister labelled the immoral gains of speculators. Others took the more conventional route of calling in the IMF to provide emergency funding as a stop-gap measure until panic subsided. Borrowing from the Fund and other multilateral agencies came, as usual, with conditions attached, but in these instances the terms were particularly controversial. Whereas borrowing countries saw themselves struggling against a short-term problem, the Fund began insisting on more fundamental kinds of reform designed to make East Asian markets, including financial markets, more open and more transparent. Talk of neo-imperialism by Western powers became commonplace as national incomes fell across the region, imports declined, and a cutthroat competition to maintain export industries ensued.

In the midst of the East Asian debacle, Russia's post-1991 experiment with frontier capitalism crashed into a wall of unsustainable foreign debt. In retrospect, it certainly seems that many foreign investors had unwisely discounted the possibility that Russia's new class of tycoons would take careful measures to spirit their own capital out of the country. By the summer of 1998, even a massive IMF loan could not bolster confidence in the value of the rouble. It also could not attract back private Russian capital invested in safe Western investments, nor could it sustain the confidence of the American and European investors in 'emerging market' funds that had recently and aggressively bought what turned out to be extremely risky securities backed by the Russian government. When the government defaulted in August and also devalued the rouble, seismic shocks were immediately felt at the core of the world's financial system. Stock markets plummeted around the world. Fearing that other emerging markets would follow Russia, panicked financiers pulled vast amounts of capital out of Mexico, Brazil, Argentina, and elsewhere.

In September 1998, Long-Term Capital Management (LTCM), a particularly prominent and highly leveraged American hedge fund with little direct exposure in emerging markets, found its heretofore extremely successful investment strategies wrecked as the crisis spread unexpectedly from Asia to Russia (Lowenstein 2001). While the consensus view among American financial market regulators would ordinarily have been to let such an entity bear the brunt of its mistakes, and even to fail, panic had by now gripped Wall Street itself. The Federal Reserve encouraged a consortium of LTCM's creditors to take over the firm's book, gradually unwind its bad bets, and replace its management. No one doubted that the full faith and credit of the US government would be available if required, but in the end this more limited emergency operation succeeded and calm gradually returned to the markets of industrial countries. When confidence in Asian emerging-market economies was finally restored a few years later, many governments moved to build up their own national monetary reserves by way of encouraging exports and discouraging imports. Those reserves were widely seen as self-insurance to provide protection in the event of future crises. Attenuating the influence of institutions like the IMF was obviously a more immediate political objective. The potentially tragic irony was that just such policies helped generate the global crisis that led to the establishment of the IMF in the first place.

For the most advanced developing countries, the situation began to improve rapidly as the new millennium dawned. With certain exceptions, access to capital markets was restored and a new era of financial globalization had apparently dawned. Foreign direct investment flows, in particular, became a major impetus to economic expansion. Beginning in the summer of 2007 and reaching its most dangerous point one year later, a new and generalized financial crisis rapidly changed the situation (see Figure 8.1 and Figure 8.2, and Table 8.1). Nothing could have underlined more boldly the urgency of finding more effective ways of preventing and managing financial emergencies and, ultimately for rendering the experiment in financial integration more legitimate.

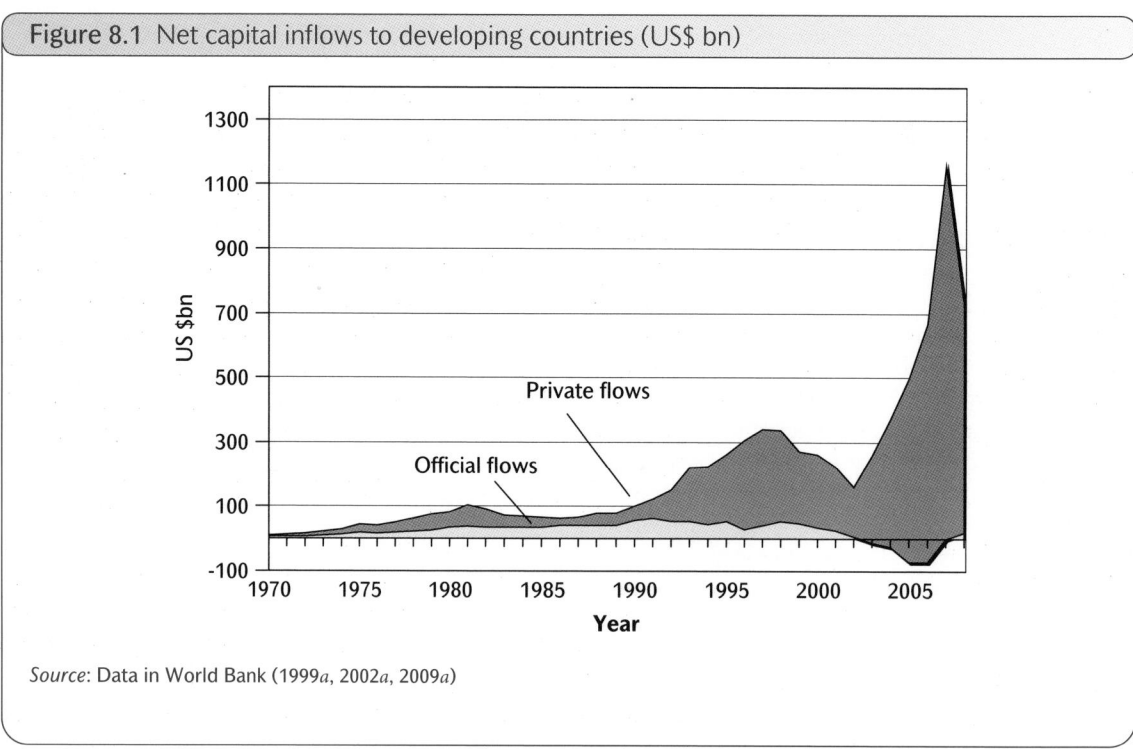

Figure 8.1 Net capital inflows to developing countries (US$ bn)

Source: Data in World Bank (1999*a*, 2002*a*, 2009*a*)

Figure 8.2 Composition of net private capital inflows to developing countries (US$ bn)

Source: Data in World Bank (1999*a*, 2002*a*, 2009*a*)

Table 8.1 Net Capital Inflows to Developing Regions, 2005–8

$ billions

	2005	2006	2007	2008e
Total	570	739	1158	707
By region:				
East Asia and Pacific	187	206	281	203
Europe and Central Asia	192	311	281	251
Latin America and the Caribbean	113	85	216	128
Middle East and North Africa	19	25	21	23
South Asia	25	72	113	66
Sub-Saharan Africa	33	40	55	36

Note: e = estimate
Source: World Bank (2009a: 40)

Key points

- Financial crises have generated policy innovations inside and among industrial states; the pattern repeated itself in many emerging-market states.

- Sovereignty remains an important legal doctrine in a globalizing economy, but in practical policy terms it is under rising pressure as border-spanning risks become ever more obvious.

Crisis Prevention

No modern financial market exists for long without common standards understood by all participants. At the most basic level, financial information must be expressed in an understandable form. Accounting, auditing, and licensing rules form the bedrock. In all but the most limited local markets, or in all but the most libertarian utopias, such rules have not been spontaneously generated. Some actor must provide the collective goods of standard setting, adjudication, reform, and, ultimately, enforcement. Even illegal markets, if they are to persist, require someone to provide those minimal requirements. In legal markets, by definition, such collective goods are provided by the final maker of binding laws. To be sure, ultimate authorities can and do delegate the responsibility to define and promote technical standards in many of the world's financial markets. But all contemporary markets that are legal rest on standards and enforcement procedures associated with governmental authority in one form or another. Even central banks that we now conventionally label 'independent', like the European Central Bank, derive their authority from constitutional arrangements or interstate treaties. Crisis prevention begins here. It is built on confidence in the long-term resilience of orderly markets.

Defining and defending public interests

Moments of financial crisis have tested this reasoning, even in recent times. International financial crises expose jurisdictional ambiguities and overlaps. But they are typically followed by new preventive measures, directly or indirectly supported by political authorities. However, they have not yet been followed by the establishment of an unambiguous global standard-setter or a global agency capable of final enforcement. The frontier of markets integrating themselves across political and legal boundaries therefore remains characterized in the final analysis by intergovernmental bodies charged with negotiating common cross-border understandings on appropriate standards and their enforcement (Bryant 2003). This is not to suggest that organizations created by private sector actors have been absent. For example, standard-setting bodies set up by accounting and other types of firms or private associations are increasingly common. In the United States, the United Kingdom, and elsewhere, governments have often been willing to let market participants attempt to reach agreement among themselves on best practices. When such attempts fail and markets are threatened with disruption, however, governments and central banks come out of the shadows.

Contemplating the ever-present possibility that a bank they regulated could fail and thereby compromise the financial system as a whole (called systemic risk), governments retained the ability either to dip into national treasuries to save it or to allow it to be liquidated in an orderly fashion. As banks expanded their international operations, regulators necessarily had to begin working with their foreign counterparts on common standards for prudential supervision and common approaches to the management of emergencies.

Over time, other kinds of financial intermediaries, like investment funds and trust companies, found ways to provide analogous services more cheaply. With the emergence of lightly regulated non-bank financial institutions in domestic and international markets in the 1960s and 1970s, the very same logic of international collaboration on standard setting and enforcement therefore spread beyond the banking sector. The provision of insurance, stock underwriting and sales, and pooled investing services had by the 1990s clearly become global businesses. To some extent, most firms in these businesses remained supervised in some sense in their home markets, but the governmental agencies licensing and overseeing them often expressly tried to limit their own responsibility for bailing them out in an emergency. That is, their licensing authorities attempted to limit the risk that firms would make imprudent judgments and take excessive risks in the knowledge that they would not be allowed to fail. As in the banking sector though, setting standards, defining enforcement responsibilities, and preventing official liabilities became more complicated as functional and geographic barriers were permitted to erode throughout the post-1970s era. Drawing a clear dividing line between public interests and private risks would rarely be a straightforward task any more (Pauly 2009).

Incipient co-ordination of regulatory and supervisory policies

Well into the 1980s, the main arenas within which financial regulators sought to co-ordinate their standard-setting and enforcement activities were easy to identify. Bilateral negotiations between national regulators and central banks were nothing new. After the fallout from the Herstatt failure spread globally through foreign exchange markets, such interaction became multilateralized through a central bankers' club organized under the institutional auspices of the Bank for International Settlements (BIS). The Basel Committee on Banking Supervision associated with the BIS (see Box 8.3) technically reports to the governors of the world's leading central banks (the so-called G10, which actually now includes more than ten members), but it continues to be the key standard-setting forum for the largest financial institutions operating across national borders, institutions that still typically have a bank at the core of complicated conglomerate structures. The prevention of future international financial crises defines the core mandate of the Basel Committee. This has led it to experiment with protocols for minimum standards for back-up capital reserves to be held by banks, and to work with other national and regional bodies to bolster the transparency and effectiveness of prudential supervision within and beyond the banking sector narrowly defined. In 2006, the most extensive and detailed effort to ensure capital adequacy came in an accord commonly dubbed Basel II. Under its terms, international lenders were encouraged to bring sophisticated risk-management techniques into the core of their internal decision-making procedures and calculations of adequate capital. The fact that this seemed to provide a new source of **competitive advantage** for the largest money-centre banks was not the only controversy engendered by the new accord. Some observers also feared that Basel II capital requirements could be 'pro-cyclical,' that is, that they could encourage banks excessively to restrict lending during recessions and imprudently to expand lending during booms. As we shall see, that fear would be justified even before the new agreement was finally implemented by key countries.

Box 8.3 Institutions for Collaboration on International Financial Policies and Practices

Bank for International Settlements (BIS) Established in 1930 to oversee Germany's war reparation payments. After the Second World War, this institution based in Basel, Switzerland, assisted European governments in their monetary and financial interactions. After the 1960s, its role in facilitating a multilateral payments system in Europe made it an obvious venue for intensifying dialogue among central bankers, now including the United States and other non-European countries, on a broad range of regulatory and supervisory issues. Today, the BIS provides a meeting venue and secretariat for several collaborative committees, including the Basel Committee of Banking Supervision.

Basel Committee on Banking Supervision Provides a forum to stimulate collaborative approaches on issues of common concern among its members, which now include Argentina, Australia, Belgium, Brazil, Canada, China, France, Germany, Hong Kong SAR, India, Indonesia, Italy, Japan, Korea, Luxembourg, Mexico, the Netherlands, Russia, Saudi Arabia, Singapore, South Africa, Spain, Sweden, Switzerland, Turkey, the United Kingdom, and the United States. The Committee has developed international standards on capital adequacy for banks and core principles for effective supervision of cross-border banking. Among other activities, it promotes its standards globally through a biennial International Conference of Banking Supervisors. The Committee also works with IOSCO and the IAIS (see below) on issues related to the supervision of financial conglomerates, including the division of responsibilities between home and host states.

Financial Action Task Force Initiated at the 1989 summit meeting of the G7 to combat money laundering. A small secretariat based in the OECD, but not technically part of that organization, it co-ordinates national efforts, now also aimed at disrupting the financing of terrorism in a world of more open markets.

Financial Stability Board (FSB) Following the international financial crises of the late 1990s, the G7 finance ministers and central bank governors brought together national financial regulators from a wide range of countries hosting important international financial centres, together with international organizations involved in financial policy matters. The Financial Stability Forum (FSF) began meeting in April 1999 and maintained a small secretariat at the BIS. In April 2009, the G20 expanded its membership to include Spain and the European Commission and transformed it into a more ambitious effort with the mandate of fostering 'macro-prudential' collaboration among central banks and financial supervisors, that is, on ensuring that the oversight of financial institutions included not only analysis of the effects of institutional failure on the system as a whole but also rigorous assessment of the effects of systemic shocks on the institutions themselves. The FSB, with a slightly expanded but still modest secretariat comprised mainly of officials seconded from central banks, was to be a vehicle for consultation across various standard-setting groups and organizations. It was to country-level link its work to the Financial Sector Assessment Programs of the World Bank and the IMF and to the Fund's surveillance operations. Particular emphasis was placed on issues related to the regulation of cross-border financial institutions, including the division of the responsibilities between home and host states.

G7/G8/G20 Dating back to informal meetings of European finance ministers after the collapse of the Bretton Woods exchange rate arrangements, regular annual meetings of financial officials and heads of government now occur under these rubrics. Originally including five members, the United States, France, Britain, Germany, Japan, Canada, and Italy in recent years also met with Russia and the European Union. The G20, which includes leading emerging market-countries like China, India, Brazil, and South Africa is set to overshadow smaller groups in the future. Meetings often involve the confidential sharing of information on financial and economic policies. Personal relationships thereby developed and reinforced can be useful when it comes to co-ordinating national policies rapidly in the face of international financial crises. There is no secretariat.

International Accounting Standards Board (IASB) and **International Federation of Accountants** Private sector bodies organized by professional accounting associations to encourage international standardization of accounting principles and auditing practices. Activities intensified during the 1970s and came to prominence in the 1990s after a series of accounting scandals in the United States and other major markets.

International Association of Insurance Supervisors (IAIS) Established in 1992 to encourage co-operation among regulators and supervisors of insurance companies. Since 1998, its secretariat has been housed in Basel, Switzerland, where it receives technical assistance from the BIS.

International Bank for Reconstruction and Development (World Bank) Also originally created at Bretton Woods (see Wade, Chapter 12, and Phillips, Chapter 13 in this volume).

International Monetary Fund (IMF) Designed at the Bretton Woods Conference, July 1944. (For details on its subsequent evolution, see Helleiner, Chapter 7 in this volume.)

International Organization of Securities Commissions (IOSCO) With a secretariat based in Montreal, Canada, IOSCO sponsors conferences and other linkages among the regulators of national stock and other securities markets. Designed to facilitate the sharing of information and best practices, it developed during the 1970s as buyers and sellers of securities increasingly moved their funds across national borders.

Organization for Economic Co-operation and Development (OECD) Evolved out of efforts after the Second World War to facilitate the use of Marshall Plan resources. Often now considered a think tank for industrial countries contemplating various forms of economic policy co-ordination.

Regional Development Banks With local mandates akin to the global development mandate of the World Bank, these multilateral organizations are now involved in providing technical advice for financial market deepening, regulation, and supervision in Africa, Latin America, East Asia, Eastern Europe, and Central Europe.

United Nations (UN) Various UN commissions, agencies, and departments, such as the Department of Economic and Social Affairs in the New York-based secretariat, have mandates to review international financial developments and seek to promote understanding among member states on issues of equity and efficiency in the global economy. In recent years, its focus has shifted to ensuring the availability of adequate financing for developing countries and to promoting internationally agreed Millennium Development Goals for poverty reduction and sustainable development (the 'Monterrey Consensus').

World Trade Organization (WTO) Having grown out of the General Agreement on Tariffs and Trade (GATT), under which national trade policies have been liberalized on a multilateral basis ever since 1948, the WTO now has growing responsibilities for trade in various services, including a widening range of financial services (see Winham, Chapter 5 in this volume).

To the extent that it can be labelled a coherent strategy, the contemporary efforts of leading states over time to prevent systemic financial collapse were mainly characterized by incremental network building. They favoured technical policy co-ordination to the extent necessary to promote the deepening integration of resilient financial markets and to extend the project safely beyond the core of the system. If agreements on standards and collaborative regulatory networks failed, two other policy instruments remained in the arsenal of states seeking to prevent financial crises from spilling over into their markets: capital controls and expanding foreign exchange reserves. In the post-1973 system, capital controls were increasingly ineffective, but they could provide breathing room in the short run. They became ever more difficult to enforce, easier to evade, disruptive to long-term investment, and susceptible to political corruption (Goodman and Pauly 1993). Nevertheless, especially in the wake of the Asian crisis, some states deployed control-like measures, including special taxes, to manage their currencies, attract desired capital flows (like loans and investments facilitating production and trade), and discourage unwanted inflows (like speculative purchases of currencies in the expectation of quick gains). If generalized, such measures would undercut the global experiment in financial integration just as surely as exchange rate manipulation would call into question the open system of trade, investment, and production that provides the ultimate rationale for the experiment itself.

The broader macroeconomic policy context

Ultimately, mutually sustainable fiscal and monetary policies in the states at the core of the world economy are required for international financial integration to succeed. Steady, sustainable growth in real economies, low inflation, and spreading prosperity defines an objective much like motherhood. Everyone favours it, no one objects to it, and the principles supporting it are impeccable. The relevant political question, however, has remained the same ever since the early 1970s. How can co-operative efforts to achieve fiscal and monetary stability be encouraged in the absence of some overarching agreement on an economic constraint, such as could theoretically be provided by a binding commitment to stable exchange rates? After 1973, leading states conceded that such a commitment could not be maintained; the most they could agree upon was a commitment to 'a stable system of exchange rates' facilitated by 'firm surveillance' by the International Monetary Fund (James 1996). (In the 1990s, the member states of the Economic and Monetary Union in Europe went further among themselves by constructing a common currency and a common monetary policy, but, significantly, not a common fiscal policy.)

Recently, the dominant problem in the global macroeconomy undercutting efforts to prevent cross-border financial crises from recurring and spreading has taken the form of rapidly expanding imbalances in the current accounts of major trading countries. In short, the United States was importing too much, saving too little, and depending for its financing needs on inflows of capital from China, Japan, Germany, and many emerging-market and developing countries. Macroeconomic policy co-ordination and adjustment in the global interest was not occurring. Instead, the US consumption engine provided the too-easy motor force for a globalizing economy. For a time, the situation looked like a happy one for all concerned. Alas, the engine soon ran too hot. Economists argue about whether excessively low interest rates early in the new millennium caused the disaster. Lax regulation, remarkably high leverage in financial intermediaries spurring illusory financial innovations (like securitized subprime mortgages), a broadly under-appreciated turn in the business cycle, and the reliance of leading states on particular sectors, like housing and finance, to sustain national prosperity—are all often now also underlined by analysts (Helleiner *et al.* 2009; Schwartz 2009; Sorkin 2009). In any case, the worst crisis since the 1930s began, not in emerging markets, but in the housing market of the United States. Early on, even the most pessimistic observers expected a version of the 'savings and loan' crisis of the late 1980s, which, though severe, proved containable within the domestic US economy. But this particular financial crisis soon went viral, and it nearly tipped the global economy into the second Great Depression (see Box 8.4).

Box 8.4 Timeline for the Crisis of 2008

17 May 2007 Following months of rising turbulence in US housing markets, combined with mounting scandals involving Fannie Mae and Freddie Mac, agencies with implicit US government backing that guarantee $5 trillion in mortgages, including many considered 'subprime', Federal Reserve Chairman Ben Bernanke states that a growing number of housing-related defaults will not seriously harm the US economy.

June 2007 Two highly leveraged ('hedge') funds owned by the investment bank, Bear Stearns, which had large holdings of subprime mortgages, report large losses and are forced to begin selling assets at distressed prices. The trouble spreads to major Wall Street firms such as Merrill Lynch, JPMorgan Chase, Citigroup, and Goldman Sachs, which had lent the funds money. Similar problems emerge in the United Kingdom.

August 2007 Early in the month, US stock markets fall sharply. 'Credit crunch' spreads around the world as subprime mortgage-backed securities are disclosed in portfolios of banks from BNP Paribas to Bank of China. To provide market liquidity, the Fed cuts inter-bank interest rates and injects nearly $100 billion into the US banking system. The European Central Bank and the central banks of Japan, England, Canada, and Australia make co-ordinated moves to provide liquidity in their own markets.

16 August 2007 Stricken by losses in investments related to US subprime mortgages, the German regional bank, SachsenLB, is rapidly sold to Germany's biggest regional bank, Landesbank Baden-Wuerttemberg. The same day, Countrywide Financial Corporation, the biggest US mortgage lender, narrowly avoids bankruptcy by taking out an emergency loan of $11 billion from a group of banks. Shortly thereafter, the UK bank, Northern Rock, admits similar difficulties and requests Bank of England assistance in the face of a run by depositors.

18 September 2007 The Fed starts cutting broader interest rates, and will continue doing so at seven straight monthly meetings and one unscheduled emergency meeting. It also agrees to start loaning money directly to Wall Street firms, rather than to commercial banks alone, and to accept troubled mortgage-backed securities as collateral.

30 September 2007 Affected by the spiraling mortgage and credit crises, Internet banking pioneer, NetBank, declares bankruptcy, and the Union Bank of Switzerland announces a loss of US$690 million in the third quarter. Six days later, US investment firm, Merrill Lynch, reports losses of $5.5 billion, which will mount to $8 billion within the next month.

2 November 2007 The US Treasury announces its long-delayed final implementation of the Basel II Accord negotiated by the Basel Committee on Banking Supervision. The aim was to set an agreed standard for risk-weighted capital requirements to offset various risks threats to bank solvency. The gathering crisis was already underlining the important risks not adequately covered by the Accord, especially the risk that extreme market conditions would limit access to normal operating liquidity. Two weeks later, the US Financial Accounting Standards Board (FASB) announces new standards for 'Fair Value Measurements' on bank balance sheets. By requiring mark-to-market accounting during a crisis, the controversial standards increase the risk that bank losses will be exaggerated.

12 December 2007 The Federal Reserve's Open Market Committee negotiates swap lines with the European Central Bank and the Swiss National Bank for up to $20 billion and $4 billion, respectively. Similar facilities, designed to assist one another in the provision of liquidity to local markets, will be extended and expanded repeatedly over the next year. Eventually, central banks from around the world, including many emerging-market countries, will participate in this evolving system.

11 January 2008 Bank of America pays $4 billion for failing Countrywide Financial, the country's biggest mortgage originator and, soon, the subject of a rising scandal involving the provision of financial favours to prominent politicians, including the chair of the Senate Banking Committee and the head of Fannie Mae.

28 January 2008 Four days after the first nationwide decline in housing prices since the 1930s is announced, the Economic Stimulus Act of 2008 is proposed in the US Congress. The next day, the House of Representatives passes a $146 billion aid package to speed up tax rebates to most taxpayers. The Senate increases the package and the legislation is sent to the President on 7 February. Six days later, Northern Rock is nationalized by the UK government.

15 March 2008 In an extraordinarily rare weekend move, the Fed provides cash, not only to commercial banks at the heart of the national payments system, but to investment banks as well. The next day, JPMorgan Chase & Co. acquires troubled Wall Street firm Bear Stearns, in a deal engineered and backstopped by the Fed. Soon thereafter, the IMF projects $945 billion in global losses from the financial crisis, and G7 finance ministers launch a review of the global financial regulatory system.

16 June 2008 The New York investment bank, Lehman Brothers, reports a loss of $2.8 billion in the second quarter. Within the firm, funds begin to flow from units overseas back to New York, a development that will cause host countries to raise serious objections. Three days later, ex-Bear Stearns fund managers are arrested by the FBI for allegedly misrepresenting the fiscal health of their funds heavily invested in subprime mortgages.

31 August 2008 German Commerzbank AG takes over Dresdner Kleinwort investment bank. Seven days later, US Treasury Secretary Henry Paulson announces a public 'conservatorship' for cash-starved Fannie Mae and Freddie Mac.

14 September 2008 Lehman Brothers, burdened by $60 billion in soured real-estate holdings, files a Chapter 11 bankruptcy petition after official attempts to arrange a rescue for the 158-year-old firm fail, and the US Treasury and Fed apparently decide that the knock-on effects will be manageable. The next day, under pressure from government officials, Bank of America acquires Merrill Lynch. The same day, New York State authorizes insurance giant, American International Group (AIG), which provides insurance for many of the securities comprised of bundled subprime mortgages, to use $20 billion from its own insurance subsidiaries for liquidity purposes.

16 September 2008 In co-ordinated operations, central banks around the world pump billions of dollars into money markets. Supposedly very safe money market investment funds shock increasingly illiquid markets when they are forced to pay clients redeeming their investments less than those clients paid in. Panic ensues, and the US government announces an unprecedented blanket guarantee for money market funds. The same day the Fed lends AIG $85 billion in exchange for nearly 80 per cent of its stock; the decision generates intense controversy from its inception, with the Fed and Treasury claiming its necessity to prevent a depression and critics seeing an ill-negotiated transfer of wealth from taxpayers to financial intermediaries. The price of gold soars by over 8 per cent, equity markets continue a broad global retreat, and governments around the world begin moving to ban the speculative short-selling of financial stocks.

21 September 2008 Goldman Sachs and Morgan Stanley, the two remaining giants in US investment banking markets, change their legal charters to become bank holding companies, thus gaining access to the emergency liquidity facilities of the Fed. Three days later, in the largest bank failure in US history, Washington Mutual collapses and with government support is sold to JPMorgan Chase.

29 September 2008 The US Senate rejects a $700 billion plan to bail out the US financial system. Bradford & Bingley of the UK is nationalized and sold to the Spanish bank, Santander. Hypo Real Estate is bailed out by banks and the government in Germany. Fortis Bank in Belgium is bailed out and then effectively taken apart by Netherlands, Belgium, and Luxembourg, and the next day, its main competitor, Dexia, is taken over by France, Belgium, and Luxembourg. Iceland begins nationalizing its biggest banks. In the US, Citigroup announces the government-backed takeover of Wachovia Bank. The Fed continues supporting markets with massive liquidity operations, while the Securities and Exchange Commission and the Financial Accounting Standards Board announce moves to relax 'mark-to-market' accounting rules. The next day, spreads on short-term inter-bank lending in global markets, normally quite low, spike to 7 per cent, their highest levels ever.

1 October 2008 The US Senate reverses itself and two days later, President Bush signs the $700 billion Emergency Economic Stabilization Act into law. Three days later, EU leaders travel to Paris for an emergency summit. During the next week, stock markets around the world record their worst week since the early 1930s. Iceland's banking system collapses, with immediate consequences for British Internet-banking depositors. Major British banks are partly nationalized; Germany, France, and other EU countries prepare decisive measures to stabilize failing local banks. Fearing a global economic collapse, central banks simultaneously slash interest rates. The fever of the crisis begins to break.

10 October 2008 G7 finance ministers and central bank governors meet in Washington and agree to co-ordinated monetary and fiscal actions to prevent the credit crisis from throwing the world into depression. Citing provisions of anti-terrorist laws, the UK government freezes Icelandic assets in a bid to force the country to compensate British depositors. Four days later, the US Treasury announces its intention to take $250 billion from the $700 billion package authorized by Congress to purchase troubled assets from US banks and the US operations of foreign banks.

22 October 2008 The House Oversight and Government Reform Committee grills executives from the country's leading credit-rating companies, who had privately acknowledged for more than a year that conflicts of interest contributed to excessively favourable ratings of mortgage-backed securities. One day later, former Federal Reserve Chairman Alan Greenspan, whose easy-money policies are now seen as sowing the seeds for the crisis, says that the inability of financial markets to correct themselves has left him in a 'state of shocked disbelief'.

10 November 2008 China announces a $586 billion stimulus package, the largest in the country's history. The US Treasury expands the bailout package for troubled insurer, AIG, to $150 billion and allows direct government investment in the company. Two days later, the Treasury loosens its structures on purchasing troubled assets and says that the bailout programme will be adapted to bolster financial intermediaries as needed.

28 November 2008 The Basel Committee on Banking Supervision provides new guidance on the valuation of assets at fair market prices, while the World Bank launches a Debt Management Facility to help developing countries prevent debt problems in the future. Meanwhile, the IMF is busy in central and eastern Europe negotiating standby arrangements with vulnerable countries from Latvia to Belarus.

1 December 2008 The US National Bureau of Economic Research announces that the economy entered a recession in December 2007. A few days later, as global investors seek the relative safety of US government debt, the yield on three-month Treasury bills briefly falls into negative territory for the first time ever. Two days later, former NASDAQ stock exchange chairman, Bernard Madoff, is charged with running a fraudulent investment business that lost at least $50 billion.

17 December 2008 The Fed lowers its base interest rates near 0 per cent and begins planning for highly unusual new measures (quantitative easing) to bolster market liquidity. Similar moves are underway at central banks in Canada, Europe, Asia, and in emerging-market nations. Two days later, President Bush announces plans to lend General Motors and Chrysler $17.4 billion to prevent their collapse.

9 January 2009 The German government takes a 25 per cent stake in Commerzbank through a €10 billion capital injection in an effort to help Commerzbank acquire Dresdner Bank. Ireland bails out Anglo-Irish Bank. A few days later, Standard & Poor's cuts the credit rating of debt issued by Greece, while Portugal, Spain, and Ireland are put on watch lists.

20 January 2009 Barack Obama is sworn in as the forty-forth president of the United States. IMF projects world economic growth to fall to just 0.5 per cent this year, its lowest rate since the Second World War.

10 February 2009 The US Treasury announces a Financial Stability Plan involving purchases of convertible preferred stock in eligible banks, the creation of a Public-Private Investment Fund to acquire troubled assets from financial institutions, expansion to $1 trillion of the Fed's Term Asset-Backed Securities Loan Facility, and new initiatives to stem residential mortgage foreclosures. One week later, a new $787 billion fiscal stimulus plan, the American Recovery and Reinvestment Act of 2009, is signed into law.

1 March 2009 The Fed and the US Treasury provide $30 billion in capital to AIG and take over two divisions of the company after it announces a $61.7 billion loss, the largest in US corporate history. Debate heats up on the effective use of US taxpayer dollars to pay AIG's obligations in full to major counterparties, including Goldman Sachs and a number of large foreign banks.

2 April 2009 G20 leaders meet in London, where they agree to convert the Financial Stability Forum (FSF), born after the Asia crisis, to the Financial Stability Board (FSB) (see Box 8.3). The heads of the FSB and the IMF are mandated to report jointly to the International Monetary and Financial Committee that brings together the finance ministers and central bank governors of all Fund members. The same day, the Financial Accounting Standards Board relaxes mark-to-market financial rules.

1 June 2009 General Motors declares bankruptcy. Many countries are by now deep in recession, and global trade flows are in decline. The Fed outlines new supervisory criteria for banks seeking to return loans and capital injections from the Treasury. President Obama proposes a massive legislative and regulatory overhaul.

17 September 2009 The US Securities and Exchange Commission approves new rules to govern rating agencies. The US Treasury announces expiration of the Guarantee Program for Money Market Funds.

9 December 2009 Finance ministers of the UK and France plan tax on windfall bonuses paid to bank executives. US Congress begins work that culminates in the sweeping Dodd-Frank Wall Street Reform and Consumer Protection Act on 21 July 2010.

11 January 2010 Fed records $46 billion profit for 2009, mainly reflecting interest payments and gains on securities purchased during the crisis. The highest earnings ever in its history are turned over to the US Treasury. Two days later, the Financial Crisis Inquiry Commission, established by the US Congress to examine the causes of the financial meltdown, holds its first public hearings. Pressure mounts for more extensive international co-ordination to reduce sovereign debts built up during the recent crisis.

Key points

- Since the collapse of the Bretton Woods exchange-rate regime, governments have attempted to co-operate more intensively to prevent financial crises.
- Fundamental macroeconomic policy choices usually condition the flow of capital across national borders, but capital flight can sometimes occur unexpectedly.

- Policy collaboration to reduce the chances that a localized financial crisis will spread has often involved talk about joint moves in fiscal and monetary policy making, but substantive movement to render global markets more resilient has occurred mainly in regulatory and supervisory arenas. The results have been mixed, and significant challenges remain.

Crisis Management and Resolution

Debt rescheduling and restructuring

When the financial obligations of a business firm become unsustainable given available resources, the classic question is whether the underlying problem is one of illiquidity or insolvency. The distinction is rarely clear-cut in practice, and one problem can easily slide into the other. In the typical case of illiquidity, creditors or investors in the firm might judge that a short-term loan or capital injection will get it through a payments crisis and enable it to find solid footing once again. In the case of insolvency, they would judge that it is no longer a going concern and that further lending would be worse than useless. One of two options might then be chosen. The firm could be taken over by its creditors and its balance sheet reorganized in an attempt to recreate some kind of viable business, or the firm's assets could be liquidated to retire as many of its liabilities as possible before finally closing its doors. In advanced capitalist systems, national bankruptcy laws exist to guide these procedures, and courts are often required to make the ultimate decisions. If Schumpeter was right and processes of creative destruction are the essence of modern capitalism, national governments use bankruptcy to clear their economic systems and enable those processes to repeat themselves. In the end, they no longer send failed entrepreneurs to debtors' prison but instead give them another chance.

Countries facing currency crises in an interdependent system are in a somewhat analogous position to a firm unable to meet its obligations. Aggregate debts become unsustainable, creditors demand repayment, and the resources available to settle accounts deteriorate in value. The national balance sheet requires adjustment. Crisis conditions may be generated by government overspending, by excessive imports, or by the building up of private-sector debt that cannot be financed domestically. Any of these situations might motivate the government to increase the rate of production of its monetary printing press. Inflation would normally be the consequence, and if the fundamental problem is one of temporary illiquidity this might provide the necessary space for internal adjustments to occur. If much of a country's debt is owed to foreigners and is denominated in foreign currency, however, such a policy may quickly deepen the problem and easily turn it into one akin to the insolvency of a business firm. Inflation in the local currency by definition pushes up the value of foreign currency liabilities. Expecting further declines in the purchasing power of the local currency, domestic as well as foreign creditors and investors rush to preserve their capital, and even to get it out of the country. A deteriorating real exchange rate makes debt repayment more costly, imported goods required to facilitate revenue-generating production become more expensive, and potential investors in future production lose confidence. The debtor government can default on its loans, or try to allow private firms under its purview to default with impunity, but then it risks cutting its economy off from future capital inflows that have no domestic substitute. The country becomes caught in the downward, vicious economic syndrome of deflation and depression. The situation in Argentina in 2001 provided a vivid example.

Obviously missing in such a scenario is a mechanism for the orderly bankruptcy of a national economy. Absent is a lender-of-last-resort, internationally agreed liquidation procedures, and a final court to replace managers and supervise the forced adjustment of the national balance sheet. This is, of course, no accident. In the conceptual extreme, the sovereignty of a state implies the absolute right both to resort to war and to default on debts. As a classic realist might argue, the ability in practice to claim such a right is in the final analysis a function of the raw power a state has in its possession to enforce its decision. In the real world, the sovereignty of particular states is compromised all the time (Krasner 1999). Unilateral defaults, payment moratoria, or standstills can be, and often are, declared by debtors. On the other hand, national assets can sometimes be unilaterally seized by aggrieved creditors.

The architects of the post-1945 system deemed economic instability to be the handmaidens of war. At Bretton Woods, therefore, they took the first steps in designing mechanisms that would limit the extent to which sovereign participants in the system would find themselves pushed to default on their debts. Time and again, from 1945 until the present moment, the main creditor states and the private financial institutions they license and regulate found themselves designing and redesigning substitutes for gunboat diplomacy, namely programmes that provide certain debtor states with the functional equivalent of last-resort lending facilities or of debt-restructuring services loosely analogous to those found in domestic bankruptcy courts. Sovereign debt reschedulings and restructurings have been common since the 1980s. International banks as well as official agencies providing export credits informally organized themselves into negotiating groups (the so-called London Club and Paris Club, respectively) to manage such arrangements. Frequently, however, the threat of default has drawn attention from creditor governments themselves.

The rise of emerging markets and their special needs

In the early post-war decades, the main economic imbalances capable of derailing the system as a whole occurred in industrial countries. They typically manifested themselves as currency crises (typically when governments sought to defend the par value of their currencies while running substantial trade deficits), so it was no coincidence that the International Monetary Fund was often enlisted either to help resolve them or retroactively to bless new currency pegs or unorthodox financial arrangements. During the 1980s and 1990s, the main crises capable of derailing the system occurred in emerging markets, and more often than not, the IMF again found itself at the centre of efforts to chart that middle path between financial anarchy and global governance. Many other institutions were eventually involved one way or another (Box 8.3). At moments of systemic danger centered on emerging markets in the 1980s and 1990s, the main creditor states shared the management burden by working through the IMF on currency crises and through the Basel Committee and ad hoc networks of central banks and finance ministries on banking crises.

The immediate objective of the IMF at such moments was to help break the psychology of fear and mistrust among its members and in the markets. Its ultimate mission, however, was to assist in stabilizing the financial underpinnings necessary for real national economies to become more deeply interdependent and more reliably prosperous through expanded trade and investment. That the IMF was not dissolved after 1973, when its members could not agree on a new exchange rate regime, reflected much more than bureaucratic inertia. Most importantly, the Fund's balance of payments financing facilities, which had grown over time in both size and flexibility, proved to be extremely convenient to its major member states. In effect, they mainly provided a mechanism for creditor states to share the burden of providing emergency financial assistance to debtors. Through the conditions attached to the use of such facilities, they could exert pressure on borrowers in a manner that would be politically difficult for individual creditor states. Moreover, the Fund's annual national and global surveillance activities offered the promise of holding all members accountable for the external consequences of their economic policy choices (Pauly 1997).

In retrospect, it is not surprising that the Fund evolved into the central crisis manager for emerging markets in a system that moved over time from one based on the interdependence of national exchange rate policies and underlying macroeconomic choices, toward one involving the deepening interaction of trade, investment, and financial policies. In this context, the leading states in the system confronted three basic choices every time one country or another found that it could not pay its bills to external customers or service its debts to external creditors:

1. They could do nothing, and risk the crisis spilling over to other countries and perhaps into their own domestic systems as well.

2. They could intervene directly by providing adequate financing from their own resources to the troubled country, and work directly with it to address the fundamental causes of the problem.

3. Or they could do the same indirectly, collectively, and more cheaply through the Fund and other collaborative institutions.

In practice, the third option often proved to be the least unattractive of the three, except for cases involving the weakest and most isolated developing countries. For countries whose periodic debt problems were widely perceived to be capable of seriously disrupting the system as a whole, the option of doing nothing, and of thereby letting markets attempt to force necessary adjustments, seldom seemed wise to actual policy-makers charged with making such a decision. Moreover, the option of exposing their own taxpayers to the unmediated hazards of crisis resolution has typically proven itself to be almost as unpalatable as bearing the political costs of unilaterally trying to impose conditions on recalcitrant debtors. The third option, therefore, nearly always found a sufficient number of advocates, in both creditor and debtor countries alike.

A New Global Architecture?

Perhaps there was a moment in time, just after the Second World War, when one could sense a window opening on a world where states would actually delegate a coherent piece of their monetary, if not fiscal, sovereignty to a technical agency with a binding, enforceable mandate. By 1973, the member states of the IMF had obviously conceded that the co-ordination of national fiscal and monetary policies could only be voluntary. How then could a reliable foundation for globalizing capitalism be constructed? If deeper financial integration remained a collective goal even as fiscal and monetary sovereignty remained sacrosanct, then those same states confronted the logically alternative necessity of co-ordinating their more technical policies and instruments aiming at preventing or, at worst, managing and resolving future financial crises. The prospect of future joint gains from routine macroeconomic policy co-ordination was not often a successful motivator. On the other hand, the prospect of catastrophic national and systemic losses did concentrate minds and held the promise of a modicum of policy collaboration (see Aggarwal and Dupont, Chapter 3 in this volume).

Key policy debates after the crises of the late 1990s revolved around the theory and practice of crisis management and resolution in emerging markets and especially around reducing the exposure of the most needy countries to excessively volatile capital flows (Eichengreen 2003; Roubini and Setser 2004). Serious reform proposals were conventionally grouped into three main categories: the unilateral, the multilateral, and the supranational (Eichengreen 2002; Bryant 2003; Woods 2006; Truman 2006).

In the first category, both conservative believers in the virtues of unfettered markets and the defenders of absolute sovereignty in developing countries join in a common cause. Crises, when they occur, are to be managed by unlucky or unwise external investors taking their lumps, and by debtor governments reverting to defaults and/or capital controls with attendant risks to their future access to external financing. In less extreme circumstances, private creditors and debtors would be left to their own devices to work out debt restructuring arrangements and to encourage reforms in national exchange rate regimes.

At the other end of the imagined policy spectrum were global institutions that would come closer to serving as the functional equivalents of domestic emergency-lending, bankruptcy, and liquidation arrangements. Two successive deputy managing directors of the IMF made such proposals, one for the Fund to be legally empowered to play the role of lender-of-last-resort and the next for the Fund to serve as a kind of ultimate bankruptcy court by overseeing a Sovereign Debt Restructuring Mechanism

(Fischer 2000; Krueger 2002; Goodhart and Illing 2002). Even in the aftermath of the Asian and Argentine crises, neither proved politically marketable. What did prove feasible was an idea in the middle position, the voluntary inclusion of 'collective action clauses' in future emerging-market bond issues. Such clauses are designed to encourage multilateral co-operation among bondholders in future situations requiring debt restructuring. By specifying in advance, for example, how defaults are to be handled, the clauses would in principle discourage individual bondholders from seeking full repayment when others were prepared to compromise and share any losses.

The debacle that began in the United States in 2007, dramatically raised the stakes involved in continuing the global experiment in financial openness and integration. Unilateral measures to manage the near-catastrophe bore the brunt of the burden. Spreading contagion was finally stopped by intensely collaborative arrangements among central banks at the core of the system, and by decisive fiscal action by national governments. Some fiscal burden-sharing occurred, for example, through the US bailout of AIG and, implicitly, through the ultimate effects of central bank asset purchases. Communication networks painstakingly constructed by key central banks in the wake of many crises had begun to prove their worth. But collaboration among the ultimate investors-of-last-resort, finance ministers and leaders making direct commitments with the resources of their citizen taxpayers, remained politically quite sensitive. Whether it can be counted upon in the future remained an open question.

The resolution of the crisis of 2008 also raised delicate questions concerning the consequences of new market expectations that many intermediaries, not least but not only those with complicated cross-border operations, were now most certainly too big or too interconnected to fail. By markedly enhancing moral hazard, governments had quite likely increased systemic risks and exacerbated market fragility. The United States and other advanced industrial states had also quite likely transformed a short-term banking crisis into a long-term fiscal problem, with negative consequences for their currencies and future living standards if official indebtedness could not soon be reined in. Moreover, although large foreign exchange reserves built up after the late 1990s had now apparently buffered China and neighbouring East Asian states from financial meltdown, the ultimate costs of that buffering could only be estimated after taking into account the political effects of fiscal stress and unemployment on the global trading system as a whole.

Like other financial crises in the post-1970s period, the recent crisis revealed the macroeconomic and macropolitical foundations of the experiment in financial market integration. In the end, the idea of cross-border financial intermediation through nationally licensed and regulated private institutions was not repudiated. The crisis therefore starkly underlined the importance of ensuring effective cross-border political collaboration and eventually of rendering such collaboration legitimate. Easier for political leaders to contemplate after the crisis were marginal adjustments in technical policies aimed mainly at prevention. This explains the new focus on the Financial Stability Board (FSB), the enhancement of the IMF's role in monitoring systemic risks and assisting weaker states, and the bolstering of bank capital adequacy and liquidity requirements in the Basel III agreement announced in September 2010.

Promoting a stable modus vivendi between national and regional impulses of competition and co-operation was a difficult task after 1945, when the United States, guided by a vision of freer trade and tightly regulated financial markets, clearly occupied the position of system leader. It is more difficult now, when raw economic and financial power is dispersing across the Americas, Europe, and Asia. The extent to which that power remains harnessed to a common purpose will be tested in the years ahead. Not coincidentally, responses to crises in financial markets will signal the answer.

Key points

- International financial crises are usually more difficult to manage than domestic crises because of jurisdictional ambiguities.

- Some basic level of cross-national co-ordination is required in crisis management and resolution; intergovernmental institutions can play a supportive role, but their main missions have typically focused on preventing the next crisis.

- Central bank networks among advanced industrial countries operated effectively during the crisis of

2008, but unilateral fiscal actions by national governments were often required to resolve the crisis. Fiscal burden-sharing occurred to a limited degree, but it remains politically quite sensitive.

- Emerging-market countries, not least, China, look set to exercise a more direct and determinative influence on the future of global financial integration.

? Questions

1. What causes financial crises, and why do some quickly spread globally?

2. What special risks are associated with cross-border finance, and how have regulators tried to respond?

3. What measures hold promise for preventing future financial crises?

4. How can international financial crises be more effectively managed?

5. How durable are any limits on crisis management and resolution?

6. How should we evaluate issues of distributive justice raised by financial market openness, both for the system as a whole and for specific countries?

→ Further reading

◼ Abdelal, R. (2007), *Capital Rules: The Construction of Global Finance* (Cambridge, MA: Harvard University Press). An insightful analysis of the normative foundations of contemporary international capital markets.

◼ Bryant, R. (2003), *Turbulent Waters: Cross-Border Finance and International Governance* (Washington, DC: Brookings Institution). A balanced exploration of the history and contemporary character of global finance by a leading economist attentive to the realities of national and international politics.

◼ Eichengreen, B. (2003), *Capital Flows and Crises* (Cambridge, MA: MIT Press). A readily accessible account of the causes and consequences of international financial crises.

◼ Flandreau, M., and Zumer, F. (2004), *The Making of Global Finance, 1880–1913* (Paris: OECD Development Centre). An excellent and nuanced study of the development of international capital markets in the first era of financial globalization.

◼ Goodhart, C., and Illing, G. (eds) (2002), *Financial Crises, Contagion, and the Lender of Last Resort* (Oxford: Oxford University Press). An enlightening assessment of the strengths and weaknesses of the institutions and practices of market governance at the global level.

■ Helleiner, E., Pagliari, S., and Zimmermann, H. (eds) (2009), *Global Finance in Crisis* (London: Routledge). A detailed and analytical survey of contemporary regulatory reforms that created the environment within which the crisis of 2007–9 played out.

■ James, H. (2009), *The Creation and Destruction of Value* (Cambridge, MA: Harvard University Press). A brilliant and historically grounded assessment of the cycles of economic and financial globalization.

■ Kindleberger, C. P. (1978), *Manias, Panics, and Crashes: A History of Financial Crises* (New York: Basic Books). A path-breaking orientation to the fragile financial underpinnings of modern capitalism.

■ Martinez-Diaz, L. (2009), *Globalizing in Hard Times: The Politics of Banking-Sector Opening in the Emerging World* (Ithaca, NY: Cornell University Press). A compelling political analysis of financial liberalization in advanced developing countries.

■ Minsky, H. (1986), *Stabilizing an Unstable Economy* (New Haven, CT: Yale University Press). The original and prescient analysis of the perils of apparently well-functioning financial markets.

■ Obstfeld, M., and Taylor, A. (2004), *Global Capital Markets: Integration, Crisis, and Growth* (Cambridge: Cambridge University Press). A detailed history of international capital mobility since the late nineteenth century by two prominent economists.

■ Pauly, L. (1997), *Who Elected the Bankers? Surveillance and Control in the World Economy* (Ithaca, NY: Cornell University Press). An examination of the development of the IMF and its principal role in the wake of twentieth-century financial crises.

■ Reinhart, C., and Rogoff, K. (2009), *This Time is Different: Eight Centuries of Financial Folly* (Princeton, NJ: Princeton University Press). A most impressive empirical examination of the history of financial crises.

■ Schwartz, H. (2009), *Subprime Nation: American Power, Global Capital, and the Housing Bubble* (Ithaca, NY: Cornell University Press). A timely examination of the roots of the 2008 crisis.

■ Sen, A. (2009), *The Idea of Justice* (Cambridge, MA: Belknap/Harvard University Press). Behind the technical discussions of globally minded financial experts lie significant issues of legitimacy and justice, and this book provides a foundation for beginning to grapple with them.

■ Sorkin, A. (2009), *Too Big to Fail* (New York: Viking). An excellent journalist's account of the unfolding crisis of 2007.

■ Stiglitz, J. E. (2006), *Making Globalization Work* (New York: W. W. Norton). Provocative critiques of the reactions of governments and international organizations to the economic disasters befalling much of the developing world in recent years, by the former chief economist of the World Bank.

■ Strange, S. (1998), *Mad Money: When Markets Outgrow Governments* (Ann Arbor, MI: University of Michigan Press). The late, great international political economist provides a rousing and contentious introduction to the policy and technical innovations that dramatically increased the volume and volatility of global financial flows.

■ Taleb, N. (2007), *The Black Swan: The Impact of the Highly Improbable* (New York: Random House). Bestseller that revived interest in the psychological aspects of market behaviour just as the crisis of 2008 began.

■ Truman, E. (ed.) (2006), *Reforming the IMF for the 21st Century* (Washington, DC: Peterson Institute for International Economics). An in-depth analysis of contemporary challenges and options for adaptation of the key multilateral instrument for crisis prevention and management in emerging markets.

■ Woods, N. (2006), *The Globalizers: The IMF, the World Bank and their Borrowers* (Ithaca, NY: Cornell University Press). A constructively critical assessment of the internal structures and major policies of the Bretton Woods twins.

LOUIS W PAULY

 Web links

■ www.imf.org/ International Monetary Fund.

■ www.worldbank.org/ The World Bank Group.

■ www.financialstabilityboard.org/ The Financial Stability Board.

■ www.un.org/esa/desa/ United Nations, Department of Economic and Social Affairs.

■ www.bis.org/ Bank for International Settlements.

■ www.oecd.org/ Organization for Economic Cooperation and Development.

■ www.g8.utoronto.ca/ and www.g20.utoronto.ca/ G8 and G20 Information Centres.

 Online resource centre

For additional material and resources, please visit the Online Resource Centre at:
www.oxfordtextbooks.co.uk/ravenhill3e/

PART 4

Globalization and its Consequences

The Logics of Economic Globalization

Anthony McGrew

9

Chapter contents

- Introduction
- A Global Economy? 'Embedded Globalization' and the Rescaling of Economic Activity
- The Logics of Economic Globalization
- The Second Age of Globalization: Another Extraordinary Episode?
- After the Crisis: The Prospects for Economic Globalization

Reader's guide

In 1987, Robert Gilpin's, *The Political Economy of International Relations* was published, a defining event in the coming of age of international political economy as a discrete field of academic enquiry. Less than two decades later, Gilpin issued a second edition, retitled *Global Political Economy*, reflecting, as noted in the book's preface, the fundamental changes that had taken place in the nature of the international economic order in the intervening period. The most significant change, he observes, is 'the globalization of the world economy' (Gilpin 2001: 3). However, the extent, significance, and consequences of this economic globalization remain hotly contested in academia and beyond. Globalization invites controversy, not least because in the wake of the financial crash of 2008, even many of its most committed advocates consider it is seriously at risk.

This chapter argues that economic globalization—understood simply as the widening, deepening, and speeding up of worldwide interconnectedness—remains a dominant feature of the contemporary world economy, although it is neither inevitable nor irresistible. It presents a systematic examination of the underlying causes or logics of economic globalization. By elucidating the principal accounts of globalization, it offers some critical judgements on which, if any, provide a convincing explanation of the globalization (and by implication deglobalization) of the world economy. Concentrating on the causes of globalization, the analysis avoids a focus upon its presumed effects or consequences—for example, on state sovereignty, patterns of inequality, or social democracy—which are taken up in later chapters of this volume (see Chapters 10, 12, and 13). The discussion instead explores the distinctive features of contemporary economic globalization and stresses the central role of politics—both local and global—in determining its future trajectory. In short, the chapter addresses four questions:

1. What is economic globalization and what are its principal features?
2. How does theory help us to explain contemporary economic globalization?
3. Is economic globalization today all that new?
4. Does the financial crisis of 2008 portend the collapse of globalization?

Introduction

In the aftermath of the cataclysmic attacks on the United States on 11 September 2001, obituaries for globalization were numerous. These momentous events, according to John Gray, heralded a new epoch in world affairs: 'The era of globalisation is over' (Naím 2002). In similar vein, John Reston Saul proclaimed 'the end of globalism', and Justin Rosenberg concluded 'the "age of globalization" is unexpectedly over' (Rosenberg 2005: 2; Saul 2005). Certainly, measured in terms of flows within the circuits of the world economy, economic globalization appeared to stall in the early part of this century. However, as later discussion illustrates, this slowdown proved a very temporary hiatus, as patterns of global economic exchange subsequently intensified, peaking with the onset of the global financial crisis in late 2008 (see Chapter 8 for a discussion of the origins and fallout from the crisis). Even before the 'Great Crash' of 2008 obituaries for economic globalization were numerous and frequent. Yet, the current 'second age of globalization' (the first age being the belle époque of 1870–1914) has proven far more resilient and socially embedded than many (even its most ardent advocates) have acknowledged. As the annual *Foreign Policy* Globalization Index noted: 'The resilience of globalization indicates that it is a phenomenon that runs deeper than

the political crises of the day' (Kearney and *Foreign Policy* Globalization Index 2005: 53). Whether, in the aftermath of the global financial crash of 2008, it continues to prove so resilient remains to be judged. For the economic historian, Harold James, the financial crisis rather dramatically signifies the end of the 'second age of globalization', as global trade, capital flows, and production have not just slowed down but actually gone into reverse. The spectre of deglobalization, as in the Great Depression era, has returned (James 2009; Roxburgh et al. 2009).

Valuable insights into the current conjuncture can be derived from examining why, despite a series of profound shocks (the East Asian crisis of 1997, the stock market crash of 2000, 9/11, to the ongoing Iraq wars in Iraq and Afghanistan), the 'second age of economic globalization' proved so resilient and enduring? Despite all these shocks, by 2007, economic globalization had attained record levels (KOF 2010). One explanation for this resilience, which is discussed in this chapter, is that economic globalization may be much more 'socially and institutionally embedded' than either its advocates or its critics have presumed (James 2001). This is not to argue that it is either inevitable or immutable, but rather to acknowledge the ways—structural, institutional political, and ideational—in which economic globalization constitutes a dominant (but not the sole) tendency in the contemporary world economy. Obituaries for the 'second age of globalization' are perhaps somewhat premature.

Since it is such a 'slippery' and overused concept within the social sciences, it is hardly surprising that globalization should engender intense debate—not to mention plain confusion. No generally accepted definition exists. It is crucial to establish from the outset, therefore, how the concept is framed within the global political economy literature. Accordingly, the first section of the chapter will address three interrelated questions, namely:

1. What is globalization?
2. Is there substantive evidence of the globalization of economic activity?

3. To what extent is globalization still the principal tendency within the contemporary world economy?

Following this analysis, the second section will identify and analyse the primary causes and the dominant theories of globalization. In doing so, it will draw an important distinction between what Rosenberg (2000) refers to as 'theories of globalization' and 'globalization theory'. Section three will draw on this discussion of causes to explore the notion of 'embedded globalization' through a comparison of its first 'golden age' (1870–1914) with the current epoch—the second age of globalization. In the concluding section, the discussion will relate the analysis of causes to an exploration of the centrality of politics and governance—both local and global—to the future trajectory of economic globalization in the aftermath of the Great Crash of 2008.

A Global Economy? 'Embedded Globalization' and the Rescaling of Economic Activity

Within the political economy literature, globalization is taken to be synonymous with a process of intensifying worldwide economic integration. Hirst and Thompson assert that: 'We can only begin to assess the issue of globalization if we have some relatively clear and rigorous model of what a global economy would be like' (Hirst and Thompson 2003: 99). This economism—that globalization can be understood solely, or even principally, as an economic phenomenon—contrasts with the broader understanding of the concept within the social science literatures (see Box 9.1). Here, globalization tends to be conceived as a multidimensional, rather than a singular, process—evident across the cultural, political, ecological, military, and social domains—which is both open-ended, in so far as it discloses no historically determinate or fixed out-

come, and complex, in that it is associated with patterns of transworld integration and fragmentation (Held et al. 1999; Keohane and Nye 2003). Underlying these different conceptions are significant methodological disagreements about how complex historical and social phenomena, such as globalization, are best analysed (Rosenberg 1995). This lack of agreement suggests the need for some conceptual caution in two significant respects: in automatically privileging the economic in accounting for globalization, but more especially in drawing general conclusions about globalization as a social process, solely from an analysis of the economic sphere. Economizing globalization, in other words, is a *conceptual* mistake. That said, few discussions of globalization can, or do, ignore its economic dimension.

ANTHONY MCGREW

Box 9.1 Globalization

Globalization is variously defined in the literature as:

1. 'The intensification of worldwide social relations which link distant localities in such a way that local happenings are shaped by events occurring many miles away and vice versa' (Giddens 1990: 21).

2. 'The integration of the world economy' (Gilpin 2001: 364).

3. 'De-territorialization—or . . . the growth of supraterritorial relations between people' (Scholte 2000: 46).

4. 'A . . . global economy . . . in which distinct national economies and, therefore, domestic strategies of national economic management are increasingly irrelevant' (Hirst and Thompson 1999: 1).

5. '[T]he international integration of markets in goods, services, and capital' (Garrett 2000*a*: 941).

Conceptually, globalization is often elided with notions of liberalization, internationalization, universalization, Westernization, or modernization (Scholte 2000). However, as Scholte argues, none of these terms capture its distinctive attributes or qualities. Within the global political economy literature, economic globalization is generally specified in reasonably precise terms as 'the emergence and operation of a single, worldwide economy' (Grieco and Ikenberry 2003: 207). It is measured by reference to the growing intensity, extensity, and velocity of worldwide economic interactions and interconnectedness, from trade, through production and finance, to migration. In this regard, it is conceived as a *process*, rather than a fixed outcome or condition, in so far as it refers to a *historical tendency* towards heightened levels of worldwide economic interconnectedness. Indeed, there is a substantive conceptual difference between the notion of a globalizing world economy, in Gilpin's terms (2001) and a fully or partially *globalized world economy* which implies a fixed state or condition of economic integration.

This distinction between process and condition (that is 'becoming' and 'being') is emphasized by Keohane and Nye, who differentiate between globalization—as a historical process—and globalism—the resulting condition at any particular historical moment (Keohane and Nye 2003). The implication is that, since globalization is neither an inevitable nor a secular tendency, it is associated, at particular historical moments, with thicker or thinner forms of globalism. Translated into the language of global political economy, globalization can be associated historically with deeper or shallower forms of worldwide economic integration.

Understood as a process, economic globalization also implies an evolving *transformation* or qualitative shift in the organization and dynamics of the world economy. Quite simply, cumulative patterns and networks of trans-border economic activity over time dissolve the separation of the world into discrete national economic units. This process makes the distinction between the domestic and world economy increasingly problematic to sustain—for academics and policy-makers alike. In other words, globalization generates emergent tendencies or systemic properties such that the world economy increasingly begins to operate as a singular system (Sayer 2000). This structural shift may be evident in, among other things, the operation of worldwide markets, the creation of transnational production networks (see Thun, Chapter 11 in this volume), and a global division of labour, together with institutionalized systems of global regulation ranging from the World Trade Organization (WTO) to the International Accounting Standards Board (IASB).

Underlying these shifts in the scale of economic organization are contemporary informatics technologies and infrastructures of communication and transportation. These have facilitated new forms and possibilities of virtual real-time worldwide economic organization and co-ordination. In the process, distance and time are being substantially reconfigured, such that, for example, economic and other shocks in one region of the world can rapidly diffuse around the globe, often with serious local consequences (see, for example, Pauly, Chapter 8 in this volume). Although geography still matters very much, it is nevertheless the case that globalization is associated with a process of *time–space compression*—literally a shrinking world—in which the sources of even very localized economic developments, from interest rate changes to corporate restructuring, may be traced to economic conditions or agents in markets on other continents.

However, a single worldwide economy is not necessarily coextensive with a universal or planetary economy. More specifically, 'worldwide' is generally taken to refer to *inter-regional or intercontinental* patterns of economic exchange and enmeshment. Accordingly, globalization is best conceived as embodying a *rescaling* of economic space manifested in the intensification of inter- or supraregional and multicontinental networks and flows of economic activity (Brenner 1999). In this respect, it is one (albeit significant) historical tendency operating within the world economy, just as regionalization, nationalization, and localization can be identified as other tendencies—whether as complementary or competing tendencies is not so obvious. As a principal tendency, globalization denotes a relative *denationalization* of economic relations as significant aspects of economic life become organized increasingly on an inter-regional or multicontinental scale transcending bounded national economic space (Held et al. 1999; Keohane and Nye 2003). This rescaling, however, is not experienced uniformly across every region or economy, since globalization is also recognizably an uneven *process*. Differential patterns of enmeshment in, or marginalization from, the worldwide economy define its 'variable geometry' (Castells 2000). Such unevenness generates a distinctive geography of inclusion and exclusion such that the notion of a worldwide or global economy is less (geographically and socially) inclusive than that of a universal or planetary economic order. The implications of this distinction, as will become clear, are highly significant for empirical assessments of economic globalization.

Having elaborated a general conception of economic globalization, its relevance and centrality to describing, understanding, and explaining the contemporary world economic order can be explored further. Two interrelated questions will be addressed:

- Is there substantive evidence of the globalization of economic activity?
- Is actually existing globalization the dominant tendency within the contemporary world economy?

Within the existing literature, there are broadly two sets of responses to these questions: the globalist and the sceptical. In short, globalists consider that world economic trends disclose significant or unprecedented levels of worldwide economic interaction, which reflect the existence of a singular world capitalist economy in which globalization is the principal tendency. By contrast the sceptics conclude, not only that the extent of globalization is highly exaggerated, but also that contrary tendencies, from growing regionalism and mercantilism to intensifying geo-economic competition, are evidence of a much more segmented and fragmented world economy than globalists acknowledge. Thus, at the height of the Great Crash in 2009, governments responded by nationalizing or subsidizing major national banks and providing state aid to beleaguered sectors of the national economy. Whilst this is an oversimplification of a more complex set of debates it is, nevertheless, a useful heuristic device for making sense of the actual historical evidence concerning the principal trends in the world economy in respect of trade, finance, production, and labour.

Trade

It is the confluence of secular trends and patterns of world trade, capital flows, transnational production, and migration that for globalists affirms the validity of the globalization tendency. As Samir Amin concludes, while economic globalization is nothing new, it has 'undeniably taken a qualitative step forward during the recent period' (1997: 31). For most of the post-war period, world trade has grown much faster than world output, and significantly so since the beginning of the 1990s (Irwin 2002; WTO 2006c). World exports, measured as a proportion of world output, were three times greater in 1998 than in 1950; the WTO estimates this ratio stood at 29 per cent in 2001 and was about 27 per cent in 2005, in comparison with 17 per cent in 1990 and 12.5 per cent in 1970 (WTO 2001a, 2006a). Despite 9/11 and the subsequent downturn in the world economy, world trade measured as a proportion of world output remained at levels well in excess of that of the 1990s until the Great Crash of 2008–9 (Kearney and *Foreign Policy* Globalization Index 2003; WTO 2003a, 2006a). World merchandise trade peaked in 2008 at almost $16 trillion compared to $10 trillion in 2005 (WTO 2009a). This is one hundred times the value of world trade in 1963. Services trade stood at $2,415 billion in 2005 and $3778 billion 2008 (compared to $365 billion in 1980, an almost 700 per cent increase) (WTO 2006c, 2009a). However, by the end of 2009, world trade had collapsed at an unprecedented rate, much faster and deeper than in the Great Depression or any subsequent postwar recession (Eichengreen and O'Rourke 2009). In comparison with 2008, the value of world trade in 2009 fell by an unparalleled 33 per cent (and volume by 22 per cent), although by late 2009 there was some evidence that trade was beginning to recover (though it remained at lower levels than in the previous decade; WTO 2009b: 3; World Bank 2010: 3, 33). All major exporters, especially Japan and China, recorded export declines in excess of 20 per cent (Wynne and Kersting 2009). At the height of the crisis, the trend in growth of world trade had not just stalled but had collapsed with such a 'remarkable degree of synchronization', that in early 2009 all the world's trading economies recorded negative trade growth (Araújo and Martins 2009).

One of the reasons that few economies escaped this collapse was because trade now involves a larger number of countries and sectors than at any time in the recent past, while developing economies now account for a growing share of world export markets (increasing from 19.2 per cent in 1970 to 32.1 per cent in 2005). They have become especially important players in trade in manufactures, and even in the services sector (Held et al. 1999; WTO 2002, 2006b; UNCTAD 2005: 11). Trade has become increasingly important to many economies, in particular to developing states, as evidenced by the growing share of national **gross domestic product (GDP)** accounted for by exports. Over the post-war period, the ratio of exports to GDP for all countries increased from 5.5 per cent in 1950 to 17.2 per cent in 1998, and for many of the major Organization for Economic Co-operation and Development (OECD) and developing states it more than doubled (Kaplinsky 2005: table 1.1). Trade now reaches deeper than ever before into more sectors of many national economies as an expanded array of goods have become tradable.

Of course, world trade remains highly concentrated, both geographically—OECD countries account for the largest proportion of world merchandise trade (some 65 per cent), and a small number of East Asian countries' for the bulk of developing countries' exports—and sectorally. In 2005, manufacturing constituted 58 per cent of total world trade (in value terms), fuels 13.9 per cent, services 20 per cent, and agriculture only 6.7 per cent (Held et al. 1999; UNCTAD 2005: 133; WTO 2006a). This concentration is hardly surprising, given that OECD countries account for the largest share of world economic output and are by far the largest economic units. Yet, since the 1990s, this dominance has become more diluted (the developed economies' market share of world merchandise exports eroded from 75 per cent in 1970 to 64.8 per cent in 2003) with the emergence of new trading powers (such as Brazil, Russia, India, and China—the so-called 'BRICs' economies) resulting from structural changes in the world economy associated with a new global division of labour (changes in countries' trade specialization in the world economy) and the intensification of worldwide competition through trade (UNCTAD 2005: 133).

Patterns of trade have altered significantly since the 1960s and particularly so in this century. A new geography of trade is emerging that reflects the changing location of manufacturing production as East Asia and other newly industrializing economies (NIEs) take on the role as the world's factories. At the same time, most OECD economies have increased their trade in services significantly and these now account for almost a quarter of their exports (WTO 2006a). Falling costs of transportation, the communications revolution, liberalization, and the growth of transnational corporations have all contributed to a new global division of labour. This restructuring is evident in the current pattern of developing country exports, in which fuels account for 18 per cent (by value), commodites 12.7 per cent, and manufactures 68.1 per cent, compared to 38.8 per cent, 26 per cent, and 31.4 per cent, respectively, in 1980 (UNCTAD 2005: 91).

In just over a quarter of a century, the share of manufactures in developing countries' exports has more than doubled. This shift has also been accompanied in recent years by a significant expansion in trade between developing economies (South–South trade) which has also almost doubled, from 22.9 per cent to 40.9 per cent of their total exports. However, this South–South trade is highly concentrated among East Asian economies, which accounted for some two-thirds of its total in 2003 (UNCTAD 2005). Even so, the NIEs are becoming increasingly important engines of global trade, such that some have argued that 'the South is gradually moving from the periphery of global trade to the centre' (UNCTAD 2004b: 1). A World Bank report similarly observes that, 'growth in the global economy will be powered increasingly by developing countries' (World Bank 2007b: xiii). In just over three decades, China has evolved from being a negligible force in global trade to the world's largest exporter in 2009, eclipsing Japan, the US, and Germany (WTO 2009a: 12).

These structural shifts constitute a new pattern of specialization (or division of labour) within the world economy, which is also associated with an intensification of economic competition (Findlay and O'Rourke 2007). In 2003, 40 per cent of manufactured imports into the OECD economies were produced in developing economies, compared with 12 per cent in 1973 (World Bank 2007b: xix). In the manufacturing sector, and also increasingly within the services sectors, the expansion of trade increases competitive pressures on domestic businesses, in both the North and the South. It is not just that OECD economies confront cheaper imports from the world's new manufacturing zones, in East Asia or Latin America, or lower-cost services from India and South Africa, but that competition among and between the OECD economies and developing economies has also intensified as production and markets become globalized.

Lower-cost imports impose greater price competition, while the dominance of intra-industry trade (trade in similar products or services) between OECD economies brings domestic business and labour into direct competition with their foreign counterparts. This development has significant distributional consequences for employment and wage levels within countries, although decomposing its effects is a complicated matter such that its implications for labour remain hotly contested (Lawrence 1996b). Seeking competitive advantage is articulated either through more efficient domestic production methods or the fragmentation of production—that is, 'slicing up the value chain' or outsourcing production such that firms draw on worldwide networks of suppliers that produce where the greatest economies of scale or efficiency gains can be realized (see Thun, Chapter 11 in this volume). Through such mechanisms, productive and competitive forces become globalized whilst economies in different regions become more tightly integrated. One recent study suggests that intra-industry and inter-firm trade accounted for at least 30 per cent of the growth of world trade in the period 1970–90 (Hummels 2001). Global trade is associated increasingly with the consolidation of a new global division of labour between North and South, which is associated with an intensification of global economic competition (Findlay and O'Rourke 2007).

In so far as dense trade flows occur between the major regions of the world economy—namely, the Asia-Pacific, North American Free Trade Agreement (NAFTA), and European Union (EU) cores—global markets in goods and services might be assumed to exist. The most obvious examples of such markets are those in key primary commodities, such as oil or wheat, which set benchmark world prices. But global markets are far from the textbook notion of the perfectly integrated market. Despite the dramatic trade liberalization since the 1960s, in which formal tariffs have become negligible (average world tariff rates almost halved from 15 per cent to 8 per cent between the 1970s and 1990s), significant non-tariff barriers to trade remain, while distance, history, and culture still continue to influence patterns of world trade (Centre for Economic Policy Reform 2002). This makes all the more remarkable both the scale and recent annual growth rates of trade—15 per cent in 2008 and averaging 12 per cent since 2000 (WTO 2006a: 3; 2009b: 3). However, much trade is conducted regionally, leading to the suggestion that the dominant tendency is one of regionalization rather than globalization (Chortareas and Pelagidis 2004: 253). This is particularly evident in the significant growth of regionalism (see Ravenhill, Chapter 6 in this volume) over recent decades. Yet, as R. E. Baldwin concludes in an exhaustive study of contemporary regional trading arrangements, there are good theoretical and empirical reasons to believe that 'multilateral and regional liberalisation [have] proceeded in tandem since 1947' (Baldwin 2006: 1487). Moreover, the increasing fragmentation of production creates significant pressures for competitive liberalization and makes it difficult to sustain any effective trade bloc 'when part of your wall encompasses the enemy camp' (Baldwin 2006: 1495). Despite regionalism, there is also evidence of a tendency for price differentials for traded goods to narrow, as might be expected in

a global market place (IMF 2002: 122). Studies suggest that distance is no longer as crucial a determinant of patterns of world trade as in the past (Coe et al. 2002). Nor, too, does regionalism appear to be producing a segmentation of the world economy into separate regional markets. Although patterns of regional trade present a complex picture, *intra-regional* trade as a proportion of world merchandise trade, at an estimated 36 per cent, was lower in 2001 than it was throughout the 1990s (WTO 2001a: 6). As Table 6.4 (Ravenhill, Chapter 6 in this volume) indicates, the evidence does not demonstrate a secular trend towards the regional segmentation of the world economy. On the contrary, it is rather inconclusive, since in the case of both the European Union and Japan *inter*-regional trade rose between 1990 and 2000, but remained constant for NAFTA, while the growth of *intra*-regional trade outpaced the growth of inter-regional trade in several regions during the same period. Since 2000, the pattern is similarly inconclusive (UNCTAD 2004a; WTO 2005). These macro-regional trends also conceal the relative strategic importance to many economies of specific commodities in inter-regional compared to intra-regional trade (for example, oil). In a world of fragmented production, intimate connections exist between intra-regional and inter-regional trade activity, but these are often obscured in aggregate trade data. For example, the growth of regional trade among East Asian economies reflects principally trade in intermediate products that are then assembled (now predominantly in China) for export as finished goods to OECD markets in Europe and the US (UNCTAD 2005: 136–8).

Of course, formally, under WTO rules—which have acquired almost universal application—regional arrangements must be compatible with the principles of the multilateral trade regime (see Ravenhill, Chapter 6 in this volume). This institutionalization of global rule-making and adjudication in trade matters marks a seminal development in the political construction of a truly global trade system. Through its very existence and functioning, the WTO defines a global regulatory framework that effectively constitutes the normative and legal foundations of global markets and their operation. In this respect, global markets are not just spontaneous constructions, but partly the product of the regulatory activities of multilateral bodies such as the WTO, not to mention the expanding role of transnational private merchant law (the new *lex mercatoria*) (Gill 1995; Cutler 2003). To this extent, trade globalization is not simply about trends in world trade but also about the critical importance of global and transnational trade authorities in the *constitution* of global markets.

Finance

Until comparatively recently, international finance was considered to be principally an adjunct to trade, a necessary mechanism enabling the international exchange of goods and services (Eichengreen 1996; Germain 1997). This direct association between finance and trade began to dissolve in the nineteenth century. By the twenty-first century, it became irrelevant, or at best marginal. Daily turnover on foreign exchange markets more than doubled, from $590 billion in 1989 to $1,210 billion in 2001, increasing to an unprecedented $3,500 billion in 2008 but declining to $2,900 billion (estimate) in 2009 (by comparison daily world exports were approximately $43 billion in 2008) (*BIS Quarterly Review* 2001; Grieco and Ikenberry 2003: 214; BIS 2007: 1). As a multiple of world merchandise trade, annual foreign exchange turnover in 1973 was equivalent to twice the value of annual world trade, but by 2008 it was equivalent to more than sixty times the value of annual world trade (Held and McGrew 2002: 48). This activity, facilitated by instantaneous global communications, is conducted around the clock between the world's major financial centres on each continent. A worldwide foreign exchange market operates determining the value of traded currencies, influencing the level of key financial variables such as national interest rates, and enabling the rapid movement of capital around the globe.

Following the significant liberalization of national financial markets since the 1980s, the level and geographical scope of global capital flows expanded enormously until the Great Crash of 2008. By comparison with trade, which exhibited a compound growth rate of almost 10 per cent over the period 1964–2001, trans-border financial flows grew at a compound rate of almost 19 per cent (Bryant 2003: 141). To put this in context, Bryant calculates for the period 1964–2001 that, if the growth of international bonds—a form of securitized international lending/borrowing measured here in terms of stocks not flows—had been at an equivalent level to the growth rate of all OECD economies, stocks of international bonds would be valued at some $776 billion, only 11 per cent of the actual $7.2 trillion in 2001 (Bryant 2003: 142). Similar patterns are evident for all other types of trans-border capital flows, from international issues of shares—which expanded from $8 billion in the 1980s to a peak of $300 billion in 2000, subsequently surpassed in 2005 ($307.5 billion); to cross-border trading in derivatives—which grew (measured in gross value) from $618.3 billion in 1986 to $4,224 billion in 2001 and more than doubled to $10,605 billion in 2005 (equivalent to the annual value of world merchandise trade); and trans-border bank lending—which increased more than tenfold from $2,095 billion in 1983 to over $30,000 billion in 2008, but contracted to $25,000 billion in 2009 (Held et al. 1999: ch. 4; BIS 2003, 2005, 2006, 2009; Bryant 2003: 140; *BIS Quarterly Review* 2005, 2009).Global capital flows fluctuated between 2 and 6 per cent of world GDP over the period 1980–95, but by 2006 stood at 15 per cent of world GDP and at $17.2 trillion were three times the gross level of 1995 (IMF 2010a). However, during the financial crisis of 2008–9, global financial flows reversed as banks and other financial institutions pursued a 'flight to safety', rapidly reducing international exposure by repatriating capital on a dramatic scale (*BIS Quarterly Review* 2009). In particular, total cross-border capital flows collapsed in 2008, falling by some 82 per cent from $10.5 trillion (2007) to $1.9 trillion (2008), whilst global banks not only stopped lending but drastically cut their exposure to international loans (from $4.9

trillion in 2007 to $1.3 trillion in 2008) (Roxburgh et al. 2009: 13). Lending to emerging markets and overall global capital flows declined to levels well below those of the previous decade, such that Roxburgh suggests that, 'Financial globalization has reversed, with capital flows falling by more than 80%' (Roxburgh et al. 2009: 7).

As with trade, the bulk of capital flows (some 66 per cent) is accounted for by the major OECD economies. While these inter-regional flows have intensified—64 per cent of trans-border investments in stock markets is intercontinental—this trans- nationalization is not replicated everywhere (IMF 2003). Trans-border financial flows are highly uneven, such that while most emerging market economies have acquired increasing access to world financial markets, many of the poorest economies remain subject to, rather than active participants in, the operations of these markets (*BIS Quarterly Review* 2005). Capital flows to developing states have fluctuated considerably since the 1970s, peaking in the mid 1990s prior to the East Asian crash and subsequently falling back, although by 2007 they had reached a new high (IMF 2003; World Bank 2007*b*: 15; World Bank 2010). The distribution of these flows is concentrated significantly among the principal emerging market economies of Latin America, East Asia, and the European transition economies. Geography and history still exert an influence on capital flows, although there is much less evidence of regionalization (Thompson 2006). Of course, this is not to conclude that the dynamics and volatilities of trans-border financial activities have no bearing on those on the world's periphery, for few economies can insulate themselves against the consequences of financial contagion in a real-time global financial system (Desai 2003).

Despite the unevenness of trans-border capital flows, the evidence suggests that, since the 1980s, there has been a significant integration of financial markets (Taylor 1996; Lane and Milesi-Ferretti 2003; Obstfeld and Taylor 2004). Financial integration is a matter of degree, or a tendency, expressed in relative measurements of greater or lesser intensity. It is assessed by a variety of measures

(including stocks and flows of capital; asset and interest rate price convergence; synchronization of stock markets; and national business cycles), with the consequence that: 'In attacking the problem of measuring [global] market integration, economists have no universally recognized criteria to turn to' (Obstfeld and Taylor 2004: 47). Not to mention the problem that different measures often lead to different conclusions. Not surprisingly, this has produced a considerable debate as to the scale and economic significance of financial globalization assessed in relation to tendencies towards the convergence, deepening, and institutionalization of worldwide financial activity, performance, and regulation (Watson 2001; Obstfeld and Taylor 2004).

Obstfeld and Taylor's (1998, 2003, 2004) econometric studies, among others, identify a narrowing of interest-rate differentials between the major OECD economies after 1960 (they returned to their pre-1914 levels), as might be expected under conditions of high capital mobility and openness (Obstfeld and Taylor 1998, 2003, 2004; Fujii and Chinn 2001; Goldberg et al. 2003). Although short of complete convergence, international differentials remain comparable to those within most national economies (for a given financial asset) while they persist for much more limited periods than in the past, an outcome that might be expected in the context of 24-hour global financial trading (Fujii and Chinn 2001; Goldberg et al. 2003; Obstfeld and Taylor 2004). In contrast, Feldstein and Horioka's classic study (1980) concluded that levels of national savings and national investment appeared to be highly correlated (see Hay, Chapter 10 in this volume), indicating significant barriers to financial integration (Feldstein and Horioka 1980). This finding has also been confirmed by other studies such that in much of the orthodox literature it is regarded as a 'stylized but very robust fact' (Obstfeld and Taylor 2004: 62).

For orthodox economists, these findings present something of a puzzle, in so far as the relative ease of global capital mobility should theoretically imply low (rather than the observed *high*) correlations between domestic savings and domestic investment.

Accordingly, the Feldstein–Horioka puzzle has attracted much attention as a measure of global financial mobility and integration. A broad range of recent studies have 'solved' the puzzle, in that they provide significant empirical evidence that the savings–investment correlation appears to have weakened since the 1990s—a period of intense trans-border capital flows (Coakley et al. 1998; Abbott and De Vita 2003; Banerjee and Zanghieri 2003; Coakley et al. 2004; Giannone and Lenza 2004). Other studies have questioned the methodological and theoretical robustness of the Feldstein–Horioka puzzle, rather than the empirical findings, as a measure of capital mobility and integration (Baxter and Crucini 1993; Taylor 1996; Hoffmann 1998). These suggest that the observed correlations—probably a product of the theoretical assumptions and econometric modelling—are not inconsistent with high capital mobility, and as such are an imperfect measure of global financial integration.

Other measures, such as the stock of foreign assets as a proportion of world GDP, indicate a much less ambiguous conclusion in so far as this increased from 6 per cent in 1960 to 25 per cent in 1980, and to 92 per cent in 2000 (Obstfeld and Taylor 2004: 55). Similarly, flows of capital as a share of GDP have grown since the 1960s, although they have not necessarily returned to the levels of the belle époque (Obstfeld and Taylor 2004: 60). Furthermore, there is considerable evidence that capital controls—legal restrictions on capital flows—have declined significantly since the 1970s for OECD states, and the 1980s for most developing economies (and were associated with the shift to a floating exchange rate regime) (Obstfeld and Taylor 2004: 165). Bryant accordingly concludes in his study of global finance that, 'the analogy of nearly autonomous national savings [and investment] reservoirs is no longer appropriate' (Bryant 2003: 152). Capital is by no means perfectly mobile in so far as global financial markets are imperfect. Even so, the dominant tendency has, nevertheless, been in the direction of greater, rather than lesser, (uneven) financial integration.

Tendencies towards financial integration have also been accompanied by processes of financial deepening (measured in terms of contagion effects, or the synchronization of financial markets and national business cycles) (Obstfeld and Taylor 2004). Finance pervades the operation and management of all modern economies, representing for many—to borrow Hilferding's (1910/1981) vocabulary—a new epoch of 'finance capitalism'. To the extent that national financial systems are increasingly integrated (in real time) with global capital markets, the consequences of financial crisis or volatility abroad is magnified and diffused rapidly at home. Both the unprecedented rapidity with which the 2008 financial crisis spread across the globe and its dramatic consequences for almost all economies, as production and trade collapsed, reflect the significant deepening of global financial integration over the last three decades.

Whether in crisis or normalcy, there is also much evidence to suggest that major stock markets and stock market returns have become increasingly synchronized since the 1970s (Longin and Solnik 1995; Bekaert et al. 2005).

This synchrony in financial market movements across the globe is not uniform, since local conditions do make a difference; moreover, it is more evident at times of crisis. Nevertheless, it denotes the heightened significance of global financial conditions for domestic financial stability, and vice versa (Eichengreen 2002). Indeed, M. Bordo and T. Helbling, in a study of business cycles over the last 120 years, points to evidence of a 'secular trend towards increased synchronization' (Bordo and Helbling 2003: 42). This process of financial deepening arises out of the interaction between the greater 'financialization' of national economies and its overlapping with global financial activity. Evidence of this is to be found during the 1990s, for example, in increased foreign holdings of national public debt—in the Eurozone an increase from 16 to 30 per cent, and in the United States from 19 per cent to in excess of 35 per cent at the time of writing—not to mention increased foreign holdings of shares, private financial assets, and the almost doubling of the ratio of foreign assets to national GDP for most OECD economies (Held et al. 1999; IMF 2002; Mosley 2003). In 2005, foreigners owned some 50 per cent of the total stock of US Treasury Bonds, enabling the US to maintain both lower interest rates than would otherwise be the case, and to fund its historic twin deficits (fiscal and balance of payments) (Warnock and Warnock 2006: 1–4). Furthermore, although many studies have pointed to the 'home bias' effect, which refers to investors' preference for domestic assets, such that the international diversification of investment portfolios appears to be relatively low (in the US, foreign equities constitute around 12 per cent of total holdings), recent studies have qualified these findings (Thompson 2006). Cai and Warnock, for example, demonstrate that this finding in part is a product of how home bias is measured, especially a failure to distinguish the kinds of domestic assets purchased (Cai and Warnock 2006). When such distinctions are made, they 'nearly eliminate the home bias puzzle' (Cai and Warnock 2006: 3).

Associated with this financial deepening is a process of institutionalization as the organization and infrastructures of trans-border finance become regularized and systematized through the activities of (public and private) global agencies and networks. This institutionalization is evident in the enormous expansion of multinational banking—for example, HSBC, 'the world's local bank'—as well as the surveillance and global standard-setting activities of the International Monetary Fund (IMF), Bank for International Settlements (BIS), and the multiplicity of official and private trans-border networks, from the Financial Action Task Force to the International Accounting Standards Board (IASB) (see Pauly, Chapter 8 in this volume). It is through the operation of these institutions that the essential infrastructure of global financial markets is developed and extended, from the Society for the Worldwide Interbank Transactions (SWIFT) global financial inter-bank payments system to mechanisms for managing sovereign 'bankruptcy'. In the process,

the global or inter-regional integration of financial markets is reinforced.

Production

Although data on trans-border capital flows include foreign direct investment (FDI), political economists usually focus separately on FDI, since it denotes effectively the globalization of production (see Thun, Chapter 11 in this volume). Outsourcing production around the world is now widespread in the most dynamic industrial sectors. Indeed, both investment in overseas production facilities (FDI) and production fragmentation (that is, the outsourcing of production to foreign independent third parties integrated within transnational production chains or networks), have increased dramatically since the 1970s (UNCTAD 2002, 2006b, 2009b). Driving and dominating this process is the transnational corporation (TNC). By comparison with the 1990s, transnational production rather than trade has become the principal means of servicing foreign markets. Transnational corporations account (at the time of writing) for more than 25 per cent of world production, 80 per cent of world industrial output, approximately 40 per cent of world merchandise trade, and 10 per cent of world GDP (compared to 7 per cent of world GDP in 1990) (Gilpin 2001: 289; UNCTAD 2001, 2003, 2006b). They have become important determinants of the location and organization of production and services in the world economy, especially within the most advanced and dynamic economic sectors, integrating and reordering business activity between and within the world's three principal economic regions and their associated hinterlands. These developments are characterized by, among other factors: an increased scale and scope; processes of transnational economic restructuring; and the consolidation of a new global division of labour.

Since the 1970s, flows of FDI have not only become more geographically diffuse, but also much more intense (Dunning 2000; UNCTAD 2001; for further discussion, see Thun, Chapter 11 in this volume). At the start of the twenty-first century, total world (inward) FDI reached a new peak of $1,409.6 billion, almost four times the level of 1995 and over six times that of a decade earlier (UNCTAD 2001: 3; 2006*b*). After 2001, annual FDI flows initially declined with the slowdown in the world economy, but subsequently increased to a new record of $1,979 billion in 2007 compared to an average of $548 billion in the period 1994–9 (UNCTAD 2003: 2; 2006*b* : 2; 2009*b*: 3). In the wake of the Great Crash, FDI declined by 14 per cent to $1,697 billion (2008) and at a much faster rate than throughout the post-war period (UNCTAD 2009*b*). Moreover, FDI between advanced economies has declined at a much faster rate than to developing and emerging economies, which immediately after the crisis increased their share of total FDI to 43 per cent (UNCTAD 2009*b*). This decline involved extensive global divestments as the manufacturing and financial sectors restructured their worldwide activities with the consequence that for some economies, notably the UK and Ireland, net FDI proved negative as divestments exceeded inward investment flows (UNCTAD 2009*b*: 14). By the end of 2009, FDI to all countries had collapsed by some 44 per cent in comparison with 2008 levels (UNCTAD 2009*b*: 14). Some estimates indicate the scale of collapse in FDI to be even worse with FDI to developing countries at some 30 per cent of 2008 levels (Roxburgh et al. 2009: 21). Even so, FDI remains considerably in excess of that of two decades earlier, and until 2008 had grown at rates in excess of world GDP growth, exports, and overall capital investment (UNCTAD 2006*b*: 7). From 2003 onwards, growth in FDI was associated with a mergers and acquisition (M&A) boom, as the pressures for global corporate consolidation intensified. This boom exceeded a previous historic high in 2000, with record deals to the value of $3,900 billion in 2006 (*Financial Times* 2006: 1).With the global credit crunch, funds for M&A rapidly declined by some 35 per cent in 2008 and by over 50 per cent in 2009 (Roxburgh et al. 2009: 15; UNCTAD 2009*b*: 14).

Flows of FDI reflect the 'trend towards integration on ever larger geographical scales . . . Supply chains have extended to new areas of the globe and integrated formerly distinct regional production activities' (UNCTAD 2002: 13). Indeed, until the crisis, significant annual flows (more than $10 billion) reached more than fifty countries (including twenty-four developing economies), compared to seventeen (and seven developing economies) in 1985 (UNCTAD 2001: 4).This is a consequence of a variety of factors, including proximity to new markets and technological shifts in the capacity to organize and manage production at a distance (Dicken 2003). However, it is no longer simply manufacturing production that is on the move, but increasingly, with the digitization of information and communications advances, the provision of services, such as call centres, information processing, and legal and banking services (Held et al. 1999: ch. 5; UNCTAD 2001: 6).

Widely diffused as it is, both flows and stocks of FDI nevertheless remain concentrated among and within the major OECD economies, although less so in the last decade (see Thun, Chapter 11 in this volume). Moreover, official FDI flows significantly understate actual levels of foreign investment, since some estimates indicate it constitutes only 25 per cent of the total of such productive investment abroad (Held et al. 1999: 237). While some FDI reaches every continent, it remains highly uneven in its dispersion—but this is changing. In 2000, OECD economies were the destination for some 80 per cent of FDI (inflows), the source of 88 per cent of FDI (outflows), 86 per cent of the world stock of (outward or exported) FDI, and 67 per cent of the world stock of (inward) FDI (UNCTAD 2006*b*: 7). However, as M. Obstfeld and A. M. Taylor observe, 'this trend may have turned, with FDI to poorer countries increasing in magnitude, and, importantly, reaching a more widely dispersed group of recipient countries' (Obstfeld and Taylor 2004: 83). Recent years have witnessed a significant change in the pattern of inward and outward FDI flows—with almost a doubling of the share accounted for by developing economies (inward from 17.5 per cent in 1990 to 43 per cent in 2008; and outward 6.9 per cent and 12.3 per cent, respectively)—and in FDI stocks (inward from 20.7 per cent in 1990 to 27.2 per cent in 2005; and outward 8.3 per cent to 11.9 per cent, respectively) (UNCTAD 2006b : 2, 7; 2009b: 4–5). This exceeds quite significantly the average shares of FDI invested in or by developing countries throughout the 1990s. Developing economies, particularly in East Asia, are both an increasingly significant destination for, as well as source of, FDI. Such trends are likely to be magnified in future years as emerging economy markets continue to grow more rapidly than mature economies. Whilst there remains a heavy concentration of investment within and between the European Union, the United States, and Japan as the largest economies—and between these economies and the NIEs of Asia, Latin America (to a lesser extent), and the East European transition economies—this is being diluted. This concentration has been conceived variously as triadization or regionalization, but this misrepresents the complex matrix of intra-regional and inter-regional flows of FDI and networks of production (Dunning 2000; Dicken 2003). It is the very clustering of FDI around the three major economic regions combined with the intensity of inter-regional flows that reinforces the dynamic of global productive integration.

In linking the dynamics of economies, FDI is also associated with processes of economic restructuring. Although the notion of 'footloose capital' is very much a cliché, the consequences of the mobility of capital are evident in structural changes across many OECD economies and the rise of NIEs in Asia and Latin America (Rowthorn and Wells 1987; Castells 1996; Kapstein 2000; Hoogvelt 2001; Dicken 2003). There is much debate, both about the significance of the deindustrialization of OECD economies in recent decades, and its causes (Piore and Sabel 1984; Krugman 1994; Wood 1994; Lawrence 1996b; Rodrik 1997; Burtless et al. 1998; Schwartz 2001). Although the impact of globalization, as opposed to technological change, on the decline of manufacturing employment in many OECD economies is disputed, there is general agreement that capital mobility and, increasingly, outsourcing nevertheless play a significant role in their continuous economic transformation. Deindustrialization in these economies is linked directly with the industrialization of many developing economies as production is shifted to lower-cost locations, both through expanded FDI but increasingly through outsourcing arrangements (which require no capital input) (Rowthorn and Wells 1987; Wood 1994; Lawrence 1996b; Rodrik 1997; Munck 2002; UNCTAD 2002; 2006b; Dicken 2003). This is not to argue that the mobility of productive capital is unconstrained, since it is not. Proximity to local markets, institutional factors, and productivity calculations limit the potential for industrial capital to relocate abroad, either rapidly or at all. Nevertheless, over time, the cumulative impact of such mobility, along with the expansion of trade, has contributed to major structural changes in the world economy.

Among the most obvious of these structural changes is the evolution and consolidation of a new worldwide division of labour. A significant shift has occurred in the location of manufacturing production, from OECD economies outwards to NIEs in East Asia, Latin America, and other parts of the developing world (Gilpin 2001: 140). Some estimates suggest that between 1977 and 1999 alone, some 3 million US manufacturing jobs were lost as production relocated abroad, but with the contraction in employment almost four times greater than the expansion of employment in developing regions (Harrison and McMillan 2006: 40–1). To a more limited extent, a similar trend is evident in the services sector, most notably in back-office functions, customer services, data and information processing, and so on (WTO 2001a, 2006b). At the same time, the raw material sector has declined, measured as a proportion of world FDI and trade, such that many developing economies have entered, or seek to enter, the manufacturing business. As a result of these shifts, the geography of world economic activity has been transformed in recent years, with important consequences for the distribution of productive power and wealth, and ultimately for the politics of global economic relations (Gilpin 2001; Crafts and Venables 2003). This is patently evident with the rise of China, India, and Brazil as key players in the global political economy.

A second, and related, structural change has been the intensification of transnational and inter-regional competition for market share, technological advantage, and rapid product innovation. Such competition is no longer necessarily best conceived as occurring simply between self-contained national economic units, but, rather, increasingly between firms and businesses in different regions of the globe, in so far as the new geography of world economic activity links distant markets through the operations of giant multinational corporations (MNCs) and inter-regional production networks (Gilpin 2001: 180–2). Economic and corporate competition becomes globalized, since it transcends regions, biting deeper into national economies and magnifying the consequences of local conditions and differences (Held et al. 1999: ch. 5). Domestic competition between supermarket chains for agricultural produce, for example, turns farmers both at home and abroad into direct competitors. Given the existence of instantaneous communications, it is not only the scope but also the rapidity with which global competition evolves that contributes significantly to its intensity (Harvey 1989; Castells 1996).

A third significant change is in the nature of production processes, particularly in manufacturing but also in services, which is not captured effectively by flows or stocks of FDI. Outsourcing, or the cross-border fragmentation of production, is increasingly a key means by which production in many sectors is located and relocated abroad to realize efficiency and competitive gains (although it tends to be concentrated in the low-valued-added segments of the production cycle or service provision) (Dicken 2003; Kaplinsky 2005). Since it requires minimal capital investment or ownership, but rather involves collaborative or contractual relationships between producers and a range of suppliers, it is increasingly open to a much wider range of economic agents,

from small publishing houses to major transnational corporations. Outsourcing relies on complex trans-border production chains, within and between regions of the world economy, such that, paradoxically, it involves the global integration of productive processes through their increasing geographical fragmentation or dispersion (Gereffi and Korzeniewicz 1994). The significant reliance on production chains presents a challenge to orthodox conceptions of the world economy as constituted by discrete national economic spaces, since it suggests a better depiction (although messier but perhaps more accurate) of a networked global economy — what, in the context of trade, Baldwin (2006) refers to as the spaghetti or noodle-bowl analogy (Castells 2000; Brenner 2004; Sassen 2006). It is also evident that the speed and synchronized collapse of world trade in 2008–9, according to Baldwin, is a result of global integration of production such that, 'Today, Factory Asia is online' (Baldwin 2009). One of the consequences of the Great Crash has been to highlight the vulnerabilities of global supply chains provoking some rethinking of the limits to outsourcing.

Labour migration

In comparison to capital and goods, labour is relatively immobile. That said, labour flows (especially unskilled) are geographically extensive and, in terms of direction, reflect an almost mirror image of capital flows in so far as they have become primarily South *to* North (Held et al. 1999; Castles and Miller 2002; Chiswick and Hatton 2003). As an International Organization for Migration (IOM) report noted, 'no country remains untouched by international migration' (IOM 2005: 381). Outward flows of people are predominantly a developing country phenomenon and, despite greater restrictions, they are, surprisingly, on a scale of the mass migrations of the early twentieth century (Chiswick and Hatton 2003: 74). Though complex in origin and destination, inter-regional (as opposed to intra-regional) migration expanded enormously over the period 1950–2000 (Chiswick and Hatton 2003). In 2005, migrants totalled around 190 million of the world's population, more than twice the level of 1970 (at 82.5 million), making up some 3 per cent of the global workforce, but 9 per cent of the workforce in the developed world (Freeman 2006: 2). Inward migration is somewhat concentrated, in that 75 per cent of migrants were domiciled in just twenty-three countries in 1970, and only twenty-eight countries by 2000 (IOM 2005: 382). Furthermore, migration tends to be an increasingly urban phenomenon, in so far as migrants concentrate in major urban areas (for example, 23 per cent of Parisians, 28 per cent of Londoners, and 30 per cent of the population of Abidjan, Ivory Coast, were born abroad), where there are more employment opportunities. Today, 50 per cent are female, whereas in the past, migrants were overwhelmingly male (Freeman 2006: 4–5). Skilled labour migration from South to North is also on the increase, linked to skills gaps and demographic trends in the North. Significantly, too, the huge expansion of temporary workers moving between world regions, facilitated by low-cost transport infrastructures, is additional to these official figures, and is of growing importance to certain sectors (for example, in construction and agriculture) within many developed economies (for example, in the US, the UK, and even in South Africa, which annually hosts 100,000 guest workers) (Freeman 2006: 8).

These developments reflect tendencies towards the integration of distant labour markets (Silver 2003). Such tendencies might be expected to produce some convergence in wage rates (both within the North, and between it and the South) most particularly for the skilled, but overall a growing divergence between rates for skilled and unskilled workers, given the preponderance of the latter among migrants and within the South. There is some evidence to confirm such trends, although the causal role of migration — as opposed to other factors such as trade, technology, or capital mobility — is debated (Galbraith 2002; Firebaugh 2003; Lindert and Williamson 2003). One incontrovertible trend, however, is the growing

scale and importance of remittances by migrants, which quadrupled between 1990 and 2004, and which for many labour-exporting countries in the South has become 'an increasingly important source of foreign exchange' (UNCTAD 2006a: 100). According to UNCTAD estimates, the level of migrants' remittances in 1990 was about 50 per cent of total official aid flows, or on a similar scale to FDI flows from North to South. Today, it far exceeds the value of aid flows, and for many countries also exceeds flows of FDI (for example, remittances to India in 2005 totalled $20.5 billion, compared to inward FDI of $11.9 billion) (UNCTAD 2006a: 100). However, migration, too, has been considerably impacted by the Great Crash, as demand for foreign workers has succumbed to rising unemployment and more stringent immigration controls amongst host nations. As a result, 2009 wage remittances by foreign workers declined, too, but by a relatively modest 6.1 per cent from a 2008 record of $338 billion (World Bank 2010: 38).

Globalization: still the dominant tendency?

Whether these historical trends are indicative of the integration of the world economy or its growing segmentation or implosion, continues to be a subject of intense debate, most especially in the aftermath of the Great Crash of 2008. Although there is fairly widespread agreement among students of global political economy that, in the period since 1945 — and in particular since the 1980s — there has been a remarkable intensification of trans-border economic activity, nevertheless this is subject to divergent interpretations and explanations (Gordon 1988; O'Brien 1992; Castells 1996; Dicken 2003; Held et al. 1999; Hirst and Thompson 1999; Gilpin 2001; Hoogvelt 2001 — for further discussion, see Hay, Chapter 10 in this volume). Whatever the scale and significance of economic globalization, as the brief discussion of regionalization and segmentation suggests, it is not the sole tendency operating within the contemporary world economy. Indeed, those of a more sceptical persuasion give much greater emphasis to these contrary trends. Consequently, they contest the assumption that globalization has been or remains the dominant tendency in the world economy (see Box 9.2). In doing so, they mount a rigorous challenge to the very idea that globalization accurately describes the historical trajectory of the world economy. Two related theses inform this sceptical analysis. The first stresses the real existing limits to any process of global economic integration; and, the second, the highly exaggerated nature of contemporary economic globalization in much of the existing literature, or as Stiglitz refers to it, 'the overselling of globalization' (Stiglitz 2005).

Box 9.2 Sceptical Argument

1. Globalization is exaggerated and far from historically unprecedented.

2. The world economy was much more integrated and open during the belle époque of 1870–1914, when interest rates, commodity prices, and wages showed significant signs of convergence.

3. Regionalization and triadization, not globalization, are the dominant tendencies in the contemporary world economy.

4. The 'Great Crash' of 2008 and responses to it demonstrate both the limits to globalization and the primacy of BRICs (Big and Really Imperial Countries; James uses this term instead of the usual BRICs—Brazil, Russia, India, China) to the effective operation of global markets (James 2009: 182).

5. Globalization is primarily an ideology or policy discourse that serves to legitimize the interests of dominant political and business interests in expanding their power.

Studies of the significant impacts of history, geography, borders, culture, and politics on worldwide economic integration largely conclude that these remain fundamental barriers to effective economic globalization. Distance, borders, and market segmentation continue to matter (Feldstein and Horioka 1980; Gordon 1988; Boyer and Drache 1996; Burtless et al. 1998; Garrett 1998a; Weiss 1998; Rieger and Leibfried 2003). Gravity models of international trade (a form of regression analysis) which take into account geographic distance, demonstrate an almost exponential decline in trade activity as the distance between trading partners increases (Carrere and Schiff 2004; Thompson 2006). Moreover, border and home bias effects (which measure economic divergence between countries and the tendency of investors or consumers to buy domestic assets/goods, respectively) do not appear to be diminishing. For example, there appears to be very little evidence of a significant trend towards international financial diversification. The implication is that, if globalization was the dominant

tendency today, much higher levels of trade and financial flows might be expected, as well as much greater economic convergence, than presently exists (Thompson 2006). Globalization in these respects is therefore considerably overstated.

In addition, the sceptics suggest a more critical interrogation of international economic trends since the 1970s would attest to increasing segmentation rather than integration of the world economy (Ruigrok and Tulder 1995; Berger and Dore 1996; Boyer and Drache 1996; Hirst and Thompson 1999; Hay 2000; Rugman 2000). As argued by Hay (Chapter 10 in this volume), the dominant patterns in the world economy over recent years have been the increasing regionalization and triadization of economic activity. This is evident, not just in trade-flow patterns, but has also been reinforced by the recent huge expansion in the numbers of preferential trade agreements (agreements between groups of states, each of which give preferential access to the others' markets) covering an increasing proportion of world trade (Crawford and Florentino 2005; Ravenhill, Chapter 6 in this volume). This segmentation of the world economy along regional lines, and the continuing dominance of OECD economies, accounts for the absence of the substantive global economic convergence that might be expected under conditions of globalization. It might therefore be concluded convincingly that regionalization or segmentation, rather than globalization, of the world economy is the dominant tendency today, or, as Thompson concludes, that the system is 'one poised between "globalization" and supranational "regionalization"' (Hay 2000; Thompson 2006).

Few would dispute that there are limits to globalization. Economic globalization here is conceived as a much more complex process than simply a juggernaut of world economic unification, in which distance and borders, along with the weight of history and ties of culture are effectively annihilated in the construction of a single global economic space. As noted above, it is associated with processes of global economic integration and fragmentation, inclusion and exclusion, and convergence and divergence. National and local economies, to varying degrees, are embedded in global economic networks and systems while, to varying degrees, national and local factors mediate their impact. Distance, borders, and national differences do still matter—but perhaps not quite to the extent that some sceptics assert. Recent studies of the effect of borders on economic interactions suggest they are much less significant than earlier studies have claimed—with only either moderate or negligible impacts on trade flows (Anderson and van Wincoop 2001; Gorodnichenko and Tesar 2005). Moreover, as noted previously, the evidence does not suggest that there exists a significant home bias in financial markets (the Feldstein–Horioka puzzle) or portfolio investment. Indeed, the evidence points to the fact that the savings–investment and home bias puzzles, if not solved, are today significantly less puzzling than they were in the 1980s (Baxter and Crucini 1993; Anderson and van Wincoop 2001). Even the most advanced national economies are not as perfectly integrated as orthodox economic theory suggests

should be the case, since sub-regional and sectoral divergences continue to matter. In this respect, indicative limits to globalization are not incompatible with the notion of the world economy as being imperfectly, rather than perfectly, integrated.

Since few economies (apart from Myanmar and North Korea) are significantly isolated, autarchy—the pursuit of national self-sufficiency as an economic strategy—appears defunct as national economic fortunes cannot be decoupled entirely from the dynamics of the world economy. This is evident in the manner and speed with which regional crises or slowdowns in world economic activity have a wide and rapid impact across the globe (Bordo and Helbling 2003; Pauly, Chapter 8 in this volume). Furthermore, as the earlier discussion noted, inter-regional flows of trade, capital, and migrants have increased significantly over recent decades. As one leading economic historian has put it, since 1950, 'Interrelations between the different parts of the world economy have greatly intensified' (Maddison 2001: 125). This is not to argue that regionalization and concentration of economic activity are not occurring, but rather to conclude that they are not the dominant trends shaping the world economy. Neither are they necessarily incompatible with economic globalization, since in several respects they reinforce it (Schirm 2002). As Baldwin argues, in a world of fragmented production, the political economy of regionalism produces an inherent tendency towards trade globalism (Baldwin 2006). Regionalization can magnify the consequences of inter-regional economic integration (and vice versa). The concentration of inter-regional flows within the OECD triad is principally evidence of the unevenness of economic globalization rather than triadization or regionalization per se. That globalization has not measured up to the ideal of neoclassical economic theory, which posits a perfectly integrated world market (of price and income convergence), is readily explicable to theorists of imperfect markets/competition and of institutional economics (Gilpin 2001). Except for the most ardent advocates of neo-liberal economics, few would argue that economic globalization can be assessed solely by measures of economic convergence, because the most pronounced phase of global economic convergence, as economic historians note, was the inter-war period, paradoxically a period of unprecedented deglobalization, when economies rapidly converged, but towards economic collapse (Dowrick and DeLong 2003).

As Garrett remarks, 'No matter how many different numbers are presented . . . the growth of international economic activity in the past 30 years remains staggering' (Garrett 2000a: 947). A global economy is in the making, constituted by, and through, the infrastructures and dynamics of economic globalization. This process of economic integration, however, is highly uneven, to the extent that it is associated both with economic convergence and divergence, as different economies/sub-regions/sectors are integrated differentially into this world economic order. Neither is it inevitable nor is it irreversible, as the Great Crash of 2008 reminds us. Indeed, as very recent trends disclose, there can be little doubt that, in key respects, economic globalization has experienced a sudden and dramatic reversal. However, for students of global political economy, the critical issue yet to be determined is whether this reversal is cyclical or structural: that is, whether it is simply a temporary hiatus or constitutes a decisive break with the last three decades. In short, does it portend incipient deglobalization?

The eminent economic historian, Harold James, observes that, 'Financial crises are the catalyst for turning the globalization cycle' (James 2009: 231). The sheer scale of the collapse in global finance, trade and FDI in the Great Crash of 2008 and the unprecedented national responses designed to prevent another Great Depression, James concludes, arguably represent the turning of that cycle: 'In 2009 we can already say that the last great globalization was financial' (James 2009: 144). As 'state capitalism', with its protectionist impulses, asserts itself in the heartlands of global capitalism, the Washington Consensus (WC) appears to have given way to the 'Beijing consensus' (Altman 2009). Combined

with the national economic adjustments which in subsequent years will be necessary to correct the global imbalances (in trade and finance) which many, such as Wolf, argue were at the root of the Great Crash of 2008, the prospects for a rapid recovery of economic globalization—as at the turn of the twenty-first century—appear dramatically muted (Wolf 2008). Although by 2010 there was some evidence of the beginnings of a recovery in trade and financial flows it was limited (World Bank 2010). As James concludes, '. . . the globalization cycle will resume, but not immediately' (James 2009: 277). Even so, the Great Crash of 2008 and its aftermath provide little support for the principal arguments of the sceptics. Both in terms of its severity and the synchronized rapidity with which its contagion effects permeated all economies, the Great Crash demonstrated, contrary to much sceptical opinion, just how integrated the world economy had become in the last three decades. Furthermore, the aftermath of the Great Crash has confirmed the structural shift in the global economy towards Asia and the emerging market economies, which rely significantly on globalization as a development and growth strategy. In this respect, the future structural adjustments that will be essential to correcting global imbalances may just as well be associated with a Third Wave of globalization, driven by emerging economies, than necessarily with an incipient deglobalization (World Bank 2007b). It is therefore both too simplistic and too premature to read the current conjuncture as necessarily a prelude to incipient deglobalization. Nor is the historical comparison with the 1930s epoch entirely appropriate, given that the Great Crash exhibited unique features, not least the unprecedented global co-ordination of immense national stimulus packages (Temin 2010). Whether, in the aftermath of the Great Crash of 2008, economic globalization is subject to a 'great reversal', a 'great moderation' or a 'great rejuvenation' has yet to be determined. That said, there is considerable evidence to conclude that up until the Great Crash of 2008, globalization was the dominant, although not the sole, tendency in the world economy. Regionalization (and segmentation) have been largely complementary, as opposed to competing tendencies (Baldwin 2006). How this 'second age of globalization' is to be explained will be the focus of the next section. In elucidating some of the driving forces behind globalization, it will offer some further analytical and historical insights into the current conjuncture and its consequences for economic globalization.

Key points

- Globalization is not a singular process, but its economic dimension is critical.
- Economic globalization defines the principal trend in the contemporary global economy.
- It is associated with growing but uneven worldwide economic integration.

- Regionalization and segmentation are not necessarily incompatible with economic globalization.
- Economic globalization peaked just before the Great Crash of 2008 and reversed through 2009. Whether this portends a more permanent reversal, moderation or revival of economic globalization remains an open question.

The Logics of Economic Globalization

Identifying the causes of economic globalization is a difficult and tricky intellectual task. Difficult because there are multiple dynamics at work, and tricky because the very notion of causation raises some thorny philosophical issues. Casting the latter aside for the moment, it is important to be clear about what is being explained here: in other words, it is necessary to identify whether the focus is on the *general* determinants of economic globalization, or the determinants of the most recent phase of economic globalization, i.e. the 'second age of globalization'. Explaining one is not quite the same as explaining the other (Robertson 2003). Given the story so far, the focus will be primarily, but not exclusively, upon the latter. The complexity of contemporary economic globalization is such that the search for a single, determinate logic is likely to prove unsuccessful since 'in explaining social change no single and sovereign mechanism can be specified' (Giddens 1984: 243).

In crude terms, the literature distinguishes between thick or thin conceptions of causation. In its thickest sense, causality implies determination in so far as causes are considered both necessary and/or sufficient to bring about an event or given social phenomenon (Mellor 1995: 6). Thus, technology, it is often argued, is the cause of globalization, because technology is sufficient to bring it about, and globalization could not have occurred in its absence. Thinner conceptions of causation refer to dispositions, in the sense of the conditions, tendencies, or factors that make given events or social phenomena more rather than less likely or probable (McCullagh 1998: 173). So, the liberalization of national economies, following the political revolution of neo-liberalism in the 1980s, can be viewed as a cause of economic globalization to the extent that it made it more, rather than less, probable, and thereby not simply a historical accident or arbitrary development. The thinnest conceptions of causation emphasize the contingency of history—that it could readily be otherwise—in that globalization is the product of the coincidence of unique circumstances and the specific interventions of social agents. However, since many complex social phenomena, such as economic globalization, involve a multiplicity of causes, few theories of globalization develop either a rigidly determinist or a contingent explanatory account. Before examining these theories in some detail, it will be helpful to analyse the principal logics of globalization.

Principal logics

Explanations of economic globalization tend to focus on three interrelated factors or social forces, namely: *technics* (technological change and social organization); *economics* (markets and capitalism); and *politics* (ideas, interests, and institutions). Since they are so closely interrelated, the principal methodological problem for analysts lies in unbundling the causal mechanisms involved (Garrett 2000*a*). Distinguishing them analytically is the first step. This will be followed in a subsequent section by an exploration of how some of the principal theories combine and configure these three causal logics in their explanatory accounts of contemporary economic globalization.

Technics is central to any account of globalization, since it is a truism that, without modern communications infrastructures in particular, a worldwide economy would not be possible. All writers refer to the transformation in communications and transport technologies and the way in which this has 'shrunk the globe'. 'Action at a distance' increasingly transcends national borders, not to mention continents, so that time and space are compressed. In this process, the distinction between domestic economic activity and global economic activity becomes less easy to sustain as global markets evolve. Rather than the liberalization of national economies driving globalization, it can be argued that technological change drives liberalization, especially in the financial sector (Garrett 2000*a*). Modern communication technology not only provides the infrastructure of a real-time global economy but also facilitates new forms of transnational and global economic organization, from production through to regulation.

This informatics revolution has underwritten, not only the infrastructure of an evolving global economy, but, also, according to Dicken and others, a 'global shift' (Dicken 2003). This is expressed in the combined move towards service-based or post-industrial economies within the advanced core of the world economy, and the associated rise of industrial economies in the developing world. To paraphrase Giddens, 'technology is inherently globalizing' in so far as contemporary economic globalization is conceived as a product of the second industrial revolution—the logic of the informatics age.

Crucial as technology is to any account of economic globalization, so, too, is its specifically *economic* logic. This is discussed in two distinct sets of literature: that of orthodox economics, which explains globalization in terms of market dynamics; and that of radical political economy, which explains it in terms of the imperatives of capitalism. In the case of the former, globalization is considered to be a direct consequence of market competition whether, as in the case of trade, in terms of the operation of comparative or strategic advantage, or in relation to transnational production in terms of imperfect competition or the product cycle (Dunning 1993; Gilpin 2001).

The structure and functioning of markets is conceived as being central to understanding the competitive dynamics that lead inevitably to the globalization of economic activity. Drawing on both neoclassical and new economic theories, the principal concern is identifying the specifically economic logic—understood in terms of the pursuit of profit, wealth, and market position—which explains the process of global economic integration and the location or distribution of economic activity (see Box 9.3). By contrast, radical political economy draws on the Marxist tradition that locates economic globalization in the expansionary and universalizing logic of modern capitalism. This expansionary logic is a product of capitalism's structural contradictions—the tendency for overproduction combined with the relative impoverishment of workers—and its insatiable requirement for capital accumulation; that is, profit. Economic globalization is driven by the continual search among the corporate sector for new markets, cheaper labour, and new sources of profitability; a process facilitated and encouraged by governments and the agencies of global economic governance, as they work to reproduce the very system on which their political legitimacy partly depends (Callinicos 2003). In short, the specifically economic logic of globalization arises from both the dynamics of markets and the dynamics of capitalism.

Box 9.3 Economic Theory and Globalization

1. Neoclassical theory explains globalization in terms of comparative advantage, market forces, and economic convergence.

2. Free trade involves economies trading what they have a comparative advantage or efficiency in producing, thus in theory maximizing both national and global welfare.

3. Market forces and global competition ensure that similar goods and services are produced efficiently and at a minimum cost.

4. Market convergence ensures that prices and interest rates in a globalizing economy become increasingly equalized or differences increasingly narrowed.

5. New trade theory, locational theory, and the theory of imperfect competition explain why perfectly competitive global markets do not exist, and why market segmentation (differences and the lack of complete convergence) occurs even in a globalizing world economy.

Politics—shorthand here for ideas, interests, and institutions—constitutes the third logic of economic globalization. Almost all accounts of contemporary globalization make reference to the rise and dominance of neo-liberal ideology throughout the OECD world, along with its associated policies of liberalization, deregulation, and privatization—that is, the infamous 'Washington Consensus'. If technology provides the physical infrastructure of economic globalization, it is the significant movement towards 'market-driven politics' (Leys 2001)—greater emphasis on laissez-faire capitalism—that provides its ideological infrastructure.

Irrespective of the party holding office, the dominant political trend since the 1970s in OECD states has been towards the liberalization of national economies and the easing of restrictions on capital mobility. This has enabled—some might argue, driven—the creation of more integrated global markets and the globalization of production. Governments, or rather states, have been central to the process of economic globalization. They have been instrumental in establishing the necessary national political conditions and policies—not to mention vital regional and global institutions, agreements, and policies—essential to its advancement. Promoted and advocated by a powerful configuration of domestic and transnational coalitions and lobbies, economic globalization is very much a political construction or project. It depends on a particular configuration of social and political forces, both national and transnational, to sustain or accelerate its momentum against the background of an established but rising anti-globalization political backlash.

Central to the politics of the current globalization project is the hegemonic power and role of the United States, as the world's sole hyper-power. To the extent that a liberal world economic order, as Gilpin (2001) and others argue, is a by-product of US global dominance, then shifts in US strategic interests and domestic politics will have significant consequences for economic globalization. On the other hand, to the extent that the relative economic power of the United States has been eroded in recent years, the politics of globalization has become far more complex, not to say shaped, by the interplay between the principal global economic players — G8 plus new economic powers, international organizations, and transnational corporations — as well as the agencies of transnational civil society. In sum, contemporary economic globalization has an underlying political logic in so far as it is the product of political ideology; national or international public policy; and the interests and interactions between states, global institutions, and national and transnational social forces.

In different measure and combination, these three logics — technics, economics, and politics — inform the principal theories of globalization to be found in the existing literature. All theories, to differing degrees, draw upon these three logics in identifying the causal mechanisms of contemporary economic globalization. How they do so is explored in the following section.

Principal theories

As Rosenberg (2000) observes, there are many theories of globalization — its causes and dynamics — but little substantive globalization theory. This distinction is important in that it suggests that any notional globalization theory must be parasitic upon, if not entirely subservient to, the 'grand theories' of social science. To date, no discrete or singular globalization theory — which seeks to provide a coherent and systematic account of its causes, consequences, and developmental trajectory — can be said to exist. Nor is there any singular theory

of globalization, only a proliferation of schools and analyses. Accordingly, the emphasis here will be on identifying distinctive theories of globalization, with subsequent elaboration and critical examination of their principal formulations.

Few convincing accounts of economic globalization, given its complexity, locate its origins in a single causal logic. However, existing theories do make judgements either about the relative significance or configuration of different causal logics, in effect privileging some over others in their explanatory narratives. Along the continuum from thicker to thinner forms of causal explanation, accounts vary according to whether they give preference to the structural, the conjunctural, or the contingent sources of economic globalization.

Broadly speaking, structural explanations are thick causal accounts because they tend towards the deterministic: they highlight the imperatives or developmental logic of social and economic systems. Thus, structuralist accounts of economic globalization explain it in terms of the imperatives or drivers of technological advance and/or capital accumulation. Globalization is considered almost an *inevitable* consequence of either modern technologically advanced societies — recall Giddens' dictum that 'modernity is inherently globalizing' — or the expansionary imperatives of capitalism. While structuralist accounts can answer the why and how questions of globalization — why it came about, and how — they are less valuable in explaining its specific historical form (what kind?) or timing (why now?) (see Table 9.1).

Table 9.1 Economic Globalization: Types of Theory

	Causal mechanism	Primary concepts
Structural	Imperatives of domestic and international systems	Imperatives Inevitability Determinate
Conjunctural	Emergent properties of confluence of separate logics and circumstances	Conditional Tendencies Dispositions
Constructivist	Ideas and discourses as constitutive	Contingent Incidental Indeterminate

In contrast, conjunctural explanations are much better at explaining its timing and its form as well as its more historically specific causes. Conjunctural accounts, which are causally thinner than structural explanations, pay more attention to the confluence of particular historical circumstances, trends, and events, which together combine to produce a given social phenomenon at a specific point in time and in a given form. As McCullagh (1998: 178) summarizes it, 'the cause of an event is a conjunction of things which together have a tendency to produce a certain kind of outcome'. Thus, contemporary economic globalization can be understood as a consequence of a multiplicity of tendencies (technological, economic, and so on), interacting with particular historical conditions and policies (for example, the end of the Cold War), to produce its distinctive (neo-liberal) form. Rather than stressing the inevitability of globalization, conjunctural explanations stress its conditionality.

Finally, accounts that stress the contingency of economic globalization emphasize its causal indeterminacy—the absence of a fully specified causal mechanism. Although such explanations may be less relevant to answering the 'why' question, they are particularly pertinent to addressing 'how, when and what' type questions. As such, these might be considered thin, rather than thick, causal accounts of economic globalization because they stress its almost *incidental* or *consequential* (rather than inevitable or conditional) origins. Attention therefore tends to be focused much more on the role of ideas—economic globalization as an idea or prevailing discourse—rather than seeking to identify specific causal connections within the empirical evidence of economic trends (Schirato and Webb 2003: 21; see also Hay, Chapter 10 in this volume). Accordingly, it can be argued that understanding the social or discursive construction of economic globalization is just as—some would say, more—important as identifying underlying causal patterns in the empirical data.

Structural theories of economic globalization can be distinguished in respect of how far they privilege domestic or global structures. Those that emphasize the primacy of domestic structures locate the sources of economic globalization in the nature and dynamics of modern societies. Since the nineteenth-century French philosopher Claude Saint-Simon wrote of the universalizing logic of industrial societies, the primacy of technology as the motor of globalization has figured prominently in the political economy literature. This thesis is to be found, in more nuanced and less deterministic formulations in the work of Ohmae (1990), Strange (1998*b*), Rosecrance (1999), and Garrett (2000*a*), among others.

Technology is privileged in such explanations, not simply because it has shrunk the globe, but also because it is often conceived as the principal dynamic of social change in advanced societies. Just as the technological revolution of industrialism transformed European agricultural societies, so today the information revolution is transforming the nature of production and social organization. In this 'virtualization' process, to borrow Rosecrance's (1999) label, borders no longer define the boundaries of national economic space, while distance becomes a less significant or costly barrier, although not entirely irrelevant, to the organization of production and economic activity. Moreover, this technological revolution enables firms and national economies, irrespective almost of geographic location, to exploit their comparative economic advantage and specialize further in the production and trading of those goods and services at which they are most efficient. Technological change, in other words, brings in its wake both economic and political change in the form of globalized markets and the liberalization of economies. Since continual technological innovation is a structural (recursive) feature of modern (and modernizing) societies, then economic globalization, notwithstanding its cyclical fluctuations, is an inevitable feature of the contemporary global political economy.

That technology is a necessary requirement of economic globalization is not doubted, but for Marxist theorists (historical materialists) it is by no means a sufficient explanation. It is the capitalist form of the economy that is the crucial explanatory factor, not technology, which is subservient to the dynamics of capitalist accumulation and competition. Wood (2003: 14–15) summarizes this argument well: 'Capitalism . . . is driven by certain systemic imperatives, the imperatives of competition, profit-maximization and accumulation . . . globalization is their result rather than their cause.' The sources of globalization are therefore located in the necessary requirement of capitalism constantly to acquire new markets and to produce more efficiently in order to sustain levels of profitability and reproduce itself. Cultivating global markets and producing abroad to maximize profits and corporate efficiency are the consequence of the structural imperatives and contradictions of capitalist economies rather than technological innovation per se.

Moreover, these expansionary tendencies are shaped by intensifying economic competition and the resulting concentration of economic power in huge national and transnational corporations that can readily exploit new technologies and economies of scale to produce more efficiently and compete more effectively, both at home and abroad. Liberalization and the rolling back of the state, reinforced by the disciplines of global institutions such as the WTO and IMF, are conceived ultimately as responses to these developments rather than their author. Such accounts do not deny the importance of political agency or the strategic action of states and other social forces, but, rather, assert that in the very last event these are of only partial relevance in explaining economic globalization (though they are highly relevant to understanding the particular form it takes; for example, Empire in the nineteenth century versus Corporate globalization in the twentieth).

In so far as the main engines of capitalist globalization are located in a small number of OECD economies, there is some disagreement as to whether the contemporary period is best described as a renewed phase of capitalist imperialism, a distinctly new form of globalized capitalism system, or a historically novel, global capitalist empire (Hardt and Negri 2000; Callinicos 2003; Gill 2003; Wood 2003). Irrespective of how it is characterized, the principal logic of contemporary economic globalization is located, in Marxist theory, firmly with the imperatives of capitalist development.

Beyond these domestic-level explanations, other structural theories give priority to international or global system-level structures. Within all the major schools of theory in global political economy—realist, liberal, and Marxist—frequent emphasis is placed on the role of hegemony—or the dominance or pre-eminence of a single power or superpower—in creating and maintaining the conditions for an open world economy, and so economic globalization. In effect, the hierarchical structure of power relations in the global political economy creates the necessary conditions for economic globalization. Despite their otherwise radically different theoretical positions, Gilpin, Ikenberry, and Wallerstein all assert that hegemony is an essential condition for the development and perpetuation of a globalizing world economy (Wallerstein 1983; Gilpin 1987; Ikenberry 2001). Without a hegemonic power capable of establishing a stable and managed world order, through both persuasion and coercion, economic globalization would be little more than an ideal. It is hegemony that makes an open world economy possible. That said, it is also an essential precondition of economic globalization that the hegemonic power is a liberal-capitalist power and thus has a material interest in creating and sustaining a liberal world economic order as opposed to a world empire. In this respect, hegemonic theory is entirely compatible with domestic level structural accounts, which consider economic globalization as a consequence of the imperatives of capitalist accumulation and market forces. However, to the extent that the hegemonic power becomes predatory or unilateralist, the necessary conditions for economic globalization will be eroded.

By contrast, the relative decline of the hegemon, as Keohane (1984) suggests, may have little impact, to the extent that globalization becomes institutionally embedded. Under current conditions, the reassertion of US hegemony is likely to hamper, if not undermine, economic globalization if

Washington pursues a unilateralist or predatory agenda; or will reinvigorate it if it seeks to advance the further liberalization of the world economy. Of course, theory also points to the limits, contradictions, and ultimate erosion of hegemonic power, suggesting that economic globalization has to be understood primarily as a historical phenomenon (Gilpin 1981).

Whereas structural theories explain economic globalization as a path-dependent outcome of systemic — whether domestic or international — imperatives, by contrast *conjunctural* accounts are rooted in a more context-dependent analysis. This is not to suggest that structural forces or tendencies are ignored — on the contrary, they form the context of any historical analysis — but, rather, they are combined with a greater attention to the unique configuration of political, social, national, and global conditions that precipitated contemporary economic globalization. There is also a greater recognition of the role of strategic action by governments or other key agencies, and the interaction between social forces, political institutions, and ideas in advancing or constraining processes of global economic integration. Rather than an inevitability, economic globalization is understood as being 'rooted in history and shaped by particular political, social and cultural conditions . . . a conjunctural correlation of forces that are subject to reversal' (Petras and Veltmeyer 2001: 46). Among the most comprehensive studies in this context is Castells's three-volume study of the rise of 'global informational capitalism' (Castells 1996, 1997, 1998).

Castells sets out to explain the most recent phase of economic globalization, which he dates to the 1980s, rather than to produce a generalizable account of economic globalization per se. Castells identifies the principal sources of this new belle époque in the profound restructuring of the major capitalist economies, itself a response to the economic and political crises of the 1970s (Castells 2000). This period was characterized by historic shifts in the technological, economic, and political spheres that, while insufficient in themselves to forge a new epoch of globalization, in conjunction they provided the vital conditions in which it could flourish. Just as two atoms of hydrogen combine with one atom of oxygen to produce a new substance called water, so, by analogy, the specific configuration and conjunction of developments in these three spheres — technics, economics, and politics — gave rise to the current epoch of globalization. In other words, globalization emerged out of — in more technical language, is an emergent property of — the particular confluence of historical conditions in the technological, economic, and political domains (Sayer 2000: 12). What, then, were these significant developments?

According to Castells, they were, respectively: the information technology revolution; capitalist restructuring; and the political hegemony of the neo-liberal project (Castells 2000: prologue). Tracing these developments to the dissipation, in the 1970s, of the post-war system of managed capitalism, Castells identifies in the informatics revolution of the 1980s a new production paradigm that facilitated a process of global economic restructuring. Overseas manufacturing production became more technically feasible as well as economically necessary. Production began shifting abroad while the major economies became increasingly service-based (post-industrial) or, in Castells' language, 'informational'. This deindustrialization in the core economies was accompanied by industrialization in its hinterlands. However, as Castells argues, this:

> Restructuring of business firms, and the new information technologies, while being at the source of globalizing trends, could not have evolved, by themselves, toward a networked global economy without policies of de-regulation, privatization, and the liberalization of trade and investment.

(Castells 2000: 147)

Politics — but, more specifically, the advocacy and implementation of neo-liberal (market-enhancing) ideas, policies, and institutional (both national and global) reforms — played a significant role in this process to the extent that he argues that: 'The decisive agents in setting up a new global economy were governments, and, in particular, the governments of the wealthiest countries, the G7, and their ancillary institutions' (Castells 2000: 137). The advance of this political project was also greatly assisted by the collapse of communism and thus any feasible political alternative to the capitalist model of development. For Castells, the emergence of a historically unique 'global informational capitalism' that has 'the institutional, organizational, and technological capacity to work as a unit in real time, or in chosen time, on a planetary scale', can be traced to the specific historical conjuncture of technological, economic, and political circumstances of the 1980s (Castells 2000: 104).

Castells' analysis of globalization is among the most comprehensive and sophisticated. However, as with other conjunctural accounts (Scholte 2000; Gill 2003), it is vulnerable to the criticism that in advocating an essentially multi-causal account, it simply avoids specifying a coherent or convincing causal mechanism. In simpler language, since almost every key factor is regarded as a cause of globalization, by definition, nothing in particular can be said to be its specific cause. To critics, conjunctural accounts do not so much explain — that is, identify a causal mechanism or mechanisms — so much as provide a rich description of economic globalization.

This judgement is a little harsh because it presumes a strongly scientific or positivistic model of causation identified with some determinate causal mechanism. By contrast, historical or interpretative models of causation readily acknowledge such causal complexity (McCullagh 1998; Sayer 2000; Benton and Craib 2001). Nevertheless, a more fundamental problem is that conjunctural analyses fail to accept, although they imply, the essential indeterminacy or contingency of complex social phenomena, such as globalization, and thus cannot really claim adequately to explain it (Wendt 1998).

Economic globalization refers, both to a process of growing material interconnectedness, as well as to the 'idea' or consciousnesses of that process. Obviously, the two are interrelated but in quite complex ways. *Social constructivist* analyses are far more interested in the idea of economic globalization, and why it has become such a pervasive discourse or way of talking and theorizing about the world economy. Although they do not discount the relevance of globalization's material manifestations — in terms of flows of trade and investment — social constructivists are far more interested in its ideational or discursive construction. In this respect, they argue, to paraphrase A. Wendt, that globalization is what states and others make of it, rather than a preordained or objective condition, and as such is a largely contingent phenomenon (Wendt 1992).

Rather than seeking to identify the causal mechanisms that generate globalization, constructivists seek to explore how widely shared ideas or discourses of economic globalization are constitutive of — that is, make real or give intersubjective meaning to — the very process itself; for example, the popular discourse or idea of globalization as an inevitable or irresistible juggernaut of social change (see Box 9.4). In simple terms, there can be no economic globalization without the idea or discourse of economic globalization. This is not to argue that globalization is simply a product of the collective imagination. On the contrary, it is largely to acknowledge that in naming or identifying these material trends in the world economy as a process of 'economic globalization', that very process becomes socially or discursively constructed and is thus given intersubjective meaning. Social constructivism, therefore, has an important bearing upon how globalization is interpreted and understood, both within the academy and beyond. Accordingly, to make sense of globalization, it is first necessary to deconstruct or unpack the dominant ideas or discourses that inform how it is generally interpreted or conceived, and the extent to which such ideas or discourses reflect or misconstrue contemporary world economic trends.

Box 9.4 Causal and Constitutive Theory

1. Causal theories refer to explanations that identify specific or general causal mechanisms which can be said to be both necessary and/or sufficient to produce the social effects or social phenomenon that are the object of analysis.

2. Constitutive theories refer to explanations that demonstrate how ideas, values, and beliefs or discourses about the world construct 'reality' and thus constitute, in part, the very social phenomenon under investigation.

3. An intense debate exists as to whether causal and constitutive theories are different or similar kinds of explanations and, thus, whether in effect reasons can be considered, in the strictest sense, to be causes.

As Petras and Veltmeyer (2001: 11) observe, 'Globalization is both a description and a prescription,' and as such, it serves as both an explanation . . . and an ideology that currently dominates thinking, policy making and political practice.' Those studies that have drawn on the insights of this kind of social constructivist methodology generally tend to conclude that the genesis and diffusion of the 'idea of economic globalization' is more important to understanding and explaining the contemporary economic condition than is a rigorous assessment of the actual empirical trends (Hay and Watson 1998; Rosamond 2001; Schmidt 2002; Hay, Chapter 10 in this volume). For the constructivists, the evidence is less important than the fact that to the extent that states, social forces, and international agencies perceive and understand the world principally within the discourse of globalization, they reproduce and perpetuate it to a large extent irrespective of what the empirical evidence discloses. There are also very good reasons why they do so, and in this context political interest and motivations — the power of political agency — becomes of critical importance. Irrespective of the objective existence of globalization, it is incontrovertible that the *idea* of economic globalization plays a crucial role in co-ordinating, communicating, and legitimating a range of diverse political projects, from the politics of the Third Way to the politics of the New Right (Schmidt 2002). Economic globalization, in such accounts, is therefore distinguished by its essential *contingency* more so than its inevitability. It is as much, if not more of, an ideational, rather than material, phenomenon. As such, it is not so much determined by collective ideas but rather constituted by, and through, them, with significant consequences for the politics of globalization (see Hay, Chapter 10 in this volume).

Making sense of the logics of economic globalization

How are these different accounts of the causes of economic globalization to be reconciled? Do these distinctive types of theory offer competing or complementary explanations? Is a 'grand theory' of economic globalization attainable? Such questions flow naturally from an examination of the theoretical pluralism that is the hallmark of global political economy. If there is no singular theory of globalization this is partly, but not exclusively, a consequence of the fact that there is no universally accepted set of criteria — or epistemology — against which the validity of theories of global political economy can be judged. This does not mean that rational judgements cannot be made as to which theories present a more or less convincing account of globalization, but simply that such judgements cannot in any meaningful sense establish their 'truth' — or its true causes. Quite simply, the problem is that, as within the social sciences more generally, an appeal to the evidence or the 'facts' of globalization largely proves inconclusive, since the 'facts' are often compatible with competing theories. That is, theories are underdetermined. Thus, for example, the evidence discussed in the first part of this chapter supports theories that identify both technology and politics as the principal cause of globalization. Accordingly, rather than seeking the unattainable grail of objective truth, a more productive approach may be to explore whether or how these three distinctive types of theory might be conjoined and so contribute to a more comprehensive understanding and explanation of the logics of economic globalization (see Table 9.2).

In a very interesting article, Eric Helleiner (1997) seeks to realize precisely that goal. Drawing on the scholarship of Fernand Braudel, a renowned social historian, Helleiner concludes that to understand and explain economic globalization as a historical and social process, it is necessary to adopt and combine different temporal perspectives. These distinct temporal perspectives reflect the different pace of historical time: from the *longue durée* of centuries over which change can appear to have a glacial momentum, shaped as it is by deeper social structures and recurrent patterns of socioeconomic organization, through the *epochal*, or conjunctural in which the pattern of socioeconomic change over several decades seems to prefigure the emergence of a new era or social formation, to *l'histoire événementielle*, or contemporaneous, in which social agents—from individuals to governments—are daily engaged in reacting to, or in seeking to shape, events and circumstances as they perceive and interpret them. As Helleiner (1997: 95) suggests, these 'three temporal perspectives are useful not just in describing economic globalization, but also in understanding and explaining it'.

A direct correspondence may be observed between these temporal perspectives and the three types of theory elaborated in the preceding section: the *longue durée* is associated with structural accounts; the epochal with the conjunctural; and the contemporaneous with constructivism.

As Gilpin (2001: 364) observes, 'globalization has been taking place for centuries'. Understood as a process of secular historical development, economic globalization might therefore best be explained through the medium of structural theories

that locate its causes in the dynamics of enduring systems or recurrent patterns of socioeconomic organization. Thus, economic globalization can be understood as an intrinsic feature of the modern age: of modern societies and the modern international state system or, to use a grand term, modernity. Conceived from a temporal vantage point of the *longue durée*, economic globalization appears as a chronic or persistent—although by no means linear—historical trend that, as Helleiner (1997: 95) comments, 'also makes it seem an almost irreversible one'. To understand and explain economic globalization therefore requires some account of the deeply embedded structures of the global political economy—capitalism, industrialism, hegemony, and so on—which are its underlying drivers. At one level, such accounts are essential, since, while they cannot explain its specific historical features or rhythms, they do offer insights into why economic globalization has been a recurring feature of the global political economy for many centuries.

In contrast, particular historical epochs of intensifying global economic integration, like that of today, are better explained by conjunctural theories. Such theories seek principally to account for the cyclical and historical rhythms of economic globalization: how and why it accelerates or contracts at different historical moments, and the specific configuration it takes—from empire to global markets. In doing so, such accounts emphasize discontinuity, rather than continuity (as in structural accounts) with the past. Thus, the entire debate about whether contemporary globalization is unprecedented by comparison with the belle époque is indicative of an epochal or conjunctural perspective. Understood from such a perspective, the origins of contemporary economic globalization are to be located in a particular conjuncture of factors and forces within a specific historical context. This provides a different frame of reference from the structural, as it suggests that economic globalization is 'also a clearly reversible process' because the conjuncture of forces that hold it together at any given moment may (or will) eventually

Table 9.2 Economic Globalization Summary: Types of Theories and Forms of Explanation

	Principal methodological focus	Causal mechanisms	Focus	Indicative account of globalization
Structural	Focus on organizing principles of domestic and international systems Holistic analysis Emphasis on dynamics or 'laws' of the social totality	Tends towards (economic, technological or political) determinism Emphasis on inevitability, irresistible forces Path-dependent outcomes	Why and How questions	Ohmae (1990)/Rosecrance (1999)—technics primary causal logic Woods (2003)—imperatives of capitalism Gilpin (1987)/Wallerstein (1983)—political imperatives of hegemony—globalization as Americanization
Conjunctural	Unique configuration of social forces and historical circumstances Political decisions and forces	Emphasis on tendencies and conditional factors Confluence of events and circumstances Emergent properties	How, When and What form	Castells (1996, 1997, 1998, 2000)—global informational capitalism product of conjuncture of technics, economics and political developments in 1980s
Constructivist	Role of ideas crucial in shaping how agents view and act on the world Discourse of globalization—globe talk—constructs the way the world is understood and acted on by social agents Discourse of economic globalization constitutes it rather than simply mirrors it	Constitutive rather than causal explanation—globalization is made real through discourse Emphasis on motivations, interests, ideas and political agency	When and What form	Schmidt (2002)—how the discourse of globalization came to play the crucial role in co-ordinating, communicating, and legitimating European government economic strategies in the 1990s

dissipate (Helleiner 1997: 95). Conjunctural accounts thereby complement structural theories because they provide an explanation of globalization's episodic and discontinuous evolutionary pattern, offering specific insights into what drives it forward (or backwards) at particular moments in history.

Finally, from a contemporaneous perspective, Helleiner notes that economic globalization 'often appears as a political weapon used and promoted by certain groups' as 'a project in which the local is increasingly "globalized" . . . in an active and deliberate way' (Helleiner 1997: 96). Constructivist explanations that emphasize motivations, strategic actions, and the political struggles over globalization offer significant insights into its contemporaneity. Such accounts complement both structural and conjunctural theories because they can explain how and why economic globalization comes to be constructed through the multiplicity of actions of, and interactions between, individual and collective (political and economic) subjects or agents, from consumers to corporations, and protestors to politicians. From this contemporaneous perspective, economic globalization appears decidedly contingent or fluid. Constructivism privileges the explanation of the motives, interests, ideas, and institutions that are constitutive of such action. In providing this, constructivist theories of economic globalization—which emphasize its essential contingency—function to correct those marked tendencies in structural and conjunctural accounts that play down the significance of social agency—ideas, motivations, and choices. In doing so, the former very much complements the latter.

For much the same reason that economic globalization is considered causally complex, necessitating a multi-causal analysis, so, too, following Helleiner (1997: 102), must it also be conceived as a 'layered' historical process; that is, 'taking place at several different historical speeds'. Accordingly, understanding and explaining the current phase of economic globalization requires a causal analysis that is not only sensitive to its multiple logics—technics, economics, and politics—but also to its multiple speeds—the *longue durée*, epochal, and contempraneous. No single theory, or account, of economic globalization meets, or is ever likely to meet, such demanding requirements (Rosenberg 2000). This should not induce academic despondency, because, as has been argued, by drawing on philosophically compatible structural, conjunctural, and constructivist accounts a more systematic and layered analysis of economic globalization is entirely feasible, even if this falls short of the explanatory properties of an ideal globalization theory.

Key points

- Economic globalization is conceived as having three logics: technics, economics, and politics.

- There are three main types of theory associated with economic globalization: structural, conjunctural, and constructivist.

- These can be distinguished in terms of their distinctive causal terms: imperatives, tendencies, and contingency.

- Understanding globalization as a historical process involves examining it in terms of three speeds of social change: the *longue durée*, the epochal, and the contemporaneous.

- The three theories of globalization correspond with each of these three speeds, explaining economic globalization from a different temporal perspective.

- The three theories of economic globalization are therefore in principle complementary, producing a layered explanation from its structured to its contingent origins.

The Second Age of Globalization: Another Extraordinary Episode?

Remarking on a previous epoch of global economic transformation, John Maynard Keynes wrote of 'an extraordinary episode in the economic progress of man', in which 'the internationalization of . . . economic and social life . . . was nearly complete' (quoted in Grieco and Ikenberry 2003: 206). Many of his liberal contemporaries, such as Norman Angell, associated (what later became known as) this belle époque (1870–1914) with the emergence of a new world order in which war was becoming increasingly unthinkable (McGrew 2002). The guns of August 1914 brutally suppressed such liberal idealism. This first age of liberal, or more accurately, imperial, global economic integration has acquired totemic status in the current debates about globalization. For those of a sceptical persuasion, it is the gold standard against which the many empirical claims concerning contemporary economic integration can be debunked (Hirst and Thompson 1999). By contrast, for those persuaded that until the Great Crash of 2008 the world was in the grip of the second age of globalization, it has become the benchmark against which to validate its historically unprecedented features. This has given rise to a voluminous literature of comparative economic history, dissecting and contrasting the two great ages of globalization in the search for conclusive — or rather, elusive — evidence as to which can lay claim to being the more 'globalized' (see Table 9.3). The real significance of this enterprise, however, is more political than historical. Because the critical issue is not the comparative scale of globalization so much as what the comparison discloses about the limits to, or scope for, national politics under conditions of global economic integration. Or, as Bordo, Eichengreen, and Irwin put it, 'why globalization a century ago did not create the same dilemmas as now' (Bordo et al. 1999).

For Gilpin, 'although globalization had become the defining feature of the international economy at the beginning of the twenty-first century', the current world economy, in comparison with the belle époque, remains considerably less globalized and integrated (Gilpin 2001: 3). This is a view shared with other economic historians (for example, O'Rourke and Williamson 1999). The implication is that, far from being unprecedented, economic globalization today is essentially a return to the developmental trajectory of the world economy inaugurated by the birth of the industrial age. In their study of global finance, Obstfeld and Taylor identify a more differentiated picture in which, on some measures (gross capital flows and stocks of foreign capital), globalization is considerably greater today; on others it has converged with pre-1914 levels (interest rate differentials, national savings, and investment correlations); and on yet others still it is below that of the pre-1914 era (flows of capital to the South and net capital flows) (Obstfeld and Taylor 2004). In contrast, for Gilpin (2002), and O'Rourke and Williamson (1999) among others, the world economy still has some way to go in order to achieve the comprehensive levels of global capital, trade, commodity, and labour market integration of the pre-1914 era (O'Rourke and Williamson 1999; Gilpin 2002). As O'Rourke and Williamson (1999: 2, 14) emphasize,

> By 1914, there was hardly a village or town anywhere on the globe whose prices were not influenced by distant foreign markets, whose infrastructure was not financed by foreign capital, whose engineering, manufacturing, and even business skills were not imported from abroad, or whose labour markets were not influenced by the absence of those who had emigrated or by the presence of strangers who had immigrated.

Table 9.3 Epochal Shifts in Globalization Since 1820

Epoch	Intercontinental commodity market integration		Migration and world labour markets		Integration of world capital markets
	Change in price gaps between continents	Why they changed	How migrant shares changed in receiving countries	Why they changed	what happened to integration (Feldstein–Horioka Slope Coefficient)
1820–1914	Price gaps cut by 81%	72% because of cheaper transport; 28% because of pre-1870 tariff cuts	Migrant shares rise	Passenger transport costs slashed, push and pull (immigration policies remain neutral)	60% progress from complete segmentation towards market integration
1914–50	Gaps double in width, return to 1870 level	New trade barriers only	Migrant shares fall	Restrictive immigration policies	Reversion to complete market segmentation
1950–2000, especially since 1970	Price gaps cut by 76%, now lower than in 1914	74% because of policies freeing trade; 26% because of cheaper transport	Migrant shares rise	Transport costs drop, push and pull again (no net change in immigration policies)	60% progress from complete segmentation towards market integration
Overall 1820–2000	Price gaps cut by 92%	18% because of trade policies; 82% because of cheaper transport	No clear change in US migrant shares, but rises elsewhere	Policy restrictions, offsetting transport improvements	60% progress from complete segmentation towards market integration

Source: Lindert and Williamson (2003)

and

" involved the most extensive wage and living standard convergence the Atlantic economy has ever seen. "

Indeed, Hoogvelt describes the current era as one of the implosion of global economic activity as it has become increasingly concentrated in the OECD and a handful of NIEs by comparison with the age of empire (Hoogvelt 2001). The implication is that the significance of the second age of economic globalization is considerably exaggerated and thus its consequences have been significantly overstated, particularly with respect to national politics and the continuing centrality of state power to the proper functioning of the world economy (Hirst and Thompson 1999; see also Hay, Chapter 10 in this volume). This, in some respects, has become the orthodox view.

As many economic historians acknowledge, however, whether this second age of economic globalization is more intensive than the belle époque cannot be determined definitively (Obstfeld and Taylor 2003). Many recent studies suggest that, on most measures, recent levels of global economic integration are comparable with, if not more so, the period of the belle époque (Geyer and Bright 1995; Bordo et al. 1999; Lindert and Williamson 2001; Maddison 2001; Taylor 2002; Findlay and O'Rourke 2007) (see Table 9.3). As Bordo et al. conclude, 'the globalization of commodity and financial markets is historically unprecedented' (1999: 56). In particular, while financial integration 'measured in terms of net flows as a percentage of GDP is quite similar in the post-1975 and pre-1914 periods, gross flows are greater today', while the correlation between domestic savings and investment (the Feldstein–Horioka puzzle) is now at 'the levels of the pre-1914 period' (Bordo et al. 1998: 17, 3). By comparison, as Findlay and O'Rourke observe, by the end of the twentieth century, 'the ratio of world trade to GDP was higher than ever before in history' (Findlay and O'Rourke 2007: 525). Table 9.3

identifies some of the comparative features of the different historical ages of globalization. It broadly confirms what Dowrick and DeLong, two leading economic historians, conclude that: 'It is hard to argue today that there is any dimension . . . save that of mass migration in which we today are less "globalized" than our predecessors at the end of World War I' (2003: 191).

That said, the second age of economic globalization displays some profound *qualitative* differences from that of the pre-1914 era. Most notable are real-time world financial markets; the breadth and depth of trade and financial cross-border activity; the speed of economic exchange; the scale of gross economic flows of goods, and short-term as opposed to long-term capital; the institutionalization of economic relations at an inter-regional level through global and regional organizations, MNCs, and transnational regulatory bodies; and, finally, the fact that twenty-first-century globalization is experienced much more unevenly than in the belle époque (Geyer and Bright 1995; Deibert 1997; Held et al. 1999; Garrett 2000a; Scholte 2000; Obstfeld and Taylor 2004). Bordo et al. note, too, that 'while net [capital] flows as a percentage of GNP a century ago may have been comparable to those of the present day, the breadth of international capital market integration is greater today' (Bordo et al. 1998: 26). Both the sources and destinations of capital flows today are far more diversified than in the pre-1914 era, while 'gross asset and liability positions were very close to net positions before 1914, in contrast to today where most major industrial countries are both major creditors and debtors' (Wilkins 2003; Bordo 2005: 10). In terms of economic structure, there are profound differences in relation to the global division of labour. The first age of globalization involved deindustrialization on the periphery and industrialization at the core, while the second age has entailed the reverse. This second age of economic globalization undoubtedly displays many unique attributes — from the scale of short-term capital flows to transnational production — and a 'secular trend towards increased synchronization' of national business cycles, as disastrously evident in the Great Crash of 2008. Combined, these trends produce novel political and economic dilemmas for all governments, but most especially democratic states (Eichengreen 1996; Rodrik 1997; Bordo and Helbling 2003: 431). As Garrett concludes, 'global market integration is qualitatively different and deeper today' (Garrett 2000*a*).

What, then, is to be made of the second age of economic globalization? If not historically unprecedented, it is certainly more than comparable to that of the belle époque—although today it is uniquely configured and constituted. As a consequence, 'Globalization today raises new issues of governance not just because it is conjoined with . . . [democratic political systems] . . . but because the economic phenomenon itself is different: integration is deeper and broader than a hundred years ago' (Bordo et al. 1999: 3–4). Some of the implications of this for the politics and governance of globalization is the focus of subsequent chapters (especially Hay, Chapter 10 in this volume).

After the Crisis: The Prospects for Economic Globalization

How might this examination of the distinctive qualities and underlying causes of economic globalization contribute to understanding its future prospects in the aftermath of the Great Crash of 2008? Drawing on the preceding analysis, two broad arguments can be made.

First, as the previous discussion has highlighted, economic globalization is much more socially and institutionally 'embedded' than its many sceptics have acknowledged. Until the Great Crash, it had proven far more resilient than even many of its advocates believed would be the case. This is not to argue, as is the tendency with structural theories of economic globalization, that it is either inevitable or irreversible. On the contrary, agency and politics still matter, even though both may be highly constrained by the logic of global capitalism. As the immediate events of the Great Crash demonstrated, politics almost everywhere was dominated by the requirement to stabilize the global political economy and to prevent a slide into global depression. This reflected, in part, just how deeply embedded the second age of globalization had become to the functioning of all modern economies.

Second, as Castells (2000: 147) argues, economic globalization has always been 'politically constituted'. Politics, in other words, provides the ideological, institutional, and motivational resin that binds together the social and political forces that have facilitated, fuelled, and benefited from the current epoch of economic globalization. The future trajectory of globalization will therefore depend critically upon how the domestic and international politics of this embedded globalization evolves in the aftermath of the Great Crash. So far, the protectionist and anti-globalization backlash has been limited, by comparison with a decade earlier, and political support for globalization has not diminished dramatically. In so far as globalization is what politicians and social forces wish to make of it, then its future trajectory is also associated with the struggle over its discursive construction: the struggle for globalization's soul (Dryzek 2006). As James remarks, 'systemic financial crises like the worldwide catastrophe of the 1930s cause [political] paradigms to shift in ways that threaten to unravel globalization' (James 2009: 179). Accordingly, the future trajectory of economic globalization is wholly speculative. That it is so is both a source of intellectual despair and a huge relief. Despair, since it reaffirms the explanatory weakness of existing theories, and relief because it confirms that the future remains to be made, even if not within conditions of free choice, to paraphrase Karl Marx. In the aftermath of the Great Crash, more than ever before, politics will define the future trajectories of globalization and the global economy, hopefully for the better, but quite possibly for the worse.

? Questions

1. What are the principal causes of globalization?

2. Is economic globalization a product of politics or of capitalism, or both?

3. 'Technics makes globalization.' Discuss.

4. In what sense, if any, do constructivist theories provide a convincing account of the origins of economic globalization?

5. Which is the more convincing: the globalist or the sceptical analysis of economic globalization?

6. Outline the globalist case, and critically evaluate it with reference to the historical evidence.

7. Why does it matter if the world economy was more economically integrated in the belle époque?

8. How does Braudel's analysis help us to understand the logics of economic globalization?

9. Critically assess the argument that economic globalization is simply a political project.

10. 'Economic globalization is much more limited than many realize' (Gilpin 2001). Critically assess this proposition with reference to contemporary global economic trends.

→ Further reading

■ Castells, M. (2000), *The Rise of the Network Society* (Oxford: Blackwell). This is now a contemporary classic account of the political economy of globalization, comprehensive in its analysis of the new global informational capitalism.

■ Dicken, P. (2007), *Global Shift: Mapping the Changing Contours of the World Economy*, 5th edn (London: Sage). This is an excellent introduction and comprehensive account of the new global division of labour and the globalization of production in the world economy.

■ Garrett, G. (2000), 'The Causes of Globalization', *Comparative Political Studies*, 33/6: 945–91. A really interesting and thorough exploration of the causal dynamics of globalization written from a rather orthodox political economy position, but, nevertheless, critical of much of the contemporary sceptical analysis.

■ Giddens, A. (1990), *The Consequences of Modernity* (Cambridge: Polity Press). A classic statement of the rootedness of globalization in the long-term historical processes of modernization or modernity. It is less a political economy than a historical sociological account of globalization which takes it seriously as a transformative force.

■ Gilpin, R. (2001), *Global Political Economy* (Princeton, NJ: Princeton University Press). A more sceptical view of economic globalization which, although taking it seriously, conceives it as an expression of Americanization or American hegemony.

■ Held, D., and McGrew, A. (2007), *Globalization/Anti-Globalization* (Cambridge: Polity Press). A comprehensive examination of the academic and political controversies surrounding globalization.

■ Hirst, P., Thompson, G., and Bromley, S. (2009), *Globalization in Question*, 3rd edn (Cambridge: Polity Press). An excellent and sober critique of the hyperglobalist arguments, it is thoroughly sceptical about the globalization thesis, viewing recent trends as a return to the belle époque and heavily shaped by states.

■ James, H. (2009), *The Creation and Destruction of Value: The Globalization Cycle* (Cambridge, MA: Harvard University Press). An excellent analysis of the sources and consequences of the Great Crash for contemporary globalization.

■ Robertson, R. (2003), *The Three Waves of Globalization: A History of Developing Global Consciousness* (London: Zed Books). A very good account of globalization as a long-term historical process driven by a combination of economic and political factors.

■ Rosenberg, J. (2000), *The Follies of Globalization Theory* (London: Verso). A very erudite and rigorous critique of the globalization literature which, although sceptical about its wilder claims, considers that globalization can only be understood from a historical materialist perspective.

■ Scholte, J. A. (2005), *Globalization: A Critical Introduction*, 2nd edn (Basingstoke: Palgrave). An excellent introduction to the globalization debate, from its causes to its consequences for the global political economy, from within a critical political economy perspective.

■ Wood, E. M. (2003), *Empire of Capital* (London: Verso). A novel reworking of the classical Marxist account of imperialism which takes globalization seriously as a new phase of capitalist development accompanied by a unique form of empire.

Web links

■ www.isn.ethz.ch/linkslib   Good links to security and global economy nexuses.

■ www.wto.org   Official WTO site, with useful material about its policies and data on world trade.

■ www.theglobalsite.ac.uk   Good site for the globalization debate and related links.

■ www.tradeobservatory.org   Unofficial site operated by non-governmental organizations (NGOs) critical of the WTO and economic globalization.

■ www.polity.co.uk/global   Good site for the globalization debate and many good links.

■ www.rgemonitor.com   Excellent site for a whole range of material on global economy and economic globalization.

■ www.indiana.edu/~ipe/ipesection   Good site for general material on IPE.

■ www.nber.org   Excellent studies of economic globalization in National Bureau of Economic Research (NBER) Working Paper series.

Online resource centre

For additional material and resources, please visit the Online Resource Centre at:
www.oxfordtextbooks.co.uk/ravenhill3e/

10

Globalization's Impact on States

Colin Hay

∗ Reader's guide

There is no topic more controversial in the field of global political economy than the impact of globalization on the accountability, autonomy, capacity, and sovereignty of the nation state. Arguably, the democratic character of governance in contemporary societies is at stake is such debates. This chapter reviews the extensive controversy which surrounds such questions, focusing attention on the principal mechanisms in and through which globalization is seen to impact upon the nation state and the empirical evidence which might either substantiate or question the existence of such mechanisms. It provides a detailed assessment of the case for and against the globalization thesis, examining the extent to which global economic integration might be seen to restrict the parameters of domestic political autonomy. It concludes by considering the complex and sometimes paradoxical relationship between globalization, democracy and the nation state.

Introduction

It is over thirty years since Charles Kindleberger boldly proclaimed that: 'the nation state is just about through as an economic unit' (1969: 207). Since then, we have witnessed a remarkable profusion of apocalyptic predictions of the demise of the nation state. In such accounts, globalization is invariably cast in the role of prosecutor, judge, jury, and executioner. Yet, despite such doom-laden prognoses, government expenditure continues to account for a significant and, in many cases, rising share of gross domestic product (GDP), whilst the nation state remains the principal focus of political identification and the principal locus of political debate and contestation in an interdependent world. Given this seeming paradox, it is perhaps not surprising that the question of the impact of globalization on the development of the state has become a subject of considerable interest and intense controversy. Opinions range widely.

Though perhaps less influential than it once was, the view that globalization is in the process of, or has already, precipitated a terminal crisis of the nation state is still widespread. Others see such apocalyptic claims as wild and unfounded extrapolations from anecdotal evidence. Proponents of such a view, they suggest, confuse a crisis of the *form* of the nation state for a crisis of the nation state per se. Yet others see globalization as a process driven by states that has, in many cases, served to strengthen and certainly to increase the significance of state intervention for economic performance. Still others question the role of globalization in such dynamics, suggesting either that globalization—though real—has little to do with the developmental trajectory of the nation state or that the claim that we have witnessed a systematic process of globalization is itself mythical. Finally, there are those who suggest that the very *idea* of globalization as a harsh and non-negotiable economic constraint has itself exerted a powerful influence in confining the political ambitions of elected officials to those consistent with the pervasive neo-liberal orthodoxy. It is this, rather than globalization per se, they suggest, that has given rise to the impression of a waning of the nation state's autonomy, capacity, and sovereignty.

Much more than academic pride is at stake in such debates. For, whether or not we see globalization as restricting the parameters of political choice domestically, and whether or not we see the nation state as having a present or, indeed, a future will have a very significant bearing on the space for political autonomy we perceive there to be. This, in turn, has significant consequences for the extent to which we might legitimately hold elected officials accountable for their conduct in office. Given the significance of the issues we are dealing with, it is important to proceed with a certain degree of caution.

We should perhaps be wary of accepting uncritically, as many have, that globalization leaves states (and the governments which give effect to state power) with no alternative other than to capitulate to the demands and desires of mobile investors. For to do so, is effectively to deny the possibility of the democratic governance of economic processes in contemporary societies, certainly at the national level. In other words, there is a certain danger that in accepting over-hastily an influential conception of the inevitable demise of the nation state's capacity and autonomy, we provide a convenient alibi for politicians keen to justify otherwise unpalatable social and economic reforms by appeal to the harsh economic realities of a global age. Maybe our politicians deserve such an alibi; maybe the constraints of the global economy are so exacting and all-pervasive as to warrant the appeal to such a 'logic of no alternative'; maybe these are valid and defensible conclusions. The crucial point for now is that we cannot allow ourselves to accept at face value such claims without a detailed consideration—both theoretical and empirical—of the arguments for and against such a view.

Though space does not permit a fully comprehensive exploration of the relevant issues, it is my aim in what follows to survey the existing literature in this area and, in so doing, to provide a basis for such an assessment. It is important to emphasize at the outset, however, that there is no agreed or emerging consensus on globalization's impact upon the state—and such debates are only further complicated by the recent global financial crisis. Commentators are divided and they are likely to remain divided. As we shall see, this is—at least in part—due to the rather slippery nature of the term globalization itself, which has come to mean a range of rather different things to a range of different analysts.

The chapter proceeds in four sections. In the first of these, I seek to establish a few necessary preliminaries, distinguishing in particular between the politics of globalization and the globalization of politics. In the second, I identify the principal mechanisms in and through which globalization is seen to impact upon the nation state before turning, in the third, to the empirical evidence which might either substantiate or question the existence of such mechanisms. In the final section, and by way of a conclusion, I consider the complex and sometimes paradoxical relationship between globalization, democracy, and the nation state, looking both at the impact of globalization on states and the state's impact on globalization.

The Globalization of Politics and the Politics of Globalization

It is crucial at the outset that we distinguish between the globalization of politics and the politics of globalization. This is particularly important, given the tendency—especially prevalent amongst international/global political economists—to talk about globalization as if it were a transparent, self-sustaining, and purely economic dynamic (on the dangers of such 'economism' see also Teivainen 2002). It is a key contention of this chapter that globalization is not a tendency that is furthered or, indeed, countered in the *absence of political actors*. As such, it has a politics that must be a central ingredient of any adequate account of its development.

By the *globalization of politics*, I refer to the displacement of political capacities and responsibilities from the national and/or regional levels to the genuinely global level, through the development of institutions of global governance.

By the *politics of globalization*, I refer to the politics of the process of globalization itself, to the political drivers of globalization and to the consequences of such a process for political conflict, practice, and the distribution of political responsibility.

Whether, and to what extent, we observe a globalization of politics is a matter of empirical judgement. It is likely to relate, amongst other things, to our evaluation of the extent and significance of genuinely global institutions of governance, the relative significance of regional institutions, and the degree to which the emergence of global institutions might be seen to give rise to a politics independent of and irreducible to that between discrete nation states or regions. Yet, whatever specific judgement we reach—and, again, opinion varies considerably (compare, for instance, Archibugi 2003; Buzan et al. 1998; Krasner 1999)—we must acknowledge that if globalization exists at all, and even if it is confined exclusively to the economic and cultural spheres, it has a politics. Whilst we may well deny the globalization of politics, then, unless we deny globalization itself we cannot deny the *politics* of globalization. It is with the latter that this chapter is principally concerned.

More specifically, I shall focus on three analytically separable, but nonetheless interconnected, dimensions of the politics of globalization:

1. The implications and consequences of globalization (whether economic, political, or cultural) for the capacity and autonomy of the nation state.

2. The interpretation of the opportunities and constraints associated with globalization and the

consequent appeal made, in political contexts, to the language of globalization (often, as we shall see, to justify social and economic reforms).

3. The role of political actors, particularly state actors, in the political 'authoring' of globalization and the processes which either sustain or impede its development.

The first of these might be seen as the *structural* dimension, relating as it does to the constraints and opportunities of the external environment for domestic political actors. The second relates to the *ideational* dimension and, more specifically, to the way in which political actors understand the constraints and opportunities that the external environment presents to them. The third relates to the *intentional*, *strategic*, or *agential* dimension—to the

role of political actors in the creation and recreation of the very external environment in which they find themselves. Together, they suggest an approach to the question of the impact of globalization on the state and the state's impact on globalization in which political actors are always present, in which the ideas they hold about their environment shapes their political conduct, and in which they are never unburdened of the constraints (and opportunities) of the environment they have created (for a further elaboration, see Hay 2002*b*: 253–60).

Such a perspective is applied, in the pages that follow, to a series of more substantive issues and controversies. These might together be taken to comprise an agenda for a consideration of the politics of globalization (see Box 10.1).

Box 10.1 The Politics of Globalization: Key Controversies

- The extent to which globalization might be seen to diminish the autonomy and 'perforate' the sovereignty of the nation state (on 'perforated sovereignty' see Duchacek 1990; Jessop 2002).

- The extent to which globalization might be seen to establish powerful tendencies towards global political convergence and homogenisation.

- The extent to which it is right to identify a globalization of political problems—the proliferation of issues that require a response in the form of concerted global action.

- The extent to which we can point to a parallel globalization of political solutions and the corresponding emergence of more or less dedicated institutions, mechanisms, and processes of *global governance*.

- The extent to which we can identify the global diffusion of 'best practice' policy solutions (or potential solutions) and/or policy models in the form of the transfer of ideas about 'good' practice between nations (whether by choice or imposition).

- The extent to which globalization might be seen to promote the development of a global polity or *cosmopolis* capable of transcending the state (see, for example, Archibugi 2003; Zolo 1997).

Each set of issues, as we shall see, reveals a separate and distinct politics of globalization. By drawing attention to the multifaceted politics of globalization in this way, my aim is to contribute to the attempt to restore political (and one might

hope democratic) scrutiny and accountability to processes more conventionally seen as economic and inexorable—and, consequently, as not subject to political deliberation (see, more generally, Hay 2002*a*).

Key points

- The impact of globalization on the autonomy, capacity, and sovereignty of the nation state is much disputed.

- It is important to distinguish between the politics of globalization (the political drivers of the process of globalization) and the globalization of politics (the displacement of political responsibilities and capacities from the level of the nation state through the emergence of institutions and processes of global governance). Globalization has a politics, whether or not politics has become globalized.

- It is equally important to distinguish between and to acknowledge the structural, ideational, and strategic dimensions of the process of globalization. The first of these relates to the constraints and opportunities presented by globalization; the second to the way in which those structural factors are understood; the third to the role of political actors is 'authoring' the process of globalization itself.

Globalization and the Crisis of the Nation State

If we are to assess the impact (if any) of globalization on the viability of the nation state, we must first identify the principal mechanisms in and through which globalization is held, in conventional accounts, to limit the capacity, autonomy, and sovereignty of the nation state. Before doing so, however, it is perhaps important to emphasize that most strong variants of the globalization thesis—which present the nation state as a casualty of globalization—tend to do so without pointing directly or explicitly to the mechanism or mechanisms involved (see, for instance, Ohmae 1990, 1995; Reich 1992). At best, it seems, they treat the existence of such mechanisms as self-evident. What we tend to see, instead, is what Andreas Busch (2000: 34) refers to as 'casual empiricism'—the anecdotal appeal to, and extrapolation from, single pieces of evidence which appear to confirm the general tenor of the argument being advanced.

At times, however, casual empiricism gives way to 'casual theoreticism'. Here, tangential reference is made to the increased bargaining power and/or mobility of capital in an era of globalization. In so doing, 'hyperglobalists' appeal, whether they are aware of it or not, to mechanisms derived from neoclassical open economy macroeconomic models (for reviews of the relevant literature, see Obstfeld and Rogoff 1996; Rødseth 2000; Ugur 2001). This is an important point and gives a first clue as to the character of the hyperglobalization thesis. For it serves to indicate that, for such authors, it is *economic* globalization that is the principal factor limiting the capacity and autonomy of the state in the contemporary context. In short, economic globalization gives mobile international investors the upper hand over domestic political authorities.

Without going into any technical detail, it is useful to examine further such open economic macroeconomics models. In particular, it is important that we:

1. Establish the assumptions on which such models are predicated.

2. Assess the plausibility of such assumptions.

3. Consider the sensitivity of the conclusions derived from such assumptions (for the viability or otherwise of the nation state) to modifications in the initial premises from which they are derived.

The hyperglobalization thesis

Arguably, the key factor determining the inevitability of state retrenchment for hyperglobalists is the heightened mobility of capital. The logic to which they appeal is, in fact, very similar to that elaborated by Adam Smith in 1776:

> The . . . proprietor of stock is properly a citizen of the world, and is not necessarily attached to any particular country. He would be apt to abandon the country in which he is exposed to a vexatious inquisition, in order to be assessed a burdensome tax, and would remove his stock to some country where he could either carry on his business or enjoy his fortune at his ease. A tax that tended to drive away stock from a particular country, would so far tend to dry up every source of revenue, both to the sovereign and to the society. Not only the profits of stock, but the rent of land and the wages of labour, would necessarily be more or less diminished by its removal.
>
> (Smith 1776/1976: 848–9; cited in Swank 2002: 245).

Updated and restated in more familiar terms, the argument goes something like this. In closed national economies, such as those which (supposedly) characterized the early post-war period, capital is essentially immobile and national in character; it has no 'exit' option. In such an environment, governments can impose punitive taxation regimes upon unwilling and relatively impotent national capitals with little cost to the domestic economy (save, except, for the tendency for capitalists to hoard rather than to reinvest their profits). With open economy conditions, such as are conventionally held to characterize the contemporary era, this is no longer the case. Capital may now exit from national economic environments at minimal cost (indeed, in most neoclassical-inspired models, at zero cost).

Accordingly, by playing off the regulatory regimes of different economies against one another, capital can ensure for itself the highest rate of return on its investment. *Ceteris paribus*, capital will exit high-taxation regimes for low-taxation regimes, comprehensive welfare states for residual states, highly regulated labour markets for flexible labour markets, and economies characterized by strict environmental regulations and high union density for those characterized by lapse environmental standards and low union density. The clear prediction would be that capital will seek out the high-growth regimes of, for instance, newly industrializing economies (NIEs) (like Malaysia, for instance) unencumbered by a powerful environmental lobby, burdensome welfare traditions, rigid labour market institutions, and correspondingly higher rates of taxation.

The process pits national economy against national economy, in an increasingly intense competitive struggle. States must effectively clamber over one another in an ever -more frenzied attempt to produce a more favourable investment environment for mobile ('footloose') foreign direct investors than their competitors. Yet, this is not a one-shot game—and an early influx of foreign direct investment (FDI) only increases the dependence of the state upon its continued 'locational competitiveness'. If investment is to be retained in such an environment, states must constantly strive to improve the investment opportunities they can offer relative to their competitors. Any failure to do so can only precipitate a haemorrhaging of invested funds, labour shedding and, in turn, economic crisis. A neo-Darwinian survival of the fittest effectively guarantees that states must internalize the preferences of capital, offering ever more attractive investment incentives, ever more flexible labour markets, and ever less restrictive environmental regulations, if they are not to be emptied of investment, economic activity, and employment. Big government, if not perhaps the state itself, is rendered increasingly anachronistic—a guarantor, not of the interests of citizens or even consumers, but a sure means to disinvestment and economic crisis.

Little wonder, then, that the hyperglobalization thesis tends to predict 'social dumping', 'competitive deregulation', and a race to the bottom in terms of social and environmental standards, a process lubricated by the 'deregulatory arbitrage' of footloose and fancy-free transnational corporations.

The policy implications of such an account are painfully clear. As globalization serves to establish competitive selection mechanisms within the international economy, there is little choice but to cast all regulatory impediments to the efficient operation of the market on the bonfire of welfare institutions, regulatory controls (for instance, of the banking sector), and labour market rigidities.

Plausible, familiar, and compelling though such a logic may well appear, it serves us well to isolate the assumptions on which it is predicated. For, as we shall see, it is these, rather than any inexorable process of globalization, which ultimately summon the crisis of the nation state. They are principally fivefold, and each can be challenged on both theoretical and empirical grounds (see Box 10.2).

Box 10.2 Core Assumptions of the 'Hyperglobalization' Thesis

1. That capital invests where it can secure the greatest net return on that investment and is possessed of perfect information of the means by which to do so.

2. That markets for goods and services are fully integrated globally and that, consequently, national economies must prove themselves internationally competitive if economic growth is to be sustained.

3. That capital enjoys perfect mobility and the cost of 'exit' (disinvestment) is zero.

4. That capital will invariably secure the greatest return on its investment by minimizing its labour costs in flexible labour markets and by relocating its productive activities in economies with the lowest rates of corporate taxation.

5. That the welfare state (and the taxation receipts out of which it is funded) represent nothing other than lost capital to mobile asset holders and have no positive externalities for the competitiveness and productivity of the national economy.

Each of these premises is at best dubious, at worst demonstrably false. Such assumptions, it should perhaps be noted, are not justified in neoclassical economics in terms of their accuracy, but because they are convenient and make possible abstract quasi-mathematical modelling. That defence, whatever one thinks of it, is simply not available to proponents of the hyperglobalization thesis whose borrowings from neoclassical economics rarely extend past the assumptions to the algebra.

Consider each assumption in turn. Whilst it may seem entirely appropriate to attribute to capital the sole motive of seeking the greatest return on its investment, the political and economic history of capital provides little or no support for the notion that capital is blessed either with complete information or even with a relatively clear and consistent conception of what its own best interest is. Moreover, as the political economy of the advanced

capitalist democracies demonstrates well, capital has a history of resisting social and economic reforms which it has later come both to rely upon and actively to defend (see, for example, Swenson 2000).

The second assumption is, again, a convenient fiction, used in neoclassical macroeconomics to make possible the modelling of an open economy. Few, if any, economists would defend the claim that markets for goods or services are fully integrated or clear instantly. Indeed, the degree of integration of such markets is an empirical question and, as such, an issue to which we return in the next section.

If the first two assumptions are problematic, then the third is demonstrably false, at least with respect to certain types of capital. For, however mobile portfolio capital may appear in a digital economy, the same is simply not the case for capital invested in infrastructure, machinery, and personnel. Consider inward foreign direct investment. Once attracted to a particular locality, foreign direct investors acquire a range of non-recuperable or sunk costs—such as their investment in physical infrastructure, plant, and machinery. Consequently, their exit options become seriously depleted. Whilst it is entirely 'rational' for foreign direct investors to proclaim loudly their mobility, exit is perhaps most effective as a threat.

What this in turn suggests is that predictions of the haemorrhaging of invested capital from generous welfare states are almost certainly misplaced. A combination of exit threats and concerns arising from the hyperglobalization thesis about the *likelihood* of exit may well have had an independent effect on the trajectory of fiscal and labour market reform. But there would seem no a priori reason to hold generous welfare state and high corporate taxation burdens incompatible with the attraction and retention of foreign direct investment. As we shall see in greater detail in the next section, this is precisely what we observe from the empirical record. Not only have the most generous welfare states consistently proved the most attractive locations for inward foreign direct investors (Locke and Kochan 1985; Swank 2002), but volumes of foreign direct investment (expressed as a share of GDP) are, in fact, found to be positively correlated with levels of corporate taxation, union density, labour costs, and the degree of regulation of the labour market (Cooke and Noble 1998; Dunning 1988; Traxler and Woitech 2000; Wilensky 2002: 654–5). As Duane Swank notes,

> contrary to the claims of the international capital mobility thesis . . . the general fiscal capacity of democratic governments to fund a variety of levels and mixes of social protection and services may be relatively resilient in the face of internationalisation of markets.

(Swank 2002: 276)

Here, it is perhaps instructive to note that, despite a marked tendency for direct corporate taxation to fall in recent years in line with the predictions of such neoclassical-inspired models, the overall burden of taxation on firms has, in fact, remained remarkably constant, rising marginally since the mid 1980s (Kiser and Laing 2001; Steinmo 2003).

No less problematic, are assumptions four and five—that capital can only compete in a more intensely competitive environment on the basis of productivity gains secured through tax reductions and cost-shedding (through rationalization, downsizing, and the flexibilization of labour), and that the welfare state is, for business, merely a drain on profits. Such assumptions reflect a narrowly Anglo-US conception of competitiveness—and, as we shall see presently, are difficult to reconcile with the empirical evidence. Though ever more influential, the hyperglobalization thesis extrapolates wildly and inappropriately from labour-intensive sectors of the international economy in which competitiveness is conventionally enhanced in this way, to the global economy more generally. It fails to appreciate that foreign direct investors in capital-intensive sectors of the international economy are attracted to locations like the Northern European economies, neither for the flexibility of their labour markets nor for the cheapness of the wage and non-wage labour costs that they impose, but for the access they provide to a highly skilled, reliable, and innovative labour force. High wages and high non-wage labour costs (in the form of payroll taxes) would seem to be a price many multinational corporations regard as worth paying for a dynamic and highly skilled workforce.

At this point, it might be objected that the above paragraphs relate principally to the investment behaviour of foreign direct investors and not to financial market actors. This is a valid point. Indeed, although the hyperglobalization thesis has rather more to say about the former, it has much to say about the latter, too.

Its assumptions about finance capital and financial markets are similar to those about productive/invested capital and markets in goods and services. Yet, the small differences are significant. Referring again to Box 10.2, the first assumption applies equally to invested and investment capital and is equally problematic. Yet, whether it is accurate or not, arguably matters rather less in the case of portfolio capital. For such investors do not need to act rationally or with perfect information in order to inflict considerable damage on the currencies against which they may be tempted to speculate and the stocks and shares they may be tempted to dump—as the influential literature on 'irrational exuberance' and 'herding instincts' in financial markets makes very clear and as the experience of the global financial crisis perhaps confirms (see, for example, Shiller 2001, 2008). Assumption two also applies equally to financial markets and to those in goods and services (see Pauly, Chapter 8 in this volume). All are assumed global and perfectly integrated. This may seem like a more plausible assumption to make of financial markets but, as we shall see in the next section, as an empirical claim it is not easily reconciled with the available evidence. Assumption three, though problematic for productive/invested capital as already discussed, again seems more plausible for portfolio investors. Stocks and shares can certainly be traded, and assets swapped from one denomination to another, in the flickering of a cursor. Yet, whether this *potential* is reflected in the actual behaviour of financial markets is, again, an empirical question and the subject of some debate. This, too, is discussed further in the next section. Assumptions four and five are not directly relevant to finance capital, but they can be adapted to financial actors. Hyperglobalists tend to assume that portfolio investors have a clear interest in, and preference for, strong and stable currencies backed both by implacable independent central banks with hawkish anti-inflationary credentials and governments wedded in theory and in practice to fiscal moderation and prudence. Any departure from this new financial orthodoxy, it is assumed, will precipitate a flurry of speculation against the currency and a haemorrhaging of investment from assets denominated in that currency. Governments provoke the wrath of the financial markets at their peril. This, again, is an intuitively plausible proposition that would seem to be borne out by a series of high-profile speculative flurries against 'rogue' governments. It is, however, an empirical claim and, as we shall see later, one that a growing body of scholarship reveals to be considerably at odds with the empirical evidence.

As the above paragraphs perhaps serve to indicate, the theoretical case against the hyperglobalization thesis is strongest with respect to the assumptions made about productive/invested capital. Its assumptions about investment/portfolio capital, if perhaps overly simplistic, are, on the face of it, more plausible. Yet, they give rise to a series of substantive claims and predictions which have prompted an important empirical challenge to the thesis. This provides the principal focus for the next section. Before turning to such issues, however, it is important that we first consider the implications of the hyperglobalization thesis for the question of convergence prior to examining an alternative and rather more political account of the origins of the contemporary crisis of the nation state.

Convergence, dual convergence, or divergence?

Through attempts to enhance competitiveness like labour market flexibility, welfare retrenchment, and the intensification of tax competition between states, the hyperglobalization thesis predicts a simple convergence amongst previously distinct 'models' or 'varieties' of capitalism—on an Anglo-US or liberal ideal type. This can be represented schematically (see Figure 10.1).

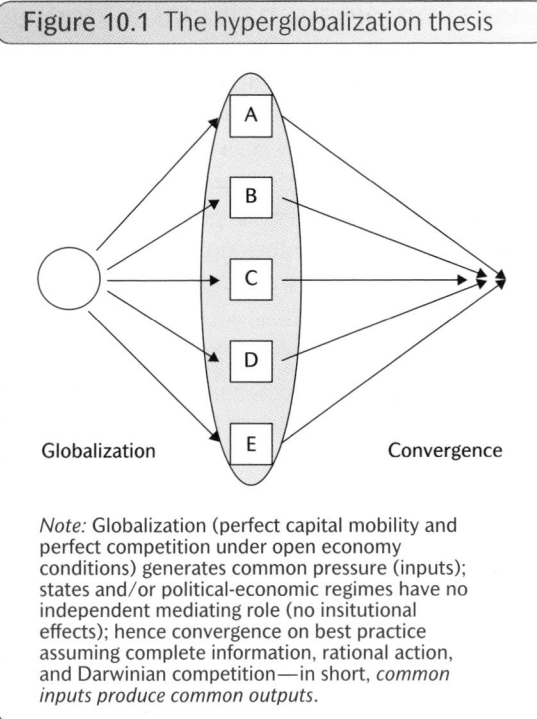

Figure 10.1 The hyperglobalization thesis

Note: Globalization (perfect capital mobility and perfect competition under open economy conditions) generates common pressure (inputs); states and/or political-economic regimes have no independent mediating role (no insitutional effects); hence convergence on best practice assuming complete information, rational action, and Darwinian competition—in short, *common inputs produce common outputs.*

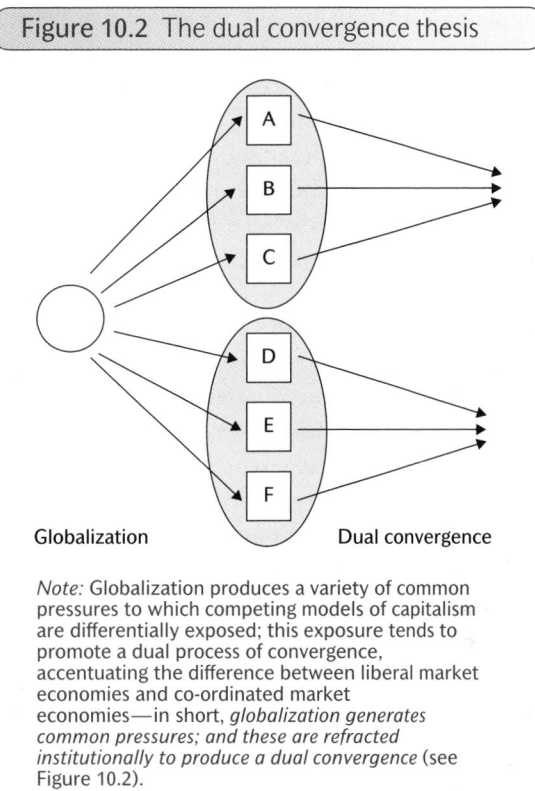

Figure 10.2 The dual convergence thesis

Note: Globalization produces a variety of common pressures to which competing models of capitalism are differentially exposed; this exposure tends to promote a dual process of convergence, accentuating the difference between liberal market economies and co-ordinated market economies—in short, *globalization generates common pressures; and these are refracted institutionally to produce a dual convergence* (see Figure 10.2).

Globalization is the driving force, unleashing an intense competitive struggle between contending models of capitalism. It exposes all economies (A–E in Figure 10.1) to common pressures, which, in turn, produce common outcomes. Since liberal models of capitalism best approximate the preferences of mobile capital for open markets, low taxation regimes, and light regulation, they rapidly establish themselves as the model to be emulated. Convergence on this Anglo-US ideal type is held to be rapid, lubricated by capital's exit from more highly regulated regimes.

Influential though this simple convergence thesis is, it is not as unquestioned as it once was. An alternative and increasingly influential account points to a rather more complex process of 'dual' or 'co-convergence', again driven by globalization (see above).

In this contending account, more attention is paid to the role of institutional factors in mediating the state's response to globalization. Models of capitalism are differentiated by virtue of the rather different institutions they embody. In the now conventional classification, *liberal market economies* (such as the US and the UK) and *co-ordinated market economies* (such as Germany, Sweden, and the Netherlands) are contrasted (Hall and Soskice 2001).

The competitive pressures unleashed by globalization may make similar demands of these institutions (such as balanced budgets, flexible labour markets, and the control of inflation), but these can be delivered in different ways in different institutional domains. Consequently, the 'varieties of capitalism' approach, as it has come to be known, predicts not a simple or singular process of convergence on the liberal (or Anglo-US) model, but a complex or dual convergence in which capitalist polities cluster ever more closely around the liberal and co-ordinated ideal types (Hall and Soskice 2001; see also Garrett 1998*b*, 2000*b*; Iversen et al. 2000; Kitschelt et al. 1999).

In its sensitivity to institutional variations amongst different models of capitalism and in its recognition that common external pressures need not translate into common outcomes, the 'varieties of capitalism' approach represents a considerable advance on the hyperglobalization thesis. Yet, in a number of significant respects it, too, is problematic (see also Blyth 2003; Goodin 2003; Hay 2004; Watson 2003).

1. It may, unwittingly, borrow too much from the hyperglobalization thesis in presenting globalization as the principal agent of convergence (paying insufficient attention to the often regional character of processes of economic integration and/or to the differential exposure of economies to globalization, for instance).

2. In drawing a rigid and rather static distinction between liberal and co-ordinated market economies, it is not perhaps as sensitive to institutional diversity as it might be (see also Crouch and Streeck 1997).

3. It makes a series of empirical predictions/claims about dual convergence, which are, at best, contestable—as we shall see in the following section.

Finally, in the wake of the recent global financial crisis, it might well be asked whether the liberal market economies (whose propensity to generate asset-price bubbles has been so cruelly exposed and which now look like the key source of systemic risk within the global financial system) can be seen as models of adaptation to globalization (Hay 2009).

Global problems, national solutions?

Thus far, we have tended to focus exclusively upon mechanisms identifying *economic* globalization as the key determinant of the contemporary crisis of the nation state. Yet, arguably altogether more plausible, is a rather more political mechanism. Strictly speaking, this does not so much point to the diminished capacity and sovereignty of the state in an era of globalization, as to the globalization of the problems with which the nation state is confronted—and its inability to deal with such problems. Indeed, it points to the more general lack of the political capacity to deal with genuinely global problems and risks that results from the continued ascendancy of the nation state as a political unit.

The classic example here, is the problem of high-consequence global environmental risks (Beck 1992; Giddens 1990). This is well expressed in the so-called **tragedy of the commons**, first identified by Garrett Hardin (1968). Hardin provides an intuitively plausible and all too compelling model of the seemingly intractable problem of environmental degradation in contemporary societies. The systematic exploitation and pollution of the environment, it is argued, is set to continue since individual corporations and states, despite a clear collective interest, choose not to impose upon themselves the costs of unilateral environmental action. Their logic is entirely rational, though potentially catastrophic in its cumulative consequences. Such actors know that environmental regulation is costly and, particularly in an open international economy, a burden on competitiveness. Accordingly, in the absence of an international agency capable of enforcing the compliance of all states and all corporations, the anticipation of free riding is sufficient to ensure that corporations and states do not burden themselves with additional costs and taxes. The long-term effects for the environment are all too obvious, preventing as it does, a global solution to a genuinely global problem.

The extent to which the narrowly perceived self-interest of states and governments can subvert the development of effective mechanisms and institutions of global governance is well-evidenced by the Bush administration's withdrawal from the 1997 Kyoto Protocol (committing signatories to staged reductions in greenhouse gas emissions); and, for its critics, by the fact that such a protocol, even if fully implemented, would only serve to reduce slightly the pace of an ongoing process of environmental degradation.

This is a most important example, and a number of broader implications might be drawn from it (see Box 10.3).

Box 10.3 The Implications of the 'Tragedy of the Commons'

1. The 'tragedy of the commons' is, effectively, a modern-day morality tale. It is indicative of a more general disparity between the need for and supply of effective institutions and mechanisms of global governance. For, whilst it is easy to point to genuinely global problems requiring for their resolution co-ordinated global responses, it is far more difficult to find examples of the latter.

2. As this perhaps suggests, the 'tragedy of the commons' is not really a story of the crisis of the nation state at all. For, it is the continued capacity of many (if perhaps not all) states to behave unilaterally and to veto international agreements that precludes the appropriate globally co-ordinated collective response. In other words, political globalization (effective and authoritative institutions of global governance) is impeded by the retention of the nation state's sovereignty. This is less a crisis of the nation state, then, than a crisis produced by the resilience of the nation state.

3. Whilst the proliferation of genuinely global political problems does point to the incapacity of a system of sovereign states to deal with the challenges it now faces, it does not indicate any particular incapacity of states to deal with the problems and issues they have always dealt with. This is, then, less of a story of a loss of capacity than of the proliferation of issues which the nation state has never had the capacity to deal with.

4. Finally, and rather perversely, the disparity between the need for and supply of global solutions to global problems is merely exacerbated by economic globalization. For this has served to drive states, at pain of economic crisis, to elevate considerations of competitiveness over all other concerns, including environmental protection. There is a clear and obvious danger that the narrow pursuit of short-term economic advantage will come at the long-term price of a looming environmental, economic, and political catastrophe.

Key points

- Many of the strongest versions of the globalization thesis fail to specify the mechanism by which globalization might be seen to limit the capacity, autonomy, and sovereignty of the nation state.

- Nonetheless, a variety of such mechanisms have been posited. These are principally economic in character and often rely upon stylized assumptions about the behaviour of capital drawn from open economy neoclassical economics. These assumptions can be questioned theoretically and empirically.

- The hyperglobalization thesis predicts a simple convergence between 'models of capitalism' under conditions of (economic) globalization; the more recent 'varieties of capitalism' perspective predicts a more complex process of dual convergence. There are theoretical problems with both sets of predictions.

- The nation state has always suffered from a limited capacity to deal with genuinely global problems; such problems are proliferating. The 'tragedy of the commons' provides a compelling model of the consequences of this lack of capacity, pointing to the need for effective and democratic institutions of global governance.

Globalization and State Retrenchment: The Evidence Assessed

As suggested in the previous section, the hyperglobalization thesis tends to present a theoretical, indeed, largely hypothetical, argument for the contemporary crisis of the nation state. If its assumptions are accepted, then the predicted crisis of the nation state is little more than a logical inference. Yet, as we have seen, there may be good theoretical grounds for challenging some of these assumptions and with them the claimed inevitability of the state's loss of capacity, autonomy, sovereignty, and legitimacy. In the end, however, these are empirical questions—and it is to the empirical evidence itself that we must turn if we are to assess the validity of the hyperglobalization thesis and to assess the impact, if any, of globalization on states. It is to this task that we now turn. We begin first by considering the dependent variable.

The dependent variable: state retrenchment

It is perhaps appropriate to begin with the simplest data which most directly addresses the contemporary condition of the state. If the state were to experience a potentially terminal crisis, we might expect to see clear evidence of systematic state retrenchment. Moreover, we would expect this to be most pronounced in highly open economies whose public spending had traditionally accounted for a high proportion of gross domestic product. Table 10.1 presents data on government expenditure expressed as a proportion of gross domestic product for a number of developed countries from the 1960s, conventionally the point of departure for political economies of globalization.

The evidence itself is fairly unequivocal. These, for the most part extremely open and developed economies, show little sign of systematic retrenchment in the so-called era of globalization. Indeed, in response to the global financial crisis, their levels of public spending are rising—and in a number of cases (notably, many of the Anglo-liberal economies such as New Zealand, the UK, and the US), current levels of state expenditure are at their historic peak. There is certainly some evidence in the last two decades or so of a decline in the proportion of GDP devoted to public spending. Though invariably greatest where unemployment has fallen most, this is consistent with the predictions of the hyperglobalization thesis to some extent. Yet, what is perhaps more important is that in each and every case, the size of the state (as expressed as a share of GDP) has increased considerably over the period, peaking in most cases in the early to mid 1990s and, in the Anglo-liberal economies, today.

Of course, state expenditure is not the only means of gauging quantitatively the role of the state. Figure 10.3 presents time-series data on the proportion of the total workforce employed directly by the state since the 1960s.

Again, the evidence is unequivocal. This period, the much-vaunted era of globalization, has witnessed the development of the largest states the world has ever seen and there is little evidence in this data series of this trend being reversed. That said, the global financial crisis has had the effect of driving up levels of public debt—and it is likely that the next decade will see some scaling back of the public sector (and, hence, public employment) in the advanced liberal democracies.

Table 10.1 Government Expenditure as a Share of GDP

	AUL	AUS	BEL	CAN	DEN	FIN	FRA	GER	IRE
1960	22.1	32.1	34.6	28.9	24.6	26.6	34.6	32.0	28.0
1965	25.6	37.9	36.5	29.1	29.6	30.8	38.4	36.3	33.1
1970	25.5	39.2	42.1	35.7	40.2	30.5	38.9	37.6	39.6
1975	32.4	46.2	51.3	40.7	47.5	38.4	43.5	47.1	46.5
1980	34.1	48.5	58.7	41.5	56.2	39.4	46.2	46.9	50.8
1985	38.5	51.7	62.3	47.1	59.3	45.0	52.2	47.5	54.8
1990	37.7	49.4	55.3	47.8	58.6	46.8	49.9	45.7	41.4
1996	37.2	56.1	52.6	46.6	58.7	59.8	54.5	49.3	39.1
2000	35.2	52.2	49.2	41.1	53.3	48.3	51.6	45.1	31.3
2005	34.8	50.1	52.2	39.9	52.5	50.3	53.4	46.2	33.7
2009	37.5	52.7	54.0	43.6	57.7	56.2	55.5	47.7	45.0
Net growth[a] (%)	70	46	56	51	135	111	60	49	61
Growth to peak (%)	74	75	80	65	158	125	60	54	96
Decline from peak (%)	2.5	6.1	13	8.8	2.7	6.0	–	3.2	18

	ITA	JAP	NTL	NOR	NZL	SWE	SWZ	UK	USA
1960	30.1	18.3	33.7	32.0	26.9	31.1	17.2	32.6	27.2
1965	34.3	18.6	38.7	34.2	–	36.0	19.7	36.4	27.2
1970	34.2	19.3	45.5	41.0	–	43.7	21.3	39.3	31.6
1975	43.2	27.3	55.9	46.6	–	49	28.7	46.9	34.6
1980	45.6	32.7	62.5	49.4	38.1	65.7	29.7	44.6	33.6
1985	50.8	32.7	59.7	45.6	–	64.3	31.0	46.2	36.4
1990	53.6	32.3	57.5	54.9	41.3	60.8	30.9	42.3	36.6
1996	52.5	36.7	49.4	48.5	41.1	62.9	35.3	42.2	36.6
2000	46.1	39	44.2	42.3	39.2	57.0	35.1	36.6	33.9
2005	48.1	38.4	44.8	42.3	39.1	54.0	35.3	44.1	36.2
2009	51.7	41.6	50.3	44.4	42.4	56.2	33.9	52.1	41.5
Net growth[a] (%)	72	127	49	39	58	81	97	60	53
Growth to peak (%)	78	127	85	72	58	111	105	60	53
Decline from peak (%)	3.5	–	20	19	–	14	4.0	–	–

Notes: AUL = Australia; AUS = Austria; BEL = Belgium; CAN = Canada; DEN = Denmark; FIN = Finland; GER = Germany; IRE = Ireland; ITA = Italy; JAP = Japan; NTL = Netherlands; NOR = Norway; NZL = New Zealand; SWE = Sweden; SWZ = Switzerland; UK = United Kingdom; USA = United States

[a] Net growth here refers to the percentage increase in the share of GDP devoted to government expenditure

Source: Calculated from OECD, *Economic Outlook*, (various years)

Figure 10.3 Government employment: as a share of total employment

Note: AUL = Australia; BEL = Belgium; CAN = Canada; DEN = Denmark; FIN = Finland; GER = Germany; ITA = Italy; JPN = Japan; NOR = Norway; SW = Sweden; UK = United Kingdom; US = United States
Source: Calculated from Huber et al. (2004)

It would certainly seem that globalization is compatible with a far higher level of state expenditure than the hyperglobalization thesis would seem to imply. This presents something of a paradox: a widely accepted conception of state crisis and retrenchment which seems to stand in some tension to the available empirical evidence. There are at least four potential solutions to this conundrum, each with rather different implications:

1. That the conventional wisdom on the subject is, indeed, correct, that 'big government' represents an ultimately unsustainable drain on competitiveness in an era of globalization, but that the institutional form of the state has become so entrenched and embedded as to make its reform and retrenchment an incremental process down which we are now only slowly embarking on. (Though perhaps the most plausible defence of the 'crisis of the nation state' thesis, this argument is rarely made in the existing literature. It might, however, draw inspiration from the work of historical institutionalists who

have consistently pointed to the inertial nature of complex institutions like the state; see, especially, Pierson 1994, 1996.)

2. That the conventional wisdom, though somewhat overstated, is basically correct, since the aggregate empirical evidence, in fact, masks the actual degree of retrenchment. Once we control for demographic and other 'welfare inflationary' pressures (such as higher levels of unemployment and the near exponential growth in health care costs since the 1960s), observed state expenditure is, in fact, substantially below that we would anticipate were consistent levels of generosity and coverage to have been maintained (Barr 1998; Esping-Andersen 1996a, 1996b; Rhodes 1996, 1997; Hay and Wincott forthcoming). We have not witnessed, nor should we expect to witness, a terminal crisis of the nation state, but we have already experienced a significant process of state retrenchment driven by globalization.

3. That whilst the aggregate evidence may, indeed, mask the real degree of retrenchment that has

occurred, the conventional wisdom is still wrong since there is no a priori reason to hold globalization responsible for such retrenchment and/or no consistent evidence of a historically unprecedented process of globalization in recent years (Hirst and Thompson 1999; Wilensky 2002).

4. That, in expecting globalization to precipitate a terminal crisis of the state, the conventional wisdom is simply inaccurate. Far from representing a drain on competitiveness, the state is the very condition of competitiveness in an ever more competitive international/global market (Weiss 1998). Globalization does not discriminate principally between states on their size but on their effectiveness in promoting and sustaining international competitiveness. Consequently, whilst we might expect to see convergence on best practice between states, we should not expect to see a withering of the state itself (Cerny 1995, 1997).

As this already serves to indicate, there are a number of ways of rehabilitating an albeit somewhat 'respecified' variant of the globalization thesis in the light of the above evidence. We can probably reject the notion that globalization has precipitated a terminal crisis of the nation state. Yet, the evidence considered thus far is by no means incompatible with the claim that globalization circumscribes the parameters of domestic political choice and is the principal determinant of the state's developmental trajectory. If we are to assess that claim, then we need to turn our attentions from the dependent variable (the extent of state retrenchment) to the independent variable (the process of globalization itself). Before doing so, however, it is important that we first consider one remaining aspect of the dependent variable—the question of convergence.

The dependent variable: convergence or dual convergence

Having originally placed their emphasis upon the crisis and transcendence of the nation state as a political unit responsible for regulating an economic

jurisdiction (Ohmae 1990, 1995), proponents of the hyperglobalization thesis now more frequently cast institutional and policy convergence as the dependent variable (Gray 1998; Parker 1998; Teeple 1995). Globalization remains the independent variable and is depicted as a stable equilibrium and as an entirely non-negotiable external economic imperative which exposes all economies within the global system to near identical pressures and challenges. In a highly competitive environment in which only the fittest survive, successful adaptation will rapidly be emulated, resulting in a powerful tendency to convergence.

As we have seen, the institutional sensitivity of the 'varieties of capitalism' approach appeals to a similar logic (and an identical independent variable), in predicting a rather different outcome—a more complex process of dual convergence around liberal and co-ordinated market economic models.

To what extent are these contending predictions borne out by the empirical evidence? Since we might consider convergence with respect to any number of potential dependent variables, this is a somewhat contentious issue that we cannot hope to do full justice to here. Space prevents an exhaustive survey. Nonetheless, we would once again expect the convergence or co-convergence theses to be most relevant to the most developed and most open economies in the world system. Moreover, given that welfare expenditure is most frequently described in the globalization literature as the kind of unnecessary indulgence which can no longer be afforded in an era of heightened competition amongst nations, we might expect to find the strongest evidence of convergence or co-convergence amongst European welfare states.

Yet, the evidence simply does not bear out that expectation (see also Hay 2003; Hay and Wincott forthcoming). Limits of space allow us only to consider social transfer payments (expressed as a percentage of GDP). These are, in essence, a measure of basic welfare expenditure. For ease of comparison, they are here standardized at 100 for 1960. Precisely because these are standardized measures, they are bound to show

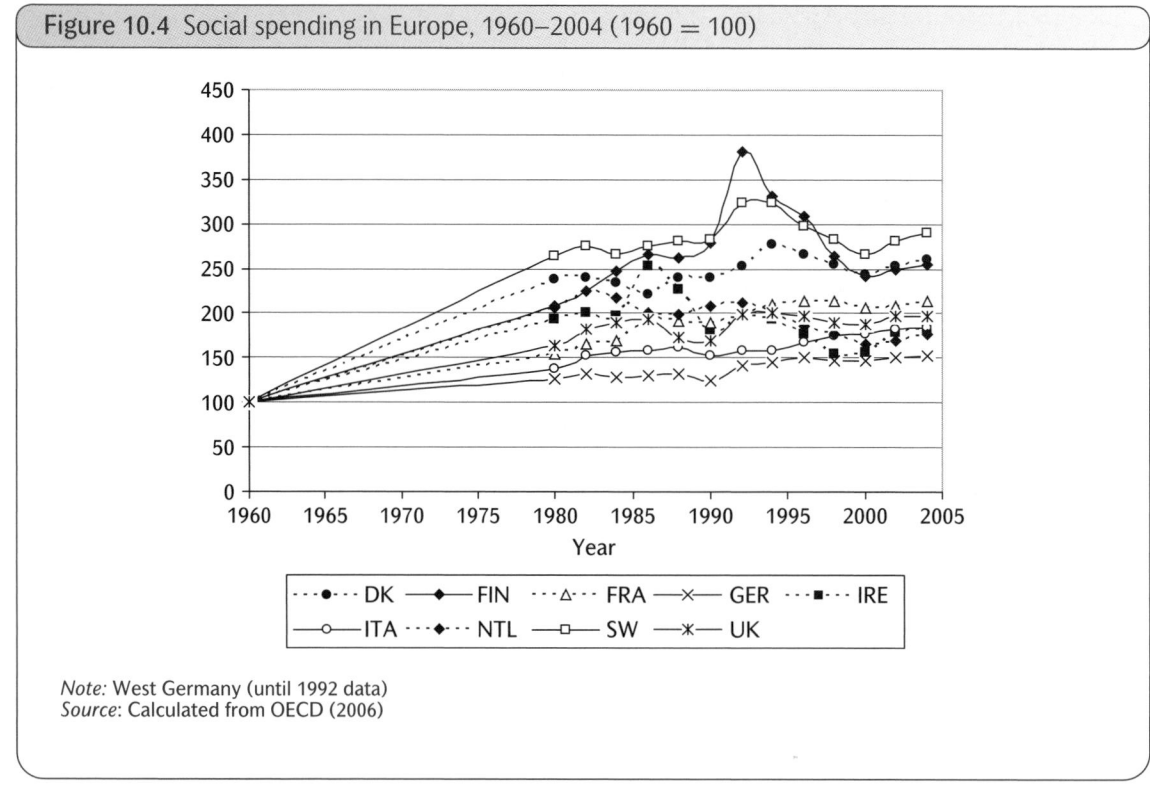

Figure 10.4 Social spending in Europe, 1960–2004 (1960 = 100)

Note: West Germany (until 1992 data)
Source: Calculated from OECD (2006)

an initial divergence. Yet, the convergence thesis would lead us to expect that initial divergence to be checked considerably by the 1980s and 1990s. It would predict, in short, an oval shaped distribution. And the co-convergence thesis would predict the emergence of two clusters—one grouped around Germany, the other grouped around the UK.

Neither prediction is borne out by the evidence (see Figure 10.4). Instead, consistent paths are mapped out from the 1960s which social models continue to follow for the most part to the present day. The wide initial variance in growth rates is sustained over time. This is not a story of systematic welfare retrenchment, nor is it a story of the diminishing distinctiveness of regime types—which seem, if anything, to be reinforced over time. Indeed, it is the Nordic welfare states that have grown the most. Under globalization, it

would seem, the most generous welfare states have thrived.

Second, we might consider the raw unstandardized data itself—i.e., social transfers expressed as a share of GDP. To aid the analysis, European welfare regimes are here grouped in terms of the conventional threefold classification. The *Nordic* regime type refers to Sweden, Denmark, Finland, and Norway; the *conservative* regime type refers to Germany, the Netherlands, Italy, and France; and the *liberal* regime type to the UK and Ireland.

Again, it seems, the evidence is in some tension with the predictions of the existing literature (see Figure 10.5). For, far from being associated with welfare retrenchment, the period of (supposedly) most intensive globalization has been associated with the consolidation—not the retrenchment—of the most generous welfare states the world has ever known. In recent years, social expenditure has been

Figure 10.5 Social spending of EU Member States, 1995–2007 (as percentage of GDP) by regime type

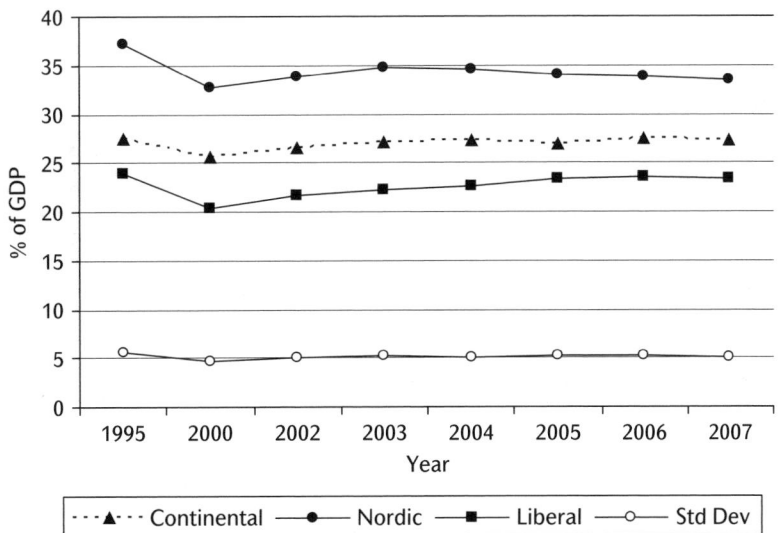

Source: European Commission (2007)

stable, with little or no evidence of convergence either between geographical clusters or between individual welfare states (the standard deviation of social expenditure for the EU25 remains almost constant over time). This is, above all, a picture of continuity rather than change. The Nordic regimes remain the most generous, the Continental European regimes the next most generous, with little to choose between the Anglo-liberal, the Southern European, and east central European in terms of total social expenditure. Much has been going on in the political economy of the EU25 during this time, but their levels of welfare state investment have remained remarkably constant.

Of course, we cannot infer from such evidence that globalization is not an agent of convergence or co-convergence, merely that the evidence considered here is not consistent with such a claim. It is also important to note that, even were this a valid inference to draw, it would be wrong to conclude that globalization has no impact on the nation state.

For, if globalization serves, as some have suggested, to increase the sensitivity of economic performance to the *quality* of public policy (see, for instance, Weiss 1998), then there is no particular reason to expect either a crisis of the state or convergence. Moreover, if, as is widely assumed, globalization generates common pressures for neo-liberalization and this has been more enthusiastically embraced in regimes already characterized by their liberalism, we might expect to see at least an initial period of divergence.

But, what evidence is there of a historically unprecedented phase of globalization capable of generating such pressures? We turn now to the independent variable.

The independent variable: globalization

As already noted, proponents of the hyperglobalization thesis have rarely felt the need to defend the intuitively plausible claim that we live in a fully integrated global economy. Casual and anecdotal appeals to supporting evidence largely exhausts the empirical content of this literature. Yet, in recent years, a more rigorous and systematically evidential assessment of patterns of economic integration has emerged. Its authors invariably draw a rather different set of conclusions. Thus, on the basis of an exhaustive (if not uncontroversial) assessment of the empirical evidence, sceptics such as Paul

Hirst and Grahame Thompson (1999) conclude that globalization is, in fact, a rather inaccurate description of existing patterns of international economic integration and cannot credibly explain the development of the state in recent years (for an important critical response to their work see Held et al. 1999).

The principal claims of this literature are summarized in Box 10.4 and discussed in more detail in the following pages.

Box 10.4 The Empirical Case against the Globalization Thesis

1. Although the period since the 1960s has seen the growing openness of national economies (such that imports plus exports are equivalent to a growing proportion of gross domestic product), there is still some considerable way to go before figures of prior to the First World War are likely to be exceeded (Bairoch 1996; Hirst and Thompson 1999).

2. There continues to be a positive and, indeed, strengthening relationship between public spending (as a share of gross domestic product) and economic openness (Cameron 1978; Katzenstein 1985; Garrett 1998b; Rodrik 1996, 1997).

3. There is no inverse relationship, as might be expected, between the volume of inward foreign direct investment and levels of corporate taxation, environmental and labour market regulations, generosity of welfare benefits or state expenditure as a share of gross domestic product (Cooke and Noble 1998; Dunning 1988; Traxler and Woitech 2000; Wilensky 2002).

4. Trade and international flows of capital (such as foreign direct investment) tend to be extremely concentrated within the core 'triad' (of Europe, North America, and Pacific Asia), providing evidence of regionalization and 'triadization', but hardly of globalization (Frankel 1997; Hirst and Thompson 1999; Petrella 1996).

5. The pace of economic integration is higher *within* regions (such as Europe, North America or Pacific Asia) than it is *between* regions, suggesting that regionalization rather than globalization is the overriding dynamic in the process of international economic integration (Frankel 1997; Hay 2004; Kleinknecht and ter Wengel 1998; Ravenhill, Chapter 6 in this volume).

6. Financial integration has failed to produce the anticipated convergence in interest rates which one would expect from a fully integrated global capital market (Hirst and Thompson 1999; Zevin 1992);

7. Financial integration has failed to produce the anticipated divergence between rates of domestic savings and rates of domestic investment which one would expect in a fully integrated global capital market—the so-called Feldstein-Horioka puzzle (Feldstein and Horioka 1980; see also Epstein 1996: 212–15; Watson 2001).

8. Though the liberalization of financial markets has certainly increased the speed, severity, and significance of investors' reactions to government policy, capital market participants appear far less discriminating or well-informed in their political risk assessment than is conventionally assumed (Mosley 2003; Swank 2002). Consequently, policy-makers may retain rather more autonomy than is widely accepted.

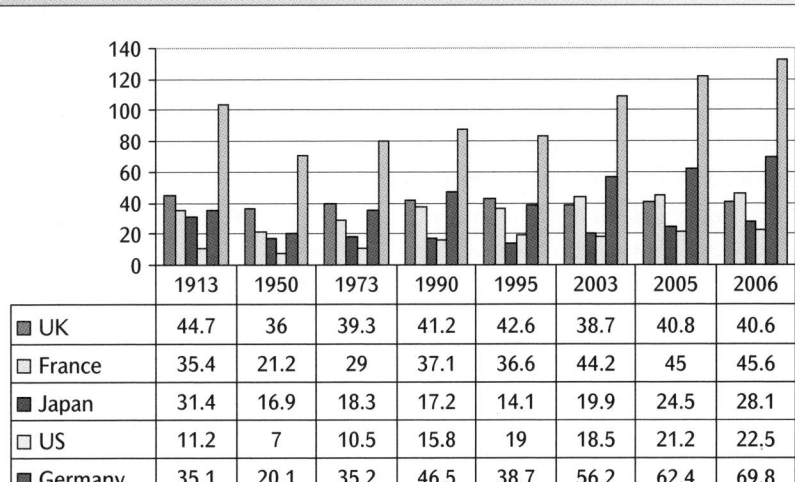

Figure 10.6 Ratio of merchandise trade to GDP at current prices

	1913	1950	1973	1990	1995	2003	2005	2006
■ UK	44.7	36	39.3	41.2	42.6	38.7	40.8	40.6
□ France	35.4	21.2	29	37.1	36.6	44.2	45	45.6
■ Japan	31.4	16.9	18.3	17.2	14.1	19.9	24.5	28.1
□ US	11.2	7	10.5	15.8	19	18.5	21.2	22.5
■ Germany	35.1	20.1	35.2	46.5	38.7	56.2	62.4	69.8

Source: Calculated from Maddison (1987: table A-23); Hirst, Thompson, and Bromley (2009: 34); World Bank (2002c, 2005a, 2009c); World Development Indicators Database available at http://data.worldbank.org/data-catalog

The comparative history of global economic integration

It is conventional, as already noted, to date the current era of globalization from the 1960s. And it is certainly the case that if we plot economic data from the early 1960s to the present day, we see clear evidence of an almost exponential increase in trade and capital flows (expressed as shares of global GDP). Yet, it would be wrong to infer from this the development of an unprecedented integration of the global economy, without first considering the history of economic integration.

If we do that, then what becomes very clear is the sensitivity of the conclusions drawn by proponents of the globalization thesis to their preferred start date. If we extend the time frame, choosing as a starting point the late nineteenth or early twentieth century, a rather different picture emerges. Consider, first, economic openness with respect to trade (the value of imports plus exports expressed as a share of GDP) (see Figure 10.6).

As Hirst and Thompson note,

" apart from the dramatic differences in the openness to trade of different economies demonstrated by these figures . . . the startling feature is that trade to GDP ratios were consistently higher in 1913 than they were in 1973 . . . Even in 1995 . . . the US was the only country that was considerably more open than it was in 1913.

"(1999: 27)

True, the composition of trade in, say, 1913, is likely to be remarkably different from that in 1973 or 1995, reflective in the case of the UK, the Netherlands, and France of a strongly colonial dimension. Nonetheless, in inviting a closer examination of the character and not just the quantity of trade, Hirst and Thompson provide a powerful challenge to the conventional literature. It should, however, be noted that, since 1995, levels of world economic integration have, indeed, surpassed those experienced during the latter half of the nineteenth century.

The data with respect to capital flows reveal a similar pattern. Between 1870 and 1914, international capital flows between the G7 economies averaged some 4 per cent of GDP, peaking at around 6 per cent in 1914. Between 1914 and 1970, they declined to 1.5 per cent of GDP. Since 1970, they have charted a consistent upward trajectory, rising to 3 per cent of GDP by the early 1990s. Yet, they still have a long way to go to reach the figures of the period prior to the First World War (Hirst and Thompson 1999: 28, figure 2.4; Bairoch 1996: 184; Lewis 1981; Turner 1981). In quantitative, if not perhaps in qualitative terms, the current period is not unprecedented or, indeed, unsurpassed.

In sum, then, whilst from the mid 1970s there has been an increasing trend towards financial and trade integration, economic openness was greater in the years before the First World War than in the 1990s.

'Stateness' and openness

Arguably more significant, and certainly less contested, are recent attempts to reproduce and update David Cameron's (1978) groundbreaking study of the covariance of economic openness and public expenditure. Such findings are particularly damaging to the globalization orthodoxy which predicts a strong inverse correlation between 'stateness' and openness—high levels of state expenditure (expressed as a proportion of GDP) *should* suppress the globalization of the domestic economy.

What Cameron demonstrated in a now famous paper published in the *American Political Science Review* in 1978, was a strong positive correlation between trade openness and social protection, funded through taxation. In other words, international economic integration seemed to go hand in hand with comprehensive social provision. Moreover, openness was also positively correlated with social democratic tenure, union power, and the degree of regulation of the labour market.

More damaging still to the orthodox globalization thesis has been more recent research in this vein by, amongst others, Peter Katzenstein (1985), Geoffrey Garrett (1998*b*) and Dani Rodrik (1996, 1997). What these authors demonstrate is that the

strength of the correlation between openness and government expenditure in OECD countries has only grown in subsequent decades. For proponents of the hyperglobalization thesis, this takes some explaining. Yet, for Rodrik, it is easily explained:

> What should we make of this? I will argue that the puzzle is solved by considering the importance of social insurance and the role of government in providing cover against external risk. Societies that expose themselves to greater amounts of external risk demand (and receive) a larger government role as shelter from the vicissitudes of global markets. In the context of the advanced industrial economies specifically, this translates into more generous social programmes. Hence the conclusion that the social welfare state is the flip side of the open economy!

(Rodrik 1997: 53)

Rodrik's is, of course, not the only possible explanation. Equally plausible, is that high levels of state expenditure are a result of success in international markets—a consequence rather than a condition of the globalization of the domestic economy. Yet, whichever way round it is, economic openness would seem far more compatible with state expenditure than is conventionally assumed.

The determinants of inward foreign direct investment

As we saw in an earlier section, orthodox accounts of globalization tend to make a series of clear and more or less plausible assumptions about the preferences and interests of mobile investors. Such assumptions, as was shown, are directly responsible for the influential thesis that states enhance their locational competitiveness to foreign direct investors by offering targeted investment incentives, eliminating labour market rigidities, reducing the burden of corporate taxation, and ensuring that environmental regulations are not overly restrictive. Alter the assumptions, and a rather different set of inferences (and consequent policy implications) follow.

Recent scholarship, which examines the *revealed* preferences of foreign direct investors as exhibited in actual investment decisions (rather than making a priori assumptions about such preferences), challenges the globalization orthodoxy in important respects. Particularly notable here, is the work of Cooke and Noble on the geographical distribution of foreign direct investment from the US (1998). This work contains a number of significant findings, each troubling to proponents of the hyperglobalization thesis:

1. It is direct market access and/or proximity to market that is the single greatest determinant of investment location. Inward direct investors value, above all else, geographical proximity to a substantial and affluent market. Consequently, the greatest single predictor of the volume of inward investment is total income within a 1,000-kilometre radius of the investment site.

2. Once access and proximity to market are controlled for, educational attainment/skill level is the most critical factor in determining the attractiveness of an industrial relations regime. Yet, the effect is complex and not as anticipated. As Cooke and Noble note, 'with respect to investments in low-skill-low-wage countries, the evidence indicates that US multinational corporations have sought to match lower work-force education with the limited labour skill requirements of operations that get located in low-skill-low-wage countries . . . [A]cross low-wage-low-skill countries US multinationals invest more in locations with the lowest levels of education' (1998: 596). This much is consistent with the hyperglobalization thesis. Yet, 'in contrast, it appears that, in matching the high labour skills requirements of operations located in high-skill-high-wage countries, US multinationals invest more in countries with both higher average education levels and higher hourly compensation costs' (1998: 596). This reveals a globally segmented market for inward investment, in which it is only developing countries that are compelled

to compete in terms of labour costs. Investors, it would seem, are perfectly prepared to pay the price of the highly trained and appropriately skilled workforce that (some) developed economies are capable of providing.

3. Moreover, and in seeming confirmation of this, it is not just the quantity (duration or level of attainment) of education that is important. Though it is difficult to gauge empirically, the evidence strongly supports the thesis that it is the *quality* and not the *cost* of skilled labour that is the key determinant of investment behaviour. Again, it would seem, cost (direct or indirect) is no impediment to investment if the perceived return provides adequate compensation for that cost. Thus, skill and productivity differences between economies make a significant and additional difference in attracting inward investment. Comparing the UK and Germany, Cooke and Noble explain, 'both have comparable average years of education . . . but substantially different average hourly compensation costs . . . Germany's unmeasured skill base has garnered about $2.3 billion more in US FDI per industry than has the UK's unmeasured skill base . . . high-skill-high-wage countries that further enhance skill levels can attract significant additional US foreign direct investment' (1998: 602).

4. The conclusion is clear, 'countries need not encourage . . . wage restraint, since high hourly compensation costs do not reduce . . . foreign direct investment, provided these costs are matched by higher skills and productivity' (1998: 602).

This, and other evidence like it (see, for instance, Dunning 1988; Traxler and Woitech 2000; Swank 2002; Wilensky 2002), seriously challenge both the assumptions on which the hyperglobalization thesis is predicated and the predictions it makes about exit from highly regulated labour market regimes with generous welfare states funded out of taxation receipts.

Globalization or 'triadization'

In the highly contentious political economy of globalization, perhaps no issue is more controversial than the geographical character of the process of international economic integration that we have witnessed since the 1960s. It is, in particular, the challenge posed to the conventional wisdom by the recent work of arch globalization sceptics, Paul Hirst and Grahame Thompson (1996, 1999), that has provided the central focus of attention and controversy (see also Allen and Thompson 1997; Petrella 1996: 77–81; and, for a flavour of the critical responses, Held and McGrew 2002: 38–57; Perraton et al. 1997).

Hirst and Thompson, along with a growing crescendo of 'sceptics', have questioned the extent to which the term globalization accurately characterizes both the pattern of economic integration within the international political economy today or the trajectory of relations of economic integration and interdependence since the 1960s. Rather than a process of globalization, they suggest, a process of 'triadization' is and has been underway (1996: 2, 63–7). By triadization, they refer to the selective and uneven process of deepening economic integration between the 'triad' economies; and by the 'triad' economies they refer to North America, South East Asia, and Europe. In short, some economies are more globalized than others and this must ultimately lead us to challenge the appropriateness of the appellation 'globalization'. For a significant and rising proportion of international economic activity is conducted within and between the triad economies. This is true of trade, foreign direct investment, and finance. For Hirst and Thompson, then, the developmental path of the international economy is far more accurately characterized by pointing to the effects of two separate processes:

1. A more general process of intra-regional economic integration or 'regionalisation' (discussed in more detail presently).
2. A more specific process of inter-regional economic integration drawing the triad economies

into an ever denser web of complex interdependencies.

The appeal, and, indeed, much of the novelty, of Hirst and Thompson's work when first published was its reliance on a substantial body of empirical evidence. Until their contribution, the innumerable empirical assertions made in the literature on globalization were largely unsubstantiated or defended only in a loose and anecdotal sense. Indeed, Hirst and Thompson's iconoclastic claim was that such assertions simply could not be defended evidentially. In so doing, they pointed to the far from global character of flows of trade, investment, and finance. Space does not permit a detailed exploration of this evidence. Suffice it to say that, between 1991 and 1996, over 60 per cent of all flows of foreign direct investment were conducted within and between the triad economies and, in 1995, over 75 per cent of the accumulated stock of foreign direct investment was located within the same triad bloc (Hirst and Thompson 1999: 71; see also Brewer and Young 1998: 58–60). Between 1980 and 1991, the figures were almost identical (Hirst and Thompson 1996: 68). The triadic concentration in the accumulated stock of outward foreign direct investment is even more pronounced (see Figure 10.7). The more recent trends does, show a sizeable growth in inbound foreign direct investment destined for the less developed economies. Yet this is largely due to the opening up of the Chinese economy.

Moreover, in 1996, despite accounting for only 14.5 per cent of the world's population, these economies accounted for some two-thirds of global exports (Hirst and Thompson 1999: 73). This figure is only marginally lower than that for 1992 (70 per cent). Yet, it is significantly greater than that for either 1990 (64 per cent), 1980 (55 per cent), or 1970 (61 per cent) (Hirst and Thompson 1996: 69; Petrella 1996: 79). Finally, as Riccardo Petrella notes, 'during the 1980s, the triad accounted for around four-fifths of all international capital flows . . . [whilst] the developing countries' share fell from 25 per cent in the 1970s to 19 per cent' (1996: 77).

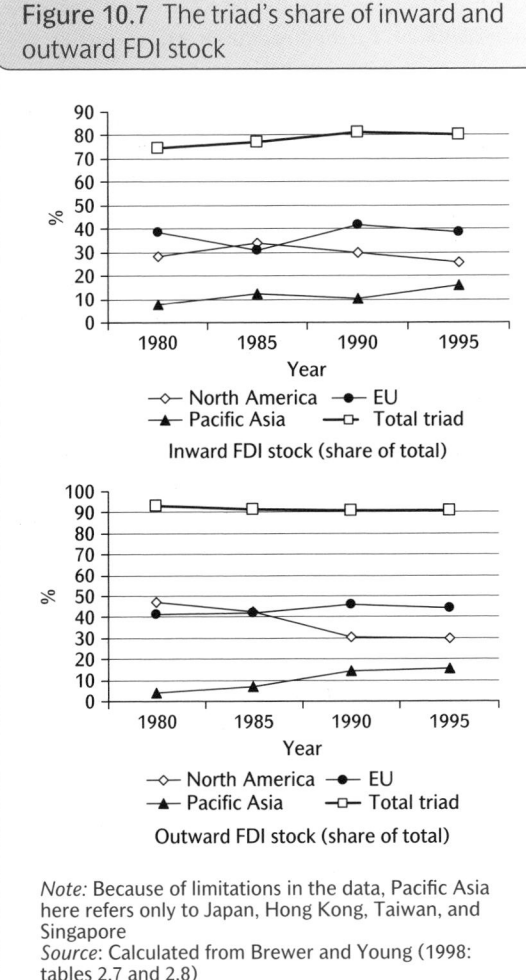

Figure 10.7 The triad's share of inward and outward FDI stock

Inward FDI stock (share of total)

- North America
- EU
- Pacific Asia
- Total triad

Outward FDI stock (share of total)

- North America
- EU
- Pacific Asia
- Total triad

Note: Because of limitations in the data, Pacific Asia here refers only to Japan, Hong Kong, Taiwan, and Singapore
Source: Calculated from Brewer and Young (1998: tables 2.7 and 2.8)

little more than economic openness (as witnessed by greater volumes of trade, investment, and financial flows as a share of global GDP), then globalization is certainly underway but it is unlikely to have the effects so frequently attributed to it. This is the challenge that the sceptics present — one, it would seem, that is largely borne out by the empirical evidence.

Globalization or regionalization?

Hirst and Thompson's (1996) emphasis, particularly in the first edition of *Globalization in Question*, is on the process of 'triadization' and hence on a series of inter-regional processes of economic integration linking North America, East Asia, and Europe. Yet, as indicated above, this rests on the prior identification of a more general tendency towards regionalization (within, and, indeed, beyond, the triad economies). In fact, in the second edition of *Globalization in Question*, the significance of triadization is somewhat downplayed as, on the basis of a reexamination and updating of the available evidence, regionalization now emerges as the pervasive tendency within the international economy (Hirst and Thompson 1999: esp. 99–103). Here, again, Hirst and Thompson's work provides a powerful statement of a developing consensus amongst sceptical voices.

Yet, it is the work of Jeffrey Frankel that is perhaps the most comprehensive on the question of regionalization (see, especially, Frankel 1997, 1998). On the basis of a detailed examination of the empirical record, he demonstrates that, with respect to trade, any tendency to globalization or even *inter*-regional economic integration has been swamped by the rapid growth in *intra*-regional integration. Due largely to the growth of preferential trading arrangements at the regional level, intra-regional trade accounts for an ever-growing share of global economic activity, suggesting once again that globalization is in fact an increasingly inaccurate characterization of both the process of economic integration and the resulting pattern of economic interdependencies (see Figure 10.8).

How much damage this does to the globalization thesis depends, to a considerable extent, on what one takes that thesis to be. Indeed, arguably the debate is largely semantic (see also Scholte 2000: 14–20). Sceptics such as Hirst and Thompson and Petrella adopt a rather more exacting definition of globalization, it seems, than many of the hyperglobalization theorists. If, to count as evidence of globalization, processes have to be either genuinely global in scope or operative in unleashing such dynamics, then globalization poorly characterizes the condition and trajectory of the international economy. If, on the other hand, globalization means

Figure 10.8 Intra-regional trade as a proportion of total trade

Note: EU-12 = Belgium (and Luxembourg), Denmark, France, Germany, Greece, Ireland, Italy, Netherlands, Portugal, Spain, and United Kingdom; NAFTA = US, Canada, and Mexico; East Asia = ASEAN-6 (Brunei, Indonesia, Malaysia, Philippines, Singapore, and Thailand), plus China, Hong Kong, Japan, South Korea, and Taiwan; MERCOSUR = Argentina, Brazil, Paraguay, and Uruguay; APEC = East Asia-11, plus NAFTA-3, plus Australia, Chile, New Zealand, and Papua New Guinea; Andean Community = Bolivia, Columbia, Ecuador, Peru, and Venezuela
Source: Calculated from Frankel (1997: 22–4)

exception of East Asia, the effect is one of trendless fluctuation or further regionalization, rather than globalization.

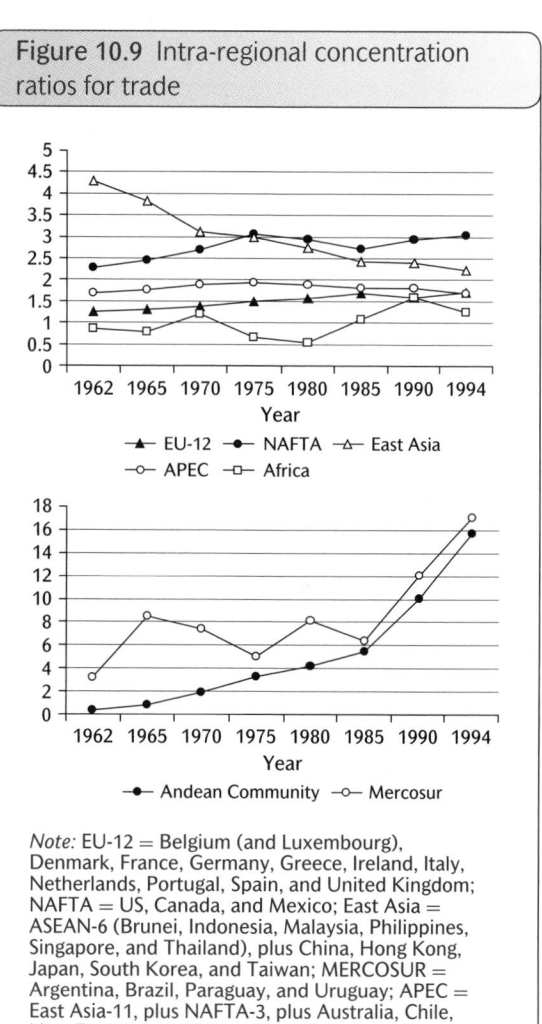

Figure 10.9 Intra-regional concentration ratios for trade

Note: EU-12 = Belgium (and Luxembourg), Denmark, France, Germany, Greece, Ireland, Italy, Netherlands, Portugal, Spain, and United Kingdom; NAFTA = US, Canada, and Mexico; East Asia = ASEAN-6 (Brunei, Indonesia, Malaysia, Philippines, Singapore, and Thailand), plus China, Hong Kong, Japan, South Korea, and Taiwan; MERCOSUR = Argentina, Brazil, Paraguay, and Uruguay; APEC = East Asia-11, plus NAFTA-3, plus Australia, Chile, New Zealand, and Papua New Guinea; Andean Community = Bolivia, Columbia, Ecuador, Peru, and Venezuela.
Source: Calculated from Frankel (1997: table 2.3)

Such findings have been replicated for foreign direct investment flows to and from Europe (Hay 2004; Kleinknecht and ter Wengel 1998). Whilst this provides strong evidence of regionalization, it does not exhaust the case against the globalization thesis. Arguably, rather more discriminating empirically is data on the regional concentration of trade. As Frankel explains, 'to obtain a useable measure of regional concentration, we need to adjust the intraregional trade share by a measure of each group's importance in world trade' (1997: 25–6). This is achieved by dividing each regional grouping's trade share (as shown in Figure 10.8) by that region's share of total world trade. The resulting index of intra-regional concentration, again, reveals a pervasive regionalization tendency. For, in a globalizing world, we would expect the value of such intra-regional concentration ratios to fall consistently over time. As Figure 10.9 makes very clear, with the sole

Finally, so-called gravity models have been used to examine the sensitivity of trade and, indeed, foreign direct investment to distance for a number of European countries (Hay 2003, 2004; see

Box 10.5 for further details). A gravity model predicts that trade (and/or foreign direct investment) will decay exponentially with distance. In an era of globalization, in which transportation costs have been diminished and barriers to trade eliminated, we would expect to see the decreasing sensitivity of trade (and investment) to distance. Accordingly, the gravity model should become ever less effective in predicting patterns of trade (and investment). Yet, unremarkably perhaps given the evidence discussed above, far from showing a consistent pattern of globalization since the 1960s, the gravity model becomes an ever better fit to the data.

This demonstrates, once again, a pervasive regionalization tendency in which trade and investment become more not less sensitive to geographical distance. European economies, it would seem, have experienced a consistent and ongoing process of deglobalization since the 1960s as the process of European economic integration has accelerated. As Figure 10.9 would suggest, similar tendencies would appear to be underway in many, if perhaps not all, regions within the international economy. As this suggests, globalization is a tendency that has, in the majority of cases, been swamped in recent decades by a regionalizing counter-tendency.

Box 10.5 Gravity Models: The Sensitivity of Trade to Distance

Within a gravity model, trade is assumed to be associated positively with the 'size' of the economies between which it is transacted (usually expressed in terms of their respective shares of global GDP) and to be associated negatively with the distance between them. Geographically proximate countries will trade more with one another than those separated by great distances, just as those economies which account for a substantial share of global GDP will tend to trade more with one another than smaller economies.

The basic model can be written as an equation of the following form:

$$\log T_{ij} = a + b \log(GDP_i/P_i) + c \log(GDP_j/P_j) - d \log(D_{ij}) + \ldots.$$

where T_{ij} is the volume of trade between countries i and j; GDP_j/P_j is the GDP per capita of country j; D_{ij} is the distance between country i and j.

Capital market integration and interest rate convergence

Thus far, we have examined evidence principally relating to trade and foreign direct investment and it is important that we now turn our attention to the degree of integration (or globalization) of financial markets. It is often assumed that, even if the case against the globalization thesis is credible with respect to trade and foreign direct investment (for the reasons discussed above), the thesis is rather more robust with respect to financial markets and, moreover, that the effects of financial market integration on the autonomy of the nation state are most pronounced (see, for instance, Cerny 1995,

1997). Yet, as we shall see, recent evidence casts some doubt on this claim, too.

The first surprising piece of empirical evidence for proponents of the globalization thesis, is the observed failure of interest rates to converge. In a fully integrated capital market, a common international rate of interest on short-term and long-term loans would emerge almost instantaneously, for fairly obvious reasons. All things being equal, borrowers will seek out the lowest rate of interest available to them, just as investors will seek the highest rate of return (and, hence, interest) on their investments.

Yet, as numerous commentators have noted, and despite some controversy about which precise index to use and what specific inferences to draw from such evidence, interest rate differentials persist and show little sign of being eroded (Bayoumi and Rose 1993; Frankel 1991; Kasman and Pigott 1988; Osler 1991; and for a review, Simmons 1999: 57–61). Moreover, as Robert Zevin has argued, 'every available descriptor of financial markets in the late nineteenth and early twentieth century suggests that they were more fully integrated than they were before or have been since' (1992: 51–2).

This is an important observation which again draws our attention to the less than totally unprecedented character of the contemporary phase of economic integration. This is relatively easily accounted for. Quite simply, capital market integration occurred (to the extent that it did occur) far earlier than most have assumed. This is why there is no clear contemporary evidence of (further) interest rate convergence. As Hirst and Thompson suggest, 'the coming of the electronic telegraph system after 1870 in effect established more or less instantaneous information communications between all the major international financial and business centres' (1999: 37–8). The shift in the 1870s from ships to telegraph was far more significant than that from telegraph to telematics in the 1970s.

Savings and investment correlations: the 'Feldstein–Horioka' puzzle

Interest rate convergence is not the only index of financial globalization. In a perfectly integrated capital market, we would expect to see a clear divergence of domestic savings and investment rates. In a system of closed and bounded national economies, these should correlate absolutely (or very closely). In a genuinely open economy (a perfectly integrated capital market), we would expect the correlation to break down as investors become genuinely global, sourcing their investments from around the world. Indeed, we would expect the correlation to fall to zero (Feldstein and Horioka 1980; see also Bayoumi 1997: 17–19). Consequently, a persistent correlation between domestic savings

and investment levels provides strong evidence of a lack of integration of capital markets.

What do we observe? The evidence is again relatively unambiguous. As a large number of commentators have noted, national savings–investment correlations show no consistent pattern of decline in the 1980s and 1990s (Bayoumi 1990; Epstein 1996; Feldstein 1983; Feldstein and Bacchetta 1991; Feldstein and Horioka 1980; Tesar 1991). As Hirst and Thompson suggest, this 'testifies to the continued robust relative autonomy of financial systems' (1999: 38). Indeed, the 'savings retention coefficient' (the proportion of incremental savings invested domestically) remains at 67 per cent for the period 1991–5 (Obstfeld 1993).

This, again, is an important finding and one that continues to trouble international macroeconomists, for whom it remains something of a paradox even after more than two decades. The 'Feldstein–Horioka puzzle', as it has come to be known, has given rise to an extensive literature and considerable controversy (for reviews of which see Bayoumi 1997: 30–53; Obstfeld and Rogoff 1996: 161–4; Rødseth 2000: 163–4). Unremarkably, a series of challenges have been mounted to the notion that it provides clear evidence of the lack of integration of capital markets. Yet, as we shall see, none of these caveats is ultimately devastating:

1. As a number of commentators have noted, aggregate indices of national investment do not discriminate between public and private investment (see, for instance, Bayoumi 1990). Savings–investment correlations might, then, mask a decrease in the savings–investment correlation for private investors. This is certainly accurate, yet the effect is likely to be relatively small; the essential paradox remains.

2. If, as Hirst and Thompson conjecture, there was 'no significant difference between the return on financial investment' from one economy to the next, 'then we might not expect a large redistribution of capital relative to savings' (1999: 40). Consequently, domestic savings–investment relations might prove persistent. Under such

conditions, we would be wrong to infer low levels of capital market integration. Yet, though plausible, the empirical evidence does not bear this out. For, although there was, indeed, some convergence in returns on investment in the 1970s between the developed economies, this has given way to subsequent divergence (Hirst and Thompson 1999: 41). Again, the paradox remains.

3. In growing desperation, perhaps, international macroeconomists have increasingly turned to hypothetical solutions to the paradox. If, they suggest, the global economy had experienced a productivity shock, we would expect profitability to increase. This would result, in turn, in an increased propensity for both savings and investment. Under such conditions, the anticipated correlation between savings and investment would be spurious, at least in terms of the degree of capital market integration—as it would be generated in the absence of domestic investment being sourced from domestic savings (Ghosh 1995; Rødseth 2000: 164). This hypothetical solution to the paradox is both plausible and ingenious, but it is significantly compromised by the fact that such productivity shocks are both relatively rare and, generally, short-term in nature. The persistent and seemingly long-term character of domestic savings–investment correlations (first observed in 1980) would suggest that a productivity shock is simply not responsible for the Feldstein–Horioka paradox.

4. Finally, and rather more plausibly, it has been suggested that economists have tended to draw the wrong (or, at least, an exaggerated) inference from the persistence of domestic savings–investment correlations. For, whilst in a perfectly integrated textbook capital market we might expect such correlations to tend to zero, in a real-world capital market, even a highly integrated one, we would expect some correlation to persist (Watson 2001). Real markets are not perfectly integrated, nor are they likely to become so. Whether this provides the elusive

'solution' to the 'Feldstein–Horioka puzzle' or merely demonstrates further the dubious nature of the premises which continue to inform influential understandings of globalization (as reflected in unrealistic expectations about the degree of capital mobility we should expect to see) is a moot point.

The expressed and exhibited preferences of financial market actors

A persistent theme of this chapter has been the disparity between the a priori theoretical assumptions made in the conventional literature about the preferences of economic actors (principally investors) and the *actual* preferences of such actors (as revealed in their conduct). We have seen how the behaviour of foreign direct investors is rather different in 'reality' from that attributed to them in much of the existing literature. The same is equally true of financial investors, however more intuitively plausible the conventional assumptions may seem for such actors.

Here, the recent work of Layna Mosley (2003) is especially notable. Mosley's work is unique in the existing literature in its attempt to gauge empirically both the *expressed preferences* of market participants through an extensive series of interviews with fund managers, and the *revealed preferences* of market participants through a detailed statistical analysis of their investment decisions. Her conclusions are extremely important and do some considerable damage to the conventional wisdom.

Though the liberalization of financial markets has certainly increased the speed, severity, and significance of investors' reactions to government policy, capital market participants appear far less discriminating or well informed in their political risk assessment than is conventionally assumed. For advanced capitalist democracies, the range of government policies considered by market participants in making investment decisions is, in fact, extremely limited. As Mosley explains,

> Governments are pressured strongly to satisfy financial market preferences in terms of overall inflation and government budget deficit levels but retain domestic policymaking latitude in other areas. The means by which governments achieve macropolicy outcomes, and the nature of government policies in other areas, do not concern financial market participants . . . [G]overnments retain a significant amount of policy autonomy and political accountability. If, for domestic reasons, they prefer to retain traditional social democratic policies, for instance, they are quite able to do so.

(Mosley 2003: 305)

This is a most important finding, all the more so given the methodological rigour of the study from which it derives. It would seem to support Duane Swank's own important findings. On the basis of a detailed statistic analysis, he demonstrates the existence of a complex interaction effect between welfare state expenditure, on the one hand, and international capital mobility, on the other. When budgets are in balance, capital market liberalization produces a positive effect on welfare effort; when budgets are moderately in deficit there is no effect; and when budget deficits exceed 10 per cent of GDP, the effect becomes negative. As Swank concludes, contrary to the prevailing consensus,

> rises in international capital openness, or exposure to international capital markets, do not exert significant downward pressure on the welfare state at moderate levels of budget imbalance [and] when budget deficits don't exist, some expansion of social protection is possible even in the context of international capital mobility'.

(2002: 94)

It would seem that the constraints imposed by financial market integration on domestic political autonomy, certainly in the advanced capitalist economies, have been grossly exaggerated. Yet, the picture is not an undifferentiated one. For developing countries, as Mosley again demonstrates in considerable detail, financial market participants are rather more exacting in the demands they make of government policy and correspondingly more severe in the constraints they impose.

Key points

- There is little evidence of systematic state retrenchment at the hands of globalization.
- There is little evidence of systematic convergence or dual convergence between models or varieties of capitalism under conditions of globalization.
- The impact of globalization of the nation state suggested in the hyperglobalization thesis has been challenged empirically by a number of authors. They

have pointed to the less than unprecedented degree of integration of the global economy today, the positive correlation between openness and public spending, the factors which attract foreign direct investors, the regional and triadic character of international trade and investment, the far from fully integrated character of financial markets, and the investment behaviour of financial market actors.

Conclusions

What are we to make of this? Well, the overall picture that emerges is rather more complex than that we began with. Whilst the economic processes usually labelled 'globalization' have led to a greater degree of economic integration than at any point in the post-war period, current levels of economic interdependence are neither unprecedented historically nor perhaps as genuinely 'global' as is invariably assumed.

The impact of such processes on the capacity, autonomy, and sovereignty of the state is also complex. For, whilst there is certainly some evidence of state retrenchment in recent years, especially once one controls for the higher demands placed upon welfare states by demographic change and higher rates of unemployment, there would seem to be no clear evidence that globalization is the driver of this retrenchment. Indeed, the evidence reviewed in the previous section would strongly suggest that the constraints imposed upon domestic political autonomy by heightened levels of economic integration (with respect to trade, foreign direct investment, or finance) have been grossly exaggerated. Yet, this does not mean that globalization has had no impact on the nation state — merely, that we need to be extremely cautious in attributing state retrenchment today to globalization.

Rather more plausible, and sadly overlooked in much of the existing literature, is the impact of *ideas* about globalization. If it is conceded that policy-makers increasingly view the world they face through a series of assumptions about globalization, then their conduct in office is likely to be shaped significantly by those assumptions. Arguably, then, the idea of globalization may be more influential in shaping the developmental trajectory of the nation state today than the *reality* of globalization (see Box 10.6).

This raises an important point about democratic legitimacy and accountability today. For, it is all very well to argue that state autonomy remains essentially intact in an era of globalization.

But, if such autonomy is perceived to have been eroded by all credible candidates for political office, then such autonomy is purely hypothetical. Whilst globalization may not have narrowed the field of democratic choice itself, the idea of globalization may well have done so — as parties across the political spectrum converge on a set of prudent economic and social policies designed to appease footloose multinational investors. Arguably, this has much to do with the widespread contemporary disaffection with liberal democratic regimes (see, for instance, Pharr and Putnam 2000; Hay 2007). Democracy is no less a casualty in such a scenario. This makes the public scrutiny of influential assumptions and ideas about globalization a most urgent political priority. It establishes, once again, the phenomenal importance of the ongoing controversy which surrounds the question of globalization's impact on the state.

One final point might also be noted. Whilst there is, in fact, little evidence for the thesis that the nation state's capacity and autonomy has been significantly eroded by virtue of globalization, it is, nonetheless, the case that globalization poses a series of problems for the nation state which it has never had the capacity to deal with. We have seen, and are likely to continue to see, a proliferation of interlinked and genuinely global political, economic, and, above all, environmental problems requiring, for their resolution, effective institutions of global governance. This final point is perhaps the most troubling of all. It is certainly tempting to dismiss globalization as a myth or as a process with minimal impact upon the historical capacities of the state. Yet, the problem of the lack of the political capacity to deal with urgent global problems in an effective and democratic way remains. The challenges we face are essentially twofold:

Box 10.6 The Role of Ideas about Globalization: Tax Competition between States

Consider tax competition between states. The hyperglobalization thesis suggests that in a globalized context characterized by the heightened mobility of capital, vicious competition between states will serve to drive down the level of corporate taxation. Accordingly, any failure on the part of a state to render its corporate taxation levels competitive in comparative terms, through tax cuts, will result in a punitive depreciation in net revenue as capital exercises its mobility to exit. If governments believe the thesis to be true, or find it to their advantage to present it as true, they will act in a manner consistent with its predictions, thereby contributing to an aggregate depreciation in corporate taxation—whether they are right to do so or not.

To elaborate, were we to envisage a (hypothetical) scenario in which the hyperglobalization thesis were accurate, the free mobility of capital would, indeed, serve to establish tax competition between fiscal authorities seeking to retain existing investment levels whilst enticing mobile foreign direct investors to relocate (see Figure 10.10). The price of any attempt to buck the trend is immediate capital flight with consequent effects on budget revenue. In such a scenario, any rational administration aware (or assuming itself to be aware) of the mobility of capital will cut corporate taxes with the effect that no exit will be observed (Scenario 1). Any administration foolish enough to discount or test the mobility of capital by retaining high levels of corporate taxation will be rudely awakened from its state of blissful ignorance or stubborn scepticism by a rapid exodus of capital (Scenario 2). In a world of perfect capital mobility, then, the learning curve is likely to prove very steep, indeed.

Were we to assume instead that we inhabit a world in which the mobility of capital is much exaggerated and in which capital has a clear vested interest in threatening exit, the scenario unfolds rather differently. Here, fiscal authorities lulled into accepting the hyperglobalization thesis by the (ultimately hollow) exit threats of capital will cut rates of corporate tax, (falsely) attributing the lack of capital flight to their competitive taxation regime (Scenario 3). Yet, were they to resist this logic by calling capital's bluff, they might retain substantial taxation

Figure 10.10 The idea of globalization

Hyperglobalization thesis true:
high taxation leads to
capital flight

Does the government believe the hyperglobalization thesis (or seek advantage from presenting it as true)?

Y: corporate tax cuts; no exit (Scenario 1)

N: no corporate tax cuts; exit (Scenario 2)

Hyperglobalization thesis false:
high taxation leads to the
hollow threat of
capital flight

Does the government believe the hyperglobalization thesis (or seek advantage from presenting it as true)?

Y: corporate tax cuts; no exit (Scenario 3)

N: no corporate tax cuts; no exit (Scenario 4)

receipts without fear of capital flight (Scenario 4). The crucial point, however, is that whilst politicians believe the hyperglobalization thesis—and act upon it—we cannot differentiate between Scenario 1 (in which the thesis is true) and Scenario 3 (in which it is false). Though in Scenario 1, globalization is a genuine constraint on political autonomy and in Scenario 3 it is merely a social construction, the outcomes are the same. As this suggests, it is ideas about globalization rather than globalization per se that affects political and economic outcomes. This makes the role of international institutions in the dissemination of ideas about globalization especially significant.

Source: adapted from Hay (2002*b*: 202–4)

1. To find ways of designing effective and democratic institutions of global governance capable of commanding political support and legitimacy.
2. To find ways of passing responsibility and, indeed, sovereignty from a system of nation states that still provides the focus of political identification and citizenship to such institutions.

At the point at which we prove ourselves capable of responding to both of these challenges, we might legitimately begin to speak of a transcendence (if not perhaps a crisis) of the nation state. But that point is a very, very long way off.

? Questions

1. Is there, or has there been, a crisis of the nation state?
2. What is meant by the globalization of politics and has it occurred?
3. What mechanisms can be pointed to suggesting a clear link between globalization and state retrenchment?
4. What are the key assumptions of the hyperglobalization thesis? Are they plausible?
5. Is globalization an agent of convergence, dual convergence, divergence, or continued diversity?
6. How does the model of the 'tragedy of the commons' illuminate the problem of global governance?
7. Assess the evidence for state retrenchment.
8. What impact has globalization had on the development of the nation-state?
9. Are the constraints on the autonomy and capacity of the nation state arising from globalization largely real or imagined?

→ Further reading

 Cerny, P. G. (1997), 'Paradoxes of the Competition State: The Dynamics of Political Globalization', *Government and Opposition*, 32/2: 251–74. The clearest exposition of a highly influential 'competition state' thesis.

■ Garrett, G. (2000*b*), 'Shrinking States? Globalization and National Autonomy', in N. Woods (ed.) *The Political Economy of Globalization* (Basingstoke: Palgrave). A clear and comprehensive survey of the existing literature and supporting evidence by an influential commentator.

■ Hirst, P., and Thompson, G. (1999), *Globalization in Question*, 2nd edn (Cambridge: Polity Press). The definitive statement of the case against the globalization orthodoxy.

■ Jessop, B. (2002), *The Future of the Capitalist State* (Cambridge: Polity Press). The product of almost two decades of scholarship, this is perhaps the single most important work on the condition of the state today. Though dense and at times difficult, it rewards close reading.

■ Mosley, L. (2003), *Global Capital and National Governments* (Cambridge: Cambridge University Press). An exceptionally important recent addition to the existing literature, and a comprehensive reappraisal of the conventional wisdom about the domestic political constraints issuing from financial markets.

■ Ohmae, K. (1995), *The End of the Nation State: The Rise of Regional Economies* (New York: Free Press). Though widely discredited, still the core exponent and defender of the hyperglobalization thesis.

■ Weiss, L. (1998), *The Myth of the Powerless State: Governing the Economy in a Global Era* (Cambridge: Polity Press). A clear and accessible defence of the continued centrality and importance of the nation state in an era of globalization.

 Web links

Useful searchable data sources can be found at:

■ http://data.worldbank.org/data-catalog

■ http://www.esds.ac.uk/international/support/user_guides/oecd/mg.asp

■ http://epp.eurostat.ec.europa.eu/portal/page/portal/eurostat/home/

 Online resource centre

For additional material and resources, please visit the Online Resource Centre at:
www.oxfordtextbooks.co.uk/ravenhill3e/

The Globalization of Production

11

Eric Thun

Reader's guide

Although companies have been investing abroad for centuries, the current era of globalization has created an unprecedented range of possibilities for global firms to reorganize and relocate their activities. This chapter analyses how advances in transportation and technology allow a firm to divide up a global value chain—the sequence of activities that lead to the production of a particular good or service—and how these decisions create new opportunities and challenges both for companies and the societies within which they operate. The first section of the chapter reviews the rise of global production and the forces that have led to dramatic increases in foreign direct investment (FDI) and outsourcing. The central questions for any firm involved in global production involve how to govern the value chain and where to locate different activities. The second section provides a framework for understanding these issues and the implications of the various choices. The third section applies these concepts to the case of East Asia.

Introduction

Multinational corporations (MNCs) are the most public face of globalization. Defined as firms that have operations in two or more countries, MNCs are a source of hope and promise to those who seek to harness the power of economic globalization for purposes of development, and a source of fear and opposition to those who view globalization as a threat to national sovereignty. MNCs are pervasive. In 2008, there were some 82,000 parent companies, with over 810,000 affiliates. These affiliates employed approximately 77 million people—more than twice the labour force of Germany—and accounted for one-third of total world exports of goods and service in 2008 (UNCTAD 2009b: 17). MNCs are also very tangible. They are not anonymous buyers and sellers engaged in arm's-length trade. Through FDI, they own assets and employ people in foreign countries. They are the companies behind the most powerful global brands. To populations that are being buffeted by the invisible forces of globalization, MNCs serve as very visible symbols of forces they cannot control.

Foreign investment on the part of MNCs, however, is only the tip of the iceberg that is the globalization of production. Firms such as Nike and Gap do not own the foreign factories that make their products; they use contractors who work to their specifications. Nike has slightly more than 20,000 direct employees, but its products are manufactured by more than 500,000 workers in over 700 factories in 51 countries (Locke 2003: 6). Gap bought 1 billion units of clothing in 2004, from 700 suppliers, and these suppliers owned and operated 3,000 factories in 50 countries, but Gap does not own a single factory abroad. These firms control global value chains—the sequence of activities through which technology is combined with material and labour inputs, and then assembled, marketed, and distributed (Gereffi et al. 2005: 79)—and while they wield tremendous power, it is not the result of ownership arising from FDI. Similarly, electronic giants such as Apple, Dell, and Hewlett Packard rely on specialized manufacturing firms to make their products, and focus primarily on design, marketing, distribution, and service.

Global value chains are important determinants of who gets what, when, and how in the global economy. There are two sides to the global production coin. From the perspective of 'home' countries—where the headquarters of multinational firms are located—the key question is what will be left behind when production moves abroad. Because outward investment from the home economy of a multinational will potentially be moving jobs, technology, and profits beyond national borders, it creates fears of a 'hollowing out' effect. Will outward investment and outsourcing lead to an inexorable flow of jobs, technology, and profits to lower-cost countries? Will the competition for high value-added activities lead to a convergence of economic models? From the perspective of 'host' countries—the destinations of FDI and outsourcing—the question is whether they will be able to capture the high value-added activities, or be trapped into a dependent relationship with multinational firms in which they are limited to low value-added activities. Will the foreign firms contribute to the long-term development of the local economy, or will they inhibit the development of local firms? Will the foreign firms adhere to the social, political, and environmental standards of the local society, or will they behave in an imperialistic manner and/or engage in practices that would not be allowed in their home societies?

In both cases, the questions revolve around the distribution of resources, the bargaining leverage of the states that 'host' foreign investment, and the power of multinational firms to determine who gets which part of global production, and how this influences employment, the locus of knowledge and innovation, and the creation of profits in the world economy. This chapter will analyse how advances in transportation and technology have created new opportunities to divide up a value chain, how this creates new possibilities for global firms to reorganize and relocate the various activities that they engage in, and the opportunities and challenges these changes create both for home and host states and societies.

There is nothing new about foreign investment or international production. In the sixteenth century, chartered trading companies established foreign production facilities for much the same reasons as firms did centuries later — internalization within the firm was a means of economizing on frequent transactions that inherently had to occur in a particular location, whether in order to access specific raw materials or markets. The Dutch East India Company, for example, established a saltpetre plant in Bengal in 1641, a print works for textiles ten years later, and employed 4,000 silk spinners by 1717. In an era when the full cycle of activity (export, transport, and sale of goods from home to foreign markets, import, transport, and sale of goods from foreign to home markets) could take anywhere from eighteen to thirty months to complete, hierarchical co-ordination within the firm allowed a trading company to equate supply and demand more effectively (Carlos and Nicholas 1988: 399, 403, 407).

In the nineteenth century, the Industrial Revolution spurred demand for raw materials, and companies sought to own and manage their sources of raw materials in order to reduce risk. For manufacturing companies, the result was vertical investments upstream and downstream, and a hub-and-spoke model of international production: raw materials were imported from the periphery, manufacturing took place at home, and finished goods were then distributed globally. In response to rising protectionism in the early twentieth century, firms began to make horizontal investments abroad: manufacturing capabilities were duplicated in foreign markets that were increasingly sheltered behind tariff barriers (Palmisano 2006: 128). In the 1920s and 1930s, for example, American companies such as General Motors, Ford, Firestone, Nabisco, General Foods, Hoover, ITT, and Honeywell rapidly increased the numbers of their manufacturing facilities in Europe. These were multinationals in the form that would dominate the global economy for much of the twentieth century. Certain activities, such as research and development, were concentrated in their headquarters, but other capabilities were duplicated in operations around the world. These companies pursued a multi-market strategy.

Numbers and trends

International production is not new, but its magnitude and the degree of fragmentation in global value chains is new. To an unprecedented degree, firms are able to break up their value chains and locate each discrete activity according to competitive advantage rather than geographical convenience. How can we measure the growth of global production?

One relatively straightforward indicator is the rapid increase in FDI prior to the global economic crisis that began in 2008. Between 1982 and 2008, according to the United Nations Conference on Trade and Development (UNCTAD) *World Investment Report*, the value of FDI inflows (in current prices) increased from $59 billion to $1,697 billion (UNCTAD 2009b: 3). The ratio of world FDI inflows to global gross domestic capital formation (a measure of domestic investment), increased from 2 per cent in 1980 to 12.3 per cent in 2008 (UNCTAD 2000: xv–xvi, 2009b: 255). Two trends are important to note about these massive flows. First, they were highly concentrated. Developed economies received 59 per cent of inward FDI in 2005, for instance, and the top five of these economies received almost 50 per cent of global flows (UNCTAD 2006b: xvii, 4). The major sources of FDI were also frequently the major destinations.

Second, and a related point, mergers and acquisitions (M&As) between existing firms rather than greenfield (new) investment were the dominant form of foreign investment. Just as the development of technology, regulatory changes, and new modes of finance led to a wave of corporate M&As in the United States at the end of the nineteenth century, as firms shifted from a regional to a national focus, so have the same factors led firms to adapt a global focus over the last several decades (UNCTAD 1999: xx). Increasing regional integration and the introduction of a single currency in the EU, for example, created a wave of M&A activity in Europe, and horizontal acquisitions between firms in the same industry (which, in terms of value, accounted for 70 per cent of M&A activity at the end of the 1990s) represented the quickest route to global scale and scope for firms seeking to access new markets and complementary capabilities (UNCTAD 1999: xix–xx). In short, the majority of FDI is the consolidation of corporate activity—large corporations being taken over by even larger corporations—in what is increasingly a global market for firms.

FDI has also become dramatically more important for developing countries. A developing country seeking external capital investment has four choices: official flows (from international development agencies and governments), commercial bank loans, portfolio flows (from institutional investors such as pension funds, insurance companies, and mutual funds), and FDI. Until the early 1990s, official flows were the dominant source of capital for developing countries, often in the form of loans that were made on concessional terms, but over the course of the 1990s there was a dramatic shift from public to private capital flows. This was partly the result of budgetary difficulties in developed countries, which led to a cutback in foreign aid, but it also reflected an ideological shift towards market-based approaches to public policy. By 2005, official flows to the developing world had largely dried up, and over half of the total resource flow to the developing world consisted of FDI ($334 billion). As is the case in the developed world, these flows tend to be concentrated: Brazil, China, Hong Kong, Mexico, and Singapore are consistently the five top FDI destinations in the developing world for virtually every year since 1996, and in some years can account for as much as half of the total inflow to the developing world (UNCTAD 2006b: 4–5). Developing

economies increased their share of overall FDI inflows in 2008, as the initial impact of the recession took a particular toll on investment in developed economies. The expectation, however, was that inflows to all economies would decline substantially in 2009, when the full effects of the recession were felt (UNCTAD 2009b: 5–7). Attracting FDI is important for developing countries, not just because it is the most stable form of foreign capital that is available, but as will be explained in greater detail below, because it is thought to have the potential to bring a package of benefits, including technology, managerial skills, and access to new markets.

Although FDI represents a critical element of global production, it only measures global production that takes place under foreign ownership, and neglects the outsourcing of production. Simply defined, outsourcing is the reallocation of a particular task from within one firm to another, and the two are usually separated by having different ownership (Sako 2006: 503). There is overlap between the two categories—an American firm that uses a South Korean manufacturer located in China is both outsourcing (from the perspective, of the US firm) and reliant on FDI (from the perspective of the South Korean firm)—but the distinction is important from an analytical perspective, because it points to the wide variety of governance forms in global value chains. And outsourcing need not necessarily be accompanied by any trans-border flows of capital—firms may be linked simply by 'arm's-length' purchase arrangements, or the relationship may involve, for example, the transfer of expertise from purchaser to supplier.

Unfortunately, it is very difficult to determine the value of outsourcing transactions from general trade data. One possible measure (albeit with a regional bias), is the growth of trade in intermediate goods (components that are neither raw materials nor finished products). In Asia, for example, between 1985 and 1996, the value of all parts and component imports increased by 6 per cent, and accounted for 25 per cent of all manufactured imports by 1996. Trade in telecommunications components increased from 3 billion in 1985 to 41 billion in

1996 (when components accounted for 72 per cent of imports in the product group), and the increase in trade in electronic components was only slightly less dramatic (Ng and Yeats 1999: 10). A second measure (albeit with a sectoral bias), is the dramatic rise of specialist contract manufacturers. Electronic manufacturing services (EMS) firms, for example, receive designs for a broad spectrum of electronic products from brand-name firms, import or manufacture components, assemble the products, and then export the finished goods. The industry grew from nothing in the early 1980s — when IBM began to look for key suppliers for its personal computers in 1981 — to $170 billion in revenue in 2005. Many of these companies have themselves become significant foreign investors. Flextronics — an example of one of the five largest firms in the sector — has manufacturing operations in thirty countries on five continents, employs over 50,000 people in China alone, and has revenues in excess of $15 billion. Flextronics and its competitors make 100 per cent of desktop computer motherboards, 83 per cent of laptop computers, and 33 per cent of cell phones, according to industry estimates (figures from Deagon 2006). Similarly, in the auto industry, the largest supply firms are now almost as large as the assembly firms they serve. In order to save on development costs, take advantage of supplier knowledge, and maximize economies of scale, auto assembly firms outsource the design and manufacture of entire modules of a car to large supply firms. In 1992, there were only twenty-eight US auto supply firms with annual sales between $1 billion and $5 billion, and five companies with sales higher than $5 billion. In 1998, these numbers were forty-seven and thirteen, respectively (Veloso 2000: 16). Although not quite as dramatic as in the electronics industry, the outsourcing of manufacturing was a dominant trend in the auto industry during the 1990s.

Why now?

Politics has played a key role in the expansion of global production. The liberalization of trade was a critical prerequisite for the globalization of production. When trade barriers are high, a multinational firm will invest in production facilities abroad in order to access foreign markets, but it will hesitate to relocate portions of the value chain that must be integrated with other global activities — the fragmentation of value chains requires low tariff barriers. As Gibert Winham argues in Chapter 5 of this book, the trade regime is the most prominent example of global co-operation in the era after the Second World War. Chastened by the breakdown of the global economy during the interwar period, the United States began a return to liberalism with the passage of the Reciprocal Trade Agreements Act of 1934 (RTAA). After the Second World War, the trend of increased economic liberalism continued with each successive round of the General Agreement on Tariffs and Trade (GATT), and the result was the rapid expansion of world trade. World exports increased by close to 8 per cent per annum between 1950 and 1973, and by 5 per cent for the subsequent twenty-five-year period (Ravenhill, Chapter 1 in this volume).

The move towards a liberal trade regime at the international level had a corollary at the domestic level — a general trend towards market-based policies — and this expanded the range of options for global production. As Anthony McGrew explains in Chapter 9 of this book, the neo-liberal ideology associated with liberalization, deregulation, and privatization provided the normative infrastructure for economic globalization. In Organization for Economic Co-operation and Development (OECD) states, governments across the political spectrum were instrumental in liberalizing national economies, and creating the policy and institutional frameworks that have enabled the growth of global trade and production.

Governments in the developing world used the expansion of global trade as an engine of growth. No region benefited more than East Asia. Scholars debate the extent to which economic growth in economies such as South Korea and Taiwan was the result of government-led industrial policies (Amsden 1989; Wade 1990) as opposed to market-conforming policies (World Bank 1993), but reliance on export markets was clear in all these cases. Taiwan, for example, pioneered the use of export-processing zones—industrial parks where foreign firms could enjoy preferential trade and investment policies so long as their output was intended for export markets—at the same time as Japanese manufacturers were forcing American firms to reduce their costs by moving labour-intensive activities offshore. With the encouragement of the Taiwanese government and the United States Agency for International Development (US-AID), General Instruments began manufacturing in Taiwan in 1964, and was followed over the next two years by twenty-four other American firms (Wade 1990: 94). This was in many important respects the beginning of the global manufacturing model that would dominate East Asia in the 1970s and 1980—firms from high-wage economies began to break apart their value chains and locate the manufacturing of each component according to competitive advantage. As the neo-liberal reforms took hold in China, Eastern Europe, India, and Latin America over the decades that followed, the scope of global manufacturing increased in turn.

At the same time as political changes were opening up countries to trade and investment, technology was extending the geographical reach of business, and making possible new forms of business organization. In many respects, this is an old story writ large. In the latter half of the nineteenth century, technology transformed the organization of business in the United States. As Alfred Chandler (1977: 75–80) has described, the spread of iron, coal, and machinery created the possibility of large-scale production in the United States, and the invention of the telegraph and expansion of railways created the means of communication and transportation that would allow these businesses to extend their geographical reach. These changes led to the emergence of the modern hierarchical corporation. Just as the telegraph and the railway allowed firms in the latter half of the nineteenth century to adopt a national rather than regional orientation, the improvement in transportation and technology

in the latter half of the twentieth century allowed firms to adopt a global perspective. These changes led to the fragmentation of the value chain.

The first set of changes involved new forms of transportation. An obvious development was the introduction of commercial jet services in the 1950s. Less obvious, but probably even more important for world commerce, was the introduction of standardized shipping containers. Prior to the introduction of standardized steel and aluminum containers in the late 1950s, the process of loading and unloading cargo at the point of origin, at ports along the way, and at the destination was time-consuming and fraught with the possibility of loss and damage. Containers dramatically reduced the friction of transportation in global economy. Marc Levinson (2006: 7) provides a compelling illustration: a 35-ton container of coffee-makers in Malaysia can be loaded into a container at the factory door, taken to a port and loaded onto a ship, and then transported the 9,000 miles to Los Angeles in sixteen days. A day later, the container will be on a unit train to Chicago. If the train were to carry the capacity load of one of the new mega container ships—which can carry over 8,000 six-metre-long containers—it would stretch over 37 kilometres. Once in Chicago, the container of coffee-makers is immediately transferred to a flatbed lorry headed to Cincinnati, the distribution centre for the retailer. The process is not only inexpensive—in this case, less than the price of a single first-class air ticket from Malaysia to the US—but it is also completely automated and the transfers at each juncture in the journey are seamless; human hands will not touch the contents of the container between the factory and the destination. In the late 1950s and early 1960s, transport costs were often a higher barrier to trade than were import tariffs (as high as 25 per cent of the cost of some products, according to one study), and the result was that globalization of production was not a cost-effective strategy (Levinson 2006: 9). At the time of writing, when 90 per cent of world trade is transported in shipping containers, transport in many industries is a marginal part of a company's overall cost structure. From the perspective of transport cost, it almost does not matter if a firm is doing business with a factory on the other side of town or the other side of the world.

If container shipping reduced the hurdle of transport costs, the digital revolution and the shift to modularity made it possible to separate the activities of the value chain and scatter them across the globe (see Box 11.1). The electronics industry has been at the cutting edge of the modular revolution (Baldwin and Clark 2000). Until the 1960s, the designs of the different parts of a computer system were highly interdependent, and, consequently, when any new product was introduced, the design process would have to begin again from the start to ensure that all the component parts were compatible. The result was time-consuming and expensive, because teams of engineers within a single company had to work together on each component; outsourcing was not possible, because the connections between different parts of the product design were complex and varied in arbitrary and non-obvious ways (Baldwin and Clark 2000: 171). Like craftsmen putting together a custom-built piece of furniture, the engineers had to work together, relying not on codified rules to piece together a machine but on tacit knowledge (information that cannot be written or coded in a set of instructions, but must be imparted by people working together).

Box 11.1 Modular Production

In the classic work on modularity, Baldwin and Clark (1997, 2000) define a modular system as one that 'is composed of units (or modules) that are designed independently but still function as an integrated whole' (1997: 86). The structural elements of a module are connected powerfully to each other and relatively weakly to elements in other modules of the same system (2000: 63). Every product that consists of multiple modules will have an *architecture* that specifies what modules are part of the system and what the function of each will be; *interfaces* that describe in detail how the modules will interact, connect, and communicate; and *standards* for testing the extent to which a module conforms to the design rules (1997: 86). Sako (2003) specifies how modularity fulfils different roles across the life cycle of a product. In the design phase, the principle purpose of modularity is to reduce the lead-time of the design process, and the cost of design and development. In the manufacturing phase, the objective is to increase operational efficiency by allowing the mixing and matching of standardized components, thus allowing for both the benefits of scale efficiencies and greater customization and variety. Finally, when the product is being used, consumers want a product that is easy to use, compatible with other products, easily upgraded, and easily and inexpensively maintained. The objectives of the different phases are not always compatible. The core concern of product designers, for example, will be to ensure that the design of each module is independent of other modules, and this may lead to tight interdependencies within the module. When the consumer has to make a repair, however, rather than being able to replace an individual component, he or she may find that an entire (and expensive) module must be replaced rather than an individual component.

Modularity does not inevitably lead to outsourcing, but it creates the possibility—it is difficult to outsource or separate the component parts of an integral product. Prior to the rise of mass production, for example, automobiles were made by craftsmen, and each vehicle had to be made in its entirety in a workshop because the component parts had to custom fit to each other. The workers were skilled in the principles of mechanical design and experienced with the materials with which they worked. As Womack et al. (1990) explain, production of the cars depended on the tacit knowledge of these craftsmen, and it was difficult to codify this knowledge reliably in a way that would make it readily accessible to outside firms; there was no standard gauging system, and machine tools at this point could not cut hardened steel. Because the craftsmen fitted each piece together individually, no two vehicles were exactly alike. The core innovation of Henry Ford was the development of a system that used a standard gauge and pre-hardened metal that would not warp during the manufacturing process, previously the major obstacle to standardizing the size of parts (Womack et al. 1990: 22–7).

The introduction of interchangeable parts with standard interfaces made it possible for an auto firm to replace skilled craftsmen with unskilled assembly-line workers, and to outsource production of components. The benefits of outsourcing to a supply firm can be numerous: the supplier will be a specialist in the production of a particular component, it will be able to capture greater economies of scale (since it supplies many firms), and it will give the assembler greater flexibility to concentrate on other parts of the production process.

The solution, introduced by IBM in the autumn of 1961, was to conceive of a family of computers—the System/360—that would include machines of different sizes and uses, but all of which would share the same instruction set and peripherals. A central office mandated the design rules that would determine how the different modules of the machine would interact with each other, and this allowed different teams of engineers to work independently on the aspects of each module that did not affect other modules. The shift to modularity increased the speed of the design process (because teams worked simultaneously), increased the rate of innovation (because teams could try any number of approaches, so long as they adhered to the design rules for interacting with other modules), and created the flexibility needed to meet a variety of customer needs. Paradoxically, these advances also led to the end of IBM's dominance of the industry, because outside companies could perform the same role as internal company divisions, so long as they knew the design rules—easily specified as computer code—that would make their product compatible with an IBM machine (Baldwin and Clark 1997: 85). As a result, we now take it for granted that we can download photographs from a Canon camera to a Dell computer in order to print them on an HP printer. In other industries, the interfaces between modules are not always as easy to specify, but there is also a trend towards increasing modularity. As was pointed out in the previous section, auto assembly firms have been shifting responsibilities to their suppliers to as great an extent as possible. A Volkswagen truck factory in Brazil has taken this approach to the extreme. VW established the architecture of the production process and the interfaces that connect modules, but all the manufacturing is done by suppliers (Baldwin and Clark 1997: 87).

The ability to codify design information in digital form, particularly when combined with new forms of telecommunication to transmit this information, was a key enabler of globalization. As Suzanne Berger (2006: 76) explains, new software in the 1990s increased the ability of a wide variety of firms to digitize instructions and thus codify the interfaces within a product. This created new options with respect to location. Once engineers are able to specify the 'hand-off' between two different modules within a product utilizing software, there is no longer any inherent reason why designers and production staff have to be located within the same facility. The design firm transmits the design specifications electronically to the production facility, and as long as the production facility meets the appropriate standards, it can be located anywhere. The ability to codify design information does not inevitably lead to the fragmentation of the value chain—in some industries and some regions, firms may decide that it makes sense to co-locate distinct parts of the value chain—but it does create a wider variety of possibilities than existed previously.

The ideal type of this new breed of firm, according to Samuel Palmisano (2006: 129), the CEO of IBM, is the globally integrated enterprise. In contrast to the multinational company of old, 'the emerging globally integrated enterprise is a company that fashions its strategy, its management, and its operations in pursuit of a new goal: the integration of production and value delivery worldwide'. Whereas the technical changes of the late nineteenth century resulted in a tightening of corporate control—a strict hierarchy was needed to organize rapidly expanding operations—the technical changes of the late twentieth century have resulted in tremendous fluidity. This new breed of firm is being organized by functions rather than products or geography, and every firm must decide which functions it will continue to perform; which functions it will rely on outside partners to perform; and where in the world each function will be located. The results to these decisions, of course, have important implications, not only for the competitiveness of individual firms and industries, but also for the well-being of the societies in which they operate.

Key points

- The globalization of production is not new, but the magnitude with which it takes place and the degree of fragmentation in global value chains *is* new.

- The increasing levels of global production can be measured in both the dramatic increases in FDI and the increasing importance of trade in components.

- Flows of FDI are heavily concentrated in developed economies, and dominated by mergers and acquisitions between large firms that are seeking the scale and scope that is increasingly necessary to compete in global markets.

- The increase in global production is a result of economic liberalization, improvements in transportation, and advances in technologies that facilitate modularization.

Global Value Chains: Governance and Location

In order to understand the implications of global value chains, it is necessary to distinguish between their different forms. For analytical purposes, it is useful to consider global value chains along two dimensions: governance (how to co-ordinate activities); and location (where to locate each activity). Although the two dimensions are closely linked, there are distinct scholarly literatures focused on each.

Governance

If a defining feature of economic globalization is that technology has increased the ability of firms to fragment the value chain, one of the key issues that must be understood is how co-ordination of the fragmented parts is achieved. Defined in its broadest sense, governance refers to any means of co-ordinating interdependent activities (Jessop 1998: 29). It is useful to think of the governance options for global value chains along a spectrum. At one end of the spectrum are pure market relations with foreign firms (for example, arm's-length trade relationships), and at the other end is hierarchical control of foreign operations (for example, FDI). Between these two endpoints are various forms of networks.

Traditional explanations of FDI focus on the endpoints of the governance spectrum, and transfer the classic 'make or buy' question from the domestic to a global context. As Sven Arndt and Henryk Kierzkowski (2001: 2) write, 'fragmentation is not a new phenomenon; nor is outsourcing. Both go back to the beginning of the Industrial Revolution or even predate it.' What is new is the extent to which improvements in technology have tamed the 'tyranny of distance' and made it increasingly possible to consider the global organization of industry in the same terms as domestic. One clear option is to rely on arm's-length market relationships. As Robert Gilpin (2001: 279) notes, in the ideal world of a neoclassical economist, firms would not invest abroad. If markets are operating efficiently, information is costless, there are no barriers to trade or competition, and there are no advantages to be gained from economies of scale, there would be little reason for a firm to invest abroad because trade would be the logical means of reaching foreign markets and accessing inputs. Markets are efficient, prices summarize all relevant information, and actors are motivated by self-interest rather than coercion — co-ordination is seemingly effortless.

Why does a firm decide to make rather than buy a particular product or service in the domestic context? Economists explain vertical integration and hierarchical co-ordination as a response to transaction costs. As Ronald Coase (1937) argued, there are costs associated with using a market; even for the simplest transaction, a buyer or seller must be found, a product or service evaluated, and a price negotiated. Oliver Williamson (1981: 1,545) added to this explanation the problems inherent in human nature. Bounded rationality makes it impossible for actors to foresee every contingency that might affect an agreement between two actors, hence contracts can never be complete; the problem of opportunism means that each actor has to expect the other to act, not only out of self-interest, but, potentially, with deceit and guile. In light of these assumptions, it is apparent that the costs of some market transactions are higher than others. It is necessary to identify and analyse the key dimensions along which transactions vary — the frequency with which transactions recur, the degree of complexity and uncertainty to which transactions are subject, and the degree of asset specificity — in order to determine whether hierarchical co-ordination (retaining all activities within the organization) is more appropriate than market co-ordination (Williamson 1975, 1981).

The same logic has been used to explain why firms engage in FDI rather than licensing, trade, or contractual relationships. The literature on FDI is large, but within it John Dunning's eclectic paradigm is one of the dominant strands (Dunning 1981). At its core is a transactional approach: a firm will create operations abroad when the net costs of an internal market (hierarchical co-ordination) are lower than the net cost of using arm's-length market relationships (Caves 1982). The *advantages of internalization* within the firm might stem from concerns about the costs and uncertainty of monitoring and negotiating the relationship with a licensee or contractor, or the firm might be eager to ensure that it captures all of the benefits of the advantages that it has over local firms. These *firm-specific advantages* (Dunning 1981) might involve a trademark, a particular technology or manufacturing process, economies of scale, or marketing power; or a firm might be reluctant to license such advantages to a foreign firm out of fear that it will be training a future competitor. There are costs to operating internationally — a foreign firm will rarely understand the local market as well as a domestic firm does, for example — so, a multinational firm has to ensure that it protects what advantages it does hold. In addition, there may be *location-specific advantages* to setting up operations on foreign soil as opposed to establishing trade relations. The foreign firm may gain better access to information on the marketplace, an ability to respond more quickly to changes in the market, access to unique resources or capabilities, and/or ability to avoid protectionist trade barriers. In short, the potential costs of relying on markets and arm's-length relationships to govern a global value chain are weighed against the difficulty of controlling and operating subsidiaries that are within the firm but spread across great distances and unfamiliar territory through FDI.

Although the distinction between utilizing markets and hierarchy to govern global value chains is an important one, there are a range of possibilities in between these two endpoints. Just as firms within a domestic economy can form long-term relationships that cannot be characterized completely by markets or hierarchy, global value chains can take the form of a diverse variety of networks that are neither pure markets nor hierarchy. In the 1990s, Gary Gereffi and others (Gereffi and Korzeniewicz 1994) developed the framework of the global commodity chain to distinguish between different forms of global value chains (for a comparison of the theoretical concepts of commodity chains and value chains, and the evolution of this research agenda, see Bair 2005). This approach identified different 'nodes' in a value chain—pivotal points in the production process (that is, supply of raw materials, production, export, or marketing)—with the intent of analysing how control of various nodes translated into power and profit. Gereffi distinguished between two types of commodity chains: the buyer-driven chain; and the producer-driven chain. In a buyer-driven chain, large retailers, brand-named marketers, and trading companies use various combinations of branding, design, marketing, and sales expertise to exert control over a decentralized network of supply firms often located in the developing world. As any supplier to a large retailer such as Wal-Mart or a brand such as Nike is painfully aware, these customers do not need ownership in order to exert control. In a producer-driven chain, large (and often capital-intensive) integrated enterprises play the key role in controlling forward and backward linkages—the auto industry is a classic example.

Over the following decade, a growing body of research on global value chains identified other forms of networks. Scholars distinguished between 'commodity suppliers' (firms that provided a standard product through arm's-length ties), 'captive suppliers' (firms that provide a specialized product using production equipment or processes that are dedicated to a particular customer), and 'turn-key' suppliers (firms that produce customized—and often sophisticated—products for customers using flexible production equipment that can be used for multiple customers) (Humphrey and Schmitz 2000; Sturgeon 2002).

There are clearly multiple means of co-ordinating a global value chain that involve neither markets nor hierarchy, and a key question is why one form is chosen rather than another. Gereffi et al. (2005: 87) argue that three key variables determine the organization of a global value chain: (1) the complexity of inter-firm transactions; (2) the degree to which this complexity can be codified; and (3) the extent to which the suppliers have the necessary capabilities to meet the requirements of the buyers. As with traditional attempts to explain FDI, their approach places a heavy emphasis on the nature of the transaction, but with a particular focus on how modern technology allows some transactions to be translated easily into a set of digital instructions, while others cannot. In this respect, the approach reflects the new range of opportunities that are available to firms. *Market relations* will tend to prevail when transactions are not complex, product specifications are easily specified by the buyer, and supplier capabilities can easily meet these demands. A buyer of inexpensive plastic toys, for example, can easily switch from one supplier to another, and a simple contract will suffice. *Modular value chains* will occur when the interfaces between complex modules can easily be codified, and there are suppliers capable of providing the sophisticated modules on either side of the interface. Large auto-supply firms or contract manufacturers in the electronic industry are prominent examples. *Relational value chains* involve complex transactions, product specifications that are not easily codified, and highly capable suppliers. The result is mutual dependence between firms, close relationships that involve the exchange of tacit knowledge, and relationships that are regulated through reputation, geographical proximity, and social, ethnic, and/or family ties. In *captive value chains*, both the complexity of transactions and the ability to codify this complexity is high, but the capabilities of suppliers are low. The lead firm in these cases must provide the core design elements of product and significant assistance to the supply firm, and because it does not want other customers to benefit from new supplier capabilities that may result, it seeks to lock the supplier into a 'captive' relationship. By not providing key design elements or complementary activities, for example, the supplier firm will remain dependent on the lead firm. Finally, when product specifications cannot be codified, products are complex, and highly competent suppliers cannot be found, a firm will rely on in-house capabilities and *hierarchical co-ordination* (Gereffi et al. 2005: 86–7).

Why does the form of governance matter? As Raphael Kaplinsky notes (2000: 118), if it was clear that the only losers from increased economic globalization were those who did not globalize, the solution would be straightforward—attract more FDI and promote exports. But, economic globalization has not benefited all participants: the trade/GDP of Sub-Saharan Africa increased from 51 per cent to 56.1 per cent between 1985 and 1995, at the same time as its share of global output fell (Kaplinsky 2000: 119; 2005; see also Wade, Chapter 12 in this volume). How a country inserts itself into the global economy is as important as whether or not a country does so, and a primary contribution of value chain analysis is to identify the terms under which a firm is participating in the global economy. The governance of value chains is critical, because it is an important determinant of who reaps the gains of globalization in three different respects: the distribution of profits among firms, the capabilities that firms within the chain are able to master, and the leverage points for policy initiatives (Humphrey and Schmitz 2001).

First, the distribution of gains within a value chain is determined to a great extent by barriers to entry (Kaplinsky 2000: 127). When barriers to entry are low, increased globalization can lead to a decrease in income, because competition is greater; when barriers to entry are high, a firm has the ability to dictate the terms (that is, the price it will receive and the role it will have) to others within the value chain. To an increasing extent, and in a dramatic shift from an era when manufacturing prowess was the key to successful development, power in the value chain now stems from intangibility (Kaplinsky 2000: 127). That is, a firm that depends on low wages to convert physical inputs into a physical product will consistently face downward pressure on its prices because it will face competition from

ambitious firms throughout the developing world; while a firm that depends on intangible factors such as design, brands, or marketing is able to protect its position because its skills are not easily copied (Kaplinsky 2000: 127; Bair 2005: 165). A value chain framework highlights the barriers to entry by focusing attention on the switching cost at each link in the chain. Any factor that makes it more difficult for a customer to switch from one supplier to another, whether it be the complexity of the transaction, the ability to codify the transaction, or the unique capabilities of the supplier, will increase the power (and profits) of the supplier. A supply firm that is part of a relational value chain, for example, will have far more power than a firm that is part of a captive value chain, because the relationship with the customer is characterized by mutual dependence—the customer cannot shift easily to another supplier—and this allows it to demand a higher price for its products or services.

Second, the governance of value chains is an important determinant of upgrading prospects. Upgrading is commonly defined as increasing competitiveness by capturing a part of the value chain that involves higher value-added activities. This can be achieved by increasing the breadth of functions a firm undertakes, the complexity of the product that is produced, or improving the process technology that is utilized in production (Bair 2005: 165). From a development perspective, of course, upgrading is very much the central question—what form of insertion to the global economy will provide a local economy with the strongest prospects for upgrading the capabilities, and thus future prospects, of local firms? The value chain literature highlights the benefits that firms in developing countries receive from incorporation into global value chains. The lead firms of these networks demand low cost, high quality, and good service from their suppliers, and often take an active role in transmitting best practice through the network (Humphrey and Schmitz 2001). The extent to which a lead firm within a network is willing to assist a supplier will depend on the form of governance: it is less likely to assist a supplier that can easily begin working for a competitor than it is a supplier that is enmeshed in a relational value chain.

Similarly, the literature on FDI — the hierarchical form of value chain governance — has long analysed the extent to which foreign investment is 'benign', because it complements local savings and provides management, marketing, and technological skills; or 'malignant', because it takes advantage of preferential policies and crowds out local firms (Moran 1998: 19–20). A narrow focus on how the different parts of a global value chain are governed is better at highlighting the constraints that local firms may face than it is at demonstrating how these constraints can be overcome, however. Understanding how upgrading takes place requires a perspective that incorporates both the policy environment provided by the state *and* the local context.

Third, the governance of global value chains gives insight into the degree of leverage that outside actors have — whether this be a government, international organization, or a non-governmental organization (NGO) — to influence the behaviour of firms. An NGO in the United States that is interested in promoting fair labour standards in Nike factories, for example, might have very little leverage over the factories themselves. The factories are foreign-owned, and even if progress is made within one factory, it will inevitably be only a small part of a huge, decentralized network. The real power in this value chain lies with Nike, but this is also the point of vulnerability: the very intangibility of branding that makes it difficult for other firms to imitate the success of Nike also creates a potential danger if the brand becomes associated with sweatshop labour. But as Richard Locke (2003: 7–8) argues, even the power of Nike to effect change within its own supply chain will vary. Because shoe factories tend to be large and capital-intensive — partly a result of the elimination by industrialized countries of quotas on footwear imports in the mid 1980s — Nike has long-term relationships with a relatively small number of large South Korean and Taiwanese suppliers, and the stability of these relationships facilitates the co-ordination of production processes and (sometimes) the implementation of Nike's labour code

of conduct. Nike has much looser relationships with its apparel suppliers because product cycles are short, factories tend to specialize in a particular segment, and these factories supply Nike's competitors as well as Nike. According to Locke, the different form of these relationships has the potential to alter Nike's influence with the suppliers and its ability to monitor their behaviour (Locke 2003: 9).

Location

The second key dimension along which value chains vary is location. Decisions about the governance of a value chain — whether it makes more sense to make or buy a particular product or service, for example — do not necessarily relate to decisions about location. If a firm decides that it can rely on market relationships to source a particular input — that it can 'buy' rather than 'make' — it can either *outsource* production to a firm across the street or it can *offshore* production to a firm overseas (Sako 2006: 503).

Why do value chains become global? One standard explanation is that foreign investment and offshoring are part of an evolutionary process. Raymond Vernon (1971) argued that every product followed a life cycle beginning with development, proceeding to maturity, and culminating in standardization and obsolescence. Over the course of this life cycle, the comparative advantage of a country will shift as the emphasis moves from product innovation and development — a stage when it can be highly beneficial to have designers, suppliers, and customers in close proximity — to a standardized product that competes on the basis of cost. At the time that Vernon was writing, the United States economy was the clear leader in technological and entrepreneurial resources, and it had the most affluent and demanding domestic marketplace. Firms developed new products for the domestic marketplace, eventually began to export to foreign markets, and finally, as the product matured and became standardized, they moved production offshore so as to forestall the rise of foreign competitors and preserve monopoly rents. A similar evolutionary pattern was used by scholars in East Asia to describe the relationship between foreign investment and regional development, although the focus was on leading industries rather than on products. Like geese flying in formation, industrial structures were passed from advanced economies to developing economies: a less-developed economy would initially import products in leading industries from more advanced countries, imitation and import-substitution would lead to the development of indigenous industry, and eventually the indigenous industry would advance to the point where it, too, would begin to export. As Bruce Cumings (1984: 3) argues in the case of North-East Asia,

> the cycle in given industries—textiles, steel, automobiles, light electronics—of origin, rise, apogee, and decline has not simply been marked, but often mastered in Japan; in each industrial life cycle there is also an appropriate jumping off place, that is, a point at which it pays to let others make the product or at least provide the labor. Taiwan and South Korea have historically been receptacles for declining Japanese industries.

Regional integration, in other words, is a natural impulse of economic growth and development—the leaders move into higher value-added activities as their cost structures rise, and lower-cost followers replicate the industrial structures of those ahead.

These evolutionary approaches captured a key dynamic driving foreign investment in a world in which the forces of technology and product innovation were highly concentrated and the rate of change was slow and predicable, but as Mitchell Bernard and John Ravenhill (1995) ague, these approaches have difficulty in explaining the contemporary global economy. First, in a world of rapid technical change and product proliferation, the process of product and technological maturation that is predicted by the industry–life cycle

model appears to be less and less common. Product life cycles—for example, for mobile phones—are now matters of months rather than years. Second, it is not an entire production system that an advanced country manufacturer such as a Japanese company simply boxes up and ships to a low-cost labour site, it is only a *part* of the system that is transferred, and in most circumstances it is the labour-intensive part of final assembly. The forces of innovation and the backward linkages remain behind in the advanced economy, and in the absence of an active state role to promote the development of indigenous industry in the developing economy, the result will be partial diffusion of technology, and what Bernard and Ravenhill call an intra-regional hierarchy of production. This is not to say that late developers cannot overcome their place in the hierarchy—the emergence of strong and powerful competitors from countries such as South Korea and Taiwan since the mid 1990s is evidence of this—but their success cannot be assumed. Finally, the evolutionary approach has difficulty explaining why the majority of global foreign investment is between developed economies that have very similar industrial structures. Clearly, the overseas activities of firms are not simply about accessing low-cost labour to produce outdated products.

Another way of thinking about how location drives global production is to consider the advantages that a firm seeks in any given place. Some of these advantages will be obvious—natural resources, new markets, or low-cost labour—but they may also involve factors that relate to the culture, language, or politics of a particular region. These motivating drivers of investment are the location-specific advantages of Dunning's 'eclectic' paradigm: a firm will invest abroad (assuming that there are benefits to internalization), in order to access the immobile resources of a particular place. A similar emphasis on the advantages inherent in a particular location is at the core of Michael Porter's (1990) concept of a firm's 'home base'. The home base consists of factors of production (and particularly specialized factors such as educational systems, technology and innovation systems, and infrastructure); demand conditions (the quality and quantity of the home market); related and supporting industries that are internationally competitive; and the national circumstances and context that influence the strategy, structure, and competitive practices of local firms. The interaction of these four attributes (what Porter calls the 'diamond of national advantage') leads to the creation of geographically concentrated clusters of competitive strengths that are mutually reinforcing. One of the greatest advantages of a multinational firm, according to Porter (1990: 60), is that it has the advantage of being able to combine the strengths of its own home base with other locations in its global network; at every stage of the value chain, a global firm can decide where to locate activities, to maximize the benefits of its global reach. If global value chains are the means of connecting a network of far-flung capabilities, the key then becomes a case of understanding why certain locations will vary in their ability to develop particular capabilities.

The traditional approach of comparative political economy has been to focus on the nation state, and to explain economic outcomes as a result of the relationship between domestic state institutions, patterns of industrial policy, and social actors. Successive generations of this approach analysed how national institutional structures responded to the challenges of economic adjustment in the advanced capitalist world (Katzenstein 1978, 1985; Schmitter and Lehbruch 1979; Zysman 1984). The most recent approach in this tradition has focused on systematic differences in the way that national economies are organized (Hall and Soskice 2001). Firms must co-ordinate activities with a range of economic actors—investors, other firms (suppliers and clients), the organizations that represent workers, and their own employees (in particular)—and firms that operate in liberal market economies will have very different characteristics and strengths from firms that operate in co-ordinated market economies (see Hay, Chapter 10 in this volume). This 'varieties of capitalism' approach assumes that 'the most important institutional structures—notably systems of labor market regulation, of education and training, and of corporate governance—depend on the presence of regulatory regimes that are the preserve of the nation-state' (Hall and Soskice 2001: 4). The result is a stark departure from the traditional perspective of economics on comparative advantage because the advantages of a particular location are not endowed by nature, but are the result of a complex constellation of interrelated institutions. Firms in a liberal market economy, for example, may have an advantage in activities that emphasize radical innovation; firms in a co-ordinated market economy may have an advantage in activities that require incremental innovation and manufacturing excellence. The key point from the perspective of global production, is that multinational firms have the potential to access the advantages of all systems, and in doing so they can compensate for weaknesses at home.

Although national institutions are clearly important in shaping general patterns of economic co-ordination within an economy, an exclusive focus on the nation state as the unit of analysis can obscure as much as it reveals. There is increasing evidence that, as Anwar Shah and Theresa Thompson (2002: 5) of the World Bank put it, 'nation-states are too small to tackle large things in life and too large to address small things'. National governments do not have the same degree of autonomy to shape their national economies as they did in the past. As Colin Hay explains (Chapter 10 in this volume), the extent to which globalization forces states to converge on a single economic model is the subject of fierce debate. While the resilience of distinct 'varieties' of capitalism is debated, few would question that nation states are increasingly aware of the international constraints on their economic policies. National governments that do not take into account international capital markets and foreign investors before making policy changes, for example, do so at their peril. At the same time as national governments are operating under greater constraints, decentralization—the process of devolving political, fiscal, and administrative powers to subnational units of government (Burki et al. 1999)—has been one of the dominant economic and political trends since the 1980s. This move towards decentralization started in advanced industrial nations, where free-market policy reforms were accompanied by a 'devolution revolution' that transferred authority and resources from central to local governments, and the approach was transferred to the developing world by the World Bank and development NGOs (Snyder 2001: 93).

The importance of regional economies is certainly not surprising to multinational firms that are seeking to access the best capabilities across the globe. If a firm wants to access high-tech capabilities in the United States, for example, the most capable firms are not scattered at random: they are clustered in places such as Silicon Valley in California; Route 128 outside Boston; or the Research Triangle in North Carolina. Why are national economic systems composed of disparate regional economies (Marshall 1920; Nadvi and Schmitz 1998)? One set of explanations focuses on the ability of firms in an industrial cluster to minimize transaction costs and maximize their share of specialized labour markets. For firms interested in design and technology, it is easier to identify new technologies and market trends; the flow of personnel between firms helps to disseminate knowledge; there is better access to

highly specialized types of labour; and there may be better access to capital and other key inputs in a technology cluster (McKendrick et al. 2000: 46). For firms involved with manufacturing and operations, there are also benefits to agglomeration, although they are slightly different. Firms will benefit from lower transport costs and reduced transport times; greater economies of scale; a greater ability to increase production rapidly; specialized pools of labour; better ability to monitor and co-ordinate with suppliers; and a greater ability to monitor and imitate the competition (McKendrick et al. 2000: 46). A second (and not competing) set of explanations focuses on the political and economic characteristics of a particular region. In an era in which decentralization is a dominant political and economic trend, increasingly it is local institutions that help firms overcome the co-ordination problems of development (Thun 2006). The patterns of association in a region, types of intergroup relations, political representation, and forms of economic governance (both in the present and in the past) create different opportunities and constraints for economic actors, and these differences help to explain divergent economic outcomes within a single national economy (Locke 1995; Herrigel 1996).

Key points

- The activities within global value chains can be governed by a range of mechanisms, including market co-ordination, various forms of network co-ordination, and hierarchical co-ordination. The form of value chain governance is a key determinant of how power and profits are distributed among the key actors within the value chain.

- According to Dunning's eclectic paradigm, firms will engage in FDI when there are firm-specific advantages, location-specific advantages, and advantages of internalization.

- Gereffi et al. (2005) argue that the organization of a global value chain will vary according to the complexity of inter-firm transactions, the degree to which this complexity can be codified, and the extent to which the suppliers have the capabilities needed to meet the requirements of the buyers.

- When considering where to locate different parts of the value chain, firms must consider the cost of production and the competitive strengths and weaknesses of both nations and regions.

There is no better place to analyse the trends in global production than China; the rise of China as an economic power has corresponded with the globalization of manufacturing. In the three decades since China began to make the transition to a market economy, the country has come to dominate world manufacturing, and the impact of this manufacturing juggernaut is difficult to ignore. China has a significant impact on the global prices of the inputs it sucks in to fuel its economic growth (even to the extent that manhole covers and highway railings disappear from countries on the other side of the world when Chinese commodity prices create the incentive for thieves to sell scrap metal) and the global price of the outputs it manufactures.

The impact of China on global manufacturing is difficult to overstate. From the perspective of economies that compete with it, the situation is often portrayed as grim. In 2008, the United States recorded a trade deficit of $266.3 billion with China—historically, the largest imbalance with a single trading partner—and when factories close in the United States and workers lose their jobs, China is an obvious target of political wrath.

From the perspective of multinational firms, however, the situation is very different. Although it is not the common understanding of the term, China is the 'world's factory' in the sense that much of the world's factories are operating in China; the impressive numbers that China chalks up in the global economy are thus as much a testament to foreign companies that have invested in manufacturing operations in China as they are an indication of the strength of Chinese-owned companies. The country is one of the leading destinations for global FDI. In 2008, it received an inflow of over US$100 billion in FDI (UNCTAD 2009b: 249; for reasons why Chinese FDI figures may be considerably overstated in official statistics, see Ravenhill 2006a: 661). These foreign-invested factories play a key role in Chinese manufacturing: over half of all Chinese

exports are from foreign-invested factories, and over 80 per cent of technology-intensive exports are from foreign-invested factories (Rosen 2003: 22). Multinational firms benefit from Chinese production, both when they invest in manufacturing facilities, and when they outsource production to factories that produce in China (both foreign- and Chinese-owned). Consumers benefit from the low price of manufactured goods that are exported from China.

Location and global production

The patterns of foreign investment in China reflect the complex interaction of the multiple levels of location within which a multinational firm operates—the regional, the national, and the local—and the efforts of both firms and governments to balance concerns of efficiency, equity, and sovereignty.

First, and most obviously, the investment flows have led to the integration of national economies in the region. In fact, it is more accurate to speak of China as a *regional production base* than a national production base. When China began to reform its economy at the end of the 1970s, a development approach that emphasized foreign investment had the benefit of allowing the leadership to avoid the ideologically sensitive issue of whether to allow private-sector investment within China, and it created the opportunity for China to acquire technical and managerial skills rapidly from foreign firms. Special economic zones were located initially in the mainland provinces that were across from Taiwan and Hong Kong—the primary sources of investment during the 1980s—and as preferential policies were gradually expanded to include the entire coastal region of China, Japan, and South Korea became important sources of investment as well. These countries did not transfer entire industries to China; they transferred the labour-intensive activities to China, and the subsidiaries established then imported higher value-added components from their home country.

The extent of regional integration is reflected in a dramatic increase in intra-industry trade. Between 1990 and 2005, for example, the percentage of the electronics trade between Japan and China that consisted of components increased from slightly over 10 per cent in 1990 to almost 60 per cent in 2005 (METI 2006: 25). It is estimated that two-thirds of the inputs for China's processing activities come from Hong Kong, Japan, South Korea, and Taiwan (Ravenhill 2006a: 670). At the end of 2003, according to Chinese statistics, there were a total of 28,401 Japanese-invested firms operating in China, and 27,128 South Korean-invested firms (see METI 2004: 3). In short, the United States trade deficit is with East Asia as a whole rather than with China: the high-wage economies export components to China for final assembly, and then the finished goods are exported to the United States. In 2003, China had a large trade surplus with the United States (about $125 billion), but an almost equally large deficit with its Asian trading partners (about $99 billion) (Hufbauer and Wong 2004: 3). In trade statistics, a good that is shipped from China to the United States appears as an import from China, even though the value added in China may be as little as 20–40 per cent (Ravenhill 2006a: 669).

The formation of these regional networks is driven by high costs at home, and facilitated by advances in technology. The production process in a garment factory, for example, is distinctly low-tech and labour-intensive—a factory consists of rows of women sitting at sewing machines—but the linkages between different parts of the garment value chain can be very high-tech, and these linkages create the opportunity to manage offshore production networks more effectively. Until the early 1980s, for example, textiles and garments were Taiwan's number one export (Gee and Kuo 1997: 52). During the 1980s, however, the rising cost of labour in Taiwan and a strengthening currency decreased Taiwan's competitiveness, and led Taiwanese firms either to upgrade into higher value-added activities or to move production overseas. Taiwan's apparel and accessory exports peaked in 1987 (at $5 billion), and then began a rapid decline as firms moved manufacturing to low-cost regions such as China (Gereffi and Pan 1994: 130–1). The result is what Gereffi and Pan call a triangular manufacturing system (see Box 11.2): a foreign buyer places orders with a Taiwanese firm with which it has had a long-term relationship; this firm then issues the manufacturing orders with offshore factories (that it either owns or contracts); and the final goods are then shipped to the foreign buyer (Gereffi and Pan 1994: 127).

Box 11.2 Triangular Manufacturing

Are companies always looking for low-cost labour? Not necessarily. The garment and apparel sector is a classic example of a labour-intensive industry, but actual decisions on where to locate production involves complex calculations of labour costs, quotas, and proximity to market. TW Industries, a Taiwanese garment manufacturer, is a typical example of a triangular manufacturing network (a pseudonym has been used to protect the confidentiality of an actual firm; the example is from Thun 2000). Its major customer is Gap, and because the two firms have a long history of working together, Gap continued to maintain its relationship with TW, even after most Taiwanese garment-manufacturing had relocated to less expensive regions. TW maintains its headquarters and one factory in Taiwan, and has a network of factories in China, Indonesia, and Cambodia.

The production process at TW begins when Gap uses a computer-assisted design system to send the master garment patterns via the Internet to TW headquarters. The local factory, although high-cost, is maintained to make samples—the workers are highly dependable and turnaround is quicker—and these samples are sent back to Gap via express mail. When the sample is approved, the headquarters must decide where to locate the production run. First, the cost of production is obviously important.

Wages vary considerably in TW factories: the monthly wages for a worker are $800 per month in Taiwan, $100 in a coastal province of China, $30–$40 in Indonesia, and $50–$60 in Cambodia. The cost of production is a combination of labour cost and productivity, of course, and the latter varies as well. Using the Taiwan productivity rate as an index of 100, China is 95, Indonesia 40–45, and Cambodia 55–60. Second, politics plays a key role in location decision. Prior to the elimination of the Multifibre Arrangement (MFA) in 2005, TW had to be sure to locate production in countries that had the quotas necessary for the final markets. Even after these quotas were eliminated, TW seeks to have a geographical distribution of production facilities in order to protect itself from the risk of new tariffs and quotas. Finally, the proximity to market is critical. Because clothing is influenced by fashion and trends, it can be extraordinarily time-sensitive. Much like a fruit or vegetable that will lose its value as it ages on a grocer's shelves, a piece of clothing that is yesterday's fashion must be marked down dramatically in price. As a result, speed to market is absolutely critical: saving a few cents on labour costs is a pyrrhic victory if it causes a firm to miss a trend and the product ends up in a discount outlet rather than a department store display case. The calculation will vary by product: it continues to make sense to produce high-fashion items in high-cost areas such as New York or Los Angeles; relatively fashionable items will be produced in regions where they can get to market quickly (Mexico and low-cost regions of Europe are only hours away from major markets); and relatively stable items (such as men's tee shirts and underwear) will be produced wherever costs are lowest.

Managing the technology of the production network is of critical importance. Given the fashion-sensitive nature of much of the business, retailers want to keep inventories low. In fact, the ideal would be to have a factory behind the store, because this would allow the retailer to make each item of clothing as it is purchased. It would be possible to expand production when it became apparent that an item was becoming popular, and stop production of items that were not selling—discounting would never be needed. Obviously, this is not possible, but retailers try to use information technology to keep their inventories low and their supply chains as 'lean' as possible. The objective of lean retailing is to reduce the risk of selling a perishable good by continuously adjusting the supply of products offered to consumers at retail outlets so as to match the actual level of market demand (Abernathy et al. 1999: 55). Bar code and scanning technology will track sales at a retail store, for example, and this information will be sent to a distant factory at the close of business. The factory will not only manufacture the new clothing, but will place it on hangers, complete with price tags, and then air freight it back to the retail store. In some cases, the buyer is able to use specialized software systems and the Internet to track the progress of an order through each stage of the production process.

The increasingly high-tech nature of the industry creates opportunities for Taiwanese firms because the emphasis of the global network shifts from achieving cost reductions, through savings on labour costs (a primary weakness of the Taiwanese at home), to more effective management of the production network and the consequent ability to match supply to market demand more effectively (a potential strength of Taiwanese firms vis-à-vis companies with lower labour costs).

At the same time that East Asia is emerging as a regional economy with manufacturing networks that cross national borders, *local economic clusters* are extraordinarily important in China. The factories of particular townships and villages will often specialize in a particular product, and then dominate world markets. For example, 80 per cent of the world's metallic-shell lighters come from the city of Wenzhou in Zhejiang Province. Not far away, in the town of Qiaotou, 700 family-run factories produce 15 billion buttons and 200 million metres of zippers a year—again, they are the world leaders (*China News Digest* 2006; Watts 2005). Qingxi Township in the southern city of Dongguan specializes in PC production, and has become so important in the production of monitors, motherboards, keyboards, and PC boxes that the deputy director of IBM Asia remarked that, 'If there is a traffic jam between Dongguan and Hong Kong [where the port is located], 70 per cent of the world's computer market will be affected' (Enright et al. 2005: 62). Similar clusters can be found for bicycles, domestic appliances, furniture, plastic flowers, air conditioners, and shoes—virtually any product imaginable.

The formation of these clusters is partly the result of a natural tendency on the part of firms to seek agglomeration economies, but government policy also played a key role. Over the course of the reform period in China, the central government gave increasing autonomy to local governments to shape their own economic policies, and gave them fiscal incentives to do so successfully (Oi 1992). The slate with which local governments had to work, however, was not a clean one: the economic history, the structure of government institutions, and the types of firms in a region created different sets of possibilities for different places. Small and entrepreneurial firms in Zhejiang Province benefited from a local government that supported (or at least did not obstruct) private-sector firms and the lack of competing state-owned enterprises (Whiting 2001). Firms in capital and technology-intensive industries in Shanghai benefited from a local government that invested heavily in firm development and guided the process of technology transfer from foreign-invested enterprises. Light industrial firms in Guangdong Province took advantage of local policies that favoured exporting and foreign investment from ethnic Chinese networks. In a decentralized economy environment, the role of local policy is as important as national policy in shaping the framework of opportunities and constraints within which firms must operate.

The competitive pressures that lead to regional integration in East Asia, and the opportunity to access world-class and inexpensive manufacturing capabilities in the various industrial clusters of China creates strong pressure on the *national 'varieties of capitalism'* of multinational firms that invest in China. As Hay points out in Chapter 10 of this volume, there is no topic in the field of global political economy that is more controversial than whether global capital, trade, and investment flows are leading towards a convergence of national institutions. This debate has a corollary in the literature on global production: when multinational firms and their suppliers move abroad, do they preserve certain characteristics of their home county? The characteristics of Japanese production networks, for example, are commonly perceived to be relatively closed when compared to American production networks—a result of the preferential trade relationships and cross-shareholding within Japanese corporate groups and long-term relationships between management and labour—and these characteristics have been seen as surprisingly durable when transferred abroad. The overseas subsidiaries of Japanese companies are less likely to employ local managers, less likely to rely on local sourcing (except when Japanese affiliates were located in the local economy), and less likely to transfer R&D activities to overseas affiliates (Encarnation 1999; Ernst and Ravenhill 2000; Solis 2003). According to this viewpoint, 'firms involved in global competition begin their lives under very different legal, social and political environments and histories . . . [and] while firms from different nations may eventually converge on some best practice, convergence may not happen quickly or automatically' (McKendrick et al. 2000: 9; see also Borrus and Zysman 1997). The durability of national foundations leads to unique corporate strategies, and alternate strategies lead to variation in the form of the production networks that bind regions together.

In China, both the durability of national approaches to investment and the intense pressures on these approaches are visible in the patterns of Japanese investment. When a Japanese firm begins to manufacture in China, for example, there has always been a strong tendency to continue to rely on the same Japanese suppliers. In some cases, these will be suppliers that are part of the same industrial grouping, but it will also be Japanese suppliers that have had long-term relationships with the company in Japan. During the 1990s, the bulk of Japanese investment in China followed a predictable pattern: the objective of Japanese firms was to lower costs, and, in keeping with the concept of a regional hierarchy, production was moved to China but core components and design continued to come from Japanese firms. Because the focus of these firms was on export markets, the drive to lower costs could not be at the expense of quality, and it was easier to maintain quality standards while using tried-and-true suppliers. Dalian, a city in north-eastern China, was a popular investment site because it was close to Japan and relatively easy to find workers there with Japanese-language skills. Within a decade, however, a distinct shift had begun to emerge, as investment trends moved towards the greater Shanghai region in eastern China, and the Guangdong region of southern China. In a 2002 survey of Japanese firms with investments in China, 81 per cent of the firms in eastern China and 80 per cent of the firms in southern China had plans for expansion, compared to 46 per cent in north-eastern China (Marugami et al. 2003: 24). The 2004 survey indicated that only 13 per cent of Japanese firms in north-eastern China had plans for expansion, while the percentages for eastern and southern China were just under 70 per cent and 50 per cent, respectively (although 64 per cent of Japanese electronics firms had plans to increase investments in southern China) (Marugami et al. 2005: 30, 32).

Why has the location of Japanese investments in China been shifting towards eastern and southern China? There are both push and pull elements to the shift. The push stems from competitive pressures and the consequent need to cut costs. First, Japanese investments in China are focused increasingly on access to the growing domestic marketplace—79 per cent of firms listed this as their primary motivation for increasing investment in 2002 (Marugami et al. 2003: 28). It is the world's largest market for telecommunication devices (wired and wireless) and one of the largest markets for digital consumer and computing devices (Ernst 2006). In this increasingly sophisticated market, it is often Chinese firms that are the key competitors, and they place tremendous cost pressure on foreign competitors. 'In terms of low-end products,' commented one Japanese manager, 'many Chinese companies sell them without taking into account profit margins. We can't compete with that' (Marugami et al. 2003:

39). (Chinese state-owned enterprises often focus on market share rather than profit levels, because they receive preferential access to capital from the government-dominated banking system.)

Second, the Japanese firms have to compete with multinational firms that are offshoring large parts of their manufacturing to low-cost producers in China, often at the expense of the small and medium-sized enterprises (SMEs) that have traditionally served as suppliers at home. The speed with which American firms have abandoned manufacturing in order to focus on product definition and design, software, and high-end services (Borrus and Zysman 1997; Sturgeon 2002) is perhaps not surprising given the characteristics of a liberal market economy, but South Korea, which has retained a focus on manufacturing, has been equally ruthless in opening up its manufacturing networks to non-Korean firms. In 2004, South Korea had close to 3 million SMEs—these firms employing the vast majority of workers in the manufacturing sector—and 86 per cent of these firms were subcontractors to large firms (*Hankyoreh 21* 2004). According to a survey conducted by the Federation of Small and Medium-Sized Enterprises in South Korea, the large firms demanded price cuts of 5–10 per cent annually, and there was seldom a choice—the large firms simply demanded the price cuts (*Hankyoreh 21* 2004). The options open to the SMEs are limited: they often do not have the technical ability to upgrade into new product areas, and if they move to China in an effort to cut costs, they have difficulty competing with Chinese firms. Firms such as Samsung, LG, and Hyundai have the classic firm-specific advantages (that is, brands, technology, and/or scale) that can be exploited when they move offshore, but their suppliers are not so fortunate. Although a political desire for balanced economic development and fear of a 'hollowing-out' of the South Korean economy led to pressure on the large firms to support the country's SMEs, there are limits to this benevolence. 'In an environment in which we compete with global firms,' commented a member of the Samsung Electronics purchasing team, 'it is meaningless to distinguish between domestic and foreign supply firms' (*Maeil Kyongjae* 2005). LG Electronics has been even more aggressive than Samsung, and has built up R&D capabilities in China partly in order to facilitate the development of local Chinese suppliers. Not surprisingly, given that they compete in the same environment as the Korean firms, Japanese firms find themselves under the same pressure to cut ties to higher-cost suppliers from home.

The primary reason Japanese investments in China are being pulled toward eastern and southern China is because these are the regions with the strongest component firms. As the director of the Japanese trade office in Dalian explained, it was no longer enough for Japanese firms simply to seek out low-cost labour and ready access to Japan; they were now being forced by competitive pressures to invest in the locations with the most capable component firms, and, in southern and eastern China, there are not only a wealth of Chinese component firms, but also Taiwanese and South Korean firms (Yabuchi 2000: 1). Even as wages rise in southern China, the benefits of the local industrial clusters endure. In some cities in southern China, wages increased as much as 50 per cent over the previous three years, the president of a Canon factory in Zhuhai commented in early 2007, but because labour contributes only 5 per cent of the total cost of final assembly for a product such as a digital camera, they will not relocate: 'We could go from China to Vietnam to India and then to Africa [in search of lower wages]. But that would be a slash-and-burn approach. In reality, it's not like that' (Pilling and Mitchell 2007: 7).

The industrial clusters of China represent a particularly pure version of globalization of production—they consist, not of local firms that have developed slowly over time, but primarily of highly competitive foreign firms that have co-located in China and feed off of each other's strengths—and this puts pressure on ties that were formed in the less competitive context of the home country. The large Japanese firms have slowly been opening up their networks to take advantage of the world-class capabilities that are available in China, and this puts pressure on Japanese SMEs. In the past, a parent company was forced to maintain a certain level of business with its subcontractors, and a 'treacherous' act could hinder its business with other firms, but overseas expansion to regions with highly capable supply firms creates new capabilities (JSBRI 2003: 187). According to a 2001 survey of Japanese SMEs, the parent company strategy that was having the most negative impact on their own operations was overseas expansion (JSBRI 2003: 187). The extent to which Japanese production networks open to non-Japanese firms varies both by firm and industry, and they continue to be far more closed than other national networks, but the trend is an important one. As Dieter Ernst argues (2006: 183), it signals the end of an unequal division of labour in East Asia, one in which the higher value-added activities and technology remain in Japan, and only the labour-intensive activities move offshore, the beginning of a complex process of 'hybridization' of national production networks (Ernst and Ravenhill 2000: 242).

It is worth noting that it is not only less competitive firms that lose out in this process, but also less competitive countries in the developing world. China contains the potent combination of a large market, low-cost labour, and a highly developed supply sector, and for many countries, this is a difficult combination with which to compete.

Governance and upgrading

The quantity of FDI that flows into China might make it the envy of the developing world, but it is increasingly a point of controversy within the country. Although advocates of openness argue that foreign investment would ultimately increase self-reliance, as Chinese firms gained technology and managerial capabilities, sceptics claim that Chinese firms have found it difficult to capture the gains from their participation in global production networks. In the wake of the rapid increase in inward FDI flows in the mid 1990s, the *Economic Daily* (*Jingji Ribao*), an authoritative economic paper in China, ran a series of articles that were highly critical of the impact that foreign investment was having on Chinese firms. Openness was not inherently bad, the commentary argued, 'but looking across the countries of the world, [we see] that opening up definitely cannot be without certain principles and certain limits'. It is important to 'pay attention to protecting national industries', the paper concluded (Fewsmith 2001: 173–4). Academics have similarly argued that discrimination against entrepreneurial private-sector firms in China and in favour of foreign firms and inefficient state-owned enterprises has handicapped the development of Chinese companies. Yasheng Huang and Tarun Khanna point to Wal-Mart shelves sagging with Chinese-made goods, and make the point that relatively few products with the 'Made in China' label are made by indigenous Chinese firms. 'That is because China's export-led manufacturing boom is largely a creation of FDI,' they argue. 'During the last 20 years, the Chinese economy has taken off, but few local firms have followed, leaving the country's private sector with no world-class companies to rival the big multinationals' (Huang and Khanna 2003: 74).

To what extent have Chinese firms benefited from foreign investment and integration with global production networks? The automotive industry is a good test case because it is a sector that the Chinese government targeted for development in the early 1980s, and FDI has been the primary means of promoting it. The barriers to entry in the industry are also high for a developing country. The high cost of product development in the industry and the rapid advance of technology create strong incentives for assembly firms to share development costs with global suppliers. The assemblers group products around common underbody platforms, outsource the design and production of large modules of the car to global suppliers, and then rely on these firms to supply the modules wherever in the world they decide to assemble the vehicles. Global platforms spread the costs of development more widely by creating greater economies of scale for each model, and

outsourcing passes a good portion of the design burden for individual modules on to the supply firms. These same characteristics, however, make it very difficult for a local supply firm to become an upper-tier supplier in the network of a multinational firm (Humphrey and Memedovic 2003). Tier one global suppliers (for example, firms such as Bosch, Denso, and Visteon) are often as large and powerful as their customers, and they must be able to co-operate on the design of new models with the assemblers.

The intention of the Chinese government in forming joint ventures with multinational auto firms was clear—FDI would allow the domestic auto firms to gain access to technology and managerial skills—and because of the large potential of the domestic marketplace, it was also clear that China had an enviable amount of leverage over multinational firms: foreign firms were not allowed to have a majority stake in an assembly joint venture (JV), they were often pressured to transfer large amounts of technology to their China projects, and until China joined the World Trade Organization (WTO) they were forced to rapidly increase the percentage of components that were sourced from within China.

Despite these advantages, none of the Chinese partners in these JV projects has emerged as a major auto manufacturer in its own right. Not only do the JVs still dominate automobile production in China, but the only two Chinese firms that were in the top ten auto producers in 2006 were independent firms (Chery and Geely) that had never formed joint ventures with foreign firms. The failure of the Chinese partners in JV projects to develop capabilities independent of their foreign partner would seem to support those who argue that foreign investment is not the most effective way to develop strong indigenous firms, or, at the very least, indicates that capturing the gains of foreign investment cannot be taken for granted.

But state policy clearly does matter. Local governments were generally the key actors in formulating the policy environment for firms in the auto sectors, and they pursued a variety of approaches (Thun

2006). Shanghai adapted the policies of a local developmental state. The municipal bureaucracy compensated for underdeveloped capital markets by taking charge of the process of capital accumulation and investment in supplier development. Municipal officials also co-ordinated the process of technology transfer to local firms, controlled their relationships with the assembly plants carefully to ensure that they received a steady stream of orders, and monitored their development. These supply firms grew both in size and capabilities, and began to expand outside Shanghai. Other regions, such as Beijing and Guangzhou, took a more market-based approach. The small supply firms received little help in their search for investment capital, technology, and customers. Few firms were able to capture economies of scale, and, unable to raise volume, they were also unable to lower costs. Most went bankrupt. In contrast to Shanghai, where the Chinese partner in the joint venture is currently investing in developing an independent line of vehicles, the joint ventures in Beijing and Guangzhou are completely dominated by their foreign firms (primarily from Japan and South Korea), and the Chinese partners have no aspirations to develop independent capabilities.

The recent success of independent firms is also not necessarily a repudiation of the JV strategy that dominated the industry for so long. In many respects, the new, independent firms are building on the base that the JVs created in China. Part of this strategy involves the strategic use of the supplier capabilities that the joint venture projects have developed, particularly in the greater Shanghai region. This involves the utilization, not only of suppliers having a range of technical capabilities that the independent assemblers do not, but also of designers who were trained at the JV projects and then created their own design firms. Part of this strategy involves luring Chinese engineers with long experience on the JV projects to work for a genuinely *Chinese* firm. The joint ventures served as a training ground for the auto sector and created a range of possibilities that did not exist prior to their formation. In short, the benefits of FDI do not necessarily flow directly to the Chinese partners at the JVs, but they, nevertheless, increase the local capabilities of the sector overall.

Key points

- Since the early 1980s, China has become a manufacturing powerhouse, and one of the world's leading destinations for FDI.
- China is a regional production base in the sense that a large proportion of its exports involve the processing trade: China imports higher-value goods from its more advanced neighbours, assembles these components into finished goods, and then exports these goods to final markets.
- Both the intensity of competition within China and the presence of highly capable supply firms from many countries have led to the weakening of national production networks.

Conclusion

Firms have long been a product of their immediate geography. They have always been shaped strongly by the regulatory and legal institutions of the states within which they are formed, the inputs available to them (human capital, raw materials, and components), and the nature of the markets within which they compete. The intensity of these constraints has varied over time, however. As early as the seventeenth century, firms were looking to distant countries for raw materials not available at home. In the early twentieth century, they began to relocate (and replicate) manufacturing activities in major foreign markets in order to escape protectionist trade barriers. Foreign production has been commonplace for centuries. What is new in the current era of globalization is that geographical dispersion no longer precludes global integration. Firms are able to break up their value chain in ways that were not previously possible, make a decision about where each particular activity should be located, and then integrate these far-flung activities with advanced technologies.

The globalization of production creates opportunities and challenges for both developing and developed economies. From the perspective of developing economies, the massive flows of foreign investment and the increased willingness of multinational firms to outsource production have created a range of opportunities that were not previously present. Under the right circumstances, multinational firms are willing to take offshore, not only the labour-intensive activities that have traditionally gone to the developing world, but also the higher value-added activities. There are two significant caveats, however. First, the flows of FDI are highly concentrated (and multinational firms often display a strongly herd-like mentality). Countries that have laboured to create a conducive political and legal context for investment can find themselves, through no fault of their own, with very few investors. They might be too small; there might be a shortage of supporting industries and suppliers; they might not be easily accessible; or they might be located in what is otherwise a rough and dangerous neighbourhood. This problem is particularly harsh, of course, because private investment flows have largely replaced official sources of investment capital. In this environment, the poorest countries may easily find themselves worse off than in the past. Second, in those cases that are blessed with high rates of inward FDI, the gains for the domestic

economy are far from guaranteed. Few countries are in as favourable a position as China to cope with the challenges of FDI, and yet even China continues to struggle with maximizing the benefits of foreign investment for indigenous firms. Indigenous Chinese firms often find themselves locked in a downward competitive spiral: because they usually compete in areas with low barriers to entry, competition is intense and profit margins thin, and they often have little to invest in research and development. State policy is critical, particularly the support that is given to local firms, but it must be more nuanced than in the past — investment that flows in can just as easily flow out when host governments impose conditions that are too onerous. Rather than strong-arming multinational firms into transferring technology and utilizing local suppliers, it is far more effective (and more difficult) to create a policy environment that will support the development of the capabilities that multinational firms are seeking in their supply base.

From the perspective of developed economies, the globalization of production allows firms to choose à la carte from a global menu of production sites. No longer constrained by the limitation of having to conduct all activities in one particular geographical setting, the parts of the value chain can be broken up and located separately, according to the competitive needs of any particular activity. This allows a firm to compensate for weaknesses in their home base without completely abandoning it. Although the hope is always that the higher value-added activities will remain at home, the danger is that the outflow will be too great and a hollowed-out economy will be left behind. In the case of the regional production networks of East Asia, the fears of hollowing-out in the advanced economies that surround China have not yet been realized. Quite the contrary, in fact — the combination of the growing Chinese market and the increase of imports of high value-added components into China has been an economic engine for the region. The gains, however, are not evenly distributed. It is the small and medium-sized enterprises in an economy that have the most difficulty in adjusting, and these are often the firms that provide the bulk of employment at home. Trading relationships that appear to be mutually beneficial in the aggregate can mask significant dislocation and, as in the developing countries, public policy must focus on increasing the capacity of smaller firms to take advantage of the potential gains of globalization. In the absence of balanced growth, the possibility of a backlash against globalization is all too real.

Key points

- The rise of global production creates new opportunities for developing countries, but also real risks: first, for those that are unable to attract FDI; and second, for those able to attract FDI but unable to maximize the benefits for indigenous firms.

- Similarly, in developed economies, the gains from globalization are not evenly distributed, and in the absence of effective public policy this imbalance creates the possibility of a backlash against globalization.

? Questions

1. What have been the drivers of the globalization of production since the 1980s?

2. Why do multinational firms invest in equity stakes in foreign operations rather than form trading relationships with foreign firms?

3. What is modularity, and how does it increase the opportunities for global production?

4. How does the governance of a global value chain affect the prospects for upgrading in a developing country?

5. What factors does a firm need to consider when deciding where to locate production facilities?

6. What are the benefits of industrial clusters, and why do they form?

7. Why has China emerged as the world's factory, and what are the implications of this trend?

8. From the perspective of a developing country, is a heavy reliance on FDI good or bad?

9. From the perspective of an advanced capitalist economy, is the offshoring of production good or bad?

→ Further reading

 Abernathy, F. H., Dunlop, J. T., Hammond, J. H., and Weil, D. (1999), *A Stitch in Time: Lean Retailing and the Transformation of Manufacturing* (Oxford: Oxford University Press). A detailed and fascinating account of how information technology has transformed retailing in the clothing industry.

■ Baldwin, C. Y., and Clark, K. B. (1997), 'Managing in an Age of Modularity', *Harvard Business Review*, 75/5: 84–93. A classic account of how modularity creates new possibilities for structuring industrial sectors.

■ Berger, S. (2006), *How we Compete: What Companies around the World are Doing to Make it in Today's Global Economy* (New York: Currency Doubleday). A highly readable and knowledgeable analysis of how different companies and countries are coping with the challenges created by the globalization of production.

■ Dunning, J. H. (1981), *International Production and the Multinational Enterprise* (London: Allen & Unwin). A classic work on FDI.

■ Gereffi, G., Humphrey, J., and Sturgeon, T. (2005), 'The Governance of Global Value Chains', *Review of International Political Economy*, 12/1: 78–104. This article provides a framework for analysing the structure of global value chains.

■ Kaplinsky, R. (2005), *Globalization, Poverty and Inequality: Between a Rock and a Hard Place* (Cambridge: Polity Press). This book provides a cogent analysis of why many countries have difficulty in capturing the benefits of globalization.

■ Levinson, M. (2006), *How the Shipping Container Made the World Smaller and the World Economy Bigger* (Princeton, NJ: Princeton University Press). A fascinating account of how something as simple as a shipping container transformed the global economy.

■ McKendrick, D. G., Doner, R. F., and Haggard, S. (2000), *From Silicon Valley to Singapore: Location and Competitive Advantage in the Hard Disk Drive Industry* (Stanford, CA: Stanford University Press). A detailed academic study of how decisions about location helped US firms to dominate the global hard disk drive industry.

■ Palmisano, S. J. (2006), 'The Globally Integrated Enterprise', *Foreign Affairs*, 85/3: 127–36. A concise account of the new model of global firm from the CEO of IBM.

■ United Nations Conference on Trade and Development (2006), *World Investment Report 2006: FDI from Developing and Transition Economies: Implications for Development* (New York/Geneva: United Nations). The annual UNCTAD report on investment flows.

:// Web links

■ The primary source of data on global investment flows is the United Nations Conference on Trade and Development (UNCTAD). Its publications are available at www.unctad.org. For academic research on global value chains in a variety of industries and countries, see www.ids.ac.uk/ids/global/index.html and www.globalvaluechains.org/.

Online resource centre

For additional material and resources, please visit the Online Resource Centre at:
www.oxfordtextbooks.co.uk/ravenhill3e/

12

Globalization, Growth, Poverty, Inequality, Resentment, and Imperialism

Robert Hunter Wade

✳ **Reader's guide**

The head of a Chinese family recently said to a BBC interviewer, 'You, in the West, all have washing machines, and refrigerators, and TVs. Why shouldn't we Chinese have the same?' This chapter moves towards an answer to his question, but with reference to the whole human race. It does so by assessing the free market argument, also known as the globalization or the new-liberal argument, which promises that ordinary people will enjoy substantial gains in living conditions provided their nation and the world keep moving towards free market policies and away from government 'interventionism'; and which promises, implicitly or explicitly, that the same forces will promote democracy.

One pillar of the argument is the record of the past quarter century. In this period, the global centre of gravity of economic policy shifted strongly in the direction of free market policies: governments everywhere exited from trying to change the relative prices established in free markets; trade, ideas, and people became less restricted; and a large part of the world started to function almost like a single economy. The new-liberal argument says that these changes had an egalitarian effect: inequality fell, the number of people living in poverty fell, median living conditions improved, and economic freedom expanded. So, globalization and the expanded scope of free market forces brought 'mutual benefits' between nations and classes (including *haute finance*), contrary to the standard Left assumption of 'conflicting interests'.

The argument concludes on the basis of both theory and evidence that the interests of rich countries and poor countries, dominant classes and subordinate classes, are broadly aligned in favour of free markets, thanks to the way that free markets open opportunities and allocate resources to their most efficient uses. The present income gaps between North and South, core and periphery, and rich and poor people are just lags in the catch-up of the poor world to the prosperity of the rich world, not a result of polarization inherent in the working of capitalist economies organized into nation states.

Of course, in the absence of global government, knowledge of the trends in *global* growth, poverty, and inequality is not of operational interest to any government. But the knowledge is of operational interest to the nearest we have to global economic government, namely the global economic multilaterals (GEMs) like the World Bank, the International Monetary Fund (IMF), the World Trade Organization (WTO), the Asian Development Bank. Since the 1980s, these bodies have been mandated by their member states to implement the Washington Consensus—to deregulate markets, open up national economies to cross-border trade and investment, and harmonize national regulations so as to give economic actors a global 'level playing field', undistorted by state restrictions. The globalization argument provides the intellectual legitimacy for this mandate, and warns that the mutual benefits of globalization will be at risk if countries start to backslide on market liberalization.

A lot is at stake. Here, I show that the evidence of positive trends in growth, poverty, and inequality is dappled with ambiguity. I suggest that the world economy organized as it has been since the 1980s may generate forces analogous to gravity, which hold low-income countries down, and others analogous to magnetic levitation, which hold a small number of high-income countries up (comprising around 15 per cent of the world's population); and which within countries sustain the gap between the plutocracy and everyone else.

At the end, I summarize some of the sources of bias in the pro-globalization argument, both theoretical and empirical. In particular, I highlight sources of bias in those statistics generated by the World Bank, which it uses to 'prove' the effectiveness of globalization-in-general and of its own interventions. I outline an alternative perspective on development strategy in developing countries and growth strategy in developed countries, which emphasizes the need for a political ethics beyond the new-liberal focus on freedom of choice and the rights of the individual.

> " It cannot make sense to fragment the world economy more than it already is but rather to make the world economy work as if it were the United States, or at least the European Union....The potential for greater economic integration is barely tapped. We need more global markets, not fewer, if we want to raise the living standards of the poor of the world. Social democrats, classical liberals and democratic conservatives should unite to preserve and improve the liberal global economy against the enemies mustering both outside and inside the gates. "
>
> (Wolf 2004*a*: 4)

> " The only alternatives today are to be neo-liberal or neo-idiotic. "
>
> (Franco 1996)

> " Overheating is not dangerous.... Neither Icelanders nor Americans need to worry about the trade deficit. The trade deficit only indicates that capital is flowing into countries in which the business environment is favourable for investments to pay off.... Iceland should be a model to the world. "
>
> (Arthur Laffer, celebrated conservative economist speaking during a visit to Iceland (*Morgunbladid* and *Vidskiptabladid* 2007))

> " Despite the enormity of recent events, the principles of economics are largely unchanged....Students still need to learn about...the efficiency properties of market outcomes. "
>
> (Mankiw 2009)

> " Much of this line of research appears to have such deep flaws that, at present, the results cannot be regarded as remotely reliable. "
>
> (Banerjee et al. 2006: 53)

Introduction

Climate change, ocean acidification, species extinction, resource depletion, nuclear proliferation, and cyber attacks on digital networks—these are by now well-recognized threats to the future of human civilization. Less familiar is the threat that the world economy over the next decades will function in a relatively 'exclusionary' way, that the caravan of people and countries will lengthen as the income gap between leaders and laggards grows. If this happens, our collective ability to manage existential crises like climate change and ocean acidification will also be impaired. Managing them requires a substantially higher level of multilateral co-operation than exists at present, yet co-operation fails and free riding flourishes when some major players consider the game to be stacked against them.

Data on the future is sadly lacking, but we can get traction by understanding the past. There is wide agreement on four big points:

1. Average living conditions have improved in most of the world in the past half century or so, by much more than in the previous half century. Rocketing life-expectancy has lifted much of the developing world to a 20–40–60 generational cycle (parents at 20, grandparents at 40, death at 60), and in places even 25–50–75, far from the 15–30–45 cycle which was the fate of most of mankind for centuries past. Meanwhile, the developed world is close to a 30–60–90 cycle. This improvement ranks alongside the Renaissance and the Industrial Revolution in the annals of human achievement.

2. The number of people living in extreme poverty fell in China in the quarter century between 1981 and 2005 on a scale never seen before in human history: from about 80 per cent of the population below the World Bank's international extreme poverty-line in 1981 to about 20 per cent in 2005, or 600 million people. Most of the fall took place in the 1980s, not later, due to rural pricing and land allocation reforms.

3. Between countries, the global expansion of capitalism since the Industrial Revolution of the

eighteenth century has gone with a steep rise in income inequality, described by some scholars as the Great Divergence (some say it started in the sixteenth century). Income inequality between countries is now substantially greater than inequality within countries.

4. Within countries, income distribution changed slowly during the 1950s to the 1970s (tracking changes was like watching grass grow, quipped one economist). But it became substantially more unequal during the 1980s, 1990s, and into the 2000s in most countries for which data is available, covering a majority of the world's population.

Beyond these points of agreement, the disputes are about trends in global poverty and global inequality in the past three decades—since about 1980—and the causes of these trends. Many influential voices say that the world has finally turned a corner towards convergence rather than divergence, towards less poverty and more equality. The world caravan is shortening as the laggards catch up. According to Martin Wolf, the celebrated economic columnist for the *Financial Times* and author of *Why Globalization Works* (2004*a*), 'The evidence strongly suggests that . . . inequality among households across the globe is . . . falling. There is also little doubt that not just the proportion of the world's population in extreme poverty, but the absolute numbers are falling' (2004*b*). Wolf bases his conclusion on statistics and research supplied by the World Bank, the IMF, and other related organizations.

Wolf and others understand these good trends as the result of the world economy becoming substantially more globalized after 1980 than before (markets more integrated across borders, prices less divergent); and understands the acceleration of globalization as propelled in large part by the worldwide shift towards free market or new-liberal *policies*, away from state 'intervention'. New-liberalism began to become 'global policy' around 1980, in the wake of the breakdown of the Bretton Woods

economic architecture in the early 1970s, the ascendancy of free market political movements in the United States and Britain at the end of the 1970s, and the collapse of the communist bloc in the 1980s; and has remained global policy ever since.

This chapter uses 'new-liberalism' in place of the more common 'neo-liberalism' because it is more neutral, the latter having come to be used in a way which implies an automatic negative. 'Global policy' here means policy which is developed by actors who claim to think for the world and who play an advocacy role in multiple states and transnational forums. Examples of global policy actors include the World Bank, the IMF, the WTO, the Organization for Economic Co-operation and Development (OECD), and also powerful national agencies like the US Treasury and the UK Treasury.

New-liberalism and its globalization or Washington Consensus policy agenda (Wade 2007*a*) is based on ideas formulated more than 200 years ago by Adam Smith. For Smith, as for today's conventional economists, the key to prosperity is to expand the size of the market (including through policy liberalization). Increases in market size permit more specialization in line with comparative advantage, which raises productivity, which raises the level of prosperity. Harvard professor Gregory Mankiw, author of a leading economics textbook and former Chairman of the President's Council of Economic Advisors, recently affirmed that 'Adam Smith was right when he said that "Little else is required to carry a state to the highest degree of opulence from the lowest barbarism but peace, easy taxes and a tolerable administration of justice"' (*Wall Street Journal*, 3 January 2006).

Hence, the global policy actors have enjoined the world's governments—especially those of developing countries—to place market liberalization at the centre of their (micro)economic policy agendas; augmented in the past two decades by an emphasis on improving 'governance' and curbing 'corruption'. On the other hand, they have warned against 'industrial policy' aimed at accelerating the diversification of production structures (beyond what would result from generic improvements in market institutions and beyond the economy's existing comparative advantage), such as the industrial policy practiced by the East Asian capitalist governments during their fast-growth phase. Their emphasis on expanding the scope for exchange as the key to development has led them to overlook production and technology, as seen in the lack of attention in the World Bank and in bilateral aid agencies such as the UK's Department for International Development to questions of how to upgrade production in selected manufacturing sectors and how to make trade protection work better rather than simply less (Wade 2004).

The theory that globalization has been driving improvements in growth, poverty, and inequality has prompted a range of criticisms. At the popular level, a backlash against globalization has been sweeping all the rich countries, even before the 2008 crash. A large proportion of their citizens (larger than in most developing countries) consider globalization to be a negative force, and look to government to cushion the blows they perceive to have come from opening the economy to trade with developing countries. Many NGOs and other critical analysts claim that, in the words of US union leader, Jay Mazur, '[G]lobalization has dramatically increased inequality between and within nations' (2000). The critics tend to see globalization, not as an exogenous force which no nation can escape, but as a political project of the dominant industrial–financial states, which use policies and regulations, both national and international, to tip the playing field—or structure of opportunities—in favour of themselves, their firms, their citizen-consumers, and, above all, in favour of the tiny fraction which draws its income from owning and managing capital. The architects intend the unequalizing effects of new-liberal policies within and between countries.

Each side tends to conduct the debate as if its case was overwhelming, and only an intellectually deficient or dishonest person could see merit in the other side. Martin Wolf raised the temperature by invoking 'the enemies [of globalization] mustering both outside and inside the gates', and claiming that the 'anti-globalization' argument constitutes 'the big lie', a phrase usually reserved for a Nazi propaganda technique (Wolf 2000, 2004a: 4).

Who is right? You would think that the matter could be settled by appeal to evidence. It turns out, however, that much of the evidence is not straightforward (Brune and Garrett 2005). Nevertheless, the GEMs, dominated as they are by the developed countries, still insist that the evidence favours the prescription of 'more market' across the board—with the qualification, since the crash of 2008, of tighter regulation of financial markets and temporary state intervention to stimulate economies out of recession. While organizations like the World Bank have become a little less dogmatic in their general statements over the past decade, the key test is what global actors, such as World Bank country directors, tell their borrower country counterparts, and what criteria are hard-wired into the operating procedures of global organizations. Here, it is clear that simple new-liberal economics and the Washington Consensus policy agenda are alive and kicking. As just one example, the World Bank deploys the Country Policy and Institutional Assessment (CPIA) formula to score countries by the 'goodness-for-development' of their policies and institutions, and factors the score into its lending decisions, especially in the allocation of grants and low-interest loans. One part of the formula is for the trade regime, and the scoring criteria imply that a virtually completely free trade regime is best for development; another part is for labour markets, and the criteria give the highest score to countries with the least worker protection (Wade 2010).

Figure 12.1 shows the distribution of world population by average country income. Here, incomes are measured at purchasing power parity (PPP) exchange rates rather than current market exchange rates (Box 12.1). Notice the 'twin peaks' and the 'missing middle'. One peak contains the 70 per cent of the world's population living in countries whose GDP per capita is below PPP$5,000. (The present tense here refers to the early 2000s.) The other peak is the 14 per cent who live in countries with GDP per capita above PPP$20,000 — the rich world. Only 4 per cent live in the missing middle, in countries with average incomes of between PPP$8,000 and PPP$20,000. Talk of the 'middle-income' countries can be misleading, for it suggests, wrongly, that they are 'midway' between the low- and the high-income countries. In fact, the middle-income countries fall towards the low end.

Box 12.1 Purchasing Power Parity (PPP)

Comparisons of real income or material well-being across countries are plagued with difficulties, especially when the countries have very different prices and economic structures. They need to use a common measuring rod. But measures of relative income in different countries—expressed in a common denominator such as the US dollar and determined on the basis of market exchange rates—do not accurately reflect relative purchasing power over goods and services. Exchange rates vary daily, sometimes significantly, whereas the underlying structure of production, income, and expenditure remains relatively stable. Exchange rate conversions also do not take account of the fact that the price levels between countries are very different. In particular, the prices of many not-internationally-traded services (for example, haircuts) are much cheaper in developing countries than in developed countries, and so the relative purchasing power of a unit of their domestic currency is bigger than indicated by converting the currency into the US dollar at the market exchange rate. This is what lies behind the experience of rich people in India who feel poorer when they come to Britain (their purchasing power over goods and services in Britain is less than over the same bundle at home), and poor people in Britain who feel richer when they go to India.

'Purchasing power parity' (PPP) refers to an adjustment of the market exchange rate so as to give the amount of local currency needed to buy as much as does one unit of the currency of the numeraire country, usually the US dollar. In other words, it takes countries' GDPs (physical quantities times prices in national currencies) and revalues the physical quantities using common standard international prices so as to enable comparisons of real purchasing power between countries. In principle, it allows real income comparisons, not only between America and India today, but also—with heroic assumptions—between Britain and India before the industrial revolution.

Because the price of many services and non-traded goods is lower in poor countries, the main effect of PPP adjustments to national income data is to raise the income of poor countries relative to richer ones. For example, Turkey's average income at market exchange rates (FX dollars) was 10 per cent of the EU-15's in the early 2000s and 24 per cent in PPP dollars. Sub-Saharan Africa's was 2 per cent in FX dollars and 7 per cent in PPP dollars. The development problem looks less daunting when incomes are expressed in PPP dollars.

Among the cognoscenti, purchasing power parity is a hotly contested subject, but few who use the numbers know of the controversies and the sources of error.

The calculation of PPPs is based on extensive price surveys in a sample of countries, coupled with assumptions about the comparability of goods and services across countries ('shoes', 'haircuts', 'housing units', 'education'). After the value of the items making up GDP in domestic prices is recalculated using 'international prices', it becomes possible to derive the comparable real volume—a 'quantum' expressed on a standard value basis—of all the goods and services measured by each country's GDP.

The calculations are detailed and complex, involving hundreds of thousands of pair-wise price calculations. The items have to be comparable internationally (including in quality); yet, the fact that many of them are not internationally traded makes comparability harder to judge, for which the solution is detailed product specifications—which makes the price surveys very expensive. While there is a framework and set of procedures for collecting these price and expenditure data locally, the core compilation has to be done centrally and not by national statistical agencies. The main source of the data on country prices is the International Comparison Program (ICP), launched in 1968 at the initiative of the UN Statistics Division and the Department of Economics at the University of Pennsylvania, financed by the World Bank and the Ford Foundation; hence the name of the series, the Penn World Tables (PWT). In 1975, Eurostat began to produce PPPs for EU countries, as a way to determine more fairly financial contributions to the organization and to settle country disbursements. In 1980, the OECD expanded the work to cover all OECD countries, plus countries of Eastern and Central Europe. Around 1980, the UN Statistics Division took over the task of compiling global estimates and the work of co-ordinating the collection of international price data. But in the UN the price collection effort soon languished, the head of the Statistical Office not wishing to use his budget for the work. The World Bank provided technical and financial support to the UN during this time, and took over responsibility for co-ordinating the global exercise in the early 1990s. In the mid 1990s, the World Bank (and the OECD) started to issue their own PPP numbers, using another method of aggregation (EKS) from the one used by PWT (Geary-Khamis). There are now two main series of global PPP data—PWT and the World Bank's. The series show some differences between countries' PPP-adjusted GDPs; and often more substantial differences in estimates of GDP components, such as private consumption, government consumption, and the like. The PWT numbers are more frequently used by academics than the World Bank's, in part because the PWT data provide more details on more countries for longer periods.

Dowrick and Akmal (2005) show that the PWT contains a systematic bias towards underestimating world income inequality, due to their use of a 'rich country' price structure to revalue GDP in poor countries (arising from the use of the Geary-Khamis formula that gives greater weight to those prices involved in the largest value of transactions). They urge that the term 'purchasing power parity' be used only in a generic way, with additional specification of whether the numbers come from the PWT or sources based on a different method of making the PPP adjustment.

Apart from the inherently difficult index number problems which have to be solved one way or another, there are daunting data problems. The price data is spotty in terms of geographic and temporal coverage. The government of China had never allowed a price survey in line with the ICP's criteria until 2005 (and then only partially); the government of India declined to carry one out between 1985 and 2005. For these and other important countries, the PPP numbers were obtained mostly by imputation from other countries or from updating old data. Even for sampled countries, the numbers are collected intermittently, not continuously, making statements of trends in PPP incomes across time problematic. Most of the results of the 1993–6 round of price surveys had still not been made available by the mid 2000s.

The spotty and out-of-date quality of the data reflects the institutional weakness of the International Comparison Program, which for much of its existence has hovered on the verge of collapse. While housed in the UN Statistics Division it received little support from senior officials and UN member states, on the grounds that it entailed a big additional burden on participating statistical bureaus and provided data of interest mainly to academics, not policymakers. Since the early 1990s, when the World Bank took it in, it has been carried forward by a few World Bank officials and consultants, still plagued by shortages of funding, managerial support, and data (Korzeniewicz et al. 2004). It was not able to supervise seriously countries' data collection for the 1993–6 round, and the resulting non-comparability is part of the reason why data collected in 1993–6 had not been made available by the mid 2000s.

The 2005 ICP price survey was more comprehensive than the earlier ones (146 countries participated), and used more strictly specified goods and services so as to ensure international comparability. The results, published in 2008, were a bombshell: they entailed huge revisions of developing countries' GDPs (mostly downwards) and poverty headcounts (mostly upwards, raising the global headcount of those in extreme poverty by half a billion). For example, the World Bank estimated China's PPP GDP per capita in 2005 using the pre-2005

PPP conversion factors at $6,760, India's at $3, 450. Using PPP conversion factors derived from the 2005 price survey, these figures became, *for the same year*, $4,090 and $2,220, respectively. (At market exchange rates, the figures are $1,720 and $800.) As Angus Deaton and Alan Heston remark, 'it is hard not to speculate about which previously established econometric results survive the incorporation of these revisions' (Deaton and Heston 2009).

Adding together all the problems of methodology and data, it is no surprise that, even before the 2005 results, plausibly constructed PPP incomes for China differed by a factor of two, and similarly for countries of the former Soviet Union before the 1990s. The bottom line is that confidence in trends in PPP incomes, inequality, and poverty should be limited by the certainty of wide margins of error, however uncomfortable that may be for those wishing to feed them into the econometrics compactor. The best source for understanding PPPs is Deaton (2010).

The distribution of world population by the income of individuals (based on household surveys) is much more skewed towards the tail than the distribution by countries' average income (based on national income accounts). The world average income is PPP$3,500, and 75 per cent of the world's population has less than the average. Slightly more than 40 per cent lives on less than PPP$1,000 a year ($2.73 a day). Only 10 per cent has more than about PPP$10,000.

Figure 12.1 'International income distribution': the distribution of people according to the GDP per capita of the country in which they live (year 2000)

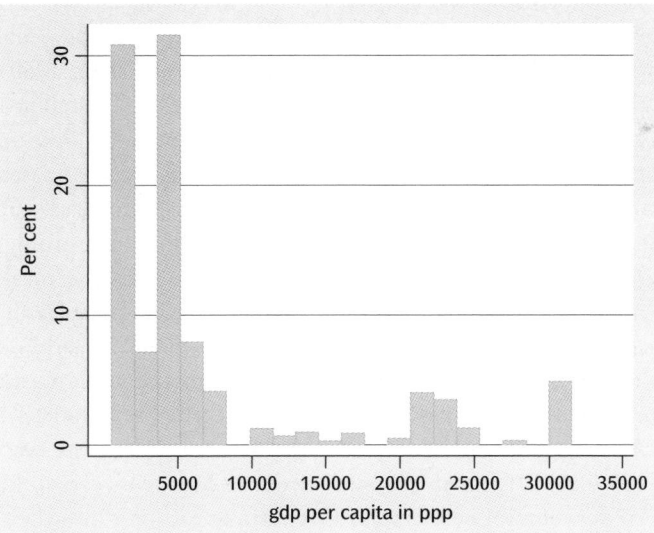

Note: GDP shown in 1995 international dollars
Source: Milanovic (2005: 129)

To get a more tangible idea of the distribution of economic hardship, we can use the number of hours of work needed for an adult male entry-level employee at McDonald's to earn the equivalent of one Big Mac. In the 'core' zone of Western Europe, North America, and Japan the figure (2007) is in the range of 15–30 minutes; in Seoul–Taipei–Singapore, 47–51 minutes; San Jose (Costa Rica) and Santiago (Chile), 1 hour 25 minutes; Shanghai 1 hour 48 minutes; Delhi 3 hours; Hyderabad (India) 3 hours 54 minutes. Remember that a job at McDonald's is well up the prestige ranking in low-income countries; most people work in less desirable jobs.

Two-hundred years ago, in the early decades of the Industrial Revolution, most of the income inequality between the world's people was due to 'class' inequality within each state, reflecting the relative equality of average incomes between states. Today, the composition of inequality between individuals has reversed: most of it is due to 'geographical' inequality in average incomes between developed and developing states and regions. Cecil Rhodes, the nineteenth-century champion of British imperialism, captured the point when he declared, 'Remember that you are an Englishman, and have consequently won first prize in the lottery of life.'

Growth and Geographical Distribution

The globalization argument implies that the period since 1980 should have experienced an increase in global economic growth, thanks to the global policy shift towards market-friendly policies and the rise in economic integration between countries. Much media commentary over the 2000s has focused on the rise of 'emerging markets', notably the BRICs (Brazil, Russia, India, and China), as though they represent the success of the post-1980s world economy. Indeed, the growth performance of the BRICs is impressive: in the decade from 1999 to 2009, in nominal dollar terms, China rose from seventh to third biggest economy, Brazil from tenth to eighth, and Russia and India joined the top twelve.

Yet this good news masks a longer-term global growth slowdown. The growth rate of world gross domestic product (GDP) per capita fell by a third between 1955–80 and 1980–2007, from an average of about 2.2 per cent to 1.7 per cent. Indeed, a majority of the world's countries (56 per cent) experienced negative growth of GDP per person in 1980–2000. Martin Wolf presents a table (2004a: table 8.1), which shows the sharp slowdown in growth of GDP per head between 1950–73 and 1973–98 in every one of the world's seven regions, except 'Asia

(excluding Japan)'. He makes no comment on the generalized slowdown or its significance for his argument that 'globalization works'.

For the OECD as a whole, and for the US, Europe, and Japan separately, the rate of growth per head fell in every decade from 1960–73, 1973–9, 1979–90, and 1990–2004. The fall in 1990–2004 is especially telling, because, by this time, the 1980s policies of squeezing inflation, deregulating, privatizing, liberalizing trade and capital movements had worked themselves through into macroeconomic stabilization and free markets; yet the promised upturn in economic growth did not appear.

In 2003 to 2008, world output grew much faster than during the previous quarter century, at about 2.3 per cent (1992–2008, 1.7 per cent). Most commentators said the rise was a long-delayed payoff from twenty-five years of liberalization and would continue for long into the future ('the end of history'). The crash of 2008 revealed that the fast growth in the earlier part of the decade was based on an unsustainable run-up of debt, especially in the US. (The Roman playwright, Plautus, got the mechanism two-thousand years ago, when he had one of his characters declare, 'I am a rich man as long as I do not repay my creditors.') The high growth rates of 2003 to 2008 are unlikely to be regained any time soon, unless again based on unsustainable debt.

The world growth trend hides large variations between regions and classes. Sub-Saharan Africa, with almost 1 billion people, had an average income in the mid 2000s barely above the level of 1980, despite most states having implemented Washington Consensus-type structural adjustment programmes for many years. Latin America, with 550 million people, experienced much the same stagnation at a higher income level. The countries of the former Soviet Union, after more than twenty years of transition to capitalism, remain at about the same average income as when the transition started. On the other hand, the North (Western Europe and North America) grew faster than these other regions, and China from the 1980s and India from the 1990s have grown very fast from a very low base.

Figure 12.2 shows the regional trends in the form of the ratio of average regional income to that of the high-income 'core'. The ratios for Latin America, Eastern Europe, and sub-Saharan Africa fell after 1980; China and 'Asia minus China and India' rose, but even by 2001 they had reached only around 15 per cent of the North's (in PPP dollars). This is far from a picture of catch-up growth. Much of the caravan has been falling even further behind.

Weighting the regional averages by regional population we get a '1:3:2' world. There are roughly 1 billion people in the high-income countries; 3 billion in countries where growth rates have been substantially faster than in the high-income countries over the past two decades, though starting from very low income levels and remaining at low levels; and 2 billion where growth rates have been lower than in the high-income countries, some of these in middle-income countries, others in low-income countries. The large majority of developing countries are in the non-catch-up category.

The brutal fact is that, after decades of self-conscious development and market liberalization, the average income for the South is still only around 15 per cent of that of the North in purchasing power parity terms, and more like 5 per cent in foreign exchange rate terms. Also, growth

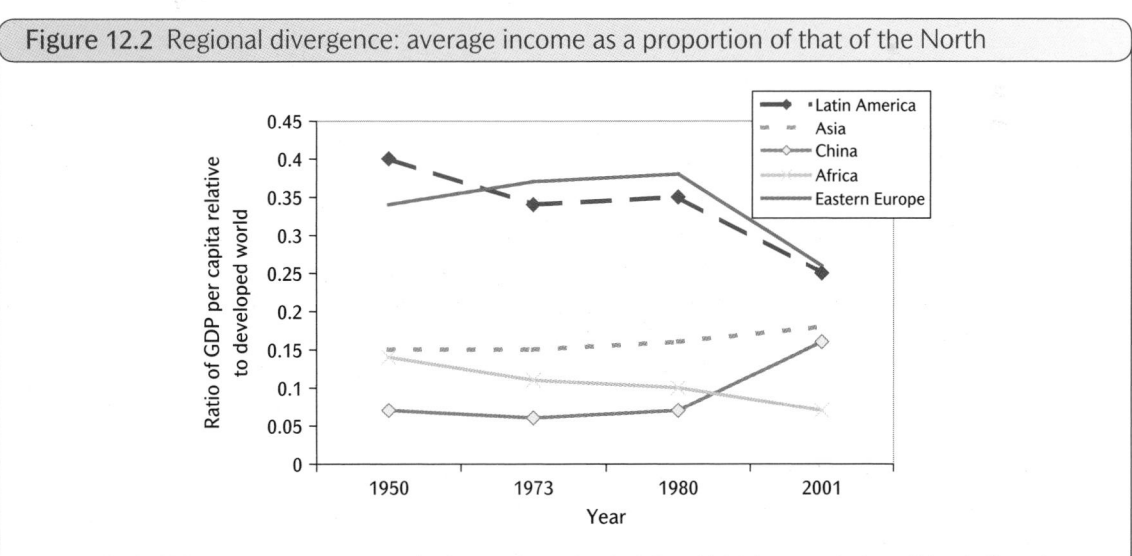

Figure 12.2 Regional divergence: average income as a proportion of that of the North

Note: Ratios in PPP values for income per capita, in 1990 Gear-Khamis dollars. 'Asia' does note include China, India, or Japan
Source: UN (2006)

in the South is much more erratic than in a typical developed country, with periods of relatively fast growth followed by deeper and longer recessions.

Of the increase in world consumption over the 1990s, a majority accrued to those already in the top 10 per cent of world income distribution—the fast growth of countries with 3 billion people notwithstanding. Figure 12.3 shows (top half) the proportion of the world's population living at each consumption level, and (bottom half) the share of world consumption accruing to each level. The dotted lines indicate 1993, the solid lines 2001. The area under the 1993 curves equals unity, while the area under the 2001 curves is larger in proportion to the increase in population and consumption between 1993 and 2001. Between these years, some 50 per cent to 60 per cent of the increase in world consumption accrued to those living on more than PPP$10,000 in 1993, around 10 per cent of the world's population; of this 10 per cent, four-fifths lived in the high-income countries and most of the rest in Latin America. The remaining 40 per cent to 50 per cent of the increase in world consumption accrued mostly to those living in 1993 on around PPP$3,000 to PPP$6,000, of whom the majority were in the burgeoning middle-class of China. Only about 10 per cent of the total increase accrued to the poorer half of the world's population. Hardly any accrued to those on less than PPP$1,000 a year ($2.73 a day). Most of the latter lived in South Asia, Africa, and China.

In short, the 'Matthew Effect' is operating, or at least the first half of it. Matthew's Gospel says, 'For unto everyone that hath shall be given, and he shall have abundance. But from him that hath not shall be taken away even that which he has.'

No surprise that the North is receiving an in-flood of legal and illegal immigrants as communications improve, for the quickest way for the average Southerner to multiply their consumption many times is to hop across a border into the North. There are many borders to choose from. Low-skilled workers coming to the North can expect even bigger relative gains than high-skilled workers. The best-paid bus drivers in the

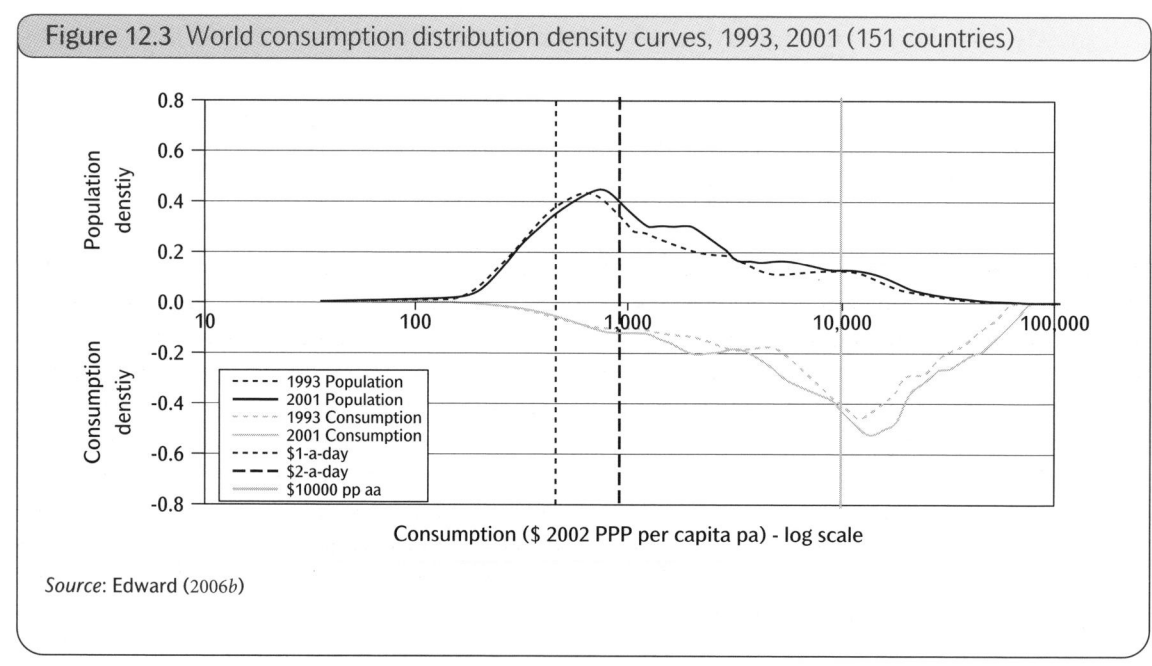

Figure 12.3 World consumption distribution density curves, 1993, 2001 (151 countries)

Consumption ($ 2002 PPP per capita pa) - log scale

Source: Edward (2006*b*)

world get thirty times the real wage of the worst paid, while the best-paid computer programmers get 'only' ten times the lowest paid, according to International Labour Organization (ILO) statistics.

Now to poverty and inequality. We have to ask about how the statistics are generated, for different methods produce different results.

Key points

- The average income for the South is still only around 15 per cent of that of the North in PPP terms, and significantly less in market exchange rate terms. This comes after five decades of self-conscious development and almost three decades of concerted market liberalization.

- There has been a major growth slowdown during the age of intensified globalization (since around 1980, in the post-Bretton Woods global economic regime) as compared with the previous two or three decades. The rate of growth of world GDP per person fell by almost half between 1960–78 and 1979–2000. For the OECD countries, output per capita grew more slowly in the period 1990–2004 than in previous decades back to 1960, despite macroeconomic stability and liberal markets.

- Growth rates varied substantially between regions. African countries performed particularly poorly; also,

from a higher starting point, many Latin American and central and East European countries. In contrast, East Asia's growth rates were the highest in the world, but from a low base.

- Between 50 per cent and 60 per cent of the increase in world consumption between 1993 and 2001 accrued to individuals with incomes of PPP$10,000 or more, constituting about 10 per cent of the world population, four-fifths of whom live in the high-income countries. Only a tiny proportion of the increase accrued to those on PPP$1,000 or less.

- The upswing in world and developing country growth rates in the first few years of the twenty-first century, which some took to be the payoff from twenty-five years of globalization, came to an abrupt end in 2008 as the Great Recession unfolded. China, India, and Brazil have been leading the global recovery since 2009. Growth has gone South, debt has gone North.

Poverty

Understood as a lack of well-being, poverty should be treated as a multidimensional phenomenon, including income, hunger, disease, lack of shelter, lack of water and sanitation, and social exclusion. Let us duck these complexities and stick to an income, expenditure, or consumption measure.

Counting the number of people living below a poverty line gives us a measure of the incidence of poverty, and we can measure trends in global poverty by summing up the total number of people living below a standard international poverty line

and tracing the number across time. Notice that while this information certainly has its uses, it is of little help on the other important question of how the benefits of growth are shared between poor and non-poor. Notice, too, that to observe poverty only through numbers on a computer screen is to miss the tragedy of truncated lives, that would be your and my tragedy if we had the bad luck to be born into the lower deciles of countries where 85 per cent of the world's population lives.

The World Bank is the main source of the poverty numbers. To get the world extreme poverty headcount, the World Bank first defines an international extreme poverty line (IEPL) for a given base year by using PPP conversion factors to convert the purchasing power of an average of the official national poverty lines of a set of low-income countries into the US dollar amount needed to have the same notional purchasing power in the United States in the same year. In its first global poverty estimation, this procedure yielded a conveniently understandable PPP$1-a-day for the base year of 1985. Then the Bank uses PPP conversion factors to estimate the amount of local currency, country by country, needed to have the same purchasing power in the same year as in the US base case. So, by this method Rs.10 may have the same purchasing power over a standard basket of goods and services in India in 1985 as US$1 in the United States in the same year. This gives an IEPL expressed in domestic currency (Rs10 per day in the Indian example).

From household surveys, the Bank then estimates the number of people in the country living on less than this IEPL in the base year. It sums up the country totals to get the world total of people living in extreme poverty. It then uses national consumer price indices to keep real purchasing power constant across time, and adjusts the IEPL for each country upwards with inflation. As well as the extreme poverty headcount (people living on less than PPP$1 a day) the Bank also estimates the ordinary poverty headcount (people living on less than PPP$2 a day). Over time, the PPP$ amounts corresponding to these initial international poverty lines have been moderately raised.

In 2008, the World Bank presented revised estimates of countries' GDPs and world poverty headcounts, based on the international price survey of 2005 (see Box 12.1). Table 12.1 summarizes the numbers before and after the revised estimates, and with and without China.

The numbers living in extreme poverty show a pronounced fall between 1981 and 2005, whether we use the pre-2005 PPP conversion factors or the ones based on the 2005 price survey. This is good news, indicating substantial progress in cutting the number of people living in extreme poverty. The bad news is that, according to the new estimates, hundreds of millions more people have been living in extreme poverty than earlier estimated, so the extreme poverty problem is much worse than

Table 12.1 Key World Poverty Numbers

	1981		2002		2005	
	Number (bn)	Percentage	Number (bn)	Percentage	Number (bn)	Percentage
Old estimate @ $1.08	1.5	41	1.1	20	0.9	17
New estimate @ $1.25	1.9	52	1.6	31	1.4	25
New estimate @ $2.50	2.7	75	3.3	62	3.1	57
Excluding China						
	1981		2002		2005	
	Number (bn)	Percentage	Number (bn)	Percentage	Number (bn)	Percentage
Old estimate @ $1.08	0.9	32	0.9	23	0.9	22
New estimate @ $1.25	1.1	40	1.2	31	1.2	28
New estimate @ $2.50	1.8	66	2.6	66	2.6	63

Note: Percentage refers to population of the developing world. 'Old' refers to PPP conversion using pre-2005 price data
Source: Chen and Ravallion 2008. See also World Bank PovcalNet (www.worldbank.org/research/PovcalNet/jsp/index)

had been thought. As the World Bank's 'poverty czars' summarize, 'While the new data suggest that the developing world is poorer than we thought, it has been no less successful in reducing the incidence of absolute poverty since the early 1980s' (Chen and Ravallion 2008: 33).

More bad news comes from the substantial increase in the number of people living on less than the scarcely generous PPP\$2.50 a day, which implies a big bunching between \$1.25 and \$2.50 a day (though the proportion of the developing world's population living on less than \$2.50 a day fell from 75 per cent to 57 per cent). People in the bunch are very vulnerable to shocks such as the steep rise in food and fuel prices after 2005, and the global economic crisis of 2008. Still more bad news comes from the fact that the fall in the number under \$1.25 a day is due entirely to China. Take China out and the number in extreme poverty increased (though the proportion still fell from 40 per cent to 28 per cent).

The geographical distribution of extreme poverty has changed. In 1981, East Asia (including China) had the highest proportion of its population in extreme poverty (78 per cent, using the new estimates for the PPP\$1.25 line), then South Asia (59 per cent), then sub-Saharan Africa (54 per cent). By 2005, the rank order was sub-Saharan Africa (51 per cent), South Asia (40 per cent), East Asia (17 per cent).

So, if we take the World Bank poverty numbers at face value, the picture is distinctly mixed. Moreover, we should not take the Bank's numbers at face value. While it almost always presents its numbers as 'without-a-doubt' it should provide health warnings in bold letters.

Large margin of error

The margin of error is large, for several reasons. First, the poverty headcount is very sensitive to the precise level of the international poverty lines. Figure 12.3 shows that the population–consumption curve is steep at the point of intersection of the \$1-a-day line, meaning that small

shifts in the line make large changes in the number of people below it. Recent research on China suggests that a 10 per cent increase in the line brings a roughly 20 per cent increase in the poverty headcount.

Second, the poverty headcount is very sensitive to the reliability of household surveys of income and expenditure. Some countries survey income, others, expenditure, and merging the results is not straightforward. The available surveys are of widely varying quality, different countries use different formats and the same country may change the format from one survey to another. For example, surveys may use different reporting periods. A study in India in the late 1990s found that switching from the standard 30-day reporting period (asking people their expenditure over the previous 30 days) to a 7-day period magically cut the number of poor by half, because the shorter recall period yields more reported income or expenditure.

Third, by far the two most important countries for the overall trend, China and India, have PPP-adjusted income figures that contain even more guesswork than for most other big countries. Because the government of China declined to participate in all the rounds of the ICP until 2005 (Box 12.1), the PPP estimations for China have been based on econometric regressions rather than real data; and those for India have been based on extrapolations from the 1985 price survey. The lack of reliable price surveys for countries accounting for over a third of the world's population—hence the lack of reliable evidence on the purchasing power of even average incomes, let alone incomes of the poor—compromises any statement about levels and trends in world poverty.

Note that other key world variables are also subject to large but unquantified margins of error. The absolute income per capita of the poorest countries is implausibly close to the survival minimum, which probably reflects substantial undercounting of agricultural, informal, and black activities. The per capita income of the richest countries may be misstated because of deficiencies in measuring inflation and quality improvements. Even as apparently solid a number as world population growth is uncertain. The World Bank's World Development Indicators for 2000 revised downwards the rate of growth of world population in 1980–90 by 40 per cent and for 1990–9 by 13 per cent, which must be one of the biggest revisions to a major world statistic ever made. Yet, the Bank made no comment on it. Many of the existing studies of world growth, poverty, and inequality are based on the unrevised population growth numbers, at cost to their reliability (Svedberg 2003).

Downward bias

Still other sources of error may bias the poverty numbers downwards, making the number of poor people seem lower than it is; and the bias may increase over time, making the trend look rosier than it is. For at least three reasons.

First, the Bank's IEPL underestimates the income or expenditure needed for an individual (or household) to avoid periods of food-water-clothing-shelter consumption too low to maintain health. And it avoids altogether the problem that basic needs include unpriced public goods like clean water and health care. The Bank's line refers to an 'average consumption' bundle, not to a basket of goods and services that makes sense for measuring poverty (though '$1-a-day' does have intuitive appeal to a Western audience being asked to support aid). Suppose it costs Rs.30 to buy an equivalent bundle of food in India (defined in terms of calories and micronutrients) as can be bought in the US with $1; and that it costs Rs.3 to buy an equivalent bundle of services (haircuts, massages) as $1 in the United States (Reddy and Pogge 2003). Current methods of calculating purchasing power parity, based on an *average* consumption bundle of food, services, and other things, may yield a PPP exchange rate of, say, PPP$1 = Rs.10, meaning that Rs.10 in India buys the equivalent average consumption bundle (food, services, etc.) as $1 in the United States. But this is misleading because the poor person, spending most income on food, can buy with Rs.10 only a third of the food purchasable with $1 in the United States. To take the IEPL for India as Rs.10 therefore biases the number of poor downwards.

We have no way of knowing what proportion of food-water-clothing-shelter needs the Bank's international poverty line captures. But we can be fairly sure that had the Bank used a basic needs poverty line rather than its present artificial one (an average of the national poverty lines of a somewhat arbitrary set of low-income countries) the number of absolute poor would rise, because the national poverty lines equivalent to a global basic needs poverty line would probably rise, perhaps by 25 to 40 per cent (this is Reddy and Pogge's estimate, the range reflecting calculations based on PPP conversion factors for 1985 and 1993, and for 'all-food' and 'bread-and-cereals' indices).

A 30 to 40 per cent increase in a basic-needs-based international poverty line would, for the reason mentioned earlier, increase the world total of people in extreme poverty by a large fraction, probably by at least 30 to 40 per cent. A study for Latin America shows that national extreme poverty rates, using poverty lines derived from calorific and demographic characteristics, may be more than twice as high as those based on the World Bank's $1-a-day line. For example, the World Bank estimated Brazil's extreme poverty rate (using its IEPL) at 5 per cent; the Economic Commission for Latin America (ECLA), using a calories-and-demography poverty line, estimated the rate at 14 per cent. Similarly, Bolivia's extreme poverty rate according to the World Bank line was 11 per cent, according to the ECLA line, 23 per cent; Chile, 4 per cent, 8 per cent; Colombia, 11 per cent, 24 per cent; Mexico, 18 per cent, 21 per cent (ECLA 2001: 51).

In view of the difficulties of defining a world-wide basic needs package, we could define a 'life expectancy poverty line' based on the pronounced kink in the relationship between individual income and individual life expectancy at around $3 a day and 72 years to 74 years. Income increases above $3 a day bring only small gains in life expectancy, increases below this figure bring substantial gains. Switching to this life expectancy poverty line increases the world poverty headcount very substantially (Edward 2006b).

In short, we can be reasonably confident that switching from the Bank's international extreme poverty line to one reflecting either the purchasing power necessary to achieve elementary human capabilities or life expectancy close to potential would substantially raise the number of people in poverty.

The second reason for suspecting that the Bank's poverty numbers make the trend look too rosy relates to the effects of changes in average consumption patterns as average incomes rise. Worldwide average consumption patterns are shifting toward services whose prices relative to food and shelter are lower in poor than in rich countries, giving the false impression that the cost of the basic consumption goods required by the poor is falling. As Indians become wealthier and consume more services relative to food, a rupee appears to buy more than it used to; and so the PPP value of Indian incomes goes up. But poor Indians continue to spend most of their income on food, and for them the purchasing power of rupees has not increased. Part of the apparent fall in the number of people below a poverty line defined in PPP-adjusted rupees is therefore a statistical illusion. This effect is amplified by the widespread removal of price controls on 'necessities' and the lowering of tariffs on luxuries.

All these problems have to be resolved in one way or another in any estimate of world poverty, whoever makes it. But the fact that the World Bank is effectively the monopoly provider, introduces a third source of possible downwards bias. The number of poor people is politically sensitive. The Bank's many critics on Right and Left like to use the poverty numbers as one of many pointers to the conclusion that it has accomplished 'precious little', in the words of former US Treasury Secretary Paul H. O'Neill. The chairman of a taskforce established by the US Congress to report on the multilateral economic organizations described the fall in the proportion of the world's population in extreme poverty from 28 per cent in 1987 to 24 per cent in 1998 as a 'modest' decline, the better to hammer the Bank (Meltzer 2001). This critique then provides a rationale for the US to control the Bank, as in the statement by the head of the US Agency for International Development (USAID), 'Whether the US way of doing things drives some multilateral institutions, I think it should, because, frankly, a lot of the multilateral institutions don't have a good track record' (*International Herald Tribune*). Understandably, the Bank highlights the fall in the poverty numbers when responding to criticism from powerful member states, in order to show that it is doing a good job. When trying to enlist support for a bold initiative (like the Comprehensive Development Framework), the Bank may play up the increase in poverty to show that it needs more support.

Here are some examples of the Bank's changes of emphasis. In 1999, the high profile *World Development Report* said that the poverty headcount was rising:

> The absolute number of those living on $1-a-day or less continues to increase. The world-wide total rose from 1.2 billion in 1987 to 1.5 billion today.
>
> (World Bank 1999b: 25)

In 2002 another report said,

> The number of people subsisting on less than $1 per day rose steadily for nearly two centuries, but in the past 20 years it has…fallen by as much as 200 million, even as the world's population has risen by about 1.6 billion.
>
> (World Bank 2002b: 3)

In 2004 the two Bank experts in charge of the poverty numbers said,

> By the frugal $1 per day standard there were 1.1 billion poor people in 2001—almost 400 million fewer than 20 years earlier.
>
> (Chen and Ravallion 2004: 141)

The enormous increase to the poverty numbers made in the wake of the 2005 ICP price survey adds to the sense of being in quicksand. Angus Deaton, one of the world experts in this subject, argues that the increase is due mostly to the statistical technique for recalibrating the IEPL; namely, the removal of India's relatively low national poverty line from the set of poverty lines whose average constitutes the IEPL (on grounds that India's average income had risen beyond a low-income threshold). Removing India therefore raised the IEPL, which raised the global poverty headcount. Having said this, Deaton also says, 'It is all very confused, at least to me' (personal communication, 27 December 2009).

Key points

- The good news is that, according to World Bank figures, the number of people living in extreme poverty (whether by the old estimates based on pre-2005 PPP conversion factors or the new ones) fell by around 25 per cent between 1981 and 2005; and the proportion of the developing world's population living in extreme poverty fell by 40 per cent to 50 per cent. The bad news is that, if China is excluded, the number in extreme poverty increased. And the number living on more than PPP$1.25 a day but less than $2.50 a day (the new extreme and ordinary poverty lines, based on the post-2005 PPP numbers) increased so much that the world total living on less than $2.50 a day increased. According to World Bank figures, more than half of the developing world's population is living on an income of less than PPP$2.50 a day.

- Despite the authoritative voice with which the World Bank delivers the poverty numbers, examination of how the numbers are constructed suggests they contain a large margin of error or indeterminacy; they probably contain a downwards bias; and may make the trend look better than it is. They may be significantly lower than the numbers that would result from the use of PPP conversion factors based more closely on the real costs of living of the poor, defined in terms of income needed to buy enough calories, micronutrients and other necessities in order not to be poor, or in order to enjoy life expectancy at the kink in the income–life expectancy curve.

- On the other hand, it is likely that the *proportions* of the world's population living in extreme poverty, and ordinary poverty, have fallen. For one thing, household surveys are more likely to miss the rich than the poor, so that their results may overstate the *proportion* of the population in poverty. For another, for all the problems with Chinese and Indian PPP income figures, we know enough about trends in other variables—life expectancy, heights, and other non-income measures—to be confident that their poverty headcounts have, indeed, fallen dramatically over the past twenty years. Moreover, the magnitude of world population increase over the past twenty years is so large that the Bank's poverty numbers would have to be *huge* underestimates for the world poverty rate not to have fallen.

- The new poverty estimates based on the 2005 ICP price survey increase the number of people living under the international extreme poverty line in 2005 by some 50 per cent, compared to the figure for the same year based on pre-2005 PPP conversions. If the new numbers are taken at face value, they suggest that the developing world is much poorer than had been thought; but that the downward trend from 1981 onwards remains equally strong. However, heroic assumptions had to be made in order to derive the numbers, and Angus Deaton claims that the increase is largely the result of the statistical technique for recalibrating the IEPL. If someone as expert in the field as Deaton says, 'It is all very confused, at least to me,' one can be forgiven for feeling confused, too. The monitoring of progress towards the first Millennium Development Goal—to halve the world extreme poverty headcount between 1990 and 2015—is hobbled by this confusion.

The world poverty headcount could move in one direction while world income inequality moves in the other. The new-liberal argument says that they have moved together: the world poverty headcount fell over the past quarter-century, and world income inequality also fell as the laggards caught up, thanks to more open markets. But in the past several years, world income distribution has become a hot topic of debate in international economics and in sociology (hotter than world poverty). Disagreement about the inequality trends should not be surprising, given the collage of economic performance by region. Different measures emphasize different parts of the collage.

Much of the debate is mathematical, far removed from people's experience of inequality, and focuses less on the 'facts' than on the measures. It turns out that the only valid short answer to the question, 'What is the trend of world income distribution?' is, 'It depends on which of several plausible measures and samples we choose.' Whereas we could get better data on the poor to the extent that the poverty headcount would command general agreement, there is no best measure of world income inequality. Different measures measure different phenomena and are useful for answering different questions.

The results vary according to which of three core measures of inequality are used: Concept 1: inter- or between-country, using average incomes (this could be called the UN General Assembly measure, one country one vote); Concept 2: inter-country, like Concept 1, but countries weighted by population; and Concept 3: inter-personal, or global, covering all the world's people as though the world was one country (Milanovic 2006).

Several other choices also affect the results. Incomes may be converted into a common numeraire using market exchange rates or PPP conversion factors. PPP numbers may be drawn from the Penn World Tables (PWT), or from the World Bank's World Development Indicators, or from Angus Maddison, or still other sources. And, of course, the sample of countries and the time period matter.

The results also depend on the choice of statistic for calculating dispersion—an integral measure over the whole distribution (such as the Gini coefficient or the Theil, see Box 12.2), or a ratio of top decile to bottom decile, or average income of a region relative to that of the North. It turns out that the use of the global Gini coefficient, the most commonly used statistic, conceals as much as it reveals.

Box 12.2 The Gini Coefficient

Income inequality is usually measured through surveys of household income. Households are then ranked from lowest to highest on the basis of income and divided into equal population groups, typically fifths (quintiles), or tenths (deciles). The share of income received by each population group is then compared with the share the population group would receive if all households received an equal share of the income.

The Gini coefficient is a number between zero and one that measures the degree of inequality in the distribution of income in a given society. The coefficient would be zero for a society in which each member received exactly the same income; it would be 1.0 for a country in which one member received all the income and the rest nothing.

For further information on measuring inequality, see the World Income Inequality Database page at www.undp.org/poverty/initiatives/wider/wiid_measure.htm

Concept 1 inequality: distribution between unweighted countries

Concept 1 gives China the same weight as Uganda. It has the great advantage that it requires very little information about each country: just GDP or GNP per capita. Of course, we should not weight countries equally if interested simply in the relative well-being of people. But we should weight them equally—treat each country as analogous to a laboratory test observation—if interested in convergence or divergence of countries rather than people. We might want to test the effects of different government policies on growth—to see whether (unweighted) countries with more open trade regimes grow faster than those with less open ones, for example.

Whatever our motivating question, the trend of Concept 1 inequality is clear (using PPP incomes): the Gini for unweighted inter-country income distribution held fairly steady from 1960 to 1980, increased steeply from 1980 to 2000, and fell from 2000 to 2007, leaving a large net increase in inequality since 1980 (Figure 12.4). Is the increase in inequality due only to the collapse of Africa? No. With Africa excluded, the Gini fell from the mid 1960s to the early 1980s, and then increased steeply.

We see the same divergence in terms of growth rates. With countries grouped into deciles by GDP per capita, the growth rate of the bottom six deciles over 1978–2000 was either negative or approximately nil, while the growth rate of the top three deciles was substantially positive (1.9 per cent a year or more) (Milanovic 2005: 53).

Concept 2 inequality: distribution between weighted countries

Concept 2 yields the desired new-liberal result of falling inequality during the era of globalization. Inter-country income inequality, using PPP/PWT

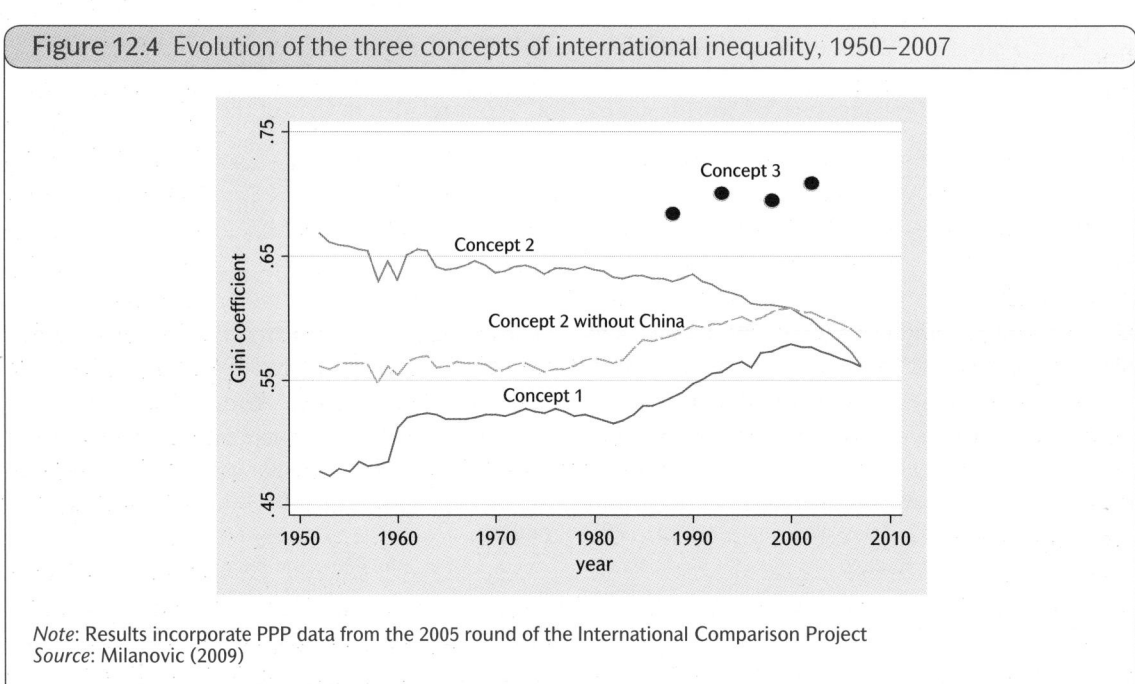

Figure 12.4 Evolution of the three concepts of international inequality, 1950–2007

Note: Results incorporate PPP data from the 2005 round of the International Comparison Project
Source: Milanovic (2009)

dollars, population weights, and the Gini coefficient, was fairly stable from 1960 to the early 1990s, and then fell right up to 2007. This is the good news: it suggests that the centuries old trend to income divergence has finally gone into reverse (Figure 12.4).

But this is a case where the global Gini conceals as much as it reveals. If we take out just one case, China, the population-weighted intercountry Gini *rises* after 1980 right up to 2000, when it, too, begins to turn down; so it goes mostly in the *opposite* direction. The conclusion is that, even with the combination of measures most favourable to the new-liberal case, falling income inequality between countries is a function of China's fast growth since the early 1980s, not a *generalized* tendency of the world system.

The other bad news is that the result also depends on the use of the Penn World Tables method of calculating PPPs. As noted (Box 12.1), Dowrick and Akmal (2005) show that the PWT method systematically understates the magnitude of inequality and overstates its fall. The bias comes through the use of an average international price structure for revaluing countries' GDPs which results from weighting countries' observed price structures by the relative global expenditure at those prices; which means that the average international price structure reflects the price structures of *rich* countries—and so values services (e.g., domestic services, haircuts) much more highly in poor countries, inflating the purchasing power of poor countries' currencies. (This is known as the Geary-Khamis method of aggregation.) When this bias is removed (for example, by switching from Geary-Khamis to the Afriat method), Dowrick and Akmal find that 'true [sic] inequality was stable or increasing slightly... over the 1980s and 90s' (2005: 226). More exactly, three out of their four measures of inequality applied to Afriat-aggregated data show an increase, one shows constancy, *none shows decline*—even when China is included.

That the trend towards falling inequality is reversed by switching from Geary-Khamis to Afriat PPPs underlines the fragility of the conclusion that

world income inequality fell since the 1980s or 1990s. Indeed, a further bias towards rich country prices—hence toward exaggerating poor countries' incomes and their convergence with rich countries—comes from the self-selection of the countries which participate in the (statistically difficult) International Comparison Program (ICP). The participating countries tend to be the statistically more advanced, able to handle the complexities; which also tend to be the richer countries. China's and India's nonparticipation, noted earlier, is part of a wider selection bias.

In any case, this Concept 2 measure—average country incomes weighted by population—is interesting only as an approximation to income distribution among all the world's people or households, regardless of which country they live in. We would not be interested in measuring income inequality in the United States by calculating the average income for each state weighted by its population if we had data for all US households.

Concept 3 inequality: interpersonal (or global) income distribution

One way to get at interpersonal or global income distribution is to take average GDPs, weight them by internal income distribution, and calculate the combined inequalities. As noted, between-country distribution, measured by the Gini, became more equal after 1980 with China included—and more unequal with it excluded.

Within-country distribution generally became more unequal. One study compared income distributions in the 1960s and 1990s in 73 countries, and found that about two-thirds of them containing about two-thirds of their population experienced an increase in inequality, while only about 10 per cent of them containing 5 per cent of their population experienced a fall (Corea and Kiiski 2001).

Another striking point is that countries tend to form high-inequality and low-inequality clusters. Most developed countries are in the low-inequality cluster (whose Gini coefficient spans the range from 0.20 to 0.33), and most developing countries are in the high-inequality cluster (0.50 to 0.65). Changes in within-country distribution tend to be small relative to these clusters, and membership of the clusters shows considerable stability through the twentieth century. Contrary to the Kuznets inverted U hypothesis, there has been little movement from the high-inequality to the low-inequality cluster as countries become richer. The US is about the most unequal of the developed countries, with a Gini in 2000 well above the upper threshold of the low-inequality cluster (Korzeniewicz and Moran 2009).

As noted, inequality between countries' average incomes has been much larger in the past several decades than inequality within countries. That is why most studies which use PPP income or consumption data and weight them by internal distribution—and which include China—show little or no increase in interpersonal (global) inequality after 1980, despite the tendency to increasing within-country inequality.

However, this method assumes that all national income reaches households and is used in welfare-enhancing ways—which is nonsense, not least because it ignores the fact that a sizeable chunk of GDP is spent on private investment or by the state, not on private consumption. In practice, this method allocates these components to households in proportion to their consumption.

A better way to get at interpersonal or global income distribution is to aggregate up from thousands of surveys of household income and expenditure. Branko Milanovic used the resources of the World Bank to do this for five-yearly intervals from 1988. His results upset the globalization champions, because he found an increase in interpersonal income inequality between 1988 and 1993, a smaller fall to 1998, and another increase to 2002, making a sizeable increase in global inequality between 1988 and 2002. Of course, this method, too, has its problems. It undercounts free public services such as education, health, and infrastructure which add to welfare but are not counted in household consumption. And there are big problems of comparability between household surveys.

As for the results of the PPP revisions based on the 2005 price data, Milanovic calculates that they raise the Gini coefficient of global interpersonal income inequality from about 0.65 to 0.70 (using only household surveys). Calculations of Concept 2 inequality also find a substantial widening between rich and poor countries.

At the least, we can say that the evidence on global interpersonal PPP income or consumption distribution, using the Gini coefficient or other integral measure, suggests that it has *not* become significantly more equal since 1980, contrary to new-liberal assertions (Dowrick and Akmal 2005; Milanovic 2005; Dikhanov and Ward 2003). A study by the Economic Commission for Latin America goes further, concluding that there is 'no doubt as to the existence of a definite trend towards distributive inequality worldwide, both across and within countries' (ECLA 2002: 85). The earlier cited evidence from population and consumption density functions for 1993 and 2001 is consistent with this stronger conclusion.

Wage rate inequality

More doubts are cast on the reality of convergence or falling inequality by trends in industrial wage inequality within countries. Wage data has the great advantage over income data that pay is a much less ambiguous variable, it has been collected systematically by the United Nations since the early 1960s, and gives many more observation points for each country than any data set on incomes. It is a useful way to get at the impacts of changes in trade policy and trade flows, or of manufacturing innovation, and the like. The disadvantage of pay data, of course, is that it treats only a small part of the economy of many developing countries, and provides only a proxy for incomes and expenditure. This is not as limit as it may seem, because what is happening to pay rates in formal-sector activity reflects larger trends, including income differences between countries and income differences within countries (since the pay of unskilled, entry-port jobs in the formal sector is closely related to the opportunity cost of time in the informal or agricultural sectors).

Pay inequality within a large sample of rich and poor countries was stable from the early 1960s to the early 1970s, then declined till about 1980–2, then increased sharply from 1980–2 to the present. The period, 1980–2, is a turning point towards greater inequality in industrial pay worldwide. The countries within continents tend to show closely correlated movements in pay dispersions, suggesting macro forces at work. These findings are awkward to reconcile with new-liberal propositions about the impact of globalization. James K. Galbraith and associates present several analyses of pay dispersions at http://utip.gov.utexas.edu.

Polarization or relative gap measures

Measures of inequality are measures of dispersion across the whole of the distribution. They can mislead by obscuring what is happening to major components and by giving more weight to what is happening in the middle than at the extremes. If China's median income fell towards India's, 'world inequality' measured by the Gini would be reduced by the smaller gap between each Chinese and each Indian, but increased by the bigger gap between each Chinese and those above. Simple 'gap' or 'polarization' measures can be more illuminating because they do not have this trade-off. They measure the income shortfall between a given country, region, or other aggregate, and a comparator. We saw one such measure earlier, the ratios of regional income to the North's (Figure 12.2). We might also take income of the top decile of the world's population over that of the bottom decile, or some variant.

Most such measures show widening gaps. For example, with countries grouped into deciles by their PPP GDP per capita, the ratio between top and bottom deciles almost doubled during the 1960–2000 period, from 19 to 1 to 37 to 1 (Milanovic 2005: 53). The polarization would be even more dramatic if we took the top 1 per cent's income over the median or over the bottom 10 per cent's.

Market exchange rate (FX) incomes

The inequality and polarization measures considered so far have all used PPP incomes. If we use market exchange (FX) incomes and Concept 2 inequality the trend is unambiguous: it increased from the 1970s to the late 1990s, when it started to fall thanks to China. See Table 12.2.

However, economists tend to insist that the question, 'What is happening to world income distribution?' should be answered only with PPP incomes, not FX incomes. Sociologists who work on these issues, on the other hand, tend to use FX incomes. National governments, too, tend to be more interested in FX incomes than PPP incomes.

It is true that FX-based income comparisons suffer from all the ways in which official exchange rates do not reflect the 'real' economy: distortions in the official rates, exclusion of goods and services that are not traded, and sudden changes in the official exchange rate driven by capital movements rather than by trade movements. In principle, PPP adjustment is better for questions about relative domestic purchasing power or, more generally, access to material welfare.

But these are not the only questions for which we may be interested in income and its distribution. We may *also* be interested in income distribution as a proxy for the relative purchasing power of

Table 12.2 Inter-country Income Distribution, PPP$ and FX$, Gini Coefficient

Incomes	1965	1980	1995	2001
PPP	0.575	0.6	0.55	0.525
FX	0.7	0.725	0.75	0.725

Note: Afriat-PPP values are in between the values in this table
Source: Korzeniewicz and Moran (2006; figure 1), based on Penn World Tables data

residents of different countries over goods and services produced in *other* countries. If we are interested in any of the questions about the impacts of one state, economy or region on others—including the capacity of developing countries to repay their debts, to import capital goods, to participate in international organizations, and the incentive for people in one country to migrate to another country—we should use FX incomes. FX incomes are a better proxy for relative power and influence, a subject of more interest to sociologists than economists.

For example, the reason why many poor small countries are hardly represented in multilateral negotiations that concern them directly is that they cannot afford the cost of hotels, offices, salaries, and consultants in places like Washington DC and Geneva, which must be paid for not in PPP dollars but in hard currency bought with their own currency at market exchange rates. Similarly for why they cannot afford to pay the foreign exchange costs of living up to many of their international commitments—hiring foreign experts to help them exercise control over their banking sectors so that they can implement their part of the anti-money-laundering regime, for example. International organizations like the World Bank and the IMF, which calculate voting shares on the basis (partly) of FX incomes, are not encouraging a switch to PPP incomes—which would substantially cut the power advantage of the rich countries.

This is why no discussion of globalization and its effects should ignore trends in FX income distribution. The trend towards an increase in inter-country and global inequality of FX incomes between 1980 and 2000 is unambiguous.

The absolute income gap

The standard measures of inequality and gaps refer to relative incomes, not absolute incomes. To see why this is misleading, take two countries: A, with a per capita income of $30,000 (e.g., US, Denmark); and, B, with a per capita income of $1,000 (Philippines, Syria). Their relative income is 30:1 and the absolute gap is $29,000. If A's per capita income increases by 1 per cent to $30,300 and B's also increases by 1 per cent to $1,010, the relative gap remains constant; but, the absolute gap widens from $29,000 to $29,290. If B jumped to 6 per cent growth while A continued at 1 per cent, the absolute gap would widen until year 35 and B would not catch up until year 70. If B grew at 4 per cent and A grew at 2 per cent, the absolute gap would widen for 140 years and catch-up would take the best part of two centuries. Even this last scenario is optimistic, because less than one in ten developing countries with more than 1 million people sustained real GDP per capita growth of 3 per cent or more from 1960 to 2000.

No one questions that world absolute income gaps have been increasing fast—as between, for example, the average income of the top 10 per cent of world income recipients (countries and individuals) and that of the bottom 10 per cent, and also between the top 10 per cent and the intermediate 60 per cent. China and India are reducing the absolute gap with the middle-income states like Mexico, Brazil, Russia, and Argentina, but not with the countries of North America, Western Europe, and Japan. If, as some evidence suggests, people commonly think about inequality in absolute rather than relative terms—those at the lower end feel more resentful and more inclined to migrate as absolute gaps increase even as relative incomes become more equal—our answer to the question, 'What is happening to income inequality?' should not be blind to absolute gaps.

Country mobility

Which way do countries move in the income hierarchy? Table 12.3 shows two state mobility matrices, for 1960–78 and 1978–2000. They divide countries into four income categories (in PPP$ per person). The 'rich' category includes the Western European, North American, and Japanese core. The 'contenders' are countries whose incomes are two-thirds or more than that of the poorest rich country (Portugal or Greece). The 'Third World' comprises countries with incomes between a third

Table 12.3 State Mobility Matrices, 1960–78 and 1978–2000 (Percentages)

	Rich	Contenders	Third World	Fourth World	Total
1960–78					
Rich	73	20	7	0	100 (41)
Contenders	14	32	36	18	100 (22)
Third World	0	5	59	36	100 (39)
Fourth World	0	0	0	100	100 (25)
1978–2000					
Rich	82	12	6	0	100 (34)
Contenders	13	6	69	13	100 (16)
Third World	3	6	28	64	100 (36)
Fourth World	0	0	5	95	100 (44)

Source: Milanovic (2005: table 7.3)

and two-thirds that of the comparator. The rest are 'Fourth World'.

The majority of states, unsurprisingly, remained in the same income category. But stability was concentrated at the extremes: at the top, few states fell into a lower income category; at the bottom, few states rose into a higher category. The middle two categories showed plenty of movement, but most of it down. Two-thirds of the states in the 'contender' and the 'Third World' categories in 1978 fell into a

lower category by 2000. Much the same exercise has been done with ten income categories and FX per capita income, yielding a similarly strong finding of downward country mobility except at the top (Ikeda 2004).

These movements invite the analogy between forces of the world economy and those of the physical universe: a gravity analogue is hindering upward mobility (and keeping internal inequality high), and a magnetic levitation analogue is holding the rich economies up (and keeping internal inequality relatively low). Brazil is a case in point. For eleven years, through the 1960s and early 1970s, it was the 'miracle' economy, on course to be the first sizeable developing country to enter the ranks of the developed countries. Then it crashed, and has remained in roughly the same position in the world income and technology hierarchy ever since; and with roughly the same very high level of income inequality. Many other middle-income countries are today also caught in a 'mid-technology trap', their firms unable to break into innovation-intensive activities or into the market for branded products, where the high profits are to be made. Malaysia is a good example. According to a recent report, Malaysia's 'technological capabilities are relatively static (and may even be declining) and . . . industrial competitiveness is marking time' (Yusuf and Nabeshima 2009: 26).

Case Studies

China and India

With 38 per cent of the world's population, China and India shape world trends. They have grown fast over the past fifteen years (India) to twenty-five years (China), if the figures are taken at face value. China's average PPP income rose from 0.3 of the world average in 1990 to 0.45 in 1998, or 15 percentage points in only eight years.

We can be sure that China and India's fast growth has reduced world poverty and inequality by more than would have been the case had they grown more slowly, and that world income distribution has become less bimodal as the bottom bulge moves out towards the 'missing middle'. About any stronger conclusion, we have to be cautious. First, recall that China and India's PPP numbers are even more unreliable than those for the average developing country. Moreover, officials in China's National

Bureau of Statistics are under strong pressure to 'toe the line' on key numbers. In October 2006, the Commissioner of the National Bureau of Statistics was arrested for 'corruption' and 'severe violation of (party) discipline' just after he announced a substantial upwards revision to GNP per capita and the growth rate. The top organs of the state had promised the US government that they would take steps to slow down China's growth, as an alternative to revaluing the yuan. Insiders consider the Commissioner's arrest to be punishment for politically incorrect revisions to official statistics.

Second, the surge of inequality within China and India partly offsets the reduction in world income inequality that comes from their relatively fast growth — though careful calculations of the relative strength of the two contrary effects have not yet been made. With respect to India, glittering shopping malls and mobile phone connections growing at the rate of 5 million a month coexist with a rate of child malnutrition twice that of Africa, and high child (especially female) mortality. The rich buy their way out of reliance on most public services, including water and electricity supply. New poverties are being created by dispossession and rising population density on limited land, at the same time that new wealth and dignities are being created at the bottom.

With respect to China, no other country has had its combination of fast average growth and fast rise of inequality since the early 1980s. Inequality is now higher than before the communists won the civil war in 1949, and higher than in the US, Russia, and Japan. China accounted for 28 of the 226 newcomers to Forbes' Billionaires list in 2008, with India adding another 19. China now has a heavier density of billionaires per unit of GDP than the European Union, though it remains way below the US.

Inequality between China's regions is probably higher than in any other sizeable country. The ratio of the average income of the richest to poorest province (Guangdong to Guizhou) rose to 4.8 by 1993 and remained at 4.8 in 1998–2001 (current yuan). The corresponding figure for India in the late 1990s was 4.2, the United States, 1.9. The large and widening gaps between regions and classes pose a serious threat to social cohesion in both China and India.

The United States and other anglophone political economies

All the countries of English settlement have experienced increases in after-tax income inequality over the past twenty to thirty years by most plausible measures of inequality. In the United States, the income of the ninetieth percentile of households was nine times that of the tenth percentile in 1970, and eleven times in 2005 (Fischer and Mattson 2009). The US is the most unequal country of the 'core' of the world economy.

The gains have accrued mostly at the very top. The highest-earning 1 per cent of Americans doubled their share of aggregate income (not including capital gains) from 8 per cent in 1980 to over 18 per cent in 2007. The top 0.1 per cent (about 150,000 taxpayers) quadrupled their share, from 2 per cent to 8 per cent. Including capital gains makes the increase in inequality even sharper, with the top 1 per cent getting 23 per cent of all income by 2007.

During the seven-year economic expansion of the Clinton administration, the top 1 per cent captured 45 per cent of the total growth in pre-tax income; while during the four-year expansion of the Bush administration the top 1 per cent captured 73 per cent (Palma 2009). This is not a misprint.

Performance-related and share-based compensation packages pushed up executive pay in the US by almost 10 per cent a year between 2003 and 2007, adjusted for inflation, compared with 0.7 percent for employees. By 2007, US corporate chief executives were paid 344 times the average worker's wage, against 42 times in 1980. Yet, much evidence shows that soaring executive pay has done little or nothing to improve company performance. It is driven, rather, by mutual backscratching between executives and boards, nonchalance of institutional shareholders like pension funds, and legislation disempowering unions.

The US now has the highest density of dollar billionaires in the world against population, and the second highest against GDP (next to Saudi Arabia); about three times the European Union's density (Forbes Billionaires list, based on market values, February 2009).

On the other hand, the typical worker earns only 10 per cent more in real terms than his counterpart twenty-five years ago, though productivity has risen much faster. Indeed, between 2000 and 2008, a time of economic boom, only workers with a professional postgraduate degree—2 per cent of the labour force—enjoyed increases in mean real money income. All other educational cohorts, including college graduates, experienced stagnation or falls.

Wealth, of course, is even more unequally distributed than income. Even those whose wealth puts them well down from the top are segregating themselves in 'gated communities', the modern version of mediaeval walled towns. In the mid 2000s, gated communities accounted for 40 per cent of new residential housing in the state of California. On the other hand, it is estimated that 25 per cent of US households in 1999 were in 'net worth asset poverty', with insufficient net worth (including house equity) to survive for three months or more without income by spending down their wealth (Caner and Wolff 2004). So, one household in four in the world's most powerful economy was persistently vulnerable to adversities such as job loss. This matters all the more because, as income inequality has risen, so also has household income volatility. American households at the end of the 1990s had an almost 20 per cent chance of seeing their income drop by more than half in the following year, more than double the probability in the 1970s.

But the increasing inequality of the past thirty years was not the dominant trend during the past century. Before 1980, the share of the very top had fallen continuously from a peak in 1929, through the Depression, the New Deal, the Second World War, and the post-war social compact, flattening out in the 1970s. However, starting around 1980, income inequality skyrocketed, regaining by the mid 2000s the level of the late nineteenth and early twentieth centuries, the era of the 'robber barons', the Great Gatsby, and labour unrest.

In Britain, the National Health Service has dampened inequalities, while the educational and housing systems have widened them. The net result is that share of the top 1 per cent of households has followed a similar trajectory as in the US, but less extreme. Overseas and homegrown billionaires flock to Britain to live and work but claim residence in an overseas tax haven, avoiding income tax. London, powerhouse of the British economy, is so unequal that a half-hour subway ride east from wealthy Kensington–Knightsbridge to poor Bethnal Green spans a sixteen-year gap in male life expectancy.

The high and rising levels of US and UK income inequality since 1980 are matched by the two lowest rates of social mobility or highest rates of transmission of economic status from one generation to the next among eight major developed countries (Blanden et al. 2005). The two societies which most advertise the virtues of free markets and open opportunities are themselves moving beyond class towards caste (Wade 2007*b*).

OECD

The upwards redistribution of the anglophone countries is part of a broader, though less extreme, pattern throughout the OECD. The OECD 90:10 ratio of after-tax income increased from 3.4 around 1980 to 3.7 around 2000. The share of labour remuneration in business revenue hovered around 70 per cent for decades after the Second World War, rose to 72 per cent by 1980, then fell steadily to 64 per cent in 2003. The share of profits rose by 8 percentage points of business revenue, an excellent result for executives and shareholders. Executives have done especially well in the anglophone economies. In the US, the top five executives in the largest 1,500 public companies saw their personal compensation double as a share of corporate profits in the decade from 1995 to 2005, from 5 per cent to 10 per cent, at cost to wage increases for ordinary workers, funding of pension plans, and reinvestment.

Even Japan's capitalism is being reinstitutionalized to twist income from labour to capital and achieve anglophone levels of income inequality. Among Japan's 5,000 biggest firms, the recovery of 1986–9 saw dividends to shareholders increase by 6 per cent, directors' salaries and bonuses by 21 per cent, and employee remuneration per capita by 14 per cent. A decade and a half later, the recovery of

2001–4 saw dividends increase by 71 per cent, directors' salaries and bonuses increase by 59 per cent, while employee remuneration fell by 5 per cent.

On the other hand, continental Western Europe and Scandinavia have experienced much less of a rise in after-tax inequality than the anglophone countries, and currently have much lower levels of inequality, even with similar or higher levels of integration into the world economy and higher levels of productivity per hour.

Key points

- The major determinant of income inequality on a world scale is the choice of measures. The income measure matters most. Studies which use market exchange rates to convert incomes into US dollars find very large income dispersions between countries and sharply rising inequality over (at least) 1980–2000. Studies which use PPP-adjusted incomes find smaller dispersions and falling, unchanged, or slower rising inequality. The distribution measure is the second most important determinant. Studies which use the Gini or other average plus PPP$ are more likely to find less change than those which measure relative gaps (share of top 1 per cent in total income, or top decile to bottom decile).

- Absolute income gaps between countries and individuals have been widening fast. The present absolute income gaps in the world economy are so large that they will go on increasing for another half-century at the least, even if developing countries experience significantly faster economic growth. Many of the negative effects of rising inequality (operating through a sense of deprivation, for example) probably hold when absolute gaps are widening, even when inequality is falling.

- Between-country income inequality (population-weighted PPP incomes, distribution measured by the Gini) fell after 1980, in line with new-liberal predictions. But those who celebrate this result often overlook the fact that it is due entirely to the

rise of China. Take China out and even the measure most favourable to the new-liberal argument shows that between-country income inequality rose between 1980 and 2000. So, falling between-country inequality is not a general tendency of the globalizing world system.

- Unweighted between-country income distribution has been widening, and the divergence in performance remains even when Africa is excluded. Since there has been a striking convergence of policy towards the new-liberal, the fact of divergence between unweighted countries is bad news for the new-liberal argument.

- Inequality within China and India has increased substantially in recent decades.

- Inequality within all English-speaking industrialized economies has increased substantially by most measures, especially between the 'mega-haves' and the rest. Throughout the OECD, capital income has risen as a share of business revenue and labour income has fallen, raising the political power of those who own capital.

- From California to India and beyond, the affluent minority is self-segregating into gated communities and private markets for health and education, undercutting democratically expressed preferences for higher-quality public services.

- The predominant pattern of mobility of states in the world income hierarchy is downwards, whichever of several comparators are used (average income of the US, the OECD, or the bottom country of the OECD). On the other hand, a small number of states are stably at the top though population aging may slowly undermine their position.

- The evidence presented above on trends in income distribution between regions, classes and individuals or households suggests that the period since 1980 might be called 'the second age of inequality', the first one being the period for several decades before 1929.

Globalization

Recall that global economic policy since the 1980s is based on the premise that 'globalization works', in the sense that as the world economy becomes more globalized, as national economies become more integrated into it, and as governments withdraw from changing relative prices set in global markets (by means of tariffs, subsidies, and the like), economic performance improves: growth rates go up, poverty goes down, inequality goes down. This is what the operational version of the theory says (as in the epigraphs), and it is confirmed by the evidence so far, according to the globalization champions. The foregoing discussion begs to differ.

But even granted that the evidence for the globalization argument is hardly watertight, the response might be Martin Wolf's: globalization has not yet gone far enough. How can we assess this claim?

Not far enough?

There is no doubt that globalization as economic integration has increased hugely over the past several decades. For example, the world trade to world GDP ratio rose from a little under 30 per cent in 1970 to a little under 60 per cent in 2001, according to the World Development Indicators. The first main reason is the end of the Cold War and the collapse of the socialist economic system, which merged two separate labour forces and investment pools into one; and at the same time, India became more open to the capitalist world economy than before. Within a short space of time, the world labour supply (workers producing for international markets) roughly doubled; and since the supply of capital remained more or less unchanged, the labour share of returns from production fell, the capital share went up.

The second main reason is technological change which permits the outsourcing of both manufacturing and services. Businesses broke up their supply chains and looked for cheap labour sites (a process sometimes called 'global labour arbitrage'). FedEx enabled companies in the US to rely on suppliers in Europe (by the late 1970s) and Asia (by the 1980s) almost as intimately as on suppliers up the road. The year 1984 was a milestone, when one day in early summer, the number of wide-bodied jets aloft over the Pacific exceeded the number over the Atlantic for the first time ever (Winchester 1991: 23). 1986 was another milestone, when Jack Welch, CEO of General Electric, created a powerful new vice president to oversee GE's international strategy, dubbing the new executive 'Mr Globalization' (Lynn 2005: 109, 161).

Not only has globalization at the level of outcomes increased hugely, globalization ideas have had a near-monopoly on policy thinking. We see their near-monopoly in the use of the word 'reform' exclusively to denote changes in a free market direction. 'Reform' of a trade regime means reducing protection, not making it work better. 'Reform' of corporate governance means increasing transparency so that investors can better evaluate the buying and selling of shares, not giving more voice to employees. 'Reform' of public enterprises means 'privatization'. 'Reform' of public services means 'outsourcing of government responsibilities' and making labour contracts 'flexible'. On the ground, policy barriers to trade and foreign investment have fallen away as part of a wider government move away from changing relative prices. For example, the world average ratio of tariff revenue to GDP fell from about 27 per cent in 1980 to 10 per cent in 2000. On the other hand, government expenditure as a share of GDP has remained fairly constant, both in developed and developing countries, a disappointment in new-liberal eyes (Cohen and Centeno 2006).

It may still be a stretch to say that most of the world is functioning as a single economy. For one thing, this ignores trends towards *macro-regional* integration, such as China–Japan, North-East — South East Asia, North America, Western Europe. Macro-regions are becoming stronger in terms of: (1) correlated fluctuations of major economic variables; (2) trade; and (3) sales of **multi-national corporations** (MNCs). (Hardly any of the top 500 MNCs have 'global' sales, even in the limited sense of at least 20 per cent in each of North America, Europe, and East Asia and less than 50 per cent in any one of them.) Nevertheless, there is no doubt that economic integration and market liberalization have already gone a long way by historical standards, which questions the argument that things would improve if only trade- and investment-to-GDP ratios rose still more.

Globalization as the key to improved national performance?

Do more globalized economies subsequently experience improved economic performance? That trade liberalization promotes higher welfare probably commands more agreement among economists than any other proposition (at least those educated in the anglophone tradition, as distinct from, say, the French tradition). The proposition appears to be supported by many cross-country studies which find that more liberal trade and investment policies generate economic dynamism. Let us consider one of the most influential, a high-profile World Bank publication called *Globalization, Growth and Poverty* (World Bank 2002b), whose weaknesses illustrate the weaknesses of this whole genre of evidence.

The study measured globalizing by *changes* in the ratio of trade to GDP between 1977 and 1997. It ranked a sample of developing countries by the amount of change. It called the top third the globalizing or more globalized countries, the remaining two-thirds, the non-globalizing or less globalized countries, and weighted countries by population. The more globalized countries had faster economic growth, no increase in inequality, and faster reduction of poverty than the less globalized. 'Thus globalization clearly can be a force for poverty reduction,' it concluded. And it attributed the increase in globalization (measured by trade) largely to trade liberalization, as in, 'The result of this trade liberalization in the developing world has been a large increase in both imports and exports.'

Not so fast. First, using 'change in the trade/GDP ratio' as the measure of globalization skews the results (Rodrik 1999). It is quite possible that 'more globalized' countries are less open than 'less globalized' countries, both in terms of trade/GDP and in terms of the magnitude of tariffs and non-tariff barriers. A country with high trade/GDP and very free trade policy would still be categorized as 'non-globalized' if its increase in trade/GDP over 1977–97 was not big enough to put it in the top one-third. On the other hand, some of the so-called globalizing countries initially had very low trade/GDP in 1977 and still had relatively low trade/GDP at the end of the period in 1997 (reflecting more than just the fact that larger economies tend to have lower ratios of trade/GDP). To call relatively closed economies 'globalizers' and economies with much higher ratios of trade/GDP and much freer trade regimes 'non-globalizers' is an Alice in Wonderland use of language.

But it yields the right result. The inclusion of India and China as globalizers—even though India at the end of the period still had relatively low trade/GDP and a trade regime with plenty of protection, and China had lots of market restrictions behind the borders—practically guarantees the conclusion that 'globalization works'. And excluding countries with high- but not fast-rising levels of trade to GDP from the globalizers, eliminates many poor countries which have had poor economic performance (Honduras and Kenya, for example).

The second problem is causality. The study finds that faster growth of trade quantities is associated with improved economic performance, and concludes that trade *policy liberalization* was key to faster trade growth. In fact, trade volumes are the outcomes of many factors, including an economy's overall growth, not only of trade policy. And they are not something that government controls directly. It turns out that there is no systematic relationship between trade policy (indicated by tariffs and non-tariff barriers) and subsequent economic growth, though this is not a conclusion the World Bank study brings out.

The only systematic relationship in the data is that governments lower trade barriers as their economies become richer. To infer that they became richer because of lowered trade barriers is like inferring that—since rich people tend to live in nice houses—you can become rich by living in a nice house.

With few exceptions, today's rich countries had high tariffs during their rapid growth phase (including the US) and then lowered trade barriers as their domestic industries became competitive. Japan through the 1950s to the 1970s and Korea and Taiwan through the 1960s to the 1980s, had fast growth of trade together with managed trade regimes. They managed trade so as to intensify the cycle of investment and reinvestment in the domestic economy; which generated rapid growth; which generated fast growth of demand for raw materials and capital goods; which prompted strategic trade liberalization (Wade 2004; Chang 2002).

More recently, China and India began to open their own markets *after* building up entrepreneurship, industrial capacity, internal integration, and fast growth behind high barriers. In 1990, China had the fifth-highest average tariffs in the world, behind Bangladesh, India, Pakistan, and Kenya, at the same time as its exports were surging. India continues to have high trade restrictions. Both countries would have got a low score on their trade regime from the World Bank and the IMF during much of their period of 'openness'.

In Latin America, Chile adopted free market policies under Pinochet in the 1970s and enjoyed substantial economic success. Economists urged other Latin American countries to follow Chile's lead, and many did. Yet, they have had poor economic performance. Take this report from Mexico, for example:

> The three main options for high school graduates—attending college, getting a job in Mexico or crossing the border illegally to work in the United States—have become tougher in the past few years . . . The result is that the generation being counted on to drive Mexico's future finds itself stuck. A historically high number of Mexicans—more than 20 million people, a fifth of the population, are 15 to 24 years old. These young people have been promised much. They are reaching working age a decade after implementation of a free trade agreement with the United States that was supposed to bring new jobs, higher wages and a better life than their parents had. They are also coming of age as Mexico moves beyond its authoritarian past. But millions are finding more obstacles than opportunities in the new democratic era.

(Jordan 2003: A15)

Something is amiss when the good pupils score the low marks and the bad pupils score the high marks.

An independent panel of economists tasked with evaluating World Bank research on development policies said of the big cross-country studies which allegedly show that free market policies constitute the ideal development model:

> We see a serious failure in the checks and balances within the system that has led the Bank to repeatedly trumpet these early empirical results without recognizing their fragile and tentative nature ... once the evidence is chosen selectively without supporting argument, and empirical skepticism selectively suspended, the credibility and utility of the Bank's research is threatened.

(Banerjee et al. 2006: 53–6)

On the other hand, while the evidence that globalization drives improvements in growth, poverty, and inequality is shaky, the evidence that globalization has not helped developing-countries-in-general to advance in manufacturing is much clearer. Manufacturing performance can be measured in terms of a country's or region's share in world manufacturing value-added. Table 12.4 shows the percentage share for developing country regions in 1980 and 2000. At first glance, the results look impressive: the share of developing countries rose from 14 per cent to 24 per cent in only 20 years. But almost all of the gain was due to East Asia (including China and excluding Japan). The other developing regions have gained little or even lost share of world manufacturing value-added. In terms of share of world manufacturing output (as distinct from value-added), Western Europe, North America, and Japan still accounted for as much as 75 per cent in 2000, and China for only 9 per cent, up from 4 per cent in 1995. As noted earlier, even an apparently advanced economy like Malaysia's, equipped with a generous array of export-oriented subsidiaries of multinational corporations, seems to be caught in a 'mid-technology trap'.

How to explain the globalization consensus?

All this raises the question: if the evidence is so shaky, why the ringing confidence in the global

Table 12.4 Regional Share of World Manufacturing Value-Added (Percentages)

	1980	2000
East Asia	4.0	14.0
Latin America and the Caribbean	6.5	5.0
South Asia	0.8	1.8
Mid East/North Africa	1.7	2.1
Sub-Saharan Africa	0.8	0.7
Total	**13.8**	**23.6**

Note: East Asia includes China and excludes Japan. Latin America and the Caribbean includes Mexico. Middle East/North Africa includes Turkey and excludes Israel. Sub-Saharan Africa includes South Africa. The table refers to manufacturing value-added, not manufacturing output
Source: Lall (2004)

policy community that new-liberal globalization is the right direction of *further* travel for the world, as in Wolf's, *Why Globalization Works*? Part of the answer comes from, 'Who gains?' By and large, the beneficiaries of a given political economy arrangement tend to argue it is good for everyone, for the reason captured in the Swahili proverb, 'Until the lions have their own historians, tales of hunting will glorify the hunters.' As noted earlier, a majority of the increase in world consumption between 1993 and 2001 accrued to those already in the top 10 per cent of world income distribution, four-fifths of whom lived in the West; and within the West, those in the top 1 per cent and top 0.1 per cent have benefited disproportionately. CEOs who saw their average compensation rise from 42 times that of the average worker in 1980 to 344 times in 2007, are keen to support the 'open' economy of which they are prime beneficiaries. And as long as the middle class had jobs and could use the soaring value of their houses to enjoy a home-equity-loan-financed vacation, its members supported the same arrangements, despite stagnant incomes.

The business community in the West, with its enormous resources, dominates the public debate about global economic policy. It commissions studies, endows think tanks and university chairs, and broadcasts appropriate findings with fanfare. All this helps to generate a normative glow around new-liberalism and globalization, which encourages the idea that 'competent', 'responsible' economists endorse new-liberal prescriptions. Then, the combination of ideology and confirmation bias puts minds to rest, as explained by former US Treasury Secretary O'Neill: 'Ideology is a lot easier because you don't have to know or search for anything. You already know the answer to everything. It's not penetrable by facts.' In this atmosphere, anyone who argues for industrial policy, higher taxation, provision of public services through public agencies, labour standards, selective protection, a currency transaction tax, and employee voice in running corporations, is suspect as incompetent or politically partisan.

The main political parties depend on the business community for finance, not on members, and present what is good for business as what is good for the nation—Centre-Left parties almost as much as those of the Right. The parties compete to win support of the mass media, which is owned for the most part by groups, like Rupert Murdoch's, aggressively committed to profit-maximization and a new-liberal agenda. No wonder that the British Labour Party, while declaring its commitment to reduce poverty, at the same time boasts its unconcern about inequality. One of its leading strategists declared, 'We are intensely relaxed about people getting filthy rich.' And Prime Minister Blair said in 2001, 'If you end up going after those people who are the most wealthy in society, what you actually end up doing is in fact not even helping those at the bottom end.'

Blair unwittingly confirmed that democracy is losing its grip to regulate market competition in line with a common good whose characteristics are defined by political debate. For many globalization champions, that is the point: the only meaningful common good or national interest is what the marketplace winners think. The British and American governments have translated this into the central mission of handing over to the private sector many of the essential functions of government—in Britain, through the private finance initiative, contracted-out services, and various forms of 'sponsorship'.

These are proximate political causes of the determining influence of new-liberal economics and the globalization consensus. What kept them in check during the long period from the 1930s to the 1970s—when income distribution in Western economies became more equal, and dramatically so in the United States—was fear of an external enemy (the Soviet Union) and internal fifth columns (trade unions), memory of the calamity brought by free market economics in the 1920s, and the need to reward the masses who fought for the nation in two World Wars. In these circumstances, ruling elites acted like an 'establishment' willing to forge class compromises in order to mobilize consent to their rule, which included measures of redistribution downwards. Social movements—the labour movement, civil rights movement, women's movement, and others—helped to force through legislation which had the effect of raising the share of income at the bottom and middle and lowering the share at the top.

All this changed in the 1980s, as the generation which had experienced the earlier calamities retired and as the angry Right came to public office determined to erode the bargaining power of trade unions and reverse the squeeze on top incomes. Political, business, and especially financial elites increasingly began to operate like an 'oligarchy', concerned to use state instruments to redistribute power and income upwards. The top UK civil servant during the Thatcher years, Sir Alan Budd, spelled it out:

> The Thatcher government never believed for a moment that [monetarism] was the correct way to bring down inflation. They did however see that this would be a very good way to raise unemployment. And raising unemployment was an extremely desirable way of reducing the strength of the working classes ... [This] has allowed the capitalists to make high profits ever since.
>
> (Palma 2009: 837)

Deprived of their adversary, Western governments and their supporters began to imagine themselves the undisputed victors and the incarnations of global progress, and began to lead Western society and the rest of the world down the globalization alley. Opening the economies of developing countries in the name of globalization and free market economics was an important part of the strategy for building profits at home, redistributing upwards, and undercutting collective bargaining. The rise of China, with its urban-biased, cheap-labour, export-oriented development model, and the willingness of its central bank to accumulate foreign exchange reserves in the form of US financial assets, meant that US consumers could continue to boost consumption and buy houses, even as their median incomes stagnated—by borrowing, ultimately from China. The recycling of dollars across the Pacific into the American credit system both preserved the globalization consensus in elite circles and maintained social stability in the American democracy, even in the face of massive concentration of income and wealth at the top—until the credit recycling part of the mechanism ruptured in 2008 (Wade 2009a, 2009c). Borrowing is the short answer to why the American 'wages crisis' produced so little public anger, until it morphed into a 'debt crisis'.

The next crisis may be the bursting of the flamboyant Chinese bubble. Fixed asset investment has risen to an eye-popping 50 per cent of GDP, as compared to 30 per cent to 35 per cent in Japan during its miracle growth decade when it achieved similar growth rates as China over the 2000s; and apartment prices have risen to a dizzying fifteen to twenty times the average household income in major cities, as compared to twelve to fifteen times in late-1980s bubble-era Japan. Two decades later Japan has still not recovered from its burst bubble, and China's crash would have further-reaching consequences for the rest of the world than Japan's did.

Key points

- The argument that globalization—seen at the national level in the form of liberalizing policy shifts and/or rising trade and investment integration into the world economy—has been driving falls in poverty and inequality does not have solid empirical support.

- The much-cited World Bank study, *Globalization, Growth and Poverty*, relies on a measure of globalization (changes in the ratio of trade to GDP) that skews the results. It also makes unwarranted assumptions about causality in the relationship between trade policy, trade growth, and economic growth.

- We can say with confidence that as countries become richer, they tend to liberalize their trade and their foreign direct investment (FDI) rules.

- The fact that countries vary substantially in after-tax inequality even when holding levels of integration into the world economy suggests that globalization is not itself a bulldozer force eliminating 'policy space' and flattening out national diversity.

- The shakiness of the evidence that new-liberal globalization is producing catch-up growth feeds back only weakly into global policy as practiced by organizations such as the World Bank and the IMF. The story is too good not to be true. It legitimizes the hugely disproportionate gains obtained by the top 10 per cent of world income distribution, by global firms based largely in the West, and by the US state which, more than others, has adopted a commitment to continuous expansion of private consumption as the basis for domestic peace. The main public-opinion-shaping media outlets are controlled by groups strongly committed to expanding the scope for private profit-seeking.

One response to this chapter is that, yes, slow long-run growth in most poor countries and a rising poverty headcount outside China are world problems, but rising national and world income inequality is not a problem as long as the poor do not become worse off than before. Some economists reduce it to a simple value judgement, as in the economist Willem Buiter's declaration, 'Poverty bothers me. Inequality does not. I just don't care.' Some say there is a trade-off between efficiency and equality, and economists should concentrate on how to increase efficiency and leave distribution to non-scientists. Still others say that unrestrained income earning at the top is a condition for improved living standards at the bottom. Inequality provides incentives for effort and risk-taking and thereby spurs efficiency and productivity, from which the poor benefit. (This is Tony Blair's argument quoted earlier, and philosopher John Rawls' more subtle proposition that increased inequality is justified if it can be demonstrated to make the poorest better off.) In any case, today's inequalities tend to be undone by tomorrow's social mobility, within and between nations. So, those who worry about inequality are just practising the 'politics of envy'.

What is the evidence? At the national level, does a rising level of income inequality cause slower or faster subsequent growth? The cross-sectional evidence gives no robust answer; there is too much 'noise', the link depends too much on the specific sources of rising inequality. Even if we found a strong relationship between inequality and subsequent growth the causality is questionable. The effect on growth might be due to whatever caused the inequality to be high rather than the inequality itself.

Correlation between income inequality and other variables is clearer. There is fairly good evidence that higher income inequality within countries goes with: (1) a higher poverty headcount and a lower contribution of economic growth to poverty reduction (lower 'growth elasticity of poverty reduction'); (2) higher unemployment; (3) higher crime; (4) lower average health; (5) weaker property rights; (6) more skewed access to public services and state rule-setting forums, and lower standards of public services; (7) lower social mobility; and (8) slower transitions to democratic regimes, more fragile democracies, more social unrest. Developed countries like the US, the UK, and Portugal, where the top 20 per cent earn seven, eight or nine times more than the bottom 20 per cent score higher on a whole range of social problems in each income category than in countries such as Sweden and Japan where the differential is only two or three times; so, even the rich cannot escape the problematic consequences of inequality in the high inequality societies. (Some of this evidence is gathered in the World Bank's, *World Development Report 2006* (2005*b*); UNDP'S *Human Development Report 2005* (2006); and Wilkinson and Pickett 2009.)

One has to remember that correlation is not causation; and that even when a correlation is statistically significant, the magnitude may be small. Also, one has to distinguish the unsurprising proposition that countries with higher income and wealth inequality have higher inequality in health, education, safety, trust, and the like, from the more surprising proposition that countries with higher income and wealth inequality have higher *average* levels of health and other social problems; and from the still more surprising proposition that cuts in income and wealth inequality are the most effective ways of reducing the average level of these social problems.

That being said, some causality from inequality to social problems makes good sense. For example, it is plausible that inequality is the friend of crime and the enemy of trust because of the inability of unskilled men in high inequality societies to play traditional male economic and social roles, including contribution to family income; and because of the perception that income differentials have no relationship to effort and social values. The crime and violence experienced in very unequal societies are just the tip of a distribution of social relationships skewed towards the aggressive end of the spectrum, with low average trust beyond the family. The relationship holds even between American states. Those with more equal income distribution, like New Hampshire, also have higher levels of social trust.

The link to political conflict is evident in China and India. Many people whose incomes are growing, nevertheless feel ever poorer — and more resentful — as they see the gap between themselves and the new money being flaunted all around them. Many others are thrown into new poverty as local officials seize their land, leaving them fuming about injustice. China's one-party state has overseen one of the biggest thefts in history, the seizure of hundreds of thousands of hectares of land in the years around the mid 2000s, prompting the biggest surge of rural violence in 2005 since the 1966–76 Cultural Revolution. In India, the Naxalite insurgency draws on widespread resentments among the poor in the northern and central zones where it operates, covering 40 per cent of India's geographic area. Resentments are also expressed through electoral politics, as seen in the electoral defeats of most political leaders seen as 'pro-business' in national and state elections in the mid 2000s.

There is evidence that higher levels of income and wealth inequality go with weaker property rights and more fragile, less accountable states. However, international development agencies like the World Bank give high priority to strengthening property rights and making governments more accountable — while they avoid inequality as too 'political'. Interestingly, the Bank's executive directors from emerging market economies with surging inequality, led by China and Russia, are the ones most opposed to the World Bank analyzing top-level inequality as distinct from poverty, on grounds that it is a 'political' issue with which the Bank, as an apolitical organization, should not concern itself.

Within Europe, Scandinavia has lower after-tax income inequality than the rest. Its 90:10 ratio increased from 2.9 around 1980 to 3.1 around 2000. Scandinavia has also shown better economic and social performance than the US and the rest of Europe by most of the important yardsticks — economic growth, labor productivity, research and development investment, product and service markets, performance in high technology and telecommunications sectors, rates of employment, physical and social infrastructure, and quality of public services (from transport to education, healthcare, and elderly care). Scandinavian countries also have rates of 'psychological distress' and mental illness roughly half those of the anglophone countries, and employees work substantially fewer hours per year. The prison population per 100,000 people is around 60–70 in Scandinavia and 85–95 in continental Europe, as compared to almost 140 in Britain, the highest in the European Union, and over 700 in the US, almost the highest in the world. A UNICEF study of child well-being in twenty-one advanced countries, found that the four Scandinavian countries had the four lowest percentages of children (0–17 years) living in households with equivalent income of less than 50 per cent of the median and were in the top seven positions in terms of child well-being; while Britain and the US had the highest percentages of children in relative poverty and the bottom two ranks in child well-being (UNICEF 2007).

Scandinavia's better performance suggests that a relatively equal income distribution is compatible with relatively high economic growth, high labour productivity, and entrepreneurial incentives. Yet, European governments and the European Commission fix on the United States as the model of virile capitalism, and look hardly at all to Scandinavia.

Japan is an ominous case of un-learning. It has had a system of welfare-oriented capitalism, with relatively equal distribution of income and wealth, good public services, and especially good education and health services for the poorer half of the population. But recall those figures of income shares in the biggest companies during the recoveries of 1986–9 and 2001–4: dividends increased by 6 per cent in the recovery of 1986–9 and 71 per cent in the recovery of 2001–4, while wages increased by 14 per cent in the first recovery and fell by 5 per cent in the second. The sharp tilt in favour of capital income results partly from changes in managers' objectives and the criteria by which they measure their performance. Once, a system of inter-company cross-holdings insulated them from shareholder pressures and an ethic of self-restraint limited top income. The unravelling of those cross-holdings, the arrival of foreign activist investors, and corporate governance legislation designed to enhance shareholder control (promulgated by the OECD) have made keeping up the share price a dominant managerial objective and success in doing so a major criterion for raising top managerial incomes. Managers who used to worry about protecting the reputation of their firm by paying good wages, and who could concentrate on managing processes and products, are becoming more concerned to manage shareholder anticipations by keeping up the share price in order to avoid takeovers. The quintessential figure of anglophone capitalism, the head-hunter, is beginning to appear; shareholder interests come increasingly to shape government economic policy; and government legislation explicitly invokes the United States as the shiny model of corporate management. This is the payoff from the coming to power in business, government, and universities of a generation of people with MBAs and PhDs in economics and corporate law soaked in the ideological assumption that new-liberal economics is like the laws of engineering, or a 'sign of God's irresistible will', as Tocqueville described the supposedly inevitable trend to ever greater equality. As yet, the change at the level of practice has not gone far. For example, the external labour market for executive talent is still rudimentary and the change in enterprise culture and managerial objectives has come about within the framework of home-grown management. Toyota, for instance, has no external directors on its board and all its

Japanese managers have been lifetime Toyota men. Nevertheless, the trend is clear: we are at the early stages of Japan's move from welfare-oriented capitalism towards devil-take-the-hindmost capitalism, accompanied by applause from those not in the hindmost.

The new-liberal argument is even less concerned about widening inequality between countries than it is about inequality within countries. Not only does it posit a sharp moral discontinuity of obligation at the national border, but it also says that nothing much can be done to reduce international inequality (short of ever-more market liberalization), because we do not have an international redistribution mechanism akin to national welfare states. But on the face of it, the more globalized the world becomes, the more that the reasons why we should be concerned about within-country inequalities also apply between countries.

Migration is an obvious case in point. The EU-15 have an average FX income 50 times higher than the average of sub-Saharan Africa, and EU territory can be reached by small boat from Africa within days. The migration incentive is a function of the FX income or wage gap as well as of the PPP gap. Commonly, migrants cut rent of expensive living space by jamming themselves into substandard accommodation and remit the savings back home where, thanks to the FX-PPP gap, their family can purchase much more than the savings could purchase in the migrant's country of residence. The inflow pressures into North America and Europe are intense and set to intensify. According to a Gallup survey, 38 per cent of the adults of sub-Saharan Africa and 23 per cent in the Middle East and North Africa would move to another country if they could. Yet, immigration is already among the two or three most emotive issues in the politics of high-income societies, with solid majorities declaring that there are already too many 'foreigners' in their midst.

Rising internal inequality in the advanced industrial countries and in the big emerging market economies like China and India may interact with rising between-country inequality to reinforce the dominance of new-liberal thinking, backed up by market-opening and standards-harmonizing trade agreements, loan conditionality, and the like. Why? Because rising internal inequality tends to reinforce the power of classes opposed to redistributive measures to expand the domestic market. Domestic capitalists are then under more pressure both to find markets abroad and to 'financialize' or 'liquify' their assets so as to be able to move in and out of markets quickly.

New-liberalism provides the common interest justification for public policies aimed at these objectives, and a much safer justification—because it is 'apolitical'—than the ones used to justify eighteenth- and nineteenth-century territorial market openings, namely nationalism, racism, Christianity, and imperialism. Yet it could properly be called a 'new imperialism' (Harvey 2005b), new

because, not being based on colonies, it operates through the combination of open economic policies and a US military apparatus with more than 700 bases around the world. The bases are intended to secure governments friendly to the US, especially in energy-rich areas. But their net effect in the Arab world and central Asia is probably to provoke armed resistance more than to provide security for the US—the resistance then justifying the need for them. The new imperialism receives remarkably little critical scrutiny, apart from marginal figures on the Left, because the clever people who flock into capital management and dominate opinion about appropriate economic—and indirectly, security—policy include very few like Maynard Keynes, who made a fortune manipulating money on behalf of Kings College, Cambridge, while also standing outside such activities and thinking for mankind.

Conclusions

This chapter began by setting out the globalization argument which profoundly shaped economic policy in most countries around the world in last decades of the twentieth century and on into the 2000s. It says, in essence, that as national governments extend the scope of exchange by adopting free market policies and institutions, so they foster a virtuous combination of higher economic growth, falling poverty, falling inequality, and—by extension—stronger democracy. Countries that are poor today can enter this virtuous combination, provided the government opens the economy to the world, bolsters private property rights, creates institutions of impersonal trust, and stands up to corruption; and provided it gets help from the 'international community'. The world economy is an open system, in the sense that all countries could conceivably enjoy the same high level of prosperity, just as all marathon runners could conceivably cross the finishing line at the same time. There

is no structural relationship between 'core', 'semi-periphery', and 'periphery'. The same basic growth strategy is appropriate for all. All governments must avoid the 'interventionism', 'protectionism', and 'import-substituting industrialization' of the 1950s and 1960s. The champions of this argument ignore contrary evidence altogether or treat it with the annoyance one might direct at a fly.

We know that the acceptance of theories is underdetermined by the evidence. Nevertheless, it is remarkable how influential this argument became, because—using two eyes rather than one—the evidence is quite ambiguous. To reiterate just one point, much of the evidence adduced for the 'globalization works' story is actually the story of China. The fact that hundreds of millions of people in China and India have moved out of extreme poverty in the past twenty years is, indeed, good news. But it does not support the idea that a general process of globalization is driving a widely distributed improvement in material living standards sufficiently fast to bring most of the caravan closer together. That economists have, nevertheless, been willing to proclaim the latter illustrates how they have become standard-bearers of an ideology which seems to imprison them.

There are broadly two criteria of 'truth' in science. One is consistency, the other, correspondence with evidence. Mathematics is the home of truth as consistency, observational sciences the home of truth as evidence. Economics contains an uneasy tension. Neoclassical economics emphasizes truth as consistency; econometrics, evolutionary economics, and behavioural economics emphasize truth as correspondence with evidence. New-liberal economics — a more ideological and anti-state version of neoclassical economics — tends to prescribe on the basis of consistent deduction from 'first principles', from simple models of atomistic rational agents and perfectly competitive markets, and to give selective inattention to data that would upset the deduced prescriptions. It is happy to affirm as universal truth that 'government failure is worse than market failure', as though this is just 'common sense'.

Its anti-state bias is consistently deduced — from a framework that excludes some of the main sources of market failure. The framework assumes that technological learning is exogenous, thereby excluding the real-world market failures in technological learning in developing countries, especially when the learning is discontinuous rather than incremental. It assumes that the willingness of individuals to supply services to the market constitutes a reciprocal demand, precluding a more than temporary gap between aggregate supply and aggregate demand. Keynesian economics displaced this assumption (often known as Says Law), but the new-liberal counter-reformation of the 1970s and 1980s restored it to the centre of mainstream thought, and, with it, the efficacy and morality of free markets. It lies behind the optimistic assumption that trade liberalization changes only the allocation of resources, not overall utilization of resources; which spirits away possible unemployment, deindustrialization, and the erosion of skills and firm-level identities.

The framework also excludes the social and political defences against the effects of these market failures, which may compound the market failure. So, the World Bank's, *World Development Report 2009: Reshaping Economic Geography* (2009*d*), says that unfortunately, 'governments intervene (usually incorrectly) to spread the benefits of economic growth more evenly across space'. It urges them not to do so, because uneven geographic development can be a primary means of stimulating economic growth. Yet it says barely a word about the evictions, dispossessions, and destruction of communities which result from capital being given precedence over people, and the crime and resistance movements (sometimes called 'terrorists') spawned by these processes.

Again, the framework bolsters its anti-state bias by implicitly assuming that developing country governments are all of a type — a 'neopatrimonial' type, in Weberian theory, where the structure of state authority is characterized by little organizational or normative separation between the public and the private domains. It is as though all developing country governments are like Nigeria's. This, too, makes it easy to declare that 'government failure is worse than market failure'.

The political economy of research and statistics

My critique of the globalization argument is partly based on the empirical conclusion that divergence may be dominating convergence in much of the world. The implications are so serious (including for international action on apparently distant issues like climate change and ocean acidification), that we should mount a co-ordinated worldwide project to get better data on poverty and inequality, just as concerns about global warming gave rise to a co-ordinated worldwide project to get better climatological data.

The World Bank is one of the key actors. It has moved from major to minor source of foreign finance for most developing countries outside Africa. But it remains an important world organization because it wields a disproportionate influence in setting the development agenda, in offering an imprimatur of 'sound finance' that crowds in other resources, and providing finance when other finance is not available. Its research and statistics are crucial to its legitimacy (Kapur 2002). Other regional development banks and aid agencies have largely given up, ceding the ground to the World Bank. Alternative views come only from a few 'urban guerrillas' in pockets of academia and the UN system (for a good example of a heterodox book from a corner of the UN system, see UNDP 2003: the WTO lobbied to prevent its publication). Indeed, so dominant is the Bank as a producer of development research and statistics that if it produced an ordinary commodity it would be liable to anti-trust action.

To see the dangers, think of two models of a research and statistical organization that is part of a larger organization working on politically sensitive subjects. The 'exogenous' model says that the research and statistics are produced by professionals exercising best judgement in the face of difficulties that have no optimal solutions, who are organizationally insulated from the tactical goals of the organization. The 'endogenous' model says that the research and statistics are produced by staff who act as agents of the senior managers (the principals). The senior managers are guided by Churchill's maxim that the truth may be 'so precious that she should always be attended by a bodyguard of lies'. They expect the wish to be mother of the thought. They expect policy-based evidence-making rather than evidence-based policy-making. They expect their researchers and statisticians to help advance the organization's tactical goals just like other staff, and select them accordingly.

The simple endogenous model does not fit the Bank; but nor does the other. The Bank is committed to an Official View of how countries should seek development; it is exposed to arm twisting by the G7 states and large developing country states; it must secure their support and defend itself against criticism. It seeks to advance its market-opening agenda, not mainly by coercing its borrowers, but more by establishing a sense that the agenda is correct because confirmed by robust empirical evidence. If it seriously qualified its argument that market liberalization is the driver of development, it would lose the support of the G7 states, Wall Street, and fractions of developing country elites.

The units of the Bank which produce statistics and research are partly insulated from the resulting pressures, especially by their membership in 'epistemic communities' of professionals inside and outside the Bank; but not wholly. The bias comes, not through management instructions to lie, but through more subtle mechanisms such as choice of statistical technique and country sample. One which yields an answer in line with the Official View is likely to be retained without much thought, one which yields a contrary answer will be subject to much scrutiny. Or the boss of a unit who wants a result that pleases senior managers or a major state but whose professionals decline to comply may bring in a consultant to write a report that affirms the 'right' answer over the heads of her professionals. (This is what happened when China's government in the late 1990s wanted the Bank to lower China's per capita income so that it could continue to be eligible for the concessions available to countries below a certain income threshold.) To deny this bias is to deny that the Bank is subject to the Chinese proverb, 'Officials make the figures and the figures make the officials'; or to Goodhart's Law, which states that any statistical regularity will tend to collapse when it is used for control purposes. Charles Goodhart was thinking of monetary policy, but the point also applies to the measurement of variables used to evaluate the performance of multilateral economic organizations. However, little is known about the balance in the Bank between autonomy and compliance, or the ability of researchers and statisticians to challenge the way that senior managers modify or misuse their results.

Some of the Bank's statistics are also provided by independent sources, which provide a check. Others, including the poverty numbers, are produced only by the Bank, and these are more subject to Goodhart's Law. The Bank should appoint an independent auditor to verify its main development statistics or cede the work to an independent agency, perhaps under UN auspices (but if done by, say, UNCTAD the opposite bias might be introduced). And it would help if the Bank and other multilateral organizations made clear the margins of error and direction of bias. They should issue health warnings that, 'Taking the figures too seriously can seriously damage your decision-making capacity.' The US National Council on Public Polls is a model. It sets principles of disclosure for its members, and the Harris Poll accompanies its findings with the warning, 'All surveys are subject to several sources of error. These include [a list of types of error],' and a statement about the magnitudes of error associated with each type.

Recently, the Bank has moved a little on the issues highlighted here. For example, having previously de-emphasized the uncertainty around the poverty numbers, the two Bank experts in charge of the poverty numbers suddenly declared, 'A cloud of doubt hangs over our knowledge about the extent of the world's progress against poverty' (Chen and Ravallion 2004: 141).

Policy implications

The arguments and evidence adduced here are a wake-up call to individuals and organizations still convinced that the private sector and market liberalization should be the microeconomic core of development strategy. Far from being rooted in evidence, meta-propositions like 'government failure is worse than market failure' derive from a distinctively anglophone world view, which has come to dominate global thinking only because two of the anglophone countries have been the norm-setting hegemonic powers for the past 150 years.

It is reasonably clear from contemporary evidence and from the nineteenth-and early-twentieth-century history of today's developed countries that states which eschew the role of nurturing their companies and encouraging sectoral diversification and technological upgrading are unlikely to rise up the world income hierarchy against the analogues of gravity (Chang 2002; Wade 2004a). An open economy with all its eggs in its 'comparative advantage' basket will lose abroad much of the spillover benefits from firms' profit-maximizing behaviour, while in a more diverse and nationally integrated economy the spillovers promote the growth of national income. Once we set aside the false dichotomies of open *or* closed economy, globalization as opportunity *or* threat, and government limited to umpiring on a level playing-field *or* government intervention to distort resource allocation, we can begin to consider the possibilities of state-sponsored directional thrust without the discussion being hijacked by a preternatural terror of governments 'picking winners' or a religious conviction that the private sector can do no wrong.

The question for policy is not whether 'globalization' is good or bad, *pace* Martin Wolf. It is how to combine the opportunities offered by international markets with co-ordinated strategies for domestic investment and institution building, so as to stimulate domestic entrepreneurs and create a more nationally integrated economy, and so as to retain some economic sovereignty within the developing country state rather than being externalized to foreign firms and foreign governments or international organizations.

However, the direction of travel of the international economic and financial regime is to shrink the space for developing country governments to undertake this role; a tendency likely to be reinforced as inequality continues to soar in the G7 states, even as these same states have long practiced disguised industrial policy themselves. (Industrial policy over the first three post-war decades set the stage for the corporate responses which made the US the leader in information technologies. Thanks to public support—largely Defense Department—IBM led on programming and computer systems, Bell Labs led on transistors, and what became the Internet was created for the Pentagon.)

The governments and civil society organizations of developing countries should therefore concert their actions so as to push back against this direction of travel, not only at the national level but also regional and multilateral levels, including in the World Trade Organization and the World Bank. The regional level is especially important as the space to build alternatives to the hub-and-spokes world economy of the twentieth century, through concerted efforts of governments, firms, and trade unions to boost the flow of trade, capital, and ideas between the erstwhile spokes — between Greater China, South Asia, South America, and the Middle East, for example.

Elsewhere, I have outlined a set of principles that might guide an alternative approach to development strategy with a more active role for the state (Wade 2003a, 2003b, 2004a: ch. 11). There is not, of course, a single alternative to the Washington Consensus. What is appropriate for middle-income, semi-peripheral economies like Malaysia and coastal China, may not be appropriate for low-income, peripheral economies like Ethiopia. Also, alternative development strategies have to be geared to the authority structure of states and to leaders' perception of the determinants of their or their group's political survival. Some states are more 'neopatrimonial' than others, some have a broader class-base than others, and both factors affect the degree to which the state is able to concentrate resources on investment (Kohli 2004). Political leaders base their survival strategies on sponsoring varying combinations of: (1) political stability; (2) rapid economic growth and diversification of production; and (3) democracy and expansion of civil society. The West is keen to promote democracy and expansion of civil society. But where political parties are weak, a democratic transition may result in business capture of the state, weakened technocracy, popular disgust of politics, and an erosion of a pre-existing growth coalition (as arguably in Malaysia and Indonesia since the Asian crisis of 1997–8). In this area of appropriate state structure, we know even less than about alternative principles of development strategy. But, certainly the contrast between the development trajectory and present-day living conditions in Seoul/South Korea and Manila/Philippines is sobering for those who believe that democracy, civil society, and a laissez-faire approach to industrial development (the Philippines' story) is the right prescription for development.

In the affluent West, the crash of 2008 has suddenly made the gap between the super-rich and the rest a pressing political issue. The conundrum is how to curb the plutocracy and its presumption of winner-takes-all, while preserving openness to ideas, people, and trade as a core political value. The solution lies in recognizing that the West has passed a turning point in human history, beyond which further increases in average income are hardly associated with improvements in the quality of life. Rather, improvements in the quality of life can be achieved by reforms in political economy institutions which generate more equality of income and wealth, in the direction of Scandinavia and Japan, not just through fiscal measures but also more indirect ones, like corporate governance reform. This also matters for climate change, for the challenge of climate change must be met while also improving the quality of life or it will not be met — until too late.

The challenge for activists is to formulate 'rules for radicals' on a world scale (Alinsky 1972) — including rules on how to foment a mutiny about the bounty, and how to shift US foreign policy away from aggressive interference in other states (how to redefine what US Secretary of State Condoleezza Rice described as 'our uniquely American realism' which teaches that it is America's 'unique opportunity' to remake the international order in its own image: Rice 2008).

The challenge for sociologists is to elucidate the mechanisms which shape the global structure of state and household stratification in income and wealth. The conventional image of development as marathon race mirrors the conventional approach to class as the outcome of individual attributes (education, place of birth, etc.). To clarify the mechanisms I have analogued as 'gravity' and 'levitation', sociologists should apply the alternative approaches to stratification which explain the economic advantages of those in privileged positions as causally related to the disadvantages of those excluded from these positions.

The challenge for economists is to adopt measures of economic activity which subtract social harm and environmental harm from social good, rather than add to it. And to design a global financial architecture which encourages growth in poor countries and at the same time stops the repeated playing out of financial crises—as global investors, disappointed with the returns they are getting, think they have found new opportunities in some country or other and rush in money, then eventually face disappointment and pull out their money, raining social costs on the former favourites. The agenda has to include regulation of private debt, caps on banks' capital, taxation of cross-border capital flows, and a requirement that financial firms keep a sizeable part of their capital in a form which automatically converts to equity as their capital position deteriorates, so as to give investors a stronger incentive to guard against reckless gambling.

The challenge for citizens in general is to put ethics back into daily life and at the centre of public debate. That means going beyond the currently dominant notions of prosperity as consumption and of freedom as freedom of choice and the rights of the individual. These notions lose their claim to constitute a universal value scheme when the derived economic policy regime, with its focus on GDP growth, helps to undermine sustainable prosperity and to produce an extremely unequal distribution of individual well-being—not to mention its effects in shifting public perceptions from appreciation of the intrinsic value of an education to a concern for its instrumental value. Or else, we could cheer on new-liberalism and the commercialization of intellectual life and await the maturing of the conditions for a socially planned economy in the spirit of Marx's dictum, 'What the bourgeoisie produces, above all, are its own gravediggers.'

? Questions

1. What arguments and evidence do liberal writers use to make the case that globalization increases growth and reduces poverty and inequality?
2. What are the advantages and disadvantages of using purchasing power parity (PPP) measures for comparing incomes across countries?
3. What are the main difficulties in measuring the number of people living in poverty?
4. What are the advantages and disadvantages of the various ways of examining the extent of inequality within and between countries?
5. How much change has there been in the global distribution of income in the last forty years?
6. Why might there be problems with the statistics that the World Bank and other international agencies use on poverty and inequality?
7. How can the new-liberal argument be tested empirically? And how do its assumptions shape its conclusions about the appropriate role of the state?
8. Should one be concerned about rising levels of inequality in the global economy?

9. What are the implications of the trends in growth, poverty, and inequality for the agendas of the multilateral economic organizations?

10. Does it make sense to apply the concept of 'imperialism' to the current world order?

→ **Further reading**

■ Brune, N., and Garrett, G. (2005), 'The Globalization Rorschach Test: International Economic Integration, Inequality and the Role of Government', *Annual Review of Political Science*, 8: 399–423. This is a short overview of different interpretations of issues discussed in this chapter.

■ Chen, S., and Ravallion, M. (2008), 'The Developing World is Poorer than we Thought, but no Less Successful in the Fight against Poverty', World Bank Policy Research Working Paper, August: 4703 (Washington, DC: World Bank). Gives key World Bank update of knowledge about global material well-being.

■ Deaton, A. (2010), 'Price Indices, Inequality and the Measurement of World Poverty', Presidential Address, American Economic Association, Atlanta, January (dated 17 January 2010). Best simple account of the purchasing power parity debate.

■ Edward, P. (2006*a*), 'Examining Inequality: Who Really Benefits from Global Growth?' *World Development*, 34/10: 1,667—95. Key evidence for the Matthew Effect.

■ Edward, P. (2006*b*), 'The Ethical Poverty Line: A Moral Quantification of Absolute Poverty', *Third World Quarterly*, 27/2: 377–93. An alternative international poverty line.

■ Galbraith, J. K. (2006), 'Global Macroeconomics and Global Inequality', in D. Held and A. Kaya (eds), *Global Inequality: Patterns and Explanations* (Cambridge: Polity Press). A non-technical discussion of inequality trends, including world wage data.

■ Kaplinsky, R. (2005), *Globalization, Poverty and Inequality: Between a Rock and a Hard Place* (Cambridge: Polity Press). An excellent overview of issues discussed in this chapter.

■ Korzeniewicz, R., and Moran, T. (2006), 'World Inequality in the Twenty-First Century: Patterns and Tendencies', in G. Ritzer (ed.), *The Blackwell Companion to Globalization* (Oxford: Blackwell). A short overview of trends in world inequality from a sociological perspective.

■ Korzeniewicz, R., and Moran, T. P. (2009), *Unveiling Inequality: A World-Historical Perspective* (New York: Russell Sage Foundation). Book-length treatment, accessible to the general reader.

■ Korzeniewicz, R., Stach, A., Patil, V., and Moran, T. (2004), 'Measuring National Income: A Critical Assessment', *Comparative Studies in Society and History*, 46/3: 535–86. The sociology of international income comparisons.

■ Milanovic, B. (2005), *Worlds Apart: Measuring International and Global Inequality* (Princeton, NJ: Princeton University Press). Magnum opus by a heterodox World Bank economist.

■ Pritchett, L. (1997), 'Divergence Big Time', *Journal of Economic Perspectives*, 11/3: 3–17. A powerful statement of the argument that inequality has been rising.

■ Reddy, S. G., and Pogge, T. W. (2003), 'How Not to Count the Poor', available at www.socialanalysis.org (accessed 26 March 2007). A detailed examination of the methodological examination of the World Bank's poverty statistics.

■ Rodrik, D. (1999), *The New Global Economy and Developing Countries: Making Openness Work* (Baltimore, MD: Johns Hopkins University Press for the Overseas Development Council). A powerful argument for development strategy that is not mainly just a liberalization strategy.

■ Svedberg, P. (2003), 'World Income Distribution: Which Way?', Institute for International Economics, Stockholm University, September. An account of the huge revision of world population figures.

■ Wade, R. (2003), 'What Strategies are Viable for Developing Countries Today? The WTO and the Shrinking of Development Space', *Review of International Political Economy,* 10/4: 621—44. An overview of the relationship between policy regimes and development space.

■ Wade, R. (2004), *Governing the Market: Economic Theory and the Role of Government in East Asian Industrialization* (Princeton, NJ: Princeton University Press). A case study of role of the state in East Asian development, and non-Washington Consensus policy prescriptions.

■ Wolf, M. (2000), 'The Big Lie of Global Inequality', *Financial Times,* 8 February. A good summary of the case that global inequality is falling.

■ Wolf, M. (2004), *Why Globalization Works: The Case for the Global Market Economy* (New Haven, CO: Yale University Press). A classic statement of the new-liberal globalization argument.

 Web links

■ http://utip.gov.utexas.edu   University of Texas Inequality Project.

■ www.unido.org/   United Nations Industrial Development Organization (UNIDO).

■ www.columbia.edu/~sr793/   Monitoring Global Poverty.

■ www.worldbank.org/poverty/   World Bank PovertyNet.

■ www.bris.ac.uk/poverty/   Townsend Centre for International Poverty Research.

 Online resource centre

For additional material and resources, please visit the Online Resource Centre at: www.oxfordtextbooks.co.uk/ravenhill3e/

13

Globalization and Development

Nicola Phillips

* Reader's guide

Despite the many accomplishments since the end of the Second World War, the problems of development in the contemporary global political economy are still of arresting proportions, and the various incarnations of a 'global development agenda' to deal with these problems have had a very mixed record. At the end of the first decade of the twenty-first century, in fact, there is still little consensus on what development actually is, let alone how it might be achieved, in either academic debates or public discourse. One of the most contested questions in this context relates to the relationship between globalization and development, and how we should understand the impact of globalization on development across the world. This chapter explores these debates. It starts by reviewing the different (and competing) ways of thinking about development that have emerged since the end of the Second World War, and showing how particular understandings of development have given rise to particular kinds of development strategies, at both the national and global levels. It goes on to consider the impacts and consequences of these strategies for development, and shows on this basis that many of the problems and failures of development have not only persisted but also worsened in the contemporary period. In this context, we move then to consider the key question of how we should understand the relationship between globalization and development, in both empirical and theoretical terms. There is a great deal at stake in this debate, in view of the centrality of globalization to both the panorama of contemporary development strategies and the prospects of achieving genuine improvements in the conditions in which large parts of the world's population live. Having summarized the various positions in the debate, I suggest that the most compelling argument is one which emphasizes and understands how conditions of 'mal-development'—or development failures—both arise from and are reinforced by globalization processes and the ways in which the global economy is governed. The chapter concludes on a speculative note, offering some observations about the likely implications for development of the global recession of the late 2000s, alongside the possible impact of the rise of China and 'the East' for the ways we will need to think about global development in the future.

Introduction

It is in some ways remarkable how little we still know, and how little consensus still exists, about the complex processes and conditions summed up in the term 'development'. The second part of the twentieth century and early part of the twenty-first century were marked by a long succession of different approaches to development, each paraded as a magic bullet that would generate growth, eliminate poverty, reduce inequality, and attain all the various goals associated with an improvement of the conditions in which huge parts of the world's population live. Yet, the record of developmental progress over this period remains very mixed. Despite the many extraordinary advances of the period since the end of the Second World War, such as unprecedented increases in life expectancy and improvements in living standards, the so-called 'Age of Development' has also bequeathed a global economy characterized by a resilience of poverty and inequalities among the world's population that are generally agreed to have increased significantly, particularly from the 1980s onwards, to reach levels which can rightly be considered to be 'without historical precedent and without conceivable justification—economic, moral or otherwise' (Pieterse 2002: 1024). Robert Hunter Wade reviewed these trends in detail in the preceding chapter.

The problems of development in the global economy thus remain of huge proportions, and in many dimensions are growing rather than diminishing. Particularly when we dig beneath the 'global' or 'regional' statistics showing overall reductions in extreme poverty levels, for instance, or increases in annual gross domestic product (GDP), we find a picture of development in which it is clear that for very large parts of the world's population, the march of globalization has not led to substantial improvements in their material or social conditions, and, indeed, in some cases led to their worsening. The global development agenda, as it evolved over the course of the twentieth century, is thus largely considered to have failed in its aspirations, and certainly failed to provide a framework for development policy that could deliver the goals of 'global development'. Despite the great fanfare to which the latest 'big idea' was unveiled around the start of the 2000s—namely, the Millennium Development Goals (MDGs) and various satellite initiatives—the global development agenda remains in a state of disarray, with few unequivocal advances on its score card, and submerged by the impact around the world of the economic and financial crisis which engulfed the later part of the decade. To complicate matters further, the extraordinary expansion of the Chinese economy and its emergence as a powerful force on the global political stage, alongside a group of other countries, has challenged the twin notions, dominant from the 1980s onwards, that: (*a*) an unequivocal embrace of 'globalization' is the surest path to growth and development; and (*b*) there is or can be an overarching framework for development informing a 'global' development agenda.

Underlying the problems of development and the shortcomings of global development policy is an enduring absence of consensus about what the causes of these trends are, and, by extension, what is to be done about them. Even more fundamentally, there is little agreement on the very basic question of what development actually is — that is, what we are referring to when we talk about development, what we are aspiring to in trying to advance it, and how we would recognize it when we saw it. The many different theories of development which have emerged in contemporary academic debates and which have informed different kinds of development strategies advance different views on all of these counts. The first task of this chapter is consequently to consider how particular ways of thinking about development have evolved in the period since the end of the Second World War, and to show and discuss how these theories of development have translated into the evolution of both the global policy agenda and local, national, and regional development strategies. Its second task is then to consider the effects and consequences of these ideas and strategies for development across the world. By reviewing both the empirical picture and competing perspectives on how to explain it, I advance the argument that the most recent phase of globalization, along with the associated policy orthodoxy, is to be judged harshly on the basis of its development outcomes and political consequences. But it is not enough simply to assert this, as many do, and move swiftly on: instead, we need to think carefully about the relationship between globalization and development, and specifically about what it is about globalization that can be said to cause or contribute directly to the problems of development that we identify as having characterized the contemporary period. The final task of the chapter is then to look forward and, necessarily speculatively, discuss the possibility that we are now moving into a new phase of global development which requires new theoretical perspectives and new policy frameworks.

Ways of Thinking about Development

Much like the term 'globalization' itself, 'development' is a word that is often bandied about in public discourse in increasingly glib and unthinking ways (Payne and Phillips 2010). It is a powerful term — one denoting a state of affairs which everyone, or nearly everyone, can easily and in some cases passionately declare themselves to be in favour of, and which can therefore be used politically to considerable advantage. Yet, few people would be able to say with much precision what the term actually means, in either abstract or concrete terms. H. W. Arndt captures this well, observing back in 1987 that, 'anyone who asked articulate citizens in developed or developing countries what they meant by this desirable objective of "development" would get a great variety of answers':

> Higher living standards. A rising per capita income. Increase in productive capacity. Mastery over nature. Freedom through control of man's environment. Economic growth. But not mere growth, growth with equity. Elimination of poverty. Basic needs satisfaction. Catching up with the developed countries in technology, wealth, power, status. Economic independence, self-reliance. Scope for self-fulfilment for all. Liberation, the means to human ascent.
>
> (Arndt 1987: 1)

He goes on to remark that 'development, in the vast literature on the subject, appears to have come to encompass almost all facets of the good society, everyman's road to utopia' (Arndt 1987: 1). This has perhaps never been more true than in the early years of the twenty-first century, when we have a bewildering array of global institutions, grand policy initiatives, less grand policy initiatives, public campaigns, civil society organizations, and individuals, all operating under the banner of 'development', but advancing either no clear conception of what it is they are aspiring to with this label, or else offering clearly competing conceptions and understandings of what the term means and how to achieve it.

Academic debates around development are also characterized by a lack of agreement—or, put in more constructive terms, a rich diversity of opinion—about how development should be conceived, how development processes should be understood to work and how development might be achieved. Each of the main theories of development that we will consider here work with different definitions of development and different diagnoses of the causes of either developmental progress or development failures. In what follows, we will review briefly the principal ways of thinking about development that have emerged since the end of the Second World War, in order then to trace in the next section of the chapter how these have been translated into particular kinds of policies, and with what effects and consequences.

But a caveat is first in order. Our focus here is on the period from the mid 1940s onwards, when the enterprise of studying development changed dramatically. The terms 'developing countries' and the 'Third World' entered public discourse, denoting somewhere that was distinct from the 'developed' world and presumed to require a separate set of policy strategies. Academic debates took a parallel turn, relocating 'development studies' as a discrete area of enquiry in the social sciences, and adhering to the notion that the study of development and the 'developing world' required its own sets of theories and a separate academic discipline for the purposes of elaborating them. Yet, the study of development has a much longer lineage. Development theory did not begin in 1945, as most studies would suggest, but rather reaches back to the periods in which the countries which came to be called the 'developed' world were themselves developing, and, indeed, much further to constitute the foundation of world history itself (Payne and Phillips 2010). Here, we can simply acknowledge this caveat, but will organize our discussion around the phase of globalization which roughly coincides with the period since the end of the Second World War.

Modernization, structuralist, and underdevelopment theories

Early phases of post-war development theory, like all others, were to a significant degree driven by the changing world order, in this case by the onset of the Cold War and the very obvious political, economic, and security shifts that accompanied it. This context yielded a very clear recognition in the US and elsewhere of the centrality of what by then was being called the 'Third World' to the effort to contain communism; the developing world became not only the physical site of conflict, but also the subject of a new preoccupation in academic and policy circles (Pakenham 1973). The development project was in an immediate sense one of 'winning over' developing countries and societies in order to divert the encroachment of socialist ideas and the influence of the Soviet Union. But, more fundamentally, it was also one of setting the developing world on a path to specifically Western-style development.

The most vigorous expression of this new development agenda was found in modernization theory—a perspective on development which evolved in the United States in this Cold War context. Its essence was an understanding of development as a 'process of social change whereby less developed societies acquire characteristics common to more developed societies' (Lerner 1972: 386). The emphasis was not only on economic change, but on a much more sweeping process of social and cultural change that would enable supposedly 'traditional' developing countries and societies both to resemble those of the purportedly advanced, developed West, and to 'catch up' with those societies in terms of levels of wealth, living standards, and, crucially, 'modernity'.

The body of modernization theory grew rapidly and became considerably varied, encompassing a range of approaches (Payne and Phillips 2010). Among the most well-known, and, indeed, harshly criticized, was the version associated most notably with W. W. Rostow (1960), in which he set out a notion of the 'stages of economic growth' through which all societies passed in a transition to modernity. These stages were identified as: traditional society; preconditions for take-off; take-off; the road to maturity; and the age of mass consumption, the latter being the indicator of a state of 'development' had been achieved. Modernization theorists in this sense conceived of development as a process with a clear endpoint, which had been achieved by those Western societies (the United States and Western Europe) that were by then considered to be 'developed'. The rest of the world was thus engaged in catching up to that condition. The other particularly influential version of modernization theory was associated with the notion of 'political development', which took development to refer to the processes by which conditions of liberal democracy were created and institutionalized. Gabriel Almond (1970), in collaboration with others such as James Coleman (Almond and Coleman 1960) and C. B. Powell (Almond and Powell 1965), was at the forefront of this theoretical effort to extrapolate an understanding of development and prescriptions for development policy from the institutional conditions which had emerged over time in the liberal democracies of the West.

Modernization theory thus advanced an approach to thinking comprehensively about development which was able to conceive of both development as a condition and development as a process of achieving—catching up to—that condition (Leftwich 2000: 33). These notions of

development (as both endpoint and 'catch-up' process) were already well established in the development theories of the nineteenth and early twentieth centuries. The early 'classical' development theories of Adam Smith, Karl Marx, and Max Weber, for instance, sought to understand how countries in Western Europe made the transition to a condition of being 'developed'. The subsequent generation of theories associated with the industrialization of the United States, Russia, and Germany, which can be grouped together as the first 'catch-up' theories, sought in this context to explain what Alexander Gerschenkron (1962) termed 'late industrialization'—that is, the problem of reacting to, and matching, those initial development processes in Western Europe (Payne and Phillips 2010). Modernization theory, in this respect, offered a clear line of continuity from these earlier phases of development theory, being concerned this time with the process of 'late-late industrialization' in the Third World. It contained a very clear idea of what a state of being developed looked like—that is, like the advanced industrialized democracies of the West—and a rather less clear but, nevertheless, central notion of how economies and societies should get there (see Box 13.1).

> **Box 13.1** Key Dimensions of Modernization Theory
>
> - Was developed in the United States in the context of the ideological rivalry of the Cold War.
>
> - Conceives of development as both an endpoint (a condition of being developed, which had already been achieved by the advanced industrialized countries) and a process of 'catching up' to that condition.
>
> - Sees the path to development as being one of 'westernization'—that is, a process of catching up by emulating the 'developed' countries, particularly in the nature and sequence of economic change and in processes of political development to put in place systems of liberal democracy.

The key characteristics of modernization theory—its ethnocentrism, the equation of modernization (development) with Westernization and its clear ideological project (Hoogvelt 1978)— generated lasting and trenchant controversy with the other major approach to development of that time. The body of 'underdevelopment theory', which encompassed most notably dependency and world systems theories, emerged as the great rival to modernization theory during the 1960s and 1970s. It unquestionably had a greater and longer-lasting impact on the ways we think about development than modernization theory, even though it was largely discredited by the time we were entering the 1980s, and certainly was trounced by the revolution in development thinking that occurred from that time onwards. But its legacy is still strongly evident in the study of global political economy, having bequeathed a 'key vocabulary' of world systems, developmental states, imperialism, neo-colonialism, and so on (Harrison 2004: 156), many of which have been central to discussions in other chapters in this book.

Unlike modernization theory, which was a distinctively US (and Western) perspective on development, underdevelopment theories had their origins in Latin America, and specifically in a group of economists clustered in the UN Economic Commission for Latin America (ECLA), based in Santiago, Chile. The most famous of them was Raúl Prebisch, who developed a 'structuralist' thesis on the relationship between the global system and the conditions of underdevelopment that he observed in the Latin American region (Prebisch 1950). He advanced the key insight that the global economic system was divided into a powerful 'centre' and weak 'periphery', and identified the ways in which what he called the **terms of trade**—that is, the ratio of export prices to import prices—worked systematically to favour the centre and disadvantage the periphery. In the periphery, export sectors were unable to generate the levels of national income required for economic development in conditions of rapid population growth, and development problems were perpetuated by the need to increase

exports in order to maintain import levels. Competition among countries exporting commodities generated a decline in export prices relative to manufactures imported from industrialized countries. The end result was seen to be the structural entrenchment of a condition of 'underdevelopment' in the periphery, in which the process of industrialization was impeded, leading to a rising gap in incomes between the two parts of the world economy.

Prebisch's insights were picked up and absorbed into more established traditions in the social sciences, specifically into 'neo-Marxist' theories which had long been concerned with notions of imperialism in the world economy. The result was a complex body of thought summed up in the label 'dependency theory', which had at its core a notion that development needed to be understood with reference to the location of economies within the world capitalist system and the interactions of the different parts of this system, and that development and underdevelopment exist in a relationship of structural symbiosis, as 'the two faces of the historical evolution of capitalism' (Sunkel 1972: 520). The obstacles to industrialization that Prebisch had identified were thus seen as rooted in the structure of the global system, which served to perpetuate underdevelopment in the periphery *as a precondition for* development in the centre. Thus, according to a classic definition,

> Dependence is a conditioning situation in which the economies of one group of countries are conditioned by the development and expansion of others. A relationship of interdependence... becomes a dependent relationship when some countries can expand only as a reflection of the expansion of the dominant countries, which may have positive or negative effects on their immediate development.

(dos Santos 1970: 231)

More and less careful versions of dependency theory emerged, but the impact of the school as a whole on ways of thinking about development during this time was unquestionably pivotal. Subsequent elaborations by André Gunder Frank and others consolidated its status as an early perspective on inequality between countries and societies, where capitalism was deemed to generate 'economic development for the few and underdevelopment for the many' (Frank 1967: 8). World systems theory subsequently took up the running, most notably elaborated by Immanuel Wallerstein (1974, 1979, 1980), who saw a world market system (what we would now call global economy) as comprising different kinds of states—core, semi-periphery, and periphery—marked by significant asymmetries and jostling for economic advantage. As such, underdevelopment theory was clearly a forerunner of many of the debates about the relationship between globalization and development, and the impact of the changing global political economy on development, in which we are interested here. Even so, both dependency and world systems theory were subjected to a barrage of criticism, justified and otherwise, to the extent that by the early 1980s they had lost much of their influence and appeal. As we will see in the next section, the failures of the strategies associated with this conception of development, alongside the success of very different development strategies in East Asia, also hastened its decline (see Box 13.2).

> ### Box 13.2 Key Dimensions of Under-development and Dependency Theory
>
> - Was pioneered in Latin America to explain continued 'underdevelopment' in that region and elsewhere.
>
> - Conceives of the world economy as divided into a powerful 'centre' and a weak 'periphery', in which the terms of trade systematically disadvantaged the periphery and perpetuated conditions of underdevelopment.
>
> - Identifies development and underdevelopment as 'the two faces of the historical evolution of capitalism' (Sunkel 1972: 520) and explores how conditions of 'dependence'—of the periphery on the centre—serve to reinforce underdevelopment and inequality.

Neo-liberalism and neo-statism

A good part of the problem for underdevelopment theories by the 1980s was, quite simply, that they were wrong-footed by events. Aside from the damage caused by the various theoretical critiques, these kinds of theories proved inadequate for understanding and explaining the key trend that was becoming visible in global development—namely, the increasing differentiation and divergence in the development trajectories of countries and economies in different parts of the world. From the 1960s onwards, the big development story was not one of underdevelopment, but rather the spectacular rise of a group of East Asian economies that came to be known as the newly industrializing economies (NIEs)—Taiwan, Korea, Singapore, and Hong Kong. Their soaring growth rates left economies in Latin America, Africa, and other developing regions in the metaphorical dust, and equally left modernization theory and, particularly, underdevelopment theory struggling for anything meaningful to say by way of explanation or theorization. In a nutshell, the rise of East Asia left the notion of a single group of countries and economies, variously termed the 'Third World', 'developing countries', 'periphery', and so on, looking entirely redundant.

Both to take account of these new trends and to conceive of the relationship between development and the processes of globalization that were accelerating at the time (which have been amply documented and discussed in other chapters in this book), the key debate that emerged from the 1970s onwards was between two schools of thought. The first was the body of theory summed up in the term 'neo-liberalism', which came to define the global development policy agenda and the panorama of development strategies across the world. The second took its cue more concretely from the East Asian experience and can be termed 'neo-statism'. The debate was not about development theories in the sense of those we have just reviewed. It was centrally about the study of political economy in the advanced industrialized world, particularly in the context of the neo-liberal revolutions under British Prime Minister Margaret Thatcher and US President Ronald Reagan, and the obsession in the 1980s about the relative performance of Anglo-American economies compared with those organized with more greater levels of state intervention in the national economy, such as Germany and Japan. But its expression in the context of development was especially vigorous, and oriented to explaining and theorizing the reasons for the divergence in performance between the 'developing regions' of the world. We will see in the next section of the chapter that the impact of these ways of thinking about development was immense, in terms of both development policies and their consequences.

Let us take neo-liberalism first—the single most influential paradigm in the contemporary period. Neo-liberal theory was, and remains, predicated on a profound cynicism about politics and, more specifically, about states. Its roots in neo-classical economics yield an assumption that individuals are motivated by self-interest, and, therefore, that politics is similarly conditioned. The intervention of states in the workings of national economies, and by extension the global economy, is therefore understood to introduce a wide range of distortions and contradictions which are deemed inimical to the pursuit of growth and development. The core contention of neo-liberalism is consequently, as David Harvey puts it (2005a: 20), that 'human well-being can best be advanced by liberating individual entrepreneurial freedoms and skills within an institutional framework characterized by strong private property rights, free markets, and free trade'. The emphasis fell on 'depoliticizing' economic activity, and development more broadly, and consolidating market-led mechanisms of organizing economies and allocating resources within them (see Gamble 2001). Crucially, these market-led mechanisms were increasingly 'global' or 'globalizing' in nature.

The era of neo-liberal development thus featured a new and distinctive emphasis on participation in the global economy, conceived both as the accommodation of increasingly unfettered global market activity and its harnessing in ways that would reap

developmental benefits. This was clearly an abrupt break with theories of underdevelopment, despite the common emphasis on the global economy and its role in shaping development. While underdevelopment theories conceived the world economy as imposing structural impediments to development, neo-liberalism understood participation in global economic activity as the prerequisite for development, and development strategy came to be understood as essentially about 'global positioning' (McMichael 2000: 15; Gore 2000). But, at the same time, neo-liberal theories continued to understand development as an inherently national process, and moreover understood the reasons for development failures as lying in internal (endogenous) factors—that is, as rooted in 'incorrect' government policies, institutional underdevelopment, and excessive state intervention in the workings of national economies (see Box 13.3).

> **Box 13.3** Key Dimensions of Neo-Liberal Development Theory
>
> - Rests on the argument that 'human well-being can best be advanced by liberating individual entrepreneurial freedoms and skills within an institutional framework characterized by strong private property rights, free markets, and free trade' (Harvey 2005a: 2).
> - Sees the path to development as requiring the consolidation of market-based mechanisms of organizing economies and allocating resources, and therefore the 'depoliticization' of economic activity.
> - Identifies engagement in the global economy as the key to propelling processes of development, while at the same time attributing development failures to 'internal' factors such as 'incorrect' government policies, institutional underdevelopment, corruption, or excessive state intervention in the economy.

The problem for neo-liberalism was that, as already noted, the big development story unfolding at the time was the rise of a group of economies which apparently contradicted this logic, characterized as they were by a very different conception of how development could and should be achieved. The centerpiece of what we call here 'neo-statism' was the notion of the 'developmental state' (Johnson 1982; also see White 1988; Woo-Cumings 1999; Kohli 2004), in which the state was recognized to shape, direct, and promote the process of economic development. Markets were in this sense 'governed' rather than 'free' (Wade 1990). The forms of 'state developmentalism' observed in East Asia offered in this view a compelling explanation of the divergence in the performance of economies in that region and those in other regions, particularly Latin America, and a way of thinking about development which was ostensibly at odds with the dominant orthodoxy of neo-liberalism. However, things were not quite that simple. Neo-liberal theory also laid a claim to the so-called 'East Asian miracle' on the basis of a very different reading of its development trajectory—one based, not on the developmental role of states, but on the supposed conformity of the economies in question with the principles of the free market. The debate is of long standing and has been amply reflected elsewhere (Wade 1990). The point for our purposes here, is that the key battleground for the rivalry between neo-liberal and neo-statist theories of development was precisely the East Asian region, and in theoretical terms the key bone of contention was the relationship between markets and states in development (see Box 13.4).

Box 13.4 Characteristics of the Japanese 'Developmental State'

1. The first priority of the state is economic development—a priority maintained consistently by the Japanese government in both the pre-war and post-war periods. Economic development is defined in terms of growth, production, and competitiveness, rather than consumption, distribution, and welfare.

2. A 'small, inexpensive but elite' bureaucracy, recruited on the basis of merit, is responsible for selecting the industries to be developed (industrial structure policy), identifying the best means of developing these industries (industrial rationalization policy), and supervising competition in the selected sectors to guarantee their economic effectiveness.

3. The legislative and judicial branches of government are restricted to the 'safety valve' functions of ensuring that the bureaucracy responds to the requirements of those groups in society on which the stability of the model rests, thus institutionalizing consultation and co-ordination between bureaucratic and business elites (the private sector) as the basis for effective policy-making. Put more pithily, 'the politicians reign and the bureaucrats rule' (Johnson 1982: 154).

4. State intervention in the economy is of a 'market-conforming' nature.

5. The bureaucracy is led by a 'pilot agency', such as the Japanese Ministry of Internation Trade and Industry (MITI), which formed the basis of Johnson's study, possessed of a wide array of functions associated with controlling and directing the process of industrial transformation.

Source: Johnson (1982)

The rivalry between these schools of thought nevertheless masks a number of key similarities between them. We need here to highlight two. First, they both conceive of development as a national process, where what 'develop' are understood to be countries or national economies. Second, in both approaches, development itself is understood to be about economic growth—only one of the large number of possibilities Arndt mentioned in the list discussed at the start of this section (see Box 13.5). While neo-liberalism and neo-statism have dominated thinking about development in the contemporary period, there have been other currents in development theory that have challenged both of these assumptions in interesting ways, some of which have been accepted into these dominant approaches, and some of which have remained on the outside.

Box 13.5 Key Dimensions of Neo-Statist Development Theory

- Was developed as a means of explaining the growth trajectory of Japan and other East Asian economies from the 1960s onwards, and the divergence between this region and other parts of the developing world.
- Advances a different understanding from neo-liberalism of the relationship between states and markets in East Asian development, emphasizing the role and importance of 'developmental states' in 'governing' markets and shaping development processes.
- Along with neo-liberalism and other development theories, also sees development as a 'national' process and prioritizes an understanding of development as economic growth.

'Human development', gender, and environmental theories

The theories grouped together in this section are unified, albeit tenuously, by a commitment to 'human' or 'people-centred' development, and later 'sustainable human development', as a direct challenge to the emphasis on development as aggregate economic growth that has characterized all of the ways of thinking about development that we have looked at thus far. The redefinition of the 'meaning of development' entailed in this commitment was summarized in an early, influential statement by the renowned economist Dudley Seers (1969: 3–4):

> The questions to ask about a country's development are therefore: What has been happening to poverty? What has been happening to unemployment? What has been happening to inequality? If all three of these have become less severe, then beyond doubt there has been a period of development for the country concerned. If one or two of these central problems have been growing worse, and especially if all three have, it would be strange to call the result 'development', even if per capita income had soared.

In this spirit, 'human development' approaches began to take shape from the 1970s onwards. Their early incarnation was as the so-called 'basic needs' approach, which rested on a core recognition that across the world, and contrary to the predictions of neo-classical economics and the neo-liberal orthodoxy, economic growth was not always associated with beneficial outcomes for the poor, either in incomes or in employment opportunities. Consequently, it was argued that special redistributive measures were required to target the poor and unemployed (Chenery et al. 1974; ILO 1976). Development in this conception emphasized the meeting of basic material needs (food, shelter, clothing), the need for access to key services (water, sanitation, health care, education), and the need for people to participate in the political and decision-making processes that affected their lives (see Streeten et al. 1982).

The approach failed to take root as a result of its unrealistic policy goals, its rejection in poor countries as a result of its 'Western' and 'Northern' flavour in the context of the ideological politics of the Cold War, and the increasing dominance of neo-liberalism. But its essence endured and reappeared in a new generation of human development theory in the 1980s and 1990s, encapsulated most notably in the work of the Nobel Prize-winning economist, Amartya Sen. Sen advanced an understanding of development as being fundamentally about the enhancement of people's 'capabilities', later reformulated as 'freedoms': stated in seductively simple terms, development was defined as 'a process of expanding the real freedoms that people can enjoy' (Sen 1999: 3). These freedoms emanate from a range of processes, including economic growth, but also social and political arrangements. Freedoms were thus understood as both the means and the ends of development. Going further, this approach emphasized the ways in which the agents of development were not governments, as in all the other theories, but ultimately people themselves, as they were granted the adequate opportunities to define their material and social circumstances—that is, their development.

Gender and environmental approaches to development echoed some of the core concerns of human development theories. Ways of thinking about development that privileged gender were varied (see Rai 2002), but were knit together by a core concern with the failures of development to bring about more egalitarian societies, the neglect of the particular needs of women in development processes, and the lack of attention to the ways in which development projects carried particular and distinctive consequences for women. Some of the most influential statements within this broad development project sought to extend the 'basic needs' approach into a 'gender needs' framework (Molyneux 1985; Moser 1989, 1993), which focused on two sets of 'gender interests': 'practical' interests associated with the satisfaction of basic material needs; and 'strategic' interests associated with the rectification of gender inequalities in such areas as political representation, educational opportunity, employment conditions, freedom from domestic violence and exploitation, and so on. These were then extended into a notion of 'empowerment' which, echoing human development approaches, was understood as increasing women's ability to secure 'their own self-reliance and internal strength' (Moser 1989: 1815). Other strands of this body of thought, which will be of particular relevance to our discussions in the next section of the chapter, emphasized the highly gendered impact of globalization processes and particular kinds of development strategies (Elson 1989, 1992, 1995; Pearson 1995; Benería 2003; Marchand 1994, 1996).

Likewise, environmental approaches emerged from the early 1970s onwards as critiques of the view of the relationship between environment and development that had prevailed in post-war growth and modernization theories, as well as neo-liberal approaches (Payne and Phillips 2010). In these latter perspectives, natural resources were not considered to pose obstacles to economic growth and there was a general optimism that technical solutions would be found that allowed human beings to 'harness nature on an ever-larger scale' (Woodhouse 2002: 141). The early critique emerged in a report commissioned by the Club of Rome, entitled *Limits to Growth* (Meadows et al. 1972), which advanced the arresting argument that the limits to growth could in fact be reached within the next century if trends in population growth, industrialization, food production, natural resource depletion, and environmental degradation continued. Gradually, the linkages between environment and development thus became a matter of global concern and had moved belatedly, along with poverty and gender, to the centre of global development debates by the end of the 1980s, clothed in the concept of 'sustainable development'. This was defined famously as 'development that meets the needs of the present without compromising the ability of future generations to meet their own needs' (World Commission on Environment and Development 1987). To this end, the ambitious call was issued for a reorientation of economic activity and development strategy to focus on human development and the needs of the poor, noting that unequal distribution of and access to resources, as well as vastly unequal patterns of resource consumption, contributed to both the perpetuation of poverty and the steady destruction of the global environment.

These three approaches, in their quite different ways, thus advance a critique of the other kinds of development theory that we have looked at in this section. They emphasize the limitations and dangers of the dominant understanding of development as a process of economic growth, and instead highlight a number of the other ways of thinking about development that we noted in the quotation from Arndt at the beginning of the section. Equally, they all take issue with the notion that what develop—the objects of development—are countries or national states and economies, in which national governments are the agents of development. Rather, they conceive of development as being about a process of improvement in the material and social conditions in which people live, and the expansion of opportunities, 'capabilities' and 'freedoms' that shape those conditions. In this sense, the meaning, process, and goals of development were all redefined to yield a focus on 'sustainable human development' (see Box 13.6).

(see Box 13.6).

> ### Box 13.6 Key Dimensions of 'Human' Development Theories
>
> - Take issue with other development theories' definition of development as growth, and instead focus on a range of indicators associated with 'human development' (poverty, inequality, unemployment, basic needs, 'capabilities', and 'freedoms', etc.) and 'sustainable development'.
>
> - Advance a 'people-centred' approach to development, where the objects of development are human beings and groups of people, not simply countries or economies.
>
> - Broaden the focus to emphasize inequalities within societies and between groups of people, not simply between countries, and incorporate not only economic inequalities but a range of social inequalities (including those based on gender).

> ### Key points
>
> - The term 'development' is used in a wide range of different ways, to mean a wide range of conditions, processes, and goals.
>
> - Different theories of development reflect differing conceptions of what development is and how it might be achieved, and entail different diagnoses of the causes of either developmental progress or developmental failure.
>
> - The period from the 1940s to the early 1980s was dominated by the controversy between modernization and underdevelopment theories, both of which had been widely discredited, for different reasons, by the end of this period.
>
> - The contemporary period (from the early 1980s) was dominated by the controversy between neo-liberalism and neo-statism in seeking to explain the key trend towards divergence in the trajectories of developing economies—a trend which challenged the validity of a notion of the 'Third World' as a single group of countries.
>
> - Both neo-liberalism and neo-statism laid claim to the 'East Asian miracle', the former interpreting it as a triumph of 'export-led growth' and conformity with the free market model, the latter as a triumph of 'investment-led development' and the importance of states in directing and mediating development processes.
>
> - Alongside these theoretical currents, 'human' or 'people-centred' theories of development challenged the emphasis on economic growth and sought to develop a wider conception of development as being fundamentally about the material and social conditions in which people live.

Development Theory in Practice

We have seen that the contemporary period has been marked by a flourishing of development theories, all advancing very different ways of thinking about what development means and how to achieve it. The important point is that many of these theories of development gave rise to very particular kinds of development strategies, both in the form of a top-down global development agenda, elaborated by a global development community, and in the form of national development strategies across the world. Our central task is to trace the translation of these different ways of thinking about development into concrete policies and strategies, and, moreover, to understand their impact and consequences. The overarching context for this discussion is that the contemporary period of development, from the end of the Second World War to the present time, has taken place in the midst of accelerating processes of globalization. All of these theories provide a different perspective on the relationship between globalization and development—both what that relationship does look like and what it should look like. Charting the evolution of development strategies over the second part of the twentieth century and the first decade of the twenty-first century thus enables us to think more clearly about the impact of globalization on development.

The mid 1940s to the early 1980s

Across the regions that constituted what at the time was called the 'Third World', the development context of the post-war period was dramatically different from that which had hitherto prevailed. First, for many, it was marked by the onset of the pivotal period of decolonization, in which African and a number of Asian states finally achieved independence from the various European powers. States in Latin America and the Caribbean had of course been through their independence struggle some time earlier, starting in the mid-nineteenth century, but it was the decolonization process of the mid-twentieth century that initiated the fundamental changes in the international political-economic landscape that defined the development project from that time forwards. Second, the experience of the Great Depression and the two World Wars prompted a reassessment, particularly in Latin America, of the virtues and dangers of the broadly laissez-faire economic policies that had been pursued up to that point, along with the wisdom of dependence on the industrialized states as markets for their exports of primary products and imports of manufactured goods. Third, demographic trends necessitated urgent attention to employment as the key goal of economic policy (Thorp 1998: 128). Finally, the world economy was defined for all developing countries by heightened protectionism in the key European and US markets, the movement towards the formation of the European Economic Community, and the establishment of new institutions under the Bretton Woods system which were dominated by the established powers and in which developing countries, by now vastly increased in number, had no means of effective participation.

This conjunction of circumstances led to two immediate priorities for development strategies. The first was to design policies that would lead to a resumption of growth, achieve the goals of industrialization, and in some cases respond to the demographic urgencies of employment creation. The second was to find ways of mitigating enduring conditions of economic dependence on the 'North' and ensuring effective participation in the new international system which was shaping the possibilities for achieving these goals. The twin imperatives were therefore of 'catching up', on the one hand, and 'breaking out', on the other (Thomas 2008: 418). The emergence of a 'North–South' dynamic in this context was reflected in the key divide in development theory of the time, namely, between modernization theory and underdevelopment theory. The former, as we have seen, viewed the purpose of development strategy as one of catching up with the developed countries by a route of emulation, particularly in matters of political system, institutional configurations, and economic orientation. For this purpose, conditioned by the strategic and ideological imperatives of the Cold War, significant amounts of aid were pumped into the developing world, particularly into regions and countries of key strategic importance. Yet, more important in modernization theory than the role of aid was its insistence that export-led growth, and hence trade, were the keys to progress for developing countries.

Underdevelopment theory gained much more traction than modernization theory across most parts of the developing world for both economic and political reasons (although, notably, it never gained much popularity in East Asia outside of the Philippines). The diagnosis of the economic impact of the Great Depression and the two World Wars led to a conviction that a new economic policy direction was required. Governments in Latin

America led the way, taking their cue directly from the structuralist theories of Prebisch and others, and advocating a turn not to export-led growth, as advocated by modernization theories and associated policy frameworks, but to 'inward-looking' development strategies. These strategies are known as import-substituting industrialization (ISI). Versions of ISI were implemented widely in Africa and South Asia as well, but its adoption as a region-wide development strategy was most pronounced in Latin America. It had three central goals:

1. Stimulating and consolidating industrialization through a more effective system of state intervention in the economy, a restructuring of economic activity away from primary products, and according much greater prominence to foreign capital over trade as the motor of capital accumulation and industrial development.

2. Politically integrating the new and expanding working classes through a programme of social reform and employment generation.

3. Achieving some degree of autonomy vis-à-vis the international economy.

In its original formulation, ISI was envisaged not as a route to excessive protectionism or self-sufficiency (autarchy), but rather as a means to the achievement of what Prebisch conceived as 'balanced growth' (Kay 1989: 37).

To these ends, ISI strategies were formulated in two phases: 'primary' ISI was associated with the domestic production of basic consumer goods, while 'secondary' or 'vertical' ISI involved the domestic production of capital- and technology-intensive manufactured products, which necessarily featured higher levels of skill intensity than the primary stages of ISI. Regional integration projects were also conceived to further the industrialization effort, primarily in order to compensate for the limited size of domestic markets and the constraints thereby imposed on both consumption and demand, and also to increase the bargaining weight of developing countries in the international system. John Ravenhill has looked in detail in his chapter at this phase of regionalism in the developing world. It suffices here

to signal the important distinction with integration initiatives being pursued at the time in the industrialized world. The premises of trade liberalization and increased competition which underpinned the latter, and were central to modernization theory, were seen to be unsuitable for the Latin American region: here, trade, it was argued, needed to be 'promoted' rather than 'freed' (Wionczek 1966: 291–5).

While inward-looking economic strategies were strongly oriented to achieving a lessening of economic dependence and greater autonomy from the advanced industrialized nations, the second, political goal of development strategy was to achieve more effective participation in the new international system. The nature of this system and the institutions that comprised it have been discussed at length in other chapters, and we do not need to recap here. The salient point for our discussions of development is that developing countries were marginalized within this new system and had few opportunities for effective participation. The Bretton Woods institutions were not set up as development institutions — indeed, they did not come to occupy that role until much later — but, rather, were focused on the needs of the industrialized countries, particularly in the context of post-war reconstruction (see Williams 1994; Woods 2006). It was not until the early 1960s that the World Bank and International Monetary Fund (IMF) began to engage on a substantial scale in lending for developing countries and to acknowledge these countries' demands for special resources. The ability of governments in developing countries to press their demands was in any case limited by the weighted voting structures that prevailed in these institutions, in which the United States occupied a position of particular privilege and veto power — as, indeed, it still does today.

The General Agreement on Tariffs and Trade (GATT) system (explored in more detail in Winham, Chapter 5 in this volume), operated similarly to marginalize developing countries. The Kennedy Round of the GATT negotiations (1964–7) was seen by governments in the developing world as illustrative of the power imbalances in the international system which left them with extremely limited bargaining power and little prospect of achieving co-operation with more industrialized countries. The main issues were, as with the financial institutions, that the GATT system made no acknowledgement of the different and special needs of developing countries, that demands for reciprocal trade liberalization took no account of the particular challenges of industrialization which necessitated protection of domestic firms and industries, and that the key sector—agriculture—remained subject to high levels of protectionism in the key markets and not open for negotiation in the GATT (see Tussie 1987). The complaints were, perhaps depressingly, exactly the same as those we hear today in the context of World Trade Organization (WTO) negotiations.

These concerns entrenched the conviction that developing countries were constrained to rely on solidarity and co-operation among themselves in order to address the disadvantageous terms on which international economic and political interactions were conducted. The non-aligned movement (NAM) and the New International Economic Order (NIEO) were the two key political movements that emerged as expressions of this goal. The NAM crystallized in 1955 following the pivotal Asian–African conference held in Indonesia, and provided a platform from which developing countries could organize themselves more effectively to participate and demand representation within international organizations. The establishment of the United Nations Conference on Trade and Development (UNCTAD) and the formation of the Group of 77 (G77), both in 1977, were the first expressions of these greater levels of political organization, the first conceived as an alternative forum to the GATT, and the second designed to afford greater participation and leverage in the UN system. Of greatest influence, however, was the NIEO movement which subsequently took shape in 1974. The call presented to the UN General Assembly for an NIEO in fact constituted a primarily political demand for the sovereignty of developing countries to be taken more seriously, along with a number of economic demands that were oriented particularly to reducing the dependence of developing economies on the international economy, reducing their vulnerability to deteriorating terms of trade for raw materials exports, and increasing their economic 'sovereignty' by enhancing control over foreign direct investment (FDI) and natural resources (Thomas 2008: 422). These concerns were articulated in a context of tumultuous change in the international political economy: the delinking of the dollar from a fixed price of gold by the US administration of Richard Nixon in 1971 effectively brought an end to the post-war Bretton Woods era of fixed exchange rates and initiated the acceleration of financial and other forms of globalization, and international oil prices quadrupled in 1973 as a result of action by the Organization of the Petroleum Exporting Countries (OPEC).

These increases in oil prices were especially damaging for oil-importing developing countries in the context of volatile commodity prices at the end of the 1970s, and were a major reason for the vast increase in borrowing among developing countries over the second part of the 1970s and early 1980s. The other reasons were related to the changing form of the ISI experiment, which, contrary to aspirations, remained dependent on inflows of foreign capital and technology. The original ECLA thesis had emphasized the importance of public capital, but in the event the model came to depend to a much greater extent on FDI. The 'classic' examples of ISI in Latin America—Argentina, Brazil, Chile, Colombia, and Mexico—were thus marked by the heavy participation of transnational corporations (TNCs) (Thorp 1998: 133–4). Peter Evans (1979) influentially used the label 'dependent development' to capture the centrality of foreign TNCs to Latin American development during this time.

The foreign capital issue was also sharpened by the explosion in liquidity in international financial markets in the late 1960s and 1970s and its availability to Latin American countries in the form of loans, credit, industrial financing, and so on, such that the ISI model in its later stages came to be driven by the massive accretion of foreign debt (see Pauly, Chapter 8 in this volume). The reasons for the implosion of ISI across Latin America and elsewhere are varied, relating both to the structural barriers ('bottlenecks') to the transition to the secondary phase of ISI and the political contradictions of the model (see Baer 1972; Phillips 2004). But it was ultimately the massive increase in borrowing across the world, and the resulting debt crisis which started in Latin America in 1982, that marked the end of experiments with these kinds of inward-looking development based on structuralist underdevelopment theory.

Yet, the failures of ISI in Latin America and elsewhere are only a part of the global picture. As noted earlier, the crisis of development in Latin America and Africa was unfolding at a time when economies in another supposedly 'developing' region — namely, East Asia — were moving in completely the opposite direction. From the early 1960s to the early 1980s, the Japanese economy, emerging from the debris of the Second World War, grew at annual rates of around 7 per cent, moving from being the world's twentieth largest exporter to the third largest, and becoming by most indicators the most successful industrialized country in the world (Pempel 1999a). During the same period, the four NIEs were also growing at annual rates of over 8 per cent. As noted earlier on in the chapter, interpretations of what came to be known as the 'East Asian miracle' vary, with both neo-liberals and neo-statists seeking to lay claim to the miracle as a vindication of their particular perspectives on development. We will turn back to these questions as we trace the story of the 1980s and 1990s. But here it is important to note that the East Asian model — as well as the notion of the developmental state that was first developed for the Japanese case but subsequently widened to other economies in the region — were strongly nationalist in their economic orientation. The emphasis on catch-up was strongly connected with a concern about the position of Asian economies in the global economy, for the purposes not only of achieving economic prosperity but also of securing a global presence and influence.

These goals were formulated in strongly nationalist terms, particularly in the Japanese context.

But this was not Latin American-style 'inward-looking development'. Rather, it was conditioned by a much more unequivocal recognition of the role of the international environment in creating the conditions for East Asian industrialization. In the 1960s, this environment, for Asia, was marked by increasing access to international finance, increasing access to the markets of the industrialized countries, and, perhaps particularly, the increasing relocation of global productive activity to low-cost sites in what was then still thought of as the 'periphery', specifically to Asia (Wade 1990). This process was captured influentially in the notion of the 'new international division of labour' (NIDL) (Frobel et al. 1980). Moreover, the Japanese and East Asian context differed dramatically from the Latin American 'dependent development' experience, inasmuch as the NIEs possessed the strength and autonomy to manage the impact inflows of foreign capital on the local economies and were therefore much less conditioned, and certainly less negatively affected, by the dominance of foreign TNCs (Haggard and Cheng 1987). The other point to note, but not to exaggerate, is that the strategic importance of the East Asian NIEs in the Cold War inclined the US to support their industrialization process during the 1960s, both through the provision of financial and technical assistance, and by providing a market for East Asian exports — an additional factor in explaining the superior performance of the NIEs relative to other Asian economies and most of Latin America and Africa (Cumings 1984; Weiss and Hobson 1995).

The point of key difference between the neo-liberals and the neo-statists, however, concerns the foundation of the East Asian model. Neo-liberals insisted on the centrality of export-led growth, often termed export-oriented industrialization (EOI), in which the formula ran along the lines of 'market-friendly policies plus export-push policies lead to export-led growth' (Wade 1996: 26). It was possible thus to pin neo-liberal stripes on the East Asian model. Leading proponents of a neo-statist interpretation, to the contrary, argue that exports were not the driving force behind growth and industrialization, but rather the result of higher investment, which leads to faster technical change and higher import levels, which in turn generate higher exports. The performance of Japan and the NIEs rested not on export orientation, but rather on 'favourable initial conditions—especially human capital and infrastructure—plus investment-led growth' (Wade 1996: 26). A rash of very detailed and influential subsequent studies, particularly of Taiwan and Korea, supported these neo-statist arguments (Wade 1990; Amsden 1989, 1990).

We can see, therefore, that this period of development—the so-called 'Age of Development'—looked very different for different parts of the developing world. We have broadly characterized the Latin American region (and, indeed, parts of sub-Saharan Africa and South Asia) as marked by experiments with ISI, but not all countries engaged in these strategies, those that did implemented different forms of ISI, timings differed, and the outcomes varied quite widely. In Chile, for example, the government of the dictator Augusto Pinochet initiated an experiment with free-market, monetarist policies from the mid 1970s onwards, substantially before the debt crisis of the early 1980s that we have for convenience taken as a chronological dividing point; the Brazilian experiment with ISI integrated certain liberalization measures into its economic strategy and the traits of state developmentalism persisted long after the generalized collapse of the model across the region. We have also talked in broad terms about the 'East Asian model', but must recognize that this did not extend to the whole of the Asian region, and the form it took was not identical across the NIEs. But, despite these huge differences between and within regions, in retrospect the period can be characterized as featuring a central role for the state in development, and this represents the primary point of contrast with the dominance of neo-liberal development strategies which gradually took root over the 1980s and 1990s.

The record of development during this time was also very mixed, casting doubt on the utility of the prevalent notions of 'core' and 'periphery', or indeed 'Third World', as homogenous categories of countries. While the East Asian NIEs experienced high growth rates, Latin America's aggregate growth performance was more modest. The story in sub-Saharan Africa was the most gloomy, with an average annual increase of only 1 per cent in per capita GDP between 1965 and 1985. More revealingly, an improvement between 1965 and 1974 gave way to a stagnation from the mid 1970s onwards, when many economies failed to cope with the increased costs of imported energy, and by the early 1980s many countries had a lower per capita GDP than before independence some twenty years earlier. Export growth was also negative in the first part of the 1980s, having been relatively healthy between 1965 and 1973. Manufactured exports declined between 1970 and 1986 for sub-Saharan African economies, while during the same period they jumped fivefold for Latin America, sixfold for the Middle East and North Africa, and thirteenfold for the East Asian NIEs (World Bank 1994: 17–18). Remember as well that, in 1965, Indonesia's GDP per capita had been lower than Nigeria's, and Thailand's lower than Ghana's (World Bank 1994: 17). What we saw over this period was thus a complete reordering of the development 'hierarchy' of developing nations, with sub-Saharan Africa sliding backwards as the East Asian NIEs surged forwards, and many other developing regions featuring at least moderate improvements in the main indicators of economic development.

The 1980s onwards

From the early 1980s onwards, we see a new phase in the global development project. This was marked by the dominance of the neo-liberal agenda, based, as we outlined earlier, on ways of thinking about development which sought the freeing of market forces and advanced a political project of 'rolling back' the state. In the advanced industrialized countries, especially the United States and the United Kingdom, neo-liberalism emerged as a specific response to the experiences of Keynesian growth strategies and welfare state policies in Europe, which by the 1970s were seen to have yielded the twin economic problems of declining growth rates and accelerating inflation (dubbed 'stagflation'), and the associated political problems of increased militancy among trade unions. In the developing world, the critique was extended as an attack on ISI and the development problems it was seen to have bequeathed: bloated states, inefficiency and corruption, hyperinflation, the debt crisis, political instability, and a laundry list of other lamentable conditions. Neo-liberal thought in this sense came to consolidate itself as what John Toye (1993) called a 'counterrevolution' in development thinking, which fundamentally shaped the process of globalization and the matter in which countries, economies, and societies participated in it.

The point at which the various currents and elements of neo-liberal thinking were brought together into a blueprint for development came at the end of the 1980s. The US economist John Williamson identified the key elements of the new global policy agenda and attached to it the label Washington Consensus (WC). The resulting framework was quickly assumed, not only to reflect the 'consensus' that had emerged in the global network of elite institutions, governments, and market actors associated with the neo-liberal orthodoxy, but also to constitute a list of what governments of countries had to do in order to 'develop'. Its elements are outlined in Box 13.7. Colin Leys put it well when he observed that, by end of the 1980s, 'the only development policy that was officially approved was not having one—leaving it to the market to allocate resources, not the state' (Leys 1996: 42).

Box 13.7 The Policy Prescriptions of the Washington Consensus

- Maintenance of fiscal discipline (budget deficits should not exceed 2 per cent of GDP).

- Reordering of public expenditure priorities (reduction and elimination of subsidies; prioritization of spending in education, health, and infrastructure).

- Tax reform (broadening of tax base; maintenance of 'moderate' marginal tax rates).

- Maintenance of positive real interest rates (to discourage capital flight and increase savings).

- Maintenance of 'competitive' exchange rates.

- Trade liberalization.

- Elimination of barriers to foreign direct investment.

- Privatization of state-owned enterprises.

- Deregulation of the economy.

- Enforcement of property rights.

Source: Williamson (1990)

From the start, the WC was presented as common sense which was immune to sensible questioning—Williamson himself famously dismissed dissenters as 'cranks'—and disseminated aggressively across the developing world. The important point is that justification for this new 'orthodoxy' was presented as coming from globalization itself. The 'structural hegemony' of global capital (Gill and Law 1989), which was the cornerstone of globalization processes, was seen to put in place a new structure of rewards and punishments in the global political

economy. Capital was understood to respond 'objectively' to particular national macroeconomic and policy conditions, to the extent that putting in place the 'right' policies—namely, those listed in the WC—was crucial for the achievement of the range of goals associated with development. Even the champion of ISI during the previous development era, ECLAC (by then the Caribbean had been added to the name of the organization), deemed 'linkages with the global economy' to be essential for Latin American countries to achieve 'sustainable changes in production patterns with social equity' (ECLAC 1995: 15–16). There was, as famously summed up by Margaret Thatcher, 'no alternative'.

The main channels of the dissemination of the new neo-liberal development orthodoxy were the international financial institutions (IFIs), and specifically the World Bank and the IMF. During the 1980s, it was structural adjustment programmes (SAPs) that ruled the day, reflecting a set of 'one-size-fits-all' policy prescriptions applied widely across Latin America and the Caribbean, sub-Saharan Africa, Eastern Europe, and other parts of the developing world. In this model, lending strategies were subject to stringent forms of conditionality—that is, continued lending was dependent on a country's conformity with a range of economic and political policy conditions attached to the loans from the IFIs. By the end of the 1980s, they were seen to have failed, particularly in view of the continued stagnation of most African economies, and resurgent inflation and hyperinflation in many Latin American economies. (The rate of 5,000 per cent in Argentina in 1989 is indicative of a situation of hyperinflation.) Indeed, the 1980s for these two regions were widely seen to be a 'lost decade' of development.

The IFIs changed tack, dropping the term 'structural adjustment' in favour of a new organizing concept—that of 'good governance'—by which the Bank sought to assert a new focus on the centrality of institutions in economic reform and development processes (World Bank 1992a; see Williams and Young 1994; Doornbos 2001). Macroeconomic stabilization (lowering inflation) and adjustment (trade liberalization, financial deregulation, privatization, and so on) remained critical, but were presented as only the 'first generation' of reforms. The 'second generation' comprised an emphasis on sweeping institutional reform for the 'modernization of the state', fiscal reform, tax reform, labour flexibilization, and so on. Whereas the days of the Bretton Woods era and the 1980s had been marked by an insistence on the 'apoliticism' of the IFIs—by which was meant that their agenda would not interfere with domestic political arrangements—the good governance agenda gave the IFIs licence to intervene in highly political ways in developing countries. The agents of the neo-liberal counterrevolution thus claimed for themselves 'an unprecedented capacity to shape the strategic direction of large parts of the world' (Payne 2005a: 59).

Key points

- From the end of the Second World War onwards, the twin goals of development were 'catching up' and 'breaking out'—that is, on the one hand, catching up with the more developed economies by achieving a resumption of growth and higher levels of industrialization, and, on the other, breaking out of enduring conditions of economic dependence on the 'North' and ensuring more effective participation and representation in the new international system.

- Underdevelopment theory gained more traction than modernization theory in the developing world, except in Asia, and led to inward-looking

- development strategies known as import-substitution industrialization (ISI).

- The NAM and NIEO reflected a conviction among developing countries that they needed greater levels of solidarity and co-operation to press their demands more effectively in the international system and key organizations such as the IFIs, the GATT, and the UN.

- The early 1980s was marked by the Latin American debt crisis, reflecting both the contradictions of ISI and the explosion in lending to developing economies.

- At the same time as inward-looking development strategies were failing in Latin America, sub-Saharan Africa, and elsewhere, the East Asian economies were achieving impressive rates of growth and moving rapidly up the economic hierarchy: from the early 1960s to the early 1980s, the Japanese economy grew at average annual rates of 7 per cent, and the East NIEs at average annual rates of around 8 per cent.

- In contrast with this success story in East Asia and modest growth in Latin America, sub-Saharan Africa slid backwards, as an improvement in economic performance from the mid 1960s to the mid 1970s gave way to a process of stagnation and decline from the mid 1970s onwards.

- As such, this period was marked by a complete re-ordering of the global development 'hierarchy'.

- From the early 1980s onwards, the landscape of development was defined by the dominance of neo-liberalism and, in particular, the dissemination of policy strategies based on the Washington Consensus across the developing world.

- The Washington Consensus was justified by its proponents on the basis of what were perceived to be the new 'demands' of globalization, particularly in matters of macroeconomic policy orientation.

- The structural adjustment programmes (SAPs) of the 1980s were seen by the end of this decade to have failed, in view of the continued stagnation of African economies, the resurgence of (hyper)inflation in Latin America, and the poor performance of other developing regions, except Asia.

- The IFIs changed tack and introduced an emphasis on 'good governance' and 'second-generation reforms', consolidating the neo-liberal 'counterrevolution' in development thinking and strategy during the 1990s.

The Crisis of the Washington Consensus

By the end of the 1990s, the neo-liberal development project was in trouble and the credibility of the WC under great strain. The record of development across Latin America, Eastern Europe and sub-Saharan Africa in particular — the main testing grounds of neo-liberal reform — was disappointing and in some cases disastrous. The Mexican 'peso crisis' of 1995, which saw the collapse of the currency following a speculative attack in the global financial markets, dealt a serious blow to the development orthodoxy. The Asian financial crisis of the late 1990s, explored by Louis W. Pauly in his chapter, similarly knocked both neo-liberalism and neo-statism onto the back foot and revealed much about the relationship between globalization and development in that region and more broadly. But let us go into a little more detail about the record of this period before exploring what it can tell us about the developmental implications of globalization.

Growth

We have already noted that the East Asian economies continued into the 1980s and 1990s with strong growth rates. The locus of that growth shifted from Japan and the NIEs to China and India over the course of this period. In the case of China, average annual GDP growth from the mid 1980s to the early 2000s stood at 9.5 per cent, increasing to 10.7 per cent by 2006 (World Bank 2007a). For India, the figures were 6 per cent from the late 1980s to the late 2000s, and 8.6 per cent in the 2003–7 period (Panagariya 2008). Both countries' trajectories featured a significant level of integration into global economic processes, at least in production and trade. But, in China especially, engagement with globalization did not extend to financial markets. Equally, both countries engaged in autarchic trade and investment policies until the late 1980s, with liberalization processes initiated only from that time. While growth rates for China and India continued uninterrupted into the 2000s, the Asian crises of the late 1990s brought a setback and new challenges for the East Asian NIEs and other economies in South East Asia.

The story elsewhere was different. In Latin America, for instance, per capita GDP grew more slowly over the 1990s than during the period between 1950 and 1980, and by 2003 was 1.5 per cent lower than in 1997 (ECLAC 2002). The World Bank's key report on Africa in the 1990s (World Bank 1994) actually seemed rather proud of what can only be thought of as a depressing picture: of the 28 countries that had engaged in structural adjustment, exactly half of them had experienced declines in the average annual growth rate of GDP per capita between 1981–6 and 1987–91, and among the half that did experience growth, the most impressive figure was an increase of around 3 percentage points during this period. Note that this does not mean GDP per capita growth rates of 3 per cent — rather, it means that the figure for the second period represents an increase of 3 percentage points on the figure for the first period, which in the majority of cases had been negative.

Trade

On the trade front, the picture was again one of divergence between developing economies, this time between those which were integrated into international trade patterns as exporters of manufactured goods (mainly the East Asian NIEs), and those which remained reliant on the export of primary commodities (mainly some smaller Latin American and sub-Saharan African economies) (Thomas 2008: 426–7). In the mid 1980s, primary products accounted for roughly the same proportion of African export revenues (around 80 per cent) as in the mid 1960s, and over the same period agricultural exports became more concentrated, with just nine products accounting for 76 per cent of exports in the mid 1980s (World Bank 1994: 18).

The obstacles to the trade strategies of the exporters of raw materials in Latin America and sub-Saharan Africa were found partly in trends in international commodity prices. In the 1980s, for example, prices collapsed for the key African export crops of cocoa, coffee (each declining by around 70 per cent), and cotton (declining by 28 per cent). But they were also found in the lack of access to the key markets. The problems of protectionism that were identified by the early structuralists and post-war policy-makers in developing countries persisted through the 1980s and 1990s, particularly in the key sector of agriculture. Government subsidies to agricultural producers in the Organization for Economic Co-operation and Development (OECD) countries fell slightly between the mid 1980s and the mid 1990s, from levels equivalent to 37 per cent of total farm receipts to around 30 per cent, but this latter figure remained unchanged by the mid 2000s. Levels in the European Union (EU) have been consistently higher than the average for the OECD, at around 34 per cent of total farm receipts, and in the early 2000s levels were higher still in Japan and Korea (around 60 per cent), and in Norway, Switzerland, and Iceland (around 70 per cent). In the early 2000s, the US was responsible for some 20 per cent of the total global agricultural subsidies, and the EU for around 40 per cent (OECD 2003, 2005).

International trade negotiations had expanded continuously to embrace a wide range of areas, including such issues as intellectual property, competition policy, or investment policy, but the area of agriculture, for many developing countries fundamental, remained essentially off the negotiating table. In this sense, while trade liberalization was central to the WC and the neo-liberal development orthodoxy, the expectation was that developing countries would unilaterally liberalize trade in key sectors (that is, with no corresponding liberalization in the developed market economies) and the structure of trade negotiations continued to fail to address the basic trade issues that were critical to their development prospects, notwithstanding the new-found preoccupation with development in the trade agenda. The ongoing marginalization of developing countries in trade negotiations themselves compounded the problems, and led a creeping situation of stalemate in the WTO agenda after the end of the Uruguay Round in the mid 1990s, which persisted throughout the 2000s (see Finger and Nogués 2002; Panagariya 2002; Narlikar 2003; Wilkinson 2006). These dynamics are explored in Winham, Chapter 5 in this volume.

Finance and investment

Much of the commentary about globalization, both enthusiastic and sceptical, notes the huge growth in private investment flows to the developing world, particularly over the course of the 1990s. By the mid 1990s, these had increased sixfold compared with 1990 levels, and were some four times greater than the peak levels reached during the lending boom of 1978–82, which, as we have seen, culminated in the Latin American debt crisis of the early 1980s. Developing economies' share of total global FDI flows stood at 40 per cent, compared with 15 per cent in 1990. Flows to these economies were dominated by FDI, largely associated with large-scale privatization processes, but portfolio investment (bonds and equities) rose sharply to account for around a third of the total. By the middle of the 1990s, private flows were also around five times greater than official (aid) flows (World Bank 1997: 9–10). Yet, the pattern is much more uneven than these figures suggest at first glance. In the mid 1990s, 95 per cent of these flows were directed to only 26 of the 166 countries classified by the World Bank as 'developing nations', although some account has to be taken of the size of economies in evaluating the relative significance of these flows and the degree of dependence on them (World Bank 1997: 12). Sub-Saharan Africa, notably, was largely bypassed by this surge in capital flows in comparison with other regions.

Such is the context of the rash of economic and financial crises in the 1990s and 2000s in the developing world—the Mexican peso crisis of 1995, the Asian financial crisis and the spread of 'contagion' to Brazil, Russia, Turkey, and elsewhere in the late 1990s, and the Argentine collapse of the early 2000s. Financial volatility was both central to the causes of these crises and a result of them. Capital flows to Latin America and the Caribbean, for instance, contracted by more than a third in 2002 alone, the decline being felt most sharply in Mexico and the Caribbean as a result of the additional impact of recession in the US economy (Phillips 2005: 339). While in some cases (Brazil, East Asia), FDI levels picked up quite quickly following the onset of crisis, in others the recovery was much slower and more partial. We will look more closely at debates surrounding the causes of these crises and contending reactions to them in the next section of the chapter. The global economic crisis of the late 2000s, meanwhile, has been declared to have marked 'the end of a growth cycle' in global FDI: by early 2009, global flows were estimated to have declined by around 20 per cent, with the impact, for once, being felt primarily in the 'developed' economies. However, UNCTAD indicated that 'the worst is yet to come' in terms of the impact on 'developing' economies, including the large and relatively powerful economies of China, India, Russia, and Brazil (UNCTAD 2009a).

Debt

The problem of indebtedness among developing countries is of long standing, but the trajectory of its increase was striking during the 1990s. The total debt stock of the net-debtor developing countries doubled during this decade to US$2.2 billion. Again at an aggregate level, the ratio of debt service payments (that is, either repayments to creditors of money owed, or payments covering some of the interest on the debt) to exports increased from 19.6 per cent in 1991 to 22.3 per cent in 1999 (Thomas 2008: 426). The problem was, and remains, most acute for the heavily indebted countries, where debt levels were equivalent to

103 per cent of total GDP between 1995 and 2000, notwithstanding a small fall since the peak of 120 per cent for 1990–4 (Thomas 2008: 426). But larger and richer developing countries also continued to struggle with high levels of indebtedness. For Argentina in 1998, for example, the ratio of total debt to foreign exchange revenues from exports reached 500 per cent, and its ratio to GDP 41.4 per cent, increasing to 50 per cent by 2000 when the economy was beginning to collapse (Mussa 2002).

The period was marked by a new phase in the global politics of debt, with the announcement in September 1996 of the Heavily Indebted Poor Countries (HIPC) initiative. This policy was not designed to eliminate debt, but, rather, had the more modest objective of reducing it to 'sustainable' levels, defined as a country's ability to meet its debt service obligations without having to resort to a rescheduling of the debt or accumulating arrears (Payne 2005*b*: 147). Forty-one countries were initially classified as HIPCs, overwhelmingly from Africa, and some progress was made over time towards reorganizing and alleviating their debt burdens. But, unsurprisingly, the HIPC initiative did not go nearly far enough for the growing concert of non-governmental organizations that began to mobilize around this issue, notably under the umbrella of the Jubilee 2000 movement which demanded the cancellation of the debt of poor countries. In mid 2005, at a summit meeting in Gleneagles, Scotland, the argument was finally accepted by the Group of Seven (G7) countries that the multilateral debt of many poor countries should be cancelled entirely (Helleiner and Cameron 2006), and the Multilateral Debt Relief Initiative (MDRI) came into being. The IMF began to provide the agreed relief from the beginning of 2006, and other institutions and governments have followed suit, on the basis of quite exacting eligibility criteria. From 2007 onwards, there were considered to be 40 countries eligible for relief. In mid 2009, the IMF estimated the total costs of MDRI relief to be around $4 billion, of which $3.4 billion had already been delivered (IMF 2009*c*).

Poverty and inequality

Trends in poverty and inequality over this period are amply documented in Robert Wade's chapter. The important points for our purposes here are simply that, in the first place, the neo-liberal development project did not yield the expected or desired results. While the proportion of the world's population living in conditions of poverty may have diminished at an aggregate level over the course of the 1990s, this improvement was almost entirely accounted for by the performance of East Asia, especially China. The population living below the $1 per day poverty line increased significantly in most other parts of the world, and the recorded increase was even greater using the $2 per day measurement (World Bank 2002*b*; Kaplinsky 2005). Second, the recurrence of economic crisis in the developing world increased very significantly the *vulnerability* of populations to poverty and destitution, along with the range of social phenomena that accompany these conditions. After the Asian financial crisis, for example, the World Bank estimated the incidence of poverty in that region to have increased by around 22 million people (Glyn 2006: 69).

The third point to add is that vulnerability to poverty has also been strongly connected with the terms on which the world's poor workers and producers participate in global production, specifically at the low-value-added ends of global value chains (GVCs). The orthodox perspective assumes a positive relationship between the enhanced integration of economies, societies, communities, and individuals into GVCs, with employment being deemed to be the key mechanism for lifting people out of conditions of poverty. The recognition of the importance of the terms on which this integration takes place leads instead to a focus on forms of 'adverse incorporation' and their implications for poverty. The pressures arising from competition between firms and the squeezing of suppliers by retailers to reduce costs and therefore maximize profit are among the characteristics of the 'normal functioning' of GVCs which produce the 'symptoms' of poverty and deprivation (Ponte 2008: 27; see Hickey and du Toit 2007; Phillips 2011).

Key points

- The development record of the contemporary period has been highly uneven across regions and countries.

- In terms of growth patterns, East Asian economies have continued to achieve high rates of GDP and GDP per capita growth, even though the Asian crisis of the late 1990s presented setbacks for many economies in the region. In Latin America, by contrast, GDP per capita grew more slowly over the 1990s than during the period between 1950 and 1980, and was 1.5 per cent lower in 2003 than in 1997. In sub-Saharan Africa, the picture was of modest improvement in some parts of the region, and a continued decline in others.

- With regard to trade, exporters of manufactured goods did rather better than those economies that remain dependent on primary products, and persistent protectionist barriers in the 'rich' countries, especially in agriculture, have impeded developmentally advantageous participation by many developing countries in the international trading system.

- Finance and investment flows to many developing economies increased significantly over the 1990s, even though sub-Saharan Africa was largely bypassed by this surge. Recurrent crises over the 1990s and 2000s have both reflected and resulted in a marked volatility of financial flows.

- The problem of indebtedness increased over the 1990s, mainly for small and poor economies but also for some large economies. The second part of the 2000s saw the initiation of multilateral debt relief for some highly indebted poor countries.

- Trends in poverty and inequality have not been consistent with the expectations of the neo-liberal orthodoxy, and need additionally to be understood in the context of the ways in which developing-country producers are affected by the reorganization of global production.

Responses to the Crisis of the Washington Consensus

Not surprisingly, explanations of the failures of the development project of the 1980s and 1990s ranged widely. The key dividing line was between those who sought explanations in internal factors and those who emphasized precisely the connections with globalization (Payne and Phillips 2010: 110–15). It was noted earlier that neo-liberal thinking conceived of development failures as being rooted in internal conditions, and as we moved into the 2000s this conviction remained unshaken. John Williamson (2003) set out the clearest statement of the view that the problem lay with the incomplete implementation of neo-liberal reforms. Others saw the Mexican crisis as a 'reality check': it was 'not that the policy recommendations that Williamson outlined are wrong, but that their efficacy—their ability to turn Argentina into Taiwan overnight—was greatly oversold' (Krugman 1995: 30). The World Bank, in a report which addressed itself specifically to the task of 'learning from a decade of reform' (World Bank 2005c), drew a long list of conclusions summarized well by Dani Rodrik (2006a: 976–7):

- Insufficient attention had been paid to stimulating the dynamic forces that lie behind the growth process.

- The objectives of economic reform did not translate into a single and unique set of policy prescriptions, but rather could be achieved in a number of ways.

- Solutions to development problems must be context-specific and the notion of 'models' for emulation was unhelpful.
- Rules had been set out in relation to government discretion in ways which introduced undue rigidities into economies and inflexibility into decision-making.
- Reform efforts needed to focus on the 'binding constraints' to development, rather than relying on a 'laundry list' of policy reforms that may or may not be appropriate.

The East Asian crisis presented more problems for both neo-liberals and neo-statists, but ultimately the same sorts of arguments emerged. Some critical explanations sought to emphasize the problems with globalization that impinged on the development experiences of the 1990s, the nature of globalized financial markets, the dynamics of crisis behaviour, and the crisis-management policies of the IMF being among the most notable of these (Wade 1998; Glyn 2006; Chang 2006; Higgott and Phillips 2000; Sachs 1998). Orthodox accounts, by contrast, took aim at levels of corruption and an excessive role for state patronage in the private sector in East Asia—famously labelled 'crony capitalism'—and the deficiencies of banking systems (Henderson 1998; Pempel 1999b; Segal and Goodman 2000; also see Kang 2002). We have noted that, up to this point, neo-liberal claims to the East Asian miracle had sought to play up the role of export-led growth and play down the issues of the role of states and the internal organization of East Asian economies, thus sidestepping the problem of having to account for the growth performance of these economies under conditions held by the neo-liberal orthodoxy to be damaging to development prospects. Now, the emphasis was reversed and the arguments that had previously been avoided were once again used to discredit the East Asian model and explain its 'failure'.

This came after a period in which even the World Bank appeared to have conceded certain ground to the neo-statists in the debate over the role of states.

The *East Asian Miracle* report of 1993, after protracted political wrangling between the Bank and the Japanese government (which was demanding from the Bank a more explicit acknowledgement of the achievements of the East Asian model), constituted the first acknowledgement of the *fact* of government intervention in East Asian successes and contained a series of mumbled concessions to the benefits of 'selective interventions' in the areas of exports and credit. But it continued staunchly to defend the Bank's line against 'industrial policy' and marshalled an array of (for many, very dubious) pieces of evidence to insist on the underlying 'market-conforming' character of the East Asian development model (World Bank 1993; see Wade 1996). The crisis of the late 1990s nevertheless allowed the Bank and other agencies to retreat quickly to much more comfortable terrain, turning these arguments around to argue, in effect, that they had been right all along.

The problems posed by the crisis of the WC more generally for the global development policy community was dealt with quite swiftly, even before the Asian crisis really took hold. The solution was found not in any radical departure from neo-liberal development thinking, but in a process of re-badging. The post-Washington Consensus (PWC) was articulated primarily by Joseph Stiglitz, one-time Chief Economist at the World Bank and subsequently self-styled critic of the WC agenda. In his diagnosis,

> [t]hat consensus all too often confused means with ends: it took privatization and trade liberalization as ends in themselves, rather than as means to more sustainable, equitable, and democratic growth…It focused too much on price stability, rather than growth and the stability of output. It failed to recognize that strengthening financial institutions is every bit as important to economic stability as controlling budget deficits and increasingly the money supply. It focused on privatization, but paid too little attention to the institutional infrastructure that is required to make markets work, and especially to the importance of competition.

(Stiglitz 1998a: 1)

The need for a 'new paradigm for development'—the PWC (Stiglitz 1998*b*, 2001)—was striking for the way it stole a good deal of the thunder from the neo-statists by emphasizing the role of state intervention in economies in order to compensate for market failures and imperfections (Payne and Phillips 2010: 148). But it went a very great deal further, Stiglitz proclaiming that the PWC was, no less, a 'development strategy [which] outlines an approach to the transformation of society'. All aspects of society (including the state, the private sector, the family, community, and individual) needed to be incorporated; it gave precedence to a focus on sustainable and equitable development; it developed the new 'buzzwords' of 'capacity-building', 'governance', 'participation', 'transparency', 'civil society', and so on, placing much greater emphasis on democratic governance than its predecessor; and it advocated reform of the IFIs and the 'global governance' of development. It also called for a greater degree of 'ownership' for developing countries of the development policies they pursued, and a correspondingly 'greater degree of humility' on the part of the IFIs—an acknowledgement that they 'do not have all the answers' (Stiglitz 1998*b*: 15). The barrage of criticisms was predictable—primarily, that the PWC represented no significant break from the WC (Standing 2000; Rodrik 2002; Fine 2001). Particularly important for our purposes is the fact that the treatment of globalization remained largely untouched, with the emphasis still falling on domestic reform rather than on rethinking how the global economy worked.

While its influence was therefore limited, what is nevertheless particularly interesting about the PWC, is the way in which it coincided with the more explicit incorporation into the global development agenda of the concerns advanced by proponents of a 'human development' approach. This was not a new development, inasmuch as by the early 1990s the work of Sen and others at the United Nations Development Programme (UNDP) had found a central place in the global development agenda, particularly in the evolving interest in poverty reduction alongside good governance. The UNDP published the first *Human Development Report* in 1990, the centrepiece of which was the human development index, intended to provide statistical information on issues that were not covered by conventional development indicators. Issues of gender and sustainable environmental development were also brought on board, albeit selectively and partially. But the focus on human development became most pronounced in the late 1990s and early 2000s, around the same time as the PWC was being elaborated, and was encapsulated in a focus on poverty reduction as the key global development strategy for the twenty-first century.

Two key frameworks emerged for this purpose: the poverty reduction strategy papers (PRSP) approach, and the Millennium Development Goals (MDGs). The PRSP process aimed to emphasize the question of local ownership in global poverty reduction strategies, involving: (*a*) 'promoting opportunity' and pursuing 'pro-poor growth'; (*b*) 'facilitating empowerment', particularly by promoting 'good governance'; and (*c*) 'enhancing [human] security', involving such areas as health, education, and sometimes 'social safety nets' or 'social protection measures' (Craig and Porter 2003: 53–4). They have been widely seen, by supporters and detractors, as integral to a PWC-type approach to development. The MDGs were announced with considerably more fanfare as a commitment by the whole international community to achieving an ambitious set of development targets. These are set out in Box 13.8. It is not difficult to see why the MDGs have widely been seen as the practical expression of the human development approach as articulated by the UNDP, expanded to embrace also the World Bank's income poverty monitoring measures (Saith 2006; Fukuda-Parr 2004).

Box 13.8 The Millennium Development Goals

Goal 1: Eradicate extreme poverty and hunger

- Halve, between 1990 and 2015, the proportion of people whose income is less than one dollar a day.

- Achieve full and productive employment and decent work for all, including women and young people.

- Halve, between 1990 and 2015, the proportion of people who suffer from hunger.

Goal 2: Achieve universal primary education

- Ensure that, by 2015, children everywhere, boys and girls alike, will be able to complete a full course of primary schooling.

Goal 3: Promote gender equality and empower women

- Eliminate gender disparity in primary and secondary education, preferably by 2005, and in all levels of education no later than 2015.

Goal 4: Reduce child mortality

- Reduce by two-thirds, between 1990 and 2015, the under-five mortality rate.

Goal 5: Improve maternal health

- Reduce by three-quarters, between 1990 and 2015, the maternal mortality ratio.

- Achieve, by 2015, universal access to reproductive health.

Goal 6: Combat HIV/AIDS, malaria and other diseases

- Have halted by 2015 and begun to reverse the spread of HIV/AIDS.

- Achieve, by 2010, universal access to treatment for HIV/AIDS for all those who need it.

- Have halted by 2015 and begun to reverse the incidence of malaria and other major diseases.

Goal 7: Ensure environmental sustainability

- Integrate the principles of sustainable development into country policies and programmes and reverse the loss of environmental resources.

- Reduce biodiversity loss, achieving, by 2010, a significant reduction in the rate of loss.

- Halve, by 2015, the proportion of people without sustainable access to safe drinking-water and basic sanitation.

- By 2020, to have achieved a significant improvement in the lives of at least 100 million slum-dwellers.

Goal 8: Develop a global partnership for development

- Develop further an open, rule-based, predictable, non-discriminatory trading and financial system. Includes a commitment to good governance, development, and poverty reduction—both nationally and internationally.

- Address the special needs of the least developed countries. Includes: tariff and quota free access for the least developed countries' exports; enhanced programme of debt relief for heavily indebted poor countries (HIPC) and cancellation of official bilateral debt; and more generous Official Development Assistance (ODA) for countries committed to poverty reduction.

- Address the special needs of landlocked developing countries and small island developing states (through the Program of Action for the Sustainable Development of Small Island Developing States and the outcome of the twenty-second special session of the General Assembly in 1999).

- Deal comprehensively with the debt problems of developing countries through national and international measures in order to make debt sustainable in the long term.

- In co-operation with pharmaceutical companies, provide access to affordable essential drugs in developing countries.

- In co-operation with the private sector, make available the benefits of new technologies, especially information and communications.

Apart from the objections which reflect criticisms of the WC and PWC, two aspects of the MDGs are of particular interest to us in our discussions of globalization and development. First, the MDGs constituted yet another global development initiative which emanated very specifically from the rich-country development community: it was 'a donor-country interpretation of the key issues, for a donor-country audience' (Nelson 2007: 2041). Second, the MDG framework contained no mention of those issues relating to globalization, global politics, and unequal power structures. The implicit assumption was, once again, that the development problems of the world could be rectified by a global concert of governments and institutions pushing sustained market reforms in the relevant national contexts.

The record has not validated this assumption. The headline achievements of the MDGs include the reduction in global levels of extreme poverty from almost half the world's population in 1990 to slightly more than a quarter in 2005, an improvement in primary school enrollments, which reached 88 per cent in 2007, and the likelihood that the targets on reversing the spread of HIV/AIDS will be met (Hulme and Scott 2010; UN 2009b). But the aggregate figures hide the patchiness of these improvements, as well as the disparities between regions and between countries within regions. In Latin America, for instance, the headline news is of a 'remarkable' decline in poverty levels since 2002, of the order of 9.9 percentage points in the case of poverty and 6.8 points in the case of indigence, and the likelihood that the region will meet the first MDG target (ECLAC 2008: 10–11). However, the data are heavily skewed by trends in the large economies, specifically in Mexico and Brazil. Those two countries, along with Chile and Ecuador (the latter using data only for urban poverty) had already met the first MDG in 2007, with Costa Rica close behind. Progress has been made in a handful of other countries. Yet, by 2008, most countries of the region were showing few signs of approaching the targets, and many showed either no improvement at all or, in some cases, slight increases in poverty

(Phillips 2011). Most of sub-Saharan Africa remains a long way from meeting the targets. The East Asia and Pacific region has ostensibly performed better, but, here, it must be noted that, because 1990 was adopted as the baseline for measurements, the targets on poverty reduction were virtually achieved before the MDGs had even been created (Pogge 2004; Hulme and Scott 2010)! Equally, as David Hulme and James Scott remind us (citing Fischer 2010), it would be a mistake to assume that progress is attributable to the MDGs, partly for the reason that many of the advances in some parts of the world were made before the MDGs came into being, but also because progress in some instances has slowed since the introduction of the MDGs. The example they give is mortality rates of children under five years of age, which fell at an annual rate of around 3.5 per cent between 1960 and 2000, while annual progress since 2000 has been around 2.75 per cent.

The impact of the global recession of the late 2000s complicates still further the prospects for achieving the MDG targets. Speculation at the end of that decade about the likely implications of the crisis for world poverty was thoroughly alarming. The World Bank was talking of a 'development emergency', and estimating that 200 million more people would fall into extreme poverty between 2005 and 2008, and an increase in the incidence of hunger from 850 million people in 2007 to 960 million in 2009 (World Bank 2009b; also see Hulme and Scott 2010). The Inter-American Development Bank (IDB) estimated that the number of people living below the poverty line in Latin America would have increased by 7 per cent—equivalent to 12.7 million people—by 2010. Worse still, the numbers of people living in conditions of extreme poverty, or indigence, were likely to increase by 9 per cent—equivalent to 7 million people (IDB 2009).

Staying with Latin America and the Caribbean, the IDB goes further in exploring the likely impact of the looming food crisis for the region's poor. Notwithstanding the above figures relating to the economic crisis, the impact of food prices remaining high is likely to put 26 million people at severe risk of falling into conditions of extreme poverty. Chronic poverty would also be deepened substantially, particularly in food-importing countries like Haiti, Peru, and Nicaragua. Individual country profiles would show significant alteration—IDB simulations indicate for Mexico an increase in poverty of around a third of present levels, to no less than 27.5 per cent of the population. These figures are held to be significant in the context of the fairly striking progress in poverty reduction that we noted above—since 2003, around 48 million people have been lifted above the poverty line—inasmuch as we are seeing the possibility of a real slide backwards for large parts of the region's population (IDB 2008). Emerging data for other developing regions, especially sub-Saharan Africa, present similar pictures of a substantial worsening of overall poverty levels over the coming years. In all cases, the impact will be felt disproportionately by particular groups, especially the rural poor.

Key points

- Explanations of the crisis of the Washington consensus—and neo-liberal strategies more generally—were divided between those who emphasized 'internal' factors and those who emphasized factors associated with globalization.

- The East Asian crisis of the late 1990s was taken by neo-liberals to validate the development orthodoxy and used to discredit the East Asian model, even though it had just appeared to concede certain ground to the neo-statists and acknowledge the role of government intervention.

- The post-Washington Consensus (PWC) was put forward as a 'new paradigm for development' (Stiglitz 1998*b*, 2001), but was seen by critics to depart very little from the original Washington Consensus.

- The issue of poverty reduction came by the 2000s to occupy the centre of global development debates, reflected particularly in the Millennium Development Goals (MDGs) and the Poverty Reduction Strategy Papers (PRSP) framework.

- Progress towards achieving the MDGs has been very uneven, with sharp differences between countries, and the impact of the financial crisis of the late 2000s is likely significantly to set back progress.

Interpreting the Relationship between Globalization and Development

What, then, can we say about the relationship between globalization and development? The clear picture that emerges, as we indicated at the start of the chapter, is that the world's development problems remain huge, and in many cases growing. Despite the remarkable accomplishments of the 'Age of Development', in the contemporary era of globalization a very large proportion of the world's population continues to live in conditions of poverty and deprivation, inequalities between countries, societies, and people continue to increase, and the global development agenda has not put in place the conditions in which development has been able to flourish. On this much it seems that most people would be able to agree, at least in the broadest terms. Yet, participants in the debate about the impact of globalization on development are still able to occupy very distant corners and fight them, as it were, with vigour. Advocates of what Robert Wade calls the 'globalization works' story have a range of different arguments in their arsenal:

1. It is not globalization, nor the development orthodoxy constructed around it, that have failed. Rather, the issue is the failure of governments to introduce the right kinds of policies, in the right kinds of ways, and to the right extent. Institutions in many developing countries also remain too weak, corruption remains too prevalent, and political conflict too pronounced. What is needed is therefore more reform — more neo-liberalism — not less.

2. The failures of development are due to too little engagement with globalization. Poor people are those who remain 'excluded' from globalization and have not (yet) been able to harness the potential of globalization processes.

3. Financial crisis is not explained by excessive levels of 'openness' or 'vulnerability' — many of the developing economies that were affected by financial crisis over the last twenty years were not the most open. Equally, most of those affected were the ones that had adopted only a lukewarm approach to neo-liberal reform.

Advocates of the contrary perspective — that globalization has worked against development — would appeal to different arguments:

1. The problem is with the policy orthodoxy itself, which works against the goals of growth and human development, carries often devastating social consequences, heightens the vulnerability of developing countries to volatility in global markets, and has yielded a generalized picture of economic and political instability. The picture of global development during the 1945–80 period was not all rosy, but it was in many respects substantially more positive than in the period from the early 1980s onwards.

2. The policy orthodoxy has taken little or no account of the nature of the global political economy, particularly the persistent barriers to trade and the workings of global financial markets. It is the characteristics of globalized market activity that impose obstacles to development. More generally, failures of development, persistent forms of poverty, and growing levels of inequality are both generated and reinforced by globalization.

3. The recurrent financial crises are crises of globalization and generated by the behaviour of financial markets and the policies of the IFIs.

At the heart of the debate is thus a conflict between different interpretations of the dynamics which have produced such an obscene development gap between and within countries, and between different parts of the world's population. It is useful to think about this in the following terms. The orthodox view sees poverty and other signs of what we might call 'mal-development' as 'residual' phenomena — that is, they are residues of a pre-globalization era, bound to be eradicated as the benign forces of globalization spread and reach the world's poor more effectively (Kaplinsky 2005: 50–1). Branko Milanovic (2003: 667) offers a pithy summary of this view:

> It is only a slight caricaturization . . . to state that its proponents regard globalization as a *deus ex machina* for many of the problems, such as poverty, illiteracy or inequality, that beset the developing world. The only thing that a country needs to do is to open up its borders, reduce tariff rates, attract foreign capital, and in a few generations if not less, the poor will become rich, the illiterate will learn how to read and write, and inequality will vanish as the poor countries catch up with the rich.

The thrust of the alternative arguments is that the various dimensions of mal-development are instead 'relational' phenomena (Kaplinsky 2005: 51; Bernstein 1990), which arise from and are reinforced by globalization processes. The task is therefore to understand how exactly this relationship works. We have noted many of the relevant issues in this chapter, relating particularly to forms of 'adverse incorporation' into GVCs, the workings of global financial markets, fluctuations in the terms of trade, the persistence of trade rules which disadvantage certain kinds of producers and exporters, the politics of the global development agenda, the dynamics of global inequality, and so on.

What this line of reasoning suggests is that the workings of globalization unquestionably present challenges for development. But it is surely too simplistic to state baldly that 'globalization' is intrinsically 'bad' or 'good' for development. It has emerged clearly here that we need to focus on the particular form that globalization takes, and that this is to an important extent politically and ideologically determined. The neo-liberal development orthodoxy has shaped heavily the terms on

which developing economies and large parts of the world's societies participate in the global economy. The global development agenda has been based on a set of political arrangements which govern how financial markets work, which trade rules prevail, how GVCs are organized, what the lending activities of the IFIs look like, how debt is managed, and so on. The structural dynamics of global capitalism thus combine with particular political and ideological currents, and more specifically particular ways of thinking about development, to shape the evolution of the material and social conditions in which people live. It is thus possible to mount a strong argument for the importance of understanding the 'relational' dynamics of globalization and development.

Key points

- Opinion is divided on the relationship between globalization and development.
- Some argue that the persistence of poverty, the widening of inequalities, and other manifestations of 'mal-development' are due to too little engagement with globalization and a failure effectively to implement neo-liberal reform. This perspective sees the signs of mal-development as 'residual phenomena', which will be eradicated as the reach of globalization is extended and its benefits are harnessed.

- Others argue that the problem is globalization itself and the policy orthodoxy that has accompanied it in the contemporary period. They see the problems of mal-development as 'relational' phenomena, which arise from and are reinforced by globalization processes and the workings of the global economy.
- It is the latter argument which offers the most compelling perspective on the problems of development in the contemporary period.

Conclusion: A New Era of Global Development?

We conclude this chapter on a note of uncertainty and speculation. Looking to the future involves considering two big questions which are hanging in the air. First, what will have been the developmental consequences of the global economic crisis of the late 2000s? And second, what does the growth of China and the rise of the 'East' imply for the future of global development? Put together, do these two sets of conditions mean that we will be seeing a

waning, or perhaps abandonment, of the global development agenda that has prevailed to this point? Do they challenge the kinds of development thinking that have underpinned it? Are we moving into a new era of development?

The midst of a crisis is always a poor vantage point for speculating on its likely implications, and this one is no exception. On the one hand, many of the consequences for development are 'knock-on' effects which derive from a crisis which crystallized in particular parts of the global economy and spread out to other parts, and also likely to be of a long-term rather than short-term nature. On the other hand, we still lack data to help us trace and understand the emerging trends. Once statistical information for the years in question starts to become available, it may be that we will have a much better picture of the actual and likely developmental consequences.

But what we can say with some confidence even at this juncture is that it is impossible to say that the crisis is either 'good' or 'bad' for development. The picture is much more mixed than such a stark characterization permits us to understand. The trends in poverty and inequality indicators are varied, depending on whether we are talking about workers in the formal or informal sector, for instance, or about rural or urban poverty, and different kinds of economic activity have been differently affected thus far. Remittances — the money that migrant workers send home to their relatives — are falling in some parts of the world but not in others. And some economies are weathering the storm far better than others, even within the same region. Countries such as China and Brazil, for instance, are in many ways suffering serious consequences as a result of global recession, which in China has raised real concerns about large-scale social unrest. But they have, nevertheless, been able to weather the downturn more successfully than many other economies: in East Asia, for instance, the most severely affected economies were those most open to international trade (Singapore, Taiwan, Malaysia). In some respects, countries like China and Brazil also appear potentially well placed to profit from the crisis, particularly in terms of opportunities for firms to expand their transnationalization strategies or banks to emerge in global financial markets, and generally in terms of geoeconomic positioning.

Perhaps then the real issue is whether the crisis will have led to a loosening of the grip of the global development orthodoxy which has prevailed for the last thirty years or so. This is the same question that is prompted by the increased prominence of China and, in particular, the articulation by the Chinese authorities of a set of strategies across the developing regions of the world (notably Africa, the Middle East, and Latin America), designed to further the Chinese development project (see Dittmer and Yu 2010). Much has been made of the apparent challenge to the foothold of neo-liberalism and the global development agenda in this context, inasmuch as Chinese aid and loans to African nations have been made without conditionality and without regard to political issues, allowing these countries to avoid the IMF and thus undoing the grip of Western development policy. The gradual emergence of China as a significant actor in the principal institutions of global governance has also prompted discussions about the potential challenge to the global development agenda as articulated over the course of the contemporary period (Gu et al. 2008). Finally, the nature of Chinese development, contradicting as it does some of the sacred cows of neo-liberalism, has prompted questions about whether we could see space opening up for an alternative development model in other parts of the developing world.

To all of these questions, it is simply too early to know the answers. We might see nothing more than business as usual, as the crisis subsides and the march of globalization resumes. Or we might see fundamental changes emerging from a discrediting of Anglo-American neo-liberalism and the global development agenda on which it was built. We do not yet know whether the remarkable rise of China and the East will be continued, and with what implications. Yet, our challenges in many ways remain unchanged from those which have always faced students and practitioners of development. They are to think carefully and clearly about what we mean by development and how to achieve it, to develop theoretical perspectives which will enable us to understand the implications of globalization for development, and to work towards local and global strategies which will, at last, put in place the conditions which will produce something very different from the situation that Frank observed back in the 1960s, and still prevails today: 'development for the few and underdevelopment for the many'.

? Questions

1. What are the key differences between the main development theories that have emerged in the period after stheSecond World War?

2. Why were both the modernization and underdevelopment theories largely discredited by the early 1980s?

3. How important were the contributions of 'human development' theories to our understandings of what development means?

4. How did neo-liberal and neo-statist theories of development try to explain the trajectory of divergence between developing regions and countries from the 1960s onwards?

5. What was the Washington Consensus (WC) and by what means did it become implanted across the developing world in the 1980s and 1990s?

6. To what extent can the development record of the contemporary period be taken as evidence that the neo-liberal development agenda failed?

7. Explain how both neo-liberals and neo-statists were able to stake a claim to explaining and understanding the 'East Asian miracle'.

8. Does the post-Washington Consensus (PWC) really represent a 'new paradigm for development'?

9. Is it more convincing to explain the problems of contemporary development as 'residual' or 'relational' phenomena?

10. Do you think that the rise of China and the 'East' changes the way we will need to think about development in the future?

→ Further reading

■ Dittmer, L. and Yu, G. T. (2010), *China, the Developing World, and the New Global Dynamic* (Boulder, CO: Lynne Rienner). A collection of essays exploring the growing engagement of China in the global economy and other developing regions.

■ Gu, J., Humphrey, J., and Messner, D. (2008), 'Global Governance and Developing Countries: The Implications of the Rise of China', *World Development*, 36/2: 274–92. An article exploring the implications of the rise of China for the governance of global development.

■ Harvey, D. (2005), *A Brief History of Neoliberalism* (New York: Oxford University Press). A discussion of the ideology of neo-liberalism and its global significance.

■ Kaplinsky, R. (2005), *Globalization, Poverty and Inequality* (Cambridge: Polity). A detailed exploration of the 'relational' dynamics of globalization, poverty, and inequality.

■ Kay, C. (1989), *Latin American Theories of Development and Underdevelopment* (London: Routledge). A classic overview of development theories in the context of Latin America–particularly strong on structuralist and underdevelopment theories.

■ Kohli, A. (2004), *State-Directed Development: Political Power and Industrialization in the Global Periphery* (Cambridge: Cambridge University Press). A detailed comparative exploration of the role of states in development.

■ Leftwich, A. (2000), *States of Development: On the Primacy of Politics in Development* (Cambridge: Polity). A discussion of the role of states and politics in development.

■ McMichael, P. (2007), *Development and Social Change: A Global Perspective*, 4th edn (Thousand Oaks, CA: Pine Forge Press). A 'global' perspective on development with detailed historical and comparative discussions.

■ Milanovic, B. (2003), 'The Two Faces of Globalization: Against Globalization as we Know it', *World Development*, 31/4: 667–83. A useful discussion of the 'residual' and 'relational' perspectives on globalization and development.

■ Payne, A. (2005b), *The Global Politics of Unequal Development* (Basingstoke: Palgrave Macmillan). A detailed discussion of the ways in which the global politics of development shape unequal outcomes in key issue areas.

■ Payne, A., and Phillips, N. (2010), *Development* (Cambridge: Polity Press). An introduction to the key theories of development from the nineteenth century onwards.

■ Rai, S. (2002), *Gender and the Political Economy of Development* (Cambridge: Polity). An introduction to the key debates around gender and development.

■ Wade, R. (1990), *Governing the Market: Economic Theory and the Role of Government in Taiwan's Industrialization* (Princeton, NJ: Princeton University Press). An influential statement of the neo-statist position, including critical discussions of the debates surrounding East Asian development.

:// Web links

■ Multilateral institutions associated with the global development agenda:

www.worldbank.org   World Bank.

www.imf.org   International Monetary Fund.

www.ilo.org   International Labour Organization.

www.unctad.org   United Nations Conference on Trade and Development.

www.wto.org   World Trade Organization.

www.oim.org   International Organization for Migration.

www.undp.org   United Nations Development Programme.

■ Regional institutions and regional development banks:

www.iadb.org   Inter-American Development Bank.

www.adb.org   Asian Development Bank.

www.afdb.org   African Development Bank.

www.ebrd.org   European Bank for Reconstruction and Development.

www.eclac.org   United Nations Economic Commission for Latin America and the Caribbean.

www.uneca.org   United Nations Economic Commission for Africa.

www.unescap.org   United Nations Economic and Social Commission for Asia and the Pacific.

■ Research institutions and think tanks:

www.cgdev.org   Center for Global Development.

www.bwpi.org   Brooks World Poverty Institute.

www.gdnet.org   Global Development Network.

Online resource centre

For additional material and resources, please visit the Online Resource Centre at:
www.oxfordtextbooks.co.uk/ravenhill3e/

14

Globalization and the Environment

Peter Dauvergne

 Chapter contents

- Introduction: Globalization and Environmental Change
- History of Global Environmentalism
- Economic Growth, Trade, and Corporations
- A Sustainable Future? Financing and Regimes
- Conclusion

 Reader's guide

Globalization is transforming the earth's environment. Nothing is particularly contro-versial about this statement. Yet, sharp disagreements arise over the nature of this transformation. Is globalization a force of progress and environmental solutions? Or is it a *cause* of our current global environmental crisis? This chapter explores these questions by examining the debates around some of the most contentious issues at the core of economic globalization and the environment: economic growth, production, and consumption; trade; and transnational investment. It begins with a glance at the general arguments about how globalization affects the global environment. Then, to set the stage for an analysis of more specific arguments about the global political economy of the environment, it sketches the history of global environmentalism—in particular, the emergence of global environmental institutions (including regimes) with the norm of sustainable development. The last section builds on these arguments to assess the effectiveness of North–South environmental financing and global environmental regimes.

Globalization is altering the global environment. Few scholars of global environmental politics would challenge this statement (see Box 14.1). The nature of the change, however, is hotly debated. Some argue it is a source of progress and ingenuity and co-operation, of a future world with much better environmental conditions for all. Others argue it is accelerating the process of the capitalist exploitation of nature and humanity, spinning the globe faster and faster toward an ecological meltdown.

Box 14.1 Globalization

This chapter assumes that globalization is an ongoing and accelerating process that is restructuring and increasing connections among economies, institutions, and civil societies. This dynamic and multidimensional process is integrating trade, production, and finance as well as strengthening global norms and global social forces. A constellation of forces drives globalization, including new and faster technologies (such as computers) as well as the increasing dominance of capitalism and Western ideologies. In the simplest terms, it is leading to a 'world as a single place', where changes in distant lands affect people around the globe more quickly, and with greater frequency and intensity (Scholte 1997: 14; also see Scholte 2005). It is, in the words of Thomas Friedman (2002: 64),

" the integration of everything with everything else ... the integration of markets, finance, and technology in a way that shrinks the world from a size medium to a size small. Globalization enables each of us, wherever we live, to reach around the world farther, faster, deeper, and cheaper than ever before and at the same time allows the world to reach into each of us farther, faster, deeper, and cheaper than ever before. "

This does not assume the process of globalization is even or equal within or across countries. The rich in Europe and America are unquestionably benefiting far more than the poor of Africa, Asia, and Latin America. The process is also not inevitable. States and societies can resist and reverse globalization.

Globalization and a healthy planet

The optimists see globalization as a process that fosters economic growth and raises per capita incomes, both essential to generate the funds and political will for global environmental management. Optimists see other environmental benefits from globalization as well. It is promoting global integration and co-operation as well as common environmental norms and standards, which are enhancing the capacity of a system of sovereign states to manage problems such as ozone depletion and climate change. It is pushing states to liberalize trade and foreign investment, promote specialization, and eliminate subsidies, which in the past have contributed to market failures and suboptimal economic and environmental outcomes. It is enhancing the capacity of developing states to manage environmental change through the transfer of technologies, knowledge, and development assistance. And it is contributing to a host of domestic reforms to policies — such as better environmental laws, stronger institutions, and more secure property rights.

Optimists such as environmental writers Julian Simon, Gregg Easterbrook, and Bjørn Lomborg see a past full of progress and a future full of hope and socioecological triumph. There is every reason to believe that economic growth and technological progress will continue for ever. 'The standard of living,' Simon (1996: 12) argues, 'has risen along with the size of the world's population since the beginning of recorded time. There is no convincing economic reason why these trends toward a better life should not continue indefinitely.' Simon's lifetime of work has stirred a hornet's nest of environmental critics. Writers such as Easterbrook, however, see him as profound and brave. 'There was a time,' Easterbrook (1995: xxi) argues, 'when to cry alarm regarding environmental affairs was the daring position. Now it's the safe position: People get upset when you say things may turn out fine.' Writers such as Lomborg (2001, 2007) add, too, that little statistical evidence exists of a global environmental crisis—that this common misperception is more a result of media hype and non-governmental organization (NGO) fund-raising antics than real problems. 'Mankind's lot,' Lomborg (2001: 4) asserts, 'has actually improved in terms of practically every measurable indicator . . . We are not running out of energy or natural resources . . . Acid rain does not kill the forests, and the air and water around us are becoming less and less polluted.' Lomborg (2009) further adds that investing in more real and present global problems, such as curable diseases and malnutrition, will produce far better immediate and long-term results for both people and the global environment.

Simon, Easterbrook, and Lomborg are at the extreme of the optimistic end of the spectrum of opinion. Most supporters of globalization—those in governments such as the United States and the United Kingdom, and in global institutions such as the World Bank and the World Trade Organization (WTO)—emphasize the need for a practical view that looks toward future generations. These supporters argue that some degree of ecological change and loss is inevitable, but the consistent trend under globalization is towards a future that looks like Britain, France, and the United States, not one that looks like Ethiopia, Cambodia, and Guyana. History demonstrates the great strides of humanity. Just a hundred years ago, cities such as London and New York were filthy and unhealthy. Today, health conditions in virtually every city in the North are vastly improved. One of the greatest feats has been the increase in food production. In the middle of the twentieth century, close to half of the people in the South were starving. By 1970, it was less than a third; by 2009, it was less than a sixth (Lomborg 2001: 61; FAO 2008, 2009).

Just over two hundred years ago, Thomas Malthus (1798) predicted that exponential population growth would, following the laws of basic maths, inevitably surpass arithmetical food production: and mass starvation would thus ensue. Since then, many scholars, now commonly called Malthusians or neo-Malthusians, have continued to tout the same logic. Yet, optimists stress, Malthus was flat-out wrong, primarily because he discounted the ability of human ingenuity to increase agricultural yields. The Green Revolution of the 1960s saw scientists and farmers work together to produce fast-growing, pest-resistant, high-yield crops able to grow just about anywhere (with the help of irrigation, fertilizers, and pesticides). There is, as a result, plenty of food today. And it is far cheaper—global food prices have fallen by two-thirds in real terms since 1957. People starve at present because of inefficient distribution and incompetent governments, not because of insufficient global food supplies. For optimists, perhaps the most revealing statistic of all is global life expectancy: in 1900, it was a mere thirty years; in 1950, forty-six years; today, it is sixty-seven years (Lomborg 2001: 50–1, 61; World Bank 2002c; WHO 2008b: 44). Granted, such progress has demanded changes, including some global environmental changes. But, optimists stress, science and human ingenuity have time and again shown the capacity to respond with even more progress.

The view that globalization is a basically positive ecological force dominates global economic and environmental negotiations, and institutional decision-making. The debate here ranges over how best to channel globalization so as to minimize environmental damage and maximize socioeconomic progress (which, in the long run, must occur for effective global environmental management). Some argue for few, if any, restraints. Others see a need to guide globalization with national environmental agencies, and strong global norms and institutions. There are, however, many scholars and activists who challenge the core assumptions behind these views — that is, they see globalization as a core cause of the current ecological crisis.

Globalization and ecological collapse

Environmental critics of globalization worry that it is luring humanity towards a global fate not unlike that of Easter Island of three-hundred years ago, where ecological decay drove a once thriving people to violence and cannibalism in just a few centuries (Rees 2002: 249; Diamond 2005). Particularly worrying for these critics is that so-called progress and scientific reason has created, in the words of Paul Ehrlich's (1968) infamous book title, 'a population bomb', an explosion from fewer than 300 million people at the time of Christ to over 6.7 billion today (see Figure 14.1). Globalization, critics contend, is compounding the ecological impact

of more than 200,000 people being added to the planet every day. It reinforces the neoclassical economic assumption that indefinite economic growth is both possible and desirable. It assumes, too, that it is possible and logical for the South to follow the development path of the North and continue to industrialize and intensify agricultural production. The globe can barely sustain its current population. How, critics ask, can it sustain another 3 billion in 2050? How can Africa sustain an additional 1 billion people in 2050, more than double its current population?

The net effect of globalization, moreover, is to enlarge the ecological footprint of *each* person on the planet, by promoting ever more economic growth as well as cultivating an almost religious faith in the value of consumption—in the value of electronic toys, cars, and fast food (Robbins 2008)—all of which requires increasing amounts of natural resources, energy, and infrastructure to produce. The growing integration and disparities among economies are also increasing the reach and intensity of ecological shadows, which tend to shift the ecological damage of more powerful economies on to weaker economies and future generations (see Box 14.2).

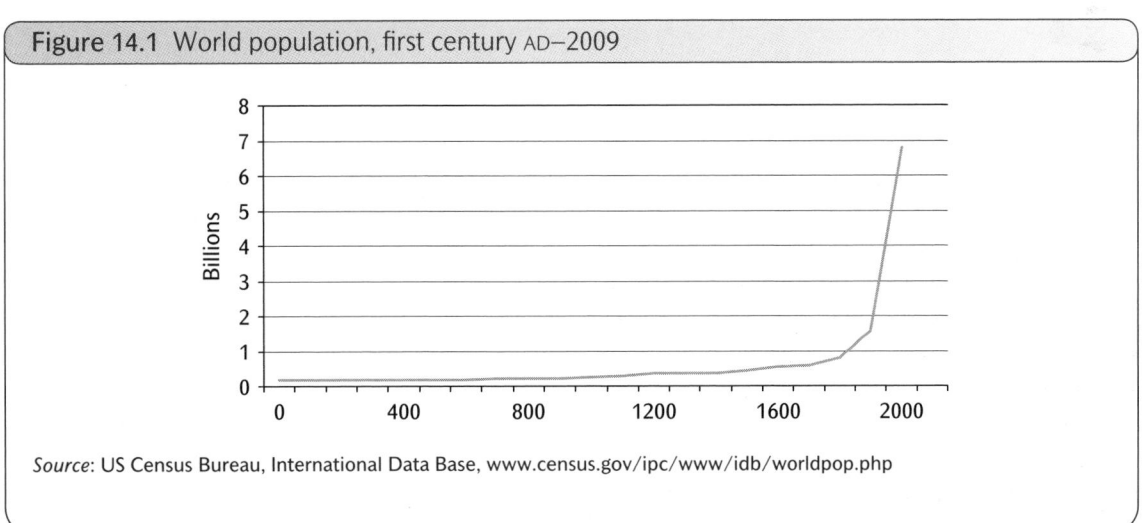

Figure 14.1 World population, first century AD–2009

Source: US Census Bureau, International Data Base, www.census.gov/ipc/www/idb/worldpop.php

PETER DAUVERGNE

Box 14.2 Ecological Footprints and Shadows

Ecological footprints

Bill Rees and Mathis Wackernagel created this concept to measure the sustainability of human lifestyles. It translates human consumption of renewable natural resources into hectares of average biologically productive land. A person's footprint is the total area in global hectares (one hectare of average biological productivity) required to sustain his or her lifestyle: food and water, clothing, shelter, transportation, and consumer goods and services. The concept allows an analyst to compare the average ecological impact of people from Africa to Australia to China to the United Kingdom to the United States. The average global ecological footprint is about 2.6 global hectares per person (as of 2006, the latest data set). There are, however, great differences across the globe. In Africa, it is about 1.4 global hectares (with a low in the Democratic Republic of Congo of 0.7) and in China it is 1.8. In contrast, the average footprint of someone in the United Kingdom is 6.1, and in the United States 9.0.

This measure also allows an analyst to compare the world ecological footprint with the total biological productive capacity of the earth. The total biocapacity of the earth in 2006 was roughly 11.9 billion hectares. Between 1961 and 1999, the world ecological footprint grew by 80 per cent, reaching 13.7 billion hectares in 1999. Today, it is over 17 billion hectares and is rising steadily. The state of the globe, according to this measure, is continuing to worsen—and the world's ecological footprint is now equal to about 1.5 planet earths. Humanity, the World Wide fund for Nature (WWF) laments, is now 'running an ecological deficit with the Earth'.

Source: Wackernagel and Rees (1996); WWF (2002): 2–4, 22–8; WWF (2006): 28–34; Global Footprint Network 2009; www.footprintnetwork.org

Ecological shadows

This concept is designed to capture the extent of the environmental impact of a nation state in jurisdictions beyond its sovereign control. Ecological shadows arise as economies, through both intentional and unintentional patterns of consumption, trade, investment, and financing, transfer the environmental harm of its citizens outside its territory. This concept is particularly useful for analysing the environmental impact of more powerful economies on weaker (dependent) economies. The United States, for example, casts a large ecological shadow over South America. Such shadows can extend down a chain of weaker economies. Japan, for example, casts an ecological shadow over Thailand, which in turn casts a shadow over neighbours such as Cambodia and Laos. Ecological shadows do not arise from straightforward North–South exploitation. Often, elites in weak economies in the South profit personally from these ecological shadows, commonly acting as the agents of the ecological destruction—for example, as miners, fishers, and loggers.

Sources: MacNeill et al. (1991); Dauvergne (1997, 2008)

Critics contend, too, that globalization is encouraging ever more economic growth and production with no real concern about unequal or unsustainable patterns of consumption. It exacerbates the ecological inequality within and between countries, and marginalizes women, indigenous peoples, and the poor. The global political economy is constructing, for critics such as William Rees and Laura Westra (2003), a world of 'eco-apartheid' and 'eco-violence'. Globalization tears, too, at the fabric of local communities, leading to 'food wars' (Bello 2009) and destroying historic patterns of trust, co-operation, and knowledge so essential to ecological and social balance (Barlow 2008; Broad and Cavanagh 2008; Cavanagh and Mander 2004; Mander and Goldsmith 2001; Shiva 1997, 2000, 2008). In short, it destroys the living environments of much of the world's people.

There can be, in the view of critics, no environmental justice or biological balance in a globalized world where the super-rich like Bill Gates and

J. K. Rowling live alongside (metaphorically, that is, in their mansions) the 1.1 billion who live on less than $1 per day, and the 2.6 billion who live on less than $2 per day. Over a billion people do not have access to clean water (UNFPA 2001: 5; WHO 2008*a*: 8). Over 1 billion people in the South suffer from chronic malnutrition (FAO 2008: 6; FAO 2009). Unhealthy environments aggravate illnesses, each year contributing to the deaths of almost 5 million children under the age of five. The future under current patterns of globalization, critics argue, is one of still greater horrors: of pandemics such as HIV/AIDS, which killed over 2 million people in 2008. Over 33 million people are now infected, with 2.7 million new HIV infections in 2008. Of those living with HIV/AIDS, two-thirds live in sub-Saharan Africa, where average life expectancy has already fallen from above 60 years to below 50 years. In Swaziland, for example, life expectancy has fallen to just 37 years, down by half since 1990 (UNAIDS 2009). What is needed, critics like Colin Hines (2000) argue, is not globalization, but localization.

The latest biological trends, critics further note, confirm the beginnings of a global Easter Island. Humans are now the dominant predator in every ecosystem (even in the seemingly limitless Pacific and Atlantic oceans), and unless strict restraints are put in place, humans will exhaust the globe's natural resources, fill its sinks, and overstep the earth's capacity to support life. Half the world's forests and wetlands are already gone. Every day another 50 to 150 species become extinct. Recent surveys of the world's oceans, say critics, are especially worrying.

One analysis of 7,800 species of wild seafood found that catches of 29 per cent of these species are now at least 90 per cent below past averages. At current harvests rates, predicts the fourteen-person team of analysts, a 'collapse' of much of the remaining commercial wild seafood will occur before 2050 (Worm et al. 2006). Another ten-year survey by Ransom Myers and Boris Worm (2003) found a 90 per cent decline in the ocean's large predatory fish — such as tuna, swordfish, marlin, cod, and flounder — since the 1950s. The waters of Ernest Hemingway's, *The Old Man and the Sea*, will soon be empty of the majestic marlin, a startling testimony, critics warn, not to the environmental consequences of the exploits of men such as Hemingway's old man, Santiago, but to the greed of industrial fishing boats plying the oceans to feed global markets.

Supporters and critics of a globalizing world, then, hold starkly different pictures of the current and future state of the global environment. The trends and statistics to support the statement 'globalization is good for the environment' seem convincing. Yet, so do the trends and statistics that say 'globalization is bad for the environment'. The truth seems to lie somewhere in the middle: globalization is producing both constructive and destructive ecological processes. The goal is to harness globalization in some way to ensure sustainability. What has the global community done so far to harness globalization and manage global environmental affairs? The next section examines the history of environmentalism with an eye on this question.

Key points

- Some perceive the net ecological impact of globalization as being positive, as a force for progress and better lives. It fosters economic growth and co-operative institutions—both of these necessary in the long run to manage the global environment.

- Others see the net impact as negative, as a force sinking the globe into a bog of ecological decay. It is accelerating the destructive process of too many

people consuming too many natural resources with no concern for equality or justice.

- Both the pro- and anti-globalization camps present persuasive data and arguments. Globalization involves multiple and complex sets of overlapping processes. Inevitably, there will be manifold and at times cross-cutting effects on the global environment.

PETER DAUVERGNE

Collective human efforts to control nature began in earnest 8,000 to 10,000 years ago, as nomadic hunters-and-gatherers in various locales began to change to settled agriculture. Great civilizations sprang up, inventing such wonders as the plough (animal drawn), the wheel, writing, and numbers. Often, nature was subsumed in the quest for human progress, and many civilizations cut down regional forests, degraded land, and polluted local waters. Environmental decay even toppled a few great civilizations, such as Mesopotamia (a land between the Tigris and Euphrates rivers, part of contemporary Iraq), where a poorly designed irrigation system gradually poisoned the agricultural land with salt. For most of the history of civilization, however, the scale of human activity has been too small to alter the global environment—that is, to induce climate change, deplete the ozone layer, empty the oceans, or destroy global biodiversity stocks.

This began to change with the dawn of the Industrial Revolution some 300 years ago. Production and energy use (including the burning of coal) began to rise rapidly. The global population of 600 million or so began to multiply. There were 1 billion people by the early 1800s; and 2 billion by the end of the 1920s. The wealthy began to extract more natural resources, more quickly, from increasingly remote parts of the globe (often through colonial administrations). Such activities strained local and regional environments. The evidence was stark. Smog in cities like London and New York killed thousands in the nineteenth and twentieth centuries. Once seemingly boundless species, like the plains bison of North America, were brought to near extinction. Some, like the passenger pigeon, a bird that once migrated through eastern North America in its millions, became extinct (in 1914).

Governments reacted to these environmental disasters with new national and regional policies. At first, these were aimed primarily at either conservation of wildlife or more effective resource management. Canada and the United States, for example, signed the Migratory Birds Treaty in 1918. Colonial powers reacted as well, putting in place policies (like sustained yield management) to try to ensure more efficient and rational resource extraction. After the Second World War, ordinary citizens began to become increasingly worried about the biological impacts of industrialization and agricultural production. Anxiety mounted after Rachel Carson's (1962) best-seller, *Silent Spring*, shocked popular consciousness with images of pesticide-laden food chains and dying ecosystems.

Worries about the health of the 'global environment' also began to emerge around this time. The picture of the earth from space, beautiful and fragile and borderless, became a compelling global ecological image. These concerns fed into the sense of the mutual economic vulnerability of post-war economies (in both the North and the South). Paul Ehrlich's 1968 best-seller, *The Population Bomb*, added a new and perturbing image: the earth left barren by an exploding population. 'In the 1970s,' Ehrlich predicted boldly, 'the world will undergo famines—hundreds of millions of people are going to starve to death' (1968: xi).

Concern over the health of the global environment continued to rise in the late 1960s and early 1970s. Experts met in 1968 at the United Nations Biosphere Conference to discuss global environmental problems. The first Earth Day was held in the United States in April 1970. Twenty million people rallied—one of the largest organized demonstrations in the history of the United States. That same year, the US government founded the Environmental Protection Agency (EPA). Canada created a Department of the Environment the following year. One outcome of this growing societal and political concern was the United Nations Conference on the Human Environment, held in Stockholm, Sweden, in June 1972.

The Stockholm Conference and the 1970s

The Stockholm Conference, organized by Canada's Maurice Strong, was the first global United Nations conference on the environment for state officials. There were 1,200 delegates from over a hundred countries. Swedish Prime Minister Olaf Palme and Indian Prime Minister Indira Gandhi were the only heads of state to attend. Russia and the communist bloc countries boycotted the conference, to protest against the exclusion of East Germany.

The North was interested initially in addressing industrial pollution, nature conservation, and population growth. The South was more worried about development, and did not want the anxieties of rich conservationists to deny poorer countries the benefits of economic growth and industrialization (an ongoing source of conflict). There were tensions, too, over who would pay, and who was responsible for solving global environmental problems. Many Southern delegates saw global capitalism as a core reason for poverty, and there was general anger that global economic institutions were pushing developing countries to export raw materials on declining terms of trade. The phrase 'the pollution of poverty' was coined at Stockholm, to express the idea that poverty was the greatest global environmental threat. Many delegates from the South called for global economic reforms to help solve the pollution of poverty.

In the end, conference delegates tried to reconcile the desire (need) for economic development in the South with the need to protect the global environment for all. Most governments came to recognize the mutual interdependence and vulnerability of North and South. The official conference documents, however, did not emphasize the Southern calls for global economic reforms. The conference produced a Declaration on the Human Environment (with twenty-six principles), an Action Plan for the Human Environment (with 109 recommendations), and a Resolution on Institutional and Financial Arrangements. These were non-binding on signatory states—and most scholars agree that Stockholm produced few practical commitments to address global environmental change.

The Stockholm Conference did, however, signal a growing concern among national governments over the global environment. It also led to a General Assembly decision to create the United Nations Environment Programme (UNEP), launched officially in 1973, with Maurice Strong (2000) as the first executive director. The United Nations Environment Programme was designed as a relatively weak global institution. Its headquarters were in Nairobi, Kenya, rather than New York or Geneva, and it was established as a co-ordinating programme with a small budget rather than as a specialized agency. This was in the interest of all sides: the North did not want to finance a large institution; and the South did not want a global institution with the power to interfere with development goals. And other United Nations agencies did not want to relinquish significant 'turf' (Elliott 1998: 11–13).

After Stockholm, the Organization of the Petroleum Exporting Countries' (OPEC) success in raising the price of oil dramatically through limiting output in 1973–4 rocked the global economy. Oil prices quadrupled, inflation soared, and economic growth became sluggish worldwide. Many developing economies, particularly those in Latin America and Africa, began to experience debt crises. This economic turbulence deflated some of the potential for more aggressive global environmental initiatives after Stockholm. The South, in particular, became even more worried about the effects on debt levels and prospects for industrial development. Still, the debate over how to handle global environmental change continued, sparked by groundbreaking books such as the Club of Rome's (1972), *Limits to Growth*, and E. F. Schumacher's (1973), *Small is Beautiful*. The global community also signed noteworthy global environmental treaties just after Stockholm. These include the Convention on the Prevention of Marine Pollution by Dumping of Wastes and other Matter (the London Convention, 1972, which came into force in 1975), and the Convention on International Trade in Endangered

Species of Wild Flora and Fauna (CITES, 1973, which came into force in 1975).

Environment slid more into the background of global affairs in the second half of the 1970s and first half of the 1980s, as conservative governments came to power in leading industrialized economies, and Southern economies sank further into debt. There was, nevertheless, a great deal of environmental activity. Scientists continued to research global environmental change. Non-governmental organizations continued to campaign and pressure governments and firms. Individual states, including some in the South, continued to establish environmental agencies. States also continued to sign and ratify global environmental agreements, such as the 1980 Convention on the Conservation of Antarctic Marine Living Resources (which came into force in 1982). The global community, too, continued to debate and make some headway on how best to manage the need for development (especially in the South) with the need for a healthy global environment. Problems such as the depletion of the ozone layer, and disasters such as the nuclear accident at Three Mile Island in 1979, the Union Carbide chemical leak in Bhopal in 1984, and the Chernobyl nuclear meltdown in 1986, added a sense of urgency. Slowly, environmental issues began to move once more up the global agenda. The debate by the mid 1980s began to focus increasingly on the concept of *sustainable development*. The publication in 1987 of the World Commission on Environment and Development (WCED) report, *Our Common Future*, synthesized and consolidated the global debates over environment and development, defining sustainable development as 'development that meets the needs of the present without compromising the ability of future generations to meet their own needs' (WCED 1987: 43).

The Brundtland Commission

The World Commission on Environment and Development, commonly known as the Brundtland Commission, was chaired by the former prime minister of Norway, Gro Harlem Brundtland. There were twenty-three members serving in an expert rather than an official state capacity — and thirteen were from the South, including from India, China, and Brazil. Among G7 countries, only France and the United Kingdom did not send representatives. The Commission's report, *Our Common Future*, commonly known as the Brundtland Report, is widely seen as a watershed in the evolution of environmental debates within the global community of state representatives. The content of the Brundtland Report is an ingenious compromise. It did not foresee any necessary limits to growth, and industrialization and natural resource production, under correct management, were viewed as being acceptable, indeed inevitable, for some countries. The report called for a transfer of environmental technologies and economic assistance to support sustainable development in the South. It called, too, for more effective controls on population growth, as well as better education and food security in the South. It portrayed poverty as a core cause of unsustainable development. The source of much of the poverty in the South, it argued, is the position of developing economies within the global structure. The best way forward, then, is to stimulate — not slow down — economic growth: not the unchecked growth of the 1960s and 1970s, however, but growth from sustainable development.

States continued to negotiate and sign global environmental treaties leading up to and after the publication of the Brundtland Report. These include the 1985 Vienna Convention for the Protection of the Ozone Layer, the 1987 Montreal Protocol on Substances that Deplete the Ozone Layer, and the 1989 Basel Convention on the Control of Transboundary Movements of Hazardous Waste and their Disposal. By the late 1980s, global environmental issues had again crept back to the top of the global agenda, culminating in a 1989 United Nations General Assembly resolution to hold the first summit of world leaders on the global environment: what became the 1992 United Nations Conference on Environment and Development (UNCED), held in Rio de Janeiro, Brazil.

The Rio (Earth) Summit

The UNCED is popularly known as the Rio or Earth Summit. It was the largest United Nations conference to date, with most countries and 117 heads of state participating. There were thousands of non-governmental representatives at the official conference as well as at a parallel NGO forum. The recommendations in the Brundtland Report and the notion of sustainable development formed the core of the debate at Rio. Most countries endorsed the Brundtland definition of sustainable development. Many developing countries, however, wanted specific assurances of transfers of environmental technologies and economic assistance from the North to support the additional costs of 'green' growth. Many Northern states, on the other hand, were reluctant to assume further financial commitments (Rogers 1993: 238–9).

The Rio Summit put environment and development on the agendas of global leaders. It reinforced, too, the Brundtland Commission's assumption that more growth was compatible with a better global environment. Two official Rio Summit documents of particular note are the Rio Declaration on Environment and Development, and Agenda 21. The Rio Declaration is a set of twenty-seven principles on the rights and responsibilities of states for environment and development. These principles include far more of the South's concerns about the right to development than the Stockholm Declaration on the Human Environment. Agenda 21 was a 300-page action programme to promote sustainable development (UN 1992).

The Rio Summit also produced the Non-legally Binding Authoritative Statement of Principles for a Global Consensus on the Management, Conservation and Sustainable Development of all Types of Forests. The original intent was to sign a legally binding forest treaty, but after irreconcilable differences arose among negotiators over the terms of an agreement, the conference settled for a

non-binding statement of principles (Brack et al. 2001: 2). Rio also opened two conventions for signature: the United Nations Framework Convention on Climate Change, and the Convention on Biological Diversity. Negotiations began, too, on a treaty on desertification. Finally, the conference established the United Nations Commission on Sustainable Development to monitor and evaluate the progress on meeting the Rio objectives.

The Rio Summit was a historic global conference, hailed by many states as a great success. Critics from all sides, however, lamented the inadequate amount of 'promised' funds—especially from the North—to implement Agenda 21. More radical environmentalists, too, attacked the Brundtland definition of sustainable development—in particular its support for more economic growth and industrialization. Among activists, there was, in addition, a general concern that the negotiators had ignored the root cause of global environmental change: the inequalities, unsustainable industrial production and growth, and over-consumption that arise from corporate globalization and free trade. That, in fact, industry captured the agenda at Rio (Chatterjee and Finger 1994), and the outcomes were little more than an incompetent doctor (the state system) slapping a Band-Aid on to a cancerous tumour (capitalism). Other critics also felt that the Rio Summit entrenched a top-down set of solutions, without nearly enough focus on the needs of local communities, or the plight of women and indigenous peoples (Shiva 1993; Lohmann 1993).

The decade after Rio saw global environmental issues again slip down the list of state priorities. States turned to the threats of terrorism, chemical and biological warfare, and global financial crises. The global community, nevertheless, kept signing and ratifying environmental treaties. The Convention on Biological Diversity, for example, was opened for signature in 1992 (and came into force in 1993). The United Nations Convention on the Law of the Sea, though first opened for signature in 1982, eventally came into force in 1994. The United Nations Convention to Combat Desertification in Those Countries Experiencing Serious Drought and/or

Table 14.1 Examples of International Environmental Agreements

Name of the agreement	Opened for signature	Entered into force	Website address
International Convention for the Regulation of Whaling	1946	1948	www.iwcoffice.org
Convention on Wetlands of International Importance Especially as Waterflow Habitat (Ramsar)	1971	1975	www.ramsar.org
Convention on the Prevention of Marine Pollution by Dumping Wastes and Other Matter (London Convention)	1972	1975	www.imo.org
Convention on the International Trade in Endangered Species of Wild Flora and Fauna (CITES)	1973	1975	www.cites.org
Convention on the Conservation of Antarctic Marine Living Resources	1980	1982, as part of the Antarctic Treaty System	www.ccamlr.org
Montreal Protocol on Substances that Deplete the Ozone Layer	1987	1989	www.ozone.unep.org
Basel Convention on the Control of Transboundary Movements of Hazardous Wastes and their Disposal	1989	1992	www.basel.int
Convention on Biological Diversity	1992	1993	www.cbd.int
United Nations Convention on the Law of the Sea (LOS)	1982	1994	www.un.org/Depts/los
United Nations Convention to Combat Desertification in Those Countries Experiencing Serious Drought and/or Desertification, Particularly in Africa	1994	1996	www.unccd.int
Stockholm Convention on Persistent Organic Pollutants (POPs)	2001	2004	www.chem.unep.ch/pops
Kyoto Protocol to the United Nations Framework Convention on Climate Change	1998	2005	www.unfccc.int

Desertification, Particularly in Africa was opened for signature in 1994 (and came into force in 1996). The Stockholm Convention on Persistent Organic Pollutants (POPs) was opened for signature in 2001 (and came into force in 2004). The Kyoto Protocol to the United Nations Framework Convention on Climate Change was opened for signature in 1998 (and came into force in 2005) (see Table 14.1).

The global community also continued to discuss and review the progress of Agenda 21 and the implementation of sustainable development, including a 1997 special session of the United Nations

General Assembly, known as the Earth Summit+5. The global community also prepared for the World Summit on Sustainable Development, eventually held in Johannesburg, South Africa, in 2002.

Johannesburg and beyond

The World Summit on Sustainable Development is popularly called Rio+10, or the Johannesburg Summit. The purpose was to evaluate the progress of sustainable development since the Rio Summit in 1992. It was also designed to establish specific targets to improve implementation of the Rio goals as well as to develop a strategy to implement the United Nations' Millennium Development Goals. The Johannesburg Summit — with over 180 nations, over 10,000 delegates, at least 8,000 civil society representatives, and 4,000 members of the press, as well as countless ordinary citizens — was even larger than the Rio Summit. Revealingly, however, only about 100 heads of state attended, fewer than at Rio.

The official documents of Johannesburg were similar to Rio and Stockholm in their broad calls for global sustainability. The two most important were the Johannesburg Declaration on Sustainable Development, a list of challenges and general commitments; and the Johannesburg Plan of Implementation, to meet these. These are non-binding, but, nevertheless, represent significant political compromises. One of the most contentious issues (as was the case too at Rio) was financing. But Johannesburg also added two equally tough topics: the impact of globalization on sustainable development as well as specific timetables/targets to meet goals (Mehta 2003: 122). The Johannesburg Declaration on Sustainable Development (2002) reflects the debates over globalization. Point 12 declares:

> The deep fault line that divides human society between the rich and the poor and the ever-increasing gap between the developed and developing worlds pose a major threat to global prosperity, security and stability.

Point 14 states:

> Globalization has added a new dimension to [global environmental problems]. The rapid integration of markets, the increasing mobility of capital and significant upsurge in investment flows around the world have opened new challenges and opportunities for the pursuit of sustainable development. But the benefits and costs of globalization are unevenly distributed, with developing countries facing special difficulties in meeting this challenge.

Was the Johannesburg Summit a success? The answer, naturally, depends on your definition of success. No doubt, like Stockholm and Rio, it helped to focus the attention of world leaders on global environmental change. The preparation and outcomes also cemented sustainable development as the core organizing concept for global and national environmental institutions, laying a strong foundation for future international environmental negotiations (for example, on climate change in Copenhagen in December 2009). Some see the outcomes as being constructive and more realistic than the outcomes of Rio. Others, though, see the conference as a symbol of the global failure to tackle sincerely global environmental problems. They see the targets and timetables as weak, and the Johannesburg Declaration as little more than a restatement of the past, doing little to promote global sustainability (Burg 2003: 116–18). These critics also see the official statements on globalization as being little more than bland and evasive whitewash. The Johannesburg Summit added yet another layer to global environmentalism, but as with Stockholm and Rio, it seems highly unlikely that it will stem the tide of ecological decay. Paul Wapner (2003: 7), in his assessment of the Johannesburg Summit outcomes, sums this up nicely: 'The strains on the earth's sources, sinks and sites have intensified dramatically since Rio and show no sign of decreasing in the near future.' In short, critics worry that environmentalism, piloted by the principle of sustainable development, is too weak to manage global environmental change. It does not, in particular, have the depth or content to restrain the ecological impacts of the globalization of production, consumption, trade, and corporations—the focus of the next section of this chapter.

Key points

- Environmental change began to accelerate some 300 years ago, after the Industrial Revolution intensified production and colonizers reached into distant lands.
- By the late 1960s, governments had begun to recognize the need to co-operate to address global environmental problems. The result was the 1972 United Nations Conference on the Human Environment.
- A global compromise gradually emerged in the 1970s and 1980s around the concept of sustainable development, as defined by the Brundtland Commission in 1987.

- The Rio Summit in 1992 set an ambitious agenda for global sustainable development. Progress, however, was slow and uneven over the following decade. Ten years later, the Johannesburg Summit endeavoured to facilitate the implementation of the Rio goals.
- The net result has left thick layers of global environmentalism (treaties, norms, and institutions) with the Brundtland Commission's concept of sustainable development at the core. Supporters see this as evidence of the global community's capacity to handle global environmental change, while critics see it as camouflage for 'business as usual'.

Economic Growth, Trade, and Corporations

What is the ecological impact of economic growth, trade, and corporations under globalization? Some see the net impact as being positive for the health of the planet. It pulls destitute people—who are prone to degrade surrounding environments to survive—out of poverty. And it raises national per capita incomes, which generate the funds, technologies, and political will to implement sustainable development. In the short run, such growth produces more food and better medical care, which in turn lengthens life expectancy and allows the global population to rise. Undeniably, this creates global ecological pressures. But, contend advocates of economic growth, this is a temporary problem. The global population will stabilize at 9 to 10 billion, probably around 2060, in part because globalization is raising the standards of living and education levels of women in the South, a development associated historically with smaller family size.

Others see economic growth and corporate globalization as core causes of the global environmental crisis. These forces are distributing environmental effects unequally, where the rich get richer and the poor remain confined in ever-worsening environments. It is also driving up per capita consumption in the South (without improving well-being) and over-consumption in the North. Already, the number of human beings is well beyond the earth's carrying capacity. The global population may well stabilize in around fifty years' time, but that is still another 3 to 4 billion people to feed, clothe, and shelter. How many earths, these critics wonder, are we planning to live on?

Which side is correct? To begin to address this question, the next section outlines the environmental arguments for more economic growth, more free trade, and more foreign investment.

Trading for growth and a better environment

A world free of poverty, say economists at institutions such as the World Bank, is critical for the long-term health of the planet. The struggle of the poor to survive is a core cause of problems such as deforestation, desertification, and unsanitary water. The poor forage for wood to cook with and to heat homes. They exhaust nearby natural resources, such as fresh water, seafood, and wildlife. They cultivate unsuitable land to grow food and earn income. And they despoil local waterways with rubbish and sewage. Stating these facts, advocates of economic growth argue, is not an attempt to assign blame. Rather, the point is far simpler: poor people have little choice if they wish to survive.

The poor and uneducated, too, tend to have more children than the rich, which creates a spiral of poverty and ecological collapse as ever more people forage for food, water, and shelter on increasingly fragile lands. This spiral occurs for many reasons besides weak economic growth. Other factors include insecure property rights, the failure of family planning, inadequate government services and regulations, trade distortions, and insufficient investment and development assistance. The downward spiral accelerates during times of slow growth — that is, during an economic recession or depression — since firms are less willing to invest in cleaner technologies, and states are less willing and less able to enforce environmental laws. A quick glance at environmental management in Asia during the 1997–9 financial crisis confirms this (Dauvergne 1999).

Admittedly, advocates note, economic growth can worsen environmental conditions in the short run. Air and water quality, for example, can deteriorate in the early stages of industrial production. Yet, in the long run, once a society harnesses sufficient per capita wealth, environmental standards will invariably rise. Advocates of economic growth commonly illustrate this with the Environmental Kuznets Curve (see Figure 14.2). This curve demonstrates that pollution (such as smog and lead) will rise along with economic growth during the early stages of industrial development. This occurs because governments focus on increasing industrial growth and national income rather than on pollution controls. Yet, this is a temporary phenomenon. Once per capita income reaches high enough levels (in the past, often between $5,000 and $8,000), pollution begins to fall (Grossman and Krueger 1995; for an overview, see Dinda 2004). This occurs partly because citizens demand

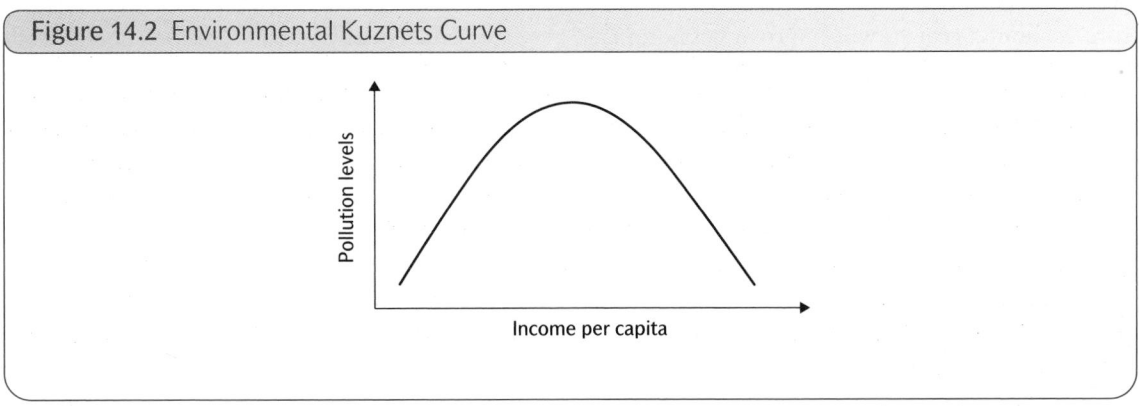

Figure 14.2 Environmental Kuznets Curve

better living environments, and partly because firms and governments now have the financial and institutional capacity to respond effectively. It arises partly, too, because strong economies naturally tend to move away from heavy industry, and toward service and information industries. The Environmental Kuznets Curve usually draws on data for industrial pollution rather than depletion of natural resources. At least one study, however, has found a correlation between lower deforestation and higher national income in Asia, Latin America, and Africa (Bhattarai and Hammig 2001).

Japan's environmental history fits the Environmental Kuznets Curve well. After the Second World War, industrial production and economic growth in Japan soared, and by the 1960s Japan was suffering from acute pollution, 'not unlike many of the heavily polluted areas of India, China, and Southeast Asia today' (Schreurs 2002: 36). Citizen protests over the health consequences of pollution escalated in the 1960s and 1970s. In response, the Japanese government brought in strict environmental regulations, and Japanese business developed new environmental technologies (McKean 1981; Broadbent 1998; Imura and Schreurs 2005). The result was a dramatic improvement in the domestic environment.

Environmental advocates of economic growth do not generally propose that states with low per capita incomes should blindly pursue economic growth. For most, the Environmental Kuznets Curve suggests two critical lessons: first, that, in the long run, economic growth will improve environmental institutions and governance; and second, that, following the logic of the Environmental Kuznets Curve, it is feasible to use measures such as ecological markets, technological advances, sound policies, and global institutions to help countries with low per capita incomes to 'tunnel' through the middle of the curve, attaining high per capita incomes with less environmental damage.

The globalization of free trade—following the principles of absolute and comparative advantage—will also help these weak economies to tunnel through the Environmental Kuznets Curve.

Free trade fosters efficient worldwide production as well as the transfer of environmental technologies and higher environmental standards from the North to the South (WTO 1999; Neumayer 2001; Lomborg 2009). It also creates incentives and price signals to ensure more efficient consumption of natural resources, supplying substitutes and more effective production technologies as scarcity rises (thus, enhancing overall resource availability). This means that humanity is able to produce more goods with fewer resources, which stimulates global economic growth and raises national per capita incomes. The extra income from efficient production is necessary, too, for sustainable development. More income means that more can be spent to preserve the environment as well as to enforce environmental regulations. World Trade Organization director-general, Mike Moore, succinctly explains the logic: 'Every WTO Member Government supports open trade because it leads to higher living standards for working families which in turn leads to a cleaner environment' (WTO 1999).

Trade liberalization, too, produces significant environmental rewards. Trade barriers distort price signals for natural resources. Prices therefore do not reflect real scarcities, availability, or pollution costs, which in turn creates waste and overconsumption. Liberalization also fosters cleaner production processes, as firms that produce goods behind trade barriers face less competition and have fewer incentives to upgrade facilities or use resources efficiently. States with more liberal trade policies are also, advocates argue, more likely to meet global environmental standards. 'Liberalized trade,' the World Bank (1992b: 67) explains, 'fosters greater efficiency and higher productivity and may actually reduce pollution by encouraging the growth of less-polluting industries and the adoption and diffusion of cleaner technologies.' Trade liberalization can further pressure producers with low environmental standards to raise these standards to gain access to markets with higher standards. This 'trading up' of environmental standards, David Vogel (1995) argues, occurred, for example, when California's strict auto emission standards pushed up standards across the United States as well as in Japan and Germany. Germany's willingness to support tougher European Union standards in part reflected its experience in the US market.

Restricting trade for environmental reasons, advocates of open trade argue, is on occasion necessary—such as to protect endangered species or to control the dumping of hazardous waste and dangerous chemicals. Yet, far more often, restricting trade on environmental grounds is illogical and counterproductive. Sound policies and incentives within an open trading structure lead to much better long-term environmental management. Green markets—where prices throughout a trade chain internalize environmental and social costs, and where consumers voluntarily pay higher prices for these products—are another effective means of promoting sustainable development.

The globalization of corporations, argue supporters, will further promote sustainable development. Transnational corporations (TNCs) transfer critical technologies, expertise, and funds into the South. Without this investment, economies stagnate, slip backwards, and sustain environmental degradation—a quick glance at North Korea or sub-Saharan Africa confirms this. Transnational corporations that invest in the South also tend to employ higher environmental standards than local laws require—what Ronie Garcia-Johnson (2000) calls exporting environmentalism. This occurs for a host of reasons: partly because of more sophisticated technologies and management techniques; partly because of pressure from states, NGOs, shareholders, and consumers; partly because of internal codes of conduct and risk-management strategies; and partly because the resulting efficiencies can provide a competitive advantage.

There is also a trend among all firms since the 1980s to 'green' operations voluntarily (Holliday et al. 2002; Makower and Pike 2009; Esty and Winston 2009). For example, Responsible Care—an environmental and safety code for the chemical industry—was established in 1985. The International Chamber of Commerce created the Global Environmental Management Initiative (GEMI) in 1990 to implement its business charter for sustainable development (Sklair 2001: 204). There was a flood of voluntary industry codes after the 1992 Rio Summit. The International Organization for Standardization (ISO) 14001 certifiable standards for environmental management have been adopted widely by business since the mid 1990s (see Box 14.3). Industry founded the World Business Council of Sustainable Development in 1995 to address 'the challenges and opportunities of sustainable development based on three fundamental and inseparable pillars: the generation of economic wealth, environmental improvement and social responsibility' (Holme and Watts 2000: 5). The Johannesburg Summit saw the business community stress the need for voluntary corporate leadership to promote sustainable development. Corporations are now embracing the principle of corporate social responsibility. Chairman and chief executive officer of AT&T, C. Michael Armstrong, explains the logic of the greening of the company: 'AT&T understands the need for a global alliance of business, society and the environment. In the 21st century, the world won't tolerate businesses that don't take that partnership seriously, but it will eventually reward companies that do' (quoted in Holme and Watts 2000: 1).

PETER DAUVERGNE

Box 14.3 ISO 14000 and ISO 14001

The International Organization for Standardization (ISO), headquartered in Geneva, advances voluntary international standards for particular products, and for environmental management. The ISO develops these standards relying on consensus and voluntary participation among ISO member countries. ISO 14000 is a series of voluntary environmental standards, including for environmental auditing, performance, labelling, and most importantly, the ISO 14001 Environmental Management System (EMS)

Standard. The ISO 14001 standard allows for certification from an external authority. By 2007, some 154,600 firms in 148 countries were certified to this standard. It requires a community or organization to implement practices and procedures that together comprise a system of environmental management. It also requires a policy to prevent pollution and continually improve environmental performance.

Source: ISO 2008; ISO 14000 Essentials, www.iso.org/iso/iso_14000_essentials

Most states and global institutions accept the need for more economic growth, more open trade, and more foreign investment. There are critics, however, many of whom see the relentless pursuit of growth, trade, and investment under globalization as a primary cause of the global environmental crisis.

Trading away the earth for unequal consumption

Critics contend that the Environmental Kuznets Curve is misleading. They see the link between growth and lower long-term pollution as being simplistic. It is possible, critics argue, for economies to get stuck along the curve, never reaching a point where pollution declines (Arrow et al. 1998; Tisdell 2001: 187). The Curve does not account for the integrity of the ecosystem as a whole, and it ignores irreplaceable losses (such as biodiversity and species loss). It discounts, too, the potential for cumulative ecological change to erupt into a sudden and uncontainable crisis. It does not address the possibility that, as the amount of one toxic substance declines, the amount of another may rise. The Curve, moreover, only works for a limited range of pollutants and resources. It fails, for example, for CO_2 emissions (the leading cause of global warming), which have been rising steadily alongside growth. Finally, a decline of a particular pollutant in one country may occur because industrial production shifts

offshore. Japan's domestic environment was able to improve, for example, partly because dirty industries shifted into South-East and North-East Asia (Hall 2002, 2009).

Environmental critics of economic growth argue further that production patterns and unequal consumption—rather than poverty—are the driving forces of global environmental decay. The earth is already beyond its carrying capacity. The push for constant economic growth under globalization, critics contend, means that industrialization, intensive agriculture, and unsustainable natural resource extraction will continue to rise. Gross domestic product (GDP) nearly tripled worldwide from 1970 to 2000 (in constant dollar terms). From 2001 to 2006, it then grew more than in any five-year period since the Second World War (World Bank 2007b). The global financial downturn of 2007–9 did slow economic growth. For critics, however, the unprecedented stimulus packages and bailouts of big banks and corporations merely confirm the unswerving faith of policy-makers in the need to keep the global economy growing. For them, the financial crisis is merely a symptom of an unsustainable and unjust global order. And government efforts to stimulate consumption and spending during this crisis have simply added to the destructive power of economic globalization.

Globalization also 'distances' production from consumption, so end users do not 'see' the ecological effects of individual purchases or disposal

(Princen 1997, 2005; Clapp 2002; Dauvergne 2008). Products like computers often become obsolete in a few years, partly because of their design. This, along with advertising, is contributing to ever higher levels of consumption in both the North and the South. Private consumption expenditures, for example, increased more than fourfold from 1960 to 2000, even though the world population only doubled during this period. Since 1950, meat consumption has increased more than fivefold, reaching over 260 million metric tons by 2009: an amount some analysts predict will exceed 420 million metric tons by 2050 (Nierenberg 2009). These rises, moreover, have not solved the gross inequalities between consumption in the South and the North. Africa's per capita consumption has been declining since the 1980s. The wealthiest one-fifth of the global population accounts for over three-quarters of total private consumption expenditures. This not only translates into far more luxury goods, but also necessities such as food. The richest 20 per cent of the world population, for example, consumes 45 per cent of all meat and fish (UNEP 2002: 35, 37). Much of this consumption, critics argue, is wasteful and excessive—creating a world where obesity is the latest crisis of the middle classes and malnutrition the everlasting crisis of marginalized peoples of the South.

Global free trade, critics contend, merely adds to the earth's unsustainable ecological burden (Daly 1993, 1996, 2002; Rees 2002, 2006). The prices of traded goods generally do not reflect the full environmental and social costs of production—the value, for example, of an old-growth tree as a source of biodiversity—leaving consumer prices far too low and consumption far too high for global sustainability. Environmental critics further argue that trade and trade agreements put downward pressure on environmental standards. This occurs because governments, in a bid to become more competitive in global markets, sometimes lower, or fail to strengthen, environmental management. Some see this as creating a race to the bottom; while others see it as leaving countries 'stuck at the bottom' (Esty 1994; Porter 1999). For many, the only solution to the ecological drawbacks of trade is to impose strict controls over trade.

Production under free trade may well become more 'efficient', critics add, but the steady increase in the production of goods overrides any environmental gains—creating, for example, a world heading toward a billion fuel-efficient cars rather than millions of fuel-inefficient cars. Global free trade, moreover, is in fact far from 'free'. Nor is it equal or fair, as highly mobile capital exploits the so-called comparative advantages of weak economies. The ideology of free trade in reality translates into patterns of exchange that exploit the labour and environments of the South and protect the interests of the North (such as farmers). The South ends up exporting unsustainable quantities of natural resources and absorbing ecological damage so that the North can prosper. Production-for-export from the South tends to rely either on unsustainable quantities of natural resources, or on dirty and unsafe factories (and, of course, cheap labour). Logging, mining, and industrial waste sites, and textile and electronic factories in Latin America, Africa, and the Asia-Pacific highlight the ecological damage of such production (Ross 2001; Jackson and Banks 2003; Ali 2004; Tienhaara 2006; Gallagher and Zarsky 2007; Pellow 2007). Global trade, critics conclude, in effect allows the North to live beyond its carrying capacity, doing so by using up the carrying capacity of the South.

Critics see corporate globalization as a fundamental cause of the escalating global ecological crisis. Transnational corporations are viewed as engines of environmental exploitation, plundering the globe's limited resources for quick profits. In particular, critics see *pollution havens* and *double standards* as real or potential threats to sustainability. A pollution haven refers to governments using low environmental standards to induce firms to invest, thus creating a haven for polluters. It does not, as David Wheeler (2002: 1) points out, 'necessarily refer to a region that is seriously polluted'. What really matters is 'the willingness of the host government to "play the environment card" to promote growth'. A double standard refers to cases where a firm applies one set of standards at home and another set overseas (generally lower standards in countries with weaker laws). Double standards are common and, most economists would agree, a normal outcome of the process of development. The case of the American TNC, Union Carbide, in Bhopal, India, the site of the worst industrial accident in history, is perhaps the best-known case of double standards (the US headquarters was responsible for the plant's design) (MacKenzie 2002; Jasanoff 2007). But there are countless others, too (Ofreneo 1993; Karliner 1997; Korten 2001; Frey 1998, 2003). The American firms, General Electric, Ford, General Motors, and Westinghouse, for example, all operate plants in Northern Mexico, thus avoiding California's much tougher regulations on toxic emissions. Critics blame these TNCs for polluting local rivers, soil, and water supplies near these plants.

There is, then, little controversy as to whether double standards exist. The existence of pollution havens, however, is hotly debated. Critics of TNCs commonly assert that corporate globalization is producing pollution havens around the globe. The process of globalization spreads these, because corporations are increasingly willing to relocate for the smallest differences in costs. Governments, meanwhile, are more likely to use lax regulations to entice investors. Most economists, however, argue that the reason for double standards is *not* a result of host governments intentionally and explicitly playing

the environment card. There are, they claim, in fact few, if any, permanent pollution havens anywhere in the world (Wheeler 2002). There are many reasons for this. For some industries, it is impractical or too risky to relocate for market or infrastructural reasons. The main reason, however, is that, for most industrial sectors, other costs, such as those for labour and technology, are far higher than environmental costs (Ferrantino 1997: 52). It therefore does not make financial sense for a firm to relocate on environmental grounds alone.

A second and much larger strand of the environmental literature, which is critical of corporations, focuses less on the differential environmental practices of firms across countries and more on practices 'on the ground'. These critics have filled libraries documenting the destructive and illegal practices of loggers, miners, oil companies, chemical companies, and agricultural companies (Clapp 2001; Dauvergne 2001; Gedicks 2001; Tacconi 2007; Clapp and Fuchs 2009). This research not only documents the activities of well-known transnational corporations, but also local and regional firms, such as Malaysian and Indonesian loggers in South East Asia and the South Pacific. Besides academics, research institutes such as the World Resources Institute and countless numbers of NGOs also research and publish such findings. This research leads popular writers such as Joshua Karliner (1997) to call the world a 'Corporate Planet', and David Korten (2001) to conclude that 'Corporations Rule the World.'

Key points

Advocates argue that the wealth from the globalization of trade and TNCs creates:
- Poverty alleviation, better education, population controls, and a stronger capacity of states and global institutions to implement sustainable development.

- Technological innovation and less harmful forms of production (for example, a shift from industry and agriculture to service and knowledge).
- Corporate investment that 'exports environmentalism' by transferring funds, new technologies, and higher standards to the South.

- Opportunities to use creative policies and incentives to tunnel through the Environmental Kuznets Curve. Critics see unequal and destructive economic growth, trade, and investment that:
  - Burden the South with unequal environmental costs and low environmental standards.
  - Allow corporations to plunder the globe's fragile ecosystems.

- Generate consumer prices that ignore environmental and social costs of production.
- Drive overconsumption in the North and unbalanced consumption in the South, putting total global consumption well beyond the earth's carrying capacity.

A Sustainable Future? Financing and Regimes

There is, then, a great divide between environmentalists who support and those who oppose globalization. Most agree, however, that it will no doubt require new consumption patterns, innovative markets, technological advances, corporate ethics, and co-operation to ensure a sustainable global economy. Reforms are, indeed, going on in all of these areas. Yet, the global community has put much of its energy into funding sustainable development, and into forming and strengthening global environmental agreements. Is sustainable development an effective core principle? Is funding sufficient? Can international agreements and sustainable development ensure globalization is a positive environmental force? Many in the global community—states and state negotiators in particular—believe in sustainable development and environmental agreements. Others, however, see them as, at best, harmless, and at worst, themselves causes of global environmental harm as the effort to reach a compromise lowers expectations, creates long delays, and ultimately contributes to ineffective policies. The next section addresses these issues, with particular attention to global environmental financing and the political economy of three international regimes: ozone depletion, climate change, and forestry.

Financing sustainable development: the Global Environment Facility (GEF)

Few deny that the South requires assistance to implement sustainable development. How else can the South find the funds and personnel to address issues such as climate change or global biodiversity? Yet, critics lament the failures of existing environmental assistance. Some see total development assistance as being far too low—far below the repeated global promise of total overseas development assistance of 0.7 per cent of gross national income. The total OECD average is just 0.28 per cent, while the United States is the lowest of the major donors, supplying a mere 0.16 per cent in 2007 (OECD 2009). Assistance for sustainable development is even lower. At the Rio Summit, for example, the North was only willing to commit to $125 billion of the $625 billion estimated as being needed to implement Agenda 21 (UNEP 2002: 17).

Other critics see development assistance as a cause of global ecological stress. They see the conditions attached to this 'aid' as a tool of donors and corporate allies to exploit labour and natural resources in the South. Multilateral donors such as the World Bank (see Park 2010; Phillips 2009) and bilateral donors such as Japan (the world's largest bilateral aid donor during the 1990s), for example, use loans to require governments to eliminate trade barriers and support foreign investors. Heavy foreign debts, these critics contend, further aggravate ecological pressures as states export natural resources to earn the foreign exchange to service and repay the debt (Rich 1994, 2000, 2009; Babb 2009).

The Global Environment Facility (GEF) is one of the few financial sources to fund specific global environmental initiatives in the South. The GEF was first set up as a pilot facility in 1991, just before the Rio Summit, becoming a permanent body formally in 1994. The GEF has three main implementing agencies—the World Bank; the United Nations Development Programme (UNDP); and the UNEP—although seven other agencies that have joined since the GEF was established also participate. The Global Environment Facility is housed formally in the World Bank; although it is functionally independent, many consider this a telling sign of the World Bank's influence over the GEF. The UNDP handles technical assistance and the UNEP co-ordinates between the GEF and global environmental agreements. Fourteen donor states and eighteen recipient states sit on the GEF Council, which has an 'open door policy' toward NGOs. The GEF finances global environmental policies and programmes in developing countries, including ozone depletion, biodiversity, climate change, and persistent organic pollutants (Streck 2001). The GEF currently supports more than 2,400 projects in over 165 countries. The total amount of GEF grants allocated by 2009 was over $8.6 billion. The GEF has also managed to leverage over $36 billion in co-financing from other sources (GEF 2009).

The GEF disburses grants and technical funds to cover the additional costs for developing countries of a project targeting a global environmental objective (such as to mitigate climate change or protect biodiversity). Some see the GEF as a critical step forward to help the South absorb the financial costs of global sustainability. Others, like Bruce Rich of the NGO Environmental Defense, have lashed out at the GEF, especially during the pilot phase: 'The formulation of the Global Environment Facility,' he argues (1994: 176–7), 'was a model of the Bank's preferred way of doing business: Top-down, secretive, with a basic contempt for public participation, access to information, involvement of democratically elected legislatures, and informed discussion of alternatives.' These critics see the GEF as little more than a financial Band-Aid that stresses top-down technological fixes rather than long-term solutions (Young 2003). These critics worry, too, that the World Bank is tying GEF grants to other World Bank loans financing projects that damage the environment. Korinna Horta of Environmental Defense states: 'The World Bank mocks the principles and policies of the GEF by hypocritically funding and mitigating environmental destruction. The GEF "greenwashes" business as usual for the Bank' (Halifax Initiative 2002; also see Horta et al. 2002).

Without doubt, funding for global sustainability is far from adequate. The global community has in some ways made more progress in developing and strengthening environmental regimes.

Explaining outcomes: the political economy of environmental regimes

The global community has put great faith in international environmental agreements to guide globalization, promote co-operation, rein in free riders, and avoid the natural drift of a system of sovereign states toward a tragedy of the commons (see Box 14.4). The number of international and regional environmental negotiations has been increasing steadily since the 1970s, and today there are over 450 multilateral environmental agreements (see Mitchell 2009 for a database of agreements; see Table 14.1 for examples).

Box 14.4 Tragedy of the Commons

Garrett Hardin (1968), in a now famous article in *Science*, drew a vivid analogy of access and historical collapse of the English commons with access and future collapse of modern-day commons (like the high seas, or the atmosphere, or an unregulated forest). Look, he says, at a grazing pasture 'open to all'. It is in the rational self-interest of a farmer to breed and graze as many animals as possible. The addition of one more animal will enhance the wealth of the owner far more than it will degrade the pasture for the owner's herd. Without controls, however, the logic of personal gain will inevitably overfill and destroy the pasture. The process is the same for all commons with rising populations and unrestricted access. 'Ruin is the destination toward which all men rush,' he argues, 'each pursuing his own best interest in a society that believes in the freedom of the commons. Freedom in a commons brings ruin to all.' The only solution, he concludes, is 'mutual coercion, mutually agreed upon by the majority of the people affected'.

An international environmental regime encompasses more than just international legal agreements. Steven Krasner's (1983: 2) definition of an international regime is the classic one: 'sets of implicit or explicit principles, norms, rules and decision-making procedures around which actors' expectations converge in a given area of international relations' (see Aggarwal and Dupont, Chapter 3 in this volume). Yet, most international environmental regimes revolve around an international agreement. Such regimes tend to evolve in four phases. They begin with the recognition of a problem, including the scientific debates about the causes and severity, and the emergence of an agenda. The science here is often speculative, especially if, as with climate change, it involves looking hundreds of years into the future. Working through the science can create decades of delay during this phase as various 'experts' make claims and counterclaims. Dramatic events, such as an oil spill or chemical leak, or a 'hole' in the ozone layer, can catalyse action toward the next stage—the negotiation of the rules and decision-making procedures. Here, coalitions of states or a powerful state such as the United States can play a critical role either in the emergence or the veto of an agreement. States may also shift gears during this phase—for example, signing an agreement then withdrawing later (by refusing to ratify, say). As with the emergence of an agenda, scientists or experts with collective policy preferences can play a key role in defining the content of an agreement (Haas 1992; Lindemann 2008). So can networks of activists who work across traditional sovereign borders (Keck and Sikkink 1998; Pellow 2007). Once an agreement comes into force, parties to the agreement need to implement policies that meet their obligations. This phase can further strengthen or weaken a regime, as many states, even those striving legitimately to meet obligations, may be unable (or unwilling) to do so for technical or political reasons. Finally, regimes continue to evolve even after implementation begins, strengthening and weakening as norms shift (or sometimes as negotiators amend the formal rules).

There is a growing literature on evaluating the effectiveness of international environmental regimes (Victor et al. 1998; Young 1999, 2002; Vogler 2000, 2003; Breitmeier et al. 2006; Mitchell 2002, 2006; Mitchell et al. 2006; Stokke and Hønneland 2007). Many global environmental regimes are weak, with little influence over the behaviour of states and firms or, if there is influence, with little impact on global ecological conditions. An array of factors can undermine regime effectiveness. Ongoing research (and resulting debates) within the scientific community can make it hard to create and maintain a scientific consensus on the causes, consequences and solutions for particular ecological problems. Corporations can exploit the resulting uncertainty common to the scientific method to further delay negotiations or weaken regimes (as well as to fund scientific research to try to prolong uncertainty).

The domestic political influence of corporations can also weaken the formal rules and procedures for international agreements, undermine international financial commitments to support compliance, and stall national implementation, even in countries with reasonable local environmental records. The priority of all states on maintaining economic growth—and the insistence of many governments in developing countries on ensuring the opportunity to one day reach the levels of economic prosperity the North currently enjoys—can also mean that international negotiators compromise and avoid strict measures entailing economic costs. These factors all shape the scope and nature of international agreements, as well as the strength of the national policies and implementing agencies designed to meet international obligations.

National agencies are generally responsible for monitoring and enforcing international environmental laws. To encourage compliance, however, parties generally submit implementation data to secretariats as well as attend regular meetings to review implementation. Some agreements also link financing to compliance (especially important in the South). The secretariats, however, often lack the staff and funds to verify data (as well as push laggards to submit). The combined total in 1999 of professional staff of the Framework Convention on Climate Change, the Convention on Biological Diversity, the Montreal Protocol, CITES, and the Convention to Combat Desertification was a mere 100 people. The combined total budget was just $43.5 million (Porter et al. 2000: 150). Both figures are tiny in comparison with the international financial institutions (IFIs) (see Winham, Chapter 5 in this volume). Non-governmental organizations also play a key role here, publicizing violations and conducting independent studies of national implementation. The NGO, Environmental Defense, for example, was 'critical' in ensuring US regulations in fact implemented the Montreal Protocol after it went into force in 1989 (Porter et al. 2000: 149).

Implementation can pose great technical and political problems for governments in the South. Often, these governments do not have the finances, personnel, or technologies to monitor and enforce environmental legislation. Systemic corruption may further hinder enforcement. The cost of compliance, too, is frequently greater in the South than in the North, as the South has less infrastructure and experience in meeting environmental obligations, although, as mentioned earlier, funds such as the ones from the GEF can help to offset the higher costs of compliance in the South. Countries in the North, however, also struggle with implementing international environmental agreements. The process of confirming scientific explanations may create long bureaucratic delays in implementation. Lobby groups and bureaucracies may work to weaken national legislation designed to meet international obligations. In democratic federations, such as Canada, the Canadian federal government may sign and ratify an agreement, but then face stiff opposition from some of the provinces, as happened after the federal government ratified the Kyoto Protocol in 2002.

For all of these reasons, then, it is a formidable challenge for state negotiators and implementers to develop and uphold an effective international environmental regime. Perhaps the most common example of a 'successful' regime is the one to reduce the production and consumption of chlorofluorocarbons (CFCs), the main cause of the depletion of the ozone layer.

Ozone depletion regime

Production and consumption of CFCs, first invented in 1928, rose quickly from the 1950s to the 1970s. The main use was in aerosols, refrigerators, air conditioners, insulation, and solvents. In 1974, Mario Molina and F. Sherwood Rowland (1974) (who went on to win the 1995 Nobel Prize in Chemistry) published an article hypothesizing that CFCs were drifting into the atmosphere, breaking apart, releasing chlorine, then reacting to deplete the ozone layer. Ozone is a molecule of three oxygen atoms able to absorb harmful ultraviolet light. The ozone layer refers to the region of high concentrations of ozone in the stratosphere.

(The stratosphere is 10–50 kilometres above the earth's surface. Below this is the troposphere, where weather occurs.) The ozone layer protects us from the harmful effects of ultraviolet radiation from the sun, which can contribute to skin cancer and cataracts, decrease our immunity to diseases, and make plants less productive.

In the decade after Molina and Rowland's seminal article, global negotiators worked slowly towards a collective consensus on the causes and consequences of ozone depletion. This effort gained momentum in 1985, after British scientists found a 'hole' (in fact, a severe thinning) in the ozone layer over Antarctica. This hole, which persisted for three months, was the size of North America. That same year, the global community signed the Vienna Convention for the Protection of the Ozone Layer, a framework convention with no legally binding targets. The 1987 Montreal Protocol on Substances that Deplete the Ozone Layer was adopted two years later, setting mandatory targets to reduce the production of ozone-depleting CFCs and halons (halons are another significant ozone-depleting substance found, for example, in fire extinguishers).

Significantly, in 1990, the South agreed to phase out consumption of CFCs and halons by 2010. The Parties to the Montreal Protocol created the Multilateral Fund for the Implementation of the Montreal Protocol to assist developing countries with implementation. This is unusual, as most international environmental agreements do not contain a funding mechanism, and instead rely on traditional development assistance and, more recently, the GEF. So far, this Fund has approved more than $2 billion to phase out the consumption of ozone-depleting substances in the South. Partly as a result, many developing countries were already 'on track' by the mid 1990s to phase out CFCs and halons ahead of schedule (Greene 1997: 329), and the South was able to reduce CFC consumption by about 60 per cent from the mid 1990s to 2004 (UNEP 2005).

Conferences of the Parties in London in 1990, Copenhagen in 1992, Montreal in 1997, and Beijing in 1999 amended and strengthened the Montreal Protocol. These conferences also added other ozone-depleting substances and accelerated the phase-out schedules. Over this time, the Vienna Convention and the Montreal Protocol became truly global agreements, and today both have over 180 Parties. The result has been a dramatic fall in global CFC production (see Figure 14.3), with only very low production levels after 2004.

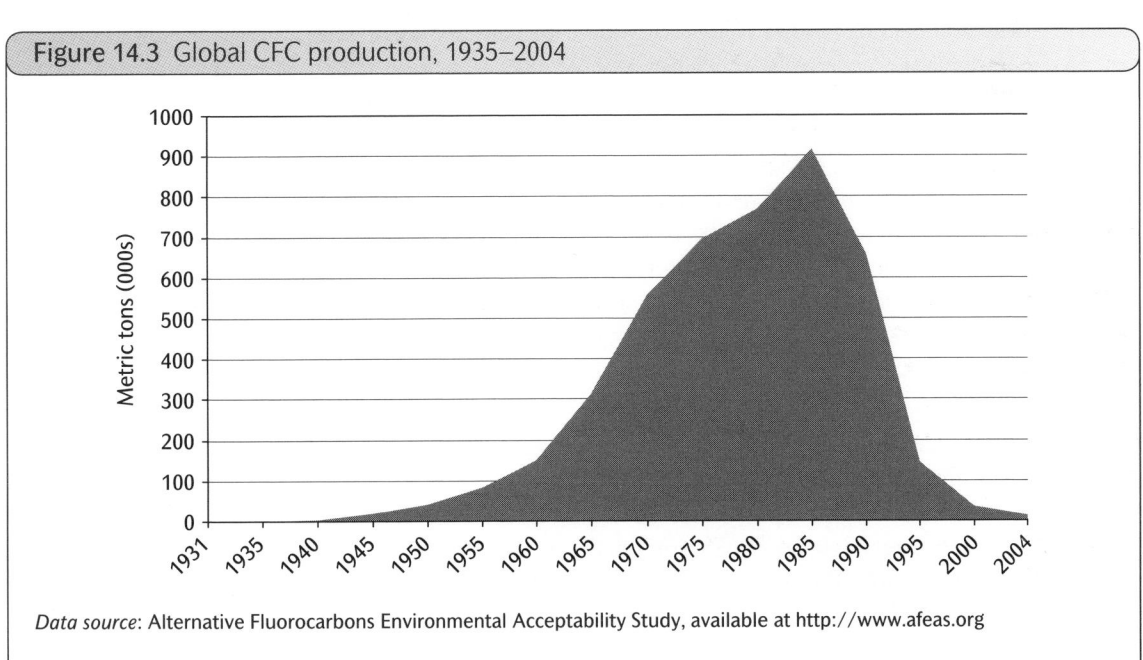

Figure 14.3 Global CFC production, 1935–2004

Data source: Alternative Fluorocarbons Environmental Acceptability Study, available at http://www.afeas.org

The damage to the ozone layer, it is important to emphasize, is still a serious problem. The long life of CFCs means that 'old' emissions are still damaging the ozone layer. The ozone hole over Antarctica broke records in September 2006 for depth and average size over a period of time (from 21–30 September). Still, the overall signs are positive, with fewer CFCs allowing the ozone layer to remain fairly stable since the mid-to-late 1990s (Barry and Phillips 2006). (The reasons for changes in ozone are complex—including sunspots, weather, and volcanoes—so, some fluctuations are natural.) The World Meteorological Organization (2006) now predicts that the ozone layer will repair itself and return to pre-1980 levels by 2065, thus preventing millions of cases of melanoma cancer and eye cataracts (UNEP 2003: 4). This is, indeed, an exceptional turnaround. 'The ozone layer regime is remarkable,' Marvin Soroos (1997: 169) argues, 'not only for the series of agreements limiting and phasing out the production and use of ozone-depleting substances but also for the broad acceptance of them and the apparent high rate of compliance with the controls.' Most other scholars would agree. Edward Parson (2003: vii) calls it a 'striking success', noting: 'With near-universal participation of nations and energetic support from industry, the ozone regime has reduced worldwide use of ozone-depleting chemicals by 95 per cent, and use is still falling.'

Yet, in many ways, this was an exceptional case, one that may well tell us little about our ability to handle future global environmental crises such as climate change. The consequences of less ozone were easy for the general public to understand, with skin cancer a particular worry in the North. The causes and solutions were also relatively straightforward. In the mid 1980s, twenty-one firms in sixteen countries were responsible for CFC production, with the North accounting for about 88 per cent of this. Especially notable, by 1986, the chemical company DuPont, the largest producer of CFCs (accounting for a quarter of global production), had decided to seek substitutes for CFCs (Grundmann 2001; Parson 2003). Two years later, DuPont announced that it would phase out production of CFCs. The shift to CFC substitutes did not harm its profits; indeed, in many ways, it gave DuPont a competitive edge as other producers soon followed suit.

Climate change regime

Most other global environmental problems involve far greater complexities and uncertainties, and will require far greater sacrifices to solve. Climate change is perhaps the most complex of all (see Dressler and Parson 2006; DiMento and Doughman 2007). Human activities are altering the relative volumes of greenhouse gases—such as carbon dioxide, methane, and nitrogen oxides—in the earth's atmosphere. Figure 14.4, for example, shows the rapid increase in global emissions of carbon dioxide during the twentieth century. The planet is warming as the 'new' atmosphere traps more heat, a process akin to rolling up a car window on a hot day. The Intergovernmental Panel on Climate Change (IPCC 2001) calculates that the mean global surface temperature rose by 0.3–0.6 degrees Celsius during the twentieth century. This may seem minor, but it was the largest rise of any century in the last millennium. And the problem appears to be getting worse. January 2000 to January 2010 was the warmest decade, and 2005 was the warmest year, since records began. One clear sign of warming is the melting polar ice caps, which have been shrinking by about 3 per cent every year since 1979.

The twenty-first century could be even hotter. The five hottest years on record are all since 1998, with the US National Aeronautics and Space Administration (NASA) predicting a new record-high temperature in 2010 with the arrival of the next El Niño (NASA 2009). Various scenarios developed by the IPCC (2007) predict a rise from the 1980–99 average surface temperature of between 1.1 and 6.4 degrees Celsius by 2100. A rise of 3 to 5 degrees Celsius would, according to NASA's Drew Shindell, 'bring us up to the warmest temperatures the world has experienced probably in the last million years' (quoted in

Figure 14.4 Global CO_2 emissions from fossil-fuel burning, cement production, and gas flaring, 1751–2006

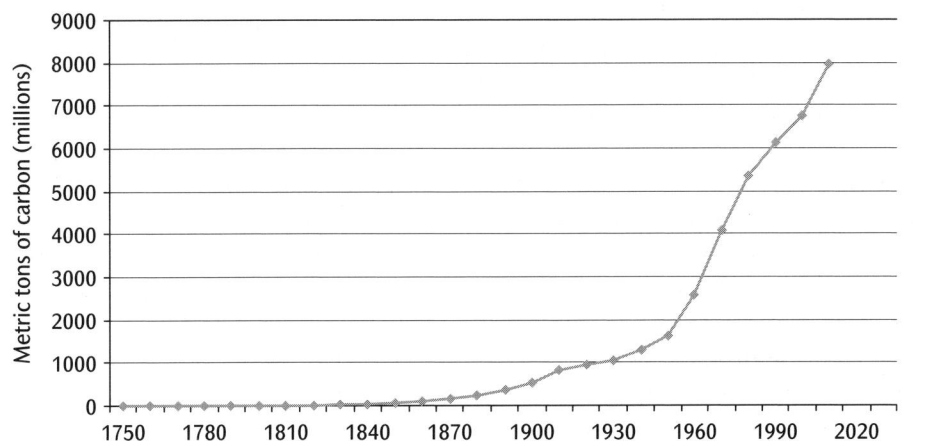

Data source: Carbon Dioxide Information Analysis Center, available at http://cdiac.esd.ornl.gov/ftp/ndp030/global. 1751_2006.ems

Zabarenko 2006). As a result, the IPCC (2007) estimates that seas could rise enough by the end of the twenty-first century to displace millions of people in low-lying coastal areas in countries such as Bangladesh and low-lying countries such as the Marshall Islands and the Maldives.

Climate change alarms environmental critics of economic globalization in particular, as the primary greenhouse gasses arise from core economic activities, such as automobiles, power plants, oil refineries, factories, agriculture, and deforestation. At the same time, many of the consequences, such as melting polar ice, rising seas, severe storms, new diseases, and drought, are beyond the lifetimes of politicians and business leaders. No doubt, to lower greenhouse gas emissions will require significant changes to global economic production and consumption patterns. It will require, too, governmental, corporate, and personal sacrifices. Replacing CFCs, these critics note, is simply not a comparable sacrifice (Paterson 1996; Newell 2000; Porter et al. 2008).

As highlighted, once again, at the Fifteenth UN Climate Change Conference in Copenhagen in December 2009, the South sees the North as being largely responsible for climate change, because developed countries accounted for three-quarters of cumulative emissions of carbon dioxide between 1950 and 1992. The North, on the other hand, often notes the need for global efforts, as carbon dioxide emissions from the South are likely to equal those from the North by 2035. Nevertheless, specific views on climate change do not split cleanly along North–South lines. The European Union, Japan, and Canada, for example, have supported global efforts to combat climate change, while the United States and Australia have remained sceptical, at times even questioning the science of global warming. Meanwhile, the states in OPEC oppose efforts to reduce the global dependence on oil while, predictably, the thirty countries in the Alliance of Small Island States support every possible effort to halt the rise of sea levels.

The 1997 Kyoto Protocol to the 1992 Climate Change Convention is the core agreement in the climate change regime. It requires developed countries (including Russia) to reduce emissions of six greenhouse gases, on average, by 5 per cent below 1990 levels between 2008 and 2012 (calculated as an average over these years). If this is achieved, emissions levels in 2010 would be about 20 per cent lower than they would have been without the Protocol. But not all governments have the same 'target'. The European Union agreed to reduce emissions by 8 per cent below 1990 levels; the United States by 7 per cent; and Japan and Canada by 6 per cent. The Russian Federation agreed to stabilize emissions at 1990 levels. Australia managed to negotiate an increase of 8 per cent above 1990 levels. Developing countries are exempt from legally binding commitments in the Kyoto Protocol, although some, like India and China, set voluntary reduction targets.

The rules of the Kyoto Protocol required it to come into force ninety days after at least fifty-five Parties, accounting for at least 55 per cent of the 1990 carbon dioxide emissions of the developed country signatories, had ratified it. This seemed unlikely to occur after the United States, which accounts for 36.1 per cent of 1990 carbon dioxide emissions of developed countries, withdrew support in 2001, and instead vowed to reduce greenhouse gases 'by 18 per cent over the next decade through voluntary, incentive-based, and existing mandatory measures' (Switzer 2004: 293). The Kyoto Protocol did, in the end, come into force in 2005 even without the United States, after Russia, which accounts for 17.4 per cent of 1990 levels, tipped the total over the 55 per cent mark. Many see this as a sign of the determination of the global community (minus the United States and Australia) to tackle climate change. Many see it, too, as a vital foundation for further international dialogue, such as the 2009 climate change summit in Copenhagen, which brought together world leaders

and negotiators from over 190 countries. Still, most analysts agree that, even with full compliance, the Kyoto Protocol will not lower greenhouse gas emissions to levels that will 'solve' climate change. More radical groups, such as Greenpeace, argue for a global emission reduction closer to 80 per cent. Almost all analysts now agree that more effective governance of climate change will require many initiatives at multiple levels, from global to local (for example, Selin and VanDeveer 2009; Okereke et al. 2009).

Forests regime

Most environmental regimes, as with ozone and climate change, contain a core international agreement. But some, like the international forests regime, are emerging without a core global treaty. The international forests regime includes the norms and principles arising from numerous global meetings since the Rio Summit to discuss the benefits and drawbacks of negotiating a global treaty for forest management. It consists, too, of the forest-related clauses of international conventions such as the ones on biodiversity, desertification, climate change, and wetlands. It also includes the sustainable forest principles of institutions such as the International Tropical Timber Organization (ITTO), and the standards of organizations such as the Forest Stewardship Council (FSC) (see Box 14.5). At the core of the regime is the concept of sustainable forest management. Humphreys (1999: 251) writes, 'The forests regime has coalesced around the core concept of sustainable forest management (SFM) and the norm that forests should be conserved and used in a sustainable manner.' Other global principles include the value of conservation, ecosystem integrity, protected areas, indigenous knowledge and values, and the participation of civil society (Humphreys 1999, 2003, 2006; also, see Cashore et al. 2004).

Box 14.5 ITTO and FSC

International Tropical Timber Organization (ITTO)

The 1983 International Tropical Timber Agreement (in force from 1985) created the International Tropical Timber Organization (ITTO), with its headquarters in Yokohama, Japan. Successor agreements were negotiated in 1994 (in force since 1997) and in 2006 (not yet in force as of January 2010). The ITTO's mandate is to facilitate consultation and co-operation among member countries that produce and consume tropical timber. There are fifty-nine members (as of 2010), representing 90 per cent of world trade in tropical timber. The organization is committed to assisting members with meeting the so-called Year 2000 Objective, which calls for members, (originally, by the year 2000), to trade only tropical timber products that originate from sustainably managed forests. (This is still being pursued, despite the passing of the target year.)

Source: ITTO website, 'About ITTO', available at www.itto.int/en/about_itto and 'ITTO Objective 2000', available at www.itto.int/en/feature01

Forest Stewardship Council (FSC)

The non-profit Forest Stewardship Council was founded in 1993 to promote more effective forest management. Its members include environmental organizations, forest industries, indigenous and community groups, and forest certification bodies. The FSC accredits and monitors organizations that certify that forest products come from 'a well-managed forest'—that is, a forest that meets the FSC's Principles and Criteria of Forest Stewardship. The FSC visits certified forests to ensure compliance. It further supports the development of regional, national, and local standards that implement these principles and criteria. The FSC logo on a wood product is ultimately designed to provide a 'credible guarantee' to the consumer 'that the product comes from a well-managed forest.'

Source: FSC website, available at www.fsc.org

Key points

- All sides agree that the South needs financial and technical support to pursue global sustainability.

- Some see current efforts—for example the GEF—as a critical lifeline for weak economies. Others see such financing as being too small to matter, and still others see global development assistance as a cause of the global environmental crisis, with states exporting natural resources to service and repay foreign debt.

- Environmental regimes are the primary global mechanism for co-ordinating environmental management across states. It is exceedingly difficult, however, to create and maintain an effective environmental regime.

- Most agree that the ozone regime has been effective, largely because the causes, consequences, and solutions of ozone depletion are straightforward.

- The climate and deforestation regimes are much weaker than the ozone regime. Advocates of regimes see this as temporary, a result of the sheer complexity and difficulty of the science, politics, and economics of climate change and deforestation. Critics, on the other hand, see weak regimes for problems such as climate change and deforestation as inevitable within the current global political economy; for some, these are not a part of the solution, but, rather, a part of the reasons for failure.

- Most advocates and critics of regimes agree, however, that solutions to climate change and deforestation will require far more than financing and regimes. Solving them will require a level of innovation, co-operation, and sacrifice never seen before in the history of global environmental politics.

Yet, global norms and principles are only a small part of the basket of rules—both formal and informal—that shape forest management. National and local leaders often ignore the concept of sustainable forest management as well as the non-binding principles of institutions such as the ITTO and FSC. The international forests regime is particularly weak and ineffective in Asia, Africa, and South America, most notably where timber profits prop up corrupt politicians, bureaucrats, and military officers. This explains in part why tropical deforestation has persisted largely unimpeded over the last few decades, despite a global outcry and repeated government promises to do better (Dauvergne 2001; Tacconi 2007).

International regimes, then, can solve global environmental problems. The history of the depletion of the ozone layer confirms this. Yet, the regimes for climate change and deforestation, for different reasons, are still largely ineffective. Supporters of regimes argue this reflects in part the complexity of the causes and consequences of these problems, as well as the need for economic sacrifices to solve them. For them, this suggests a need to work even harder to strengthen these regimes. For critics of regimes, however, the failure to slow climate change and deforestation suggests the innate limitations of regimes as a mechanism to constrain and guide economic globalization. The energy expended on seemingly endless international negotiations on climate change and deforestation, some critics argue, would be better spent elsewhere, perhaps in labs developing new technologies, or in communities developing new ethics. A few of these critics even see the focus on the development of agreements, such as an international forests convention, as a strategic move by powerful actors to delay real action and ensure that 'business as usual' continues for as long as possible (Dauvergne 2005).

Conclusion

What, then, is the nature of global environmental change in an era of globalization? Is globalization a force for environmental progress or crisis? Are global environmental regimes and the norm of sustainable development effectively channelling globalization to ensure a sustainable future? The record is mixed. For some problems, such as ozone depletion, global co-operation has indeed been effective. But for problems such as tropical deforestation, the global community appears to be making no headway at all. Perhaps the greatest environmental problem of all is climate change. Here, it also appears that global efforts are failing. Can sustainable development and regimes alone 'solve' deforestation and climate change? The answer seems clear: no. These may, indeed, help. But such great problems will require new national policies, new corporate ethics, more North–South financial transfers, innovative markets, technological advances, and new forms of co-operation. It will be a bumpy path forward: one that will, because of the nature of the global political economy and global environmental change—no doubt, most unjustly—impose the greatest hardships on the world's poorest and least powerful peoples. That much seems certain.

The chapter did not strive to convince the reader to believe in a particular set of arguments. Already far too many globalization and anti-globalization 'environmental ideologues' preach or chant at, rather than talk to, each other. The goal was instead to deepen the understanding of the range of reasonable and logical arguments about the environmental impacts of the ongoing changes to the global political economy. The hope is that, one day, those who choose to act on their beliefs—from joining the World Bank's environment team to protesting at an anti-globalization rally—will do so with the humility of knowing the complexities and uncertainties of the relationship between globalization and the environment.

? Questions

1. What, in the broadest terms, is the relationship between globalization and global environmental change?

2. What is the globalization of environmentalism? Is the overall trend positive or negative?

3. Is the Environmental Kuznets Curve a useful policy tool?

4. Which is more common: 'pollution havens' or 'exporting environmentalism'?

5. What are the effects of inequality and consumption on global environmental conditions?

6. What are the effects of trade and corporations on global environmental conditions?

7. What are the effects of financing and regimes on global environmental conditions?

8. Is there a global environmental crisis? If yes, why? If no, why?

9. Can we solve global environmental problems within the current political and economic structures? If yes, how? If no, why?

→ Further reading

■ Axelrod, R. S., VanDeveer, S. D., and Downie, D. L. (eds) (2010), *The Global Environment: Institutions, Law, and Policy*, 3rd edn (Washington, DC: CQ Press). Analyses the role of institutions, legal instruments, and policy in shaping global environmental management and change.

■ Chasek, P. S., Downie, D. L., and Brown, J. W. (2010), *Global Environmental Politics*, 5th edn (Boulder, CO: Westview Press). Introduces the academic study of global environmental politics with a focus on international agreements.

■ Clapp, J., and Dauvergne, P. (2011), *Paths to a Green World: The Political Economy of the Global Environment*, 2nd edn (Cambridge, MA: MIT Press). Maps out an original typology to classify the dominant world views regarding the impact of the global political economy on the global environment.

■ Conca, K., and Dabelko, G. D. (eds) (2010), *Green Planet Blues: Four Decades of Global Environmental Politics*, 4th edn (Boulder, CO: Westview Press). Surveys and extracts core concepts and arguments from seminal articles in global environmental politics.

■ Dauvergne, P. (ed.) (2005), *Handbook of Global Environmental Politics* (Cheltenham: Edward Elgar). Collection of original and cutting-edge articles by many of the world's premier scholars of global environmental politics.

■ Dryzek, J. S. (2005), *The Politics of the Earth: Environmental Discourses*, 2nd edn (Oxford: Oxford University Press). Analysis of the history of environmental discourses. Collection of accompanying readings is available in: J. S. Dryzek and D. Schlosberg (eds) (2005), *Debating the Earth: The Environmental Politics Reader*, 2nd edn (Oxford: Oxford University Press).

■ *Global Environmental Politics* available at www.mitpressjournals.org/loi/glep. Scholarly journal that contains the latest innovative and original research on environment and the global political economy (first issue February 2001).

■ Haas, P. M. (ed.) (2003), *Environment in the New Global Economy* (Cheltenham: Edward Elgar). A collection of sixty seminal articles on environment, globalization, and the global political economy (previously published, dating from 1944 to 2001).

■ Lipschutz, R. D. (2003), *Global Environmental Politics: Power, Perspectives, and Practice* (Washington, DC: CQ Press). A text on the politics of the global environment, that among other issues, examines green thought, capitalism, power, and international environmental policies.

■ O'Neill, K. (2009), *The Environment and International Relations* (Cambridge: Cambridge University Press). Draws on theories in international relations to provide a valuable toolkit to analyse global environmental change.

■ Pojman, L. P. and Pojman, P. (eds) (2007), *Environmental Ethics: Readings in Theory and Application*, 5th edn (Belmont, CA: Wadsworth Publishing). Balanced collection of many of the most influential articles in environmental philosophy and politics, including deep ecology, generational obligations, population, hunger, economics, and sustainability.

■ Princen, T., Maniates, M. F., and Conca, K. (eds) (2002), *Confronting Consumption* (Cambridge, MA: MIT Press). Breaks new ground in the understanding of consumption as a core problem for the global political economy.

:// Web links

■ www.unep.org   United Nations Environment Programme and www.undp.org   United Nations Development Programme. Provide entries into environment and development data and projects of the United Nations.

■ www.gefweb.org   Global Environment Facility. Outlines projects and programmes to finance protection of the global environment in developing countries.

■ www.wri.org   World Resources Institute. Source of scientific environmental research and non-governmental policy proposals. Includes agriculture, biodiversity, forests, climate change, marine ecosystems, water, and health.

■ www.iisd.org   International Institute for Sustainable Development. Monitors the proceedings of global environmental negotiations and conferences.

■ www.worldwatch.org   WorldWatch Institute. Source of data on the global environmental 'crisis'. Challenges some of the data (and interpretations) of the United Nations, World Bank, and governments.

Online resource centre

For additional material and resources, please visit the Online Resource Centre at:
www.oxfordtextbooks.co.uk/ravenhill3e/

Glossary

Absolute advantage Where a country produces one or more goods or services at lower cost than other countries.

Adjustable peg A form of international monetary system in which governments are permitted to change their currencies' exchange rates, normally fixed in value against other currencies.

Alienation A process described by Marx through which an increasingly complex division of labour deprives workers of opportunities to realize their full human potential by turning them into purely functional aspects of the broader capitalist system.

Anarchy The absence of a centralized authority in the international system capable of enforcing agreements.

Autarchy When a country attempts to maximize its self-sufficiency by minimizing contacts with the global economy.

Balance of payments An account of a country's transactions with foreign countries and international institutions in a specific period. Transactions are divided into current account, which consists of the balance of trade in goods and services plus profits and interest on overseas assets less those paid to foreign owners of domestic assets, plus net transfers such as worker remittances. The capital account consists of inflows and outflows of money for investment, and for grants and loans (and their repayment). The balance of payments is an accounting identity: the entries in the account should sum to zero with, for example, any imbalances on the current account being offset by net movements of capital.

Balance of trade *see* Balance of payments

Bounded rationality Rational decision-making in a context of incomplete knowledge.

Bretton Woods New Hampshire village where the Mount Washington Hotel is located—the site of the 1944 United Nations Monetary and Financial Conference: the birthplace of the International Monetary Fund (IMF) and the World Bank. 'Bretton Woods' is often used as shorthand for post-war international financial regimes.

Capital account *see* Balance of payments

Capital accumulation The process which gives the capitalist economy its essential dynamism: without the accumulation of capital no reinvestment can take place and therefore the economy will not grow over the long term. For writers in the Marxist tradition, capital can only be accumulated through the forced exploitation of the labouring classes.

Capital controls Restrictions placed by governments on private actors moving funds into or out of the territories they control.

Coase Theorem The argument that economic efficiency will be optimized as long as property rights are fully allocated, and completely free trade in these rights is possible.

Collaboration games A type of game where the Pareto-optimal solution the players desire may not be an equilibrium outcome; for example, the pursuit of strategies that are rational for individual players produces a suboptimal outcome, as in the Prisoner's Dilemma.

Common market A customs union that also allows free movement of factors (capital, labour) within its boundaries.

Common pool resources Goods that cannot be withheld from those that do not pay for them, and whose consumption comes at the expense of other potential consumers.

Comparative advantage Where a country is relatively more efficient at producing at least one product than others, even though it may lack absolute advantage in producing that good or service. Production according to comparative advantage enables specialization in relatively more efficient production, thereby increasing welfare.

Competitive advantage The competitive strength of an economy that derives from the capacity of its firms in various sectors. Whether government intervention can enhance an economy's competitive advantage remains a matter of considerable controversy.

Conditionality The stipulation by lenders of conditions that borrowers must meet if they are to continue to receive instalments of their loans.

Co-ordination games A type of game that typically has multiple Nash Equilibria, some of which are more preferred by one or more players.

Current account *see* Balance of payments

Customs unions Agreements between two or more countries to trade freely between themselves, and to adopt a common tariff on imports from countries outside the customs union.

Division of labour The centerpiece of Adam Smith's theoretical system in *The Wealth of Nations*, it refers to a situation in which individual workers specialize in only a small part of the production process rather than trying to undertake every work task involved in the production of a particular good. Efficiency gains materialize for the economy as a whole when workers specialize in this way and are brought together in large work teams.

Dollarization The adoption by foreign countries of the US dollar as their national currency.

Dumping A situation where a country's exports are sold in foreign markets at a price less than that at which they are sold at home.

Ecological footprint A measure (translated into hectares of average biologically productive land) of the resources required to sustain a person's lifestyle.

Ecological shadow A concept that attempts to capture the environmental impact of a country in jurisdictions beyond its sovereign control.

Economic union A common market that has also adopted common monetary and fiscal policies.

Economies of scale Realized when longer production runs enable firms to produce at a lower average unit cost.

Embedded liberalism A concept put forward by John Gerard Ruggie, following Karl Polanyi, to capture the compromise in post-war economic regimes between liberalization and the pursuit of domestic social and political objectives.

Enabling clause Formally, the 1979 Decision on Differential and More Favourable Treatment, Reciprocity and Fuller Participation of Developing Countries, it legitimizes special and differential treatment in the trade regime for less developed countries.

Environmental Kuznets Curve A graphical representation of the relationship between the level of per capita income and pollution, showing that levels of pollution initially increase with economic growth but then decline once per capita income reaches high levels.

Epistemology What knowledge is and how it is acquired.

Export-oriented industrialization Strategy for economic development based on domestic production targeted primarily at international markets.

Exporting environmentalism The use by transnational corporations in less developed economies of more environmentally friendly technologies than are required by local laws.

Externalities Consequences for societal welfare (costs and benefits) that are not captured in the market price of a good; for example, pollution is a negative externality if the producers do not pay the financial costs it imposes on society. Innovation can be a positive externality if pricing does not capture the full benefits that flow from innovators to the broader society. Externalities are a type of market failure.

Factor price equalization The process whereby trade generates a tendency for the prices of factors (capital or labour) to be equalized (a process predicted by the Stolper–Samuelson Theorem).

False consciousness A process through which the working class internalizes a misleading understanding of the true relationship between the individual and the economy, because the ideology of capitalism imposes its own understanding and, in the process of doing so, masks the objective exploitation experienced by the working class. A working class experiencing false consciousness will be led to believe that the capitalist system operates in its interests, whereas for Marx this could never be the case.

Feldstein–Horioka Puzzle In a world of unfettered capital mobility, savings will flow to those countries offering the highest interest rates, while investment will be financed from the lowest-cost source. Feldstein and Horioka, however, found in a 1980 study that national savings and domestic investment were highly correlated in sixteen OECD countries, suggesting the presence of segmented capital markets and low capital mobility.

Financial intermediaries Institutions that provide links between those with surplus savings and those who desire to use these funds for investment purposes.

Fiscal policies Government budgetary policies on taxation and expenditure.

Fixed exchange rate An exchange rate regime under which the value of a currency is tied to that of another currency, a basket of currencies, or another asset such as gold. Post-1945, the exchange rates of most currencies were valued at a specific amount of US dollars.

Foreign direct investment (FDI) The establishment by domestic firms of a foreign subsidiary, or their acquisition of a controlling interest in an existing foreign company.

Free riders Actors who fail to contribute appropriately to the cost of the goods or services from which they benefit.

Free trade area Agreements between two or more countries to remove tariff and non-tariff barriers on trade between themselves.

General Agreement on Tariffs and Trade (GATT) A 1947 agreement that became the principal component of the international trade regime following the failure of the international community to establish the International Trade Organization. Its provisions were incorporated into the World Trade Organization (WTO) when it was established in 1995.

Generalized System of Preferences (GSP) Non-reciprocal programmes of tariff preferences on selected goods for less developed countries introduced by industrialized countries after GATT in 1971 permitted a waiver of the MFN requirement to facilitate special and differential treatment for LDCs.

Gini coefficient A measure of income inequality devised by the Italian statistician, Corrado Gini. The Gini coefficient is a number between zero and one, where zero represents perfect equality (everyone has the same income), and one represents perfect inequality (one person has all the income, all others have zero). The Gini coefficient is calculated using the Lorenz curve, a graph showing the relationship between the percentage of households and the share of the country's income they receive.

Global Environment Facility (GEF) A fund established in 1991, jointly managed by the World Bank, the United Nations Development Programme, and the United Nations Environment Programme, which finances environmental projects in less developed economies.

Global value chains (GVCs) The sequence of activities involved in the production of a good or service through which technology is combined with material and labour inputs.

Gold exchange standard An international monetary system in which it is possible for central banks to convert their foreign exchange holdings into gold (one or more countries must guarantee that they will permit others to convert their currencies into gold, as the US did in the period from 1945 to 1971).

Gold standard A monetary system in which the money supply is linked directly to the country's holdings of gold; citizens are usually entitled to exchange banknotes for gold. An international gold standard is an international monetary system in which the value of all currencies is set in terms of a unit of gold, and settlement of trade imbalances occurs through the transfer of gold reserves.

Graduation The process by which less developed economies are removed from the list of countries given special trade benefits by industrialized countries once they reach a certain level of development.

Gross domestic product (GDP) The total value of goods and services produced by an economy in a specific time period.

Gross national product (GNP) Gross domestic product plus the income earned by domestic residents from investment abroad less the income earned by foreigners in the domestic market.

Heavily Indebted Poor Countries (HIPC) A grouping of the world's poorest countries, identified as those eligible for concessional assistance from the World Bank group's International Development Association and from the IMF's Poverty Reduction and Growth Facility that face an unsustainable debt situation after the full application of traditional debt relief mechanisms. A debt initiative for HIPC was proposed by the World Bank and the IMF in 1996.

Heckscher–Ohlin Model Countries will export those commodities that are intensive in the factor (land, labour, capital) in which they are best endowed.

Hegemonic stability Argument that liberal (open) international economic regimes are associated with the presence of a dominant state.

Import-substitution industrialization (ISI) Strategy pursued by less developed economies to promote industrialization by domestic production of goods previously imported (usually undertaken behind high levels of tariff protection).

Inclusive club goods Goods that can be withheld from those who do not pay for them, and whose consumption does not reduce their availability to other potential consumers.

Infant industry promotion Idea that recently established industries require protection until they are able to produce efficiently and withstand import competition from more advanced economies.

Interdependence A network of relationships among actors that is costly for any of the actors to break.

Intermediation The process whereby financial institutions link savers and investors of funds.

International Bank for Reconstruction and Development (World Bank) The original component of the World Bank group, created at the Bretton Woods conference in 1944. Subsequently, two other institutions, the International Finance Corporation (1956) and the International Development Association (1960) were added to the group. Most writers today simply refer to the group of institutions as the 'World Bank'.

International financial institutions (IFIs) the International Monetary Fund (IMF) and the World Bank.

International Trade Organization (ITO) Intended to be the third of the major post-war international economic institutions alongside the World Bank and the IMF, the ITO was stillborn when the US Congress failed to ratify the Havana Charter.

Intra-industry trade International trade in products from the same sector.

Keynesian economics A branch of economic theory associated with the work of John Maynard Keynes and his followers, suggesting that there is no automatic tendency for economies to reach an equilibrium position that sustains full employment, and that governments, through their manipulation of fiscal policies, can affect aggregate demand and reduce unemployment.

Laissez-faire An economic doctrine prescribing non-interference by the state in commercial, corporate, and competitive affairs, often associated with the dominance of market ideology. The literal translation from the French comes close to being an argument for allowing events to run their own course.

Least developed countries A UN-designated group of fifty low-income countries, membership of which is defined by per capita GDP under $750, weak human assets (a composite index of health, nutrition, and education indicators), and high economic vulnerability (a composite index based on instability of export earnings, dependence on a limited number of primary product exports, and overall size of the economy). The UN can 'graduate' countries from the category when they meet the thresholds of two of the three criteria (over $900 per capita GDP) for two successive years.

Lender of last resort A financial institution, usually the central bank, that is charged with the responsibility of providing loans to other financial institutions when they need an injection of cash—and no other institution is willing to lend to them.

Less developed countries (LDCs) A self-designated category at the WTO of countries that typically have relatively low per capita incomes, an undeveloped industrial base, and a substantial part of their population living in poverty. Often associated with the Group of 77 (G77), established on 15 June 1964 by seventy-seven developing countries signatories of the 'Joint Declaration of the Seventy-Seven Countries' issued at the end of the first session of the United Nations Conference on Trade and Development in Geneva. At the time of writing, the G77 has 130 members, including such relatively high-income economies as the Bahamas, Singapore, and South Korea.

Liquidity International liquidity comprises the total gold and foreign exchange reserves and Special Drawing Rights (that is, all international reserves acceptable to other countries) held by all countries in the international financial system.

Logrolling The practice whereby two or more legislators agree to trade their votes to support legislation in which they have no particular interest in order to gain support for legislation that they regard as more important; for example, financing of projects in their electoral districts.

Market failure A situation whereby a market does not achieve the optimal allocation of resources. Causes of market failure include the presence of public goods, externalities, and imperfect information.

Marshall Plan A US post-war programme to provide grants and loans to assist in the rebuilding of the economies of Europe and some European colonies.

Mercantilism Economic policies based on the premise that national wealth and power are best served by the state acting to increase exports and to run a balance of trade surplus (originally with the intention of accumulating precious metals).

Methodology A procedure or set of procedures used to study a subject matter.

Minilateralism Policy co-ordination among a small number of states.

Monetarism A branch of macroeconomic theory which holds that changes in the money supply affect aggregate demand for goods and services, and thus the rate of inflation.

Monetary policies Government policies on the money supply, the rate of interest, and the exchange rate.

Moral hazard A form of Market failure: the creation of a situation in which individuals or institutions are encouraged to act irresponsibly because of the guarantees (implicit or explicit) that others provide for them; for example, people with insurance may take greater risks than those without it, because they know they will receive compensation if they suffer adverse consequences from their behaviour.

Most-favoured nation principle (MFN) The principle of non-discrimination, enshrined in Article I of the GATT/WTO, that members should give all other members the most favourable trade treatment they offer to any member.

Multifibre Arrangement (MFA) A multilateral agreement (1974–94), a form of orderly marketing arrangement, limiting the exports of textiles and clothing by less developed countries to industrialized countries. Industrialized countries agreed to phase out the MFA over a ten-year period, as part of the Uruguay Round Agreements.

Multilateral Agreement on Investment (MAI) A proposal made by OECD members in 1995 for a multilateral agreement that would liberalize investment regimes, provide protection for foreign investors, and establish dispute settlement mechanisms. The talks on establishing an MAI collapsed in 1998, following disagreements among industrialized countries and opposition from many less developed countries and civil society groups.

Multilateralism Policy co-ordination by three or more states on the basis of principles that specify appropriate conduct for a class of actions.

Multinational corporation/Multinational enterprise (MNCs) *see* Transnational corporation

Nash Equilibrium A situation in game theory where all participants are pursuing their best possible strategy, given the strategies that other players have chosen; in other words, no player can improve his/her situation by changing their own strategy.

National treatment A GATT/WTO principle requiring members to offer foreign goods or services identical treatment in their markets to that they give to the same domestic good or service.

Neo-liberalism A political orientation that came to prominence in the 1980s, celebrating the desirability of market-based economic institutions and exposure to market ideology as a means of disciplining the population. It is often closely associated with policies of privatization and the retreat of the state from prominence in economic affairs.

New International Economic Order (NIEO) A list of demands by less developed economies in the 1970s that proposed a radical restructuring of international economic regimes.

Newly industrializing economy (NIE) term originally applied to the 'Gang of Four' economies of East Asia (Hong Kong, Korea, Singapore, Taiwan) that experienced rapid economic growth from the late 1960s. Subsequently sometimes applied to selected rapidly growing South East Asian and Latin American economies.

Non-tariff barriers (NTBs) (also Non-tariff measures (NTMs): A wide variety of official or unofficial devices (other than tariffs) that hinder imports into an economy; for example, quantitative restrictions, health regulations, customs procedures.

ODA Official Development Assistance, popularly referred to as foreign aid.

OEM Original equipment manufacturers. Originally used (primarily in the electronics industry) to describe a company manufacturing a product that was marketed under another company's brand name. Now also used (somewhat confusingly) to refer to companies that sell a final product under their own brand name but it is assembled from components manufactured by others; for example, Toyota, General Motors, and other auto assemblers are often referred to as OEMs.

Oligopoly An industry dominated by a few large suppliers.

Ontology The study of being, addressing the question of what is there; what are the essential features of an object.

Opportunism Decision-makers pursue their self-interest without regard for principles or the breaking of relationships with others based on trust.

Orderly marketing arrangement (OMA) An agreement between an importing country and one or more exporting countries whereby the latter pledge to limit their exports of particular products. Outlawed by the GATT Uruguay Round Agreements.

Pareto-optimal Outcomes where no actor can be better off without making others worse off. In Pareto-deficient situations, other outcomes could increase some actors' welfare without decreasing that of others.

Plaza Accord Agreement reached by the G5 at the Plaza Hotel in New York in 1985 for concerted intervention by central banks to produce a currency realignment that resulted in a depreciation of the US dollar against other major currencies.

Portfolio investment The acquisition of interest-bearing foreign securities (either government bonds or company stocks and shares) that do not in themselves give the investor management control over the foreign concern.

Private goods Goods and services that can be withheld from those who do not pay for them, and that cannot be used by others without additional production taking place.

Property rights The legal right of owners of resources to be paid for their usage; for example, fees paid to patent or copyright owners.

Public goods Goods that cannot be withheld from consumers who do not pay for them, and whose consumption does not reduce their availability to other consumers.

Purchasing power parity (PPP) A method of computing an appropriate exchange rate between currencies (rather than that determined by the market or fixed by governments), which rests on determining domestic purchasing power by calculating the price of a basket of goods in the two countries in local currencies. To compute the PPP exchange rate between the two currencies, one takes the ratio of the prices for the baskets of goods in local currencies. PPP exchange rates are often used as a means of presenting a more accurate comparison of standards of living across countries than those given by actual exchange rates.

Race to the bottom The idea that, in a globalized economy, some governments will attempt to increase their attractiveness to investors by offering minimal requirements on, for example, environmental and labour standards and taxation.

Reciprocity The principle in international trade that countries benefiting from trade liberalization by others should offer equivalent (but not necessarily identical) concessions in return.

Regime A set of international governing arrangements (including rules, norms, and procedures) that are intended to regularize the behaviour of state and non-state actors, and control its effects.

Rules of origin Regulations negotiated as part of free trade agreements that specify the conditions that goods must meet if they are to be considered as originating in a partner country (for example, that a specific share of the good's value must be added locally). Intended to prevent non-partner countries from transshipping goods to take advantage of the lower tariffs offered within a free trade agreement.

Safeguards Provisions enabling countries with problems in specific sectors or their economy more generally to seek temporary exemptions from some of their obligations in the trade regime.

Seigniorage The profit that results from the difference between the cost of producing and distributing money and the face value of that money. Originally, the difference between the face value of a coin and the cost of the metal that went into that coin.

Singapore issues The 1996 WTO ministerial meeting in Singapore began exploratory work on co-operation on policy harmonization in four areas: investment, competition, transparency in government procurement, and trade facilitation. These subsequently became known as the 'Singapore issues'.

Single undertaking The principle within the GATT/WTO that members must accept all parts of the agreement rather than signing on selectively to individual components.

Special and differential treatment Exemptions for less developed countries from some of the obligations imposed on other members of the trade regime.

Special Drawing Rights (SDR) An international reserve asset created by the International Monetary Fund in 1969. Over 30 billion SDRs have been created; these were distributed by the IMF to member countries in proportion to the size of their IMF quota. The SDR is valued in terms of a basket of sixteen major currencies.

Specific Factors Model Movement of factors of production to different uses following trade liberalization may be difficult: the effects of trade, therefore, contrary to the Stolper–Samuelson Theorem, may not benefit/harm different factors across various sectors but rather hurt/benefit *all* factors *within* the same industrial sector.

Statism An approach that treats the state as the principal actor. Characteristic not just of many realist theories of global political economy but also some that attempt to explain the economic success of North-East Asian economies.

Sterilization Efforts by monetary authorities to counter the impact of international monetary flows on domestic economic activity by issuing/selling financial instruments to reduce or increase the domestic money supply.

Stolper–Samuelson Theorem Trade benefits the owners of factors of production that are relatively abundant in an economy while lowering the returns to owners of relatively scarce factors; for example, trade for labour-rich countries such as China should benefit (their relatively abundant) labour.

Strategic trade policies Efforts by governments to promote domestic companies in international industries characterized by oligopoly through policies (for example, investment subsidies) intended to permit them to move strategically (for example, enable them to become early developers of a product).

Structural adjustment programmes (SAPs) These are often designed in association with the international financial institutions, and pursued by countries experiencing debt problems. They usually include privatization of assets, reductions in government expenditure to reduce budgetary deficits, trade liberalization, encouragement of foreign investment, and currency devaluation.

Sunk costs Costs that are difficult for investors to recover; for example, investment in physical infrastructure, plant, and machinery.

Supranational institutions International institutions to which states have ceded some of their sovereignty; for example, the European Union.

Swiss formula A method of reducing tariffs based on a mathematical equation, which results in higher tariffs being reduced more than lower ones. It was used in the Tokyo Round of GATT negotiations.

Terms of trade The price of a country's exports relative to the price of its imports.

Trade creation Where a preferential trade agreement leads to the replacement of domestic production by lower-cost imports from a party to the trade agreement.

Trade diversion Where a preferential trade agreement leads to the displacement of goods previously imported from a non-preferred trading partner by imports from a party to the preferred agreement (because these preferential imports now enter the local market at a reduced tariff).

Trade-Related Aspects of Intellectual Property (TRIPs) A Uruguay Round WTO agreement that establishes minimum levels of protection that governments must give to the intellectual property of fellow WTO members.

Trade-Related Investment Measures (TRIMs) The title of a Uruguay Round WTO agreement that prohibits governments from applying measures that discriminate against foreign companies or foreign products; for example, requirements that foreign investors must source a certain value of their inputs locally ('local content' requirements) or export a certain value of their output ('trade balancing' requirements).

Tragedy of the commons Garrett Hardin, in a paper published in *Science* in 1968, first put forward the idea that individuals rationally pursuing their self-interest where they have access to a freely available good (a 'commons') will inevitably act in a way that is collectively irrational; for example, through over-grazing a pasture.

Transaction costs The costs other than the monetary price that are involved in trading goods and services; for example, costs of search and information, bargaining and decision-making, and policing and enforcement. High transaction costs are often viewed as a significant example of externalities.

Transnational corporations (TNCs) (also Multinational enterprises) Companies that engage in Foreign direct investment; that is, which own, control, and manage assets in more than one country.

Triffin Dilemma Yale University economist Robert Triffin pointed out in a 1960 book that the Bretton Woods monetary system rested on the confidence of other countries in the gold exchange standard—that is, that they could convert their dollar holdings into gold—yet, the capacity of the US to guarantee this conversion was being undermined by dollar outflows that were the principal source of new liquidity in the system. If outflows stopped, the system would have insufficient liquidity; if they continued, confidence in the system would be undermined.

Two-level game Term coined by Robert Putnam to refer to negotiations in which governments must negotiate simultaneously at two levels: with domestic constituencies, and with one or more foreign partners.

Voluntary export restraint An agreement between an exporting and an importing country under which the exporting country agrees to limit the total (value or volume of) exports of particular products. Outlawed by the GATT Uruguay Round Agreements.

Washington Consensus (WC) Phrase coined by John Williamson to refer to the prevailing views held in the late 1980s and early 1990s by the international financial institutions and governments of most industrialized countries regarding the desirable policy agenda for less developed economies; for example, liberalization of their trade regimes, privatization of state-owned enterprises, and reduction of state intervention in the economy.

Other Useful Sources

Print

Bannock, G., Baxter, R. E., and Davis, E. (2003), *The Penguin Dictionary of Economics*, 7th edn (London: Penguin). Black, J. (2003), *A Dictionary of Economics*, 2nd edn (Oxford: Oxford University Press). Pearce, D. W. (1992), *The MIT Dictionary of Modern Economics*, 4th edn (Cambridge, MA: MIT Press).

Online

- Deardorff's Glossary of International Economics http://www-personal.umich.edu/~alandear/glossary
- Economics—Wikipedia, the free encyclopedia http://en.wikipedia.org/wiki/Economics
- *The Economist*'s Economics A–Z http://economist.com/research/Economics

References

Abbott, A. J., and De Vita, G. (2003), 'Another Piece in the Feldstein–Horioka Puzzle', *Scottish Journal of Political Economy*, 50/1: 68–89.

Abbott, K. W., and Snidal, D. (2000), 'Hard and Soft Law in International Governance', *International Organization*, 54/3: 421–56.

Abdelal, R. (2007), *Capital Rules: The Construction of Global Finance* (Cambridge, MA: Harvard University Press).

——, Blyth, M., and Parsons, C. (eds) (2010), *Constructing the International Economy* (Ithaca, NY: Cornell University Press).

Abernathy, F. H., Dunlop, J. T., Hammond, J. H., and Weil, D. (1999), *A Stitch in Time: Lean Retailing and the Transformation of Manufacturing* (Oxford: Oxford University Press).

Adler, M., Brunel, C., Hufbauer, G. C., and Schott, J. J. (2009), 'What's on the Table? The Doha Round as of August 2009', Working Paper 09-6 (Washington, DC: Peterson Institute for International Economics).

Aggarwal, V. K. (1985), *Liberal Protectionism: The International Politics of Organized Textile Trade* (Berkeley and Los Angeles, CA: University of California Press).

—— (1994), 'Comparing Regional Cooperation Efforts in Asia-Pacific and North America', in A. Mack and J. Ravenhill (eds), *Pacific Cooperation: Building Economic and Security Regimes in the Asia-Pacific Region* (Sydney: Allen & Unwin).

—— (ed.) (1998), *Institutional Designs for a Complex World: Bargaining, Linkages and Nesting* (Ithaca, NY: Cornell University Press).

—— (2001), 'Economics: International Trade', in P. J. Simmons and C. de Jonge Oudraat (eds), *Managing Global Issues: Lessons Learned* (Washington, DC: Carnegie Endowment for International Peace).

—— and Dupont, C. (1999), 'Goods, Games and Institutions', *International Political Science Review*, 20/4: 393–409.

—— —— (2002), ' "Goods, Games, and Institutions": A Reply', *International Political Science Review*, 23/4: 402–10.

Ali, S. H. (2004), *Mining, the Environment and Indigenous Development Conflicts* (Tucson, AZ: University of Arizona Press).

Alinsky, S. (1972), *Rules for Radicals: A Practical Primer for Realistic Radicals* (New York: Vintage Books).

Allen, J., and Thompson, G. F. (1997), 'Think Global, and Then Think Again: Economic Globalization in Context', *Area*, 29/3: 213–27.

Allen, M. (2003), 'Some Lessons from the Argentine Crisis: A Fund Staff View', in J. J. Teunissen and A. Akkerman (eds), *The Crisis That Was Not Prevented: Lessons for Argentina, the IMF, and Globalisation* (The Hague: FONDAD).

Almond, G. A. (1970), *Political Development: Essays in Heuristic Theory* (Princeton, NJ: Princeton University Press).

—— and Coleman, J. (eds) (1960), *The Politics of the Developing Areas* (Princeton, NJ: Princeton University Press).

—— and Powell, C. B. (1965), *Comparative Politics: A Developmental Agenda* (Boston, MA: Little, Brown).

Alt, J., and Gilligan, M. (1994), 'The Political Economy of Trading States', *Journal of Political Philosophy*, 2/2: 165–92.

Altman, R. C. (2009), 'The Great Crash, 2008', *Foreign Affairs*, 88/1: 2–14.

Amin, S. (1997), *Capitalism in the Age of Globalization* (London: Zed Books).

Amsden, A. (1989), *Asia's Next Giant: South Korea and Late Industrialization* (New York: Oxford University Press).

—— (1990), 'Third World Industrialization: "Global Fordism" or a New Model?', *New Left Review*, 182: 5–31.

Anderson, J. E., and van Wincoop, E. (2001), 'Gravity with Gravitas: A Solution to the Border Puzzle', NBER Working Paper 8079 (Cambridge, MA: National Bureau of Economic Research).

Andrews, D. M. (1994), 'Capital Mobility and State Autonomy: Toward a Structural Theory of International Monetary Relations', *International Studies Quarterly*, 38/2: 193–218.

—— (ed.) (2006), *International Monetary Power* (Ithaca, NY: Cornell University Press).

Araújo, S., and Martins, J. O. (2009), 'The Great Synchronisation: What do High-Frequency Statistics Tell us about the Trade Collapse?', 8 July, www.voxeu.org/index.php?q=node/3751

Archibugi, D. (ed.) (2003), *Debating Cosmopolitics* (London: Verso).

Arndt, H. W. (1987), *Economic Development: The History of an Idea* (Chicago, IL: University of Chicago Press).

Arndt, S. W., and Kierzkowski, S. (2001), *Fragmentation: New Production Patterns in the World Economy* (Oxford: Oxford University Press).

Arrow, K., Bolin, B., Costanza, R., Dasgupta, P., Folk, C., Holling, C. S., Jansson, B., Levin, S., Mäler, K., Perrings, C., and Pimentel, D. (1998), 'Economic Growth, Carrying Capacity and the Environment', *Science*, 268 (28 April 1995), in J. Dryzek and D. Schlosberg (eds), *Debating the Earth: The Environmental Politics Reader* (Oxford: Oxford University Press).

Arup, C. (2000), *The New World Trade Organization Agreements: Globalizing Law through Services and Intellectual Property* (Cambridge: Cambridge University Press).

Aslanbeigui, N., and Summerfield, G. (2000), 'The Asian Crisis, Gender and the International Financial Architecture', *Feminist Economics*, 6/3: 81–103.

Axelrod, R., and Keohane, R. O. (1986), 'Achieving Cooperation under Anarchy: Strategies and Institutions', *World Politics*, 38/1: 226–54.

Babb, S. (2009), *Behind the Development Banks: Washington Politics, World Poverty, and the Wealth of Nations* (Chicago, IL: University of Chicago Press).

Bachrach, P., and Baratz, M. S. (1970), *Power and Poverty: Theory and Practice* (New York: Oxford University Press).

Backhouse, R. (2002), *The Penguin History of Economics* (London: Penguin).

Baer, W. (1972), 'Import Substitution and Industrialization in Latin America: Experiences and Interpretations', *Latin American Research Review*, 7/1: 95–122.

Bair, J. (2005), 'Global Capitalism and Commodity Chains: Looking Back and Going Forward', *Competition & Change*, 9/2: 153–80.

Bairoch, P. (1996), 'Globalization Myths and Realities: One Century of External Trade and Foreign Investment', in R. Boyer and D. Drache (eds), *States against Markets: The Limits of Globalization* (London: Routledge).

Baker, A. (2006), *The Group of Seven: Finance Ministries, Central Banks and Global Financial Governance* (London/New York: Routledge).

Baldwin, C. Y., and Clark, K. B. (1997), 'Managing in an Age of Modularity', *Harvard Business Review*, 75/5: 84–93.

—— —— (2000), *Design Rules*, Vol. 1: *The Power of Modularity* (Boston, MA: MIT Press).

Baldwin, R. E. (1993), 'A Domino Theory of Regionalism', Working Paper 4465 (Cambridge, MA: National Bureau of Economic Research).

—— (1997), 'The Causes of Regionalism', *World Economy*, 20/7: 865–88.

—— (2006), 'Multilateralising Regionalism: Spaghetti Bowls as Building Blocs on the Path to Global Free Trade', *World Economy*, 29/11: 1451–518.

—— (2009), 'The Great Trade Collapse: What Caused it and What Does it Mean?', 27 November, www.voxeu.org/index.php?q=node/4304

Banerjee, A., and Zanghieri, P. (2003), 'A New Look at the Feldstein–Horioka Puzzle Using an Integrated Panel', CEPII Working Paper 2003–22 (Paris: Centre d'Etudes Prospectives et d'Informations Internationales).

—— Deaton, A., Lustig, N., Rogoff, K., with Hsu, E. (2006), 'An Evaluation of World Bank Research, 1998–2005' (Washington, DC: World Bank).

Barber, W. (1991), *A History of Economic Thought*, reprinted edn (London: Penguin).

Barlow, M. (2008), *Blue Covenant: The Global Water Crisis and the Coming Battle for the Right to Water* (New York: New Press).

Baron, H. (1988), *In Search of Florentine Civic Humanism: Essays on the Transition from Medieval to Modern Political Thought*, Vol. 1 (Princeton, NJ: Princeton University Press).

Barr, N. (1998), *The Economics of the Welfare State*, 3rd edn (Oxford: Oxford University Press).

Barry, P. L., and Phillips, T. (2006), 'Earth's Ozone Layer: Good News and a Puzzle', *Space and Earth Science*, 26 May, www.physorg.com/

Bauer, R. A., Pool, I., and Dexter, L. A. (1972), *American Business and Public Policy*, 2nd edn (Chicago, IL: Aldine Atherton).

Baxter, M., and Crucini, M. J. (1993), 'Explaining Saving–Investment Correlations', *American Economic Review*, 83/3: 416–36.

Bayoumi, T. (1990), 'Savings–Investment Correlations', *IMF Staff Papers*, 37: 360–87.

—— (1997), *Financial Integration and Real Activity* (Manchester: Manchester University Press).

—— and Rose, A. D. (1993), 'Domestic Savings and Intra-National Capital Flows', *European Economic Review*, 37/6: 1197–202.

Beason, R., and Weinstein, D. E. (1993), 'Growth, Economies of Scale, and Targeting in Japan, 1955–90', Harvard Institute for Economic Research Discussion Paper No. 1644 (Cambridge, MA: Harvard University).

Beck, U. (1992), *The Risk Society* (London: Sage).

Bekaert, G., Hodrick, R. J., and Zhang, X. (2005), 'International Stock Return Comovements', NBER Working Paper 11906 (Cambridge, MA: National Bureau of Economic Research).

Bello, W. (2009), *The Food Wars* (London and New York: Verso).

Benería, L. (2003), *Gender, Development, and Globalization: Economics As If All People Mattered* (New York: Routledge).

Benton, T., and Craib, I. (2001), *Philosophy of Social Science* (London: Routledge).

Berger, S. (2006), *How we Compete: What Companies around the World Are Doing to Make it in Today's Global Economy* (New York: Currency Doubleday).

—— and Dore, R. (eds) (1996), *National Diversity and Global Capitalism* (Ithaca, NY: Cornell University Press).

Bergsten, C. F. (1999), 'America and Europe: Clash of the Titans', *Foreign Affairs*, 78/2: 20–34.

Bernard, M., and Ravenhill, J. (1995), 'Beyond Product Cycles and Flying Geese: Regionalization, Hierarchy, and the Industrialization of East Asia', *World Politics*, 47/2: 171–209.

Bernhard, W., and Leblang, D. (1999), 'Democratic Institutions and Exchange Rate Commitments', *International Organization*, 53/1: 71–97.

Bernstein, H. (ed.) (1990), *The Food Question: Profits vs. People* (London: Earthscan).

Bhagwati, J. (1988), *Protectionism* (Cambridge, MA: MIT Press).

—— (1991), *The World Trading System at Risk* (New York: Harvester Wheatsheaf).

—— (1995), 'US Trade Policy: The Infatuation with Free Trade Areas', in J. N. Bhagwati and A. O. Krueger (eds), *The Dangerous Drift to Preferential Trade Agreements* (Washington, DC: AEI Press).

—— Brecher, R., Dinopoulos, E., and Srinivasan, T. N. (1987), 'Quid Pro Quo Foreign Investment and Welfare: A Political-Economy-Theoretic Model', *Journal of Development Economics*, 27/1–2: 127–38.

Bhattarai, M., and Hammig, M. (2001), 'Institutions and the Environmental Kuznets Curve for Deforestation: A Cross-country Analysis for Latin America, Africa and Asia', *World Development*, 29/6: 995–1010.

BIS (Bank for International Settlements) (2003), *International Banking and Financial Market Developments* (Geneva: BIS).

—— (2005), *Triennial Central Bank Survey: Foreign Exchange and Derivatives Market Activity in 2004* (Basel: BIS).

—— (2006), *OTC Derivatives Market Activity in the First Half of 2006* (Basel: BIS).

—— (2007), *Triennial Central Bank Survey: Foreign Exchange and Derivatives Market Activity in 2007* (Basel: BIS).

—— (2009), International Banking Statistics (June) (Basel: BIS).

BIS Quarterly Review (2001) (Geneva: Bank for International Settlements).

—— (2005) (Geneva: Bank for International Settlements).

—— (2009) (December) (Geneva: Bank for International Settlements).

Blackhurst, R. (1998), 'The Capacity of the WTO to Fulfill its Mandate', in A. O. Krueger (ed.), *The WTO as an International Organization* (Chicago, IL: University of Chicago Press).

Blanden, J., Gregg, P., and Machin, S. (2005), 'Intergenerational Mobility in Europe and North America', Centre for Economic Performance (London: London School of Economics).

Blaug, M. (1996), *Economic Theory in Retrospect*, 5th edn (Cambridge: Cambridge University Press).

Blonigen, B., and Feenstra, R. (1996), 'Protectionist Threats and Foreign Direct Investment', NBER Working Paper 5475 (Cambridge, MA: National Bureau of Economic Research).

Blustein, P. (2005), *And the Money Kept Rolling In (And Out): Wall Street, the IMF, and the Bankrupting of Argentina* (New York: Public Affairs).

Blyth, M. (2003), 'Same As It Never Was: Temporality and Typology in the Varieties of Capitalism', *Comparative European Politics*, 1/2: 215–26.

Bomberg, E. E., and Stubb, A. C. G. (2003), *The European Union: How Does it Work?* (Oxford: Oxford University Press).

Bordo, M. (2005), 'Historical Perspectives on Global Imbalances', NBER Working Paper 11383 (Cambridge, MA: National Bureau of Economic Research).

—— and Eichengreen, B. (2002), 'Crises Now and Then: What Lessons from the Last Era of Financial Globalization', NBER Working Paper W8716 (Cambridge, MA: National Bureau of Economic Research).

—— and Helbling, T. (2003), 'Have National Business Cycles become More Synchronized?', NBER Working Paper 10130 (Cambridge, MA: National Bureau of Economic Research).

—— Eichengreen, B., and Irwin, D. A. (1999), 'Is Globalization Today Really Different than Globalization a Hundred Years Ago?', NBER Working Paper 7195 (Cambridge, MA: National Bureau of Economic Research).

—— —— and Kim, J. (1998), 'Was There Really an Earlier Period of International Financial Integration Comparable to Today?', NBER Working Paper 6738 (Cambridge, MA: National Bureau of Economic Research).

Borjas, G. J. (1999), 'The Economic Analysis of Immigration', in O. Ashenfelter and D. Card (eds), *Handbook of Labor Economics* (Amsterdam: North-Holland).

—— Freeman, R., and Katz, L. (1996), 'Searching for the Effect of Immigration on the Labor Market', *American Economic Review*, 86/2: 247–51.

Borrus, M., and Zysman, J. (1997), 'Globalization with Borders: The Rise of Wintelism as the Future of Global Competition', *Industry and Innovation*, 4/2: 141–66.

Boughton, J. (2001), *Silent Revolution: The International Monetary Fund, 1979–1989* (Washington, DC: International Monetary Fund).

Bovard, J. (1991), *The Fair Trade Fraud* (New York: St. Martin's Press).

Boyer, R., and Drache, D. (eds) (1996), *States against Markets* (London: Routledge).

Brack, D., Calder, F., and Dolun, M. (2001), 'From Rio to Johannesburg: The Earth Summit and Rio+10', Royal Institute of International Affairs Briefing Paper New Series No. 19 (London: RIIA).

Brawley, M. (2005), *Power, Money, and Trade: Decisions that Shape Global Economic Relations* (Peterborough, Ont: Broadview Press).

Breitmeier, H., Young, O. R., and Zürn, M. (2006), *Analyzing International Environmental Regimes: From Case Study to Database* (Cambridge, MA: MIT Press).

Brenner, N. (1999), 'Beyond State-Centrism? Space, Territoriality and Geographic Scale in Globalization Studies', *Theory and Society*, 28/1: 39–78.

—— (2004), *New State Spaces: Urban Governance and the Rescaling of Statehood* (Oxford: Oxford University Press).

Brewer, T. L., and Young, S. (1998), *The Multilateral Investment System and Multinational Enterprises* (Oxford: Oxford University Press).

Broad, R., and Cavanagh, J. (2008), *Development Redefined: How the Market Met Its Match* (Boulder, CO: Paradigm Publishers).

Broadbent, J. (1998), *Environmental Politics in Japan: Networks of Power and Protest* (Cambridge: Cambridge University Press).

Brogger, T. (2008), 'Europe Scrambles as Iceland's Banks Fail', *Bloomberg.com*, 9 October, retrieved 27 April 2009 from http://www.nationalpost.com/story-printer.html?id=870988

Broz, J. L., and Frieden, J. A. (2001), 'The Political Economy of International Monetary Relations', *Annual Review of Political Science*, 4/1: 317–43.

Brune, N., and Garrett, G. (2005), 'The Globalization Rorschach Test: International Economic Integration, Inequality, and the Role of Government', *Annual Review of Political Science*, 8: 399–423.

Bryant, R. C. (2003), *Turbulent Waters: Cross-Border Finance and International Governance* (Washington, DC: Brookings Institution).

Burch, K., and Denemark, R. A. (1997), *Constituting International Political Economy* (Boulder, CO: Lynne Rienner).

Burg, J. (2003), 'The World Summit on Sustainable Development: Empty Talk or Call to Action?', *Journal of Environment and Development*, 12/1: 111–20.

Burki, S. J., Perry, G. E., and Dillinger, W. R. (1999), *Beyond the Center: Decentralizing the State* (Washington, DC: World Bank).

Burtless, G., Lawrence, R. Z., Litan, R. E., and Shapiro, R. J. (1998), *Globaphobia: Confronting Fears about Free Trade* (Washington, DC: Brookings Institution).

Busch, A. (2000), 'Unpacking the Globalization Debate: Approaches, Evidence and Data', in C. Hay and D. Marsh (eds), *Demystifying Globalization* (Basingstoke: Palgrave).

Buzan, B., Held, D., and McGrew, A. (1998), 'Realism Versus Cosmopolitanism: A Debate', *Review of International Studies*, 24/3: 387–98.

Cai, F., and Warnock, F. E. (2006), 'International Diversification at Home and Abroad', NBER Working Paper 12220 (Cambridge, MA: National Bureau of Economic Research).

Calleo, D. (1976), 'The Historiography of the Interwar Period: Reconsiderations', in B. Rowland (ed.), *Balance of Power or Hegemony: The Interwar Monetary System* (New York: New York University Press).

—— (1987), *Beyond American Hegemony* (New York: Basic Books).

Callinicos, A. (2003), *An Anti-Capitalist Manifesto* (Cambridge: Polity Press).

Calvo, G. A., and Talvi, E. (2005), 'Sudden Stop, Financial Factors and Economic Collapse in Latin America: Learning from Argentina and Chile', NBER Working Paper 11153 (Cambridge, MA: National Bureau of Economic Research).

Cameron, D. R. (1978), 'The Expansion of the Public Economy: A Comparative Analysis', *American Political Science Review*, 72/4: 1243–61.

Caner, A., and Wolff, E. (2004), 'Asset Poverty in the United States, 1984–1999', *Challenge: The Magazine of Economic Affairs*, 47/1: 5–52.

Capling, A., and Nossal, K. R. (2009), 'The Contradictions of Regionalism in North America', in R. Fawn (ed.), *Globalising the Regional, Regionalising the Global* (Cambridge: Cambridge University Press).

Carlos, A. M., and Nicholas, S. (1988), 'Giants of an Earlier Capitalism: The Chartered Trading Companies as Modern Multinationals', *Business History Review*, 62/Autumn: 398–419.

Carr, E. H. (1939/1946), *The Twenty Years' Crisis 1919–1939: An Introduction to the Study of International Relations*, 2nd edn (London: Macmillan).

Carrere, C., and Schiff, M. (2004), 'On the Geography of Trade: Distance is Alive and Well', World Bank Policy Research Working Paper 3206 (Washington, DC: World Bank).

Carson, R. (1962), *Silent Spring* (Boston, MA: Houghton Mifflin).

Carver, T., and Thomas, P. (1995), *Rational Choice Marxism* (London: Macmillan).

Cashin, P., McDermott, C. J., and Scott, A. (1999), 'Booms and Slumps in World Commodity Prices', IMF Working Paper 99/155 (Washington, DC: IMF).

Cashore, B., Auld, G., and Newsom, D. (2004), *Governing Through Markets: Forest Certification and the Emergence of Non-state Authority* (New Haven, CT: Yale University Press).

Castells, M. (1996), *The Rise of the Network Society* (Oxford: Basil Blackwell).

—— (1997), *The Power of Identity* (Oxford: Basil Blackwell).

—— (1998), *End of the Millennium* (Oxford: Basil Blackwell).

—— (2000), *The Rise of the Network Society* (Oxford: Basil Blackwell).

Castles, S., and Miller, M. (2002), *The Age of Global Migration* (Basingstoke: Palgrave).

Cavanagh, J., and Mander, J., (eds) (2004), *Alternatives to Economic Globalization: A Better World is Possible*, 2nd edn (San Francisco, CA: Berrett-Koehler).

Caves, R. E. (1982), *Multinational Enterprise and Economic Analysis* (Cambridge: Cambridge University Press).

Centre for Economic Policy Reform (2002), 'Making Sense of Globalization', CEPR Policy Paper 8 (Paris: CEPR).

Cerny, P. G. (1994), 'The Dynamics of Financial Globalization: Technology, Market Structure, and Policy Response', *Policy Sciences*, 27/4: 319–42.

—— (1995), 'Globalization and the Changing Logic of Collective Action', *International Organization*, 49/4: 595–625.

—— (1997), 'Paradoxes of the Competition State: The Dynamics of Political Globalization', *Government and Opposition*, 32/2: 251–74.

Chandler, A. D. (1977), *The Visible Hand: The Managerial Revolution in American Business* (Cambridge, MA/London: Harvard University Press).

Chang, H.-J., (2002), *Kicking Away the Ladder: Development Strategy in Historical Perspective* (London: Anthem).

—— (2006), *The East Asian Development Experience: The Miracle, the Crisis and the Future* (New York: Zed Books).

Chase, K. A. (2003), 'Economic Interests and Regional Trading Arrangements: The Case of AFTA', *International Organization*, 57/1: 137–74.

—— (2005), *Trading Blocs: States, Firms, and Regions in the World Economy* (Ann Arbor, MI: University of Michigan Press).

Chatterjee, P., and Finger, M. (1994), *The Earth Brokers: Power, Politics and World Development* (London: Routledge).

Chen, S., and Ravallion, M. (2004), 'How Have the World's Poorest Fared Since the Early 1980s?', *World Bank Research Observer*, 19/2: 141–69.

—— —— (2008), 'The Developing World is Poorer than we Thought, but no Less Successful in the Fight against Poverty', World Bank Policy Research Working Paper 4703 Washington, DC: World Bank, August).

Chenery, H., Bowen, I., and Svikhart, B. (1974), *Redistribution with Growth: Policies to Improve Income Distribution in Developing Countries in the Context of Economic Growth* (Oxford: Oxford University Press).

Chin, G., and Helleiner, E. (2008), 'China as a Creditor: A Rising Financial Power?', *Journal of International Affairs*, 62/1: 87–102.

China News Digest (2006), 'Survey of China's Second-Tier Cities', 15 June.

Chiswick, B. R., and Hatton, T. J. (2003), 'International Migration and Integration of Labor Markets', in M. D. Bordo, A. M. Taylor, and J. G. Williamson (eds), *Globalization in Historical Perspective* (Chicago, IL: Chicago University Press).

Chortareas, G. E., and Pelagidis, T. (2004), 'Trade Flows: A Facet of Regionalism or Globalisation?', *Cambridge Journal of Economics*, 28/2: 253–71.

Citrin, J., Green, D., Muste, C., and Wong, C. (1997), 'Public Opinion toward Immigration Reform: The Role of Economic Motivations', *Journal of Politics*, 59/3: 858–81.

Clapp, J. (2001), *Toxic Exports: The Transfer of Hazardous Wastes from Rich to Poor Countries* (Ithaca, NY: Cornell University Press).

—— (2002), 'What the Pollution Havens Debate Overlooks', *Global Environmental Politics*, 2/2: 11–19.

—— and Fuchs, D., (eds) (2009), *Corporate Power in Global Agrifood Governance* (Cambridge, MA: MIT Press).

Clark, W. R., and Hallerberg, M. (2000), 'Strategic Interaction between Monetary and Fiscal Actors under Full Capital Mobility', *American Political Science Review*, 94/2: 323–46.

—— and Reichert, U. N. (1998), 'International and Domestic Constraints on Political Business Cycles in OECD Economies', *International Organization*, 52/1: 87–120.

Cline, W. R. (ed.) (1983), *Trade Policy in the 1980s* (Washington, DC: Institute for International Economics).

Club of Rome (authors D. H. Meadows, D. L. Meadows, W. W. Behrens, and J. Randers) (1972), *The Limits to Growth* (New York: Universe Books).

Coakley, J., Fuertes, A.-M., and Spagnolo, F. (2004), 'Is the Feldstein–Horioka Puzzle History?', *The Manchester School*, 72/5: 569–90.

—— Kulasi, F., and Smith, R. (1998), 'The Feldstein–Horioka Puzzle and Capital Mobility: A Review', *International Journal of Finance and Economics*, 3/2: 169–88.

Coase, R. H. (1937), 'The Nature of the Firm', *Economica*, 4/16: 386–405.

—— (1960), 'The Problem of Social Cost', *Journal of Law and Economics*, 3: 1–44.

Coe, D. T., Subramanian, A., Tamirisa, N. T., and Bhavnani, R. (2002), 'The Missing Globalization Puzzle', IMF Working Paper No. 02/171 (Washington, DC: IMF).

Cohen, B. (2003), 'Can the Euro Ever Challenge the Dollar?', *Journal of Common Market Studies*, 41/4: 575–95.

—— (2007), 'The Transatlantic Divide: Why are American and British IPE so Different?', *Review of International Political Economy*, 14/2: 197–219.

—— (2008a), *Global Monetary Governance* (London: Routledge).

—— (2008b), *International Political Economy: An Intellectual History* (Princeton, NJ: Princeton University Press).

—— (2008c), 'The International Monetary System: Diffusion and Ambiguity', *International Affairs*, 84/3: 455–70.

Cohen, B. (2009), 'Striking a Nerve', *Review of International Political Economy*, 16/1: 136–43.

Cohen, J., and Centeno, M. (2006), 'Neoliberalism and Patterns of Economic Performance, 1980–2000', *Annals of the American Academy of Political and Social Sciences*, 606/1: 32–67.

Colander, D. (2001), *The Lost Art of Economics: Essays on Economics and the Economics Profession* (Cheltenham: Edward Elgar).

Condliffe, J. B. (1950), *The Commerce of Nations* (New York: W. W. Norton).

Conybeare, J. A. C. (1980), 'International Organization and the Theory of Property Rights', *International Organization*, 34/3: 307–34.

——(1984), 'Public Goods, Prisoners' Dilemmas and the International Political Economy', *International Studies Quarterly*, 28/1: 5–22.

Cooke, W. N., and Noble, D. S. (1998), 'Industrial Relations Systems and US Foreign Direct Investment Abroad', *British Journal of Industrial Relations*, 36/4: 581–609.

Cooper, A., and Momani, B. (2005), 'Negotiating out of Argentina's Financial Crisis: Segmenting the International Creditors', *New Political Economy*, 10/3: 305–20.

Cooper, R. N. (1968), *The Economics of Interdependence* (New York: McGraw-Hill).

——(1972), 'Economic Interdependence and Foreign Policy in the Seventies', *World Politics*, 24/2: 159–81.

——(1975), 'Prolegomena to the Choice of an International Monetary System', *International Organization*, 29/1: 63–97.

Corea, G., and Kiiski, S. (2001), 'Trends in Income Distribution in the Post-World War II Period', Discussion Paper 89 (Helsinki: WIDER).

Cornes, R., and Sandler, T. (1996), *The Theory of Externalities, Public Goods, and Club Goods*, 2nd edn (New York: Cambridge University Press).

Cox, R. W. (1981), 'Social Forces, States and World Orders: Beyond International Relations Theory', *Millennium: Journal of International Studies*, 10/2: 126–55.

——(1987), *Production, Power, and World Order: Social Forces in the Making of History* (New York: Columbia University Press).

——(2000), 'Explaining Business Support for Regional Trade Agreements', in J. A. Frieden and D. A. Lake (eds), *International Political Economy: Perspectives on Global Wealth and Power*, 4th edn (New York: St. Martin's Press).

——with Sinclair, T. (1996), *Approaches to World Order* (Cambridge: Cambridge University Press).

Crafts, N., and Venables, A. J. (2003), 'Globalization in History: A Geographical Perspective', in M. D. Bordo, A. M. Taylor, and J. G. Williamson (eds), *Globalization in Historical Perspective* (Chicago, IL: Chicago University Press).

Craig, D., and Porter, D. (2003), 'Poverty Reduction Strategy Papers: A New Convergence', *World Development*, 31/1: 53–69.

Crane, G. (1998), 'Economic Nationalism: Bringing the Nation Back In', *Millennium: Journal of International Studies*, 27/1: 55–75.

Crawford, J.-A., and Florentino, R. V. (2005), 'The Changing Landscape of Regional Trade Agreements', WTO Discussion Paper 8 (Geneva: World Trade Organization).

Croome, J. (1995), *Reshaping the World Trading System: A History of the Uruguay Round* (Geneva: World Trade Organization).

Crouch, C., and Streeck, W. (1997), 'Introduction: The Future of Capitalist Diversity', in C. Crouch and W. Streeck (eds), *Political Economy of Modern Capitalism* (London: Sage).

Crystal, J. (1994), 'The Politics of Capital Flight: Exit and Exchange Rates in Latin America', *Review of International Studies*, 20/2: 131–47.

——(2003), *Unwanted Company: Foreign Investment in American Industries* (Ithaca, NY: Cornell University Press).

Cumings, B. (1984), 'The Origins and Development of the Northeast Asian Political Economy: Industrial Sectors, Product Cycles, and Political Consequences', *International Organization*, 38/1: 1–40.

Cutler, A. C. (2003), *Private Power and Global Authority* (Cambridge: Cambridge University Press).

Dahl, R. A. (1963), *Modern Political Analysis* (Englewood Cliffs, NJ: Prentice-Hall).

Daly, H. (1993), 'The Perils of Free Trade', *Scientific American*, November: 50–7.

——(1996), *Beyond Growth: The Economics of Sustainable Development* (Boston, MA: Beacon Press).

——(2002), 'Uneconomic Growth and Globalization in a Full World', *Natur und Kultur*, 2/2: 3–22.

Dam, K. W. (1970), *The GATT: Law and International Economic Organization* (Chicago, IL: University of Chicago Press).

Dash, K., Cronin, P., and Goddard, R. (2003), 'Introduction', in R. Goddard, P. Cronin, and K. Dash (eds), *International Political Economy: State–Market Relations in a Changing Global Order*, 2nd edn (Basingstoke: Palgrave).

Dauvergne, P. (1997), *Shadows in the Forest: Japan and the Politics of Timber in Southeast Asia* (Cambridge, MA: MIT Press).

——(1999), 'Asia's Environment after the 1997 Financial Meltdown: The Need of a Regional Response', *Asian Perspective: A Journal of Regional and International Affairs*, 23/3: 53–77.

——(2001), *Loggers and Degradation in the Asia-Pacific: Corporations and Environmental Management* (Cambridge: Cambridge University Press).

——(2005), 'The Environmental Challenge to Loggers in the Asia-Pacific: Corporate Practices in Informal Regimes of Governance', in D. L. Levy and P. J. Newell (eds), *The Business of Global Environmental Governance* (Cambridge, MA: MIT Press).

——(2008), *The Shadows of Consumption: Consequences for the Global Environment* (Cambridge, MA: MIT Press).

Davey, W. J. (2000), 'The WTO Dispute Settlement System', *Journal of International Economic Law*, 3: 15–18.

Deagon, B. (2006), 'Electronics—Contract Manufacturing', *Investor's Business Daily*, 17 April.

Deaton, A. (2010), 'Price Indices, Inequality and the Measurement of World Poverty', Presidential Address, American Economic Association, Atlanta, 17 January.

Deaton, A., and Heston, A. (2009), 'Understanding PPPs and PPP-based National Accounts', NBER Working Paper 14499 (Cambridge, MA: National Bureau of Economic Research).

De Cecco, M. (2009), 'From Monopoly to Oligopoly: Lessons from the Pre-1914 Experience', in E. Helleiner and J. Kirshner (eds), *The Future of the Dollar* (Ithaca, NY: Cornell University Press).

De Goede, M. (2000), 'Mastering Lady Credit: Discourses of Financial Crisis in Historical Perspective', *International Feminist Journal of Politics*, 2/1: 58–81.

De Gregorio, J. (2001), 'Something for Everyone: Chilean Exchange Rate Policy Since 1960', in J. Frieden, P. Ghezzi, and E. Stein (eds), *The Currency Game: Exchange Rate Politics in Latin America* (New York: Inter-American Development Bank).

Deibert, R. (1997), *Parchment, Printing and Hypermedia* (Ithaca, NY: Cornell University Press).

de la Merced, M. J., and Sorkin, A. R. (2010), 'Report Details How Lehman Hid its Woes', *The New York Times*, 11 March, retrieved from http://www.nytimes.com/2010/03/12/business/12lehman.html?th=&emc=th&pagewanted= print.

De Marchi, N. (1999), 'Adam Smith's Accommodation of "Altogether Endless" Desires', in M. Berg and H. Clifford (eds), *Consumers and Luxury: Consumer Culture in Europe, 1650–1850* (Manchester: Manchester University Press).

Desai, P. (2003), *Financial Crisis, Contagion, and Containment* (Princeton, NJ: Princeton University Press).

Destler, I. M. (1995), *American Trade Politics*, 3rd edn (Washington, DC: Institute for International Economics).

——and Balint, P. (1999), *The New Politics of American Trade: Trade, Labor, and the Environment* (Washington, DC: Institute for International Economics).

——and Henning, R. C. (1989), *Dollar Politics: Exchange Rate Policymaking in the US* (Washington, DC: Institute for International Economics).

Diamond, J. M. (2005), *Collapse: How Societies Choose to Fail or Succeed* (New York: Viking).

Dicken, P. (2003), *Global Shift: Reshaping the Global Economic Map in the 21st Century*, 4th edn (London: Sage).

Diebold, W. (1952), *The End of the GATT* (Princeton, NJ: Princeton University Press).

Dikhanov, Y., and Ward, M. (2003), 'Evolution of the Global Distribution of Income in 1970–99', Proceedings of the Global Poverty Workshop, Initiative for Policy Dialogue, Columbia University, New York.

DiMento, J. F. C., and Doughman, P. M. (eds) (2007), *Climate Change: What it Means for us, our Children, and our Grandchildren* (Cambridge, MA: MIT Press).

Dinda, S. (2004), 'Environmental Kuznets Curve Hypothesis: A Survey', *Ecological Economics*, 49/4: 431–55.

Dittmer, L., and Yu, G. T. (2010), *China, the Developing World, and the New Global Dynamic* (Boulder, CO: Lynne Rienner).

Dooley, M. P., Folkerts-Landau, D., and Garber, P. (2003), 'An Essay on the Revived Bretton Woods System', NBER Working Paper 9971 (Cambridge, MA: National Bureau of Economic Research).

Doornbos, M. (2001), ' "Good Governance": The Rise and Decline of a Policy Metaphor?', *Journal of Development Studies*, 37/6: 93–108.

dos Santos, T. (1970), 'The Structure of Dependence', *American Economic Review*, 60/2: 231–36.

Downs, G. W., and Rocke, D. M. (1995), *Optimal Imperfection? Domestic Uncertainty and Institutions in International Relations* (Princeton, NJ: Princeton University Press).

Dowrick, S., and DeLong, J. B. (2003), 'Globalization and Convergence', in M. D. Bordo, A. M. Taylor, and J. G. Williamson (eds), *Globalization in Historical Perspective* (Chicago, IL: Chicago University Press).

——and Akmal, M. (2005), 'Contradictory Trends in Global Income Inequality: A Tale of Two Biases', *Review of Income and Wealth*, 51/2: 201–29.

Dressler, A. E., and Parson, E. A. (2006), *The Science and Politics of Global Climate Change* (Cambridge: Cambridge University Press).

Drezner, D. W. (2007), *All Politics is Global: Explaining International Regulatory Regimes* (Princeton, NJ: Princeton University Press).

——(2009), 'Bad Debts: Assessing China's Financial Influence in Great Power Politics', *International Security*, 34/2: 7–45.

Dryzek, J. (2006), *Deliberative Global Politics: Discourse and Democracy in a Divided World* (Cambridge: Polity Press).

Duchacek, I. D. (1990), 'Perforated Sovereignties: Towards a Typology of New Actors in International Relations', in H. J. Michelman and P. Soldatos (eds), *Federalism and International Relations* (Oxford: Oxford University Press).

Duffield, J. S. (2007), 'What Are International Institutions?', *International Studies Review*, 9/1: 1–22.

Dunne, T. (2001), 'Liberalism', in J. Baylis and S. Smith (eds), *The Globalization of World Politics*, 2nd edn (Oxford: Oxford University Press).

Dunning, J. H. (1981), *International Production and the Multinational Enterprise* (London: Allen & Unwin).

——(1988), 'The Eclectic Paradigm of International Production: An Update and Some Possible Extensions', *Journal of International Business Studies*, 19/1: 1–32.

——(1993), *Multinational Enterprises and the Global Economy* (Wokingham: Addison-Wesley).

——(2000), 'The New Geography of Foreign Direct Investment', in N. Woods (ed.), *The Political Economy of Globalization* (Basingstoke: Palgrave).

Dupont, C. (1998), 'European Integration and APEC: The Search for Institutional Blueprints', in V. K. Aggarwal and C. Morrison (eds), *Asia-Pacific Crossroads: Regime Creation and the Future of APEC* (New York: St. Martin's Press).

——and Hefeker, C. (2001), 'Integration Linkages: Between Trade-Offs and Spillovers', Paper presented at the Fourth Pan-European IR conference, Canterbury, United Kingdom, 8–10 September.

Durbin, A., and Welch, C. (2002), 'The Environmental Movement and Global Finance', in J. A. Scholte (ed.), *Civil Society and Global Finance* (London: Routledge).

Easterbrook, G. (1995), *A Moment on the Earth: The Coming Age of Environmental Optimism* (New York: Penguin).

ECLA (Economic Commission for Latin America) (2001), *Panorama Social De America Latina 2000–01* (Santiago: ECLA (CEPAL)).

——(2002), *Globalization and Development* (Santiago: ECLA (CEPAL)).

ECLAC (UN Economic Commission for Latin America and the Caribbean) (1995), *Policies to Improve Linkages with the Global Economy* (Santiago: ECLAC).

——(2002), *Preliminary Overview of the Economies of Latin America and the Caribbean, 2002* (Santiago: United Nations).

——(2008), *Social Panorama of Latin America: Briefing Paper* (Santiago: ECLAC).

Economist (2003), 'Special Report', 20 September.

Edward, P. (2006*a*), 'Examining Inequality: Who Really Benefits from Global Growth?', *World Development,* 34/10: 1667–95.

——(2006*b*), 'The Ethical Poverty Line: A Moral Quantification of Absolute Poverty', *Third World Quarterly*, 27/2: 377–93.

Edwards, S. (2005), 'Capital Controls, Sudden Stops and Current Account Reversals', NBER Working Paper 11170 (Cambridge, MA: National Bureau of Economic Research).

Ehrlich, P. (1968), *The Population Bomb* (New York: Sierra Club–Ballantine).

Eichengreen, B. J. (ed.) (1985), *The Gold Standard in Theory and History* (New York: Methuen).

——(1992), *Golden Fetters: The Gold Standard and the Great Depression: 1919–1939* (New York: Oxford University Press).

——(1996), *Globalizing Capital: A History of the International Monetary System* (Princeton, NJ: Princeton University Press).

——(2002), *Financial Crises and What to Do about them* (Oxford: Oxford University Press).

——(2003), *Capital Flows and Crises* (Cambridge, MA: MIT Press).

——(2009), 'Out of the Box Thoughts about the International Financial Architecture', IMF Working Paper No. 09/116 (Washington, DC: International Monetary Fund).

——and O'Rourke, K. H. (2009), 'A Tale of Two Depressions', 1 September, www.voxeu.org/index.php?q=node/3421

————(2010), 'A Tale of Two Depressions: What Do the New Data Tell us? February 2010 Update', 8 March, retrieved 21 March 2010, from http://www.voxeu.org/index.php?q=node/3421

Elliott, L. (1998), *The Global Politics of the Environment* (New York: New York University Press).

Elson, D. (1989), 'How is Structural Adjustment Affecting Women?', *Development*, 1: 67–74.

——(1992), 'Male Bias in Structural Adjustment', in H. Afshar and C. Dennis (eds), *Women and Adjustment Policies in the Third World* (London: Macmillan).

——(ed.) (1995), *Male Bias in the Development Process* (Manchester: Manchester University Press).

Encarnation, D. J. (ed.) (1999), *Japanese Multinationals in Asia: Regional Operations in Comparative Perspective* (New York/Oxford: Oxford University Press).

Enright, S., Scott, E. E., and Chang, K. (2005), *Regional Powerhouse: The Greater Pearl River Delta and the Rise of China* (Singapore: John Wiley).

Epstein, G. (1996), 'International Capital Mobility and the Scope for National Economic Management', in R. Boyer and D. Drache (eds), *States against Markets: The Limits of Globalization* (London: Routledge).

Ernst, D. (2006), 'Searching for a New Role in East Asian Regionalization: Japanese Production Networks in the Electronics Industry', in P. J. Katzenstein and T. Shiraishi (eds), *Beyond Japan: The Dynamics of East Asian Regionalism* (Ithaca, NY/London: Cornell University Press).

——and Ravenhill, J. (2000), 'Convergence and Diversity: How Globalization Reshapes Asian Production Networks', in M. Borrus, D. Ernst, and S. Haggard (eds), *International*

Production Networks in Asia: Rivalry or Riches? (London: Routledge).

Espenshade, T. J., and Calhoun, C. A. (1993), 'An Analysis of Public Opinion toward Undocumented Immigration', *Population Research and Policy Review*, 12: 189–224.

Esping-Andersen, G. (1996*a*), 'After the Golden Age? Welfare State Dilemmas in a Global Economy?', in G. Esping-Andersen (ed.), *Welfare States in Transition: National Adaptations in Global Economies* (London: Sage).

—— (1996*b*), 'Positive-Sum Solutions in a World of Trade-Offs', in G. Esping-Andersen (ed.), *Welfare States in Transition: National Adaptations in Global Economies* (London: Sage).

Esty, D. C. (1994), *Greening the GATT: Trade, Environment and the Future* (Washington, DC: Institute for International Economics).

—— and Winston, A. S. (2009), *Green to Gold: How Smart Companies Use Environmental Strategy to Innovate, Create Value, and Build Competitive Advantage*, rev. and updated edn (Hoboken, NJ: John Wiley).

European Commission (1990), 'One Market, One Money', *European Economy*, 44.

—— (2007), *European Economy*, No. 3 (Brussels: DG for Economic and Financial Affairs).

Evans, J. W. (1971), *The Kennedy Round in American Trade Policy: The Twilight of the GATT* (Cambridge, MA: Harvard University Press).

Evans, P. B. (1979), *Dependent Development: The Alliance of Multinational, State, and Local Capital in Brazil* (Princeton, NJ: Princeton University Press).

—— Jacobson, H. K., and Putnam, R. D. (eds) (1993), *Double-Edged Diplomacy: International Bargaining and Domestic Politics* (Berkeley and Los Angeles, CA: University of California Press).

FAO (Food and Agriculture Organization) (2008), *The State of Food Insecurity in the World 2008: High Food Prices and Food Security-Threats and Opportunities* (Rome: FAO).

—— (2009), 'More People Than Ever Are Victims of Hunger', News Release, www.fao.org/fileadmin/user_upload/newsroom/docs/Press%20release%20june-en.pdf

Feldstein, M. (1983), 'Domestic Savings and International Capital Movements in the Long Run and the Short Run', *European Economic Review*, 21: 139–51.

—— and Bacchetta, P. (1991), 'National Saving and International Investment', in D. B. Bernheim and J. B. Shoven (eds), *National Saving and Economic Performance* (Chicago, IL: Chicago University Press).

—— and Horioka, C. (1980), 'Domestic Savings and International Capital Flows', *Economic Journal*, 90/358: 314–29.

Fernandez, R., and Portes, J. (1998), 'Returns to Regionalism: An Analysis of Nontraditional Gains from Regional Trade Agreements', *World Bank Economic Review*, 12/2: 197–220.

Ferrantino, M. (1997), 'International Trade, Environmental Quality and Public Policy', *World Economy*, 20/1: 43–72.

Fewsmith, J. (2001), *China Since Tiananmen* (Cambridge: Cambridge University Press).

Financial Times (2006), 21 December: 1.

Findlay, R., and O'Rourke, K. H. (2007), *Power and Plenty: Trade, War, and the World Economy in the Second Millennium* (Princeton, NJ: Princeton University Press).

Fine, B. (2001), 'Neither the Washington nor the Post-Washington Consensus: An Introduction', in B. Fine, C. Lapavitsas and J. Pincus (eds), *Development Policy in the Twenty-First Century: Beyond the Post-Washington Consensus* (London: Routledge).

Finger, J. M., and Nogués, J. J. (2002), 'The Unbalanced Uruguay Round Outcome: The New Areas in Future WTO Negotiations', *The World Economy*, 25/3: 321–40.

Firebaugh, G. (2003), *The New Geography of Global Income Inequality* (Cambridge, MA: Harvard University Press).

Fischer, A. M. (2010), 'Towards Genuine Universalism within Contemporary Development Policy', *IDS Bulletin*, 41/1: 36–44.

Fischer, C., and Mattson, G. (2009), 'Is America Fragmenting?', *Annual Review of Sociology*, 35/1, 435–55.

Fischer, S. (2000), *On the Need for an International Lender of Last Resort* (Princeton, NJ: International Economics Section, Department of Economics, Princeton University).

Flandreau, M., and Zumer, F. (2004), *The Making of Global Finance, 1880–1913* (Paris: OECD Development Centre).

Fleischacker, S. (2004), *On Adam Smith's Wealth of Nations: A Philosophical Companion* (Princeton, NJ: Princeton University Press).

Foroutan, F. (1998), 'Does Membership in a Regional Preferential Trade Arrangement Make a Country More or Less Protectionist?', *World Economy*, 21/3: 305–36.

Franco, G., (1996), President of Brazil's central bank during the 1990s, *Veja*, 15 November.

Frank, A. G. (1967), *Capitalism and Underdevelopment in Latin America* (New York: Monthly Review Press).

Frankel, J. A. (1991), 'Quantifying International Capital Mobility in the 1980s', in D. Bernheim and J. Shoven (eds), *National Saving and Economic Performance* (Chicago, IL: Chicago University Press).

—— (1997), *Regional Trading Blocs in the World Economic System* (Washington, DC: Institute for International Economics).

—— (ed.) (1998), *The Regionalisation of the World Economy* (Cambridge, MA: National Bureau of Economic Research).

—— (2005), 'Contractionary Currency Crashes in the Developing Countries', CID Working Paper 117 (Cambridge, MA: Center for International Development at Harvard University).

Freeman, R. B. (2006), 'People Flows in Globalization', NBER Working Paper 12315 (Cambridge, MA: National Bureau of Economic Research).

Frey, B. S. (1984), 'The Public Choice View of International Political Economy', *International Organization*, 38/1: 199–223.

Frey, R. S. (1998), 'The Export of Hazardous Industries to the Peripheral Zones of the World System', *Journal of Developing Societies*, 14/1: 66–81.

——(2003), 'The Transfer of Core-Based Hazardous Production Processes to the Export Processing Zones of the Periphery: The Maquiladora Centers of Northern Mexico', *Journal of World-Systems Research*, 9/2: 317–54.

Frieden, J. A. (1988), 'Sectoral Conflict and Foreign Economic Policy, 1914–1940', *International Organization*, 42/1: 59–90.

——(1991), 'Invested Interests: The Politics of National Economic Policies in a World of Global Finance', *International Organization*, 45/4: 425–51.

——(1994), 'Exchange Rate Politics', *Review of International Political Economy*, 1/1: 81–98.

——(1997), 'Monetary Populism in Nineteenth-Century America: An Open Economy Interpretation', *Journal of Economic History*, 57/2: 367–95.

——Ghezzi, P., and Stein, E. (eds) (2001), *The Currency Game: Exchange Rate Politics in Latin America* (New York: Inter-American Development Bank).

——and Lake, D. (1995), 'Introduction: International Politics and International Economics', in J. Frieden and D. Lake (eds), *International Political Economy: Perspectives on Global Power and Wealth*, 3rd edn (London: Routledge).

Friedman, M. (1953), 'The Case for Flexible Exchange Rates', in M. Friedman, *Essays in Positive Economics* (Chicago, IL: University of Chicago Press).

Friedman, T. (2000), *The Lexus and the Olive Tree* (New York: Anchor Books).

——(2002), 'Techno Logic', in 'States of Discord: A Debate between Thomas Friedman and Robert Kaplan', *Foreign Policy*, 129/March–April: 64–5.

Frobel, F., Heinrichs, J., and Kreye, O. (1980), *The New International Division of Labor: Structural Unemployment in Industrialized Countries and Industrialization in Developing Countries* (Cambridge: Cambridge University Press).

Fujii, E., and Chinn, M. (2001), '*Fin de Siècle* Real Interest Parity', *Journal of International Financial Markets, Institutions and Money*, 11/3–4: 289–308.

Fukuda-Parr, S. (2004), 'Millennium Development Goals: Why they Matter', *Global Governance*, 10/4: 396–402.

Funabashi, Y. (1988), *Managing the Dollar: From the Plaza to the Louvre* (Washington, DC: Institute for International Economics).

G20 (2009a), 'London Summit— Leaders' Statement 2 April 2009' (London: G20, Communiqué, 2 April), http://www.g20.org/Documents/g20_communique_020409.pdf

——(2009b), 'Leaders' Statement: The Pittsburgh Summit, September 24–25, 2009' (Pittsburgh, PA: G20, Communiqué, September 24–5), http://www.g20.org/Documents/pittsburgh_summit_leaders_statement_250909.pdf

Galbraith, J. R. (2002), 'A Perfect Crime: Inequality in an Age of Globalization', *Daedalus*, 131/1: 11–25.

Gallagher, K., and Zarsky, L. (2007), *The Enclave Economy: Foreign Investment and Sustainable Development in Mexico's Silicon Valley* (Cambridge, MA: MIT Press).

Gallarotti, G. M. (1995), *The Anatomy of an International Monetary Regime: The Classical Gold Standard, 1880–1914* (New York: Oxford University Press).

Gamble, A. (2001), 'Neo-Liberalism', *Capital and Class*, 75: 127–34.

——and Payne, A. (eds) (1996), *Regionalism and World Order* (New York: St. Martin's Press).

Garcia-Johnson, R. (2000), *Exporting Environmentalism: US Multinational Chemical Corporations in Brazil and Mexico* (Cambridge, MA: MIT Press).

Gardner, R. N. (1969), *Sterling–Dollar Diplomacy: The Origins and the Prospects of our International Economic Order*, 2nd edn (New York: McGraw-Hill).

——(1980), *Sterling–Dollar Diplomacy in Current Perspective: The Origins and the Prospects of our International Economic Order* (New York: Columbia University Press).

Garrett, G. (1995), 'Capital Mobility, Trade, and the Domestic Politics of Economic Policy', *International Organization*, 49/4: 657–87.

——(1998a), 'Global Markets and National Politics: Collision Course or Virtuous Circle?', *International Organization*, 52/4: 787–824.

——(1998b), *Partisan Politics in the Global Economy* (Cambridge: Cambridge University Press).

——(2000a), 'The Causes of Globalization', *Comparative Political Studies*, 33/6–7: 945–91.

——(2000b), 'Shrinking States? Globalization and National Autonomy', in N. Woods (ed.), *The Political Economy of Globalization* (Basingstoke: Palgrave).

——and Lange, P. (1996), 'Internationalization, Institutions and Political Change', in R. O. Keohane and H. V. Milner (eds), *Internationalization and Domestic Politics* (Cambridge: Cambridge University Press).

——and Weingast, B. R. (1993), 'Ideas, Interests, and Institutions: Constructing the European Community's Internal Market', in J. Goldstein and R. O. Keohane (eds), *Ideas and Foreign Policy: Beliefs, Institutions and Political Change* (Ithaca, NY: Cornell University Press).

Gedicks, A. (2001), *Resource Rebels: Native Challenges to Mining and Oil Corporations* (Boston, MA: South End Press).

Gee, S., and Kuo, W. J. (1997), 'Export Success and Technological Capability: Textiles and Electronics in Taiwan Province of China', in D. Ernst, T. Ganistasos, and L. Mytelka (eds), *Technological Capabilities and Export Success* (London: Routledge).

GEF (Global Environment Facility) (2009), 'What is the GEF?', www.gefweb.org/interior_right.aspx?id=50

Gereffi, G., and Korzeniewicz, M. (eds) (1994), *Commodity Chains and Global Capitalism* (Westport, CT: Praeger).

—— and Pan, M. L. (1994), 'The Globalization of Taiwan's Garment Industry', in E. Bonacich, L. Cheng, N. Chinchilla, N. Hamilton, and P. Ong (eds), *Global Production: The Apparel Industry in the Pacific Rim* (Philadelphia, PA: Temple University Press).

—— Humphrey, J., and Sturgeon, T. (2005), 'The Governance of Global Value Chains', *Review of International Political Economy*, 12/1: 78–104.

Germain, R. (1997), *The International Organization of Credit* (Cambridge: Cambridge University Press).

Gerschenkron, A. (1962), *Economic Backwardness in Historical Perspective* (Cambridge, MA: Harvard University Press).

Geyer, M., and Bright, C. (1995), 'World History in a Global Age', *American Historical Review*, 100/4: 1034–60.

Ghosh, A. R. (1995), 'International Capital Mobility amongst the Major Industrialised Countries: Too Little or Too Much?', *Economic Journal*, 105/1: 173–80.

Giannone, D., and Lenza, M. (2004), 'The Feldstein–Horioka Fact', CEPR Discussion Paper 4610 (Paris: Centre for Economic Policy Research).

Giavazzi, F., and Pagano, M. (1988), 'The Advantage of Tying One's Hands: EMS Discipline and Central Bank Credibility', *European Economic Review*, 32/5: 1055–75.

Giddens, A. (1984), *The Constitution of Society* (Cambridge: Polity Press).

—— (1990), *The Consequences of Modernity* (Cambridge: Polity Press).

Gill, S. (1990), *American Hegemony and the Trilateral Commission* (Cambridge: Cambridge University Press).

—— (1995), 'Globalization, Market Civilization, and Disciplinary Neoliberalism', *Millennium: Journal of International Studies*, 24/3: 399–424.

—— (2003), *Power and Resistance in the New World Order* (Basingstoke: Palgrave).

—— and Law, D. (1988), *The Global Political Economy: Perspectives, Problems and Policies* (London: Harvester-Wheatsheaf).

—— —— (1989), 'Global Hegemony and the Structural Power of Capital', *International Studies Quarterly*, 33/4: 475–99.

Gilligan, M. (1997), *Empowering Exporters; Reciprocity and Collective Action in Twentieth Century American Trade Policy* (Ann Arbor, MI: University of Michigan Press).

Gilpin, R. (1975), *US Power and the Multinational Corporation* (New York: Basic Books).

—— (1981), *War and Change in World Politics* (Cambridge: Cambridge University Press).

—— (1987), *The Political Economy of International Relations* (Princeton, NJ: Princeton University Press).

—— (2001), *Global Political Economy: Understanding the International Economic Order* (Princeton, NJ: Princeton University Press).

—— (2002), *The Challenge of Global Capitalism: The World Economy in the 21st Century* (Princeton, NJ: Princeton University Press).

Global Footprint Network (2009), *Ecological Footprint Atlas 2009* (Oakland, CA: Global Footprint Network), www.footprintnetwork.org/images/uploads/Ecological_Footprint_Atlas_2009.pdf

Glyn, A. (2006), *Capitalism Unleashed: Finance, Globalization, and Welfare* (Oxford: Oxford University Press).

Goddard, R., Cronin, P., and Dash, K. (eds) (2003), *International Political Economy: State–Market Relations in a Changing Global Order*, 2nd edn (Basingstoke: Palgrave Macmillan).

Goldberg, L. G., Lothian, J. R., and Kunev, J. (2003), 'Has International Financial Integration Increased?', *Open Economies Review*, 14/3: 299–317.

Goldin, C. (1994), 'The Political Economy of Immigration Restriction in the United States, 1890 to 1921', in C. Goldin and G. Libecap (eds), *The Regulated Economy: A Historical Approach to Political Economy* (Chicago, IL: University of Chicago Press).

Goldsmith, M. M. (1990), 'Liberty, Luxury and the Pursuit of Happiness', in A. Pagden (ed.), *The Languages of Political Theory in Early-Modern Europe* (Cambridge: Cambridge University Press).

Goldstein, J. (1993), *Ideas, Interests, and American Trade Policy* (Ithaca, NY: Cornell University Press).

—— and Keohane, R. O. (eds) (1993), *Ideas and Foreign Policy: Beliefs, Institutions and Political Change* (Ithaca, NY: Cornell University Press).

Goodhart, C., and Illing, G. (eds) (2002), *Financial Crises, Contagion, and the Lender of Last Resort* (Oxford: Oxford University Press).

Goodin, R. E. (2003), 'Choose Your Capitalism?', *Comparative European Politics*, 1/2: 203–14.

Goodman, J., and Pauly, L. (1993), 'The Obsolescence of Capital Controls? Economic Management in an Age of Global Markets', *World Politics*, 46/1: 50–82.

Gordon, D. (1988), 'The Global Economy: New Edifice or Crumbling Foundations?', *New Left Review*, 168: 24–64.

Gore, C. (2000), 'The Rise and Fall of the Washington Consensus as a Paradigm for Developing Countries', *World Development*, 28/5: 789–804.

Gorodnichenko, Y., and Tesar, L. (2005), 'A Re-Examination of the Border Effect', NBER Working Paper 11706 (Cambridge, MA: National Bureau of Economic Research).

Gowa, J. (1983), *Closing the Gold Window* (Ithaca, NY: Cornell University Press).

——(1994), *Allies, Adversaries, and International Trade* (Princeton, NJ: Princeton University Press).

Graham, E., and Krugman, P. R. (1995), *Foreign Direct Investment in the United States* (Washington, DC: Institute for International Economics).

Gray, J. (1998), *False Dawn: The Delusions of Global Capitalism* (London: Granta).

Greene, O. (1997), 'Environmental Issues', in J. Baylis and S. Smith (eds), *The Globalization of World Politics: An Introduction to International Relations* (Oxford: Oxford University Press).

Greenspan, A. (2008), Testimony before the House of Representatives, Committee on Oversight and Government Reform, *Bloomberg News (online)*, October 23.

Grieco, J. M., and Ikenberry, G. J. (2003), *State Power and World Markets: The International Political Economy*, 1st edn (New York: W. W. Norton).

Grimes, W. W. (2009), *Currency and Contest in East Asia: The Great Power Politics of Financial Regionalism* (Ithaca, NY: Cornell University Press).

Grossman, G. M., and Helpman, E. (1994), 'Protection for Sale', *American Economic Review*, 84/4: 833–50.

————(1995), 'The Politics of Free-Trade Agreements', *American Economic Review*, 85: 667–90.

——and Krueger, A. (1995), 'Economic Growth and the Environment', *Quarterly Journal of Economics*, 110/May: 353–77.

Grundmann, R. (2001), *Transnational Environmental Policy: Reconstructing Ozone* (London: Routledge).

Gu, J., Humphrey, J., and Messner, D. (2008), 'Global Governance and Developing Countries: The Implications of the Rise of China', *World Development*, 36/2: 274–92.

Haas, E. B. (1958), *The Uniting of Europe: Political, Social and Economic Forces, 1950–1957* (Stanford, CA: Stanford University Press).

——(1975), *The Obsolescence of Regional Integration Theory* (Berkeley, CA: Institute of International Studies, University of California).

——(1980), 'Why Collaborate? Issue-Linkage and International Regimes', *World Politics*, 32/3: 357–405.

Haas, P. M. (1992), 'Introduction: Epistemic Communities and International Policy Coordination', *International Organization*, 46/1: 1–35.

Haggard, S. (1990), *Pathways from the Periphery: The Politics of Growth in the Newly Industrializing Economies* (Ithaca, NY: Cornell University Press).

——(1997), 'Regionalism in Asia and the Americas', in E. D. Mansfield and H. V. Milner (eds), *The Political Economy of Regionalism* (New York: Columbia University Press).

——and Cheng, T.-J. (1987), 'State and Foreign Capital in the East Asian NICs', in F. Deyo (ed.), *The Political Economy of New Asian Industrialism* (Ithaca, NY: Cornell University Press).

Halifax Initiative (2002), 'Green Band-Aid Won't Save the Environment', Press Release, 29 August.

Hall, D. (2002), 'Environmental Change, Protest and Havens of Environmental Degradation: Evidence from Asia', *Global Environmental Politics*, 2/2: 20–8.

——(2009), 'Pollution Export as State and Corporate Strategy: Japan in the 1970s', *Review of International Political Economy*, 16/2: 260–83.

Hall, P. A. (ed.) (1989), *The Political Power of Economic Ideas* (Princeton, NJ: Princeton University Press).

——and Soskice, D. (eds) (2001), *Varieties of Capitalism: The Institutional Foundations of Comparative Advantage* (Oxford: Oxford University Press).

Hankyoreh 21 (2004), no. 513, 9 June.

Hardin, G. (1968), 'The Tragedy of the Commons', *Science*, 162/3859: 1243–8.

Hardt, M., and Negri, A. (2000), *Empire* (Cambridge, MA: Harvard University Press).

Harmes, A. (1998), 'Institutional Investors and the Reproduction of Neoliberalism', *Review of International Political Economy*, 5/1: 92–121.

Harrison, A. E., and McMillan, M. S. (2006), 'Outsourcing Jobs? Multinationals and US Employment', NBER Working Paper 12372 (Cambridge, MA: National Bureau of Economic Research).

Harrison, G. (2004), 'Introduction: Globalisation, Governance and Development', *New Political Economy*, 9/2: 155–62.

Harvey, D. (1989), *The Condition of Postmodernity* (Oxford: Basil Blackwell).

——(2005a), *A Brief History of Neoliberalism* (New York: Oxford University Press).

——(2005b), *The New Imperialism* (Oxford: Oxford University Press).

Haufler, V. (1997), *Dangerous Commerce: Insurance and the Management of International Risk* (Ithaca, NY: Cornell University Press).

Hawkins, D. G., Lake, D. A., Nielson, D. L., and Tierney, M. J. (eds) (2006), *Delegation and Agency in International Organizations* (Cambridge: Cambridge University Press).

Hay, C. (2000), 'Contemporary Capitalism, Globalization, Regionalization and the Persistence of National Variation', *Review of International Studies*, 26/4: 509–31.

—— (2002a), 'Globalization as a Problem of Political Analysis: Restoring Agents to a "Process Without a Subject" and Politics to a Logic of Economic Compulsion', *Cambridge Review of International Affairs*, 15/3: 379–92.

—— (2002b), *Political Analysis* (Basingstoke: Palgrave).

—— (2003), 'What's Globalisation Got to Do with it?', Inaugural Lecture, University of Birmingham, www.polsis.bham.ac.uk/department/staff/publications/hay_inaugural.htm

—— (2004), 'Common Trajectories, Variable Paces, Divergent Outcomes? Models of European Capitalism Under Conditions of Complex Economic Interdependence', *Review of International Political Economy*, 11/2: 231–62.

—— (2007), *Why we Hate Politics* (Cambridge: Polity Press).

—— (2009), 'Good Inflation, Bad Inflation: The Housing Boom, Economic Growth and the Disaggregation of Inflationary Preferences in the UK and Ireland', *British Journal of Politics and International Studies*, 11/3: 461–78.

—— and Rosamond, B. (2002), 'Globalisation, European Integration and the Discursive Construction of Economic Imperatives', *Journal of European Public Policy*, 9/2: 147–67.

—— and Watson, M. (1998), 'Rendering the Contingent Necessary: New Labour's Neo-Liberal Conversion and the Discourse of Globalisation', *Center for European Studies Working Paper* (Boston, MA: Center for European Studies, Harvard University).

—— and Wincott, D. (forthcoming) *Welfare in the New Europe* (Basingstoke: Palgrave).

Heilbroner, R. (2000), *The Worldly Philosophers: The Lives, Times and Ideas of the Great Economic Thinkers*, rev. 7th edn (London: Penguin).

Held, D., and McGrew, A. (2002), *Globalization/Anti-Globalization* (Cambridge: Polity Press).

—— —— Goldblatt, D., and Perraton, J. (1999), *Global Transformations: Politics, Economics and Culture* (Cambridge: Polity Press).

Helleiner, E. (1994), *States and the Reemergence of Global Finance* (Ithaca, NY: Cornell University Press).

—— (1997), 'Braudelian Reflections on Economic Globalization: The Historian as Pioneer', in S. Gill and J. Mittleman (eds), *Innovation and Transformation in International Studies* (Cambridge: Cambridge University Press).

—— (2001), 'Regulating Capital Flight' , *Challenge*, 44/1: 19–34.

—— (2003), *The Making of National Money: Territorial Currencies in Historical Perspective* (Ithaca, NY: Cornell University Press).

—— (2005), 'Conclusion: The Meaning and Contemporary Significance of Economic Nationalism', in E. Helleiner and A. Pickel (eds), *Economic Nationalism in a Globalizing World* (Ithaca, NY: Cornell University Press).

—— (2006), *Towards North American Monetary Union? The Politics and History of Canada's Exchange Rate Regime* (Montreal: McGill-Queen's University Press).

—— (2009), 'The Development Mandate of International Institutions: Where Did it Come from?', *Studies in Comparative and International Development*, 44/3: 189–211.

—— and Cameron, G. (2006), 'Another World Order? The Bush Administration and HIPC Debt Cancellation', *New Political Economy*, 11/1: 125–40.

—— and Kirshner, J. (eds) (2008), 'Special Issue: At Home Abroad? The Dollar's Destiny as a World Currency', *Review of International Political Economy*, 15/3: 335–459.

—— —— (eds) (2009a), *The Future of the Dollar* (Ithaca, NY: Cornell University Press).

—— —— (eds) (2009b), 'Special Section: The Geopolitics of Sovereign Wealth Funds', *Geopolitics*, 14/2: 300–75.

—— and Lundblad, T. (2008), 'States, Markets, and Sovereign Wealth Funds', *German Policy Studies*, 4/3: 59–82.

—— Pagliari, S., and Zimmermann, H. (eds) (2009), *Global Finance in Crisis* (London: Routledge).

Helleiner, G. K. (1996), 'Why Small Countries Worry: Neglected Issues in Current Analyses of the Benefits and Costs for Small Countries of Integrating with Large Ones', *The World Economy*, 19/6: 759–63.

Henderson, C. (1998), *Asia Falling: Making Sense of the Asian Crisis and its Aftermath* (New York: McGraw-Hill).

Henning, C. R. (1987), *Macroeconomic Diplomacy in the 1980s* (London: Croom Helm).

—— (1998), 'Systemic Conflict and Regional Monetary Integration: The Case of Europe', *International Organization*, 52/3: 537–73.

—— (2002), *East Asian Financial Cooperation,* Policy Analyses in International Economics 68 (Washington, DC: Institute for International Economics).

Herrigel, G. (1996), *Industrial Constructions: The Source of German Industrial Power* (Cambridge: Cambridge University Press).

Hickey, S., and du Toit, A. (2007), 'Adverse Incorporation, Social Exclusion and Chronic Poverty', Working Paper No. 81 (Manchester: Chronic Poverty Research Centre, June).

Higgott, R., and Phillips, N. (2000), 'Challenging Triumphalism and Convergence: The Limits of Global Liberalisation in Asia and Latin America', *Review of International Studies*, 26/3: 359–79.

—— and Watson, M. (2008), 'All at Sea in a Barbed Wire Canoe: Professor Cohen's Transatlantic Voyage in IPE', *Review of International Political Economy*, 15/1: 1–17.

Hilferding, R. (1910/1981), *Finace Capital: A Study of the Latest Phase of Capitalist Development*, transl. by M. Watrick and G. Gordon (London: Routledge & Kegan Paul).

Hines, C. (2000), *Localization: A Global Manifesto* (London: Earthscan).

Hirschman, A. O. (1945), *National Power and the Structure of Foreign Trade* (Berkeley and Los Angeles, CA: University of California Press).

Hirst, P., and Thompson, G. (1996), *Globalization in Question*, 1st edn (Cambridge: Polity Press).

—— —— (1999), *Globalization in Question*, 2nd edn (Cambridge: Polity Press).

—— —— (2003), 'Globalization: A Necessary Myth?', in D. Held and A. McGrew (eds), *The Global Transformations Reader*, 2nd edn (Cambridge: Polity Press).

—— —— and Bromley, S. (2009), *Globalization in Question*, 3rd edn (Cambridge: Polity Press).

Hiscox, M. J. (1999), 'The Magic Bullet? The RTAA, Institutional Reform, and Trade Liberalization', *International Organization*, 53/4: 669–98.

—— (2002), *International Trade and Political Conflict* (Princeton, NJ: Princeton University Press).

Hobson, J. A. (1902/1948), *Imperialism* (London: Allen & Unwin).

Hoekman, B., and Kostecki, M. (1995), *The Political Economy of the World Trading System* (Oxford: Oxford University Press).

Hoffmann, M. (1998), 'Long Run Capital Flows and the Feldstein–Horoika Puzzle: A New Measure of International Capital Mobility and Some Historical Evidence from Great Britain and the United States', EUI Working Paper 1998/30 (Florence: European University Institute).

Hoffmann, S. (1966), 'Obstinate or Obsolete? The Fate of the Nation-State in Europe', *Daedalus*, 95/3: 862–915.

Holliday, C. O. Jr., Schmidheiny, S., and Watts, P. (2002), *Walking the Talk: The Business Case for Sustainable Development* (Sheffield: Greenleaf).

Holme, R., and Watts, P. (2000), *Corporate Social Responsibility: Making Good Business Sense* (Conches-Geneva: World Business Council for Sustainable Development).

Holsti, O. R. (1996), *Public Opinion and American Foreign Policy* (Ann Arbor, MI: University of Michigan Press).

Hoogvelt, A. (1978), *The Sociology of Developing Societies* (London: Macmillan).

—— (1997), *Globalisation and the Postcolonial World: The New Political Economy of Development* (London: Macmillan).

—— (2001), *Globalization and the Post-Colonial World* (Basingstoke: Palgrave).

Hörnqvist, M. (2000), 'The Two Myths of Civic Humanism', in J. Hankins (eds), *Renaissance Civic Humanism* (Cambridge: Cambridge University Press).

Horta, K., Round, R., and Young, Z. (2002), *The Global Environment Facility: The First Ten Years — Growing Pains or Inherent Flaws?* (Washington, DC and Ottawa: Environmental Defense and Halifax Initiative).

Huang, Y., and Khanna, T. (2003), 'Can India Overtake China?', *Foreign Policy*, 137/July–August: 74–81.

Huber, E., Ragin, C., Stephens, J. D., Brady, D., and Beckfield, D. (2004), *Comparative Welfare States Data Set* (Northwestern University and University of North Carolina), www.lisproject.org/publications/welfaredata/welfare access.htm

Hudec, R. E. (1975), *The GATT Legal System and World Trade Diplomacy* (New York: Praeger).

Hufbauer, G. C., and Wong, Y. (2004), 'China Bashing 2004', *International Economics Policy Briefs*, Number PB04–5/September: 1–53.

Hulme, D., and Scott, J. (2010), 'The Political Economy of the MDGs: Retrospect and Prospect for the World's Biggest Promise', *New Political Economy*, 15/2: 293–306.

Hummels, D. (2001), 'The Nature and Growth of Vertical Specialization in World Trade', *Journal of International Economics*, 54/1: 75–96.

Humphrey, J., and Memedovic, O. (2003), *The Global Automotive Value Chain* (Vienna: United Nations Industrial Development Organization).

—— and Schmitz, H. (2000), 'Governance and Upgrading: Linking Industrial Cluster and Global Value Chain Research', IDS Working Paper 120 (Brighton: Institute of Development Studies, University of Sussex).

—— —— (2001), 'Governance in Global Value Chains', *IDS Bulletin*, 32/3: 19–29.

Humphreys, D. (1999), 'The Evolving Forests Regime', *Global Environmental Change*, 9/3: 251–54.

—— (2003), 'Life Protective or Carcinogenic Challenge? Global Forests Governance under Advanced Capitalism', *Global Environmental Politics*, 3/2: 40–55.

—— (2006), *Logjam: Deforestation and the Crisis of Global Governance* (London: Earthscan).

Hundert, E. (1994), *The Enlightenment's Fable: Bernard Mandeville and the Discovery of Society* (Cambridge: Cambridge University Press).

Hymer, S. (1976), *The International Operations of National Firms* (Cambridge, MA: MIT Press).

IDB (Inter-American Development Bank) (2008), 'Countries Need To Spend More To Prevent Food Crisis From Deepening Poverty', 12 August, www.iadb.org/features-and-web-stories/2008-08/english/countries-need-to-spend-more-to-prevent-food-crisis-from-deepening-poverty-4718.html

—— (2009), 'Fact Sheet: Poverty Scenarios and the Crisis', http://idbdocs.iadb.org/wsdocs/getdocument.aspx?docnum=1885962

Ikeda, S. (2004), 'Zonal Structure and the Trajectories of Canada, Mexico, Australia, and Norway under Neo-liberal Globalization', in M. G. Cohen and S. Clarkson (eds), *Governing Under Stress: Middle Powers and the Challenge of Globalization* (London: Zed Books).

Ikenberry, G. J. (2001), *After Victory* (Princeton, NJ: Princeton University Press).

——and Kupchan, C. A. (1990), 'Socialization and Hegemonic Power', *International Organization*, 44/3: 283–315.

ILO (International Labour Organization) (1976), *Employment, Growth and Basic Needs: A One-World Problem* (Geneva: ILO).

IMF (International Monetary Fund) (2002), *World Economic Outlook: Trade and Finance* (Washington, DC: International Monetary Fund).

——(2003), *World Economic Outlook: Trade and Finance* (Washington, DC: International Monetary Fund).

——(2008), 'Global Financial Stability Report: Constraining Systemic Risks and Restoring Financial Soundness' (Washington, DC: International Monetary Fund, April) http://www.imf.org/External/Pubs/FT/GFSR/2008/01/pdf/text.pdf

——(2009a), 'Group of Twenty: Meeting of the Deputies January 31– 1 February 2009, London UK' (Washington, DC: International Monetary Fund, Note by the Staff of the International Monetary Fund), http://www.imf.org/external/np/g20/pdf/020509.pdf

——(2009b), 'Global Financial Stability Report: Navigating the Financial Challenges Ahead' (Washington, DC: International Monetary Fund, October).

——(2009c), 'The Multilateral Debt Initiative (MDRI): Factsheet', June, www.imf.org/external/np/exr/facts/mdri.htm

——(2009d), *World Economic Outlook* (Washington, DC: International Monetary Fund, October).

——(2010a), *World Economic Outlook: Trade and Finance* (Washington, DC: International Monetary Fund).

——(2010b), *World Economic Outlook Update: A Policy-Driven, Multispeed Recovery* (Washington, DC: International Monetary Fund, 26 January), http://www.imf.org/external/pubs/ft/weo/2010/update/01/pdf/0110.pdf

——(various years), *Financial Statistics Yearbook* (Washington, DC: International Monetary Fund).

Imura, H., and Schreurs, M. A. (eds) (2005), *Environmental Policy in Japan* (Cheltenham: Edward Elgar in association with the World Bank).

IOM (International Organization for Migration) (2005), *World Migration 2005: Costs and Benefits of International Migration* (Geneva: International Organization for Migration).

IPCC (Intergovernmental Panel on Climate Change) (2001), *Climate Change 2001: The Scientific Basis* (Cambridge: Cambridge University Press for IPCC).

——(2007), 'Climate Change 2007: The Physical Science Basis (Summary for Policymakers)', http://ipcc-wg1.ucar.edu/wg1/docs/WG1AR4_SPM_Approved_05Feb.pdf

Irwin, D. A. (2002), 'Long-Run Trends in World Income and Trade', *World Trade Review*, 1/1: 89–100.

——(2003), 'Explaining America's Surge in Manufacturing Exports, 1880–1913', *Review of Economics and Statistics*, 85/2: 364–76.

——and Kroszner, R. S. (1997), 'Interests, Institutions and Ideology in the Republican Conversion to Trade Liberalization, 1934–45', NBER Working Paper 6112 (Cambridge, MA: National Bureau of Economic Research).

ISO (International Organization for Standardization) (2008), *The ISO Survey: 2007*, www.iso.org/iso/survey2007.pdf

Iversen, T., Pontusson, J., and Soskice, D. (eds) (2000), *Unions, Employers and Central Banks: Macroeconomic Coordination and Institutional Change in Social Market Economies* (Cambridge: Cambridge University Press).

Jackson, J. H. (1969), *World Trade and the Law of the GATT* (Indianapolis, IN: Bobbs-Merrill).

——(1998), *The World Trade Organization: Constitution and Jurisprudence* (London: Pinter).

Jackson, R. H. (1993), 'The Weight of Ideas in Decolonization: Normative Change in International Relations', in J. Goldstein and R. O. Keohane (eds), *Ideas and Foreign Policy: Beliefs, Institutions and Political Change* (Ithaca, NY: Cornell University Press).

Jackson, R. T., and Banks, G. (2003), *In Search of the Serpent's Skin: The Story of the Porgera Gold Project* (Brisbane: Boolorong Press).

James, H. (1996), *International Monetary Cooperation Since Bretton Woods* (Washington, DC: International Monetary Fund).

——(2001), *The End of Globalization: Lessons from the Great Depression* (Cambridge, MA: Harvard University Press).

——(2009), *The Creation and Destruction of Value: The Globalization Cycle* (Cambridge, MA: Harvard University Press).

Jasanoff, S. (2007), 'Bhopal's Trails of Knowledge and Ignorance', *ISIS: An International Review Devoted to the History of Science and its Cultural Influences*, 98/2: 344–50.

Jenkins, R. (1987), *Transnational Corporations and Uneven Development* (London: Methuen).

Jessop, B. (1998), 'The Rise of Governance and the Risks of Failure: The Case of Economic Development', *International Social Science Journal*, 50/155: 29–45.

——(2002), *The Future of the Capitalist State* (Cambridge: Polity Press).

Jevons, W. S. (1871/1970), *The Theory of Political Economy* (Harmondsworth: Pelican).

Johannesburg Declaration on Sustainable Development (2002), Official Document of the 2002 World Summit on Sustainable Development, 4 September.

Johnson, C. (1982), *MITI and the Japanese Miracle* (Stanford, CA: Stanford University Press).

Jones, R. (1971), 'A Three-Factor Model in Theory, Trade, and History', in B. Jagdish, R. Jones, R. A. Mundell, and J. Vanek (eds), *Trade, Balance of Payments, and Growth* (Amsterdam: North-Holland).

Jones, V. C. (2006), 'WTO: Antidumping Issues in the Doha Development Agenda', CRS Report for Congress (Washington, DC: Congressional Research Service, Library of Congress).

Jordan, (2003), *New York Times*, 4 October: A15.

Josselin, D. (2001), 'Trade Unions for EMU: Sectorial Preferences and Political Opportunities', *West European Politics*, 24/1: 55–74.

JSBRI (Japan Small Business Research Institute) (2003), *White Paper on Small and Medium Enterprises* (Tokyo: Japan Small Business Research Institute).

Kahler, M. (1992), 'Multilateralism with Small and Large Numbers', *International Organization*, 46/3: 681–708.

Kaltenthaler, K. (1998), *Germany and the Politics of Europe's Money* (Durham, NC: Duke University Press).

Kang, D. (2002), *Crony Capitalism: Corruption and Development in South Korea and the Philippines* (Cambridge: Cambridge University Press).

Kaplinsky, R. (2000), 'Governance and Unequalisation: What Can Be Learned from Value Chain Analysis?', *Journal of Development Studies*, 37/2: 117–46.

—— (2005), *Globalization, Poverty and Inequality: Between a Rock and a Hard Place* (Cambridge: Polity Press).

Kapstein, E. B. (1994), *Governing the Global Economy: International Finance and the State* (Cambridge, MA: Harvard University Press).

—— (2000), 'Winners and Losers in the Global Economy', *International Organization*, 54/2: 359–384.

Kapur, D. (2002), 'The Changing Anatomy of Governance of the World Bank', in J. Pincus and J. A. Winters (eds), *Reinventing the World Bank* (Ithaca, NY: Cornell University Press).

—— and McHale, J. (2003), 'Migration's New Payoff', *Foreign Policy*, 139/November–December: 49–57.

Karliner, J. (1997), *The Corporate Planet, Ecology and Politics in the Age of Globalization* (San Francisco, CA: Sierra Club).

Kasman, B., and Pigott, C. (1988), 'Interest Rate Divergences amongst the Major Industrial Nations', *Federal Reserve Bank of New York Quarterly Review*, 13/3: 28–44.

Katada, S. (2002), 'Japan and Asian Monetary Regionalization: Cultivating a New Regional Leadership after the Asian Financial Crisis', *Geopolitics*, 7/1: 85–112.

Katzenstein, P. J. (ed.) (1978), *Between Power and Plenty: Foreign Economic Policies of Advanced Industrial States* (Madison, WI: University of Wisconsin Press).

—— (1985), *Small States in World Markets: Industrial Policy in Europe* (Ithaca, NY: Cornell University Press).

Kay, C. (1989), *Latin American Theories of Development and Underdevelopment* (London: Routledge).

Kearney, A. T., and *Foreign Policy* Globalization Index (2003), 'Measuring Globalization: Who's Up, Who's Down?', *Foreign Policy*, 134/January–February: 60–72.

—— —— (2005), 'Measuring Globalization', *Foreign Policy*, 148/May–June: 53–60.

Keck, M. E., and Sikkink, K. (1998), *Activists beyond Borders: Advocacy Networks in International Politics* (Ithaca, NY: Cornell University Press).

Keegan, J. (1998), *The First World War* (London: Random House).

Keohane, R. O. (1984), *After Hegemony: Cooperation and Discord in the World Political Economy* (Princeton, NJ: Princeton University Press).

—— (1997), 'Problematic Lucidity: Stephen Krasner's "State Power and the Structure of International Trade"', *World Politics*, 50/1: 150–70.

—— and Nye, J. S. (eds) (1972), *Transnational Relations and World Politics* (Cambridge, MA: Harvard University Press).

—— —— (1977), *Power and Interdependence* (Boston, MA: Little, Brown).

—— —— (2003), 'Globalization: What's New? What's Not? (And So What?)', in D. Held and A. McGrew (eds), *The Global Transformations Reader* (Cambridge: Polity Press).

Keynes, J. M. (1925), *The Economic Consequences of Mr. Churchill* (London: L. and V. Woolf).

—— (1933), 'National Self-Sufficiency', *Yale Review*, 22: 755–69.

—— (1936), *General Theory of Employment, Interest and Money* (New York: Harcourt, Brace).

Keynes, J. N. (1891/1970), *The Scope and Method of Political Economy*, reprinted 4th edn (New York: Augustus M. Kelley).

Kindleberger, C. P. (1951), 'Group Behavior and International Trade', *Journal of Political Economy*, 59/1: 30–46.

—— (1969), *American Business Abroad: Six Lectures on Direct Investment* (New Haven, CT: Yale University Press).

—— (1973), *The World in Depression, 1929–1939* (Berkeley and Los Angeles, CA: University of California Press).

—— (1975), 'The Rise of Free Trade in Western Europe', *Journal of Economic History*, 35/1: 20–55.

—— (1978), *Manias, Panics, and Crashes: A History of Financial Crises* (New York: Basic Books).

Kirshner, J. (1995), *Currency and Coercion: The Political Economy of International Monetary Power* (Princeton, NJ: Princeton University Press).

——(ed) (2003), *Monetary Orders: Ambiguous Economics, Ubiquitous Politics* (Ithaca, NY: Cornell University Press).

——(2007), *Appeasing Bankers: Financial Caution on the Road to War* (Princeton, NJ: Princeton University Press).

Kiser, E., and Laing, A. M. (2001), 'Have we Overestimated the Effects of Neoliberalism and Globalization? Some Speculations on the Anomalous Stability of Taxes on Business', in J. L. Campbell and O. K. Pedersen (eds), *The Rise of Neoliberalism and Institutional Analysis* (Princeton, NJ: Princeton University Press).

Kitschelt, H., Lange, P., Marks, G., and Stephens, J. D. (1999), *Continuity and Change in Contemporary Capitalism* (Cambridge: Cambridge University Press).

Klein, N. (2002), *No Logo* (New York: Picador).

Kleinknecht, A., and ter Wengel, J. (1998), 'The Myth of Economic Globalization', *Cambridge Journal of Economics*, 22/5: 637–47.

Knight, F. (1921), *Risk, Uncertainty and Profit* (Chicago, IL: University of Chicago Press).

Knight, J. (1992), *Institutions and Social Conflict* (Cambridge: Cambridge University Press).

KOF (2010), 'KOF Index of Globalization 2010), http://globalization.kof.ethz.ch

Kohli, A. (2004), *State-Directed Development: Political Power and Industrialization in the Global Periphery* (Cambridge: Cambridge University Press).

Koremenos, B., Lipson, C., and Snidal, D. (2001), 'The Rational Design of International Institutions', *International Organization*, 55/4: 761–99.

Korten, D. C. (2001), *When Corporations Rule the World*, 2nd edn (San Francisco, CA: Berrett-Koehler).

Korzeniewicz, R., and Moran, T. (2006), 'World Inequality in the Twenty-First Century: Patterns and Tendencies', in G. Ritzer (ed), *The Blackwell Companion to Globalization* (Oxford: Blackwell).

——and Moran, T. (2009), *Unveiling Inequality: A World-Historical Perspective* (New York: Russell Sage Foundation).

——Stach, A., Patil, V., and Moran, T. (2004), 'Measuring National Income: A Critical Assessment', *Comparative Studies in Society and History*, 46/3: 535–86.

Krasner, S. D. (1976), 'State Power and the Structure of International Trade', *World Politics*, 28/3: 317–47.

——(ed.) (1983), *International Regimes* (Ithaca, NY: Cornell University Press).

——(1985), *Structural Conflict: The Third World against Global Liberalism* (Berkeley and Los Angeles, CA: University of California Press).

——(1991), 'Global Communications and National Power: Life on the Pareto Frontier', *World Politics*, 43/3: 336–66.

——(1994), 'International Political Economy: Abiding Discord', *Review of International Political Economy*, 1/1: 13–19.

——(1999), *Sovereignty: Organized Hypocrisy* (Princeton, NJ: Princeton University Press).

Krueger, A. O. (1995), *Trade Policies and Developing Nations* (Washington, DC: Brookings Institution).

——(1999), 'Are Preferential Trading Arrangements Trade-Liberalizing or Protectionist?', *Journal of Economic Perspectives*, 13/4: 105–24.

——(2002), 'A New Approach to Sovereign Debt Restructuring', Pamphlet Series (Washington, DC: International Monetary Fund).

Krugman, P. R. (1990), 'Import Protection as Export Promotion: International Competition in the Presence of Oligopoly and Economies of Scale', in P. R. Krugman (ed.), *Rethinking International Trade* (Cambridge, MA: MIT Press).

——(1994), 'Does Third World Growth Hurt First World Prosperity?', *Harvard Business Review*, July: 113–21.

——(1995), 'Dutch Tulips and Emerging Markets', *Foreign Affairs*, 74/4: 28–44.

——and Obstfeld, M. (2000), *International Economics: Theory and Policy*, 5th edn (New York: Addison-Wesley).

Kurzer, P. (1993), *Business and Banking: Political Change and Economic Integration in Western Europe* (Ithaca, NY: Cornell University Press).

Lall, S. (2004), 'Reinventing Industrial Strategy: The Role of Government Policy in Building Industrial Competitiveness', G-24 Discussion Paper Series No. 28 (New York and Geneva: United Nations).

Landreth, H., and Colander, D. (1994), *History of Economic Thought*, 3rd edn (Boston, MA: Houghton Mifflin).

Lane, P. R., and Milesi-Ferretti, G. M. (2003), 'International Financial Integration', *IMF Staff Papers* 50/Special Issue: 82–100.

Lasswell, H. D. (1936), *Politics: Who Gets What, When, How* (New York: Whittlesey House, McGraw-Hill).

Lawrence, R. Z. (1996a), *Regionalism, Multilateralism, and Deeper Integration* (Washington, DC: Brookings Institution).

——(1996b), *Single World, Divided Nations? International Trade and OECD Labor Markets* (Washington, DC: Brookings Institution).

Leamer, E., and Levinsohn, J. (1995), 'International Trade Theory: The Evidence', in G. Grossman and K. Rogoff (eds), *Handbook of International Economics*, Vol. 3 (Amsterdam: North-Holland).

Leftwich, A. (2000), *States of Development: On the Primacy of Politics in Development* (Cambridge: Polity).

Lenin, V. I. (1917/1996), *Imperialism, the Highest Stage of Capitalism: A Popular Outline* (London: Pluto Press).

Lerner, D. (1972), 'Modernization: Social Aspects', in D. Sills (ed.), *International Encyclopedia of the Social Sciences*, Vol. 9 (New York: Collier Macmillan).

Levi-Faur, D. (1997), 'Friedrich List and the Political Economy of the Nation-State', *Review of International Political Economy*, 4/1: 154–78.

Levinson, M. (2006), *How the Shipping Container Made the World Smaller and the World Economy Bigger* (Princeton, NJ: Princeton University Press).

Lewis, A. (1981), 'The Rate of Growth of World Trade, 1830–1973', in S. Grassman and E. Lundberg (eds), *The World Economic Order: Past and Prospects* (London: Macmillan).

Leys, C. (1996), 'The Crisis in "Development Theory"', *New Political Economy*, 1/1: 41–58.

——(2001), *Market-Driven Politics: Neoliberal Democracy and the Public Interest* (London: Verso).

Lindberg, L. N. (1963), *The Political Dynamics of European Economic Integration* (Stanford, CA: Stanford University Press).

Lindemann, S. (2008), 'Understanding Water Regime Formation—A Research Framework with Lessons from Europe', *Global Environmental Politics*, 8/4: 117–40.

Lindert, P. H., and Williamson, J. G. (2001), 'Does Globalization Make the World More Unequal?', NBER Working Paper W8228 (Cambridge, MA: National Bureau of Economic Research).

————(2003), 'Does Globalization Make the World More Unequal?' in M. D. Bordo, A. M. Taylor, and J. G. Williamson (eds), *Globalization in Historical Perspective* (Chicago, IL: University of Chicago Press).

Lissakers, K. (1991), *Banks, Borrowers and the Establishment* (New York: Basic Books).

List, F. (1841/2005a), *National System of Political Economy*, Vol. 1: *The History* (New York: Cosimo Classics).

——(1841/2005b), *National System of Political Economy*, Vol. 2: *The Theory* (New York: Cosimo Classics).

——(1841/2005c), *National System of Political Economy*, Vol. 3: *The Systems and the Politics* (New York: Cosimo Classics).

Locke, R., and Kochan, T. (1985), 'The Transformation of Industrial Relations? A Cross-National Review of the Evidence', in R. Locke, T. Kochan, and M. Piore (eds), *Employment Relations in a Changing World* (Cambridge, MA: MIT Press).

Locke, R. M. (1995), *Remaking the Italian Economy* (Ithaca, NY: Cornell University Press).

——(2003), 'The Promise and Perils of Globalization: The Case of Nike', in T. A. Kochan and R. Schmalensee (eds), *Management: Inventing and Delivering its Future* (Boston, MA: MIT Press).

Lohmann, L. (1993), 'Resisting Green Globalism', in W. Sachs (ed.), *Global Ecology: A New Arena of Political Conflict* (London: Zed Books).

Lohmann, S. (1997), 'Linkage Politics', *Journal of Conflict Resolution*, 41/1: 38–67.

Lomborg, B. (2001), *The Skeptical Environmentalist* (Cambridge: Cambridge University Press).

——(2007), *Cool It: The Skeptical Environmentalist's Guide to Global Warming* (New York: Alfred A. Knopf).

——(ed.) (2009), *Global Crises, Global Solutions: Costs and Benefits*, 2nd edn (Cambridge: Cambridge University Press).

Longin, F., and Solnik, B. (1995), 'Is the Correlation in International Equity Returns Constant: 1960–1990?', *Journal of International Money and Finance*, 14/1: 3–26.

Lowenstein, R. (2001), *When Genius Failed: The Rise and Fall of Long-Term Capital Management* (London: Fourth Estate).

Lukes, S. (1974), *Power: A Radical View* (London: Macmillan).

Lynn, B. (2005), *End of the Line: The Rise and Coming Fall of the Global Corporation* (New York: Doubleday).

McCall Smith, J. (2000), 'The Politics of Dispute Settlement Design: Explaining Legalism in Regional Trade Pacts', *International Organization*, 54/1: 137–80.

McCloskey, D. (2006), *The Bourgeois Virtues: Ethics for an Age of Commerce* (Chicago, IL: Chicago University Press).

McCord, N. (1958), *The Anti-Corn Law League 1838–1846* (London: George Allen & Unwin).

McCullagh, C. B. (1998), *The Truth of History* (London: Routledge).

McDowell, L. (1997), *Capital Culture: Gender at Work in the City* (Oxford: Basil Blackwell).

McGillivray, F. (1997), 'Party Discipline as a Determinant of the Endogenous Formation of Tariffs', *American Journal of Political Science*, 41/2: 584–607.

McGinnis, M. D. (1986), 'Issue Linkage and the Evolution of International Cooperation', *Journal of Conflict Resolution*, 30/1: 141–70.

McGrew, A. (2002), 'Liberal Internationalism: Between Realism and Cosmpolitanism', in D. Held and A. McGrew (eds), *Governing Globalization: Power, Authority, and Global Governance* (Cambridge: Polity Press).

McKean, M. A. (1981), *Environmental Protest and Citizen Politics in Japan* (Berkeley and Los Angeles, CA: University of California Press).

McKendrick, D. G., Doner, R. F., and Haggard, S. (2000), *From Silicon Valley to Singapore: Location and Competitive Advantage in the Hard Disk Drive Industry* (Stanford, CA: Stanford University Press).

MacKenzie, D. (2002), 'Fresh Evidence on Bhopal Disaster', *New Scientist*, 4 December.

McKenzie, R., and Lee, D. (1991), *Quicksilver Capital: How the Rapid Movement of Wealth Has Changed the World* (New York: The Free Press).

McLaren, L. (2001), 'Immigration and the New Politics of Inclusion and Exclusion in the European Union: The Effect of Elites and the EU on Individual-Level Opinions Regarding European and Non-European Immigrants', *European Journal of Political Research*, 39/1: 81–108.

McLean, I. (2006), *Adam Smith, Radical and Egalitarian: An Interpretation for the 21st Century* (Edinburgh: Edinburgh University Press).

MacLeod, M. R. (2007), 'Financial Actors and Instruments in the Construction of Global Corporate Social Responsibility', in A. Ebrahim and E. Weisband (eds), *Global Accountabilities: Participation, Pluralism, and Public Ethics* (Cambridge: Cambridge University Press).

McMichael, P. (2000), *Development and Social Change: A Global Perspective*, 2nd edn (Thousand Oaks, CA: Pine Forge Press).

McNamara, K. (1998), *The Currency of Ideas: Monetary Politics in the European Union* (Ithaca, NY: Cornell University Press).

—— (2009), 'Of Intellectual Monocultures and the Study of IPE', *Review of International Political Economy*, 16/1: 72–84.

MacNeill, J., Winsemius, P., and Yakushiji, T. (1991), *Beyond Interdependence: The Meshing of the World's Economy and the Earth's Ecology* (New York: Oxford University Press).

Maddison, A. (1987), 'Growth and Slowdown in Advanced Capitalist Economies: Techniques of Quantitative Assessment', *Journal of Economic Literature*, 25/2: 649–98.

—— (1989), *The World Economy in the 20th Century* (Paris: Development Centre of the Organisation for Economic Co-operation and Development).

—— (2001), *The World Economy: A Millennial Perspective* (Paris: Development Centre of the Organisation for Economic Co-operation and Development).

Maeil Kyongjae [Maeil Business Newspaper] (2005), 'Global Sourcing: Samsung Electronics', 22 February.

Magee, S. P. (1980), 'Three Simple Tests of the Stopler–Samuelson Theorem', in P. Oppenheimer (ed.), *Issues in International Economics* (London: Oriel Press).

—— Brock, W. A., and Young, L. (1989), *Black Hole Tariffs and Endogenous Policy Theory* (Cambridge: Cambridge University Press).

Maggi, G. (1999), 'The Role of Multilateral Institutions in International Trade Cooperation', *American Economic Review*, 89/1: 190–214.

Makower, J., and Pike, C. (2009), *Strategies for the Green Economy: Opportunities and Challenges in the New World of Business* (New York: McGraw-Hill).

Malthus, T. R. (1798), *Essay on the Principle of Population*, 1st edn, www.econlib.org/library/Malthus/malPop.html

Mander, J., and Goldsmith, E. (eds) (2001), *The Case Against the Global Economy: And for a Turn towards Localization*, rev. edn (London: Earthscan).

Mandeville, B. (1714/1755), *The Fable of the Bees; Or, Private Vices, Public Benefits*, 9th edn (Edinburgh: W. Gray and W. Peter).

—— (1723/1997), 'Selections from *The Fable of the Bees, Volume 1*', in B. Mandeville, *The Fable of the Bees and Other Writings*, abridged and edited by Edward Hundert (Indianapolis, IN: Hackett).

Manheim, J. M. (1991), *All of the People All of the Time: Strategic Communication and American Politics* (Armonk, NY: M. E. Sharpe).

Mankiw, G. (2009), *New York Times*, 23 May.

Marchand, M. (1994), 'Gender and New Regionalism in Latin America: Inclusion/Exclusion', *Third World Quarterly*, 15/1: 63–76.

—— (1996), 'Reconceptualising "Gender and Development" in an Era of "Globalisation"', *Millennium: Journal of International Studies*, 25/3: 577–603.

Marshall, A. (1920), *Principles of Economics*, 8th edn (London: Macmillan).

Martin, L. L. (1992), 'Interests, Power, and Multilateralism', *International Organization*, 46/4: 765–92.

—— (2000), *Democratic Commitments: Legislatures and International Cooperation* (Princeton, NJ: Princeton University Press).

—— (2002) 'International Political Economy: From Paradigmatic Debates to Productive Disagreements', in M. Brecher and F. P. Harvey (eds), *Conflict, Security, Foreign Policy, and International Political Economy: Past Paths and Future Directions in International Studies* (Ann Arbor, MI: University of Michigan Press).

Martinez-Diaz, L. (2009), *Globalizing in Hard Times: The Politics of Banking-Sector Opening in the Emerging World* (Ithaca, NY: Cornell University Press).

Marugami, T., Mimura, T., Saito, K., Suzuki, M., and Kotaka, T. (2005), 'Survey Report on Overseas Business Operations by Japanese Manufacturing Companies', *JBICI Review*, No. 13 (Tokyo: Japan Bank for International Cooperation, September).

Marugami, T., Toyoda, T., Kasuga, T., and Suzuki, M. (2003), 'Survey Report on Overseas Business Operations by Japanese Manufacturing Companies', *JBICI Review*, No. 7 (Tokyo: Japan Bank for International Cooperation, August).

Marx, K. (1890/1930), *Capital: A Critique of Political Economy*, trans. from 4th German edn by E. and C. Paul (London: Dent).

—— (1973), *Grundrisse: Foundations of the Critique of Political Economy (Rough Draft)*, trans. from German edn by M. Nicolaus (Harmondsworth: Penguin).

—— and Engels, F. (1848/1948), *The Communist Manifesto* (London: Lawrence & Wishart).

Maskus, K. E. (2000), *Intellectual Property Rights in the Global Economy* (Washington, DC: Institute for International Economics).

Mazur, J. (2000), 'Labor's New Internationalism', *Foreign Affairs*, 79/1: 79–93.

Meadows, D. H., Meadows, D. L., Randers, J., and Behrens, W. W. (1972), *The Limits to Growth* (New York: Universe Books).

Mearsheimer, J. J. (1990), 'Back to the Future: Instability in Europe after the Cold War', *International Security*, 15/1: 5–56.

Mehta, S. (2003), 'The Johannesburg Summit from the Depths', *Journal of Environment and Development*, 12/1: 121–8.

Mellor, D. H. (1995), *The Facts of Causation* (London: Routledge).

Meltzer, A. (2001), 'The World Bank One Year after the Commission's Report to Congress', *Hearings before the Joint Economic Committee, US Congress*, 8 March.

Menger, C. (1871/1950), *Principles of Economics*, trans. and ed. by J. Dingwall and B. Hoselitz (Glencoe, IL: The Free Press).

Mészáros, I. (2005), *Marx's Theory of Alienation*, 5th rev. edn (London: Merlin Press).

METI (Ministry of Economy, Trade and Industry, Japan) (2000), 'The Economic Foundations of Japanese Trade Policy—Promoting a Multi-Layered Trade Policy', Ministry of Economy, Trade and Industry, www.meti.go.jp/english/report/data/g00Wconte.pdf

—— (2004), 'The Report of the Joint Study Group on the Possible Trilateral Investment Arrangements among China, Japan, and Korea' (Tokyo: METI), 29 November.

—— (2006), 'White Paper on International Economy and Trade 2006' (Tokyo: METI), June.

Milanovic, B. (2003), 'The Two Faces of Globalization: Against Globalization as we Know it', *World Development*, 31/4: 667–83.

—— (2005), *Worlds Apart: Measuring International and Global Inequality* (Princeton, NJ: Princeton University Press).

—— (2006), 'Global Income Inequality: A Review', *World Economics*, 7/1.

—— (2009), 'Global Inequality Recalculated: The Effect of New 2005 PPP Estimates on Global Inequality', World Bank Working Paper 5061 (Washington, DC: World Bank, September).

Mill, J. S. (1970), *Principles of Political Economy, with Some of their Applications to Social Philosophy* (Harmondsworth: Penguin).

Miller, J. W. (2010), 'WTO has Obstacles to Trade in Retreat', WSJ.com, 8 March, retrieved 21 March 2010, from http://online.wsj.com/article/SB10001424052748704706304575107341978847782.html?mod=WSJ_economy_LeftTopHighlights#printMode

Milner, H. V. (1997a), *Interests, Institutions, and Information: Domestic Politics and International Relations* (Princeton, NJ: Princeton University Press).

—— (1997b), 'Industries, Governments, and the Creation of Regional Trading Blocs', in E. D. Mansfield and H. V. Milner (eds), *The Political Economy of Regionalism* (New York: Columbia University Press).

Milward, A. S. (1984), *The Reconstruction of Western Europe 1945–51* (London: Routledge).

—— (1992), *The European Rescue of the Nation-State* (London: Routledge).

Minsky, H. (1986), *Stabilizing an Unstable Economy* (New Haven: Yale University Press).

Mitchell, B. R. (1992), *International Historical Statistics: Europe 1750–1988*, 3rd edn (London: Macmillan).

—— (1993), *International Historical Statistics: The Americas 1750–1988*, 2nd edn (London: Macmillan).

Mitchell, R. B. (2002), 'A Quantitative Approach to Evaluating International Environmental Regimes', *Global Environmental Politics*, 2/4: 58–83.

—— (2006), 'Problem Structure, Institutional Design, and the Relative Effectiveness of International Environmental Agreements', *Global Environmental Politics*, 6/3: 72–89.

—— (2009), 'International Environmental Agreements (IEA) Database Project (Version 2007.1), IEA Database Project, 2002–2009, http://iea.uoregon.edu

—— Clark, W. C., Cash, D. W., and Dickson, N. M. (eds) (2006), *Global Environmental Assessments: Information and Influence* (Cambridge, MA: MIT Press).

Molina, M. J., and Rowland, F. S. (1974), 'Stratospheric Sink for Chlorofluoromethanes: Chlorine Atom Catalyzed Destruction of Ozone', *Nature*, 249: 810–14.

Molyneux, M. (1985), 'Mobilization Without Emancipation? Women's Interests, the State, and Revolution in Nicaragua', *Feminist Studies*, 11/2: 227–54.

Moran, T. H. (1998), *Foreign Direct Investment and Development* (Washington, DC: Institute for International Economics).

Moravcsik, A. (1998), *The Choice for Europe: Social Purpose and State Power from Messina to Maastricht* (Ithaca, NY: Cornell University Press).

Morgenthau, H. (1948/1960), *Politics Among Nations: The Struggle for Power and Peace*, 3rd edn (New York: Knopf).

Morgunbladid and *Vidskiptabladid* (2007), 17 November.

Morse, E. L. (1976), *Modernization and the Transformation of International Relations* (New York: The Free Press).

Moser, C. (1989), 'Gender Planning and Development: Meeting Practical and Strategic Needs', *World Development*, 17/11: 1799–825.

—— (1993), *Gender Planning and Development: Theory, Practice and Training* (London: Routledge).

Mosley, L. (2003), *Global Capital and National Governments* (Cambridge: Cambridge University Press).

Motta, M., and Norman, G. (1996), 'Does Economic Integration Cause Foreign Direct Investment?', *International Economic Review*, 37/4: 757–83.

Mun, T. (1664/1928), *England's Treasure by Forraign Trade*, reset and reprinted edn (Oxford: Basil Blackwell).

Munck, R. (2002), *Globalisation and Labour* (London: Zed Books).

Mundell, R. (1961), 'A Theory of Optimum Currency Areas', *American Economic Review*, 51/3: 657–65.

Murphy, C., and Nelson, D. (2001), 'International Political Economy: A Tale of Two Heterodoxies', *British Journal of Politics and International Relations*, 3/3: 393–412.

Mussa, M. (1974), 'Tariffs and the Distribution of Income: The Importance of Factor Specificity, Substitutability, and Intensity in the Short and Long Run', *Journal of Political Economy*, 82/6: 1191–203.

—— (2002), *Argentina and the Fund: From Triumph to Tragedy* (Washington, DC: Institute for International Economics).

Muthu, S. (2008), 'Adam Smith's Critique of International Trading Companies: Theorizing "Globalization" in the Age of Enlightenment', *Political Theory*, 36/2: 185–212.

Myers, R., and Worm, B. (2003), 'Rapid Worldwide Depletion of Predatory Fish Communities', *Nature*, 423/6937: 280–3.

Nadvi, K., and Schmitz, H. (1998), 'Industrial Clusters in Less Developed Countries: Review of Experiences and Research Agenda', in P. Cadène and M. Holström (eds), *Decentralized Production in India: Industrial Districts, Flexible Specialization, and Employment* (Thousand Oaks, CA: Sage).

Naím, M. (2002), 'Post-Terror Surprises', *Foreign Policy*, 132/September–October: 95–6.

Narlikar, A. (2003), *International Trade and Developing Countries: Bargaining Coalitions in the GATT and WTO* (London: Routledge).

NASA (National Aeronautics and Space Administration) (2009), 'GISS Surface Temperature Analysis Global Temperature Trends: 2008 Annual Summation, updated 13 January 2009', http://data.giss.nasa.gov/gistemp/2008

Nelson, P. (2007), 'Human Rights, the Millennium Development Goals, and the Future of Development Cooperation', *World Development*, 35/12: 2041–55.

Neumayer, E. (2001), *Greening Trade and Investment: Environmental Protection without Protectionism* (London: Earthscan).

Newell, P. (2000), *Climate for Change: Non-State Actors and the Global Politics of the Greenhouse* (Cambridge: Cambridge University Press).

Ng, F., and Yeats, A. (1999), 'Production Sharing in East Asia: Who Does What for Whom, and Why?' World Bank Policy Research Working Paper No. 2197 (Washington, DC: World Bank).

Nicholson, J. S. (1904/1977), 'Introductory Essay', reprinted in F. List (1841/1977) *The National System of Political Economy* (Fairfield, NJ: Augustus M. Kelley).

Nierenberg, D. (2009), 'Meat Production and Consumption Continues to Grow', in *Vital Signs* (Washington, DC: Worldwatch Institute), http://vitalsigns.worldwatch.org/vs-trend/meat-production-and-consumption-continues-grow

Noble, G., and Ravenhill, J. (eds) (2000), *The Asian Financial Crisis and the Architecture of Global Finance* (Cambridge: Cambridge University Press).

Notermans, T. (2001), *Social Democracy and Monetary Union* (New York: Berghahn).

Nye, J. S., Jr. (1990), 'Soft Power', *Foreign Policy*, 80: 153–71.

Oatley, T. (1997), *Monetary Politics: Exchange Rate Cooperation in the European Union* (Ann Arbor, MI: University of Michigan Press).

—— (2006), *International Political Economy: Interests and Institutions in the Global Economy*, 2nd edn (London: Pearson Longman).

O'Brien, R. (1992), *The End of Geography: Global Financial Integration* (London: Pinter).

—— Williams, M. (2004), *Global Political Economy: Evolution and Dynamics* (Basingstoke: Palgrave Macmillan).

Obstfeld, M. (1993), 'International Capital Mobility in the 1990s', NBER Working Paper 4534 (Cambridge, MA: National Bureau of Economic Research).

—— and Rogoff, K. (1996), *Foundations of International Macroeconomics* (Cambridge, MA: MIT Press).

—— and Taylor, A. M. (1998), 'The Great Depression as a Watershed: International Capital Mobility in the Long Run', in M. D. Bordo, C. Goldin, and E. N. White (eds), *The Defining Moment: The Great Depression and the American Economy in the Twentieth Century* (Chicago, IL: Chicago University Press).

—— —— (2003), 'Globalization and Capital Markets', in M. D. Bordo, A. M. Taylor, and J. G. Williamson (eds), *Globalization in Historical Perspective* (Chicago, IL: University of Chicago Press).

—— —— (2004), *Global Capital Markets: Integration, Crisis, and Growth* (Cambridge: Cambridge University Press).

Odell, J. S. (1982), *US International Monetary Policy: Markets, Power, and Ideas as Sources of Change* (Princeton, NJ: Princeton University Press).

—— (2002), 'Making and Breaking Impasses in International Regimes: The WTO, Seattle and Doha', Paper Prepared for the Conference on Gaining Leverage in International Negotiations, Yonsei University, Seoul.

OECD (Organization for Economic Co-Operation and Development) (various years), *Economic Outlook* (Paris: OECD).

OECD (2002), Regional Trade Agreements and the Multilateral Trading System: Consolidated Report, 20 November, www.olis.oecd.org/olis/2002doc.nsf/43bb6130e5e86e5fc12569 fa005d004c/db1bbc3ddbadceeec1256c770042bc1b/$FILE/JT00 135547.PDF

—— (2003) Agricultural Policies in OECD Countries: Monitoring and Evaluation (Paris: OECD).

—— (2005) Agricultural Policies in OECD Countries: Monitoring and Evaluation 2005: Highlights, www.oecd.org/dataoecd/33/27/35016763.pdf

—— (2006), Social Expenditure Database, SOCX (Paris: OECD), www.oecd.org/els/social/expenditure

—— (2009), 'OECD Data, Table 1: Net Official Development Assistance in 2008', 30 March, www.oecd.org/dataoecd/48/34/42459170.pdf

——, WTO, and UN (2010), 'Report on G20 Trade and Investment Measures (September 2009 to February 2010)' (Paris and Geneva: OECD, WTO, UNCTAD, 8 March), http://www.oecd.org/dataoecd/22/16/44739159.pdf

Offer, A. (1989), The First World War: An Agrarian Interpretation (Oxford: Clarendon Press).

Officer, L. H. (2001), 'Gold Standard', EH.Net Encyclopedia, 1 October, http://eh.net/encyclopedia/article/officer.gold.stan dard

Ofreneo, R. (1993), 'Japan and the Environmental Degradation of the Philippines', in M. Howard (ed.), Asia's Environmental Crisis (Boulder, CO: Westview Press).

Ohmae, K. (1990), The Borderless World (London: Collins).

—— (1995), The End of the Nation State: The Rise of Regional Economies (New York: The Free Press).

Oi, J. C. (1992), 'Fiscal Reform and the Economic Foundations of Local State Corporatism in China', World Politics, 45/1: 99–126.

Okereke, C., Bulkeley, H., and Schroeder, H. (2009), 'Conceptualizing Climate Governance Beyond the International Regime', Global Environmental Politics, 9/1: 58–78.

Okimoto, D. I. (1988), 'Political Inclusivity: The Domestic Structure of Trade', in T. Inoguchi and D. I. Okimoto (eds), The Political Economy of Japan, Vol. 2: The Changing International Context (Stanford, CA: Stanford University Press).

Olson, M. (1965), The Logic of Collective Action: Public Goods and the Theory of Groups (Cambridge, MA: Harvard University Press).

Onuf, N. (1997), 'Hegemony's Hegemony in IPE', in K. Burch and R. Denemark (eds), Constituting International Political Economy (Boulder, CO: Lynne Rienner).

O'Rourke, K. H., and Williamson, J. G. (1999), Globalization and History: The Evolution of a Nineteenth-Century Atlantic Economy (Cambridge, MA: MIT Press).

Osherenko, G., and Young, O. R. (1993), 'The Formation of International Regimes: Hypotheses and Cases', in O. R. Young and G. Osherenko (eds), Polar Politics: Creating International Environmental Regimes (Ithaca, NY: Cornell University Press).

Osler, C. L. (1991), 'Explaining the Absence of International Factor-Price Convergence', Journal of Money and Finance, 10/1: 89–107.

Ostrom, E. (2000), 'Reformulating the Commons', Swiss Political Science Review, 6/1: 29–52.

—— (2003), 'How Types of Goods and Property Rights Jointly Affect Collective Action', Journal of Theoretical Politics, 15/3: 239–70.

Oye, K. A. (1985), 'Explaining Cooperation under Anarchy: Hypotheses and Strategies', World Politics, 38/1: 1–24.

—— (1992), Economic Discrimination and Political Exchange: World Political Economy in the 1930s and 1980s (Princeton, NJ: Princeton University Press).

Paarlberg, R. L. (1997), 'Agricultural Policy Reform and the Uruguay Round: Synergistic Linkage in a Two-Level Game', International Organization, 51/3: 413–44.

Pahre, R. (1999), Leading Questions: How Hegemony Affects the International Political Economy (Ann Arbor, MI: University of Michigan Press).

Pakenham, R. (1973), Liberal America and the Third World (Princeton, NJ: Princeton University Press).

Palan, R. (2003), The Offshore World: Sovereign Markets, Virtual Places and Nomad Millionaires (Ithaca, NY: Cornell University Press).

Palma, J. G. (2009), 'The Revenge of the Market on the Rentiers', Cambridge Journal of Economics, 33/1: 829–69.

Palmeter, D. N., and Mavroidis, P. C. (1999), Dispute Settlement in the World Trade Organization: Practice and Procedure (The Hague: Kluwer).

Palmisano, S. J. (2006), 'The Globally Integrated Enterprise', Foreign Affairs, 85/3: 127–36.

Panagariya, A. (2002), 'Developing Countries at Doha: A Political Economy Analysis', The World Economy, 25/9: 1205–33.

—— (2008), India: The Emerging Giant (Oxford: Oxford University Press).

Park, S. (2010), World Bank Group Interactions with Environmentalists: Changing International Organisation Identities (London: Manchester University Press).

Parker, B. (1998), Globalization and Business Practice: Managing across Boundaries (London: Sage).

Parson, E. A. (2003), Protecting the Ozone Layer: Science and Strategy (Oxford: Oxford University Press).

Pastor, R. (1980), Congress and the Politics of US Foreign Economic Policy, 1929–1976 (Berkeley and Los Angeles, CA: University of California Press).

Paterson, M. (1996), Global Warming and Global Politics (London: Routledge).

—— (2001), 'Risky Business: Insurance Companies in Global Warming Politics', *Global Environmental Politics*, 1/4: 18–42.

Pattberg, P. (2005), 'The Institutionalization of Private Governance: How Business and Nonprofit Organizations Agree on Transnational Rules', *Governance,* 18/4: 589–610.

Pauly, L. W. (1997), *Who Elected the Bankers? Surveillance and Control in the World Economy* (Ithaca, NY: Cornell University Press).

—— (2009), 'The Old and the New Politics of International Financial Stability', *Journal of Common Market Studies*, 47/5: 955–75.

Payne, A. (2005*a*), 'The Study of Governance in a Global Political Economy', in N. Phillips (ed.), *Globalizing International Political Economy* (Basingstoke: Palgrave Macmillan).

—— (2005*b*), *The Global Politics of Unequal Development* (Basingstoke: Palgrave Macmillan).

—— and Phillips, N. (2010), *Development* (Cambridge: Polity Press).

Pearson, F., and Rochester, M. (1998), *International Relations: The Global Condition in the Twenty-First Century*, 4th edn (New York: McGraw-Hill).

Pearson, R. (1995), 'Male Bias and Women's Work in Mexico's Border Industries', in D. Elson (ed.), *Male Bias in the Development Process* (Manchester: Manchester University Press).

Pellow, D. N. (2007), *Resisting Global Toxics: Transnational Movements for Environmental Justice* (Cambridge, MA: MIT Press).

Pempel, T. J. (1999*a*), 'The Developmental Regime in a Changing World Economy', in M. Woo-Cumings (ed.), *The Developmental State* (Ithaca, NY: Cornell University Press).

—— (ed.) (1999*b*), *The Politics of the Asian Financial Crisis* (Ithaca, NY: Cornell University Press).

Perraton, J., Goldblatt, D., Held, D., and McGrew, A. (1997), 'The Globalization of Economic Activity', *New Political Economy*, 2/2: 257–78.

Perroni, C., and Whalley, J. (1994), 'The New Regionalism: Trade Liberalization or Insurance?', NBER Working Paper 4626 (Cambridge, MA: National Bureau of Economic Research).

Petras, J., and Veltmeyer, H. (2001), *Globalization Unmasked: Imperialism in the 21st Century* (London: Zed Books).

Petrella, R. (1996), 'Globalization and Internationalization: The Dynamics of the Emerging World Order', in R. Boyer and D. Drache (eds), *States against Market: The Limits of Globalization* (London: Routledge).

Pharr, S. J., and Putnam, R. D. (eds) (2000), *Disaffected Democracies: What's Troubling the Trilateral Countries?* (Princeton, NJ: Princeton University Press).

Phillips, D. A. (2009), *Reforming the World Bank: Twenty Years of Trial—and Error* (Cambridge: Cambridge University Press).

Phillips, N. (2004), *The Southern Cone Model: The Political Economy of Regional Capitalist Development in Latin America* (London: Routledge).

—— (2005), 'Latin America in the Global Political Economy', in R. Stubbs and G. Underhill (eds) *Political Economy and the Changing Global* Order, 3rd edn (Oxford: Oxford University Press).

—— (2011), 'Poverty Reduction and the Role of Regional Institutions', in G. Mace, A. F. Cooper, and T. M. Shaw (eds), *Inter-American Cooperation at a Crossroads* (Basingstoke: Palgrave).

Pierson, P. (1994), *Dismantling the Welfare State? Reagan, Thatcher and the Politics of Retrenchment* (Cambridge: Cambridge University Press).

—— (1996), 'The New Politics of the Welfare State', *World Politics*, 48/2: 143–79.

Pieterse, J. N. (2002), 'Global Inequality: Bringing Politics Back In', *Third World Quarterly*, 23/6: 1023–46.

Pilling, D., and Mitchell, T. (2007), 'Japan in Yields to China's Lure', *Financial Times*, 5 April: 7.

Pinto, P. M. (2003), 'Tying Hands vs. Exchanging Hostages: Domestic Coalitions, Political Constraints, and FDI', Paper Presented at the Annual Meeting of the American Political Science Association, Philadelphia, PA.

Piore, M., and Sabel, C. (1984), *The Second Industrial Divide: Possibilities for Prosperity* (New York: Basic Books).

Pogge, T. (2004), 'The First United Nations Millennium Development Goal: A Cause for Celebration?', *Journal of Human Development and Capabilities*, 5/3: 377–97.

Polanyi, K. (1944), *The Great Transformation* (New York: Rinehart).

Ponte, S. (2008), 'Developing a "Vertical" Dimension to Chronic Poverty Research: Some Lessons from Global Value Chain Analysis', Working Paper No. 111 (Manchester: Chronic Poverty Research Centre, June).

Porter, G. (1999), 'Trade Competition and Pollution Standards: "Race to the Bottom" or "Stuck at the Bottom?"', *Journal of Environment and Development*, 8/2: 133–51.

—— Bird, N., Kaur, N., and Peskett, L. (2008), *New Finance for Climate Change and the Environment* (Washington, DC: WWF and Heinrich Böll Foundation), http://assets.panda.org/downloads/ifa_report.pdf

—— Brown, J. W., and Chasek, P. (2000), *Global Environmental Politics,* 3rd edn (Boulder, CO: Westview Press).

Porter, M. E. (1990) *The Competitive Advantage of Nations* (New York: The Free Press).

Prebisch, R. (1950), *The Economic Development of Latin America and its Principal Problems* (New York: United Nations).

Prebisch, R. (1963), *Towards a Dynamic Development Policy for Latin America* (New York: United Nations).

——(1970), *Change and Development: Latin America's Great Task* (Washington, DC: Inter-American Development Bank).

Preeg, E. H. (1970), *Traders and Diplomats: An Analysis of the Kennedy Round under the General Agreement on Tariffs and Trade* (Washington, DC: Brookings).

——(1995), *Traders in a Brave New World: The Uruguay Round and the Future of the International Trading System* (Chicago, IL: University of Chicago Press).

Princen, T. (1997), 'The Shading and Distancing of Commerce: When Internalization is not Enough', *Ecological Economics*, 20/3: 235–53.

——(2005), *The Logic of Sufficiency* (Cambridge, MA: MIT Press).

Putnam, R. D. (1988), 'Diplomacy and Domestic Politics: The Logic of Two-Level Games', *International Organization*, 42/3: 427–60.

——and Bayne, N. (1987), *Hanging Together: Cooperation and Conflict in the Seven-Power Summits* (Cambridge, MA: Harvard University Press).

Radelet, S., and Sachs, J. (2000), 'The Onset of the East Asian Financial Crisis', in P. Krugman (ed.), *Currency Crises* (Chicago, IL: University of Chicago Press).

Rai, S. (2002), *Gender and the Political Economy of Development* (Cambridge: Polity).

Raphael, D. D., and Macfie, A. L. (1982), 'Introduction', in A. Smith (1759/1982), *The Theory of Moral Sentiments*, Glasgow Edition of the Works and Correspondence of Adam Smith, ed. D. D. Raphael and A. L. Macfie (Indianapolis, IN: Liberty Fund).

Ravenhill, J. (1995), 'Competing Logics of Regionalism in the Asia-Pacific', *Journal of European Integration*, 18/2–3: 179–99.

——(2001), *APEC and the Construction of Asia-Pacific Regionalism* (Cambridge: Cambridge University Press).

——(2003), 'The New Bilateralism in the Asia-Pacific', *Third World Quarterly*, 24/2: 299–317.

——(2004), 'Back to the Nest? Europe's Relations with the African, Caribbean and Pacific Group of Countries', in V. K. Aggarwal and E. A. Fogarty (eds), *EU Trade Statistics: Between Regionalism and Globalization* (Basingstoke: Palgrave Macmillan).

——(2006*a*), 'Is China an Economic Threat to Southeast Asia?', *Asian Survey*, 46/5: 653–74.

——(2006*b*), 'The Political Economy of the New Asia-Pacific Bilateralism: Benign, Banal or Simply Bad?', in V. K. Aggarwal and S. Urata (eds), *Bilateral Trade Agreements in the Asia-Pacific: Origins, Evolution, and Implications* (London: Routledge).

——(2010), 'The "New East Asian Regionalism": A Political Domino Effect', *Review of International Political Economy*, 17/2: 178–208.

Reddy, S. G., and Pogge, T. W. (2003), 'How *Not* to Count the Poor', 26 March, www.columbia.edu/~sr793/count.pdf

Rees, W. E. (2002), 'Globalization and Sustainability: Conflict or Convergence?', *Bulletin of Science, Technology & Society*, 22/4: 249–68.

——(2006), 'Globalization, Trade and Migration: Undermining Sustainability', *Ecological Economics*, 59/2: 220–5.

——and Westra, L. (2003), 'When Consumption Does Violence: Can there Be Sustainability and Environmental Justice in a Resource-Limited World?', in J. Agyeman, R. Bullard, and B. Evans (eds), *Just Sustainabilities: Development in an Unequal World* (London: Earthscan).

Reich, R. (1992), *The Work of Nations* (New York: Vintage Books).

Reinhart, C., and Rogoff, K. (2009), *This Time is Different: Eight Centuries of Financial Folly* (Princeton, NJ: Princeton University Press).

Rhodes, M. (1996), 'Globalization and West European Welfare States: A Critical Review of Recent Debates', *Journal of European Social Policy*, 6/4: 305–27.

——(1997), 'The Welfare State: Internal Challenges, External Constraints', in M. Rhodes, P. Heywood, and V. Wright (eds), *Developments in West European Politics* (London: Macmillan).

Ricardo, D. (1817/2002), *On the Principles of Political Economy and Taxation*, reprinted version of 3rd edn (London: Empiricus Books).

Rice, C. (2008), 'Rethinking the National Interest: American Realism for a New World', *Foreign Affairs*, 87/4: 2–28.

Rich, B. (1994), *Mortgaging the Earth: The World Bank, Environmental Impoverishment, and the Crisis of Development* (London: Earthscan).

——(2000), 'Exporting Destruction', *Environmental Forum*, September–October: 32–40.

——(2009), *Foreclosing the Future: Coal, Climate and Public International Finance* (Washington, DC: Environmental Defense Fund), www.edf.org/documents/9593_coal-plants-report.pdf

Rieger, E., and Leibfried, S. (2003), *Limits to Globalization: Welfare States and the World Economy* (Cambridge: Polity Press).

Robbins, R. H. (2008), *Global Problems and the Culture of Capitalism*, 4th edn (Boston, MA: Pearson/Allyn & Bacon).

Robertson, R. (2003), *The Three Waves of Globalization: A History of Developing Global Consciousness* (London: Zed Books).

Robins, N. (2006), *The Corporation That Changed the World: How the East India Company Shaped the Modern Multinational* (London: Pluto).

Robinson, J. (1964), *Economic Philosophy*, 2nd edn (Harmondsworth: Pelican).

Rodrik, D. (1989), 'Promises, Promises: Credible Policy Reform via Signalling', *Economic Journal*, 99/397: 756–72.

——(1995), 'Political Economy of Trade Policy', in G. Grossman and K. Rogoff (eds), *Handbook of International Economics*, Vol. 3 (Amsterdam: Elsevier).

——(1996), 'Why Do More Open Economies Have Bigger Governments?', NBER Working Paper 5537 (Cambridge, MA: National Bureau of Economic Research).

——(1997), *Has Globalization Gone too Far?* (Washington, DC: Institute for International Economics).

——(1999), *The New Economy and Developing Countries: Making Openness Work* (Baltimore, MD: Johns Hopkins University Press for Overseas Development Council).

——(2002), 'After Neoliberalism, What?', Paper Presented to the Conference on Alternatives to Neoliberalism sponsored by the New Rules for Global Finance Coalition, 23–4 May, www.new-rules.org/docs/afterneolib/rodrik.pdf

——(2006*a*), 'Goodbye Washington Consensus, Hello Washington Confusion: A Review of the World Bank's *Economic Growth in the 1990s: Learning from a Decade of Reform*', *Journal of Economic Literature*, 44/4: 973–87.

——(2006*b*), 'The Social Cost of Foreign Exchange Reserves', NBER Working Paper 11952 (Cambridge, MA: National Bureau of Economic Research).

Rødseth, A. (2000), *Open Economy Macroeconomics* (Cambridge: Cambridge University Press).

Roemer, J. E. (1988), *Free to Lose: An Introduction to Marxist Economic Philosophy* (London: Radius).

Rogers, A. (1993), *The Earth Summit: A Planetary Reckoning* (Los Angeles, CA: Global View Press).

Rogowski, R., (1987), 'Trade and the Variety of Democratic Institutions', *International Organization*, 41/2: 203–23.

——(1989), *Commerce and Coalitions* (Princeton, NJ: Princeton University Press).

Rosamond, B. (2001), 'Discourses of Globalization and European Identities', in T. Christiansen, K. Jorgensen, and A. Wiener (eds), *The Social Construction of Europe* (London: Sage).

Rosecrance, R. (1986), *The Rise of the Trading State: Commerce and Conquest in the Modern World* (New York: Basic Books).

——(1999), *The Rise of the Virtual State* (New York: Basic Books).

Rosen, D. (2003), 'Low-tech Bed, High-tech Dreams', *China Economic Quarterly*, 4: 20–7.

Rosenberg, A. (1995), *Philosophy of Social Science* (Boulder, CO: Westview Press).

Rosenberg, J. (2000), *The Follies of Globalization Theory* (London: Verso).

——(2005), 'Globalization Theory: A Post Mortem', *International Politics*, 42/1: 2–74.

Rosow, S. (1997), 'Echoes of Commercial Society: Liberal Political Theory in Mainstream IPE', in K. Burch and R. Denemark (eds), *Constituting International Political Economy* (London: Lynne Rienner).

Ross, M. L. (2001), *Timber Booms and Institutional Breakdown in Southeast Asia* (Cambridge: Cambridge University Press).

Rostow, W. W. (1960), *The Stages of Economic Growth: A Non-Communist Manifesto* (Cambridge: Cambridge University Press).

Roubini, N., and Setser, B. (2004), *Bailouts or Bail-Ins? Responding to Financial Crises in Emerging Markets* (Washington, DC: Peterson Institute for International Economics).

Rousseau, J.-J. (1755/2003), 'A Discourse on a Subject Proposed by the Academy of Dijon: What is the Origin of Inequality among Men, and is it Authorized by Natural Law?', in J.-J. Rousseau, *The Social Contract and Discourses*, trans. and introduced by G. D. H. Cole, reprinted edn (London: Everyman).

Rowthorn, R., and Wells, J. (1987), *De-Industrialization and Foreign Trade* (Cambridge: Cambridge University Press).

Roxburgh, C., Lund, S., Atkins, C., Belot, S., Hu, W. W., and Pierce, M. S. (2009), 'Global Capital Markets: Entering a New Era' (McKinsey Global Institute).

Ruggie, J. G. (1982), 'International Regimes, Transactions, and Change: Embedded Liberalism in the Postwar Economic Order', *International Organization*, 36/2: 379–415.

——(1992), 'Multilateralism: The Anatomy of an Institution', *International Organization*, 46/3: 561–98.

Rugman, A. (2000), *The End of Globalization* (London: Random House, New York: Amacom–McGraw Hill).

Ruigrok, W., and Tulder, R. V. (1995), *The Logic of International Restructuring* (London: Routledge).

Sachs, J. (1998), 'The IMF and the Asian Flu', *American Prospect*, March–April: 16–21.

Saith, A. (2006), 'From Universal Values to Millennium Development Goals: Lost in Translation', *Development and Change*, 37/6: 1167–99.

Sako, M. (2003), 'Modularity and Outsourcing: The Nature of Co-Evolution of Product Architecture and Organization Architecture in the Global Automotive Industry', in A. Prencipe, A. Davies, and M. Hobday (eds), *The Business of Systems Integration* (Oxford: Oxford University Press).

——(2006), 'Outsourcing and Offshoring: Implications for Productivity of Business Services', *Oxford Review of Economic Policy*, 22/4: 499–512.

Sandholtz, W. (1993), 'Choosing Union: Monetary Politics and Maastricht', *International Organization*, 47/1: 1–39.

Sandholtz, W. and Stone Sweet, A. (eds) (1998), *European Integration and Supranational Governance* (Oxford: Oxford University Press).

—— and Zysman, J. (1989), '1992: Recasting the European Bargain', *World Politics*, 42/1: 95–128.

Sandler, T. (1992), *Collective Action: Theory and Applications* (Ann Arbor, MI: University of Michigan Press).

Sassen, S. (2006), *Territory, Authority, Rights: From Medieval to Global Assemblages* (Princeton, NJ: Princeton University Press).

Saul, J. R. (2005), *The Collapse of Globalism* (London: Atlantic Books).

Sayer, A. (2000), *Realism and Social Science* (London: Sage).

Schelling, T. C. (1960), *The Strategy of Conflict* (Cambridge, MA: Harvard University Press).

Schiff, M. W., and Winters, L. A. (2003), *Regional Integration and Development* (New York: Oxford University Press for the World Bank).

Schirato, T., and Webb, J. (2003), *Understanding Globalization* (London: Sage).

Schirm, S. A. (2002), *Globalization and the New Regionalism* (Cambridge: Polity Press).

Schmidheiny, S., and Zorraquin, F. (1996), *Financing Change: The Financial Community, Eco-Efficiency, and Sustainable Development* (Cambridge, MA: MIT Press).

Schmidt, V. (2002), *The Futures of European Capitalism* (Oxford: Oxford University Press).

Schmitter, P., and Lehbruch, G. (eds) (1979), *Trends towards Corporatist Intermediation* (Beverly Hills, CA: Sage).

Schnietz, K. (1994), 'To Delegate or Not to Delegate: Congressional Institutional Choice in the Regulation of Foreign Trade, 1916–1934', Ph.D. dissertation (Berkeley, CA, University of California).

Scholte, J. A. (1997), 'The Globalization of World Politics', in J. Baylis and S. Smith (eds), *The Globalization of World Politics: An Introduction to International Relations* (Oxford: Oxford University Press).

—— (2000), *Globalization: A Critical Introduction* (Basingstoke: Palgrave).

—— (2005), *Globalization: A Critical Introduction*, rev. and updated 2nd edn (Basingstoke: Palgrave Macmillan).

Schreurs, M. A. (2002), *Environmental Politics in Japan, Germany, and the United States* (Cambridge: Cambridge University Press).

Schubert, A. (1992), *The Credit-Anstalt Crisis of 1931* (Cambridge: Cambridge University Press).

Schumacher, E. F. (1973), *Small is Beautiful: Economics as if People Mattered* (New York: Harper & Row).

Schumpeter, J. (1954/1994), *History of Economic Analysis* (New York: Oxford University Press).

Schwartz, H. (2001), 'Round up the Usual Suspects: Globalization, Domestic Politics, and Welfare State Change', in P. Pierson (ed.), *The New Politics of the Welfare State* (Oxford: Oxford University Press).

Schwartz, H. M. (2009), *Subprime Nation: American Power, Global Capital, and the Housing Bubble* (Ithaca, NY: Cornell University Press).

Scollay, R., and Gilbert, J. (2001), *New Regional Trading Arrangements in the Asia Pacific?* (Washington, DC: Institute for International Economics).

Seers, D. (1969) 'The Meaning of Development', *International Development Review*, 11/4: 2–6.

Segal, G., and Goodman, D. (eds) (2000), *Towards Recovery in Pacific Asia* (London: Routledge).

Selin, H., and VanDeveer, S. D. (eds) (2009), *Changing Climates in North American Politics: Institutions, Policymaking, and Multilevel Governance* (Cambridge, MA: MIT Press).

Sen, A. (1999), *Development as Freedom* (Oxford: Oxford University Press).

—— (2009), *The Idea of Justice* (Cambridge, MA: Belknap/Harvard University Press).

Shah, A. and Thompson, T. (2002), 'Implementing Decentralized Local Governance: A Treacherous Road with Potholes, Detours, and Road Closures', Paper presented at 'Can Decentralization Help Rebuild Indonesia?', Andrew Young School of Policy Studies, Georgia State University, Atlanta, Georgia, 1–3 May.

Shiller, R. J. (2001), *Irrational Exuberance* (Princeton, NJ: Princeton University Press).

—— (2008), *The Subprime Solution: How Today's Global Financial Crisis Happened, and What to Do About It* (Princeton, NJ: Princeton University Press).

Shiva, V. (1993), 'The Greening of the Global Reach', in W. Sachs (ed.), *Global Ecology: A New Arena of Political Conflict* (London: Zed Books).

—— (1997), *Biopiracy: The Plunder of Nature and Knowledge* (Toronto: Between the Lines).

—— (2000), *Stolen Harvest: The Hijacking of the Global Food Supply* (Cambridge, MA: South End Press).

—— (2008), *Soil not Oil: Environmental Justice in an Age of Climate Justice* (Cambridge, MA: South End Press).

Shonfield, A. (ed.) (1976), *International Economic Relations of the Western World 1959–1971, I: Politics and Trade* (London: Oxford University Press).

Silver, B. J. (2003), *Forces of Labor: Workers' Movements and Globalization Since 1870* (Cambridge: Cambridge University Press).

Simmons, B. A. (1994), *Who Adjusts? Domestic Sources of Foreign Economic Policy During the Interwar Years* (Princeton, NJ: Princeton University Press).

—— (1999), 'The Internationalisation of Capital', in H. Kitschelt, P. Lange, G. Marks, and J. D. Stephens (eds), *Continuity and Change in Contemporary Capitalism* (Cambridge: Cambridge University Press).

Simon, J. L. (1996), *The Ultimate Resource 2* (Princeton, NJ: Princeton University Press).

Sinclair, T. (1994), 'Between State and Market', *Policy Sciences*, 27/4: 447–66.

Singh, A., and Zammit, A. (2000), 'International Capital Flows: Identifying the Gender Dimension', *World Development*, 28/7: 1249–68.

Skidelsky, R. (2003), 'Keynes's Road to Bretton Woods: An Essay in Interpretation', in M. Flandreau, C.-L. Holtfrerich, and H. James (eds), *International Financial History in the Twentieth Century* (Cambridge: Cambridge University Press).

——(2009), *Keynes: The Return of the Master* (New York: Public Affairs).

Sklair, L. (2001), *The Transnational Capitalist Class* (Oxford: Blackwell).

Smith, A. (1759/1982), *The Theory of Moral Sentiments*, Glasgow Edition of the Works and Correspondence of Adam Smith, ed. D. D. Raphael and A. L. Macfie (Indianapolis, IN: Liberty Fund).

——(1776/1976), *An Inquiry into the Nature and Causes of the Wealth of Nations* (Oxford: Oxford University Press), www.econlib.org/library/Smith/smWN.html

——(1776/1981), *An Inquiry into the Nature and Causes of the Wealth of Nations*, Glasgow Edition of the Works and Correspondence of Adam Smith, ed. R. H. Campbell and A. Skinner (Indianapolis, IN: Liberty Fund).

Snidal, D. (1985a), 'Coordination versus Prisoners' Dilemma: Implications for International Cooperation and Regimes', *American Political Science Review*, 79/4: 923–42.

——(1985b), 'The Limits of Hegemonic Stability Theory', *International Organization*, 39/4: 579–614.

Snyder, R. (2001), 'Scaling Down: The Subnational Comparative Method', *Studies in Comparative International Development*, 36/1: 93–110.

Solis, M. (2003), 'On the Myth of *Keiretsu* Network: Japanese Electronics in North America', *Business and Politics*, 5/3: 303–33.

Sorkin, A. (2009), *Too Big to Fail: The Inside Story of How Wall Street and Washington Fought to Save the Financial System—And Themselves* (New York: Viking).

Soroos, M. S. (1997), *The Endangered Atmosphere* (Columbia, SC: University of South Carolina Press).

Soros, G. (1997a), 'The Capitalist Threat', *Atlantic Monthly*, February.

——(1997b), Letter to the Editor, *Atlantic Monthly*, May.

——(1998), *The Crisis of Global Capitalism* (New York: Public Affairs).

Spero, J. (1980), *The Failure of the Franklin National Bank* (New York: Columbia University Press).

Standing, G. (2000), 'Brave New Worlds? A Critique of Stiglitz's World Bank Rethink', *Development and Change*, 31/4: 737–63.

Stasavage, D. (2003), 'When Do States Abandon Monetary Discretion? Lessons from the Evolution of the CFA Franc Zone', in J. Kirshner (ed.), *Monetary Orders: Ambiguous Economics, Ubiquitous Politics* (Ithaca, NY: Cornell University Press).

Steans, J., and Pettiford, L. (2001), *International Relations: Perspectives and Themes* (Harlow: Pearson Education).

Stein, A. A. (1982), 'Coordination and Collaboration: Regimes in an Anarchic World', *International Organization*, 36/2: 294–324.

Steinmo, S. (2003), 'The Evolution of Policy Ideas: Tax Policy in the Twentieth Century', *British Journal of Politics and International Relations*, 5/2: 206–36.

Stiglitz, J. E. (1998a), 'Towards a New Paradigm for Development: Strategies, Policies and Processes', Prebisch Lecture at UNCTAD, Geneva, 19 October.

——(1998b), 'More Instruments and Broader Goals: Moving Toward the Post-Washington Consensus', World Institute for Development Economic Research Annual Lecture, Helsinki, 7 January.

——(2001), 'An Agenda for Development in the Twenty-First Century', in A. Giddens (ed.), *The Global Third Way Debate* (Cambridge: Polity).

——(2005), 'The Overselling of Globalization', in M. M. Weinstein (ed.), *Globalization: What's New?* (New York: Columbia University Press).

——(2006), *Making Globalization Work* (New York: W. W. Norton).

Stokke, O. S., and Hønneland, G. (eds) (2007), *International Cooperation and Arctic Governance: Regime Effectiveness and Northern Region Building* (New York: Routledge).

Stolper, W., and Samuelson, P. A. (1941), 'Protection and Real Wages', *Review of Economic Studies*, 9: 58–73.

Strange, S. (1986), *Casino Capitalism* (Oxford: Basil Blackwell).

——(1988), *States and Markets* (London: Pinter).

——(1994), *States and Markets*, 2nd edn (London: Pinter).

——(1998a), 'International Political Economy: Beyond Economics and International Relations', *Economies et Sociétés*, 34/4: 3–24.

——(1998b), *Mad Money: When Markets Outgrow Government* (Ann Arbor, MI: University of Michigan Press).

Streck, C. (2001), 'The Global Environment Facility—A Role Model for International Governance?', *Global Environmental Politics*, 1/2: 71–94.

Streeten, P., with Burki, S. J., Ul Haq, M., Hicks, N., and Stewart, F. (1982), *First Things First: Meeting Basic Human Needs in Developing Countries* (New York: World Bank/Oxford University Press).

Strong, M. (2000), *Where on Earth are We Going?* (Toronto: Knopf).

Sturgeon, T. (2002), 'Modular Production Networks: A New American Model of Industrial Organization', *Industrial and Corporate Change*, 11/3: 451–96.

Sunkel, O. (1972), 'Big Business and "Dependencia": A Latin American View', *Foreign Affairs*, 50/3: 517–31.

Svedberg, P. (2003), 'World Income Distribution: Which Way?', Institute for International Economics Seminar Paper 724 (Stockholm: Stockholm University).

Swank, D. (2002), *Global Capital, Political Institutions and Policy Change in Developed Welfare States* (Cambridge: Cambridge University Press).

Swenson, P. (2000), *Capitalists against Markets* (Oxford: Oxford University Press).

Switzer, J. V. (2004), *Environmental Politics: Domestic and Global Dimensions,* 4th edn (Belmont, CA: Thomson/Wadsworth).

Tacconi, L. (ed.) (2007), *Illegal Logging: Law Enforcement, Livelihoods and the Timber Trade* (London: Earthscan).

Tasca, H. J. (1938), *The Reciprocal Trade Policy of the United States* (New York: Russell & Russell).

Taylor, A. M. (1996), 'Domestic Saving and International Capital Flows Reconsidered', NBER Working Paper 4892 (Cambridge, MA: National Bureau of Economic Research).

—— (2002), 'Globalization, Trade and Development: Some Lessons from History', NBER Working Paper 9326 (Cambridge, MA: National Bureau of Economic Research).

Taylor, M. (1987), *The Possibility of Cooperation* (Cambridge: Cambridge University Press).

Teeple, G. (1995), *Globalization and the Decline of Social Reform* (Toronto: Garamond Press).

Teivainen, T. (2002), *Enter Economism, Exit Politics* (London: Zed Books).

Temin, P. (2010), 'The Great Recession and the Great Depression', NBER Working Paper 15645 (Cambridge, MA: National Bureau of Economic Research).

Tesar, L. L. (1991), 'Saving, Investment and International Capital Flows', *Journal of International Economics,* 31/1: 55–78.

Thomas, C. (2008), 'Globalization and Development in the South', in J. Ravenhill (ed.), *Global Political Economy*, 2nd edn (Oxford: Oxford University Press).

Thompson, G. (2006), 'The Supra-national Regionalization of the International Financial System: How Far and With What Prospects?', Paper prepared for the GARNET Conference, Amsterdam, 28–30 September.

Thorp, R. (1998), *Progress, Poverty and Exclusion: An Economic History of Latin America in the 20th Century* (Baltimore, MD: Johns Hopkins/Inter-American Development Bank).

Thun, E. (2000), 'Growing Up and Moving Out: Globalization in the Taiwanese Textile/Apparel and Automotive Sectors', MIT IPC Working Paper 00–007 (Cambridge, MA:

Industrial Performance Center, Massachusetts Institute of Technology), June.

—— (2006), *Changing Lanes in China: Foreign Direct Investment, Local Governments, and Auto Sector Development* (New York: Cambridge University Press).

Tichenor, D. J. (2002), *Dividing Lines: The Politics of Immigration Control in America* (Princeton, NJ: Princeton University Press).

Tienhaara, K. (2006), 'Mineral Investment and the Regulation of the Environment in Developing Countries: Lessons from Ghana', *International Environmental Agreements: Politics, Law and Economics*, 6/4: 371–94.

Tisdell, C. (2001), 'Globalization and Sustainability: Environmental Kuznets Curve and the WTO', *Ecological Economics*, 39/2: 185–96.

Toye, J. (1993), *Dilemmas of Development*, 2nd edn (Oxford: Blackwell).

Traxler, F., and Woitech, B. (2000), 'Transnational Investment and National Labour Market Regimes: A Case of "Regime Shopping"?', *European Journal of Industrial Relations*, 6/2: 141–59.

Tribe, K. (1995), *Strategies of Economic Order: German Economic Discourse, 1750–1950* (Cambridge: Cambridge University Press).

Triffin, R. (1960), *Gold and the Dollar Crisis* (New Haven, CT: Yale University Press).

Truman, E. (2006), 'A Strategy for International Monetary Fund Reform', *Policy Analyses in International Economics* 77 (Washington, DC: Institute for International Economics).

Tullock, G. (1983), *The Economics of Income Distribution* (Boston, MA: Kluwer-Nijhoff).

Turner, P. (1981), 'Capital Flows in the 1980s: A Survey of Major Trends', *BIS Economic Papers*, No. 30 (Geneva: Bank for International Settlements).

Tussie, D. (1987), *The Less Developed Countries and the World Trading System: A Challenge to the GATT* (London: Frances Pinter).

Tyers, R., and Anderson, R. K. (1992), *Disarray in World Food Markets* (Cambridge: Cambridge University Press).

Ugur, M. (ed.) (2001), *Open Economy Macroeconomics: A Reader* (London: Routledge).

UN (United Nations) (1992), *Agenda 21: The United Nations Programme of Action from Rio* (New York: United Nations).

—— (2006), *World Economic and Social Survey 2006: Diverging Growth and Development* (New York: United Nations).

—— (2009*a*), 'Report of the Commission of Experts of the President of the United Nations General Assembly on Reforms of the International Monetary and Financial System', 21 September, www.un.org/ga/econcrisissummit/docs/FinalReport_CoE.pdf

—— (2009*b*) *The Millennium Development Goals Report 2009* (New York: UN).

UNAIDS (2009), *AIDS Epidemic Update* (UNAIDS), http://data.unaids.org/pub/Report/2009/2009_epidemic_update_en.pdf

UN Commission on Transnational Corporations (1978), *Transnational Corporations in World Development: A Re-Examination* (New York: UN Publications).

UNCTAD (United Nations Conference on Trade and Development) (1979), *Multilateral Trade Negotiations: Evaluations and Further Recommendation Arising Therefrom*, UNCTAD v (UN Doc. TD/227).

—— (1999), *World Investment Report 1999: Foreign Direct Investment and the Challenge of Development* (Geneva: UNCTAD).

—— (2000), *World Investment Report 2000: Cross-Border Merqers and Acquisitions and Development* (Geneva: UNCTAD).

—— (2001), *World Investment Report: Promoting Linkages* (Geneva: UNCTAD).

—— (2002), *World Investment Report 2002: Transnational Corporations and Export Competitiveness* (Geneva: UNCTAD).

—— (2003), *World Investment Report 2003: FDI Policies for Development: National and International Perspectives* (Geneva: UNCTAD).

—— (2004*a*), *Development and Globalization: Facts and Figures* (Geneva: UNCTAD).

—— (2004*b*), 'The New Geography of International Economic Relations', TD/B/51/6 Trade and Development Board, 51st Session, Geneva, 4–15 October, GE.04–52426.

—— (2005), *Trade and Development Report 2005: New Features of Global Interdependence* (Geneva: UNCTAD).

—— (2006*a*), *Trade and Development Report 2006: Global Partnership and National Policies for Development* (Geneva: UNCTAD).

—— (2006*b*), *World Investment Report 2006: FDI from Developing and Transition Economies: Implications for Development* (Geneva: UNCTAD).

—— (2009*a*), 'Global FDI in Decline due to the Financial Crisis, and a Further Drop Expected', *UNCTAD Investment Brief*, 1, www.waipa.org/pdf/InvestmentBriefs/Investmentbrief_01_2009.pdf

—— (2009*b*), *World Investment Report 2009: Transnational Corporations, Agricultural Production and Development* (Geneva: UNCTAD).

Underhill, G. (1994), 'Introduction: Conceptualizing the Changing Global Order', in R. Stubbs and G. Underhill (eds), *Political Economy and the Changing Global Order* (Basingstoke: Macmillan).

UNDP (United Nations Development Programme) (2003), *Making Global Trade Work for People* (London: Earthscan).

—— (2006), *Human Development Report 2005: International Cooperation at a Crossroads: Air, Trade and Security in an Unequal World* (New York: UNDP).

UNEP (United Nations Environment Programme) (2002), *Global Environment Outlook 3* (London: Earthscan).

—— (2003), 'Backgrounder: Basic Facts and Data on the Science and Politics of Ozone Protection', www.unep.org/ozone/pdf/Press-Backgrounder.pdf

—— (2005), 'Basic Facts and Data on the Science and Politics of Ozone Protection', November Media Release (Nairobi: UNEP).

UNFPA (United Nations Fund for Population Activities) (2001), *The State of the World Population 2001. Footprints and Milestones: Population and Environmental Change* (New York: UNFPA).

UNICEF (United Nations Children's Fund) (2007), 'Child Poverty in Perspective: An Overview of Child Well-being in Rich Countries', Report Card 7 (Florence: UNICEF Innocenti Research Centre).

van der Pijl, K. (1998), *Transnational Classes and International Relations* (London: Routledge).

van Dormael, A. (1978), *Bretton Woods: The Birth of a Monetary System* (London: Macmillan).

van Staveren, I. (2002), 'Global Finance and Gender', in J. A. Scholte (ed.), *Civil Society and Global Finance* (London: Routledge).

Vaubel, R. (1986), 'A Public Choice Approach to International Organization', *Public Choice*, 51/1: 39–57.

—— (1991), 'The Political Economy of the International Monetary Fund', in R. Vaubel and T. D. Willett (eds), *The Political Economy of International Organizations: A Public Choice Approach* (Boulder, CO: Westview Press).

Veloso, F. (2000), 'The Automotive Supply Chain Organization: Global Trends and Perspectives', MIT Working Paper (Cambridge, MA: MIT).

Verdier, D. (1994), *Democracy and International Trade: Britain, France, and the United States, 1860–1990* (Princeton, NJ: Princeton University Press).

Vernon, R. (1971), *Sovereignty at Bay* (New York: Basic Books).

—— (1995), 'The World Trade Organization: A New Stage in International Trade and Development', *Harvard International Law Journal*, 36: 329–40.

Victor, D., Raustiala, K., and Skolnikoff, E. (1998), *The Implementation and Effectiveness of International Environmental Commitments: Theory and Practice* (Cambridge, MA: MIT Press).

Viner, J. (1928/1989), 'Adam Smith and Laissez-Faire', in J. M. Clark, P. H. Douglas, J. H. Hollander, G. R. Morrow, M. Palyi, and J. Viner, *Adam Smith, 1776–1926: Lectures to Commemorate the Sesquicentennial of the Publication of* the 'Wealth of Nations' (New York: Augustus M. Kelley Publishers).

Viner, J. (1948), 'Power Versus Plenty', World Politics, 1/1: 1–29.

——(1950), The Customs Union Issue (New York: Carnegie Endowment for International Peace).

Vogel, D. (1995), Trading Up: Consumer and Environmental Regulation in a Global Economy (Cambridge, MA: Harvard University Press).

Vogler, J. (2000), The Global Commons: Environmental and Technological Governance, 2nd edn (Chichester: John Wiley).

——(2003), 'Taking Institutions Seriously: How Regime Analysis Can be Relevant to Multilevel Environmental Governance', Global Environmental Politics, 3/2: 25–39.

Wackernagel, M., and Rees, W. (1996), Our Ecological Footprint: Reducing Human Impact on the Earth (Gabriola Island, British Columbia: New Society Publishers).

Wade, R. (1990), Governing the Market: Economic Theory and the Role of Government in Taiwan's Industrialization (Princeton, NJ: Princeton University Press).

——(1996), 'Japan, the World Bank, and the Art of Paradigm Maintenance: The East Asian Miracle in Political Perspective', New Left Review, 217: 3–36.

——(1998), 'The Asian Debt-and-Development Crisis of 1997–?: Causes and Consequences', World Development, 26:8:1535–53.

——(2003a), 'What Strategies Are Viable for Developing Countries Today? The WTO and the Shrinkage of Development Space', Review of International Political Economy, 10/4: 621–44.

——(2003b), 'The Invisible Hand of the American Empire', Ethics and International Affairs, 17/2: 77–88.

——(2004), Governing the Market: Economic Theory and the Role of Government in East Asian Industrialization (Princeton, NJ: Princeton University Press).

——(2007a), 'The Washington Consensus', in International Encyclopedia of the Social Sciences (New York: Macmillan).

——(2007b), 'Economic Liberalism and the "Outward Alliance" of State, Finance and Big Companies: A Perspective from the United Kingdom', in P. Bowles, H. Veltmeyer, S. Cornelissen, N. Invernizzi, and K.-L. Tang (eds), National Perspectives on Globalization: A Critical Reader (Basingstoke: Palgrave Macmillan).

——(2009a), 'From Global Imbalances to Global Reorganizations', Cambridge Journal of Economics, 33/4: 539–62.

——(2009b), 'Iceland as Icarus', Challenge, 52/3: 5–33.

——(2009c), 'The Global Slump: Deeper Causes and Harder Lessons', Challenge, 52/5: 5–24.

——(2010), 'Is the Globalization Consensus Dead?' in N. Castree, P. Chatterton, N. Heynen, W. Larner, and M. Wright (eds), The Point is to Change it: Geographies of Hope and Survival in an Age of Crisis (Oxford: Wiley-Blackwell).

Walker, R. B. J. (1993), Inside/Outside: International Relations as Political Theory (Cambridge: Cambridge University Press).

Wall Street Journal (2006), 3 January.

Wallace, H. (2000), 'The Policy Process: A Moving Pendulum', in H. Wallace and W. Wallace (eds), Policy-Making in the European Union, 4th edn (Oxford: Oxford University Press).

——, Wallace, W., and Pollack, M. A. (eds) (2005), Policy-Making in the European Union (Oxford: Oxford University Press).

Wallerstein, I. (1974), The Modern World System, Vol. I (New York: Academic Press).

——(1979), The Capitalist World-Economy: Essays (Cambridge: Cambridge University Press).

——(1980), The Modern World System, Vol. 2 (New York: Academic Press).

——(1983), Historical Capitalism (London: Verso).

Walras, L. (1874/1984), Elements of Pure Economics: Or the Theory of Social Wealth, trans. W. Jaffé (Philadelphia, PA: Orion Editions).

Waltz, K. N. (1979), Theory of International Politics (Reading, MA: Addison Wesley).

Wapner, P. (2003), 'World Summit on Sustainable Development: Toward a Post-Jo'burg Environmentalism', Global Environmental Politics, 3/1: 1–10.

Warnock, F. E., and Warnock, V. C. (2006), 'International Capital Flows and US Interest Rates', NBER Working Paper 12560 (Cambridge, MA: National Bureau of Economic Research).

Watson, M. (2001), 'International Capital Mobility in an Era of Globalization: Adding a Political Dimension to the "Feldstein–Horioka Puzzle"', Politics, 21/2: 81–92.

——(2003), 'Ricardian Political Economy and the Varieties of Capitalism Approach: Specialisation, Trade and Comparative Institutional Advantage', Comparative European Politics, 1/2: 227–40.

——(2005), Foundations of International Political Economy (Basingstoke: Palgrave Macmillan).

Watts, J. (2005), 'The Tiger's Teeth', The Guardian, 25 May.

WCED (World Commission on Environment and Development) (1987), Our Common Future (Oxford: Oxford University Press).

Webb, M. (1995), The Political Economy of Policy Coordination: International Adjustment Since 1945 (Ithaca, NY: Cornell University Press).

Weber, M. (1913/1958), 'The Social Psychology of the World Religions', in H. H. Gerth and C. Wright Mills (eds), *Max Weber: Essays in Sociology* (New York: Oxford University Press).

Weingast, B., Shepsle, K., and Johnsen, C. (1981), 'The Political Economy of Benefits and Costs', *Journal of Political Economy*, 89/4: 642–64.

Weiss, L. (1998), *The Myth of the Powerless State: Governing the Economy in a Global Era* (Cambridge: Polity Press).

——and Hobson, J. M. (1995), *States and Economic Development: A Comparative Historical Analysis* (London: Polity).

Wendt, A. (1992), 'Anarchy Is What States Make of It', *International Organization*, 42/2: 391–422.

——(1995), 'Constructing International Politics', *International Security*, 20/1: 71–81.

——(1998), 'On Constitution and Causation in International Relations', *Review of International Studies*, 24/5: 101–17.

Whalley, J. (1999), 'Why Do Countries Seek Regional Trade Agreements?', in J. Frankel (ed.), *The Regionalization of the World Economy* (Cambridge, MA: National Bureau of Economic Research).

Wheeler, D. (2002), 'Beyond Pollution Havens', *Global Environmental Politics*, 2/2: 1–10.

White, G. (ed.) (1988), *Developmental States in East Asia* (London: Macmillan).

Whiting, S. H. (2001), *Power and Wealth in Rural China* (Cambridge: Cambridge University Press).

WHO (World Health Organization) (2008a), *The World Health Report 2008—Primary Health Care (Now More Than Ever)* (Geneva: WHO).

——(2008b), *World Health Statistics: Part 2 Global Health Indicators* (Geneva: WHO).

Wilensky, H. L. (2002), *Rich Democracies: Political Economy, Public Policy and Performance* (Berkeley, CA and Los Angeles, CA: University of California Press).

Wilkins, M. (2003), 'Conduits for Long Term Foreign Investment in the Gold Standard Era', in M. Flandreu, C.-L. Holtfrerich, and H. James (eds), *International Financial History in the Twentieth Century: System and Anarchy* (Cambridge: Cambridge University Press).

Wilkinson, R. (2006), *The WTO: Crisis and the Governance of Global Trade* (London: Routledge).

——and Pickett, K. (2009), *The Spirit Level: Why More Equal Societies Almost Always Do Better* (London: Allen Lane).

Williams, D., and Young, T. (1994), 'Governance, the World Bank and Liberal Theory', *Political Studies*, 42/1: 84–100.

Williams, M. (1994), *International Economic Organizations and the Third World* (Hemel Hempstead: Harvester Wheatsheaf).

Williamson, J. (1990), 'What Washington Means by Policy Reform', in J. Williamson (ed.), *Latin American Adjustment: How Much Has Happened?* (Washington, DC: Institute of International Economics).

——(2003), 'Overview: An Agenda for Restarting Growth and Reform', in J. Williamson and P.-P. Kuczynski (eds), *After the Washington Consensus: Restarting Growth and Reform in Latin America* (Washington, DC: Institute for International Economics).

——(2009), 'Understanding Special Drawing Rights (SDRs)', Policy Brief Number PB09-11 (Washington, DC: Peterson Institute for International Economics, June).

Williamson, O. E. (1975), *Markets and Hierarchies, Analysis and Anti-Trust Implications: A Study in the Economics of Internal Organization* (New York: The Free Press).

——(1981) 'The Modern Corporation: Origins, Evolution, Attributes', *Journal of Economic Literature,* 19/4: 1537–68.

Winch, C. (1998), 'Listian Political Economy: Social Capitalism Conceptualised?', *New Political Economy*, 3/2: 301–16.

Winchester, S. (1991), *Pacific Rising* (New York: Prentice-Hall).

Winham, G. R. (1986), *International Trade and the Tokyo Round Negotiation* (Princeton, NJ: Princeton University Press).

——(1998a), 'Explanations of Developing Country Behaviour in the GATT Uruguay Round Negotiation', *World Competition*, 21/3: 109–34.

——(1998b), 'The World Trade Organization: Institution-Building in the Multilateral Trade System', *World Economy*, 21/3: 349–68.

Wintrobe, R. (1998), *The Political Economy of Dictatorship* (Cambridge: Cambridge University Press).

Wionczek, M. (1966), 'Requisites for Viable Economic Integration', in M. Wionczek (ed.), *Latin American Economic Integration: Experiences and Prospects* (New York: Praeger).

Wolf, D., and Zangl, B. (1996), 'The European Economic and Monetary Union: "Two-Level Games" and the Formation of International Institutions', *European Journal of International Relations*, 2/3: 355–93.

Wolf, M. (2000), *Financial Times*, 8 February.

——(2004a), *Why Globalization Works* (New Haven, CT: Yale University Press).

——(2004b), 'States are Cure and Disease', Special Report: World Economy, *Financial Times*, 1 October.

——(2008), *Fixing Global Finance* (Baltimore, MD: Johns Hopkins University Press).

——(2009), 'Why President Obama Must Mend a Sick World Economy', *Financial Times*, 21 January.

Womack, J. P., Jones, D. T., and Roos, D. (1990), *The Machine That Changed the World* (New York: Harper Perennial).

Woo-Cumings, M. (ed.) (1999), *The Developmental State* (Ithaca, NY: Cornell University Press).

Wood, A. (1994), *North–South Trade, Employment and Inequality* (Oxford: Oxford University Press).

Wood, E. M. (2003), *Empire of Capital* (London: Verso).

Woodhouse, P. (2002), 'Development Policies and Environmental Agendas', in U. Kothari and M. Minogue (eds), *Development Theory and Practice: Critical Perspectives* (Basingstoke: Palgrave).

Woods, N. (2003), 'Order, Justice, the IMF and the World Bank', in R. Foot, J. L. Gaddis, and A. Hurrell (eds), *Order and Justice in International Relations* (Oxford: Oxford University Press).

——(2006), *The Globalizers: The IMF, the World Bank and Their Borrowers* (Ithaca, NY: Cornell University Press).

World Bank (1992a), *Governance and Development* (Washington, DC: IBRD).

——(1992b), *World Development Report 1992* (New York: Oxford University Press).

——(1993), *The East Asian Miracle: Economic Growth and Public Policy* (Oxford: Oxford University Press).

——(1994), *Adjustment in Africa: Reforms, Results, and the Road Ahead* (Washington, DC: IBRD).

——(1997), *Private Capital Flows to Developing Countries: The Road to Financial Integration* (Washington, DC: IBRD).

——(1999a), *Global Development Finance* [electronic resource] (Washington, DC: International Bank for Reconstruction and Development/The World Bank), computer disks; 3 1/2 in.

——(1999b), *World Development Report 1999/2000: Entering the 21st Century* (Washington, DC: World Bank).

——(2000), *Trade Blocs* (New York: Oxford University Press).

——(2002a), *Global Development Finance: Financing the Poorest Countries* [electronic resource] (Washington, DC: World Bank), 1 CD-ROM; 4 3/4 in.

——(2002b), *Globalization, Growth, and Poverty: Building an Inclusive World Economy* (New York: Oxford University Press).

——(2002c), *World Development Indicators 2002* (Washington, DC: World Bank).

——(2005a), *World Development Indicators 2005* (Washington, DC: World Bank).

——(2005b), *World Development Report 2006: Equity and Development* (New York: World Bank and Oxford University Press).

——(2005c), *Economic Growth in the 1990s: Learning from a Decade of Reform* (Washington, DC: IBRD).

——(2007a), *East Asia & Pacific Update: Ten Years After Asia's Financial Crisis*, April, http://siteresources.worldbank.org

——(2007b), *Global Economic Prospects: Managing the Next Wave of Globalization, 2007* (Washington, DC: World Bank).

——(2009a), *Global Development Finance* (Washington, DC: World Bank).

——(2009b), *Global Monitoring Report: A Development Emergency* (Washington, DC: World Bank).

——(2009c), *World Development Indicators 2009* (Washington, DC: World Bank).

——(2009d), *World Development Report 2009: Reshaping Economic Geography* (Washington, DC: World Bank).

——(2010), *Global Economic Prospects 2010: Crisis, Finance, and Growth* (Washington, DC: World Bank).

World Commission on Environment and Development (1987), *Our Common Future* (Oxford: Oxford University Press).

World Meteorological Organization (2006), 'New Report Projects Later Recovery of Ozone Layer', Press Release WMO No. 757, 18 August (Geneva/Nairobi: World Meteorological Organization).

Worm, B., Barbier, E. B., Beaumont, N., Emmett Duffy, J., Folke, C., Halpern, B. S., Jackson, J. B. C., Lotze, H. K., Micheli, F., Palumbi, S. R., Sala, E., Selkoe, K. A., Stachowicz, J. J., and Watson, R. (2006), 'Impacts of Biodiversity Loss on Ocean Ecosystem Services', *Science*, 314/5800, 3 November: 787–90.

Wright, C., and Rwabizambuga, A. (2006), 'Institutional Pressures, Corporate Reputation, and Voluntary Codes of Conduct: An Examination of the Equator Principles', *Business and Society Review*, 111/1: 89–117.

WTO (World Trade Organization) (1999), *WTO, Trade and Environment*, Special Studies 4 (Geneva: WTO), Press Release, www.wto.org/english/tratop_e/envir_e/stud99_e.htm

——(2000a), 'Mapping of Regional Trade Agreements: Note by the Secretariat', Committee on Regional Trade Agreements, WT/REG/W/41 (Geneva: World Trade Organization) 11 October, www.wto.org/english/tratop_e/region_/wtregw41_e.doc (chart 2: 5).

——(2000b), 'Overview of the State of Play of WTO Disputes', Informal Paper (Geneva: WTO).

——(2001a), *World Trade Report* (Geneva: WTO).

——(2001b), 'WTO Successfully Concludes Negotiations on China's Entry', WTO Press Release (PRESS/243), 17 September.

——(2002), *World Trade Report* (Geneva: WTO).

—— (2003a) *Annual Report* (Geneva: WTO).

—— (2003b), 'Decision Removes Final Patent Obstacle to Cheap Drug Imports', WTO Press Release, PRESS/350/Rev. 1, 4 September.

—— (2003c), *World Trade Report* (Geneva: WTO), www.wto. org/english/res_e/booksp_e/anrep_e/world_trade_report_ 2003_e.pdf

—— (2005), *World Trade Report 2005: Exploring the Links between Trade, Standards and the WTO* (Geneva: WTO).

—— (2006a), *International Trade Statistics 2006* (Geneva: WTO).

—— (2006b), *Report (2006) of the Committee on Regional Trade Agreements to the General Council*, WT/REG/17, http://docsonline.wto.org/

—— (2006c), *World Trade Report 2006: Subsidies, Trade and the WTO* (Geneva: WTO).

—— (2008), 'European Communities— Regime for the Importation, Sale and Distribution of Bananas', www.wto.org/ english/tratop_e/dispu_e/cases_e/ds27_e.htm

—— (2009a), *World Trade Report 2009: Trade Policy Commitments and Contingency Measures* (Geneva: WTO).

—— (2009b), *International Trade Statistics 2009* (Geneva: WTO).

—— WTO (2009c), 'European Communities— Measures Concerning Meat and Meat Products (Hormones)', www.wto.org/english/tratop_e/dispu_e/cases_e/ds26_e.htm

—— (2010), 'Regional Trade Agreements: Facts and Figures', www.wto.org/english/tratop_e/region_e/regfac_e.htm

WWF (World Wide Fund for Nature) (2002), *Living Planet Report 2002* (Gland, Switzerland: WWF), www.panda.org/ downloads/general/LPR_2002.pdf

—— (2006), *Living Planet Report 2006* (Gland, Switzerland: WWF).

Wynne, M. A., and Kersting, E. K. (2009), 'Trade, Globalization and the Financial Crisis', *Economic Letter— Insights from the Federal Reserve Bank of Dallas*, 4/8, www.dallasfed. org/research/eclett/2009/e10908.htm

Yabuchi, M. (2000), 'Changing Determinants for Manufacturing Investment: The Availability of Parts', *JETRO China Newsletter*, 6/149: 1–2.

Yandle, B. (1984), 'Intertwined Interests, Rent Seeking and Regulation', *Social Science Quarterly*, 65/4: 1002–12.

Young, O. R. (ed.) (1999), *The Effectiveness of International Environmental Regimes: Causal Connections and Behavioral Mechanisms* (Cambridge, MA: MIT Press).

—— (2002), *The Institutional Dimensions of Environmental Change: Fit, Interplay, and Scale* (Cambridge, MA: MIT Press).

Young, Z. (2003), *A New Green Order: The World Bank and the Politics of the Global Environment Facility* (London: Pluto Press).

Yusuf, S., and Nabeshima, K. (2009), *Tiger Economies under Threat* (Washington, DC: World Bank).

Zabarenko, D. (2006), '2005 Was Warmest Year on Record: NASA', *Reuters*, 24 January.

Zaller, J. (1992), *The Nature and Origins of Mass Opinion* (New York: Cambridge University Press).

Zevin, R. (1992), 'Are World Financial Markets More Open? If so, Why and with What Effects?', in T. Banuri and J. B. Schor (eds), *Financial Openness and National Autonomy: Opportunities and Constraints* (Oxford: Oxford University Press).

Zhou Xiaochuan (2009), 'Reform the International Monetary System', 24 March, People's Bank of China, Beijing, www.pbc.gov.cn/english/detail.asp?col=6500&id=178

Zimmermann, H. (2002), *Money and Security: Troops, Monetary Policy and West Germany's Relations with the United States and Britain 1950–71* (Cambridge: Cambridge University Press).

Zolo, D. (1997), *Cosmopolis: Prospects for World Government* (Cambridge: Polity Press).

Zürn, M. (1992), *Interessen und Institutionen in der internationalen Politik. Grundlegung und Anwendung des situationsstrukturellen Ansatzes* (Opladen, Germany: Leske & Budrich).

Zysman, J. (1984), *Governments, Markets and Growth: Financial Systems and the Politics of Industrial Change* (Ithaca, NY: Cornell University Press).

Index